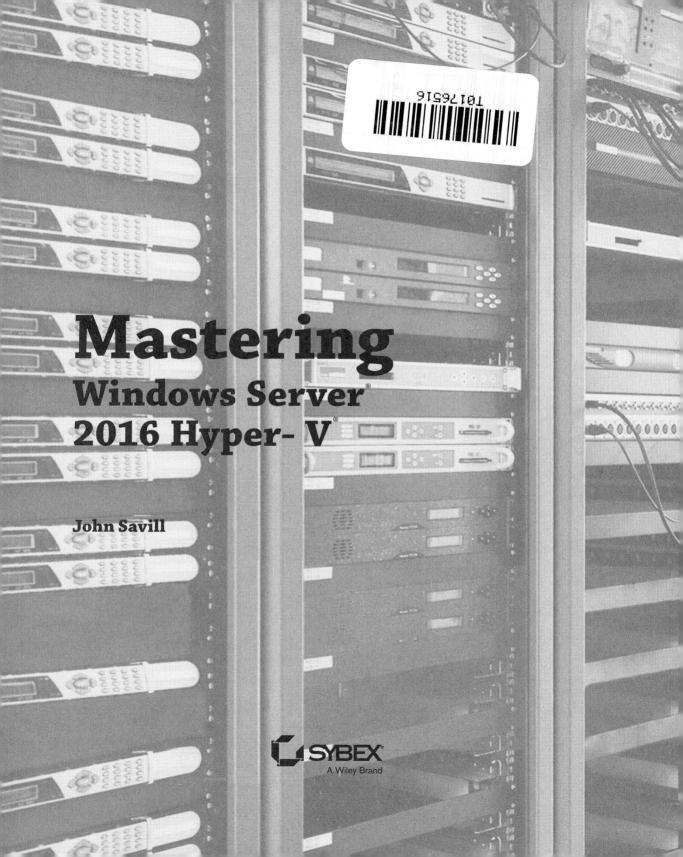

Mastering
Windows Server®
2016 Hyper- V®

John Savill

SYBEX®
A Wiley Brand

Senior Acquisitions Editor: Kenyon Brown
Development Editor: Gary Schwartz
Production Editor: Christine O'Connor
Copy Editor: Sharon Wilkey
Editorial Manager: Mary Beth Wakefield
Production Manager: Kathleen Wisor
Executive Editor: Jim Minatel
Book Designers: Maureen Forys, Happenstance Type-O-Rama and Judy Fung
Proofreader: Nancy Carrasco
Indexer: Ted Laux
Project Coordinator, Cover: Brent Savage
Cover Designer: Wiley
Cover Image: dotshock/Shutterstock

For general information on our other products and services or to obtain technical support, please contact our Customer Care Department within the U.S. at (877) 762-2974, outside the U.S. at (317) 572-3993 or fax (317) 572-4002.

Wiley publishes in a variety of print and electronic formats and by print-on-demand. Some material included with standard print versions of this book may not be included in e-books or in print-on-demand. If this book refers to media such as a CD or DVD that is not included in the version you purchased, you may download this material at http://booksupport.wiley.com. For more information about Wiley products, visit www.wiley.com.

Library of Congress Control Number: 2016959384

10 9 8 7 6 5 4 3 2 1

For my wife, Julie, and my children,
Abby, Ben, and Kevin. My everythings.

Acknowledgments

I could not have written this book without the help and support of many people. First I need to thank my wife, Julie, for putting up with me for being busier than usual the last six months and for picking up the slack as always—and for always supporting the crazy things I want to do. My children, Abby, Ben, and Kevin, always make all the work worthwhile; they can turn the worst, most tiring day into a good one with a smile and a laugh.

Of course, the book wouldn't be possible at all without the Wiley team: senior acquisitions editor Kenyon Brown, development editor Gary Schwartz, production editor Christine O'Connor, copy editor Sharon Wilkey, and proofreader Nancy Carrasco.

Many people have helped me over the years with encouragement and technical knowledge, and this book is the sum of that. The following people helped out on specific aspects of this book, and I want to thank them and give them the credit they deserve for helping make this book as good as possible (if I've missed anyone, I'm truly sorry): Theo Thompson, Mathew John, Jake Oshins, Chris Huybregts, Neil Peterson, Jim Wooldridge, Steven Ekren, Michael Gray, Darren Moss, Claus Joergensen, Dean Wells, Nir Ben Zvi, Andrew Mason, Jian Yan, Simon Gurevich, Shivam Garg, Elden Christensen, Jason Messer, Taylor Brown, Manish Jha, Shon Shah, Pradeep Reddy, Don Stanwyck, Greg Cusanza, Paul Kimbel, Scott Willwerth, and Tim Aranki.

About the Author

John Savill is a technical specialist who focuses on Microsoft core infrastructure technologies including Windows, Hyper-V, System Center, and anything that does something cool. He has been working with Microsoft technologies for 20 years. He is the creator of the highly popular NTFAQ.com website and a senior contributing editor for Windows IT Pro magazine. He has written seven previous books covering Windows, Azure, Hyper-V, and advanced Active Directory architecture. When he is not writing books, he writes magazine articles and white papers; creates many technology videos, which are available on his YouTube channel, www.youtube.com/ntfaqguy; and presents online and at industry-leading events, including TechEd, Ignite, and Windows Connections. When he was writing this book, he had just completed running his annual series of Master Classes, which include classes on Azure, Hyper-V, PowerShell, and the complete Microsoft stack. John also has online courses on Pluralsight and O'Reilly.

Outside technology, John enjoys cardio and weight training. In fact, while writing this book, he was training for his third full Ironman triathlon in Chattanooga, Tennessee.

John tries to update his blog at www.savilltech.com/blog with the latest news of what he is working on and also tweets at @NTFAQGuy.

Contents at a Glance

Contents

Introduction

The book you are holding is the result of 20 years of experience in the IT world and over 15 years of virtualization experience that started with VMware and includes Virtual PC and now Hyper-V. My goal for this book is simple: to help you become knowledgeable and effective when it comes to architecting and managing a Hyper-V-based virtual environment. This means not only understanding how Hyper-V works and its capabilities, but also knowing when to leverage other technologies to provide the most complete and optimal solution. That means leveraging System Center and Microsoft Azure, which I also cover because they relate to Hyper-V. I also dive into some key technologies of Windows Server that bring benefits to Hyper-V.

Hyper-V is now a mature and widely adopted virtualization solution. It is one of only two x86 server virtualization solutions in Gartner's leader quadrant. In addition to being used by many of the largest companies in the world, Hyper-V powers Microsoft Azure, which is one of the largest cloud services in the world.

Hyper-V is a role of Windows Server. If you are a Windows administrator, you will find Hyper-V management fairly intuitive, but there are still many key areas that require attention. I have structured this book to cover the key principles of virtualization and the resources that you will manage with Hyper-V before I cover installing and configuring Hyper-V itself and then move on to advanced topics such as high availability, replication, private cloud, and more.

I am a strong believer in learning by doing, and therefore I highly encourage you to try out all of the technologies and principles I cover in this book. You don't need a huge lab environment. For most topics, you could use a single machine with Windows Server installed and 8GB of memory to enable a few virtual machines to run concurrently. Ideally, though, having at least two servers will help with the replication and high-availability concepts. In this book, sometimes you'll see step-by-step instructions to guide you through a process, sometimes I link to an external source that already has a good step-by-step guide, and sometimes I link to videos that I have posted to ensure maximum understanding. With Windows 10, Hyper-V is included in the box, so even without any kind of server, it is possible to explore many of the Hyper-V technologies.

I have created an application that is available for various platforms: Mastering Hyper-V 2016. It provides easy access to the external links, videos, and code samples that I use in this book. As you read each chapter, check out the application to find related content. The application can be downloaded from www.savilltech.com/mhv. Using the various platform stores also allows me to update it over time as required. Please get this application, as I will use it to add videos based on reader feedback that are not referenced in the main text and include additional information where required.

Who Should Read This Book

I am making certain assumptions regarding the reader:

◆ You have basic Windows Server knowledge and can install Windows Server.

◆ You have basic knowledge of PowerShell.

◆ You have access to a Hyper-V server to enable a test implementation of the many covered technologies.

This book is intended for anyone who wants to learn Hyper-V. If you have a basic knowledge of virtualization or a competing technology, such as VMware, that will help, but it is not a requirement. I start off with a foundational understanding of each technology and then build on that to cover more-advanced topics and configurations. If you are an architect, a consultant, an administrator, or really anyone who just wants better knowledge of Hyper-V, this book is for you.

At times I go into advanced topics that may seem over your head. In those cases, don't worry. Focus on the preceding elements that you understand, and implement and test them to solidify your understanding. Then, when you feel comfortable, come back to the more advanced topics. They will seem far simpler once your understanding of the foundational principles is solidified.

What's Inside

Here is a glance at what's in each chapter:

Chapter 1: Introduction to Virtualization and Microsoft Solutions   This chapter focuses on the core value proposition of virtualization and how the datacenter has evolved. It covers the key changes and capabilities of Hyper-V in addition to the role System Center plays in a Hyper-V environment. I cover the types of cloud services available and how Hyper-V forms the foundation of private cloud solutions.

Chapter 2: Virtual Machine Resource Fundamentals   This chapter covers the core resources of a virtual machine, specifically architecture (generation 1 and generation 2 virtual machines), processor, and memory. You will learn about advanced configurations to enable many types of operating system support along with best practices for resource planning.

Chapter 3: Virtual Networking   This chapter covers one of the most complicated aspects of virtualization, especially when using the new network virtualization capabilities in Hyper-V. This chapter covers the key networking concepts, how to architect virtual networks, and how to configure them. I also cover networking using System Center Virtual Machine Manager (SCVMM) and how to design and implement network virtualization v2 that is introduced in Windows Server 2016.

Chapter 4: Storage Configurations   This chapter covers the storage options for Hyper-V environments, including the VHD and VHDX formats, plus capabilities in Windows Server 2016 that help manage direct attached storage, including Storage Spaces Direct and Storage Replica. You will learn about storage technologies for virtual machines such as iSCSI, Virtual Fibre Channel, and shared VHDX; their relative advantages; as well as the storage migration and resize functions.

Chapter 5: Managing Hyper-V   This chapter walks you through the installation of and best practices for managing Hyper-V. The basics of configuring virtual machines, installing operating systems, and using the Hyper-V Integration Services are all covered. Strategies for migrating from other hypervisors, physical servers, and other versions of Hyper-V are explored.

Chapter 6: Maintaining a Hyper-V Environment   This chapter focuses on the tasks required to keep Hyper-V healthy after you've installed it, which includes patching, malware protection, backup, and monitoring. Key actions, such as taking checkpoints of virtual machines, setting up service templates, and performance tuning are covered.

Chapter 7: Failover Clustering and Migration Technologies   This chapter covers making Hyper-V highly available by using Failover Clustering, and it includes a deep dive into exactly what makes a cluster tick, specifically when running Hyper-V. Key migration technologies such as Live Migration, Shared Nothing Live Migration, and Storage Migration are explored in addition to configurations related to mobility outside a cluster and placement optimization for virtual machines.

Chapter 8: Hyper-V Replica and Cloud Orchestration   This chapter shifts from high availability to a requirement of many organizations today: providing disaster-recovery protection in the event of losing an entire site. This chapter looks at the options for disaster recovery, including leveraging Hyper-V Replica, orchestrating failovers with Microsoft Azure in the event of a disaster, and using Azure as the DR target location.

Chapter 9: Implementing the Private Cloud, SCVMM, and Microsoft Azure Stack   This chapter shows the many benefits of the Microsoft stack to organizations, beyond just virtualization. This chapter explores the key benefits of a private cloud and describes what a private cloud using Microsoft technologies looks like. Key components and functional areas, including the actual end-user experience and how you can leverage all of System Center for different levels of private cloud capability, are all covered. The Microsoft Azure Stack solution is introduced and its key capabilities explored.

Chapter 10: Containers and Docker   This chapter focuses on the new Windows and Hyper-V container technologies available in Windows Server 2016. This chapter dives into the architectural components and management with Docker.

Chapter 11: Remote Desktop Services   This chapter shifts the focus to another type of virtualization, virtualizing the end-user experience, which is a critical capability for most organizations. Virtual desktop infrastructure is becoming a bigger component of the user environment. This chapter looks at the types of desktop virtualization available with Remote Desktop Services, with a focus on capabilities that are enabled by Hyper-V, such as advanced graphical capabilities with RemoteFX.

Chapter 12: Microsoft Azure IaaS, Storage, and Networking   This chapter explores the capabilities of one of the biggest public cloud services in the world, which is powered by Hyper-V. This chapter covers the fundamentals of Microsoft Azure and how to create virtual machines in Microsoft Azure. The chapter also covers the networking options available both within Microsoft Azure and to connect to your on-premises network. I examine the migration of virtual machines and how to leverage Azure Storage. Ways to provide a seamless management experience are also explored.

Chapter 13: Bringing It All Together with a Best-of-Breed Cloud Solution   This chapter brings together all of the technologies and options to help architect a best-of-breed virtualization and cloud solution.

Don't forget to download the companion Windows Store application, Mastering Hyper-V, from www.savilltech.com/mhv.

The Mastering Series

The Mastering series from Sybex provides outstanding instruction for readers with intermediate and advanced skills in the form of top-notch training and development for those already working in their field and clear, serious education for those aspiring to become pros. Every Mastering book includes the following elements:

◆ Skill-based instruction, with chapters organized around real tasks rather than abstract concepts or subjects

◆ Self-review test questions, so you can be certain that you're equipped to do the job right

How to Contact the Author

I welcome feedback from you about this book or about books you'd like to see from me in the future. You can reach me by writing to john@savilltech.com. For more information about my work, visit my website at www.savilltech.com and follow me on Twitter at @NTFAQGuy.

Sybex strives to keep you supplied with the latest tools and information that you need for your work. Please check the Sybex website at www.sybex.com/go/masteringhyperv2016, where we'll post additional content and updates that supplement this book should the need arise.

Chapter 1

Introduction to Virtualization and Microsoft Solutions

This chapter lays the foundation for the core fabric concepts and technologies discussed throughout not just this first part of this book, but the entire book. Virtualization has radically changed the layout and operation of the datacenter, and this datacenter evolution and its benefits are explored.

Microsoft's solution for virtualization is its Hyper-V technology, which is a core part of Windows Server, and it is also available in the form of a free, stand-alone hypervisor. The virtualization layer is only part of the solution. Management is just as critical, and in today's world, the public cloud is also a consideration. Thus a seamless management story with compatibility between your on- and off-premises resources provides the model implementation.

In this chapter, you will learn to:

◆   Articulate the key value propositions of virtualization.

◆   Understand the differences in functionality between the various versions of Hyper-V.

◆   Differentiate between the types of cloud services and when each type is best utilized.

The Evolution of the Datacenter

Many books are available that go into a great amount of detail about the history of datacenters, but that is not the goal of the following sections. Instead, I am going to take you through the key changes that I have seen in my 20 years of working in and consulting about datacenter infrastructure. This brief look at the evolution of datacenters will help you understand the challenges of the past, why virtualization has become such a key component of every modern datacenter, and why there is still room for improvement.

One Box, One Operating System

As recent as 10 years ago, datacenters were all architected in a similar way. These huge rooms with very expensive cabling and air conditioning were home to hundreds, if not thousands, of servers. Some of these servers were mainframes, but the majority were regular servers (although today the difference between a mainframe and a powerful regular server is blurring). Although the processor architecture running in these servers may have been different—for example, some were x86 based, some Alpha, some MIPS, some SPARC—each server ran an operating system (OS) such as Windows, Linux, or OpenVMS. Some OSs supported different processor architectures, while others were limited to a specific architecture. Likewise, some processor architectures would dictate which OS had to be used. The servers themselves may have been freestanding, but as technology advanced, servers got smaller and became rack mountable, enabling greater compression of the datacenter.

UNDERSTANDING X86

Often, the term *x86* is used when talking about processor architecture, but its use has been generalized beyond just the original Intel processors that built on the 8086. *x86* does not refer only to Intel processors, but it is used more generally to refer to 32-bit operating systems running on any processor leveraging x86 instruction sets, including processors from AMD. *x64* represents a 64-bit instruction set extension processor (primarily from Intel and AMD), although you may also see *amd64* to denote 64-bit. What can be confusing is that a 64-bit processor is still technically x86, and it has become more common today simply to use *x86* to identify anything based on x86 architecture, which could be 32-bit or 64-bit from other types of processor architecture. Therefore, if you see *x86* within this book, or in other media, it does not mean 32-bit only.

Even with all this variation in types of server and operating systems, there was something they had in common. Each server ran a single OS, and that OS interacted directly with the hardware in the server and had to use hardware-specific drivers to utilize the available capabilities. In the rest of this book, I focus primarily on x86 Windows; however, many of the challenges and solutions apply to other OSs as well.

Every server comprises a number of resources, including processor, memory, network, and storage (although some modern servers do not have local storage such as blade systems, and instead rely completely on external storage subsystems). The amount of each resource can vary drastically, as shown in the following sections.

PROCESSOR

A server can have one or more processors, and it's common to see servers with two, four, or eight processors (although it is certainly possible to have servers with more). Modern processors use a core architecture that allows a single processor to have multiple cores. Each core consists of a discrete central processing unit (CPU) and L1 cache (very fast memory used for temporary storage of information related to computations) able to perform its own computations. Those multiple cores can then share a common L2 cache (bigger but not as fast as L1) and bus interface. This allows a single physical processor to perform multiple parallel computations and actually act like many separate processors. The first multicore processors had two cores (dual-core), and this continues to increase with eight-core (octo-core) processors available and a new "many-core" generation on the horizon, which will have tens of processor cores. It is common to see a physical processor referred to as a *socket*, and each processor core referred to as a *logical processor*. For example, a dual-socket system with quad-core processors would have eight logical processors (four on each physical processor, and there are two processors). In addition to the number of sockets and cores, variations exist in the speed of the processors and the exact instruction sets supported. (It is because of limitations in the continued increase of clock speed that moving to multicore became the best way to improve overall computational performance, especially as modern operating systems are multithreaded and can take advantage of parallel computation.)

Some processors also support *hyperthreading*, which is a means to split certain parts of a processor core into two parallel computational streams to avoid wasted processing. Hyperthreading does not double computational capability, but it generally gives a 10 to 15 percent performance boost. Typically with hyperthreading, this would therefore double the number of logical processors in a system. However, for virtualization, I prefer not to do this doubling, but this does not mean that I turn off hyperthreading. Hyperthreading may sometimes help, but it certainly won't hurt.

IS THERE A BIG AND A LITTLE THREAD WITH HYPERTHREADING?

Hyperthreading enables two streams of execution on a single processor core, and you often hear numbers such as a 15 percent performance improvement. This leads to the belief that there is the main thread on the core and then a little "mini-me" thread that has a smaller capability. This is not true. With hyperthreading, a single core has some components duplicated, enabling two sets of logical state per core. Typically, during a thread of execution, the core is not fully utilized for various reasons, such as when a particular instruction stream uses only specific types of ALU (Arithmetic Logic Unit), leaving others unused, and more commonly when a cache miss occurs that causes the thread execution to stall while data is fetched. With hyperthreading and the two sets of logical state, if one thread is stalled because of a cache miss, the chances are good that the other thread can execute. This, therefore, keeps the core better utilized and improves the overall performance, and this is where the 15 percent performance gain comes from. Notice that both threads are equal and which one does more work just depends on how busy they are kept, the type of computations, the frequency of cache misses, and so on.

Earlier versions of Windows supported different processor architectures, including MIPS, Alpha, PowerPC, and more recently Itanium. However, as of Windows Server 2012, the only supported processor architecture is x86 and specifically only 64-bit from Windows Server 2008 R2 and above. (There are still 32-bit versions of the Windows 8/8.1 client operating system.)

Prior to Windows Server 2008, there were separate versions of the hardware abstraction layer (HAL), depending on whether you had a uniprocessor or multiprocessor system. However, given the negligible performance savings on modern, faster processors that were specific to the uniprocessor HAL on single-processor systems (synchronization code for multiple processors was not present in the uniprocessor HAL), this was removed, enabling a single unified HAL that eases some of the pain caused by moving from uni- to multiprocessor systems.

MEMORY

The memory resource is generally far simpler, with fewer variations. Some memory supports error-correcting code (ECC), which provides resiliency against the most common types of internal corruption, and memory has different speeds. However, for most environments, the memory consideration is simply how much there is! Generally, the more memory, the better, and with only 64-bit versions of Windows Server, there are no longer considerations around the maximum amount of memory that can be used by an operating system (a 4GB limit exists for 32-bit operating systems).

STORAGE

Storage falls into one of two buckets: internal or external. If the storage is internal (direct-attached storage, or DAS), the disks are local to the server and attached via a technology such as SCSI, SATA, or SAS. (Even if the storage is in an external storage enclosure but is connected via one of these means, it is still considered direct-attached.) Alternatively, the storage is external, such as storage that is hosted on another server or on a storage area network (SAN) or on network-attached storage (NAS). Various protocols may be used for external storage access that offer either file-level or block-level access to the storage.

File-level access enables the requesting server to access files on the server, but this is offered over a protocol that hides the underlying filesystem and actual blocks of the file on disk. Examples of file-level protocols are Server Message Block (SMB) and Network File System (NFS), typically offered by NAS devices.

Block-level access enables the requesting server to see the blocks on the disk and effectively mount the disk, format the mounted disk with a filesystem, and then directly manipulate blocks on the disk. Block-level access is typically offered by SANs using protocols such as iSCSI (which leverages the TCP/IP network) and Fibre Channel (which requires dedicated hardware and cabling). Typically, block-level protocols have offered higher performance, and the SANs providing the block-level storage offer advanced features, which means that SANs are typically preferred over NAS devices for enterprise storage. However, there is a big price difference between a SAN and potentially the dedicated storage hardware and cabling (referred to as *storage fabric*), and an SMB device that leverages the existing IP network connectivity.

The line between types of storage is also blurring greatly, especially with modern hyperconverged systems that contain both compute and the storage for workloads. Windows Server 2016 includes Storage Spaces Direct (S2D), which enables direct-attached storage in cluster nodes to be aggregated together and utilized as cluster storage. This is commonly referred to as a *VSAN technology* in the industry. When combined with other Windows Server storage features, using direct-attached storage no longer means compromising features and performance.

The hardware for connectivity to storage can vary greatly for both internal storage, such as SCSI controllers, and external storage, such as the host bus adapters (HBAs), which provide the connectivity from a server to a Fibre Channel switch (which then connects to the SAN). Very specific drivers are required for the exact model of storage adapter, and often the driver version must correlate to a firmware version of the storage adapter.

In all components of an environment, protection from a single point of failure is desirable. For internal storage, it is common to group multiple physical disks together into arrays that can provide protection from data loss due to a single disk failure, a redundant array of independent disks (RAID). Windows Server also has other technologies that are covered in later chapters, including Storage Spaces. For external storage, it is possible to group multiple network adapters together into a team for IP-based storage access. For example, SMB, NFS, and iSCSI can be used to provide resiliency from a single network adapter failure, and for non-IP-based storage connectivity, it is common for a host to have at least two storage adapters, which are in turn each connected to a different storage switch (removing single points of failure). Those storage adapters are effectively joined using multipath I/O (MPIO), which provides protection from a single storage adapter or storage switch failure. Both the network and storage resiliency configurations are very specific and can be complex.

Finally, the disks themselves have different characteristics, such as size and speed. The higher availability of SSD storage and its increase in size and reduced cost is making it a realistic component of modern datacenter storage solutions. This is especially true in tiered solutions, which allow a mix of fast and slower disks, with the most used and important data moved to the faster disks. Disk speed is commonly measured in input/output operations per second, or IOPS (pronounced *eye-ops*). The higher the IOPS, the faster the storage.

The storage also contains the actual operating system (which can be local or on a remote SAN using boot-from-SAN capabilities).

NETWORKING

Compute, memory, and storage enable a server to perform work, but in today's environments, that work often relies on work done by other servers. In addition, access to that work from clients and the communication between computers is enabled through the network. To participate in an IP network, each machine has to have at least one IP address, which can be statically or automatically assigned. To enable this IP communication, a server has at least one network adapter, and that network adapter has one or more ports that connect to the network fabric, which is typically Ethernet. As is true when connecting to storage controllers, the operating system requires a driver specific to the network adapter to connect to the network. In high-availability network configurations, multiple network adapters are teamed together, which can be done in many cases through the driver functionality or in Windows Server 2012 using the native Windows NIC Teaming feature. Typical networking speeds in datacenters are 1 gigabit per second (Gbps) and 10Gbps, but faster speeds are available. As with IOPS for storage, the higher the network speed, the more data that you can transfer and the better the network performs.

How Virtualization Has Changed the Way Companies Work and Its Key Values

I spend quite a lot of time talking about resources and how they can vary, and where specific drivers and configurations may be required. This is critical to understand because many benefits of virtualization derive directly from the complexity and variation in all of the resources available to a server. Figure 1.1 shows the Device Manager output from a server. Notice all of the very specific types of network and storage hardware.

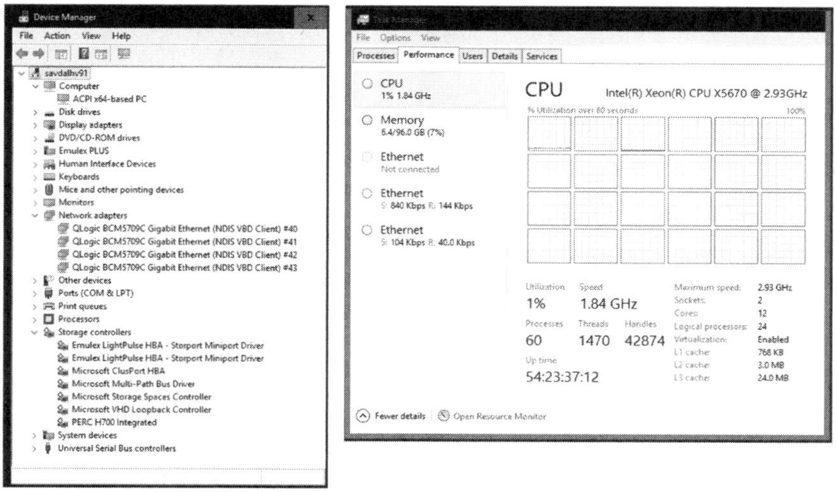

FIGURE 1.1
The Device Manager view of a typical physical server, with Task Manager showing some of its available resources

All of these resources are specific to the deployed operating system and are not easy to change in normal physical server deployments. If the boot disk from a server is placed in a different server with a different motherboard, network, or storage, there is a strong possibility the server will not boot, and it certainly will lose configuration settings and may not be able to use the hardware in the new server. The same applies to trying to restore a backup of a server to different hardware. This tight bonding between the operating system and the hardware can be a major pain point for organizations when they are considering resiliency from hardware failure but also for their disaster-recovery planning. It's necessary to have near identical hardware in the disaster-recovery location, and organizations start to find themselves locked into specific hardware vendors.

Virtualization abstracts the physical hardware from that of the created virtual machines. At a high level, virtualization allows virtual machines to be created. The virtual machines are assigned specific amounts of resources, such as CPU and memory, in addition to being given access to different networks via virtual switches. They are also assigned storage through virtual hard disks, which are just files on the local filesystem of the virtualization host or on remote storage. Figure 1.2 shows a high-level view of a virtualized environment.

FIGURE 1.2
A high-level view of a virtualization host and resources assigned to virtual machines

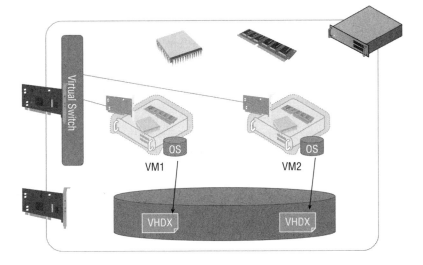

Within the virtual machine, an operating system is installed such as Windows Server 2016, Windows Server 2008, Windows 10, or a Linux distribution. No special process is needed to install the operating system into a virtual machine, and it's not even necessary for the operating system to support virtualization. However, most modern operating systems are virtualization-aware today and are considered "enlightened" to be able to understand virtualized hardware directly. The operating system installed in the virtual machine, commonly referred to as the *guest operating system*, does not see the physical hardware of the server but rather a set of virtualized hardware that is completely abstracted from the physical hardware.

Figure 1.3 shows a virtual machine (VM) that is running on the physical server shown in Figure 1.1. Notice the huge difference in what is visible. All of the same capabilities are available—the processor capability, memory (I assigned the VM only 12GB of memory, but up to 1TB can be assigned), storage, and networks—but it is all through abstracted, virtual hardware that is completely independent of the physical server on which the virtual machine is running.

FIGURE 1.3
A virtual machine running on a physical server

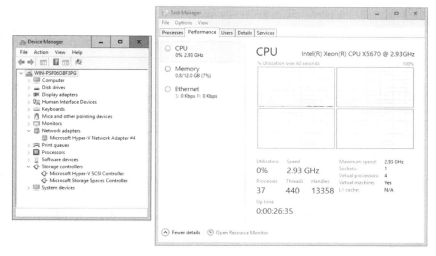

With virtualization, all virtualized operating system environments and their workloads become highly mobile between servers. A virtual machine can be moved between any two servers, provided those servers are running the same version of the hypervisor and have enough resource capacity. This enables organizations to be more flexible with their server hardware, especially in those disaster-recovery environments that now allow any hardware to be used in the disaster-recovery location as long as it runs the same hypervisor. When a backup needs to be performed, it can be performed at the hypervisor level and then at restoration, provided the new server is running the same hypervisor version. As long as this is the case, the virtual machine backup can be restored and used without additional reconfiguration or manual repair.

The next major pain point with physical servers is sizing them—deciding how much memory they need, how many processors, how much storage (although the use of SANs has removed some of the challenge of calculating the amount of local storage required), how many network connections, and what levels of redundancy. I spent many years as a consultant, and when I was specifying hardware, it always had to be based on the busiest possible time for the server. It was also based on its expected load many years from the time of purchase, because organizations wanted to ensure that a server would not need to be replaced in six months as its workload increased.

This meant servers would be purchased that had far more resources than required, especially processor resources; it was typical to see a server running at 5 percent processor utilization with maybe a peak of 15 percent at its busiest times. This was a huge waste of resources and not optimal resource utilization. However, because each OS instance ran on its own box, and often server-class hardware comes in only certain configurations, even if it was known that the processor requirement would not be high, it was not possible to procure lower-specification hardware. This same overprocurement of hardware applied to the other resources as well, such as memory, storage, and even network resources.

In most environments, different services need processor resources and memory at different times, so being able somehow to combine all of the resources and share them between operating system instances (and even modify the amounts allocated as needed) is key, and this is exactly what virtualization provides. In a virtual environment, the virtualization host has all of the resources, and these resources are then allocated to virtual machines. However, some resources such as processor and network resources can be shared between multiple virtual machines, allowing for a much greater utilization of the available resource and avoiding the utilization waste. A single server that previously ran a single OS instance with a 10 percent processor usage average could run 10 virtualized OS instances in virtual machines with most likely only additional memory being required in the server and higher IOPS storage. The details of resource sharing are covered in future chapters, but resources such as those for processors and networks can be shared between virtual machines concurrently; resources like memory and storage can be segregated between virtual machines, but they cannot actually be shared because you cannot store different pieces of information in the same physical storage block.

The best analogy is to consider your Windows desktop that is running a single OS and likely has a single processor, but that is able seemingly to run many applications all at the same time. You may be streaming a movie with Internet Explorer, sending email with Outlook, and editing a document in Word. All of these applications seem to be running at the same time, but a processor core can perform only one computation at a time (ignoring multicores and hyperthreading). In reality, though, the OS is time-slicing turns on the processor and giving each application a few milliseconds of time each cycle. With each application taking its turn on the processor very quickly, it appears as if all applications are running at the same time.

A similar concept applies to network traffic, except this time there is a finite bandwidth size and the combined network usage has to stay within that limit. Many applications can send/receive data over a shared network connection up to the maximum speed of the network. Imagine a funnel. I could be pouring Coke, Pepsi, and Dr. Pepper down the funnel, and all would pour at the same time, up to the size of the funnel. Those desktop applications are also assigned their own individual amounts of memory and disk storage. This is exactly the same for virtualization, except instead of the OS dividing up resource allocation, it's the hypervisor allocating resources to each virtual machine that is running but uses the same mechanisms.

Building on the previous benefit of higher utilization are scalability and elasticity. A physical server has a fixed set of resources that are not easily changed, which is why physical deployments are traditionally overprovisioned and architected for the busiest possible time. With a virtual environment, virtual machine resources can be dynamically changed to meet the changing needs of the workload. This dynamic nature can be enabled in various ways. For resources such as processor and network, the OS will use only what it needs, which allows the virtual machine to be assigned a large amount of processor and network resources because those resources can be shared. So while one OS is not using the resource, others can. When it comes to resources that are divided up, such as memory and storage, it's possible to add them to and remove them from a running virtual machine as needed. This type of elasticity is not possible in traditional physical deployments, and with virtualization hosts generally architected to have far more resources than in a physical OS deployment, the scalability, or maximum resource that can be assigned to a virtualized OS is much larger.

The consolidation of operating system instances onto a smaller number of more powerful servers exposes additional virtualization benefits. With a reduced number of servers that are more powerful but more highly utilized, organizations see reduced datacenter space requirements, which leads to energy savings and ultimately cost savings.

Many organizations have long struggled with a nontechnical aspect of their datacenters, and that is licensing. I cover licensing in detail later in this chapter, but when you have thousands of individual servers, each running a single operating system, it can be hard to track all of the licenses and hard to know exactly what version you need based on the capabilities required. Most important, it costs a lot of money. With virtualization, there are ways to license the virtualization hosts themselves and allow an unlimited number of virtual machines, making licensing of the OS and management software far more cost-effective.

Another challenge with a single operating system per physical server is all the islands of resources that you have to manage. Every server has its own local storage, and somehow you have to protect all of that data. Utilizing centralized storage such as a SAN for every physical server is possible but typically cost prohibitive. It's not practical to purchase Fibre Channel HBAs (cards that enable connectivity to Fibre Channel switches), Fibre Channel switches to accommodate all of the servers, and all of the cabling. Take those same servers and reduce the number of physical servers even tenfold using virtualization, and suddenly connecting everything to centralized storage is far more realistic and cost effective. The same applies to regular networking. Implementing 10Gbps networking in a datacenter for 100 servers is far more possible than it is for one with 1,000 servers.

On the opposite side of the scale from consolidation and centralization is the challenge of isolating workloads. Consider a branch location that for cost purposes has only a single server to host services for the local workers. Because there is only a single server, all roles have to run on a single OS instance without virtualization, which can lead to many complications in configuration and supportability. With virtualization, that same server can host numerous virtual machines, with each workload running in its own virtual machine, such as a virtual machine running a domain controller and DNS, another running file services, and another running a line-of-business (LOB) service. This allows services to be deployed and isolated to standard best practices. Additionally, many remote offices will deploy two virtualization servers with some kind of external storage enclosure that can be connected to both servers, or with Windows Server 2016, another option would be to deploy four servers with internal storage and leverage Storage Spaces Direct for clustered storage. This enables virtual machines to be moved between the servers, allowing high availability, which brings us to the next benefit of virtualization.

Physically deployed services that require high availability must have some native high-availability technology. With virtualization, it's still preferred to leverage the service's native high-availability capabilities, but virtualization adds options and can provide solutions where no native capability exists in the virtualized service. Virtualization can enable virtual machines to move between physical hosts with no downtime using Live Migration, and it can even provide disaster-recovery capabilities using technologies such as Hyper-V Replica. Virtualization also allows simpler backup and recovery processes by allowing backups to be taken of the entire virtual machine.

Consider the process of deploying a new service on a physical server. That server configuration has to be specified, ordered, delivered, and installed in the datacenter. Then the OS has to be installed and the actual service configured. That entire process may take a long time, which lengthens the time it takes to provision new services. Those delays may affect an organization's ability to respond to changes in the market and react to customer requirements. In a virtual environment, the provisioning of a new service consists of the creation of a new virtual machine for that service; with the right automation processes in place, that could take minutes from start to finish, instead of weeks. Because resources are pooled together in a virtual infrastructure, it is common always to run with sufficient spare capacity available to allow for new services to be provisioned as needed, and as the amount of free resources drops below a certain thresh-old, new hardware is purchased and added to the virtual infrastructure ready for additional services. Additionally, because the deployment of a new virtual machine does not require any physical infrastructure changes, the whole process can be completely automated, which helps in the speed of provisioning. By removing many manual steps, the chances of human error are removed, and with a high level of consistency between deployed environments comes a simpli-fied supportability process.

Finally, I want to touch on using public cloud services such as Microsoft Azure Infrastructure as a Service (IaaS), which allows virtual machines to be hosted on servers accessed over the Internet. When using virtualization on premises in your datacenter, and in this case specifi-cally Hyper-V, you have full compatibility between on and off premises, making it easy to move services.

There are other benefits that are specific to virtualization, such as simplified networking infrastructure using network virtualization, greater quality-of-service (QoS) controls, meter-ing, and more. However, the benefits previously mentioned are generally considered the biggest wins of virtualization. To summarize, here are the key benefits of virtualization:

- ◆ Abstraction from the underlying hardware, allowing full mobility of virtual machines

- ◆ High utilization of resources

- ◆ Scalability and elasticity

- ◆ Energy, datacenter space, and cost reduction

- ◆ Simplification and cost reduction for licensing

- ◆ Consolidation and centralization of storage and other resources

- ◆ Isolation of services

- ◆ Additional high-availability options and simpler backup/recovery

- ◆ Speed of service provisioning and automation

- ◆ Compatibility with public cloud

Ultimately, what these benefits mean to the organization is either saving money or enabling money to be made faster.

History of Hyper-V

So far in this chapter, I have not used the word *Hyper-V* very much. I have focused on the challenges of traditional datacenters and the benefits of virtualization. I now want to start looking at the changes to the various versions of Hyper-V at a high level since its introduction. This is important because it will not only enable you to understand the features available in your Hyper-V deployments if you are not yet running Windows Server 2016 Hyper-V, but also show the great advancements made with each new version. All of the features I talk about are covered in further detail throughout this book, so don't worry if the following discus-sion isn't detailed enough. I provide a high-level explanation of what they are in this part of the chapter.

I'll start with the first version of Hyper-V, which was introduced as an add-on after the Windows Server 2008 release. Hyper-V was not an update to Microsoft Virtual Server, which was a virtualization solution Microsoft acquired as part of the Connectix acquisition. Microsoft Virtual Server was not well adopted in many organizations as a virtualization solution because it was a type 2 hypervisor, whereas Hyper-V is a type 1 hypervisor. There are numerous definitions, but I think of them quite simply as follows:

Type 2 Hypervisors A type 2 hypervisor runs on a host operating system. The host operating system manages the underlying hardware; the type 2 hypervisor makes requests to the host operating system for resources and to perform actions. Because a type 2 hypervisor runs on top of a host OS, access to all of the processor rings of operating systems running in the virtual machine is limited, which generally means slower performance and less capability.

Type 1 Hypervisors A type 1 hypervisor runs directly on the bare metal of the server and directly controls and allocates resources to virtual machines. Many type 1 hypervisors take advantage of a Ring −1, which is present on processors that support hardware virtualization to run the hypervisor itself. This then allows virtual machines still to be able to access Ring 0 (kernel mode) of the processor directly for their computations, giving the best performance while still allowing the hypervisor management of the resource. All modern datacenter hypervisors are type 1 hypervisors.

It is important at this stage to realize that Hyper-V is absolutely a type 1 hypervisor. Often people think that Hyper-V is a type 2 hypervisor because of the sequence of actions for installation:

1. Install Windows Server on the physical host.

2. Enable the Hyper-V role.

3. Configure and manage virtual machines through the Windows Server instance installed on the physical host.

Someone might look at this sequence of actions and how Hyper-V is managed and come to the conclusion that the Hyper-V hypervisor is running on top of Windows Server; that is not the case at all. When the Hyper-V role is enabled on Windows Server, changes are made to the boot configuration database to configure the hypervisor to load first, and then the Windows Server operating systems runs on *top* of that hypervisor, effectively becoming a pseudo virtual machine itself. Run the command bcdedit /enum on a Hyper-V host, and it shows that the hypervisor launch type is set to automatically launch.

The Windows Server operating system becomes the management partition for the Hyper-V solution. The hypervisor itself is quite compact and needs to be as light as possible, so it's focused on interacting with compute and memory resources and controlling access for virtual machines to avoid introducing latencies in performance. The management partition works for the hypervisor, and it is tasked with various items, such as hosting worker processes to communicate with virtual machines, hosting drivers for storage and network adapter interactions, and more. However, all of the virtual machines are running directly on the hypervisor and not on the host operating system that was installed. This is best shown by looking at the Hyper-V architecture in Figure 1.4, which clearly shows the hypervisor running in Ring −1 and both the management partition and all the virtual machines running side by side on the hypervisor. The management partition does have some additional privileges, capabilities, and hardware access beyond that of a regular virtual machine, but it is still running on the hypervisor.

FIGURE 1.4
Hyper-V architecture

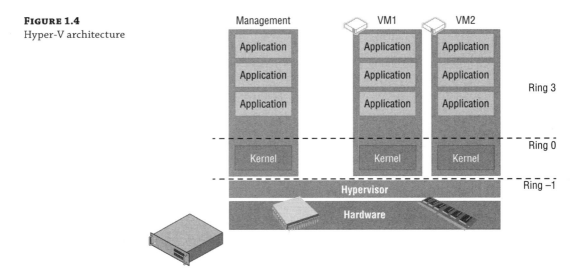

WHAT IS A PARTITION?

In the discussion of the history of Hyper-V, I referred to a management partition. The hypervisor runs directly on the hardware and assigns different amounts of resources to each virtual environment. These virtual environments can also be referred to as *partitions*, because they are partitions of the underlying resource. Because the management partition is not a true virtual machine (because not all of its resources are virtualized) and it has privileged access, it is referred to as the *management partition* or the *parent partition*. Although it can be confusing, it's also common to see the management partition referred to as the *host* because it is the OS closest to the hardware and is directly installed on the server. Sometimes virtual machines are referred to as *child partitions* or *guest partitions*.

Windows Server 2008 Hyper-V Features

The initial version of Hyper-V provided a solid foundation for virtualization and a fairly limited set of additional capabilities. As with all versions of Hyper-V, the processors must support hardware-assisted virtualization (AMD-V or Intel VT) and also Data Execution Prevention (DEP). Although Hyper-V is available only on 64-bit versions of Windows Server, it is possible to run both 32-bit and 64-bit operating systems. The initial version of Hyper-V included the following key capabilities:

◆ Up to 64GB of memory per VM

◆ Symmetric multiprocessing (SMP) VMs (up to four virtual CPUs [vCPUs] each). However, the exact number differed depending on the guest operating system. For example, four vCPUs were supported on Windows Server 2008 SP2 guests, but only two were on Windows Server 2003 SP2. The full list is available at:

    http://technet.microsoft.com/en-us/library/cc794868(v=ws.10).aspx

◆ Virtual Hard Disk (VHD) format for virtualized storage up to 2TB in size with multiple VHDs supported for each VM on either a virtual IDE controller or a virtual SCSI controller. VMs had to be booted from a VHD attached to a virtual IDE controller, but data VHDs could be connected to a virtual SCSI controller with higher performance through the virtual SCSI controller. Only 4 devices could be connected to the IDE controller (2 to each of the 2 IDE controllers), while each of the 4 virtual SCSI controllers supported up to 64 devices, each allowing up to 256 VHDs attached via the virtual SCSI.

◆ Leveraged failover clustering for high availability

◆ Ability to move virtual machines between hosts in a cluster with minimal downtime using quick migration. Quick migration worked by pausing the virtual machine and saving the device, processor, and memory content to a file on the cluster storage. It then moved that storage to another host in the cluster, reading the device, processor, and memory content into a newly staged virtual machine on the target and starting it. Depending on the amount of memory in the virtual machine, this may have meant minutes of downtime and the definite disconnect of any TCP connections. This was one of the biggest weaknesses of the Windows Server 2008 Hyper-V solution.

◆ Supported VSS (Volume Shadow copy Service) live backup of virtual machines. This allowed a backup to be taken of a virtual machine from the host operating system. The VSS request for the backup was then communicated to the virtual machine's guest operating system through the Hyper-V Integration Services to ensure that the application data in the VM was in an application-consistent state and suitable for a backup.

◆ The ability to create VM snapshots, which are point-in-time captures of a virtual machine's complete state (including memory and disk). This allowed a VM to be rolled back to any of these snapshots. The use of the term *snapshots* was confusing, because the term is also used in the backup VSS nomenclature, but in this case it's referring to snapshots used in the backup process, which are different from VM snapshots. In Windows Server 2012 R2, VM snapshots are now called *checkpoints* to help remove this confusion.

◆ Pass-through disk access for VMs was possible even though not generally recommended. It was sometimes required if VMs needed access to single volumes greater than 2TB in size (which was the VHD limit).

◆ Integration services available for supported guest operating systems, allowing capabilities such as heartbeat, mouse/keyboard interaction, backup services, time synchronization, and shutdown

◆ Multiple virtual networks could be created with support for 10Gbps and VLANs.

Windows Server 2008 R2 Changes

While Windows Server 2008 Hyper-V offered a solid foundation and a reliable solution for a v1, several limitations stopped Hyper-V from being seriously considered in many environments, among them the ability to move virtual machines between hosts in a cluster with no downtime. There were two challenges for Hyper-V to enable this:

◆ The VM had to be paused to enable the memory, processor, and device state to be saved to disk.

◆ NTFS is not a shared filesystem and can be mounted by only one OS at a time, which means that when a virtual machine moves between hosts in a cluster, the logical unit number, or LUN (which is a block of storage from a SAN), must be dismounted from the source host and mounted on the target host. This takes time.

Windows Server 2008 R2 solved both of these challenges. First, a new technology called Live Migration was introduced. Live Migration enabled the memory of a virtual machine and the virtual machine's state to be replicated to another host while the virtual machine was still running and then switched over to the new host with no downtime. I cover this in detail in Chapter 7, "Failover Clustering and Migration Technologies," but the technology worked at a high level using the following steps:

1. A container VM was created on the target host using the existing VM's configuration.

2. The memory of the VM was copied from the source to the target VM.

3. Because the VM was still running while the memory was copied, some of the memory content changed. Those dirty pages were copied over again. This process repeated numerous iterations, with the number of dirty pages shrinking by a magnitude each iteration, so the time to copy the dirty pages shrank greatly.

4. Once the number of dirty pages was very small, the VM was paused and the remaining memory pages were copied over along with the processor and device state.

5. The VM was resumed on the target Hyper-V host.

6. A reverse unsolicited ARP was sent over the network, notifying routing devices that the VM's IP address was moved.

The whole process can be seen in Figure 1.5. You may be concerned about Step 4, the VM being paused for a copy of the final few pages of dirty memory. This is common across all hypervisors and is necessary; however, only milliseconds of time are involved, so it's too small to notice and well below the TCP connection time-out, which means no connections to the server would be lost.

FIGURE 1.5
A high-level view of the Live Migration process

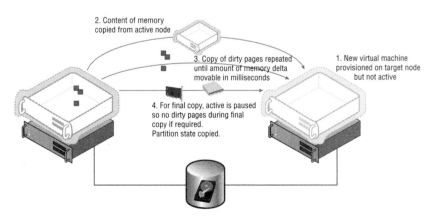

Live Migration solved the problem of pausing the virtual machine to copy its memory between hosts. It did not, however, solve the problem that NTFS couldn't be shared, so the LUN containing the VM had to be dismounted and mounted, which took time. A second new technology solved this problem: *Cluster Shared Volumes*, or CSV.

CSV allows an NTFS-formatted LUN to be available simultaneously to all hosts in the cluster. Every host can read and write to the CSV volume, which removes the need to dismount and mount the LUN as VMs move between hosts. This also solved the problem of having to have one LUN for every VM to enable each VM to be moved independently of other VMs. (The LUN had to move when the VM moved, which meant that if other VMs were stored on the same LUN, those VMs would also have to move.) With CSV, many VMs could be stored on a single CSV volume, with VMs running throughout all hosts in the cluster. Behind the scenes, CSV still leverages NTFS, but it controls the writing of Metadata to the volume to a single host for each CSV volume to avoid any risk of NTFS corruption. This is also explained in detail in Chapter 7.

With Live Migration and CSV technologies working in unison, the ability to move a virtual machine between hosts in a cluster with no downtime was now possible and removed a major obstacle to the adoption of Hyper-V. Windows Server 2008 R2 included other enhancements:

◆ A processor compatibility mode that allowed a virtual machine to be migrated between different versions of the same processor family. When a guest OS started within a virtual machine, it would commonly query the processor to find out all of the instruction sets available, as would some applications, and those instruction sets would possibly be used. If a virtual machine was then moved to another host with a different processor version that did not support that instruction set, the application/OS would crash when it tried to use it. Download Coreinfo from:

    http://technet.microsoft.com/en-us/sysinternals/cc835722.aspx

    and execute it with the -f switch. This will show which instruction sets are supported on your processor. When the processor compatibility feature was enabled for a virtual machine, the high-level instruction sets were masked from the VM so it did not use them, allowing the VM to be moved between different versions of the processor.

◆ Hot-add of storage to the SCSI bus. This enabled additional VHDs to be added to a virtual machine without shutting it down.

◆ Network performance improvements, including support for jumbo frames, Virtual Machine Queues (VMQs), and allowing the use of NIC Teaming implemented by network drivers

◆ If the processor supported it, Second Level Address Translation (SLAT), which allowed the processor to own the mapping of virtual memory to physical memory, therefore reducing overhead on the hypervisor. SLAT is used by Hyper-V when available.

Windows Server 2008 R2 Service Pack 1

It's not common for a service pack to bring new features, but Windows Server 2008 R2 had one key feature missing, and this was the ability to change dynamically the amount of memory available to a virtual machine. SP1 for Windows Server 2008 R2 added the Dynamic Memory feature, which was different from how other hypervisors handled memory optimization.

Dynamic Memory worked by configuring a starting amount of memory and a maximum amount of memory. Hyper-V would then monitor the actual amount of memory being used within the virtual machine by processes via the integration services. If the amount of available memory dropped below a certain buffer threshold, additional memory was added to the virtual machine if it was physically available. If a virtual machine no longer needed all of its memory, some was reclaimed for use with other virtual machines. This enabled Hyper-V to achieve great optimization of VM memory and maximize the number of virtual machines that could run on a host.

The other new technology in Service Pack 1 was RemoteFX, based on technologies obtained through the Calista Technologies acquisition. The RemoteFX technology was focused on Virtual Desktop Infrastructure (VDI) deployments running on Hyper-V and making the VDI experience as rich as possible no matter the capabilities of the client device. RemoteFX consisted of three technologies to offer this rich capability:

◆ The first was the ability to virtualize a GPU (Graphical Processing Unit) in the Hyper-V server and then assign virtual GPUs to virtual machines. This works in a similar way to how CPUs are carved up between virtual machines. Once a virtual machine was assigned a vGPU, the OS within that VM could perform native DirectX processing using the GPU, allowing graphically rich applications to run, such as videoconferencing, Silverlight and Flash applications, and any DirectX application. As a demonstration, I installed Halo 2 in a RemoteFX-enabled virtual machine and played it over the network; you can see this at http://youtu.be/CYiLGxfZRTA. Without RemoteFX, some types of media playback would depend on the capability of the client machine, and certainly any application that required DirectX would not run. The key item is that all the graphical rendering is on the Hyper-V host's GPU and not on the local client.

◆ The second technology was related to the rich graphical capability and was an updated codec that was used to compress and uncompress the screen updates over the network.

◆ The final technology enabled USB device redirection at a port level. Typically, with Remote Desktop Protocol (RDP), certain types of devices could be used in remote sessions, such as a keyboard, a mouse, a printer, and some devices with an inbox such as a scanner. However, many other types of devices and multifunction devices would not work. RemoteFX USB redirection enabled any USB device to be used in a remote session by redirecting at a USB port level all USB request blocks (URBs).

Note that the last two components of RemoteFX, the codec and USB redirection, are not Hyper-V features but rather updates to RDP. I cover them because they are part of the RemoteFX feature family and complete the remote client experience.

The combination of Dynamic Memory and RemoteFX made Hyper-V a powerful platform for VDI solutions, and Dynamic Memory on its own was useful for most server virtual machines as well.

Windows Server 2012 Hyper-V Changes

Windows Server 2012 put Hyper-V to the top of the list of the true top hypervisors by closing nearly every gap it had with other hypervisors and leapfrogging the competition in many areas. This entire book focuses on many of the changes in Windows Server 2012, but here I call out some of the biggest improvements and new features.

One of the key reasons for the huge advancement of Hyper-V in Windows Server 2012 was not only the big focus on virtualization (to enable Hyper-V to compete and win against the competition) but also the success of Microsoft's public cloud service, Azure. I briefly cover the types of cloud services later in this chapter and in far more detail later in the book, but for now, realize that Azure is one of the largest public cloud services that exists. It powers many of Microsoft's cloud offerings and runs on Windows Server 2012 Hyper-V. All of the knowledge Microsoft gained operating Azure and the enhancements it needed went into Windows Server 2012, and the engineering teams are now cloud-first focused, creating and enhancing technologies that are then made available as part of new Windows Server versions. This is one of the reasons the release cadence of Windows Server has changed to an annual release cycle. Combining the development for the public and private cloud solutions makes Hyper-V a much stronger solution, which is good news for organizations using Hyper-V.

SCALABILITY

The first grouping of changes relates to scalability, which previously was one of the weakest areas. Windows Server 2008 R2 did not change the scalability of virtual machines from Windows Server 2008 (although there were some modest improvements to the Hyper-V host limits). Windows Server 2012 made some big changes, as shown in Table 1.1.

TABLE 1.1:   Scalability Changes from Windows Server 2008 R2 to Windows Server 2012

ATTRIBUTE	WINDOWS 2008 R2	WINDOWS 2012	IMPROVEMENT
Logical processors on hardware	64	320 (640 without Hyper-V role)	> 5x
LP:VP ratio	8:1 (12:1 for Windows 7 VDI)	No limit	
Physical memory	1TB	4TB	4x
Virtual processors per host	512	2,048	4x
Virtual processors per virtual machine	4	64 (includes NUMA awareness)	16x
Memory per virtual machine	64GB	1TB	16x
Active virtual machines per host	384	1,024	2.5x
Maximum cluster nodes	16	64	4x
Maximum cluster virtual machines	1,000	8,000	8x
Maximum VHD size	2TB	64TB (with VHDX)	32x

Some of the new scalability limits may seem ridiculously large: 64TB virtual hard disks, 1TB of memory in a single VM, and even 64 vCPUs in a single VM. But the point now is that almost any workload can be virtualized with Windows Server 2012 Hyper-V. To illustrate this capability to virtualize almost any workload, Microsoft released a statement that more than 99 percent of the world's SQL Server deployments could now run on Windows Server 2012 Hyper-V. One aspect that is important to the 64TB VHDX scalability is that it removes most scenarios of having to use pass-through storage, which maps a virtual machine directly to raw storage. The goal of virtualization is to abstract the virtual machine environment from the physical hardware. Directly mapping a virtual machine to physical storage breaks this abstraction and stops some features of Hyper-V from being used, such as checkpoints, Live Migration, and Hyper-V Replica. In all my years of consulting, I have never seen an NTFS volume 64TB in size. In fact, the biggest I have heard of is 14TB, but a 64TB limit means that VHDX scalability would not limit the storage workloads that could be virtualized.

Why Most Volumes Are Less Than 2TB

In most environments, it's fairly uncommon to see NTFS volumes greater than 2TB. One reason is that master boot record (MBR) partitioning had a limit of 2TB. The newer GUID Partition Table (GPT) removed this limitation, but volumes still stayed at around 2TB. Another reason concerns the unit of recoverability. Any set of data is typically restricted to the amount of data that can be restored in the required time frame. Legacy backup/restore solutions that were tape based could limit how large data sets would be, but modern backup/restore solutions that are primarily disk-based remove this type of limit.

The number one reason for limits on volumes is a corruption occurring on the NTFS volume. If a corruption occurs, the ChkDsk process must be run, which takes the volume offline while the entire disk is scanned and problems are repaired. Depending on the disk subsystem and its size, this process could take hours or even days. The larger the volume, the longer ChkDsk will take to run and the longer the volume would be offline. Companies would limit the size of volumes to minimize the potential time a volume would be offline if ChkDsk had to be run. In Windows Server 2012, ChkDsk has been rearchitected to no longer take the volume offline during the search for errors. Instead, it has to take the disk offline only to actually fix the problems discovered during an online scan. The maximum possible offline time for a volume is now 8 seconds, no matter how large the volume. With this change, we can expect to see larger NTFS volumes as organizations adopt Windows Server 2012 and above.

Also important to note about scalability is that only very large virtual machines can be created with tens of virtual processors, but the non-uniform memory access (NUMA) topology is passed to the virtual machine, enabling the most optimal levels of performance. This scalability applies to both Windows guest operating systems and Linux, as Figure 1.6 shows with a 64 vCPU Linux virtual machine. Also note in the figure the awareness of the NUMA nodes. This was another investment area in Windows Server 2012: making Linux a first-class guest operating system. Nearly every feature of Hyper-V worked equally for Windows guests and Linux guests.

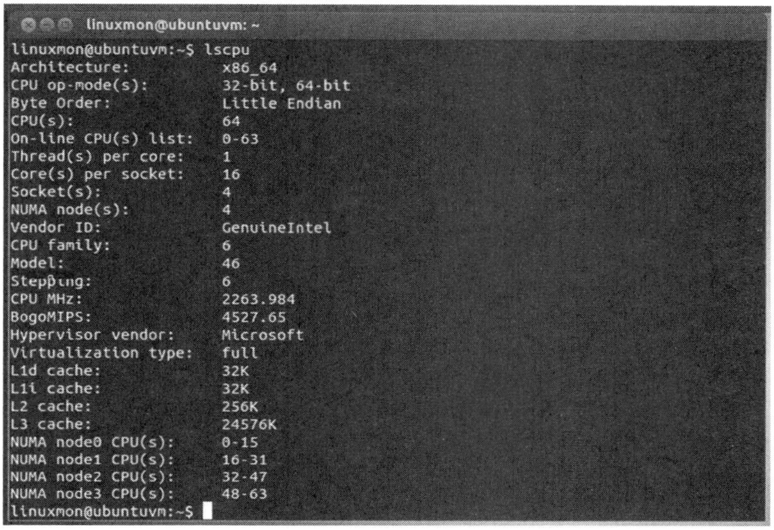

FIGURE 1.6
Linux virtual machine
running on Windows
Server 2012 Hyper-V
with 64 vCPUs

```
● ● ●   linuxmon@ubuntuvm: ~
linuxmon@ubuntuvm:~$ lscpu
Architecture:          x86_64
CPU op-mode(s):        32-bit, 64-bit
Byte Order:            Little Endian
CPU(s):                64
On-line CPU(s) list:   0-63
Thread(s) per core:    1
Core(s) per socket:    16
Socket(s):             4
NUMA node(s):          4
Vendor ID:             GenuineIntel
CPU family:            6
Model:                 46
Stepping:              6
CPU MHz:               2263.984
BogoMIPS:              4527.65
Hypervisor vendor:     Microsoft
Virtualization type:   full
L1d cache:             32K
L1i cache:             32K
L2 cache:              256K
L3 cache:              24576K
NUMA node0 CPU(s):     0-15
NUMA node1 CPU(s):     16-31
NUMA node2 CPU(s):     32-47
NUMA node3 CPU(s):     48-63
linuxmon@ubuntuvm:~$ █
```

MOBILITY AND AVAILABILITY

As virtual machines became more scalable, the workloads that could be virtualized increased exponentially, which makes keeping the virtual machines available even more important. Windows Server 2012 made great advancements to the mobility and resiliency of virtual machines. Windows Server 2008 R2 had introduced Live Migration as a means to move virtual machines between nodes in a cluster that had shared storage. Windows Server 2012 took this to the next level by allowing multiple concurrent Live Migrations, which it would autoscale based on available bandwidth and would queue until they could be performed based on network bandwidth availability.

A big shift for Hyper-V architecture options was support of SMB 3 for the storage of virtual machines. This allows Hyper-V virtual machines to be run from SMB 3 file shares, enabling a new file-based storage option. This change made it possible for Windows Server 2012 file-share clusters to be used as the shared storage for Hyper-V environments in addition to any NAS or SAN solutions that support SMB 3. By using SMB 3 as the storage for virtual machines, an additional type of Live Migration was enabled, SMB Live Migration, which enabled virtual machines to be moved between *any* two Windows Server 2012 Hyper-V hosts, even if they were not part of a cluster. The Live Migration and SMB Live Migration processes remained similar, except that the handles and locks to the files on the SMB share are transferred between hosts as part of the SMB Live Migration process.

Storage Live Migration was introduced with Windows Server 2012 Hyper-V. It allows all of the storage-related items of a virtual machine to be moved between supported storage mediums with no downtime to the virtual machine. This included the virtual machine's configuration files, checkpoint data, smart paging files, and virtual hard disks. Any and all of these can be moved with no interruption to the virtual machine's availability. While this was an important feature to have because it was available in other virtualization solutions, its use must be accompanied with extreme caution. Consider the amount of I/O required to move the storage of a virtual machine, both reading from the source and writing to the target. If a storage subsystem is having performance issues, which is a reason to want to move the virtual machine, then performing a storage migration would add substantial I/O load and would likely worsen the situation in the short term. It is, however, an important feature to have and enables the true "Wow" mobility feature of Windows Server 2012, Shared Nothing Live Migration.

The ability to move a virtual machine without any constraints is the utopian goal of any virtualization solution: to be able to move a virtual machine between any hosts in the datacenter and between different storage subsystems without any downtime using only a 1Gbps network connection. Windows Server 2012 delivers this in Windows Server 2012 with Shared Nothing Live Migration. Shared Nothing Live Migration allows a virtual machine to be moved between stand-alone hosts, from a cluster to a stand-alone, from a stand-alone to a cluster, or from cluster to cluster without any interruption to virtual machine communication. A Storage Live Migration is performed first if required to move the storage of the virtual machine to the destination. Then it is synchronized while the memory of the virtual machine is copied, and synchronized again before the virtual machine is flipped and started on the destination. Being able to move virtual machines anywhere in the datacenter with no downtime is a useful capability, but the same cautions related to Storage Live Migrations apply—understand the impacts of moving virtual machines.

Mobility is important for moving virtual machines in planned scenarios to enable hardware and software maintenance on hosts without affecting the availability of virtual workloads. Beyond that, though, is making services available in unplanned events such as power outages, host crashes, and natural disasters. Windows Server 2012 greatly improved Failover Clustering, which is the backbone of Hyper-V high availability. However, what many customers asked for was a disaster-recovery (DR) feature that would allow an asynchronous replication of virtual machines from one datacenter to another. Hyper-V Replica provides this capability exactly, allowing the virtualized storage of a virtual machine to be replicated to a DR location Hyper-V server every 5 minutes in addition to providing numerous failover options, including the ability to test failover without impacting production replication. I cover high availability and disaster recovery in great detail later in the book, and I don't consider Hyper-V Replica the answer to all DR situations. Hyper-V Replica, which provides asynchronous replication between a primary VM and a replica VM, is one available tool that works well in specific scenarios.

WHY IS ASYNCHRONOUS REPLICATION A GOOD THING FOR DISASTER RECOVERY?

Typically, synchronous is best for any kind of replication. With synchronous replication, a change made to the primary store is not committed until it is also written to the secondary store. For the best assurance of data integrity and to ensure no loss, this is a good thing. However, synchronous replication has a substantial cost. The connectivity required for synchronous replication needs to be resilient and fast enough, with a low enough latency to ensure that the performance of the primary workload is not negatively affected. For the replication of a virtual machine across datacenters, only the highest levels of connectivity would enable the storage replication without affecting the primary workload. Although these solutions are possible, they are typically part of SAN solutions, which are usually costly. With asynchronous replication, the primary workload is not affected, and the changes are replicated to the secondary store as quickly as possible or on a fixed interval. This achieves a good level of protection without requiring very fast, low-latency network connections, but it is not real-time replication. In the event of an unplanned failover to the DR site, a few minutes of data may be lost, but in a true disaster, a few minutes of state loss is typically accepted. Asynchronous brings disaster recovery to all workloads rather than just the tier 1 services that can utilize SAN-level synchronous replication.

OTHER CAPABILITIES

Windows Server 2012 Hyper-V introduced many other capabilities that greatly change virtual environments:

◆ Virtual Fibre Channel support that allows virtual machines to communicate directly with Fibre Channel–connected SANs, which is a necessity for guest clustering scenarios that need shared storage and cannot use iSCSI

◆ Network virtualizing that enables complete abstraction of the network viewed by virtual machines from the physical network fabric, enabling complete isolation between virtual environments and also enabling environments to span multiple datacenters without having to modify IP configuration

◆ SR-IOV(Single Root I/O Virtualization) and dynamic VMQ for the highest level of virtual machine network performance

◆ Improvements to Dynamic Memory

When I created presentations for Windows Server 2012 Hyper-V, I used a single slide that showcased the majority of the new Hyper-V features (Figure 1.7) and, as noted, all of the new capabilities, none of which affected the ability to live-migrate virtual machines. These technologies are all covered throughout this book.

FIGURE 1.7
The major new features of Windows Server 2012 Hyper-V

Hyper-V in Windows Server 2012

- No VP:LP limits
- 64TB VHDX
- 64-node clusters
- 4,000 VMs per cluster and 1,000 VMs per node
- 32 vCPUs and 1TB of RAM per VM
- Offloaded Data Transfer (ODX)
- BitLocker Cluster Shared Volumes (CSV)
- Virtual Fibre Channel
- Storage spaces and thin provisioning
- SMB support
- Native NIC Teaming
- Software QoS and hardware QoS with DCB
- Dynamic VMQ and SR-IOV
- Extensible switch
- PVLAN
- Network virtualization (GRE and IP-rewrite)
- Concurrent Live Migrations
- Live Migration queuing in box
- Live storage move
- Shared Nothing Live Migration
- Hyper-V replica
- New CPU instruction support

- VM import raw XML file. Auto "fix up"
- NUMA topology presented to guest
- Predictive failure analysis (PFA) support
- Isolate HW errors and perform VM actions
- Storage and network metering
- Average CPU and memory metering
- Persistent metrics
- Live VHD merge (snapshot)
- Live new parent
- 4K disk support
- Anti-affinity VM rules in cluster
- VMConnect for RemoteFX
- PowerShell for everything
- DHCP guard
- Router guard
- Monitor mode
- Ipsec task offload
- VM trunk mode
- Resource pools (network and storage)
- Maintenance mode
- Dynamic memory 2.0 (min, start, max)
- Better linux support (part of linux distros)

I have focused on the changes to Hyper-V so far. However, many other changes in Windows Server 2012 enabled Windows Server 2012 to be an even better foundation for many Hyper-V services, such as changes to Failover Clustering, the new SMB 3 protocol, configuration levels that enable a server to be switched between server core and server via a GUI without having to reinstall, native NIC Teaming, Server Manager, PowerShell v3, and much more. In addition, I cover the non-Hyper-V features of Windows Server throughout this book where appropriate and where they bring value to a virtual experience.

Windows Server 2012 R2

I look at Windows Server 2012 Hyper-V as a whole new generation of Hyper-V from the previous versions. It took Hyper-V to new levels of scalability and functionality and made it a true enterprise hypervisor, bringing in major new technologies such as Hyper-V Replica, Network Virtualization, SMB 3 usage, and Live Migration. I look at Windows Server 2012 R2 as the continued advancement of the Hyper-V technology, refining many of the capabilities based on the feedback of enterprises that deployed Windows Server 2012 Hyper-V. Many organizations will welcome the 2012 R2 enhancements.

No scalability changes were made in Windows Server 2012 R2. I think most people would agree that the scalability of Windows Server 2012 meets today's and tomorrow's requirements. The focus was on improving the utilization of environments and fully embracing the technologies that companies were utilizing.

GENERATION 2 VIRTUAL MACHINE

The format of virtual machines has not really changed since the first version of Hyper-V. Ten years ago, virtual machines required a lot of emulated hardware, because operating systems didn't natively understand virtualization. This is no longer true today. Nearly all modern operating systems understand virtualization and the synthetic types of resources available, making the emulated hardware previously required for compatibility not required.

Windows Server 2012 R2 introduces a new type of virtual machine, a generation 2 virtual machine, which removes all of the legacy emulated hardware previously present and shifts to a UEFI-based (User Extensible Firmware Interface) virtual machine exclusively using synthetic SCSI (allowing virtual machines to now boot from the synthetic SCSI) and network adapters (including PXE boot from a synthetic network adapter). Generation 1 virtual machines are still available, and there is no real performance improvement of a generation 1 vs. generation 2 virtual machine after the OS is installed and running, but a generation 2 virtual machine will install and boot faster.

STORAGE ENHANCEMENTS

One feature that did not make Windows Server 2012 Hyper-V was the capability to dynamically resize a VHDX attached to a running machine. For some organizations, just adding VHD/VHDX files to a running virtual machine was not sufficient. 2012 R2 Hyper-V supports the dynamic resizing of VHDX files attached to the virtual machine's SCSI controller. This dynamic resizing supports both increasing the size and reducing the size, provided sufficient unpartitioned space exists within the VHDX file.

VHDX files can be shared among multiple virtual machines in 2012 R2 Hyper-V; and these shared VHDX files, which are hosted on Cluster Shared Volumes or a scale-out file server, are seen to the virtual machines as shared SAS storage and can be used as shared storage within the virtual machine for guest clustering scenarios. This removes the previous requirement to use iSCSI or virtual Fibre Channel to enable shared storage within virtual machines for guest clustering purposes.

Resource metering was introduced in 2012 Hyper-V for processor, memory, and network, but not storage (other than the amount of storage used). In Windows Server 2012 R2, the resource metering is expanded to give more detail on the I/O profiles of storage, including average IOPS and data read and written. 2012 R2 also allows QoS to be used with storage to restrict the maximum IOPS of each individual virtual hard disk and also can alert administrators if the IOPS drops below a certain threshold.

MOBILITY AND AVAILABILITY

Live Migration in Windows Server 2012 may seem to be the perfect solution, covering all scenarios, but in 2012 R2, it has been made more efficient. The Windows 2012 Live Migration method of copying memory over the networks specified for Live Migration is still available in 2012 R2. However, the default now utilizes compression, which reduces the amount of data sent over the network, thus reducing Live Migration durations potentially by a factor of five at the expense of some extra CPU cycles to both compress the memory at the source and decompress at the target. Another option is to utilize SMB Direct as the transport. This may not seem like a good option initially, but the goal is to use it if the network adapters support remote direct memory access (RDMA), which allows it to be used; SMB Direct will be faster than even compressed Live Migration, but it uses almost no CPU. Windows Server 2012 R2 also allows Live Migration from Windows Server 2012, which allows organizations to migrate from 2012 to 2012 R2 without downtime for virtual machines.

Hyper-V Replica is also enhanced to allow different choices for the frequency of the asynchronous replication of the storage changes. The 5-minute frequency from Windows 2012 Hyper-V is still available, but additional options of 30 seconds and 15 minutes are also now offered (see Figure 1.8). Extended Hyper-V Replica can be configured, allowing a replica to be created of a replica. Note that the extended replica is sourced from the existing replica and not from the original virtual machine. This is a useful capability for organizations using Hyper-V Replica within a datacenter who also want an additional replica in a separate datacenter for true DR.

FIGURE 1.8
Extended Hyper-V Replica allows different replication intervals between the replicas

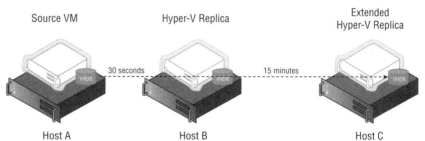

Source VM   Hyper-V Replica   Extended Hyper-V Replica

30 seconds   15 minutes

Host A   Host B   Host C

OTHER CAPABILITIES

One major new feature in Windows Server 2012 R2 is the inclusion of a network virtualization gateway, which is critical to allowing different virtual networks to communicate and also to be able to communicate with the physical network fabric. Prior to 2012 R2, a hardware gateway was required, and there really were not many of them.

In 2012 R2, it's possible to export virtual machines and virtual machine checkpoints while they are running, enabling a simple cloning process that can be useful, especially in development and testing environments.

More capabilities were added for Linux virtual machines, including Dynamic Memory, live backup offering file consistency, and Hyper-V Replica IP reconfiguration during failover.

Activation can be a pain point in virtual environments. In Windows Server 2012 R2 Hyper-V, if the Hyper-V host is running Datacenter edition and is activated, then any Windows Server 2012 R2 virtual machine (Essentials, Standard, or Datacenter) on the server will automatically activate. No need for KMS (Key Management Service) or Active Directory–Based Activation (ADBA). If the VM leaves the host, it will deactivate. The only required action is to use the Automatic Virtual Machine Activation key in the guest OS, which can be found at the following location:

```
http://technet.microsoft.com/en-us/library/dn303421.aspx
```

Windows Server 2016

Windows Server 2016 continues the evolution of Windows and Hyper-V with a key theme of the cloud fabric that drives a number of innovations, including how applications are hosted and security. Providing a platform that can host the latest "born-in-the-cloud applications" while being used on premises, in Azure, and by hosting partners is central to the Windows Server 2016 release.

Windows Server 2016 makes some major changes to the scalability of the hypervisor host and the VMs as shown in Table 1.2.

TABLE 1.2:   Windows Server 2016 Scalability Improvements

RESOURCE MAXIMUM	WINDOWS SERVER 2012/2012 R2	WINDOWS SERVER 2016
Physical (host) Memory	4 TB	24 TB (6x improvement)
Physical (host) Logical Processor	320	512
VM Memory	1 TB	12 TB (12x improvement)
VM vCPUs	64 vCPUs	240 vCPUs (3.75x improvement)

```
https://blogs.technet.microsoft.com/windowsserver/2016/08/25/windows-server-
scalability-and-more/
```

CONTAINERS AND NESTED VIRTUALIZATION

Containers provide a sandbox for creating applications; these containers can contain the application, configuration, and details of dependencies such as libraries and runtimes. This enables simple and consistent deployment of applications, isolation from other applications, centralized management and storage, in addition to granular resource control.

Containers have been available in Linux distributions for a while and have gained adoption with Docker, which offered a standardized management solution, container technology, and library. Windows Server 2016 brings container technology to Windows for Windows applications in two types: Windows Containers and Hyper-V Containers that, while utilizing the same container technology, enable a deployment time choice to be made as to the level of isolation required for the application: user mode or kernel mode isolation. Management can be performed using PowerShell or Docker.

Enabling the kernel-mode isolation capability via Hyper-V Containers requires creating virtual machines that previously would have been impossible if the container host OS was a virtual machine, as creating a VM within a VM (nested virtualization) was not possible. Windows Server 2016 enables nested virtualization for Hyper-V Containers and general nested virtualization needs.

SHIELDED VMS

Shielded VMs provide protection for the data and state of the VM against inspection, theft, and tampering from administrator privileges. Shielded VMs work for generation 2 VMs that provide the necessary Secure Boot, UEFI firmware, and virtual TPM (Trusted Platform Module) (vTPM) 2 support required. While the Hyper-V hosts must be running Windows Server 2016, the guest operating system in the VM can be Windows Server 2012 or above and, shortly after the Windows Server 2016 release, Linux guest VMs.

A new Host Guardian Service instance is deployed in the environment, which will store the keys required to run shielded VMs for authorized Hyper-V hosts if they can prove that they're healthy through various types of attestation. A shielded VM provides the following benefits:

◆ BitLocker-encrypted disks

◆ A hardened VM worker process (VMWP) that helps prevent inspection and tampering

◆ Automatically encrypted Live Migration traffic as well as encryption of its runtime state file, saved state, checkpoints, and even Hyper-V Replica files

◆ No console access in addition to blocking PowerShell Direct, Guest File Copy Integration Components, and other services that provide possible paths from a user or process with administrative privileges to the VM

OTHER CAPABILITIES

Windows Server 2016 provides two distinct groups of new capabilities for Hyper-V: those that are part of the Hyper-V role and those that the Hyper-V role will benefit from. Both are equally important in many scenarios, but there is a definite theme of enabling Windows Server 2016 and Hyper-V to be the definitive platform for the cloud on-premises, in hosting partners, and in Microsoft's own Azure public cloud for Windows and Linux workloads. Customers will have a choice of how to deploy their services without having to change how they write their applications and complete hybrid options.

When first considering the Hyper-V role specifically, there is a new VM hardware version available, version 7, that enables the new features discussed in the rest of this section. A version 7 virtual machine can be used only on a Windows Server 2016 host and uses a new binary VMCX configuration file instead of the old XML-based configuration that was prone to corruption. Generation 2 VMs can now have memory and network adapters hot-added and removed, providing more flexibility in VM resource configuration. Virtual TPMs are also now available for generation 2, hardware version 7 VMs, enabling high-security features such as shielded VMs and BitLocker. Linux VMs can now use the Secure Boot feature initially introduced for Windows VMs in Windows Server 2012 R2.

When looking at the rest of Windows Server 2016, many of the features, while usable by many technologies, certainly have Hyper-V as the focus role that will benefit from the technology. The new Nano Server deployment option for Windows Server, which features a completely refactored architecture that is a fraction of the size of a Server Core deployment, is the recommended option for cloud fabric servers, Hyper-V servers, and file servers, in addition to born-in-the-cloud application servers. Nano Servers are quick to deploy, require less patching and rebooting, and have no real local interface, but they can be managed remotely in rich ways. Windows Server 2016 has new builds released at a far greater pace than the regular once-every-two-years frequency to which we have grown accustomed. To enable easy adoption of new builds, rolling upgrades will be supported that allow a mix of Windows Server 2016 builds in a single cluster, and this functionality also extends to Windows Server 2012 R2, allowing organizations to add Windows Server 2016 nodes in their existing Windows Server 2012 R2 clusters. Major new storage technologies enable new types of replication and new ways to use direct-attached storage in cluster nodes.

Licensing of Hyper-V

The most painful aspect of most virtual environments is understanding the licensing of the hypervisor, the operating systems running in the virtual machines, and the management software. I don't want to go into great detail about licensing in this book because, despite new licensing agreements, special combinations of licensing still exist through agreements with programs such as Server and Cloud Enrollment (SCE) and the legacy Enrollment for Core Infrastructure (ECI). For most organizations, the licensing is simple with Windows Server 2012 and above; however, changes in Windows Server 2016 are important to understand.

One Operating System (Well Two, but Really One) with Windows Server 2012 and 2012 R2

Prior to Windows Server 2012, numerous versions of Windows Server existed—Web, Standard, Enterprise, and Datacenter—and each version had different capabilities and different limits and were licensed differently. That all goes away in Windows Server 2012 and above; for medium and large companies, there are only two versions of Windows Server: Windows Server 2012 R2 Standard and Windows Server 2012 R2 Datacenter. Both versions are *exactly* the same:

◆ They have the same limits, both supporting 64 processor sockets, 640 logical processors (320 with Hyper-V role enabled), and 4TB of memory.

◆ Both have the same roles and features; for example, even Standard has Failover Clustering.

◆ They are essentially bit-for-bit the same operating system, other than that each shows different versions in the About menu option and different background wallpaper.

◆ Both are licensed in two-socket increments, and all sockets in the server must be licensed. If a server has four sockets, then two licenses of either Standard or Datacenter must be purchased.

The difference between Standard and Datacenter is in operating system environments (OSEs), or virtual instances for each license. This is the number of virtual machines running Windows Server that are included as part of your license: Standard allows two virtual instances per license, and Datacenter allows unlimited instances. From a virtualization environment perspective, this is a big difference. For each Standard license, I can run two virtual machines running Windows Server, while with Datacenter, I can run an unlimited number of virtual machines. Standard edition is now targeted at physically deployed operating system instances or very light virtualization, while Datacenter is targeted at virtualization hosts.

It is possible to stack licenses—for example, buying three Standard licenses for a server would allow me to run six virtual machines running Windows Server (each Standard license allows two "slots," with each "slot" supporting a Windows Server virtual machine), which would be cheaper than buying a Datacenter license. However, complications will occur if you want to move virtual machines between hosts.

Consider Figure 1.9, which shows two Hyper-V hosts in a remote office that needs only six virtual machines. The option shown in the example is using three copies of Windows Server Standard on one server and a single copy on the other server, and this is allowed. However, suppose you want to move the virtual machines to the other server, as shown in Figure 1.10, to perform maintenance on the first server. This can be done, but it requires moving two of the Windows Server Standard licenses between physical hosts. License mobility allows the movement of licenses only every 90 days, which means that you could move the virtual machines and the licenses, but you would not be able to move the virtual machines back for 90 days.

FIGURE 1.9
Using stacked Standard licenses for virtual machines

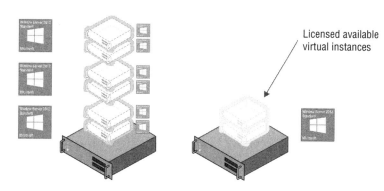

Licensed available virtual instances

FIGURE 1.10
Moving Standard licenses to enable licensed virtual machine migrations

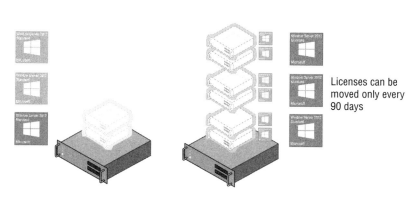

Licenses can be moved only every 90 days

To allow free movement of the virtual machines, the high watermark of virtual machines ever present on the hosts would need to be used to calculate the required number of licenses, which would therefore be three copies of Standard on both servers, as shown in Figure 1.11. Now consider having 8, 10, or 20 virtual machines and having clusters of 16 or even 64 hosts. The unlimited number of virtual machines that accompanies the Datacenter edition makes much more sense, as shown in Figure 1.12. Using Datacenter enables highly dense deployments of virtual machines without you needing to worry about the licensing of the virtual machines.

FIGURE 1.11
Required Standard licensing to enable virtual machine mobility

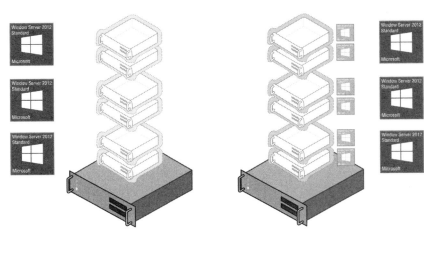

FIGURE 1.12
Using Datacenter to enable an unlimited number of virtual machines on the hosts for full mobility

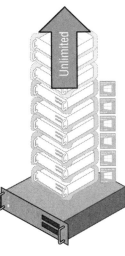

It's important to realize that the use of Standard or Datacenter is not related to Hyper-V specifically, but rather the licensing of the operating systems running inside the virtual machines, and the same would apply to any hypervisor, such as XenServer or ESX.

This is an important point. Standard vs. Datacenter relates to the number of virtual instances running the Windows Server operating system. If you need to run something other than Windows Server (for example, Linux virtual machines or Windows Client virtual machines such as for a VDI environment), then these virtual instances do not apply and you need to license those operating systems to whatever licensing scheme is required. There is no limit to the number of virtual machines that you can run on Windows Server Standard Hyper-V, and it would be possible to have hundreds of virtual machines running Linux or Windows Client without the need to use Datacenter or have multiple Standard licenses.

In fact, there is another option if a virtual environment needs to run Linux or Windows Client exclusively, and no virtual instance rights for Windows Server are required. Microsoft makes available Microsoft Hyper-V Server, which is a free download from Microsoft that is designed for environments that don't wish to run Windows Server virtual machines and don't need the virtual instance rights included with the Standard or Datacenter edition, making it perfect for Linux and VDI environments. Microsoft Hyper-V Server is updated with each version of Windows Server, making the version that's currently available Microsoft Hyper-V Server 2012 R2, and it has all of the same capabilities of the version of Hyper-V that is available in Windows Server, but only the Hyper-V role is included. It cannot be a file server or a domain controller or be used for any other role, nor can the graphical interface or server management tools be installed; it runs in the Server Core configuration level.

Windows Server 2016 Changes to Licensing and Versions

While the virtual OSE rights of Standard and Datacenter remain the same for Windows Server 2016, there are two major changes:

◆ There are differences in features between the Standard and Datacenter SKUs.

◆ Windows Server has moved to per core licensing instead of per socket.

STANDARD VS. DATACENTER

The introduction of changes in functionality between Standard and Datacenter may concern some readers that the technology they currently enjoy in the Standard edition will be missing in Windows Server 2016. However, that is not the case. No functionality is being removed from the Standard SKU of Windows Server 2016, but rather some of the new features in the 2016 version will be available only in the Datacenter SKU, specifically:

◆ Enterprise storage features, specifically Storage Spaces Direct and Storage Replica

◆ New network virtualization stack inspired and consistent with Azure

◆ Shielded VMs

Other features, such as Nano Server, containers, clustering changes, and everything else unless otherwise stated will be common to both the Standard and Datacenter SKU.

Windows Server 2016 Licensing

The per socket licensing of Windows Server 2012 (at least two-sockets are licensed for any node and purchased in two-socket increments) struggles in two major ways for modern deployments:

◆ Modern processors have an increasing number of cores, with the new many-core processors featuring more than 50 cores per socket. This would result in staggering numbers of VMs running on hosts with a single datacenter license, which does not make business sense for Microsoft.

◆ Cloud providers such as Azure and other hosters operate services based on vCPUs assigned to VMs where no actual physical sockets are visible, which makes any licensing based on sockets incompatible. A move to per socket licensing enables consistent and simple licensing across hybrid environments.

SQL Server 2012 made the switch to per core licensing, and this continues with Windows Server 2016 and System Center 2016. Both Standard and Datacenter are sold in two-core pack licenses with the following rules:

◆ Every socket must be licensed for at least eight cores (four two-core packs).

◆ Every server must be licensed for at least sixteen cores (eight two-core packs).

◆ Every core must be licensed.

If you compare this to the 2012 model, it is consistent; every server had to be licensed for at least two sockets, and most servers had processors with eight cores or less. Therefore, provided your servers have processors with eight cores or less, your licensing costs for Windows Server 2016 will be the same as with Windows Server 2012 R2. If you have processors with more, you should work with your Microsoft account representative, as there may be options to make the transition seamless. For customers with licensing and enterprise agreements, there will be grants of eight two-core packs for each existing two-socket Windows Server 2012 R2 license. If processors have more than eight cores, then the deployment may be under-licensed and additional two-core license packs may need to be purchased.

For Datacenter, an unlimited number of OS instances running Windows Server continue to be granted. However, the stacking of Standard changes. For Windows Server 2016, two OS instances running Windows Server are granted if all cores are licensed, but this is different. In Windows Server 2012, if you had a four-processor server, you would buy two copies of Standard (two processors each) to cover all sockets, and each came with two OS instance rights, giving four in total. Additional two-socket licenses could be purchased to get two more OS instances. For Windows Server 2016, if you have a four-socket server with eight cores each (or fewer cores—every socket still has to be licensed for eight cores, remember), you would need to buy sixteen two-core licenses (the financial equivalent of two old licenses) but you have covered the cores only once and you get two Standard OS instances for Windows Server, half the number of OS instance rights. If you wanted to stack Standard to get another two OS instance rights, you would have to license *every* core again, buying another sixteen two-core licenses. This is a major change; however, while this sounds daunting, very few organizations stack Windows Server Standard on servers with more than two sockets. Nevertheless, if you are one of those organizations, you should start conversations with your Microsoft account representative now. Stacking on systems with sixteen cores or less will work the same as Windows Server 2012.

Microsoft has a good licensing document that I recommend reading:

```
http://download.microsoft.com/download/7/2/9/
7290EA05-DC56-4BED-9400-138C5701F174/
WS2016LicensingDatasheet.pdf
```

Table 1.3 shows the number of two-core packs required, based on the number of sockets and the cores per socket in a system. It also indicates that extra licensing for Windows Server 2016 may be required (denoted with an exclamation point), if you have two sockets or more with more than eight cores per socket.

TABLE 1.3: Licensing Cost Changes for Windows Server 2016 vs. Windows Server 2012 R2

		PHYSICAL CORES PER PROCESSOR				
		2	**4**	**6**	**8**	**10**
Procs per server	**1**	8	8	8	8	8
	2	8	8	8	8	10 !
	4	16	16	16	16	20 !

Microsoft 2016 Licensing Datasheet

Choosing the Version of Hyper-V

Given the information in the previous section, determining which version of Hyper-V is required is a fairly simple decision. While it is technically possible to mix Standard and Datacenter in a single cluster, this makes tracking licensing complex. I use the following criteria to decide which version of Hyper-V I need in a virtual environment:

◆ If the virtual machines will all be running non–Windows Server operating systems, use the free Microsoft Hyper-V Server.

◆ If the environment will be running only a few virtual machines with no plans to expand and with limited mobility required, then the Standard edition of Windows Server can be used. However, with the new stacking changes in Windows Server 2016 Standard, it is likely to be used only where very low numbers of virtual machines are needed with 16 cores or less, unless you are willing to incur additional costs above the current Windows Server 2012 R2 costs.

◆ If there will be more than a few virtual machines with future growth possible and full mobility of virtual machines required, use the Datacenter edition of Windows Server.

The Role of System Center with Hyper-V

The capabilities of the Hyper-V features that I described previously in this chapter are impressive, but it's important to realize that this is just for virtualization. Yes, Hyper-V is powerful and can enable almost any required scenario, but virtualization is the foundation and not the complete solution.

A production environment of any kind needs management services, and virtualization adds requirements to those management capabilities. For Windows Server and Hyper-V, the management solution is System Center. While it is possible to deploy Hyper-V without System Center in a small, limited capacity, it is required for any enterprise deployment. System Center comprises various components, and each is separately deployed and offers its own discrete capabilities. Moreover, while deployment of the entire System Center product offers numerous benefits, some organizations will deploy only certain components. For organizations wanting to deploy a true cloud with consistent capabilities with Azure, they can deploy Microsoft Azure Stack, which takes the Azure code and brings it on-premises running on top of Hyper-V.

Azure Stack is delivered in a prescriptive way with specific requirements and configurations and delivered at a rapid pace. System Center enables more flexible configurations, as you can manage all aspects of the environment, but with that comes more complexity. System Center will continue to run in a long-term servicing model with releases every couple of years. Chapter 9, "Implementing the Private Cloud, SCVMM, and Microsoft Azure Stack," details how System Center and Microsoft Azure Stack are leveraged. I briefly introduce all the components of System Center here because they will be discussed and used in the chapters preceding Chapter 9. Figure 1.13 shows the full System Center product.

FIGURE 1.13
Components of
System Center

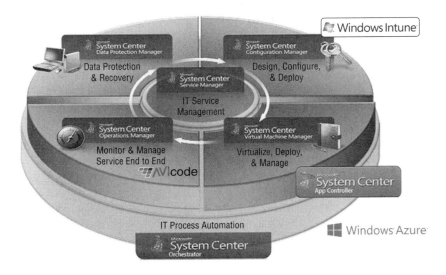

System Center is licensed in exactly the same way as Windows Server. It can be purchased in the Standard or Datacenter edition. The versions are identical except for the number of virtual instance rights: two for Standard and unlimited for Datacenter. It is licensed in two-socket increments for Windows Server 2012/2012 R2 and two-core increments for the 2016 version, which makes it easy to know how many and of what type of System Center licenses you need for your Windows Server environment. Typically, it will match your Windows Server licenses, and there are combination licenses available, such as ECI, which licenses Windows Server and System Center together.

It is important to note that System Center has been updating functionality throughout the Windows Server 2012/2012 R2 waves via update rollups (URs), which contain not only fixed but also new features. An example is a UR with added support for Azure IaaS in the SCVMM console.

Many organizations also extend System Center to the cloud with Operations Management Suite (OMS). OMS provides capabilities for on-premises and cloud-hosted systems that can integrate with System Center. OMS runs in the cloud without local infrastructure requirements, making it available to manage any workload, anywhere, and it can take advantage of the huge compute capabilities of the cloud. Some examples of capability include the following:

◆ Insights into your environment including log analysis from Windows and Linux systems and trend analysis of systems helping plan resources. This data can be gained through an OMS agent or through connectivity to Operations Manager.

◆ Automation allowing PowerShell to execute in the cloud

◆ Backup and recovery solutions

◆ Security and auditing through network, host, and audit inspection in addition to threat analysis

Long-term and even day-to-day management capabilities may be available in OMS. However, today OMS is best utilized with System Center; System Center manages the day-to-day, while OMS focuses on activities related to analytics and trend analysis.

System Center Configuration Manager

Moving through the products shown in Figure 1.13, I'll start with System Center Configuration Manager (SCCM). SCCM provides capabilities to deploy operating systems, applications, and OS/software updates to servers and desktops. Detailed hardware and software inventory and asset intelligence features are key aspects of SCCM, enabling great insight into an entire organization's IT infrastructure. SCCM 2012 introduces management of mobile devices such as iOS and Android through ActiveSync integration with Exchange and a user-focused management model. One key feature of SCCM for servers is settings management, which allows a configuration of desired settings to be defined (such as OS and application settings) and then applied to a group of servers (or desktops). This can be useful for compliance requirements.

Configuration Manager is closely aligned with the Windows client OS. As Windows 10 has shifted to being delivered at a frequent interval (approximately every four months in the new Windows as a Service paradigm), so too must Configuration Manager, in order to enable new Windows 10 functionality to be managed.

Configuration Manager has shifted to a naming convention of <year><month> to denote the version. For example, Configuration Manager 1511 represents the version released in November 2015 to coincide with the Windows 10 1511 release. Post Windows Server 2012 R2, Configuration Manager has added native support for mobile devices such as iOS and Android, where integration with Microsoft Intune is not possible or desired, in addition to new service plans that help manage the deployment of new branches of Windows 10 to groups of machines as they are released.

System Center Virtual Machine Manager and App Controller

Next in the circle of products in Figure 1.13, you see System Center Virtual Machine Manager (SCVMM). It gets a lot of attention in this book, but essentially it's the virtualization-specific management functionality across multiple hypervisors and gives insight and management into storage and network fabric resources. SCVMM allows the creation and deployment of virtual machine templates and even multitier services. It also lights up several Hyper-V features, such as network virtualization. App Controller provides a rich Silverlight web-based self-service interface for management of private and public cloud resources that, while useful, is removed in the 2016 version in favor of the Azure Pack interface.

SCVMM 2016 adds support for new Windows Server 2016 features such as Nano Server deployment and management, the new network virtualization stack, shielded VMs, and guardian host management in addition to simplifying the management of virtual environments.

System Center Operations Manager

System Center Operations Manager (SCOM) provides a rich monitoring solution for Microsoft and non-Microsoft operating systems and applications and also for hardware. Any monitoring solution can tell you when something is broken, and yes, SCOM does that. But its real power is in its proactive nature and best practice adherence functionality. SCOM management packs are units of knowledge about a specific application or component. For example, there is an Exchange management pack and a Domain Name System (DNS) for Windows Server management pack. The Microsoft mandate is that any Microsoft product should have a management pack that is written by the product team responsible for the application or operating system component. All of the knowledge of those developers, the people who create best practice documents, is incorporated into these management packs, which you can then just deploy to your environment. Operations Manager will raise alerts when potential problems are detected or when best practices are not being followed. Often customers object that when first implemented, Operations Manager floods them with alerts. This could be for various reasons (perhaps the environment has a lot of problems that should be fixed), but often Operations Manager will be tuned to ignore configurations that perhaps are not best practice but are nevertheless accepted by the organization.

Many third parties provide management packs for their applications and hardware devices. When I think about "it's all about the application" as a key tenant of the private cloud, the Operations Manager's ability to monitor from the hardware, storage, and network all the way through the OS to the application is huge, but it goes even further in Operations Manager 2012.

System Center Operations Manager 2012 introduced several changes, but two huge ones were around network monitoring and custom application monitoring. First, Microsoft licensed technology from EMC called SMARTS, which enables a rich discovery and monitoring of network devices. With the network discovery and monitoring functionality, Operations Manager can identify the relationship between network devices and services to understand, for example, that port 3 on this switch connects to server A. Then, if a switch problem occurs, Operations Manager will know the affected servers. CPU and memory information, among other types of information, is available for supported network devices.

The other big change was the acquisition by Microsoft of AVIcode, which is now Application Performance Monitoring (APM) in Operations Manager 2012. APM provides monitoring of custom applications without any changes needed by the application. APM currently supports .NET applications and Java Enterprise Edition (JEE).

Like SCVMM, Operations Manager 2016 investments include supporting all of the new Windows Server 2016 features but also extending monitoring support for LAMP stack, Azure, Office 365, and more. Additionally, Operations Manager has focused significant effort on easing the workload for administrators in understanding what management packs (MPs) are needed and if new versions are available. This now surfaces as Updates and Recommendations in the Operations Management console that will advise on new MPs and updates to MPs that will bring benefit to the environment. Additionally, the amount of "alert noise" (large numbers of alerts that muddy the data being viewed and therefore obstruct the viewing of alerts that you really care about) has been reduced, with more intuitive tuning via tune management packs.

System Center Data Protection Manager

System Center Data Protection Manager (DPM) is Microsoft's best-of-breed backup, continuous data protection, and recovery solution for key Microsoft workloads, including SharePoint, SQL Server, Dynamics, Exchange, Hyper-V, file services, and desktops. DPM allows granular recovery of information within the supported options for the product, including end-user self-recovery in certain scenarios. DPM can be useful in the private cloud, in the protection of the environment. DPM can back up and protect the Hyper-V servers, the SQL databases that are used by most of the System Center 2012 components, the management servers running the System Center infrastructure, and all of the virtual machines running on Hyper-V that are created.

DPM supports backing up at the Hyper-V server level, and that backup request will be passed by Hyper-V to the virtual machines. That allows the virtual machines to ensure that information on disk is in a backup-ready state so when the virtual machine is backed up, the integrity and usability of that backup can be ensured.

I do want to be clear; just because you can back up at the Hyper-V level does not mean that you should back up only at the Hyper-V level. If you want granular restoration capabilities of applications like SharePoint, SQL Server, and Exchange, you need to have the DPM agent installed within the virtual machine and actually be backing up from the VM directly, to enable DPM to have the knowledge of the application configuration and data.

System Center 2016 DPM adds support for the backup for VMware VMs in addition to better leveraging modern storage capabilities such as Storage Spaces Direct and even protect-shielded VMs. ReFS (Resilient File System) is utilized to streamline the creation of recovery points by utilizing ReFS cloning, therefore greatly increasing the number of sources that can be protected per DPM server and reducing the amount of storage required.

System Center Service Manager

I'll spend more time on System Center Service Manager (SCSM) in a later chapter, but think of it as the configuration management database (CMDB) for the entire infrastructure, which is another ITIL key capability. Service Manager is shown in the center of the rest of the System Center components for a good reason. It has connectors into all of the surrounding components, receiving feeds of information that it consolidates into a single view of everything related to an asset (such as a computer or person), giving a single point of truth for the entire organization.

Service Manager has capabilities commonly associated with a help desk solution, such as logging incidents, problems, and change requests, but it also handles change management and release management in addition to providing a powerful workflow engine to enable your organization's processes such as approvals to be replicated in Service Manager.

The key item that I focus on later is the service catalog, which provides the organization with the ability to request services, including services for software and virtual infrastructures. Organizations often have a help desk solution already in place, but realize that Service Manager is far more than a ticketing system. It can be implemented and integrated with another ticketing solution, all the while leveraged for its other powerful capabilities and CMDB functionality.

A welcome change in Service Manager 2016 is a new HTML5-based self-service portal that was previously a huge pain point for using Service Manager. Service Manager also integrates tightly with OMS.

System Center Orchestrator

System Center Orchestrator is the result of an acquisition of a product called Opalis, which has been renamed System Center Orchestrator as part of System Center 2012. Orchestrator provides two key capabilities that, as with Service Manager, I dive into in more detail in a later chapter.

First, Opalis was acquired because it had connectivity to many of the major datacenter applications and systems that exist, which with the acquisition now includes the Microsoft solutions. Integration packs exist for many systems and provide activities that are specific to the integration pack target, but Orchestrator can talk to targets that don't have integration packs, using many types of communication, including WMI, SSH, PowerShell, SNMP, and many more.

Second, Opalis had powerful runbook automation capabilities that leveraged all of this connectivity. Runbooks that were typically manually actioned by IT administrators and business users can be migrated to Orchestrator using an easy-to-use flowchart-type interface and can be completely automated. One shortcoming of Orchestrator is the limited capabilities of integration packs that would often result in having to use .NET activities to use PowerShell commands to complete functionality.

A PowerShell-based alternative is also provided, Orchestrator Service Management Automation (SMA), which enables standard PowerShell modules to be used as part of runbooks instead of the Orchestrator proprietary integration packs. It is Orchestrator SMA that is the future of Orchestrator and provides the greatest consistency with Azure Automation.

It is because of these capabilities that Orchestrator is shown as the foundation of the System Center product. All of the other System Center components can leverage Orchestrator for action requests made to other systems and complex processes. Orchestrator can talk to the rest of System Center, enabling automation of processes that use many components of System Center and other systems through a single runbook.

Clouds and Services

This book's primary focus is on Hyper-V, but the big technology investment area today is around various types of clouds and various types of capabilities offered "as a Service." I focus on several of these throughout the book, but in this section I provide a high-level summary of the types of clouds and "as a Service" offerings commonly seen, so they will make sense as I discuss their principles and use in later chapters.

There are two primary types of clouds: private and public. Virtualization focuses on services related to compute, such as creating, configuring, and running the virtual machines, but it does not focus on the storage or network fabrics that are major pieces of the datacenter. Virtualization does not help abstract the underlying resources from how they may be provisioned, and quotas to create resources are allocated to business units and users. Virtualization does not provide self-service capabilities and workflows to the clients. Cloud services enable this by providing rich management technologies that build on the virtualization foundation and enable intuitive, scalable, and controlled services that can be offered beyond just the IT team. With cloud services, different resources from the datacenter can be grouped together and offered to different groups of users with well-defined capabilities and capacity. There are many more benefits, and I go into more detail throughout this book.

Cloud services that are offered using an organization's internal resources are known as *private clouds*. Cloud services that are offered external to the organization, such as from a hosting partner or even solutions such as Microsoft Windows Azure, are called *public clouds*.

Within these clouds, different types of services can be offered, and typically these are seen from public cloud providers. There is, however, a movement of these types of services being offered in an organization's private cloud to its various business units, especially IaaS. There are three primary types of services: infrastructure as a service (IaaS), platform as a service (PaaS), and software as a service (SaaS). For each type, the responsibilities of the nine major layers of management vary between the vendor of the service and the client (you). Figure 1.14 shows the three types of service and a complete on-premises solution.

FIGURE 1.14
The key types of management and how they are owned for the types of cloud service

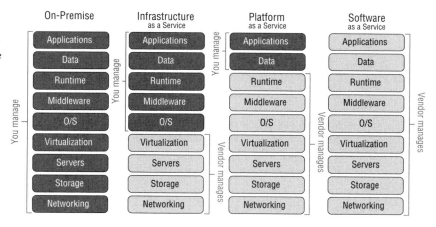

IaaS can be thought of as a virtual machine in the cloud. The provider has a virtual environment, and you purchase virtual machine instances. You then manage the operating system, the patching, the data, and the applications within. Examples of IaaS are Amazon Elastic Compute Cloud (EC2) and Azure IaaS, which give organizations the ability to run operating systems inside cloud-based virtual environments.

PaaS provides a framework in which custom applications can be run. Organizations need to focus only on writing the very best application within the guidelines of the platform capabilities, and everything else is handled. There are no worries about patching operating systems, updating frameworks, backing up SQL databases, or configuring high availability. The organization just writes the application and pays for the resources used. Azure is a classic example of a PaaS.

SaaS is the ultimate in low maintenance. The complete solution is provided by the vendor. The organization has nothing to write or maintain, other than configuring who in the organization should be allowed to use the software. A commercial example of SaaS is Hotmail, a messaging service on the Internet. An enterprise example is Office 365, which provides cloud-hosted Exchange, SharePoint, and Lync services all accessed over the Internet with no application or operating system management for the organization.

Ideally, for the lowest management overhead, SaaS should be used, then PaaS if SaaS is not available, and then IaaS if PaaS is not an option. SaaS is gaining a great deal of traction with services such as Office 365, but PaaS adoption is fairly slow. The primary obstacle for PaaS is that applications have to be written within specific guidelines to be able to operate in PaaS environments. Many organizations have many custom applications that cannot be modified or don't have the budget to change the application, which is why IaaS is so popular. With IaaS, an existing virtual machine on-premises can fairly painlessly be moved to the IaaS solution. In the long term, I think PaaS will become the standard for custom applications, but it will take a long time, and I think IaaS can help serve as the ramp to adopting PaaS.

Consider a multitiered service that has a web tier, an application tier, and a SQL database tier. Initially, all of these tiers would run as IaaS virtual machines. The organization may then be able to convert the web tier from IIS (Internet Information Services) running in an IaaS VM and use the Azure web role, which is part of PaaS. Next the organization may be able to move from SQL running in an IaaS VM to using SQL Azure. Finally, the organization could rewrite the application tier to directly leverage Azure PaaS. It's a gradual process, but the reduced overhead and increased functionality and resiliency at the end state is worth it.

As will be explored in this book, a key Microsoft differentiator is its hybrid capability to enable organizations to have a complete choice when deploying services, without having to change how they architect and create applications. When using Microsoft Azure Stack on-premises, an organization can write an application on the Azure Resource Manager (ARM) model and deploy it on-premises, to the public cloud, or to a hosting partner that leverages Microsoft Azure Stack. If a JSON (Java Script Object Notation) template is created to deploy a service to ARM, it can be deployed on-premises, to a hosting partner, or to Azure without modification. Typically, organizations will not pick one, but will utilize all of the options in the scenario where a particular type of hosting makes the most sense.

The Bottom Line

Articulate the key value propositions of virtualization. Virtualization solves the numerous pain points and limitations of physical server deployments today. Primary benefits of virtualization include consolidation of resources, which increases resource utilization and provides OS abstraction from hardware, allowing OS mobility; financial savings through less server hardware, less datacenter space, and simpler licensing; faster provisioning of environments; and additional backup and recovery options.

Master It How does virtualization help in service isolation in branch office situations?

Understand the differences in functionality between the different versions of Hyper-V. Windows Server 2008 introduced the foundational Hyper-V capabilities, and the major new features in 2008 R2 were Live Migration and Cluster Shared Volumes (CSV). Windows 2008 R2 SP1 introduced Dynamic Memory and RemoteFX. Windows Server 2012 introduced new levels of scalability and mobility with features such as Shared Nothing Live Migration, Storage Live Migration, and Hyper-V Replica in addition to new networking and storage capabilities. Windows 2012 R2 Hyper-V enhances many of the 2012 features with generation 2 virtual machines, Live Migration compression and SMB support, new Hyper-V Replica replication granularity, and Hyper-V Replica Extended replication. Windows Server 2016 builds on this with shielded VMs providing new levels of security for virtual environments, containers for new ways to deploy and manage applications, and other features and management enhancements.

Master It   What is the largest virtual machine that can be created on Windows Server 2012 Hyper-V, and does this change for Windows Server 2016 Hyper-V?

Master It   What features were enabled for Linux virtual machines in Windows Server 2016 Hyper-V?

Differentiate between the types of cloud service and when each type is best utilized.   There are three primary types of cloud services: software as a Service (SaaS), platform as a service (PaaS), and infrastructure as a service (IaaS). SaaS provides a complete software solution that is entirely managed by the providing vendor, such as a hosted mail solution. PaaS provides a platform on which custom-written applications can run, and it should be used for new custom applications when possible because it minimizes maintenance by the client. IaaS allows virtual machines to be run on a provided service, but the entire OS and application must be managed by the client. IaaS is suitable where PaaS or SaaS cannot be used and in development/test environments.

Chapter 2

Virtual Machine Resource Fundamentals

This chapter covers the primary building blocks of a virtual machine: the motherboard, processor, memory, and storage resources. You will look at the mechanics behind how these building blocks are virtualized on the physical host and explore the configuration options available for each of the virtualized resources when it's assigned to a virtual machine. You will also take a look at the advantages and limitations of the options in the different common usage scenarios. By thoroughly understanding the fundamentals of virtual machine resources, you will be able to correctly architect the optimal virtual machine configuration based on the requirements available. You will also understand why the many other technologies are needed and how they should be utilized when they are explained later in this book.

In this chapter, you will learn to:

- ◆ Describe how the resources of a virtual machine are virtualized by the hypervisor.

- ◆ Use processor and memory advanced configuration options.

- ◆ Explain the difference between VHD/VHDX and pass-through storage.

Understanding VMBus

Before we get into virtual machine resources, this section covers the Hyper-V architecture in more detail than the high-level overview provided in Chapter 1, "Introduction to Virtualization and Microsoft Solutions." It is important to understand how the various resources for virtual machines are engineered and enabled. Figure 1.4 in Chapter 1 shows the hypervisor running directly on the hardware, with all of the virtual machine resource access serviced through the hypervisor. If you look carefully at the figure, I deliberately showed only the processor and memory resources being managed by the hypervisor. Other resources must be available for a fully functioning environment, such as storage and networking. The mechanisms to communicate with the processor and memory in a system are quite standardized, removing the need for many different sets of code to handle the different types of processors and memory found in a system.

This is not the case with storage controllers and network devices. Each vendor typically has its own specific implementation and must provide a driver to enable the operating system to correctly communicate with the hardware. There are thousands of these drivers for Windows, with most written by the independent hardware vendor (IHV). All of these types of storage and networks need to be usable by Hyper-V, and therefore the drivers need to be available. Type 1 hypervisors have two architectures: monolithic and microkernelized, as shown in Figure 2.1.

FIGURE 2.1
The monolithic and microkernelized hypervisors

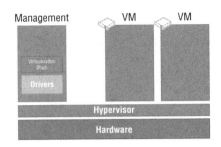

Monolithic hypervisor

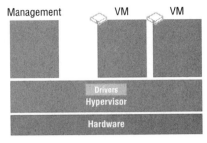

Microkernelized hypervisor

With a *monolithic hypervisor,* the drivers responsible for communication with the hardware sit in the actual hypervisor, which is a fairly complex kernel, basically a mini operating system. The virtual machines access the hardware via these specialized device drivers, which results in very good performance because the virtual machines can go directly to all hardware via these drivers in the hypervisor.

There are issues, however, with a monolithic hypervisor approach. The first is that these shared drivers are specifically written for the hypervisor, which limits the hardware that is supported by a monolithic hypervisor; and virtualization solutions that use a monolithic hypervisor typically have a small hardware compatibility list. This shared driver base leads to the main concern, which is security and stability. With a shared driver for all of the virtual machines, if a malware driver was placed in the hypervisor, all of the partitions would be vulnerable to attack and snooping. Furthermore, if a driver is updated in the hypervisor that has an issue, it will cause problems for all of the virtual machines.

Consider the Windows ecosystem, with its huge number of hardware partners and thousands of storage controllers and network adapters that organizations may wish to use. Trying to create hypervisor drivers for all of the hardware would not be practical, and drastically reducing the supported hardware when using Hyper-V would also not be popular. Thus Microsoft chose the *microkernelized hypervisor* model, and this is why there is a Windows Server management/parent partition. With the microkernelized hypervisor model used by Hyper-V, all of the Windows drivers created by vendors for their hardware can still be used and run in the management partition, removing the need for Hyper-V-specific drivers and not reducing the range of hardware usable with Hyper-V. This also keeps drivers out of the hypervisor, removing the security and stability concerns that relate to a monolithic hypervisor.

In fact, the hypervisor really just governs the allocation of CPU cycles and RAM and no other types of devices, such as storage and network. The parent partition hosts a virtualization stack that includes management components running in normal user mode. The Virtual Machine Management Service (VMMS) manages the state of virtual machines and launches the virtual machine worker processes (VMWPs). There's one for each child partition running, and it controls the state changes of the child partition, enables certain types of emulated hardware, and enables management activities such as stopping and starting.

Figure 2.2 shows Task Manager running on a Hyper-V server with a single vmms.exe instance, and many vmwp.exe instances that correspond to each VM. In the background is a PowerShell command, which helps identify the worker process for a specific virtual machine. You need the parent partition along with the hypervisor to do anything useful such as creating child partitions. While you can install the hypervisor on its own, it won't do much without a Windows Server parent partition.

FIGURE 2.2
Task Manager showing a single vmms.exe instance and many vmwp .exe instances

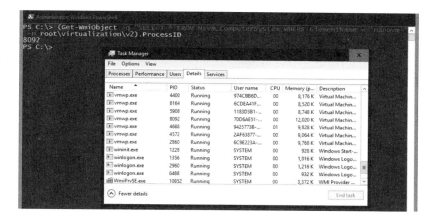

Components also run in kernel mode, such as the virtual machine bus (VMBus), which enables communication between virtual service providers (VSPs) that allow support for non-CPU and memory hardware such as storage and networking. Each VSP corresponds to numerous virtual service clients (VSCs) running in the child partitions; for example, we have a virtual service provider and consumer for a network, a pair for storage, and so on. When a child partition wishes to access hardware resources that are not CPU or memory, its VSC makes a request to the VSP hosted in the VMBus on the parent partition, and the VSP performs the actual communication to the physical hardware.

This is shown in Figure 2.3, which is an updated version of Figure 2.1 to show more clearly how the various types of hardware resources are serviced. The VMBus is not shared between all of the child partitions, and there is one channel between each child and the parent, so no communication or data can be seen by other child partitions running on the same server. This VMBus does not incur any significant performance penalty, even though child partitions wanting to access hardware now essentially communicate via the VSC to a VSP on the VMBus hosted on the parent partition, which communicates with the hardware. This is because the VMBus is a pure memory bus running at a kernel level, so there is practically no latency introduced. By using this model, Microsoft keeps the hypervisor small and secure while still allowing full hardware support for the breadth of the Microsoft hardware ecosystem.

FIGURE 2.3
Hyper-V VMBus
architecture

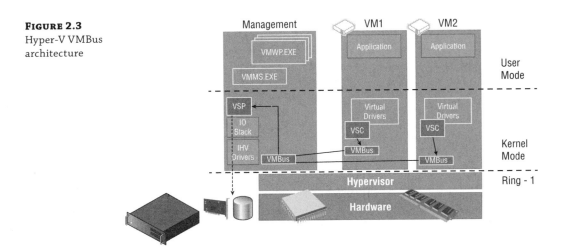

The parent partition hosts all of the VM support components that are not part of the hypervisor. If the parent partition reboots or is unavailable, none of the child partitions are available either. The Hyper-V solution has components that I do not show in Figure 2.3, to avoid confusion. A virtualization infrastructure driver (VID, vid.sys) runs in the parent kernel mode and enables management services to the VMMS and VMWP that run in the user mode. The VID talks to the Windows Hypervisor Interface Library (WinHv) that communicates directly with the hypervisor via the hypercall interface, which communicates with the WinHv that runs in each VM (winhv.sys). There are a lot of moving parts, but generally you don't need to know about them. Things just work. It is, however, important to understand the VMBus and the role it plays in enabling very fast access to nonprocessor and nonmemory resources via the parent partition.

The Anatomy of a Virtual Machine

Consider the fundamental objectives of a virtualization environment. One objective is to enable multiple operating system instances to execute simultaneously on a single physical system, which enables the many benefits covered in Chapter 1. Another objective is to divide up and share the resources available on the physical host to many virtual machines, which act as their own, self-contained systems that are completely isolated from the other virtualized systems running on the host. Each virtual machine believes it is the sole user of the hardware on which it is running. Within each virtual machine, an operating system is installed, and into that operating system, applications are installed and configurations implemented to enable services to the organization.

Operating systems are written to run on hardware and expect certain components to be present that can be interacted with, such as the computer's BIOS, storage controller, input/output systems, and network device. Drivers are included in the operating system to see certain types of devices, such as network and storage controllers, to enable installation and startup of the operating system. It's also possible to add drivers for hardware that does not have drivers included as part of the operating system. This fundamental presence of hardware components does not apply to a virtual machine. The entire environment of a virtual machine is synthetic, with abstracted resources allotted to the virtual machine and many resources utilizing the VMBus, as previously explained. However, the key aspects of a computer must be present for an operating system to install and function. Note that when using SR-IOV networking configurations or Discrete Device Assignment (DDA) in Windows Server 2016, physical hardware is mapped directly to a VM. These are specialized configurations, however, and the core resources of the VM, such as chipset, processor, and memory, are still virtualized.

Generation 1 Virtual Machine

All of the synthetic resources and devices that are exposed by Hyper-V provide the highest level of performance and functionality, but if an operating system cannot natively use them, that operating system cannot be installed or started on that synthetic hardware. Even today with Hyper-V, many Windows 2000, Windows 2003, and Windows XP virtual machines are running virtualized, and these operating systems are not virtualization aware. The use of the VMBus architecture within a guest operating system requires deep integration with other operating system components; it's not as simple as installing an additional storage or network driver during installation.

It is therefore often required to provide certain types of hardware as emulated, which means Hyper-V components provide to virtual machines what appear to be standard types of hardware, such as an Intel 82371AB/EB IDE controller, an Intel 21140 Ethernet adapter, a PS/2 keyboard and mouse, and a complete virtual motherboard with BIOS. Behind the scenes, though, the Hyper-V solution is running code to pretend that this hardware exists. Providing emulated hardware requires an additional workload in the hypervisor, predominantly provided by the worker process for the virtual machine, vmwp.exe.

Remember that vmwp.exe runs in the user mode space of the parent partition, which means as emulated hardware is used, its performance will be poorer than the synthetic equivalents (which run purely in kernel mode and don't have the additional overhead of emulating physical pieces of hardware). The emulated hardware requires many context switches between user mode and kernel mode for the actual real hardware communications via the management partition's I/O stack, and the communication path is far more convoluted. Additionally, the interface to the emulated devices assumes things about a physical machine. For instance, setting up an IDE transfer involves seven I/O port writes, each of which is a separate round-trip to the emulator in the vmwp.exe and a huge performance penalty. This performance penalty is why synthetic hardware is always preferred over emulated hardware, but sometimes there isn't a choice, and for some types of hardware that is rarely used or primarily triggered by the user, the difference in performance is not noticeable (consider mouse or keyboard type hardware).

The term *generation 1 virtual machine* may be completely new to you. Prior to Windows Server 2012 R2 Hyper-V, it would have just been called a virtual machine. There is now a new type of virtual machine, which I cover in the section, "Generation 2 Virtual Machine," and that is why there is now a name distinction. Consider the generation 1 virtual machine as the virtual machine that you have known and loved since Windows Server 2008 Hyper-V, but with a few improvements. Unless you are deploying all brand-new virtual machines on Windows Server 2012 R2 with the latest operating systems, you will continue to use generation 1 virtual machines for some time, and this is not a problem at all. Remember that generation 1 virtual machines not only fully support the VMBus and synthetic hardware, but also provide support for emulated hardware when required.

VIRTUAL MOTHERBOARD AND BIOS

At the core of a virtual machine is the virtual motherboard and the basic input/output system (BIOS). This provides the environment needed to initially start the virtual machine, choose the boot device, and hand over control to the operating system installed. Microsoft uses the American Megatrends BIOS for the virtual machines.

However, you don't access the BIOS of a virtual machine in the same way that you access the BIOS of a physical machine (for example, by pressing the Esc or Delete key). Instead, the options related to BIOS startup and boot order are configured through the virtual machine properties using the BIOS area, as shown in Figure 2.4. Notice that the figure shows that the Num Lock state can be set as well as the types of boot devices supported in a generation 1 virtual machine (CD, IDE, legacy network adapter, and floppy). The types of network adapters are covered in the next chapter, but for now know that a legacy network adapter is an emulated network adapter instead of the synthetic network adapter that utilizes the VMBus. Typically, you *never* want to use the legacy network adapter except for a very specific use case, booting over the network.

FIGURE 2.4
The BIOS configurations possible for a generation 1 virtual machine. The boot order can be changed using the Move Up and Move Down buttons.

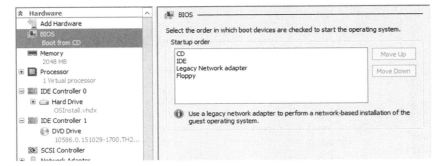

Many other system devices are enabled in the guest operating system through the virtual motherboard provided by Hyper-V. They can be seen in the System Devices section in Device Manager (`devmgmt.msc`), but typically you won't interact with these items.

WHAT ABOUT THE TIME?

A physical motherboard has a small battery and a real-time clock (RTC) to track time. But the way most operating systems work is to read the time from the RTC at startup and then use their own internal routines to calculate passed time. The problem for a virtual machine is that the routines used to calculate time do not work correctly, because of the way virtual machine resources are delivered, which means time drifts in a virtual machine.

To solve this problem, Hyper-V uses a time synchronization integration service that keeps the time correct within the virtual machine. You could see some time anomalies when a virtual machine is first booted or resumed from a saved state or checkpoint (point-in-time saved view of a virtual machine), but these should quickly be resolved after the time synchronization integration service loads, which will correct the issue. Even if the virtual machine is in a different time zone or is part of a domain that synchronizes time from domain controllers, you should leave the time synchronization integration service enabled. The time synchronization service will work well with other time sources. Run the w32tm /query /source command to check the time source for your operating system. A Hyper-V virtual machine should show the following:

```
C:\>w32tm /query /source
VM IC Time Synchronization Provider
```

The guidance for domain controllers has changed over the years. The recommendation was to disable time synchronization completely and then to disable only part of the service with the following command:

```
reg add HKLM\SYSTEM\CurrentControlSet\Services\W32Time\TimeProviders↵
\VMICTimeProvider /v Enabled /t reg_dword /d 0
```

Once again, though, the recommendation is to just disable the time synchronization integration service completely, as documented in the time service section at the following location:

```
http://technet.microsoft.com/en-us/library/virtual_active_directory_domain_
controller_virtualization_hyperv(WS.10).aspx
```

My recommendation is to check back regularly, but fundamentally, Hyper-V has gotten better at controlling the drift, hence minimizing the time synchronizations needed for virtual machines that already synchronize from another source.

IDE Controller

I cover processors and memory in great detail later in this chapter. The other "must have" component for a system is storage (technically, you don't need a network, though a system is typically not very useful without one). Generation 1 virtual machines must boot from storage connected to the IDE controller, which as previously explained emulates an Intel 82371AB/EB IDE controller. This enables almost any operating system to be installed in a Hyper-V virtual machine, because the Intel 82371AB/EB IDE controller is common and the driver is built into every major operating system.

Two IDE controllers are provided in a generation 1 virtual machine: IDE controller 0 and IDE controller 1. Each IDE controller can have up to two devices attached, which can be a hard drive or a DVD drive. Typically, the only time a DVD drive is used is when there is an option to install the operating system into a new virtual machine by attaching an operating system installation ISO to the drive, although mapping to a physical DVD drive in the host is also possible. It's also possible to install or update the Hyper-V Integration Services, which were provided as an ISO prior to Windows Server 2016, but they are now delivered through Windows Update to the guest OS.

Two IDE controllers with two devices each allows a maximum of four storage devices to be connected, which may seem limited. In most virtual machines, you will use the IDE controller only for the boot hard disk, and all data drives will be connected to the synthetic SCSI controller instead.

Something seemingly obvious may be occurring to you. In this chapter, I have been continually saying that emulated hardware is bad, that it is provided by a user mode process (vmwp.exe) in the parent partition (which gives poor performance), and wherever possible, to avoid using it. Now I'm saying every single Hyper-V virtual machine has to boot from a hard disk attached to the emulated IDE controller. Doesn't that mean every virtual machine will have terrible disk performance for the operating system disk? Yes, a little, but mostly no, because the architects of Hyper-V did something very clever with the IDE controller.

The IDE controller had to emulate a common IDE controller to provide compatibility with all operating systems in which the components needed to use synthetic, VMBus-enabled devices that would not natively be available. Once an operating system is installed in a Hyper-V virtual machine, one of the first steps is to install Hyper-V Integration Services, which enlightens the operating system to its virtualized state and allows it to leverage the synthetic devices available via the VMBus. Integration Services also enables tighter integration between Hyper-V and the operating system, such as time synchronization, data exchange, backup services, shutdown, and more. Once the integration services have been installed and loaded, the IDE controller switches under the covers from being an emulated IDE device to being a synthetic device that uses the VMBus and the VSC/VSP model via a component in the guest called the *fast pass filter* (storflt). It therefore matches the performance of the synthetic SCSI controllers that are also available. This means that provided Hyper-V Integration Services is installed, there is no performance difference between using the IDE or SCSI controller in a virtual machine after the operating system has booted. The SCSI controller does offer additional functionality, which is why its use is still preferred for assets such as data disks.

SCSI Controller

By default, a generation 1 virtual machine does not have a SCSI controller, but up to four SCSI controllers can be added to a virtual machine by using the Add Hardware area of the virtual machine's property page, as shown in Figure 2.5. Once a virtual machine has four SCSI controllers, the option to add SCSI controllers will be grayed out. The SCSI controller is a pure synthetic device fully leveraging the kernel, in-memory VMBus, which gives essentially the highest, bare-metal storage performance. The term *bare-metal* refers to a system that does not use virtualization. When something is compared to bare metal, the comparison is to a nonvirtualized environment. In this case, studies have shown that there is no performance loss from using storage attached to the SCSI controller as compared to the raw performance capabilities of the underlying storage.

FIGURE 2.5
Adding a SCSI controller to a generation 1 virtual machine

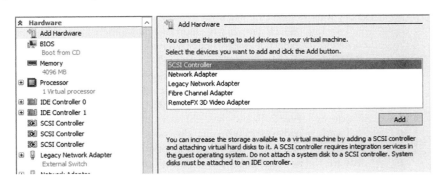

Each SCSI controller supports up to 64 hard drives attached, which equates to a maximum of 256 disks attached via the SCSI bus. Like the IDE controller, those hard disks can be virtual hard disks or mapped to physical hard disks on the host (pass-through storage). The SCSI controller also supports the hot-add/hot-plug of disks to a running virtual machine, which is a capability not available on the IDE controller. The SCSI controller offers even more functionality in Windows Server 2012 R2:

◆ Shared VHDX between multiple virtual machines

◆ Dynamic resizing of VHDX files

Always use SCSI-connected disks where possible in the virtual machine and restrict use of IDE-connected disks to the operating system and DVD drive.

COM PORTS

Generation 1 virtual machines include two COM ports, COM 1 and COM 2, which can be connected to a named pipe either local to the Hyper-V host or on a remote computer. The use of COM ports is generally deprecated, and it is typically restricted to certain types of guest kernel debug scenarios.

USB PORTS

If you are looking at a virtual machine settings dialog box, you may wonder where USB devices are found. How do you map a USB device attached to the Hyper-V host directly through to a virtual machine? You won't find it, and the reality is you don't want to find it.

There are two scenarios for USB devices to be accessed in a virtual machine:

◆ As part of a user's session to a virtual machine

◆ Always available to the virtual machine—for example, a USB dongle that must be available for a piece of software or service to function

Hyper-V does not allow the pass-through of a USB-attached device on a host to a virtual machine. This would break the desired abstraction of the virtual machine from the hardware and therefore stop virtual machine mobility. This does not mean there are not solutions, though.

For the first scenario, a USB device available as part of a user's session on a virtual machine, the solution is to use the Remote Desktop Protocol (RDP) capability to pass a locally attached USB device on the user's local device directly through to the remote virtual machine. With Windows Server 2012 and the RemoteFX technology, it is possible to redirect almost any USB device over RDP.

The second scenario, for a USB device always to be connected to a virtual machine even when a user is not logged on, requires the use of third-party solutions that enable USB over IP. The solutions work by having a physical server that has all of the USB devices connected to it and runs a service that enables the USB devices to be accessed remotely over IP. The virtual machines then run a client piece of software that connects to the USB device over IP and looks to the VM like a local USB device. The benefit to these types of solutions is that the virtual machine can still be moved between hosts without losing connectivity to the USB device. Many solutions are available, but the two I have seen in customers' environments are described at the following locations:

```
www.silexamerica.com/products/connectivity-solutions/device-networking/usb-
parallel-connectivity/sx-ds-3000wn/
www.digi.com/products/usb/anywhereusb#overview
```

Generation 2 Virtual Machine

Earlier I made a statement, "Each virtual machine believes it is the sole user of the hardware on which it is running," and the point was that the operating system was unaware it was running on a hypervisor, which is why there was so much emulated hardware in a generation 1 virtual machine. The various PS/2 keyboard and mouse devices, the IDE controller, the legacy network adapter for PXE boot, PCI controllers, and so on were required so that operating systems could work in a virtual environment, because they were inherently ignorant to virtualization, unable to natively use virtualized or synthetic devices.

This was true when virtualization was first introduced and needed to support operating systems such as Windows NT 4 and Windows 2000, but the reality for modern operating systems such as Windows Server 2012 and even recent Linux distributions is that they natively understand virtualization and are fully virtualization enlightened. They can use virtual devices without additional drivers installed and don't require "physical hardware" elements to be present. Modern operating systems are designed to run in physical and virtual environments.

The generation 2 virtual machine was introduced in Windows Server 2012 R2 Hyper-V. It is focused on the new generation of operating systems that are natively enlightened to virtualization and don't require the emulated components such as IDE controllers, PS/2 I/O devices, COM ports, legacy network adapters, floppy drives, and all the other emulated motherboard components (such as PCI-to-ISA bridge). A generation 2 virtual machine removes these emulated components to offer a simpler, streamlined virtual machine that also enables the latest operating system features by switching from BIOS to a Unified Extensible Firmware Interface (UEFI) such as Secure Boot (enabled by default). Secure Boot ensures a secure handoff from the UEFI to the operating system without any other party, such as malware, injecting itself between the hardware and the operating system. In Windows Server 2012 R2, Secure Boot worked for Windows guest operating systems, while in Windows Server 2016, this support extends to Linux guest operating systems as well.

Generation 2 virtual machines can boot from SCSI controller–connected hard disks and DVD drives and also from the synthetic network adapter to enable PXE boot scenarios. There is no IDE controller, floppy drive, or legacy network adapter option for a generation 2 virtual machine.

No COM ports are available via the Hyper-V Manager graphical interface, either. If a COM port is required in a generation 2 virtual machine for remote kernel debugging, one can be added using the `Set-VMComPort` PowerShell cmdlet. However, better options exist for virtual machines than using a serial port, such as using synthetic debugging. If the COM port has no named pipe associated at boot time, the COM port will not be visible in the virtual machine. Remember also that kernel debugging is not compatible with Secure Boot, so if you need to perform kernel debugging (and many of us won't!), then turn off Secure Boot by using `Set-VMFirmware -EnableSecureBoot Off`.

In Figure 2.6, you see a generation 1 virtual machine next to a generation 2 virtual machine showing Device Manager and also the BIOS mode and version. Notice the large amount of hardware that is not present in a generation 2 virtual machine, because this hardware is not required for an operating system that is natively virtualization enlightened.

FIGURE 2.6
Generation 1
compared to
generation 2
hardware

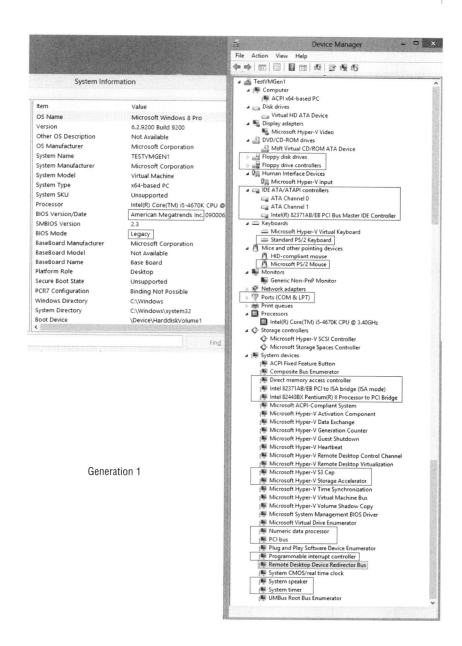

Generation 1

FIGURE 2.6
(*CONTINUED*)

Generation 2

At the time of this writing, the following operating systems can be installed in a generation 2 virtual machine:

◆ Windows Server 2012

◆ Windows Server 2012 R2

◆ Windows Server 2016

◆ Windows 8 64-bit

◆ Windows 8.1 64-bit

◆ Windows 10 64-bit

◆ Certain Linux distributions that are 64-bit with native UEFI support and the Hyper-V SCSI controller, such as Ubuntu 14.04

The biggest restriction is the need for the operating system to natively fully support UEFI, which is not available prior to Windows 8/Windows Server 2012, and only the 64-bit versions of Windows support UEFI. For a good overview of UEFI support with Windows, see:

```
http://msdn.microsoft.com/en-us/windows/hardware/gg463149.aspx
```

The main benefits to using a generation 2 virtual machine are the ability to boot from the synthetic SCSI controller or network device, and the minimized risks associated with boot-time malware (by leveraging the UEFI Secure Boot capability). In Windows Server 2016, the new virtual TPM and shielded VM functionality are available for only generation 2 VMs. Installing and booting an operating system take less time on a generation 2 virtual machine compared to a generation 1 virtual machine, but after the virtual machine has booted, there is no performance difference. The choice of generation 1 vs. generation 2 is made when the virtual machine is created and cannot be changed. A single Hyper-V server can have a mix of generation 1 and generation 2 virtual machines.

When deciding to use generation 1 or generation 2, my advice is to use generation 2, if you do not need backward compatibility with Windows Server 2012 Hyper-V. Compatibility is not required with other public cloud services either, such as Windows Azure Infrastructure as a Service (IaaS), which at the time of this writing does not support generation 2 virtual machines; this will change over time.

CONVERTING A GENERATION 1 VIRTUAL MACHINE TO GENERATION 2

The question of converting a generation 1 virtual machine to a generation 2 virtual machine comes up often, but the reality is that you don't need to do this in most cases. Generation 1 virtual machines will continue to work and perform the same as a generation 2 virtual machine. But what if you really want to make this conversion? You can't, or at least not without a huge amount of work.

A generation 1 virtual machine is BIOS based, which equates to a certain disk configuration such as an NTFS system partition. A generation 2 virtual machine is UEFI based and uses a FAT32 system partition. This alone prohibits moving virtual hard disks between generation 1 and generation 2 virtual machines. Also remember that generation 1 machines boot from the IDE controller, and generation 2 machines boot from the SCSI controller.

The only way to move from generation 1 to generation 2 is to boot the virtual machine from Windows PE, capture the partitions to a WIM file, and then redeploy to a generation 2 virtual machine. This amount of effort, however, is not worth the benefit. Generation 2 is best saved for new virtual machines.

VMCX Configuration File

Prior to Windows Server 2016, the configuration for a virtual machine was stored in an XML file that was readable in an XML or text editor. The file could also be edited to make changes to the configuration outside supported mechanisms, such as Hyper-V Manager and the Hyper-V PowerShell cmdlets, which could lead to problems. Additionally, because of the text-based nature of the file, it was susceptible to corruption if an unplanned power outage or loss of access to storage occurred.

Windows Server 2016 moved to a new binary-based configuration file, the VMCX file, in addition to a new VMRS file that contains resource state data for the VM. The VMCX file cannot be read through a text editor, and it is resilient to corruption from storage or power failures.

The correct method for viewing and modifying configuration is through the aforementioned Hyper-V management tools. However, it is possible to dump out the configuration of the VMCX file using PowerShell. The best method I have found is to create a temporary object that contains a copy of the configuration in the VMCX file. It is then possible to view all of the data from within the temporary object that is a copy of the VMCX configuration. For example:

```
$tempVM = (Compare-VM -Copy -Path .\yourvmcxfile.vmcx -GenerateNewID).VM
```

You can examine all of the key properties by using the following:

```
$tempVM | select *
```

It is also possible to view specific collections that are part of the object, such as network adapters and disks. For example:

```
$tempVM.NetworkAdapters
$tempVM.HardDrives
$tempVM.FibreChannelHostBusAdapters
```

If you type **$tempVM** and press Tab, PowerShell will show all of the options available to you.

VM Configuration Versions

Each version of Hyper-V introduces a new VM configuration version that exposes the new capabilities. Windows Server 2016 introduces the new VM configuration version 8. Table 2.1 shows the various configuration versions available for each version of Hyper-V.

TABLE 2.1:   VM Configuration Versions by Windows Server Version

HYPER-V VERSION	VM CONFIGURATION VERSIONS SUPPORTED
Windows Server 2008	1
Windows Server 2008 SP1	2
Windows Server 2008 R2	3
Windows Server 2012	4
Windows Server 2012 R2	5 (and 4 to enable Live Migration from 2012, but once migrated, it is automatically upgraded to version 5)
Windows Server 2016	8 and 5

Note that Windows Server 2016 supports both 8 and 5, as 5 may be required for pre-2016 compatibility. New VMs created on 2016 will use the new VM configuration version 8, while VMs created on 2012 R2 will maintain version 5 unless they are manually converted. When a VM is converted to the new VM configuration version, its XML-based configuration is converted to the binary VMCX format and a VMRS file is created for the runtime state.

This conversion can be done using Hyper-V Manager or PowerShell. Figure 2.7 shows the configuration version update context menu option for a configuration version 5 VM that was imported from Windows Server 2012 R2.

FIGURE 2.7
VM configuration
upgrade using Hyper-V
Manager

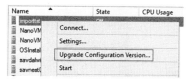

To perform the conversion using PowerShell, use the following:

```
Update-VMVersion -Name "<VM name>" -Confirm:$false
```

Note that after a VM configuration version is upgraded to 8, the conversion cannot be reversed back to a 5. Therefore, before upgrading a VM to version 8, make sure that there is no need for backward compatibility.

Processor Resources

With the core fabric of a virtual machine understood, it's time to move on to the processor, which is one of the most interesting and used resources for a virtual machine. It's important to understand some of the terminology related to processor resources and how this relates to virtualization and Hyper-V.

There is a difference between the number of processors, cores, and logical processors and the amount of memory supported by Windows Server and that supported by Hyper-V. With new processors having multiple processing cores, and technologies such as hyperthreading adding more complexity to understanding processors, a review of logical and virtual processors is important.

Motherboards have one or more sockets, which can have processors installed. This is why the terms *socket* and *processor* are sometimes used interchangeably. Each processor has one or more processing cores. Early processors had only one core, but multicore processors became predominant starting with dual-core processors, then quad-core, and today there are 10-core processors available. Each core acts like a separate processor with the ability to perform its own execution of program instructions, though the cores share a common bus interface and certain types of processor cache, as explained in Chapter 1.

In many types of program instruction execution, not all of the core's execution resources are utilized, so Intel introduced a hyperthreading technology. This technology makes a single processor core look like two processor cores, known as logical processors, and allows two instruction threads to run on each processor core. This increases overall throughput by allowing the processor to switch between the two instruction threads to keep the cores busy; it's common for instruction threads to stall while waiting on a resource. With hyperthreading, if one thread stalls, the other thread can be executed. There is still only a single execution resource on the core, so hyperthreading does not double performance; the improvement varies, but between a 10 to 15 percent performance improvement is an accepted value.

Figure 2.8 shows Task Manager on one of my Windows Server 2012 R2 boxes. It has two Intel Xeon processors, which are eight-core processors, and has hyperthreading enabled. Notice that the socket count is 2 and the core count is 16, while the logical processor count is 32 because the hyperthreading splits each core into two logical processors.

FIGURE 2.8
Task Manager in
Logical Processor view
showing the physical
processors and logical
processor details

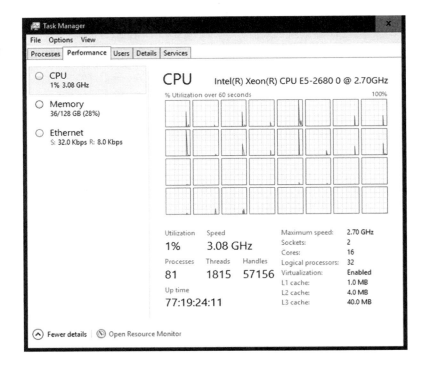

Prior to Windows Server 2012, the various SKUs (editions) of Windows Server had different capabilities and scalability . This changed with Windows Server 2012. Windows Server 2012 Standard and Datacenter have the same scalability and capabilities, supporting up to 320 logical processors addressable by the hypervisor and 4TB of memory. Each virtual machine can be allocated up to 64 virtual processors. These scalability numbers did not change with Windows Server 2012 R2 Hyper-V, because they didn't need to. With the Windows Server 2012 Hyper-V scalability capability of 64 vCPUs per virtual machine, Microsoft found that more than 99 percent of the world's SQL Server instances could now be virtualized on Hyper-V. Windows Server 2016 introduces feature differences between the Standard and Datacenter SKUs, but the scalability is the same for both and remains unchanged from Windows Server 2012.

Having multiple logical processors is useful for virtualization. To benefit from many logical processors on a normal system, the applications being used have to be written to take advantage of multiple threads of execution. Alternatively, many applications would be used at the same time, and the operating system would distribute them over the available logical processors. With virtualization, each virtual machine is assigned a certain number of virtual processors (vCPUs), which then map to logical processors. A single logical processor can be used by multiple virtual processors, because the logical processor's capacity is divided among the virtual processors as computations are required. This works in a similar manner to the time slicing that occurs between applications in an operating system sharing the processors. As virtual processors need to perform computations, they are scheduled on an available logical processor.

Prior to Windows Server 2012, there was a supported ratio of 8 virtual processors for every 1 logical processor (8:1) for all workloads except for Windows VDI environments, where a ratio of

12:1 was supported. This was stipulated to ensure that hosts were not overcommitted in terms of virtual processors assigned to virtual machines. For example, with a ratio of 8:1, if a system had a total of 8 logical processors, then up to 64 vCPUs could be assigned in total for all of the virtual machines running on that host. Note that a single virtual machine can never be assigned more virtual processors than the number of logical processors present in the server. Taking the same 8 logical processors, this means that a single virtual machine could not have more than 8 virtual processors assigned. However, I could have 8 virtual machines, all with 8 virtual processors (or any other smaller combinations, providing the total does not exceed 64 virtual processors). The supportability ratio of virtual processors to logical processors was removed in Windows Server 2012. If you test the environment and it works, then it will be supported by Microsoft. You still cannot have more virtual processors in a virtual machine than logical processors that exist in the server. A Hyper-V host supports up to 2,048 virtual processors.

Even though the supported ratio has been removed, this does not mean that careful planning is not required when architecting your Hyper-V environment. Virtualization cannot magically enable more processing resources than are physically available. For virtual machines with very low CPU utilization, such as around 10 percent, planning on 8 virtual processors to 1 logical processor would be fine and would yield an average utilization of around 80 percent on the physical core. If virtual machines have high processor utilization, a ratio of 8:1 would yield poor performance, because virtual machines constantly wait for cycles on the physical cores.

Some applications, such as SQL Server and Exchange, have their own supported ratios of virtual processor to logical processor, which can be as low as 1:1. I cover this in more detail later in this chapter. Because of the fairly low additional performance that hyperthreading actually yields, though, I prefer to count processor cores only when thinking about my virtual-to-physical ratios. If I have a Hyper-V host with 4 processor cores, I would consider 32 my maximum number of virtual processors, even if hyperthreading was enabled. Figure 2.9 shows a high-level view of mapping of physical processors to cores to logical processors to virtual processors.

FIGURE 2.9
A view of logical processor to virtual processor mapping

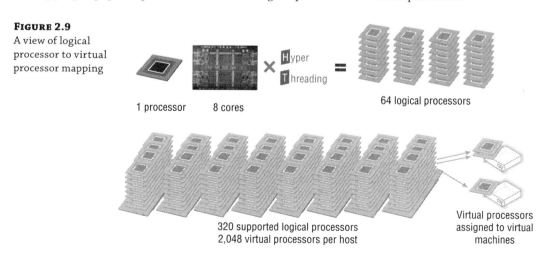

1 processor   8 cores   64 logical processors

320 supported logical processors
2,048 virtual processors per host

Virtual processors assigned to virtual machines

Note that there is no concept of processor affinity in Hyper-V. You cannot force a certain virtual processor always to map to the same logical processor. That could lead to poor performance while waiting for the processor to be available, and it also breaks the goal of abstracting the virtual resource from the physical resource.

SHOULD I TURN OFF HYPERTHREADING?

Hyperthreading causes no harm and may help performance—unless it pushes the number of logical processors above 320, which is the maximum number supported by Hyper-V. If hyperthreading results in more than 320, those logical processors provided by hyperthreading could be used instead of physical cores by the hypervisor. Therefore, if hyperthreading pushes the number of logical processors above 320, turn it off in the servers' BIOS/UEFI.

Virtual Processor to Logical Processor Scheduling

How a virtual machine's virtual processors are assigned to logical processors for computations is interesting. Consider the simplest possible scenario: a single virtual processor on a virtual machine. When the virtual processor needs to perform a computation, the hypervisor schedules the computation to an available logical processor, as shown in Figure 2.10.

FIGURE 2.10
A virtual processor from a single-processor VM assigned to a logical processor on the host

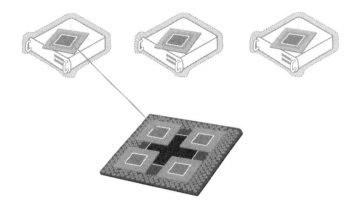

This gets more complicated for a virtual machine with multiple virtual processors, a symmetric multiprocessing (SMP) environment. The problem is that operating systems believe that all of their processors are available to run at the same time, because the operating system would exclusively own the hardware and can allow interdependencies between different computations on different processors. This is a problem in a virtual environment, because many virtual processors are using the same logical processors. Therefore, the virtual processor scheduler in the hypervisor could have a problem.

Consider Figure 2.11, where two of the virtual machines now have multiple processors. If the processor scheduler has to schedule all of the virtual processors in a VM to logical processors at the same time, the virtual processor scheduler suddenly becomes inefficient. Even virtual processors not currently doing work would be scheduled on the logical processor as a set, and none of the virtual processors in a VM can be scheduled until there are an equal number of logical processors available to ensure that the computations for the VM can take place simultaneously. Consider a heavily used server and that virtual machines can have up to 64 virtual processors. Trying to group and schedule processors in this way is highly problematic. This type of scheduling is known as *gang scheduling*, because when a multiprocessor virtual machine needs to schedule a processor, all of the virtual processors are "ganged" together and scheduled together against the available logical processors.

FIGURE 2.11
A virtual machine with multiple virtual processors being scheduled to the available logical processors

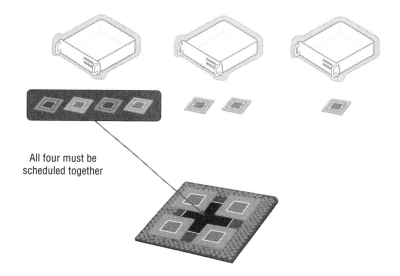

All four must be scheduled together

Here's a great analogy: Consider going out to dinner with a group of friends. You sit down, open the menu, and know exactly what you want to eat. You then proceed to sit there for 15 minutes until everyone else has decided what they will order, because you have to all order at the same time. You are, in essence, gang scheduled.

Nobody has been able to create a perfect gang scheduler that does not lead to delays and inefficiencies. It is because of this gang scheduling that with some hypervisors, you need to minimize the number of virtual processors per virtual machine as much as possible.

Hyper-V does not use gang scheduling and instead takes an alternate approach to handling multiprocessor virtual machines and the scheduling to logical processors. Remember, the problem is that operating systems believe that all of their processors are available to run at the same time. Rather than trying to work around this problem, Microsoft fixed the operating system kernel itself so that the operating system no longer assumes that all processors will be scheduled at the same time. This enables Hyper-V to schedule virtual processors from a multiprocessor virtual machine independently of each other, which allows virtual processors to be scheduled only as they have workload. This is known as *free processor scheduling*. This fix was made in Windows Server 2008, which is why Windows Server 2000 supports only a single processor. A targeted change was made to the kernel in Windows Server 2003 Service Pack 2 and Windows XP Service Pack 3, which allows for two virtual processors to be configured. Because gang scheduling is not used with Hyper-V, there is no guidance to limit the number of virtual processors in a virtual machine. Having lots of idle processors still carries some overhead, but it is fairly minimal and has nowhere near the impact of a hypervisor that uses gang scheduling. In my lab environment, nearly all my virtual machines have two processors, and some have eight.

Using the same dinner analogy for Hyper-V would allow you to order dinner whenever you were ready and then get your food. This would be, however, poor dining etiquette on your part and would likely get you excluded from future dinner events and subject you to lots of future solo dining.

The exact number of virtual processors supported for each guest operating system for Hyper-V is documented and updated at https://technet.microsoft.com/library/mt126119.aspx, but the primary numbers are shown in Table 2.2. Note that Windows Server 2000 and Windows Server 2003 are not listed on the Microsoft site because they are no longer supported operating systems; only one processor was supported for Windows Server 2000 and two for Windows Server 2003.

TABLE 2.2: Maximum Number of Virtual Processors

OPERATING SYSTEM	NUMBER OF VIRTUAL PROCESSORS
Windows Server 2008 R2 and above	64
Windows Server 2008 SP2	4
Modern supported Linux distributions (RHEL 5.9+, SUSE 11 SP2+, Ubuntu 12.04+)	64
Windows 8 and above	32
Windows 7	4
Windows Vista SP2	2

It's important to understand that gang scheduling is not bad; rather, there's just not an efficient algorithm to use it at this time. In the future, a perfect algorithm may be created, and then I would not be surprised to see Hyper-V implement some type of gang scheduling.

Processor Assignment

When assigning processors to a virtual machine, between 1 and 64 (or the number of logical processors in the system) can be assigned. Additionally, it is possible to set three other values that help control the processor resource usage. These are Virtual Machine Reserve (Percentage), Virtual Machine Limit (Percentage), and Relative Weight:

Virtual Machine Reserve (Percentage) The amount of the processor that is reserved for this virtual machine and therefore always available. If a host has 4 logical processors and the virtual machine has 1 virtual processor and the reserve is set to 50 percent, then it means that half of one of the logical processors is always available to this virtual machine. Note that it does not mean it's the same core or all from the same core, but the hypervisor will ensure that the virtual machine always has the equivalent of half of a logical processor of processing available to this virtual machine. If the virtual machine is not using the full reserve, other virtual machines may access the processor resource. However, as soon as the virtual machine with the reserve needs the CPU, it will take priority and be guaranteed its full allocation. The Percent Of Total System Resources value shows what percentage of the overall system resources the reserve that's assigned equates to. If a virtual machine has been assigned 8 virtual processors with a 25 percent reserve and the server has 16 logical processors in total, this means that the percent of total system resources reserved is 12 percent (12.5 percent, really).

Virtual Machine Limit (Percentage)   The maximum amount of processor that the virtual machine can use. The default is 100 percent, which means that this virtual machine can use the entire resources of the allocated processors. Note that in times of resource contention, the virtual machine may not get a full 100 percent, but it will always get its reserve amount.

Relative Weight   Used to determine the importance of a virtual machine getting shares of the CPU time in times of resource contention. For example, a virtual machine with a weight of 200 would get twice the number of CPU cycles that a virtual machine with a weight of 100 would get.

Although the number of processors of a virtual machine cannot be changed after the virtual machine has been started, it is possible to modify the Virtual Machine Reserve (Percentage), Virtual Machine Limit (Percentage), and Relative Weight values while the virtual machine is running. This enables you to tweak processor resources for a virtual machine dynamically. This would let you assign extra processors to a virtual machine than normally would be required, but you can set the Virtual Machine Limit (Percentage) value to something like 50 percent so that only half the capacity could be used. If more processor is required while the virtual machine is running, that value can be increased. Typically, operating systems will not "waste" processor resources, so this type of limiting usually is not required, unless you have a heavily overcommitted system or a virtual machine with rogue processes.

SOLVING "HANGING" PROBLEMS FOR VERY LARGE HYPER-V VIRTUAL MACHINES

For a virtual machine with more than 32 virtual processors, I would sometimes see the virtual machine hang within 30 seconds of logging on (the same time Server Manager started and used processor resources). After investigation, I found that the problem was that a large number of the logical processors in the Hyper-V host had gone into a C3 sleep state, which is a deep sleep state to save power when the processor is idle. The problem seemed to be caused by all of these logical processors trying to wake at the same time and getting into contention with each other. The solution for me was simply to disable the C3 sleep state on my processors on the Hyper-V host by using the following command:

```
reg.exe add HKLM\System\CurrentControlSet\Control\Processor /v Capabilities ↵
/t REG_DWORD /d 0x0007e066
```

Then I would reboot the server, and my problem was solved.

Windows Server Hyper-V has another processor-related setting that is set per virtual machine. This setting is "Migrate to a physical computer with a different processor version." It is not possible to migrate a virtual machine between Intel and AMD processors by using migration technologies, because of the completely different architecture and instruction sets of the processor. However, by default you also can't migrate between servers with different versions of the same processor family. Although both servers may have Intel processors, the different processors may have different capabilities, features, and instructions, which is a problem because some applications perform tests when they start to check the capabilities of the processor. If an application checks the processor and decides that it has a certain set of instructions and is then moved using migration technologies to a server with a different processor that does not support a particular instruction, when the application makes the call, the application may crash. To resolve this problem, Hyper-V adds the ability to hide many higher-level functions of processors in the guest operating systems. You can move guest operating systems between nodes in a cluster even if the processor versions are different, because the virtual operating systems are exposed only to the generic instructions that are present in all versions of the processor family. The functionality does not scan the processors and expose the lowest common set of functionality of all of the processors in the cluster; it just limits to a generic basic set lower than all of the processors in the cluster. Do not enable this setting unless you know that you will need the ability to move between hosts with different versions, because hiding the instructions of the processor may cause a performance impact to applications and services that would otherwise use those instructions to improve performance. This can also be set using PowerShell with the following command:

```
Set-VMProcessor -CompatibilityForMigrationEnabled $true
```

The exact instructions that are hidden when this setting is enabled are shown in Table 2.3.

TABLE 2.3:   Process Features Hidden with Processor Compatibility Enabled

INTEL PROCESSORS	AMD PROCESSORS
SSSE3, SSE4.1, SSE4.2, POPCNT, Misaligned SSE, XSAVE, AVX	SSSE3, SSE4.1, SSE4.A, SSE5, POPCNT, LZCNT, Misaligned SSE, AMD 3DNow!, Extended AMD 3DNow!

Prior to Windows Server 2012 Hyper-V, there was also a setting to enable running older operating systems, such as NT 4, but this option has been removed from the Hyper-V manager graphical user interface. The problem for older operating systems is that modern processors return more information about the capabilities than can be handled by the operating system, and it will blue screen (this was fixed in Windows NT 4 SP6). This option can still be set, but it must be configured using PowerShell:

```
Set-VMProcessor -CompatibilityForOlderOperatingSystemsEnabled $true
```

A great way to understand these two settings is by leveraging the Coreinfo utility from Sysinternals, which can list all features for a processor. You'll find it at the following location:

http://technet.microsoft.com/en-us/sysinternals/cc835722.aspx

When running Coreinfo on a processor without any compatibility enabled, I see all the features available for the operating system. An enabled feature shows an * instead of a -. When I run Coreinfo on the same virtual machine but after setting CompatibilityForMigrationEnabled, all of the items in bold change from * to -, which means that they are now hidden, as shown in the following listing. In this example, SSSE3, SSE4.1, SSE4.2, and POPCNT were hidden. Running with CompatibilityForOlderOperatingSystemsEnabled removed the entire Logical Processor to Cache Map section from the returned data, which means that it was hidden from the operating system. It is important to use these features only when required, because you are removing capability from the processor, which you don't want to do unless you absolutely have to.

```
S:\Tools>coreinfo

Coreinfo v3.2 - Dump information on system CPU and memory topology
Copyright (C) 2008-2012 Mark Russinovich
Sysinternals - www.sysinternals.com


Intel(R) Xeon(R) CPU          E5530  @ 2.40GHz
Intel64 Family 6 Model 26 Stepping 5, GenuineIntel
HTT             *       Hyperthreading enabled
HYPERVISOR      *       Hypervisor is present
VMX             -       Supports Intel hardware-assisted virtualization
SVM             -       Supports AMD hardware-assisted virtualization
EM64T           *       Supports 64-bit mode

SMX             -       Supports Intel trusted execution
SKINIT          -       Supports AMD SKINIT

NX              *       Supports no-execute page protection
SMEP            -       Supports Supervisor Mode Execution Prevention
SMAP            -       Supports Supervisor Mode Access Prevention
PAGE1GB         -       Supports 1 GB large pages
PAE             *       Supports > 32-bit physical addresses
PAT             *       Supports Page Attribute Table
PSE             *       Supports 4 MB pages
PSE36           *       Supports > 32-bit address 4 MB pages
PGE             *       Supports global bit in page tables
SS              *       Supports bus snooping for cache operations
VME             *       Supports Virtual-8086 mode
RDWRFSGSBASE    -       Supports direct GS/FS base access

FPU             *       Implements i387 floating point instructions
MMX             *       Supports MMX instruction set
```

```
MMXEXT          -       Implements AMD MMX extensions
3DNOW           -       Supports 3DNow! instructions
3DNOWEXT        -       Supports 3DNow! extension instructions
SSE             *       Supports Streaming SIMD Extensions
SSE2            *       Supports Streaming SIMD Extensions 2
SSE3            *       Supports Streaming SIMD Extensions 3
SSSE3           *       Supports Supplemental SIMD Extensions 3
SSE4.1          *       Supports Streaming SIMD Extensions 4.1
SSE4.2          *       Supports Streaming SIMD Extensions 4.2


AES             -       Supports AES extensions
AVX             -       Supports AVX instruction extensions
FMA             -       Supports FMA extensions using YMM state
MSR             *       Implements RDMSR/WRMSR instructions
MTRR            *       Supports Memory Type Range Registers
XSAVE           -       Supports XSAVE/XRSTOR instructions
OSXSAVE         -       Supports XSETBV/XGETBV instructions
RDRAND          -       Supports RDRAND instruction
RDSEED          -       Supports RDSEED instruction


CMOV            *       Supports CMOVcc instruction
CLFSH           *       Supports CLFLUSH instruction
CX8             *       Supports compare and exchange 8-byte instructions
CX16            *       Supports CMPXCHG16B instruction
BMI1            -       Supports bit manipulation extensions 1
BMI2            -       Supports bit manipulation extensions 2
ADX             -       Supports ADCX/ADOX instructions
DCA             -       Supports prefetch from memory-mapped device
F16C            -       Supports half-precision instruction
FXSR            *       Supports FXSAVE/FXSTOR instructions
FFXSR           -       Supports optimized FXSAVE/FSRSTOR instruction
MONITOR         -       Supports MONITOR and MWAIT instructions
MOVBE           -       Supports MOVBE instruction
ERMSB           -       Supports Enhanced REP MOVSB/STOSB
PCLULDQ         -       Supports PCLMULDQ instruction
POPCNT          *       Supports POPCNT instruction
SEP             *       Supports fast system call instructions
LAHF-SAHF       *       Supports LAHF/SAHF instructions in 64-bit mode
HLE             -       Supports Hardware Lock Elision instructions
RTM             -       Supports Restricted Transactional Memory instructions


DE              *       Supports I/O breakpoints including CR4.DE
DTES64          -       Can write history of 64-bit branch addresses
DS              -       Implements memory-resident debug buffer
DS-CPL          -       Supports Debug Store feature with CPL
```

```
PCID              -      Supports PCIDs and settable CR4.PCIDE
INVPCID           -      Supports INVPCID instruction
PDCM              -      Supports Performance Capabilities MSR
RDTSCP            -      Supports RDTSCP instruction
TSC               *      Supports RDTSC instruction
TSC-DEADLINE      -      Local APIC supports one-shot deadline timer
TSC-INVARIANT     -      TSC runs at constant rate
xTPR              -      Supports disabling task priority messages

EIST              -      Supports Enhanced Intel Speedstep
ACPI              -      Implements MSR for power management
TM                -      Implements thermal monitor circuitry
TM2               -      Implements Thermal Monitor 2 control
APIC              *      Implements software-accessible local APIC
x2APIC            -      Supports x2APIC

CNXT-ID           -      L1 data cache mode adaptive or BIOS

MCE               *      Supports Machine Check, INT18 and CR4.MCE
MCA               *      Implements Machine Check Architecture
PBE               -      Supports use of FERR#/PBE# pin

PSN               -      Implements 96-bit processor serial number

PREFETCHW         *      Supports PREFETCHW instruction


Logical to Physical Processor Map:
*-  Physical Processor 0
-*  Physical Processor 1

Logical Processor to Socket Map:
**  Socket 0

Logical Processor to NUMA Node Map:
**  NUMA Node 0

Logical Processor to Cache Map:
*-  Data Cache          0, Level 1,   32 KB, Assoc   8, LineSize  64
*-  Instruction Cache   0, Level 1,   32 KB, Assoc   4, LineSize  64
*-  Unified Cache       0, Level 2,  256 KB, Assoc   8, LineSize  64
*-  Unified Cache       1, Level 3,    8 MB, Assoc  16, LineSize  64
-*  Data Cache          1, Level 1,   32 KB, Assoc   8, LineSize  64
-*  Instruction Cache   1, Level 1,   32 KB, Assoc   4, LineSize  64
-*  Unified Cache       2, Level 2,  256 KB, Assoc   8, LineSize  64
```

```
 -*  Unified Cache      3, Level 3,     8 MB, Assoc  16, LineSize  64

Logical Processor to Group Map:
**  Group 0
```

NUMA Support

Consider the ability to now have virtual machines with 64 virtual processors and up to 1TB of memory. I don't know of a physical processor with 64 logical processors on the market today, even with hyperthreading, which means that a virtual machine with more virtual processors than can be provided by a single processor will receive resources from multiple physical processors. A multiprocessor motherboard has multiple sockets where processors can be installed and a corresponding number of memory slots directly linked to each of the sockets. A processor and the memory that is directly attached and managed by the processor is known as a *non-uniform memory access (NUMA)* node. There is typically a 1:1 relationship between sockets and NUMA nodes, although some of the latest hardware does have more than one NUMA node per socket. A motherboard with four sockets would normally have banks of memory for each socket and would therefore have four NUMA nodes. A processor can access the local memory in its NUMA node faster than nonlocal memory, which means that for best performance, processes running on a processor should use memory within that processor's NUMA node.

Windows Server 2012 introduced a new set of configurations for virtual machine processors, NUMA, but the reality is that you should never touch these. Most likely bad things will happen, and Hyper-V will make the right configurations for your environment without any manual intervention. However, I do want to cover the purpose of these settings and why NUMA is important. Note that Windows Server 2008 R2 Hyper-V host was NUMA aware and would always try to ensure that virtual processors and memory were assigned within the same NUMA nodes, but this NUMA topology was not made available to the virtual machine, which wasn't a problem considering virtual machines could have only four vCPUs and were therefore not likely to use more than one NUMA node.

Operating systems are aware of the NUMA nodes and the configuration that enables the most optimal resource usage. With the large virtual machines possible in Hyper-V, the NUMA topology is also projected to the virtual machine, which is known as *virtual NUMA* or *vNUMA*. vNUMA uses the standard ACPI (Advanced Configuration and Power Interface) Static Resource Affinity Table (SRAT), which means that the NUMA topology should be usable by any NUMA-aware operating system, including Linux. This NUMA awareness is also a benefit for enterprise applications, such as SQL, MySQL, and IIS, which utilize resources based on NUMA configuration.

VIRTUAL MACHINE NUMA CONFIGURATION

Figure 2.12 shows the NUMA configuration options available for the processor configuration of a virtual machine. These options are hidden away for good reason. In nearly all scenarios, you should not change these values. Hyper-V will do the best job of setting the right NUMA topology based on the physical Hyper-V host. In a few scenarios, however, you may need to change these values, which are related to the number of processors, memory, and number of nodes on a single socket.

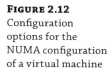

FIGURE 2.12
Configuration
options for the
NUMA configuration
of a virtual machine

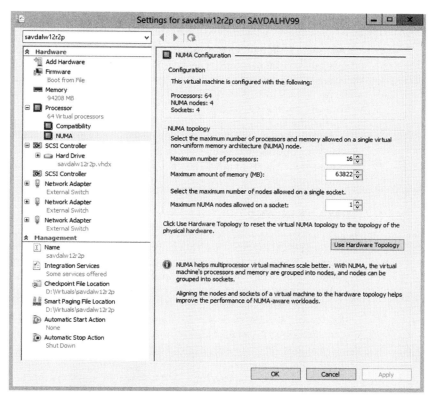

Consider a large Hyper-V environment with many types of servers. The physical servers have different NUMA topologies, and virtual machines may be live-migrated between the servers. In this case, the NUMA configuration should be changed to match the smallest NUMA topology among all of the servers to which the virtual machine may be migrated. For example, suppose I have two servers:

♦ Server 1 NUMA topology: Maximum number of processors is 16, and maximum amount of memory is 63822.

♦ Server 2 NUMA topology: Maximum number of processors is 8, and maximum amount of memory is 22720.

If a virtual machine is created on Server 1, that is the NUMA topology that will be configured for the virtual machine. If the virtual machine is then moved to Server 2, the VM will have incorrect NUMA configuration and will not have optimal resource assignments, because what it believes is a single NUMA node actually spans multiple NUMA boundaries. It therefore makes sense to set the NUMA topology of the virtual machine manually to match that of Server 2. Hopefully in the future, the management solutions for Hyper-V will look at all of the nodes in a cluster and automatically configure virtual machines with a NUMA topology that matches the smallest NUMA configuration in the cluster. At the time of this writing, this does not occur.

Additionally, in most clusters, the hosts all have the same NUMA topology, so in practice this is not a big issue.

Another challenge with automated NUMA configuration is that with Shared Nothing Live Migration, virtual machines can be migrated outside a cluster. No management solution could consider that. For most scenarios, virtual machines are created on the server upon which they will run, which means that they will have the most optimal configuration and no manual actions are necessary.

Notice the Use Hardware Topology button. If you change the settings and realize that you don't know the original values, you can click this button and the values will be reset back to the Hyper-V recommended values for that server.

Note that if a virtual machine uses Dynamic Memory, the vNUMA is disabled for the virtual machine.

NUMA SPANNING

As previously discussed, the best performance comes from processes running on processor cores using local memory within the NUMA node rather than having to "span" NUMA nodes. Spanning means that the memory required is connected to another processor; it's known as *foreign memory* or *remote memory*, and it has a higher latency than local memory. NUMA spanning configurations come in two types: configuration at a host level and configuration at a virtual machine level.

By default, Windows Server 2012 enables NUMA spanning at the host level. This provides the most flexibility, because virtual machines can access and use memory in any NUMA node. But it also may result in lower performance, compared to forcing virtual machines to use memory on the same NUMA node as the processor cores. By disabling NUMA spanning at the host level, you disable it for all virtual machines on the host and you ensure that virtual machines' virtual NUMA nodes are backed by memory from one NUMA node giving the best performance. However, it could also mean that virtual machines might not be able to start if the required amount of memory for the VM is not available on a single NUMA node. It also means that you may not be able to live-migrate virtual machines to other nodes if the target node cannot satisfy the NUMA requirements.

The NUMA spanning option should be changed only when you, as an administrator, feel comfortable with NUMA and the implications of disabling and have an additional management suite that can help ensure the best configuration. In reality, the best practice should be to leave NUMA spanning enabled, and that is what I recommend. To disable NUMA spanning, open the Hyper-V Settings page and deselect the NUMA spanning option, as shown in Figure 2.13.

FIGURE 2.13
Changing the NUMA spanning option for a Hyper-V server

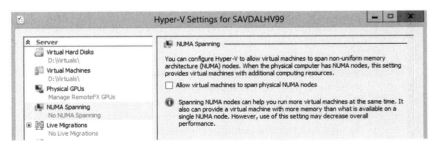

Note that System Center Virtual Machine Manager allows NUMA spanning to be configured per virtual machine. Behind the scenes, this means manually configuring virtual machine assignments to specific NUMA nodes, but this is not something you would ever want to try to perform manually. If you value having your workload always perform predictably, and you accept that your virtual machine may not start when memory is fragmented, turn off spanning for that guest. If you value having your workload start up predictably, with perhaps nonoptimal performance, leave spanning turned on. It's probably the right choice for most people once again to leave NUMA spanning enabled for most virtual machines.

Note that whether NUMA spanning is enabled or disabled, the hypervisor will always make a best effort to be as efficient as possible and schedule the virtual processor on the appropriate physical NUMA node, backing the memory of the virtual machine. Hyper-V will also make an effort not to fragment memory among multiple NUMA nodes if at all possible. NUMA spanning allows a way out only if there is no other option but to fragment. However, if no logical processor in the physical NUMA node is available, the hypervisor may temporarily schedule the virtual processor to a remote logical processor in another NUMA node. Running a virtual processor on a remote NUMA node is still more efficient than not running it at all if no local NUMA node resource is available. Again, NUMA spanning does not change this behavior. The NUMA spanning configuration is primarily controlling whether the memory for a virtual NUMA node can be sourced from multiple physical NUMA nodes if necessary (which is NUMA spanning enabled).

Memory Resources

When you're looking at resources used in virtual environments, memory is the other major type of resource, along with the processor, that typically dictates the number of virtual machines that can be supported on a host. While logical processors are shared by virtual processors via rapid context switching, the same technique does not work with memory. The context—the content of memory itself—cannot be swapped in and out fast enough to simulate simultaneous execution.

For Windows 2008 and Windows Server 2008 R2 before Service Pack 1, the amount of memory that was assigned to a virtual machine could not be modified while the virtual machine was running. If a Hyper-V server had 16GB of memory, and assuming 1GB was kept for the Windows Server parent partition, then 15GB could be assigned to virtual machines running on the server. That 15GB could be consumed by 1 virtual machine with 15GB of memory assigned, or 30 virtual machines each using 512MB of memory.

In this model, each virtual machine must be assigned the most memory it will ever need. At any specific point in time, however, much of this memory may be unneeded. For example, half of the VMs on a host may require their full assignment, but the other half may be experiencing an idle period and not require anywhere near their full allotment of memory. This can lead to a lot of wasted memory during normal utilization, which reduces the number of virtual machines that can be hosted on each server.

Dynamic Memory

Windows Server 2008 R2 Service Pack 1 introduced a new memory optimization feature, *Dynamic Memory*. This new technology allows the amount of memory allocated to a virtual machine to increase and decrease based on the amount of memory the processes running in the guest operating system need at any given moment in time. Dynamic Memory is different from memory overcommit used by other hypervisors. Memory overcommit strategies tell the VM that it has a very large amount of memory in the hopes that not all VMs try to write to all of the visible memory. If that were to happen, memory would have to be swapped with other storage—say compressed memory, shared memory, or disk data—which can drastically impact VM performance.

Dynamic Memory uses three settings for each virtual machine: an initial, a maximum, and (in Windows Server 2012 and beyond) a minimum amount of memory. Hyper-V can intelligently add or remove memory to or from a virtual machine based on its real-time demand for memory and memory availability on the host. The virtual machine is initially allocated the amount of memory defined as the startup RAM, and then based on how the processes inside the virtual machine are using the memory, additional memory is allocated if available, possibly reallocated from other virtual machines with a lesser need or removed from the virtual machine.

Figure 2.14 shows the dialog box for configuring memory in Windows Server 2012. Note that if the Enable Dynamic Memory check box is not selected, the virtual machine uses static memory and will use the amount defined in the Startup RAM setting. Selecting Enable Dynamic Memory allows the Dynamic Memory setting to be changed. The value defined in Startup RAM is still used as the initial amount of memory, but Minimum RAM and Maximum RAM values are also available. Maximum RAM is the size to which the memory for the virtual machine can grow. The default Maximum RAM is 1,048,576MB; the maximum Hyper-V allows. However, this can be configured to a more reasonable limit based on the expected and tolerated memory use, to prevent depriving other virtual machines of memory if things go wrong and memory use grows unchecked. Minimum RAM was introduced in Windows Server 2012, and it allows configuration of the virtual machine to shrink below its Startup RAM value. This is useful if you have an application that needs a certain amount of memory to launch initially but then no longer needs that amount.

FIGURE 2.14
Configuring Dynamic Memory settings for a virtual machine

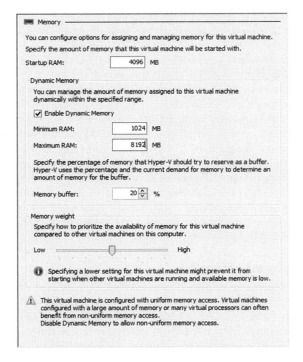

Also in the figure are options to set a percentage of memory to use as a buffer and to use a memory slider to set the memory priority compared to other virtual machines running on the host. The memory buffer allows you to keep extra memory assigned to the VM beyond its immediate need. This accomplishes two things. First, it's not desirable to let the operating system totally exhaust all memory before adding more RAM, which may take a few seconds to be added and used. In those few seconds, the performance of the virtual machine could be severely adversely affected, and it would have started to page out pages of memory to its pagefile. The *pagefile* is a file on disk that can be used by an OS's virtual memory manager to store pages from RAM temporarily when physical memory is low. This can deteriorate performance because disk is much slower to use than RAM. Second, it provides extra memory to be used for cache and other memory consumers that use otherwise available memory behind the scenes.

To avoid this memory starvation and provide extra memory for caches, Dynamic Memory provides some memory beyond a virtual machine's instantaneous demand, up to the Maximum RAM setting (that is, Hyper-V will never assign more than Maximum RAM). By default, this amount is 20 percent of demand. When the virtual machine has less than this available memory percentage, then more memory is added if physically available in the Hyper-V host to bring the virtual machine back to the desired percentage of available memory. The memory buffer can be changed to a desired amount based on the needs of the virtual machine, and it can be modified while the virtual machine is running.

The other slider is used to set a priority of memory allocation in times when there is not enough physical RAM available to meet all of the desired amounts for the VMs. Just as with CPU allocation, a VM with a higher memory priority will receive additional memory before VMs of a lower priority.

One aspect of Dynamic Memory that makes it special in terms of its memory optimization technique is how the decision to add or remove memory is made. I used the word *intelligently* earlier because Dynamic Memory does not just give more memory to a virtual machine if its free memory is low, but rather it's based on how much memory the workload needs. Figure 2.15 shows part of a Task Manager view of a Windows Server 2008 R2 server that has 8GB of RAM. At first glance, this virtual machine has only 4MB of free memory, so it would seem to need more. But this is not the case.

FIGURE 2.15
An operating system with only 4MB of free memory but still plenty of available memory

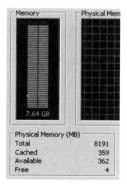

Windows XP, Windows Server 2003, and earlier operating systems tried to use as little memory as possible, and so it was common to see systems with large amounts of free memory. Windows Vista, Windows Server 2008, and later operating systems use all of the memory that they can use for cache purposes, to help improve performance by preloading programs into memory. If memory is available, it makes sense to use it to try to improve performance. Leaving memory free does not benefit anyone, which is why it's rare to see a high Free Memory value on Windows Server 2008 and above. It is because nearly all memory is always used that memory overcommit technologies such as Allocate on First Write (which assigns memory as the virtual machine writes data) don't work well with modern operating systems and why Hyper-V does not use that memory optimization technique. The memory used for caching can be used by applications whenever needed, so the memory used for cache is largely still available, and therefore looking at free memory is fairly meaningless. We need to consider the available memory (which includes most of the memory being used for cache), which can be seen in Figure 2.15 as well.

Dynamic Memory uses the commit value for memory to identify the amount of memory that is used, and therefore its memory demand, and it is key to the intelligence it brings to memory allocation. Hyper-V Integration Services has a Dynamic Memory virtual service client (VSC) in the guest OS that communicates with its corresponding virtual service provider (VSP) in the parent partition to report its use of memory and specifically its amount of available memory. Based on the amount of available memory in the guest, the desired memory buffer configured for the virtual machine and the amount of physical RAM available in the host additional memory may be allocated to the guest. This type of intelligent memory allocation is possible only because of the guest OS insight provided by the Dynamic Memory VSC. It would not be possible if the hypervisor was looking only at which memory is being used by a virtual machine externally, because it would not be possible to tell whether the memory was being used by an application or just for disposable purposes like pre-caching.

While adding memory to a virtual machine is fairly simple—more memory is simply presented to the guest OS for it to consume—the process of removing memory that is no longer needed is more complex. You can't just take memory away from a guest operating system's memory manager and expect it to continue to function. The guest was probably using the memory (remember that little memory is actually free in a modern operating system) and, even it was truly free, the guest expects it to be usable in the future. Moreover, even if memory could be taken from a virtual machine, it would be difficult to know what memory is safest to take back! Hyper-V uses a process called *ballooning* to get around these problems and remove memory.

Ballooning is a clever way to get the guest operating system to decide which memory it no longer needs and discontinue use of that memory. A "balloon" of memory is allocated by a kernel mode device driver under Hyper-V's control. When Hyper-V wants memory back from a Dynamic Memory VM, it requests the balloon driver to allocate memory inside that VM. The driver, running inside the guest OS, allocates the memory and grows the "balloon" to a certain size. When a modern OS receives a memory allocation request, it uses insight into existing memory content and workload activity to decide where that memory can best come from. Free memory, cache memory, and unused or inactive application memory are all typical targets. If none of those are available, the guest OS may choose to page out memory content to the guest OS pagefile to generate free memory. The key is that the guest OS, rather than an outside process that does not understand how memory is being used, gets to decide intelligently which pages should be given in the most unobtrusive way, with the least hit to performance. Once the memory is allocated to the balloon driver, these addresses are communicated to the virtualization manager, which tells the hypervisor it can now effectively unmap those address ranges from physical RAM because the balloon driver will never actually touch them and no other part of the guest OS is allowed to touch them. The memory has been reclaimed by Hyper-V, and it can be used with other virtual machines.

If the virtual machine needs additional memory in the future, the VM management can "deflate" the balloon, either fully or by a certain amount. Physical RAM is provided by Hyper-V at its previous locations, and then the balloon driver frees the previously allocated RAM back to the guest OS. This process is shown in Figure 2.16.

FIGURE 2.16
The inflation of the balloon driver to allow Hyper-V to reclaim memory from a virtual machine

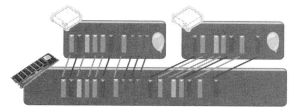

Balloon driver is deflated and not allocated any memory in the guest.

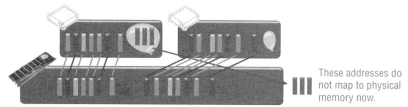

These addresses do not map to physical memory now.

Hyper-V under memory pressure sets a desired size for the balloon driver in the virtual machine. The balloon driver requests the memory from the guest and as allocated reports the pages to Hyper-V, allowing the memory to be unmapped from physical.

It is still critical to understand and plan placement of virtual machines based on expected memory usage and to set realistic maximum values. Poor planning will result in the host running out of memory and virtual machines not getting enough RAM.

While Dynamic Memory is great for client operating systems in Virtual Desktop Infrastructure implementations, it also works well for many server workloads. I've seen many organizations use Dynamic Memory on all types of server workloads like file servers, domain controllers, System Center servers, and more, and get huge memory savings. Using Dynamic Memory can enable running many more virtual machines on a server, thanks to the optimized use of memory.

Some types of services need special consideration when using Dynamic Memory, and others should not use it. I've included some of the main ones in the following list. Ultimately check with the application vendors for their support of Dynamic Memory:

◆ Linux VMs were not able to utilize Dynamic Memory until the release of Windows Server 2012 R2, which provides updated Linux Integration Services. This allows recent distributions of Linux to leverage Dynamic Memory, but older releases without updated Integration Services may not be able to do so.

◆ The Exchange 2010 and above Mailbox server role checks the amount of memory when the mailbox server starts and then does not recheck it. So Exchange will not take advantage of additional memory if it's added to the virtual machine after the mailbox service has started.

◆ The Enterprise SKU of SQL Server supports the hot-add of memory into the operating system, which is how SQL Server treats Dynamic Memory. For SQL Server to leverage additional memory, you must be running the Enterprise SKU of SQL Server. With SQL Server Enterprise edition, the physical memory is checked every second. If the memory has increased, the target memory size for SQL Server is recalculated, which is how the additions from Dynamic Memory will be seen. Because SQL Server has its own caching mechanisms regarding free memory, the buffer percentage should be set to 5 percent for a SQL Server virtual machine instead of the default 20 percent.

◆ Like SQL Server, Java also has its own caching mechanisms. The buffer percentage should be set to 5 percent for virtual machines running Java workloads instead of the default 20 percent.

It should be clear that Dynamic Memory is not a memory overcommit technology. Dynamic Memory gives a virtual machine an initial amount of memory and then, as the virtual machine uses the memory for processes, additional memory is added if available in the host. This assures the best use of memory while not running the risk of overcommitting the amount of memory available to virtual machines.

The maximum amount of memory that can be assigned to a virtual machine with Windows Server 2012 Hyper-V is 1TB. One other memory-related setting is available for a virtual machine: the Smart Paging file location. Smart Paging files were necessary because of the change in Windows Server 2012 that introduced the Minimum RAM configuration memory option for a virtual machine. The new minimum RAM capability introduces a potential problem. Consider the following scenario on a host that is fully utilized from a memory perspective:

1. A virtual machine has been running for a period of time, and the amount of physical RAM allocated is set to its Minimum RAM value, 512MB. The additional memory it was allocated when it started (startup RAM, which was 1GB) has been taken by Hyper-V through the balloon driver process.

2. The virtual machine is restarted or the host is restarted.

3. To restart, the virtual machine needs 1GB of memory, but it has only 512 MB available. In this worst-case scenario, the Hyper-V host has no spare memory, and no memory can be reclaimed from other virtual machines running on the host.

This one and only scenario is where the new Smart Paging feature is utilized:

◆ The virtual machine is being restarted (also caused by host restart).

◆ There is no available physical memory.

◆ No memory can be reclaimed from other virtual machines running on the host.

At this time, a Smart Paging file will be created for the virtual machine in the location specified in the configuration of the virtual machine and will be used by the virtual machine as memory to complete startup. As soon as possible, that memory mapped to the Smart Paging file will be ballooned out, and the Smart Paging file will be no longer used and deleted. The target time to stop using the Smart Paging file is as soon as possible and no longer than 10 minutes. The Smart Paging feature is used only to provide reliable restart of virtual machines, and it is not used to provide overcommit after boot.

WHY PAGE SHARING IS NOT USED BY HYPER-V

When virtualization technologies are used, it's common to run many operating system instances (often similar versions) on one physical piece of hardware. On my main server, I have 18 virtual machines all running Windows Server 2012 R2. The operating system version is the same, which means that a large part of their memory content will have the same data as other virtual machines running the same guest operating system.

The idea of page sharing is storing only duplicate pages of memory from all of the virtual machines once stored in physical RAM, basically single-instance storage for virtual machine memory. One way this can work is that a process in the hypervisor looks at every page of memory for every virtual machine, creates a hash value for each page of memory, and then compares the hash values. If a duplicate hash is found, a bit-by-bit comparison of the memory pages is performed to make sure that the memory pages really are identical, and then the content is stored only once in memory and the duplicate virtual machine page addresses point to the singly stored page. We are now sharing the page. This seems like a great idea, but for many reasons it doesn't work well with newer operating systems, Windows Server 2008 and later.

First, page sharing works best on empty pages. However, as you saw in the previous section with Windows Vista and above, memory is rarely left empty and is used to cache as much as possible.

Second, memory pages are getting bigger—much bigger. In the past, memory pages were 4KB, so finding 4KB pages now with the same content across operating systems is quite possible, and there-fore physical memory space will be saved. Processors have supported large memory pages for a long time now, and a 2MB memory page size is commonly recommended, which is what Windows Vista and Windows Server 2008 and above use by default (along with newer Linux operating systems). The chances of finding duplicate 2MB memory pages is slight, which is why as operating systems adopt large memory pages, memory sharing technologies lose their benefit.

Another factor is that Windows Vista and above use address space load randomization, a security technology that loads key components of the Windows kernel and user space into 1 of 256 possible locations. This makes it harder for malware to attack the kernel based on the components' location in memory, because the locations will vary on different instances of the OS and at each reboot. Duplicate instances of the same operating system will not have the same content in the same locations for this memory content, which will minimize the effectiveness of page sharing, but this is only for a small part of the operating system content.

Runtime Memory Resize

Dynamic Memory is a powerful feature that is the perfect solution for many scenarios in which the memory assigned to a VM should vary based on the actual utilization within the guest operating system. In some instances, however, this fluctuating memory assignment is not appropriate. Consider a hosting provider that has to plan resource allocation carefully and bill based on certain resources provisioned to customers. A VM whose memory allocation constantly changed would make planning difficult and billing complicated. At the same time, the flexibility for customers to change the memory of a VM as required without a restart of the VM is beneficial. This is just one example where this functionality is useful; there are many others, but the key point is to give more control and granularity of memory configuration.

Windows Server 2016 introduces the Runtime Memory Resize capability, also known as hot-add/remove memory. As the name suggests, it is the ability to add and remove memory for a running VM completely separate from Dynamic Memory. In fact, Dynamic Memory and runtime memory resize are mutually exclusive. If you utilize Dynamic Memory, you cannot manually adjust the assigned memory for a VM via runtime memory resize. The requirements for runtime memory resize are as follows:

◆ The guest must be running Windows 10 or Windows Server 2016 with Linux support for hot-add of memory for most recently released distributions but not hot-remove. Changes to the kernel mode memory manager in Windows 10/2016 enable memory to be removed (unplugged) or added (plugged) from an operating system that is not present pre-Windows 10/2016.

◆ Dynamic Memory is not used for the VM.

◆ Can be a generation 1 or generation 2 VM

◆ The amount of memory added to a VM cannot exceed that which is available on the host.

◆ A VM cannot have more memory removed than is currently available within the VM; that is, memory that is marked as in use by a process cannot be released. This is different from Dynamic Memory, which could force a guest OS to page memory to disk to release the required amount of memory to the balloon driver. This can be thought of in a similar way as shrinking an NTFS partition—you can shrink a disk down by only the amount of free space. To shrink a disk further, you would have to delete data. To remove more memory from a VM than is currently available in the VM, you would have to free up memory by stopping applications and services

Behind the scenes, when a Windows 10 or Windows Server 2016 VM starts that is not configured with Dynamic Memory, the VM still utilizes the Dynamic Memory VSC, which is started automatically, and all memory in the VM is configured as hot-pluggable. This enables the memory to be removed in the future via the kernel mode memory manager if required based on future configuration, as the kernel understands that the memory is volatile and that access to it could change. Note that while memory is discussed in terms of hot-add and remove, the memory is all synthetic and there is no concept inside the VM of emulating addition and removal of sticks of memory. The guest OS is fully enlightened.

The memory configuration can be altered for the running VM at any time through Hyper-V Manager, PowerShell, and so on. This will result in the VM worker process (VMWP) for the VM communicating to the API in the kernel of the VM via the Dynamic Memory VSC, and the memory change will be implemented via the addition or removal of memory pages. Inside the guest, the amount of memory currently allocated will be seen, which is different from Dynamic

Memory that would always show the high watermark of memory assigned. When memory is removed, the amount of memory visible inside the VM will decrease.

The ability to hot-remove memory from Windows 10 and Windows Server 2016 is also utilized by Dynamic Memory, and ballooning is no longer used, as actually removing the memory is more efficient and useful for the guest OS. Ballooning is still used by Dynamic Memory for pre-Windows 10/2016 operating systems that do not support hot-remove of memory.

When using this functionality, I have already mentioned that you cannot remove more memory from a VM than is available and not being used, and you cannot add more memory than is available in the host. If you attempt to remove more memory from a VM than is available, then the maximum amount of memory that can be removed will be taken from the VM, and you will receive an error message that the memory change was only partially completed. If you attempt to add more memory than is available, the same will occur; as much memory as is available will be added, and an error message will indicate that the memory change was only partially completed. An example of this error is shown in Figure 2.17.

FIGURE 2.17
Error message when a memory change can be only partially completed

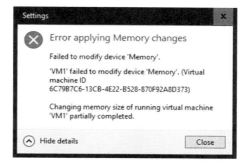

One major difference with runtime memory resize and Dynamic Memory is that vNUMA still works with runtime memory resize, which is not the case with Dynamic Memory. This was a big priority for the Hyper-V team not to break the benefits of vNUMA to the workloads running inside the VMs.

The addition of runtime memory resize does not remove the benefit of Dynamic Memory. Dynamic Memory provides automatic rebalancing of memory between VMs, based on the need of the processes running inside the VM, which typically vary over time. Dynamic Memory is still the best option for many workloads. The more granular, manual configuration via runtime memory resize is a better fit for hoster-type scenarios or where memory assignment must be strictly controlled but modification may be required.

Virtual Storage

I previously covered the IDE controller and the SCSI controller, which support storage to be attached. There are primarily two types of storage: virtual hard disks and pass-through storage. Before I even start discussing the technologies, I want to be clear: *always use virtual hard disks!* While pass-through storage was required in some scenarios in Windows Server 2008 R2 Hyper-V, it should never be needed with the new VHDX format in Windows Server 2012 Hyper-V, so don't use it. I will, however, cover it briefly for completeness.

Processor and memory are important resources to virtual machines, but storage is also critical. There are ways to enable a Windows Server 2008 R2 and above Hyper-V virtual machine to boot from a SAN by attaching to the LUN from the Hyper-V host and then mapping the disk directly to the VM using the pass-through disk capability of Hyper-V. In most cases, though, virtual machines will have some dedicated storage.

VHD

The most common and recommended storage for a virtual machine is the use of a virtual hard disk, which prior to Windows Server 2012 was the VHD format. In Windows Server 2008 R2, the VHD format is a core part of the operating system, and from a performance analysis, there is only a negligible difference from using a pass-through disk. VHDs can be mounted using Windows Server 2008 R2 and above disk management tools, and physical computers can boot from VHDs using the Boot from VHD feature available in Server 2008 R2 and Enterprise and above versions of Windows 7.

A VHD can be up to 2TB in size, and several types of VHDs are available:

Dynamically Expanding   This is the most popular format. The virtual hard disk is created using a minimal amount of disk space. As the disk is used, the file expands on the filesystem to accommodate the data written to the disk, up to the size specified as the size for the virtual hard disk. This option is the most efficient use of the disk space, because space is not used on the physical hard drives unless needed. In Windows Server 2008, there was a performance penalty with dynamic disks, such as when a write was performed, the file had to grow. However, the VHD implementation was rewritten in Windows Server 2008 R2, and this performance penalty is negligible. A dynamically expanding disk does not shrink if data is deleted unless a compact operation is performed. This type of disk is also commonly referred to as *thinly provisioned*, because it starts off thin and grows as data is written to it.

Fixed Size   In this case, the size specified for the virtual hard disk is allocated and used when the disk is created. If a 127GB fixed-size virtual hard disk is created, a 127GB VHD file is created on the Hyper-V server. This is likely to lead to a less fragmented virtual hard disk.

Differencing   A differencing hard disk is linked to a parent virtual hard disk and stores only the changes from the parent hard disk. As writes are made, the differencing (child) disk will have the writes committed, while read operations will be sourced from the parent VHD unless an update was made to the original data or its new data, in which case the data will be read from the differencing disk. Once a VHD becomes a parent disk, it becomes read-only. A differencing disk has the name of AVHD instead of VHD and will grow as data is written, behaving similarly to a dynamic disk.

Figure 2.18 gives an overview of the types of VHD and how they function.

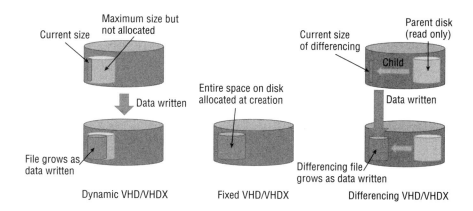

FIGURE 2.18
The key types of
VHD disks

Although there is little performance difference between a dynamic and fixed VHD in
Windows Server 2008 R2, the recommendation for production environments is to use a fixed
VHD. The primary reason is that when dynamic VHDs are used, there is always the possibility
that the underlying storage runs out of space, so as the dynamic VHD tries to grow, it will fail,
causing unpredictable results. If systems have well-defined processes to monitor disk space
usage and alert as required, then the use of dynamic VHDs in production may be possible.
VHD is a published standard by Microsoft, and it is used by other vendors, like Citrix. The
specification can be found on the Microsoft Download Center website; just search for "VHD
specification" at www.microsoft.com/download.

Virtual machines can have numerous VHDs attached to them, but a single VHD cannot be
used by multiple virtual machines at the same time. Hyper-V supports both an IDE bus and a
SCSI bus to connect VHDs to virtual machines. While the IDE bus must be used for DVD drives
and the disk from which the virtual machine will boot, for all other VHDs, the SCSI bus is
recommended for best performance and maximum flexibility.

It is possible to perform conversions between dynamic and fixed VHDs using Hyper-V
Manager and command-line tools. The conversion process creates a new VHD and copies over
the content from the source VHD to the target.

VHDX

The VHDX format was introduced in Windows Server 2012 to address some of the scalability
and, to a lesser extent, performance challenges of the VHD implementation. VHD can still be
used in Windows Server 2012 Hyper-V, but the recommendation is always to use VHDX unless
backward compatibility is required with Windows Server 2008 R2 Hyper-V or, at the time of this
writing, Windows Azure IaaS (which currently supports only VHD).

The same capabilities for VHD apply to VHDX, such as Boot from VHDX, the three types of
VHDX (dynamic, fixed, and differencing), and native mounting and use within Windows Server
2012. VHDX builds on VHD, and it provides new scalability and options.

VHDX supports a maximum virtual hard disk size of 64TB, 32 times that of the VHD format. In all my years of consulting with the largest companies in the world, I have never seen

an NTFS volume bigger than 14TB. There is no workload that could not be contained within the new VHDX format, removing the few cases where pass-through storage was previously required because of size limitations with VHD. While it is true that the new ChkDsk features introduced in Windows Server 2012 will allow larger NTFS volumes because volumes can now have any corruption fixed with only seconds of downtime instead of hours or days, I still don't believe it will be common for any organization to require single volumes bigger than 64TB.

VHDX also leverages an improved logging mechanism for updates to the VHDX Metadata, which protects against corruption in the case of unplanned events such as power loss. In addition, VHDX features the ability to have custom Metadata stored, which can be useful to store user notes about a virtual hard disk. The TRIM function is supported for VHDX files, which allows space to be reclaimed, provided the hardware is TRIM-compatible.

VHDX files automatically align with the underlying physical structure of the disk, giving the most optimal performance, and also leverage larger block sizes for dynamic and differencing disk, giving better performance. When you're using dynamic VHDX files, the performance difference is even more negligible than with VHD, making dynamic the default choice when provisioning new VHDX files. However, the same guidance with VHD does apply if you don't have a good monitoring solution in place; to ensure that you don't run out of physical disk space, you would still use fixed VHDX format.

When VHDX is combined with the SCSI controller in Windows Server 2012 R2, the VHDX can be dynamically resized while being used by a running virtual machine, allowing the disk to be expanded and even shrunk, provided there is sufficient unpartitioned space in the volume.

VHDX files can also be shared by multiple virtual machines in Windows Server 2012 R2 that are stored on a cluster shared volume or provided by a scale-out file server. I cover this and dynamic resize in more detail in Chapter 4, "Storage Configurations."

If you have VHD disks, they can be converted to VHDX using Hyper-V Manager via the Edit Disk action and using the Edit Virtual Disk Wizard, which allows the Convert action. An alternative is using PowerShell with the `Convert-VHD` cmdlet, as in the command `Convert-VHD .\test.vhd .\test.vhdx`.

Creating a Virtual Hard Disk

Virtual hard disks can be created in various ways. Using Hyper-V Manager, you can create disks using the New – Hard Disk option, which I will walk you through in the following steps. Additionally, the same wizard is launched if you choose to create a new virtual hard disk on a disk controller within a virtual machine settings dialog box.

1. Select the New – Hard Disk option from Hyper-V Manager.

2. Click Next to open the New Virtual Hard Disk Wizard introduction screen.

3. Select the type of disk format: VHD or VHDX. Always use VHDX if possible. Click Next.

4. Select whether the disk is fixed size (the default if VHD is selected on the previous screen), dynamically expanding (the default if VHDX is selected on the previous screen) or differencing, and click Next.

5. Select a name for the new virtual hard disk and location, and then click Next.

6. If a fixed or dynamic disk is being created, you can use the Configure Disk screen to choose a size for the new disk or to copy the content from an existing physical or virtual hard disk, as shown in Figure 2.19. The default size is 127GB, but you should change this to meet your needs. Click Next.

FIGURE 2.19
Selecting the size or source content for a new virtual hard disk

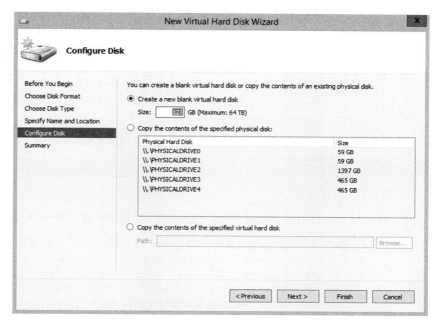

7. A summary of the choices will be shown. Click Finish to create the new virtual hard disk.

Also in Hyper-V Manager is the Edit Disk action, which when launched allows a virtual hard disk to be selected and then have actions such as the following performed on it:

Compact   Reduces the size of the virtual hard disk. This is useful if large amounts of data within the virtual hard disk have been deleted and the dynamic disk should have physical space reclaimed.

Convert   Allows conversion between virtual hard disk formats (VHD/VHDX) and between provisioning type (fixed/dynamic). The conversion works by creating a new virtual hard disk and copying the content so that it will consume extra space on disk during the conversion process and may take a long time.

Expand   Expands the capacity of a virtual hard disk.

The Inspect Disk action in Hyper-V Manager gives the basic information about a selected virtual hard disk, as shown in Figure 2.20. For a dynamic virtual hard disk, it shows its maximum size as well as the amount of space currently used on disk.

FIGURE 2.20
The basic information about a virtual hard disk shown by the Inspect Disk option

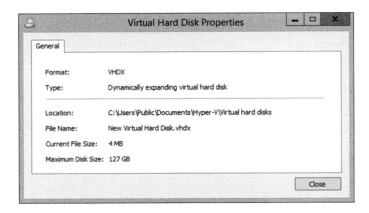

While graphical tools are highly intuitive for automation, a scripting language is typically leveraged, and PowerShell is the command-line interface and scripting language of choice for Microsoft.

Here are some of my favorite PowerShell commands related to virtual hard disks. Note that you do not have to specify whether a disk is VHD or VHDX. Simply setting the file type to VHD or VHDX lets the commands know the type of virtual hard disk to create. I'll show you later in the book how to create new virtual hard disks as part of a virtual machine creation.

Here's the command to create a fixed VHDX file:

```
New-VHD -Path D:\Virtuals\newfix.vhdx -Fixed -SizeBytes 10GB
```

To create a dynamic VHDX file, use this command:

```
New-VHD -Path D:\Virtuals\newdyn.vhdx -Dynamic -SizeBytes 1TB
```

The command to create a differencing VHDX file is as follows:

```
New-VHD -ParentPath D:\Virtuals\newfix.vhdx '
-Path D:\Virtuals\newdif.vhdx -Differencing '
-SizeBytes 1000000000
```

Here is the command to create a VHDX using very large block sizes:

```
New-VHD –Path D:\Virtuals\LargeBlockSize.vhdx –BlockSizeBytes 128MB '
–LogicalSectorSize 4KB –SizeBytes 1TB
```

A virtual hard disk can be added to a virtual machine by using the Add-VMHardDiskDrive PowerShell cmdlet, as in this example:

```
Add-VMHardDiskDrive -VMName Demo1 -Path D:\Virtuals\newdyn.vhdx '
-ControllerType SCSI
```

Pass-Through Storage

As I mentioned, one storage option is to use a pass-through disk, whereby a virtual machine has connectivity mapped directly to physical disks. However, this requires the physical disk to be used exclusively by a single virtual machine. The benefits of abstracting the virtual machine from hardware are lost, because the virtual machine is now directly linked to a physical piece of hardware. Other features, such as using checkpoints that provide a point-in-time saved state of a virtual machine, are not possible.

The Hyper-V host cannot access a disk that is passed through to a VM. It becomes exclusively usable by the virtual machine. The disk must be offline on the Hyper-V host to be connected to a virtual machine. Pass-through disks may be used for very high I/O applications like SQL Server, but this is typically not required given the continued improvements in VHDX performance. Prior to VHDX, the use of pass-through storage was required for a volume larger than 2TB because of the VHD size limit, but this is no longer a limiting factor because of VHDX.

Discrete Device Assignment

SR-IOV is a part of the PCI Express specification. It allows you to separate the controlling aspects of a device from the data-moving aspects of the device, so that the device appears on the PCI Express bus multiple times (once for the control plane and once for each data plane). When you use this for NIC (Network Interface Card), it allows each VM to have its own path directly to the NIC, and for the NIC to have a direct path to the VM's memory. No software needs to get in the way. To make this all happen, the hypervisor has to build a virtual network switch and let the NIC run part of it. The software switch still exists, but the individual data paths in the NIC can bypass it.

In Hyper-V, these individual data planes (called *virtual functions*, for reasons dating back 20 years) aren't modeled as full virtual NICs. The virtual NIC is handled in software and most, but not all, of the networking traffic is offloaded to the virtual function. You can see this, by the way, in the guest VM by looking at the vNIC and the virtual function. They have the same MAC address. The virtual function can't function entirely by itself, though, and at times during a VM's life cycle (while it's in the middle of Live Migration, for instance), all the traffic goes through the software path. This is in contrast to most other hypervisors, by the way, which send all traffic through the virtual function and don't build a software path beside it, foregoing things like Live Migration, VM checkpoints, and anything else that can't work with a piece of actual hardware exposed to the VM.

Windows Server 2016 expands on this idea of mapping hardware directly to a VM with *Discrete Device Assignment (DDA)*. DDA enables PCI Express–connected devices to be connected directly through to virtual machines. This can be useful in certain scenarios. For example, certain types of storage (especially NVMe devices) and even graphics adapters may not typically work with applications via RemoteFX, because of unrecognized drivers for applications or because of the limited features exposed via RemoteFX that are limited historically to DirectX primitives (although this improves with Windows Server 2016 with OpenCL and OpenGL support). When using DDA, the hardware is passed through directly to the VM, and therefore the hardware's IHV drivers are used instead of generic virtual device drivers. The decision to use RemoteFX vs. DDA really comes down to using DDA when you need native drivers and the best possible performance, and using RemoteFX vGPU when you need scale.

To use DDA, the system must support Access Control Service, which enables the secure pass-through of a PCI Express device. Additionally, the host must support SLAT (a base requirement for Hyper-V 2016) and interrupt remapping (Intel VT-d2 or AMD I/O MMU).

To test whether your machine supports DDA, execute the following PowerShell, which will also identify all hardware that could be used with DDA and therefore assigned to a VM:

```
wget https://raw.githubusercontent.com/Microsoft/Virtualization-↵
Documentation/master/hyperv-samples/benarm-powershell/DDA/survey-dda.ps1 ↵
-OutFile survey-dda.ps1
.\survey-dda.ps1
```

Microsoft has an excellent article that walks through the output of this script in great detail:

```
https://blogs.technet.microsoft.com/virtualization/2015/11/20/
discrete-device-assignment-machines-and-devices/
```

Note that when using DDA, the devices cannot also be used in the host or shared between VMs. The devices are directly passed through to a VM. This also means Live Migration of the VM would not be possible, because the VM is directly bound to hardware in a specific host. This is different from SR-IOV, which does not block Live Migration. The lack of Live Migration is a major concession, and this functionality will be used in only very specific scenarios. However, in those scenarios, the ability to directly map PCIe devices is a huge benefit. Additionally, a critical point: it's really difficult to pass an entire device through to a guest without exposing the whole machine to denial-of-service attacks. Almost every device can be tricked into generating errors on the bus that will bring the entire machine down with odd messages about hardware failure. So DDA should be used only for VMs that the administrator has complete trust in. In practice, the DDA-enabled VMs should probably be part of the hoster's infrastructure, not something that the tenant gets to use. Note that this may give you pause, because Azure uses this exact functionality with its N-series VMs that expose NVIDIA cards to VMs. However, Microsoft and NVIDIA performed extensive penetration testing, resulting in a safe method to enable this functionality in Azure.

The host must be running Windows Server 2016. However, the guest OS can be Windows Server 2016, Windows Server 2012 R2, Windows 10 (1511 and above), and certain Linux distributions. This is the technology that will be leveraged to enable the N-series VMs in Azure that have GPU capabilities by directly mapping GPUs to Azure VMs.

To use DDA, you need first to unload the default driver from the device you wish to map to a VM, dismount the device from the management OS, and then you can map it to a VM. The following script, which will dismount NVMe devices on the system, making them available to VMs, is from this article:

```
https://blogs.technet.microsoft.com/virtualization/2015/11/19/
discrete-device-assignment-description-and-background/
```

```
# get all devices which are NVMe controllers
$pnpdevs = Get-PnpDevice -PresentOnly | Where-Object {$_.Class -eq ↵
```

```
"SCSIAdapter"} | Where-Object {$_.Service -eq "stornvme"}

# cycle through them disabling and dismounting them
foreach ($pnpdev in $pnpdevs)
{
        disable-pnpdevice -InstanceId $pnpdev.InstanceId -Confirm:$false
        $locationpath = ($pnpdev | get-pnpdeviceproperty ↵
DEVPKEY_Device_LocationPaths).data[0]
        dismount-vmhostassignabledevice -locationpath $locationpath
        $locationpath
}
```

The output of the script will include the devices that were identified and unmounted. These devices can also now be seen by executing the `Get-VMHostAssignableDevice` cmdlet, which includes a property named `LocationPath`. It is the `LocationPath` that you specify when mapping a device to a VM via DDA using the `Add-VMAssignableDevice` cmdlet, for example:

```
PS C:\> Get-VMHostAssignableDevice

InstanceID : PCIP\VEN_144D&DEV_A820&SUBSYS_1F951028&REV_03\4&368722DD&0&0010
LocationPath : PCIROOT(40)#PCI(0200)#PCI(0000)
CimSession : CimSession: .
ComputerName : SAVDALHVFX
IsDeleted : False

PS C:\> Add-VMAssignableDevice -LocationPath ↵
"PCIROOT(40)#PCI(0200)#PCI(0000)" -VMName TestVM
```

To remove a device from a VM, use `Remove-VMAssignableDevice` with the same parameters as the Add cmdlet. There is no graphical interface to manage DDA—you must use PowerShell. Remember that since this is direct mapping of a device to a VM, if special drivers are needed for the hardware, these will need to be installed in the VM guest OS, and you will no longer be able to live-migrate the VM.

When mapping an NVMe storage device to a VM using DDA, no additional configuration is required. However, if you are mapping a graphics device that tends to have a lot of memory, memory-mapped I/O space will not be available for the guest OS to map and use the memory of the graphical device. You will need to reconfigure the VM. The exact amount of memory that needs to be mapped will depend on the graphics device, and it can be seen by examining the Resources tab of the device in Device Manager, as shown in Figure 2.21. You can modify the low and high memory space for VMs by using the -`LowMemoryMappedIoSpace` and -`HighMemoryMappedIoSpace` parameters of the `Set-VM` cmdlet. This is explained in detail in this article:

```
https://blogs.technet.microsoft.com/virtualization/2015/11/23/
discrete-device-assignment-gpus/
```

The article also points out that you should enable the guest to control the caching by setting -`GuestControlledCacheTypes` `$true` via `Set-VM`. All of these configurations require the VM to be shut down.

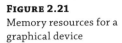

FIGURE 2.21
Memory resources for a
graphical device

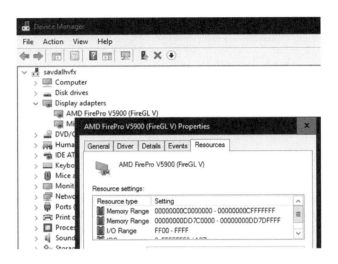

The Bottom Line

Describe how the resources of a virtual machine are virtualized by the hypervisor. The hypervisor directly manages the processor and memory resources with Hyper-V. Logical processors are scheduled to satisfy computer requirements of virtual processors assigned to virtual machines. Multiple virtual processors can share the same logical processor. Virtual machines are assigned memory by the hypervisor from the memory available in the physical host. Dynamic Memory allows memory to be added and removed from a virtual machine based on resource need. Other types of resources, such as network and storage, are provided by the management partition through a kernel mode memory bus known as a VMBus. This allows existing Windows drivers to be used for the wide array of storage and network devices typically used.

Master It How is Dynamic Memory different from Memory Overcommit?

Correctly use processor and memory advanced configuration options. The compatibility configuration of a virtual machine processor should be used when a virtual machine may be moved between hosts with different versions of the same processor family. The processor compatibility option hides higher-level features from the guest operating system, enabling migrations without downtime to the virtual machine. Processor reserve and limit options ensure that a virtual machine coexists with other virtual machines without getting too many or too few resources. Dynamic Memory configurations allow the startup, minimum, and maximum amounts of memory for a virtual machine to be configured. It's important to note that the maximum amount of memory configured is available only if sufficient memory exists within the host.

Master It When should the NUMA properties of a virtual machine be modified?

Explain the difference between VHD/VHDX and pass-through storage.   VHD and VHDX files are virtual hard disks that are files on a filesystem or share accessible to the Hyper-V host. They provide abstraction of the storage seen by the virtual machine and the underlying physical storage. Pass-through storage directly maps a virtual machine to a physical disk accessible from the host, which limits Hyper-V functionality and breaks one of the key principles of virtualization: the abstraction of the virtual machine from the physical fabric.

Master It   Why would VHD still be used with Windows Server 2012 Hyper-V?

Chapter 3

Virtual Networking

This chapter covers the networking elements that enable virtual machines to communicate with each other and with the rest of your environment. Features that are specific to virtual machines are covered, as well as network technologies in the operating system that can bring additional benefit.

Windows 2012 introduced network virtualization, which started to close the remaining gap between virtualization and the goal of complete abstraction of the virtual machine from the underlying fabric. This goal is fully realized with version 2, introduced in Windows Server 2016. Network virtualization allows virtual machines to be abstracted from the physical network fabric, allowing complete isolation between virtual networks and the ability to use IP schemes independently of the physical network fabric. This technology is covered in detail, along with all of the various options available to you.

In this chapter, you will learn to:

- ◆ Architect the right network design for your Hyper-V hosts and virtual machines by using the options available.

- ◆ Identify when to use the types of gateways.

- ◆ Leverage SCVMM for many networking tasks.

Virtual Switch Fundamentals

A typical server has one or more network adapters that are configured with an IPv4 and IPv6 address, either statically or dynamically, using services such as Dynamic Host Configuration Protocol (DHCP). The server may be part of a VLAN to provide isolation and control of broadcast traffic. It may require different network connections to connect to different networks, such as a separate, nonrouted network for cluster communications between servers in a failover cluster, a separate network for iSCSI traffic, a separate management network, and so on. With virtualization, the requirements for network connectivity are just as important as they are for a physical server. However, additional options are available because multiple server instances exist on a single physical asset. Moreover, in some cases, they need to communicate only with each other and not externally to the virtualization host.

Three Types of Virtual Switches

Virtual machines have numerous virtualized resources. One type is the virtual network adapter (as discussed in the previous chapter, two types of network adapters are available for a generation

1 virtual machine, but their connectivity options are the same). One or more virtual network adapters are added to a virtual machine, and then each virtual adapter is attached to a virtual switch that was created at the Hyper-V host level. A Hyper-V host can have many virtual switches created. Three types of virtual switches are available: external, internal, and private, as shown in Figure 3.1.

FIGURE 3.1
The three types of virtual switches available in Hyper-V

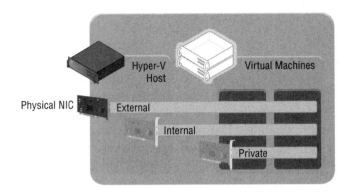

EXTERNAL VIRTUAL NETWORKS

External virtual networks are bound to a physical network card in the host. Virtual machines have access to this physical network via the physical NIC, which is linked to the external switch to which the virtual network adapter is connected. Virtual machines on the same virtual switch can also communicate with each other. If they are on different switches that can communicate through the physical network (that is, through routing), then they can also communicate. Each virtual machine sees a virtual network device, and the Hyper-V host still sees the network adapter; however, it will no longer use it. The network device on the Hyper-V host is the physical NIC, which is bound only to the Hyper-V extensible virtual switch, which means that it is being used by a Hyper-V virtual switch.

It is also possible when creating a virtual switch to enable the Hyper-V host itself, the management OS, to continue using the network adapter even though it has been assigned to a virtual switch. Sharing the adapter works by creating a virtual network adapter in the management partition that is connected to the Hyper-V virtual switch so that all communication still goes through the virtual switch, which exclusively owns the physical network adapter. In Windows Server 2012 and above, it's possible to create multiple virtual network adapters in the management partition, which opens new configuration options and scenarios that I cover later in this chapter. If you have only a single network adapter in the Hyper-V host, you should definitely select the option to share the network adapter with the management operating system. This option can be enabled or disabled at any time after the external switch has been created.

INTERNAL VIRTUAL NETWORKS

Internal virtual networks are not bound to a physical NIC and so cannot access any machine outside the physical server. An internal network is visible to the Hyper-V host and the virtual machines, which means that it can be used for communication between virtual machines and between virtual machines and the Hyper-V host. This can be useful if you are hosting services on the management partition, such as an iSCSI target, that you wish the virtual machines to be able to use. On both the Hyper-V host and virtual machines, a network device is visible that represents the internal virtual network.

CREATING A NAT FORWARDING SWITCH

Windows Server 2016 (and Windows 10) introduces a new mode for the internal switch, which is as a Network Address Translation (NAT) forwarding switch. In this mode, the switch acts like a regular internal switch, providing connectivity between VMs on the host and the host itself. Additionally, however, the VMs can access the external networks connected to the host through NAT functionality. Furthermore, port forwarding can be configured on the host IP so that certain traffic is forwarded to a VM on the internal switch. This is useful when testing and using containers.

To create a new internal switch and enable it for NAT, use the following:

```
New-VMSwitch -SwitchName "NATSwitch" -SwitchType Internal
New-NetIPAddress –IPAddress 192.168.1.1 -PrefixLength 24 `
-InterfaceAlias "vEthernet (NATSwitch)"
New-NetNat –Name NATnetwork -InternalIPInterfaceAddressPrefix 192.168.1.0/24
```

To create a NAT static-forwarding rule to send traffic directed to the host to a VM, use the following:

```
#Map the host IP to port 80 on VM 192.168.1.10 through switch
Add-NetNatStaticMapping -NatName NATnetwork -Protocol TCP `
-ExternalIPAddress 0.0.0.0 `
-InternalIPAddress 192.168.1.10 -InternalPort 81 -ExternalPort 81
```

PRIVATE VIRTUAL NETWORKS

Private virtual networks are visible only on virtual machines, and they are used for virtual machines to communicate with each other. This type of network could be used for virtual machines that are part of a guest cluster. The private network could be used for the cluster network, provided that all hosts in the cluster are running on the same Hyper-V host.

In most cases, an external switch is used, because most virtual machines require communications beyond the local Hyper-V host, with internal and private networks used in testing and niche scenarios, such as the guest cluster that is confined to a single host. However, most likely, if you were creating a production guest cluster in virtual machines, you would want them distributed over multiple Hyper-V hosts to protect against a host failure, in which case an external switch would be required.

A single physical network adapter can be bound only to a single external switch, and in production environments it's common to use NIC Teaming on the Hyper-V host. This allows multiple network adapters to be bound together and exposed to the operating system as a single teamed network adapter, which provides resiliency from a network adapter failure as well as aggregated bandwidth that enables higher-speed communications. (There are many caveats around this, which I cover later in this chapter.) A teamed network adapter can also be used and bound for an external switch with Hyper-V, giving all of the virtual network adapters connected to that switch additional resiliency.

If you have numerous network adapters in a host and they connect to different networks (which may, for example, use VLANs to isolate traffic), then, if virtual machines need access to those networks, you would create multiple external virtual switches, with each bound to the physical network adapter connected to one of the networks. It may seem obvious, but virtual machines can communicate only with the other services that are available on that physical network or can be routed via that network. Effectively, you are expanding the connectivity of the physical network adapter to virtual machines via the virtual switch.

Many virtual machines can be connected to the same virtual networks, and one nice feature is that if multiple virtual machines on the same Hyper-V host are connected to the same external network and communicate over that network, the traffic never goes to the physical network adapter. The Hyper-V networking stack is smart enough to know that the traffic is going to another VM connected to the same switch and directly passes the traffic to the VM without ever touching the physical network adapter or physical network.

When you start creating virtual switches, it's important to use a consistent naming scheme across all hosts for the switches. This is important because when a virtual machine is moved between Hyper-V hosts, it looks for a virtual switch with the same name as its existing virtual switch connection on the target host. If there is no matching virtual switch, the virtual network adapter will become disconnected—and therefore the virtual machine will lose connectivity. Consistent naming is critical in failover clusters, where virtual machines can freely move between cluster nodes. With the Windows Server 2012 and above capability of moving virtual machines between any host with no shared resources and no downtime, it's important to have consistent virtual switch naming between all Hyper-V hosts. Take some time now to think about a good naming strategy and stick to it.

It's also possible to create access control lists, called *extended port access control lists*, within the virtual switch to allow and block communication between virtual machines connected to the switch based on IP address, protocol, and port. Additionally, stateful rules can be created to allow communication only when certain conditions are met. Microsoft has a detailed walkthrough on using the ACLs at the following location:

```
http://technet.microsoft.com/en-us/library/dn375962.aspx
```

When using Software Defined Networking v2, even richer sets of traffic control are available through the built-in datacenter firewall and other types of extensions.

Creating a Virtual Switch

When the Hyper-V role is enabled on a server, you are given an option to create an external switch by selecting a network adapter on the host. If you choose this option, a virtual switch will already be present on the host and will be automatically configured to allow the management operating system to share the adapter so that an extra Hyper-V virtual Ethernet adapter will be present on the Hyper-V host. In general, I prefer not to create the virtual switches during Hyper-V role installation but to configure them post-installation. Also, as you will read later, if your deployment is a production deployment and you're using System Center, then Virtual Machine Manager can do all of the switch configuration for you. I will, however, walk you through manually configuring virtual switches:

1. Launch Hyper-V Manager.

2. Select the Virtual Switch Manager action from the actions pane.

3. In the navigation pane, select New Virtual Network Switch, and in the details pane, select the type of virtual switch to create. In this case, select External and click the Create Virtual Switch button.

4. Replace the default New Virtual Switch name with a meaningful name that matches the naming standard for the switches that you have selected, such as, for example, External Switch. Optionally, you can enter notes.

5. If the switch type is external, you must select the specific network adapter or the NIC team that will be bound to the virtual switch from the list of available network adapters on the system, as shown in Figure 3.2. Note that you can change the type of switch on this screen by selecting another type of network, such as internal or private. Also note that network adapters/teams bound to other switches are still listed, but the creation will fail if they are selected.

FIGURE 3.2
Primary configuration page for a new virtual switch

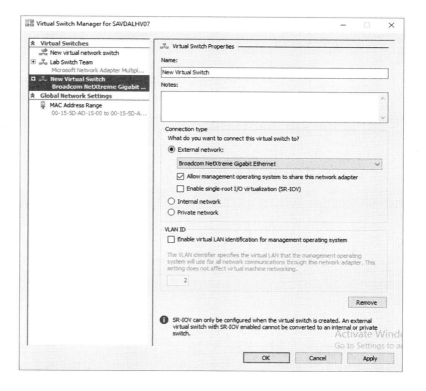

By default, the Allow Management Operating System To Share This Network Adapter option is enabled. This option creates the virtual network adapter on the management partition, enabling the Hyper-V host to continue accessing the network through the new virtual switch that is bound to the network adapter. However, if you have a separate management network adapter or if you will create it manually later, then disable this option by deselecting the check box. If you uncheck this box, you will receive a warning when the switch is being created that you will lose access to the host unless you have another network adapter used for management communication. The warning is shown to protect you from disabling any way to communicate with the host.

6. If you plan to use SR/IOV, select the Enable Single-Root I/O Virtualization (SR-IOV) check box. This cannot be changed after the switch is created. (SR-IOV is covered later in this chapter. It's a technology found in newer, advanced networking equipment and servers that allows virtual machines to communicate directly with the networking equipment for high-performance scenarios.)

7. If you selected the option to allow the management operating system to use the network adapter, you can set the VLAN ID used by that network adapter on the host operating system through the VLAN ID option by selecting the Enable Virtual LAN Identification For Management Operating System check box and then entering the VLAN ID. Note that this does not set the VLAN ID for the switch but rather for the virtual network adapter created on the management partition.

8. After selecting the options, click the OK button to create the switch. (If you unchecked the option to allow the management operating system to use the adapter, the warning displays at this point.)

Creating switches is also possible using PowerShell. The following commands create an external (without sharing with the management operating system), an internal, and a private switch and then list switches that are of type External:

```
#Create new external (implicit external as adapter passed)
New-VMSwitch -Name "External Switch" -Notes "External Connectivity" `
-NetAdapterName "VM NIC" -AllowManagementOS $false
#Create new internal (visible on host) and private (vm only)
New-VMSwitch -Name "Internal Switch" -SwitchType Internal
New-VMSwitch -Name "Private Switch" -SwitchType Private
```

After creating a switch, you can view it through the Virtual Switch Manager and modify the properties. A virtual switch's type can be changed at any time unless it is an external virtual switch with SR-IOV enabled. In that case, its type cannot be changed without deleting and re-creating it. Virtual network adapters can be connected to the switch through the properties of the virtual network adapter.

Extensible Switch

The Hyper-V *extensible switch* provides a variety of capabilities that can be leveraged by the virtual network adapters connected to the virtual switch ports, including features such as port mirroring, protection from rogue DHCP servers and router advertisements, bandwidth management, support for VMQ, and more. However, although this specific set of capabilities covers the majority of scenarios and customer requirements, it might not cover every requirement that various clients may have. Those familiar with VMware may have heard of the Cisco Nexus 1000V, which is available for ESXi and essentially replaces the VMware switching infrastructure completely. The Cisco Nexus 1000V is the only model that VMware supports, and the challenge is that not many vendors have the resources available to write a complete virtual switching infrastructure. Microsoft went a different direction in Windows Server 2012.

Windows Server 2012 introduced the extensible switch for Hyper-V. The extensible switch enables third parties to plug into the Hyper-V virtual switch at various points without having to replace it completely, thus making it far easier for organizations to bring additional value. It was common to have the ability to add functionality into the Hyper-V switch, such as enhanced packet-filtering capabilities, firewall and intrusion detection at the switch level, switch forwarding, and utilities to help sniff data on the network. Consider that Windows already has a rich capability around APIs and interfaces for third parties to integrate with the operating system, specifically Network Device Interface Specification (NDIS) filter drivers and Windows Filtering Platform (WFP) callout drivers. The Hyper-V extensible switch uses these exact same interfaces that partners are already utilizing, making it possible for vendors to easily adapt solutions to integrate directly into the Windows 2012 and above extensible switch. InMon's sFlow monitoring extension allows great trending analysis of traffic, NEC has OpenFlow extension, and 5nine Software has a complete firewall extension for the Hyper-V extensible switch.

The Hyper-V switch has four specific types of extensions, which are listed in Table 3.1.

TABLE 3.1:   Types of Extensions for Hyper-V Virtual Switch

EXTENSION	PURPOSE	EXAMPLES	EXTENSIBILITY COMPONENT
Network packet inspection	Inspecting network packets, but not altering them	Network monitoring	NDIS filter driver
Network packet filter	Injecting, modifying, and dropping network packets	Security	NDIS filter driver
Network forwarding	Third-party forwarding that bypasses default forwarding	Virtual Ethernet Port Aggregator (VEPA) and proprietary network fabrics	NDIS filter driver
Firewall/intrusion detection	Filtering and modifying TCP/IP packets, monitoring or authorizing connections, filtering IPsec-protected traffic, and filtering RPCs	Virtual firewall and connection monitoring	WFP callout driver

Multiple extensions can be enabled on a virtual switch, and the extensions are leveraged for both ingress (inbound) and egress (outbound) traffic. One big change from Windows Server 2012 is that in Windows Server 2012 R2, the Hyper-V Network Virtualization (HNV) module is moved into the virtual switch instead of being external to the virtual switch. This enables switch extensions to inspect both the provider and customer headers and therefore work with network virtualization. (You'll learn more on this later, but for now: the *provider header* is the packet that enables Network Virtualization to function across physical networks, and the *customer header* is the IP traffic that virtual machines in a virtual network see.). The move of the Network Virtualization module also enables third-party forwarding extensions such as the

Cisco Nexus 1000V to work with Network Virtualization, which wasn't the case in Windows Server 2012. And yes, Cisco has a Nexus 1000V for Hyper-V that works with the Hyper-V switch instead of completely replacing it. This is important because many organizations use Cisco networking solutions, and the Nexus 1000V enables unified management of both the physical and virtual network environment through the Cisco network management toolset.

The Windows Server 2012 R2 extensible switch also supports hybrid forwarding, which allows packets to be forwarded to various forwarding agents based on the packet type. For example, suppose the Cisco Nexus 1000V extension (a forwarding agent) is installed. With hybrid forwarding, if network virtualization traffic is sent through the switch, it would first go through the HNV module and then to the forwarding agent, the Nexus 1000V. If the traffic was not network virtualization traffic, the HNV module would be bypassed and the traffic sent straight to the Nexus 1000V.

Figure 3.3 best shows the extensible switch and the way that traffic flows through the extensions. Notice that the traffic flows completely through all layers of the switch twice; once *inbound* into the switch (which could be from a VM or from external sources) and once *outbound* from the switch (which could be to a VM or to an external source).

FIGURE 3.3
How traffic flows through the extensible switch and registered extensions for the inbound path

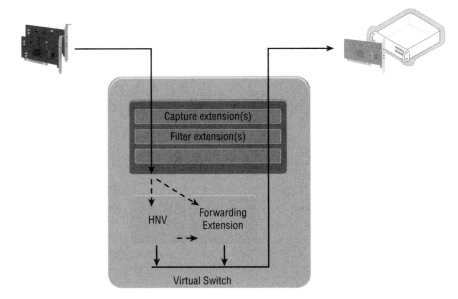

Extensions to the switch are provided by the third parties, installed onto the Hyper-V server, and then enabled per virtual switch. The process to enable an extension is simple. Open the Virtual Switch Manager, select the virtual switch for which you want to enable extensions, and then select the Extensions child node of the virtual switch. In the extensions area of the dialog box, select the check box for the extension(s) you wish to enable. That's it! The extensions are now enabled. In Figure 3.4, you can see the various extension types. Two are not part of standard Hyper-V: Microsoft VMM DHCPv4 Server Switch Extension and sFlow Traffic Monitoring. When enabled, the sFlow Traffic Monitoring extension sends trending information and more to the sFlowTrend tool for graphical visualization and analysis. The Microsoft VMM DHCPv4 Server Switch Extension is a filter that, when it sees DHCP traffic, intercepts the requests and utilizes IP pools within Virtual Machine Manager to service DHCP requests over the virtual switch instead of using standard DHCP services, enabling VMM to manage all IP configuration.

FIGURE 3.4
Enabling extensions for a virtual switch in Hyper-V

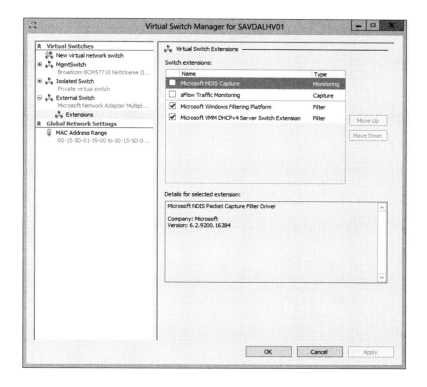

Windows Server 2016 adds a new built-in extension, the Microsoft Azure VFP Switch Extension. The Virtual Filtering Platform, originally developed for Azure, enables the Azure-like functionality for the Windows Server 2016 network virtualization solution, known as *Software Defined Networking v2* (*SDNv2*). Ordinarily, without the VFP, the Windows Server 2016 VM Switch is more of a shell, and it is the addition of the VFP (which is implemented as a forwarding extension) when SDNv2 is enabled on the switch that lights up most of the new 2016 features such as these:

◆ Address virtualization for virtual networks

◆ Virtual IP to dynamic IP translation for the software load balancer (Network Address Translation, or NAT)

◆ Access control lists that utilize programmable rule/flow tables enabling per packet actions

◆ Metering and quality of service (QoS)

◆ Security mechanisms

The VFP performs all of the processing and acts as the brain and its own virtual switch inside the Hyper-V VMSwitch. Figure 3.5 shows its architecture.

FIGURE 3.5
The VFP place with
the VMSwitch

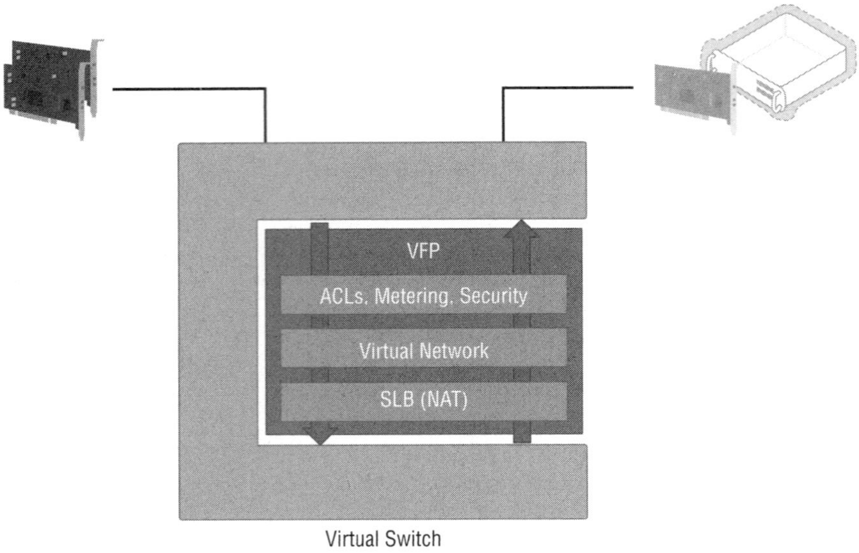

Virtual Switch

The layers of the VFP are implemented and actioned as separate flow tables that define the rules affecting the incoming packets from the physical NIC. A *flow table* consists of the traffic flow and certain types of policies—for example, all traffic to a certain subnet and then an action that varies depending on the policy type used by the flow table. This action could be to encapsulate the packet and send to a certain address (VNet), to apply a certain type of NAT (SLB), or even to block the packet (ACLs), as shown in Figure 3.6. Note that although the figure shows three types of policies, others exist, such as routing tables and port-mirroring tables.

The flow tables are implemented in a specific order; the virtual network rules that govern how packets will be encapsulated and handled between the virtual network and physical network are implemented first, then the software load-balancing rules and NAT, and then finally the ACLs to control whether traffic is allowed to get to a particular VM. The VFP is also used for outbound traffic from the VM, with the layers implemented in reverse order (ACLs, then SLB NAT, and finally the virtual network). The order of application is logical: For incoming traffic, the IP address has to first be mapped to the virtual network address space by removing the encapsulation, which currently would be addressed using the datacenter address space; then any NAT has to be performed, which ensures that all of the packets are now in the virtual network address space; and finally, ACLs can be applied. All of these flow tables are populated with policies from the network controller which is another new SDNv2 component inspired by Azure that is covered in more detail later in this chapter.

Applying all of these layers of rules to every packet would incur a significant performance penalty. To remediate this, the VFP implements a table-typing algorithm; a hash-lookup flow-caching table is generated for each flow (connection), and the complete set of rules are stored. This means that only the first packet for any flow goes through all of the rules (which could be complex). Subsequent packets from the same flow would find a match in the flow-caching table and apply those actions. Say that the final ACL discards the traffic after going through all of the rules. By caching the result for all future packets, no processing needs to be performed for packets that are ultimately deleted anyway. This is shown in Figure 3.6, and it is what enables the VFP to support the fast network speeds that are used in today's datacenters—40Gbps and beyond. Additionally, the use of the VFP does not block any offloads to the NIC, which is critical to ensure optimal performance.

FIGURE 3.6
The flow-caching hash lookup used in the VFP

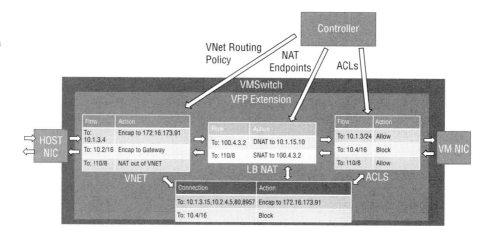

VLANs and PVLANS

In most datacenters, widespread use of virtual LANs (VLANs) is common. VLANs allow you to isolate traffic without using physical separation—for example, by using various switches and network adapters for the different types of isolated networks. Although physical separation works, maintaining the additional physical infrastructure is costly in terms of hardware, power, and even cooling in the datacenter. Managing large numbers of isolated physical network topologies also can be complex.

Understanding VLANs

A *VLAN* is a layer 2 technology that primarily adds the capability to create partitions in the network for broadcast traffic. Normally, networks are separated by using devices such as routers, which control the transmission of traffic between segments (a local area network, or LAN) of the network. However, a VLAN allows a single physical network segment to be virtually partitioned so that VLANs cannot communicate with each other, and broadcast traffic such as ARP (to resolve IP addresses to MAC addresses) would not cross VLANs.

Here's a great example that explains the broadcast boundary nature of a VLAN: Say you have ten machines plugged into a single switch, and one of those machines is a DHCP server. All nine of the other machines plugged into that switch are able to get an IP address from the DHCP server. If VLANs are configured, and the DHCP server and a few of the machines are put in a specific VLAN, then only the machines in the same VLAN as the DHCP server can get an

IP address from the DHCP server. All of the other machines not part of that VLAN can't contact the DHCP server and would require another method for IP configuration.

Additionally, through network hardware configuration, it is possible for a single VLAN to cross physical network segments and even locations, allowing machines that are physically distributed to act and communicate as if they were on a single physical network segment. The VLAN is, at a high level, creating virtual LANs that are abstracted from the physical location. For VLANs to communicate with each other, layer 3 technologies (IP) are used for IP-level routing.

By partitioning communication and broadcast traffic, VLANs provide the following key features to an environment that make VLANs an attractive technology to implement:

Separate Broadcast Domains This seems obvious, but separate broadcast domains can be a huge benefit for larger networks that have an amount of broadcast traffic that may be causing network performance issues. This also enables a single network to be divided into separate networks as required.

Isolation between Machines VLANs enable partitions between groups of servers, which may be required in scenarios such as different departments, Internet-facing networks, hosting providers to separate clients, and more.

Administrative Help With VLANs, it's possible to move servers between locations but maintain their VLAN membership, avoiding reconfiguration of the host.

Separation of Physical Networks from Virtual Networks This enables virtual LANs to span physical network segments.

Typically, a VLAN and IP subnet has a one-to-one mapping, although it is possible to have multiple subnets within a single VLAN. Remember, though, that a VLAN represents a broadcast boundary; a single subnet cannot cross VLANs because, by definition, an IP subnet represents a group of machines with direct communication that rely on broadcasts for translating IP addresses to MAC addresses using ARP.

While VLANs seem like a useful technology, and they are, their configuration has some drawbacks and complexity. First, consider a typical datacenter network switch configuration with numerous racks of servers. Typically, two types of switches are involved: servers within a rack connect to the top-of-rack (ToR) switch in each rack and then connect to aggregation switches. The configuration in Figure 3.7 shows three VLANs in use by Hyper-V servers for different virtual machines, which in this example are VLANs 10, 20, and 30. Notice that machines in VLAN 10 span racks, which requires configuration of the VLAN in not just the ToR but also aggregation switches. For VLANs 20 and 30, all of the VMs are in the same rack, so while the ports from the hosts in the rack to the ToR require access for VLANs 10, 20, and 30, the aggregation switches will see only VLAN 10 traffic passed to them. As a result, only VLAN 10 has to be configured.

Notice in Figure 3.7 that single ports can be configured to allow traffic from different VLANs. (Ports between switches are known as *trunk ports*, because they are configured for all of the VLAN traffic that has to be passed between them.) However, even normal ports to a host can be configured to allow multiple VLANs, which is especially necessary with virtualization, as different virtual machines on a single host may be part of different VLANs. Realize that even in this basic configuration with only two racks, the VLAN configuration can require changes on the network infrastructure at multiple points, such as the ToRs and aggregation switches.

FIGURE 3.7
Three VLANs in a two-rack configuration. For redundancy, each ToR has a connection to two separate aggregation switches.

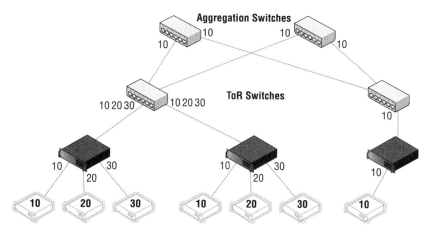

Imagine now that a new virtual machine is required for VLAN 20. There is no capacity in the first rack, so the virtual machine must be created in the second rack, as shown in Figure 3.8. This requires changes to the second rack ToR and both aggregation switches. Now imagine that you have hundreds of racks and hundreds of VLANs. This type of VLAN change can be very complex and take weeks to implement, because all of the VLAN configuration is static and requires manual updating, which makes the network a bottleneck in provisioning new services. You've probably heard of some VLAN configuration problems, although you might not have known they were VLAN configuration problems. Some of the major "outages" of Internet-facing services have been caused not by hardware failure but by changes to network configuration that "went wrong" and take time to fix, specifically VLANs! Suppose that you wish to use Live Migration to easily move virtual machines between hosts and even racks; this adds even more complexity to the VLAN configurations to ensure that the virtual machines don't lose connectivity when migrated.

FIGURE 3.8
New VM in VLAN 20 added to the host in the second rack, and the changes to the switch VLAN configuration required

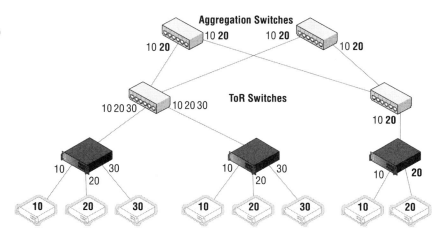

TAGGED VS. UNTAGGED CONFIGURATION

One thing regarding VLANs confused me when I first started with network equipment (well, lots of things confused me!), and that was whether to configure ports as tagged or untagged. Both are options when configuring a port on a switch.

When a port is configured as *tagged*, that port expects the traffic to already be tagged with a VLAN ID. This means that the VLAN must be configured at the host connected to the port or at a VM level running on the host. Additionally, for a tagged port, it is possible to configure inclusions and exclusions for the VLAN IDs accepted on that port. For example, a port configured as tagged may be configured to allow only VLAN ID 10 through. A trunk port would be configured with all of the VLAN IDs that needed to be passed between switches.

When a port is configured as *untagged*, that port does not require traffic to be tagged with a VLAN ID and will instead automatically tag traffic with the default VLAN ID configured on the port for traffic received from the host and going out to other hosts or switches. For inbound traffic to the switch going to the host, the VLAN ID is stripped out and the packet is sent to the host. On many switches, all ports are configured by default as untagged with a VLAN ID of 1.

To summarize:

Tagged The port expects traffic to be tagged when receiving.

Untagged The port expects traffic to not be tagged and will apply a default VLAN ID. Any traffic that has a VLAN tag will be dropped.

Another limitation with VLANs is the number of VLANs that can be supported in an environment, which is 4,095, because the VLAN ID in the header is 12 bits long, and one VLAN ID is not usable. So 4,095 is the theoretical number, but most switches limit the number of usable VLANs to 1,000. This may still seem like a lot, but if an organization is a host with thousands of clients, then the 1,000 limitation, or even 4,095, would make it an unusable solution. Also, remember the complexity issue. If you have 1,000 VLANs over hundreds of servers, managing them would not be a pleasant experience!

VLANs and Hyper-V

Even with the pain points of VLANs, the reality is that you are probably using VLANs, will still use them for some time even when using Network Virtualization, and want to use them with your virtual machines. It is completely possible to have some virtual machines in one VLAN and other virtual machines in other VLANs. While there are different ways to perform configuration of VLANs, with Hyper-V there is really one supported and reliable way to use them and maintain manageability and troubleshooting ability:

◆ Configure the switch port that is connected to the Hyper-V host in tagged mode and configure it to have inclusions for all of the VLAN IDs that will be used by VMs connected to that host. Another option is to run the port essentially in a trunk-type mode and allow all VLAN IDs through the port to avoid potential configuration challenges when a new VLAN ID is used by a VM on the host. Definitely do not configure the port as untagged with any kind of default VLAN ID. I cannot stress this enough. If a switch port is configured as untagged and it receives traffic that is tagged, that traffic will be dropped even if the VLAN ID matches the VLAN the port has been configured to set via the untagged configuration.

◆ Do not set a VLAN ID on the physical NIC in the Hyper-V host that is used by the virtual switch that will be connected to the virtual machines.

◆ If you are using NIC Teaming, have only a single, default mode team interface configured on the team.

◆ Run all communications through the Hyper-V virtual switch and apply the VLAN ID configuration on the virtual switch ports that correspond to the virtual network adapters connected to the virtual switch.

This process makes configuring a VLAN simple. The only VLAN configuration performed in the Hyper-V environment is within the properties of the virtual network adapter, as shown in Figure 3.9, where I set the VLAN ID for this specific network adapter for the virtual machine. The Set-VMNetworkAdapterVlan PowerShell cmdlet can also be used to set the VLAN ID for a virtual network adapter, as in the following example:

```
Set-VMNetworkAdapterVlan –VMName test1 –Access –VlanId 173
```

FIGURE 3.9
Setting the VLAN ID for a virtual machine's network adapter

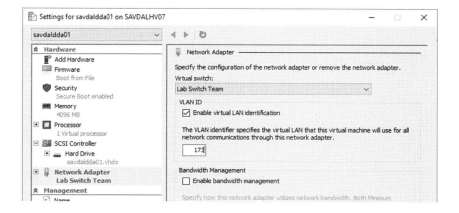

If you refer back to Figure 3.2, something might seem confusing: the option to configure a VLAN ID on the virtual switch itself. Does this setting then apply to every virtual machine connected to that virtual switch? No. As the explanation text in the dialog box explains, the VLAN ID configured on the virtual switch is applied to any virtual network adapters created in the management OS for the virtual switch, which allows the management OS to continue using a physical network adapter that has been assigned to a virtual switch. The VLAN ID configured on the switch has no effect on virtual machine VLAN configuration.

Note that if you do not require different VLAN IDs within the Hyper-V environment, and all virtual machines effectively will use the same VLAN ID, then no VLAN configuration is required at the Hyper-V host or virtual machine level. Simply use untagged at the switch and configure whatever VLAN ID you wish all traffic to be tagged with as the default. You use the previous configuration when you need different VLAN IDs for the various virtual machines and management OS. The only exception to this is when using RDMA and utilizing traffic-class tagging with Data Center Bridging (DCB). While the specification indicates that traffic-class tagging without a VLAN is legal, many switches do *not* support this and require a VLAN tag. Therefore, if you plan to use RDMA with traffic tagging, you should use a tagged configuration and specific VLANs.

PVLANs

With all of the scalability limitations of VLANs, you may wonder how large organizations and hosters specifically handle thousands of clients. This is where private VLANs (PVLANs) are a key feature. Through the use of only two VLAN IDs that are paired, PVLANs enable huge numbers of environments to remain isolated from each other.

PVLANs enable three modes, as shown in Figure 3.10: isolated, community, and promiscuous. The primary mode used with PVLANs is *isolated*; no direct communication is possible between hosts that are in isolated mode, but they can talk to their gateway and therefore out to the Internet and other promiscuous resources. This mode is useful if there are many tenants that have only one host/VM each. Think about that large hosting company that hosts millions of VMs that don't need to communicate with each other, or a hotel with 1,000 rooms. Also consider many workloads behind a load balancer that don't need to communicate with each other. Using PVLANs stops the servers behind the load balancer from being able to communicate with each other, which provides protection if one of them were compromised in some way, making it useful for Internet-facing workloads. PVLANs are a great way to isolate every port from every other with only two VLANs required.

FIGURE 3.10
PVLAN overview and the three types

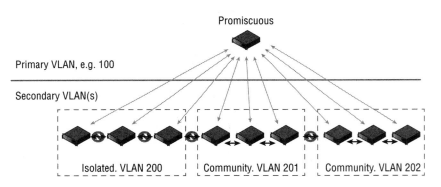

Community mode enables multiple hosts in the same community to communicate with each other. However, each community requires its own second VLAN ID to use with the shared primary VLAN ID. Finally, hosts in *promiscuous* mode can communicate with hosts in isolated or community mode. Promiscuous PVLANs are useful for servers that are used by all hosts— perhaps they host a software share or updates that can be used by all.

Hyper-V supports all three PVLAN modes, but this is not exposed through the graphical Hyper-V Manager. Instead, all configuration is done in PowerShell by using the Set-VMNetworkAdapterVlan cmdlet. Remember that each VLAN can be used as the primary VLAN of only one isolated PVLAN, so ensure that different VLANs are used as the primary for your isolated PVLANs. Note that the same secondary VLAN can be used in multiple isolated PVLANs without a problem. The following configurations are some that you will perform for PVLAN via PowerShell.

To set a VM in isolated mode, use this command:

```
Set-VMNetworkAdapterVlan -VMName testvm -Isolated -PrimaryVlanId 100 `
 -SecondaryVlanId 200
```

Use this command to set a VM in community mode (note that the secondary VLAN ID sets the community for the VM):

```
Set-VMNetworkAdapterVlan -VMName testvm2 -Community -PrimaryVlanId 100 `
-SecondaryVlanId 201
```

Use this command to set a VM in promiscuous mode (note that the secondary VLAN is now a list of all VLAN IDs used in the community and for the isolated):

```
Set-VMNetworkAdapterVlan -VMName testvm3 -Promiscuous -PrimaryVlanId 100 `
-SecondaryVlanIdList 200-400
```

To check the configuration of a virtual machine, use the `Get-VMNetworkAdapterVlan` cmdlet, as in this example:

```
Get-VMNetworkAdapterVlan -VMName testvm | fl *
```

The preceding commands assume that a virtual machine has a single network adapter, which essentially changes the configuration for the entire virtual machine. If a virtual machine has multiple network adapters and you wish to configure only one of the virtual network adapters, then pass the specific network adapter to the `Set-VMNetworkAdapterVlan` cmdlet. For example, the following command sets the VLAN for the virtual network adapter with the MAC address (remember, you can view the MAC addresses of all the virtual machines' NICs with the command `Get-VMNetworkAdapter -VMName "VMName"`). This command lists all of the adapters for the VM, narrows the list down by the one that matches the passed MAC address, and then passes that adapter to the `Set-VMNetworkAdapterVlan` cmdlet:

```
Get-VMNetworkAdapter -VMName "VMName" `
| where {$_.MACAddress -like "00155DADB60A"} `
| Set-VMNetworkAdapterVlan -Isolated -PrimaryVlanID 100 -SecondaryVlanId 200
```

Some configuration of PVLANs is also possible using SCVMM, but only isolated mode is supported, and not promiscuous or community mode. If you are using SCVMM and wish to have promiscuous and community mode virtual machines, you will need to continue using PowerShell for those virtual machines. To use SCVMM for isolated mode, you use a fairly simple configuration:

1. Open the Virtual Machine Manager interface, open the Fabric workspace, and select Networking ➤ Logical Networks.

2. Select the Create Logical Network action.

3. For VMM on the Settings page of the Create Logical Network Wizard dialog box, select the Private VLAN (PVLAN) networks option, as shown in Figure 3.11, and click Next.

4. On the Network Site page of the wizard, add a site as usual. However, you will enter both a primary and secondary VLAN ID, as shown in Figure 3.12. Multiple rows can be added, each a separate isolated PVLAN if needed. When virtual networks are created later, each virtual network can be linked to a specific isolated PVLAN. Click Next.

FIGURE 3.11
Enabling a PVLAN by
using SCVMM on a new
logical network

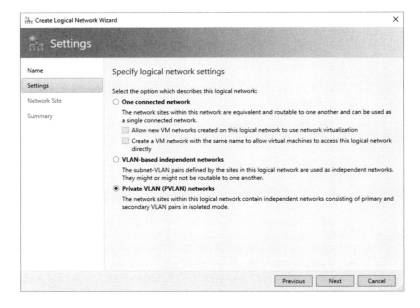

FIGURE 3.12
Using SCVMM to
create multiple iso-
lated PVLANs that use
the same secondary
VLAN ID

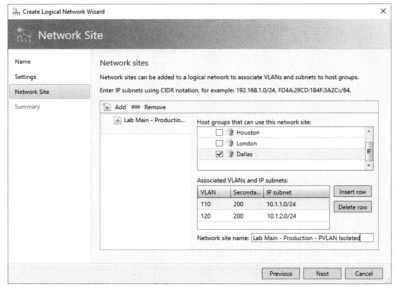

5. Click Finish to create the new PVLAN isolated configuration.

Here are the same PowerShell commands for SCVMM to create the isolated PVLAN configuration that matches the configuration previously performed using the SCVMM graphical
interface:

```
$logicalNetwork = New-SCLogicalNetwork -Name "test" `
-LogicalNetworkDefinitionIsolation $true `
```

```
 -EnableNetworkVirtualization $false -UseGRE $false -IsPVLAN $true

$allHostGroups = @()
$allHostGroups += Get-SCVMHostGroup `
 -ID "b08d9191-5890-4edf-a067-8ab63baf5946"
$allSubnetVlan = @()
$allSubnetVlan += New-SCSubnetVLan -Subnet "10.1.1.0/24" -VLanID 110 `
 -SecondaryVLanID 200
$allSubnetVlan += New-SCSubnetVLan -Subnet "10.1.2.0/24" -VLanID 120 `
 -SecondaryVLanID 200

New-SCLogicalNetworkDefinition -Name "Lab Main-Prod-PVLAN Isolated" `
 -LogicalNetwork $logicalNetwork -VMHostGroup $allHostGroups `
 -SubnetVLan $allSubnetVlan -RunAsynchronously
```

It's important that all of the physical switch ports are configured correctly for the VLANs used as part of a PVLAN configuration, or traffic will not flow between hosts correctly. Although VLANs are used heavily in many environments, most organizations won't use PVLANs that are aimed at specific scenarios requiring large numbers of hosts/virtual machines that cannot talk to each other. The good news is that they are all supported with Hyper-V.

How SCVMM Simplifies Networking with Hyper-V

Although SCVMM is covered in detail later in the book, I've already mentioned its use numerous times in this chapter and I'm about to discuss it a lot more as it moves from being an optional management technology to being the *only* practical way to implement some technologies. In this section, I discuss some fundamental SCVMM logical components and how to get up and running with them quickly, including deploying some of the components already covered in this chapter the "SCVMM way."

When you consider the configuration performed with Hyper-V, it really consisted of creating a virtual switch that was tied to a physical network adapter, and the way you named the virtual switch could indicate what it would be used for. However, if that switch connected to an adapter that connected to a switch port that supported different VLANs for different networks, then there was no way to convey that and manage it effectively. Also, there was no concept of separating the network seen by the virtual machines from that defined on the Hyper-V server. Additionally, on each Hyper-V server, the virtual switch configuration and any extensions were manually configured. Things get a lot more complicated when virtual switches are used for multiple virtual network adapters on the management operating system, as you'll see when you look at a more converged network infrastructure later this chapter.

SCVMM introduces quite a few new concepts and constructs that initially may seem a little overwhelming. However, they are fundamentally designed to let you model your physical networks, your switch, and your network configurations on the Hyper-V hosts and then model a separate abstracted set of definitions for networks available to virtual machines. These constructs can broadly be divided into those that model connectivity and those that model capability.

Let's build these constructs out and then walk through a configuration for a new deployment. One key point ideally is to perform all of your configuration through SCVMM for your Hyper-V host. Install the Hyper-V role with no virtual switches and do nothing else. Don't create virtual switches, don't create NIC teams, don't start creating virtual machines. The best experience is to define the configuration in SCVMM and let SCVMM perform all of the configuration on the hosts.

One important point for networking—whether for physical hosts, for virtualization with Hyper-V, or using SCVMM—is proper planning and design. You need to understand your physical network topology and your requirements, and then translate this to your virtual network infrastructure. This becomes emphasized with SCVMM because SCVMM networking components force you to do this planning; you need to model your network within SCVMM by using its various networking architectural components to achieve desired results. There are three primary groups of activities that are undertaken when networking with SCVMM:

1. *Discovery.* Understand the network requirements of your datacenter and your virtual environments. This may require asking questions of the network teams and the business units to find out the types of isolation required, the address spaces to be used, and the types of networks that exist and need to be leveraged. Do certain types of traffic require guaranteed bandwidth, which would dictate the use of separate networks or use QoS technologies?

2. *Design.* Take the information that you have discovered and translate it to SCVMM architectural components. Consider any changes to process as part of virtual environments. This may be an iterative process because physical infrastructure such as hardware switches may limit some options and the design for the virtual network solution may need to be modified to match capabilities of physical infrastructure.

3. *Deployment.* Configure SCVMM with a networking design and deploy the configuration to hosts, virtual machines, and clouds.

SCVMM Networking Architecture

The first architectural component for SCVMM is the logical network, which helps model your physical network infrastructure and connectivity in SCVMM. Consider your virtualization environment and the networks to which the hosts and the virtual machines will need to connect. In most datacenters, at a minimum you would see something like Figure 3.13.

FIGURE 3.13
Common networks seen in a datacenter with virtualization

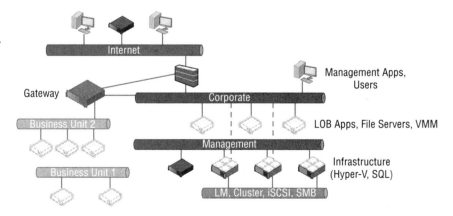

In this common datacenter, the various types of networks have different connectivity, different capabilities, and different routing available. The networks may require isolation from each other by using various technologies, which is explained in more detail later. Remember, these are just examples. Some datacenters will have many more. Here are the types of networks you could have:

The Internet   You may have customers or users who access the network via the Internet and connect to the Internet through various routes, so systems with Internet connectivity will likely need to be modeled as a separate network.

Corporate   This is usually the primary network in your company where users physically reside and will connect to the various services offered, such as line-of-business (LOB) applications, file servers, domain controllers, and more. Additionally, administrators may connect to certain management systems via systems available on the corporate network, such as your VMM server. The VMM environment needs to model the corporate environment so that virtual machines can be given connectivity to the corporate environment to offer services.

Management   Infrastructure servers typically are connected on a separate management network that is not accessible to regular users and may not even be routable from the corporate network.

Special Networks   Certain types of servers require their own special types of communications, such as those required for cluster communications, Live Migrations, iSCSI, and SMB storage traffic. These networks are rarely routable and may even be separate, isolated switches to ensure desired connectivity and low latencies or they may use separate VLANs. Some organizations also leverage a separate network for backup purposes.

Business Units/Tenants/Labs   Separate networks may be required to isolate different workloads, such as different business units, different tenants (if you are a hoster), and lab/test environments. Isolation can be via various means, such as VLANs, PVLANs, or network virtualization. These networks may require connectivity out to the Internet, to other physical locations (common in hoster scenarios where a client runs some services on the hoster infrastructure but needs to communicate to the client's own datacenter), or even to the corporate network, which would be via some kind of gateway device. In Figure 3.13, Business Unit 2 requires connectivity out of its isolated network, while Business Unit 1 is completely isolated with no connectivity outside of its own network.

Each type of network would be modeled as a logical network in SCVMM. Additionally, an organization may have different physical locations/datacenters, and SCVMM allows you to define a logical network and include details of the sites where it exists along with the configuration required at each site, known as a *network site*.

For example, suppose an organization has two locations, Dallas and Houston, and consider just the management network in this example. In Dallas, the management network uses the 10.1.1.0/24 subnet with VLAN 10, while in Houston, the management network uses the 10.1.2.0/24 subnet with VLAN 20. This information can be modeled in SCVMM by using network sites, which are linked to a SCVMM host group and contained within a logical network. This enables SCVMM to assign not just the correct IP address to virtual machines based on location and network but also the correct VLAN/PVLAN. This is a key point. The logical network is modeling the physical network, so it's important that your objects match the physical topology, such as correct IP and VLAN configuration.

Note that a network site in a logical network does not have to reflect an actual physical location but rather a specific set of network configurations. For example, suppose that I have a management network that uses two physical switches, and each switch uses a different VLAN and IP subnet.

I would create a single logical network for my management network and then a separate site for each of the network configurations, one for each VLAN and IP subnet pair.

A network site can be configured with just an IP subnet, just a VLAN, or an IP subnet/VLAN pair. You need to configure IP subnets for a site only if SCVMM will be statically assigning IP addresses to the site. If DHCP is present, no IP subnet configuration is required. If VLANs are not being used, a VLAN does not need to be configured. If DHCP is used in the network and VLANs are not used, you do not have to create any network sites.

After the sites are defined within a logical network, IP pools can be added to the IP address subnet that's defined, which enables SCVMM to configure virtual machines with static IP addresses as the virtual machines are deployed. If DHCP is used in the network, there is no need to configure IP pools in SCVMM or even specify the IP subnet as part of the site configuration. DHCP would be leveraged for the IP assignment, but if you don't have DHCP, then creating the IP pool allows SCVMM to handle the IP assignment for you.

The IP assignment is achieved by modifying the Sysprep answer file with the IP address from the SCVMM IP pool as the virtual machine template is deployed. When the virtual machine is deleted, SCVMM reclaims the IP address into its pool. Even if DHCP is primarily used in the network, if you are using features such as load balancing as part of a service, SCVMM has to be able to allocate and track that IP address, which requires the configuration of an IP pool. If no IP pool is created for a network site, SCVMM configures any virtual machines to use DHCP for address allocation. Both IPv4 and IPv6 are fully supported by SCVMM (and pretty much any Microsoft technology, because a Common Engineering Criteria requirement for all Microsoft solutions is support for IPv6 at the same level as IPv4).

At a high level, this means the logical network models your physical network and allows the subnet and VLANs to be modeled into objects and then scoped to specific sites, which can also include static IP address pools for allocation to resources such as virtual machines and load-balancer configurations. This is shown in Figure 3.14, with a management logical network that has two network sites, Dallas and Houston, along with the IP subnet and VLAN used at each location. For Dallas, an IP pool was also created for the network site to enable static IP configuration. Houston uses DHCP because no IP pool was created for the Houston network site within the logical network.

FIGURE 3.14
High-level view of logical networks

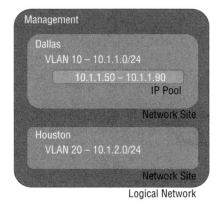

When planning your logical networks, try to stay as simple as possible. You should not have hundreds of logical networks. You should have fewer that contain different network sites that reflect the various network configurations within the type of network that is represented by the logical network. Microsoft has a good blog on designing logical networks at

```
http://blogs.technet.com/b/scvmm/archive/2013/04/29/
logical-networks-part-ii-how-many-logical-networks-do-you-really-need.aspx
```

The information can be summarized as follows:

1. Create logical networks to mirror the physical networks that exist.

2. Create logical networks to define the networks that have specific purposes.

3. Identify logical networks that need to be isolated and identify the isolation method.

4. Determine required network sites, VLANs, PVLANs, and IP pools required for each logical network and deploy them.

5. Associate logical networks to host computers.

Logical Switch

Earlier in this chapter, we created a virtual switch, and as part of that configuration options were available as well as the ability to enable certain extensions. Although it is possible to perform a manual configuration on a server-by-server basis, this can lead to inconsistencies and inhibits automatic deployment of new Hyper-V hosts. SCVMM has the logical switch component, which acts as the container for all virtual switch settings and ensures a consistent deployment across all servers using the logical switch. The automatic configuration using the logical switch is not only useful at deployment, but SCVMM will continue to track the configuration of the host compared to the logical switch, and if the configuration deviates from that of the logical switch, this deviation will be flagged as noncompliant, and that can then be resolved. This may be important in terms of ensuring compliance enforcement in an environment. If the logical switch is updated (for example, a new extension is added), all the Hyper-V hosts using it will automatically be updated.

Logical switches use port profiles, which are another SCVMM architectural construct that has two types: virtual port profiles and uplink port profiles.

A *virtual port profile* enables settings to be configured that will be applied to virtual network adapters attached to virtual machines or created on the management host OS itself. This can include offload settings such as the settings for VMQ, IPsec task offloading, and SR-IOV, and security settings such as those for DHCP Guard. It can also include configurations that may not be considered security related, such as guest teaming and QoS settings such as minimum and maximum bandwidth. Built-in virtual port profiles are provided in SCVMM for common network adapter uses, many of which are aimed at virtual network adapters used in the host OS. Figure 3.15 shows the inbox virtual port profiles in addition to the Security Settings page. Once a virtual port profile is used within a logical switch and the logical switch is deployed to a host, if the virtual port profile configuration is changed, the hosts will be flagged as noncompliant because their configuration no longer matches that of the virtual port profile. The administrator can easily remediate the servers to apply the updated configuration.

FIGURE 3.15

Viewing the security settings for the built-in Guest Dynamic IP virtual port profile

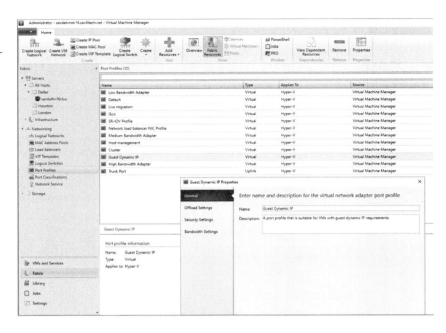

An *uplink port profile* defines the connectivity of the virtual switch to logical networks. You need separate uplink port profiles for each set of hosts that require the same physical connectivity (remember that logical networks define the physical network). Conversely, anytime that you need to restrict logical networks to specific hosts in the same location or need custom connectivity, you will require different uplink port profiles. Logical networks can be selected that will be available as part of the uplink port profile and NIC Teaming configuration, when used on hosts that will assign multiple network adapters. No inbox uplink port profiles are supplied because their primary purpose models the logical networks that can be connected to, and by default there are no logical networks. If a change is made to the uplink port profile definition (for example, adding a new VLAN that is available), SCVMM will automatically update all of the virtual switches on the Hyper-V hosts that use the uplink port profile via a logical switch with the new VLAN availability or any other settings within the uplink port profile.

Putting all of these components together does require additional up-front work. However, the long-term deployment and manageability of the environment becomes much simpler and can help you identify misconfigurations or problems in network connectivity.

The logical switch is a Live Migration boundary for SCVMM's placement logic. Note that a logical switch can be deployed to many hosts, it can stretch clusters, and so on. However, SCVMM needs to ensure that the same capabilities and connectivity are available when virtual machines are moved between hosts, and so the SCVMM placement logic will not allow Live Migration to hosts using a different logical switch. If you have a scenario requiring different logical switches in the environment (for example, if you require different extension configurations), then a Live Migration would not be possible and may be a reason for those hosts not to use the logical switch and instead perform the switch configuration directly on the Hyper-V hosts; this type of switch is known as a *standard switch*. Standard switches are fully supported within SCVMM, and their deployment and configuration occur via Hyper-V Manager or SCVMM.

If you had an existing Hyper-V server with virtual switches defined that will be standard switches in SCVMM, there was no way to convert them to logical switches prior to SCVMM 2016. A new option in SCVMM 2016, however, allows a standard switch to be converted to a logical switch. This conversion is facilitated through the properties of the host in the Fabric workspace: Select the Virtual Switches tab, select the standard switch, and then, at the bottom of the details, there is a button to convert to a logical switch. Click the button, select a logical switch that is equivalent to the connectivity, and the switch will be converted to a logical switch on the host.

It is also still possible to delete the standard switches and then re-create the switches as logical switches via SCVMM. To delete the standard switches, you would need to evacuate the host of virtual machines, which typically means that you have a cluster. However, with Windows Server 2012 and above, you can also move virtual machines with no downtime by using Shared Nothing Live Migration between any Hyper-V hosts, provided that they have a 1Gbps network connection. Of course, none of this should be required if you ensure that all configuration is done through SCVMM initially after planning out the logical networks, logical switches, and all other components before deploying Hyper-V hosts.

VM NETWORKS

While the logical network provides the modeling of the networks available in the environment and the desired isolation, the goal for virtualization is to separate and abstract these logical networks from the actual virtual machines. This abstraction is achieved through the use of VM networks, which is another networking architectural component in SCVMM. Through the use of VM networks, the virtual machines have no idea of the underlying technology used by the logical networks—for example, whether VLANs are used on the network fabric. Virtual machine virtual network adapters can be connected to only a VM network. When Network Virtualization is used, the customer address (CA) space is defined as part of the VM network, allowing specific VM subnets to be created as needed within the VM network.

In some scenarios, the isolation provided by VM networks might not be required—for example, when Direct Access to the infrastructure is required (such as if your SCVMM server is running in a virtual machine) or when the network is used for cluster communications. It is possible to create a no-isolation pass-through VM network that directly passes communication through to the logical network. The VM network is present only because a virtual machine network adapter needs to connect to a VM network. If a logical network has multiple sites defined, then when a virtual machine is deployed, it will automatically pick the correct IP subnet and VLAN configuration at deployment time based on the location to which it's being deployed. Users of self-service-type portals are exposed to VM networks but not the details of the underlying logical networks.

PORT CLASSIFICATIONS

Port classifications are assigned to virtual machines and are the containers for port profile settings. The benefit of the port classification is that it acts as a layer of abstraction from the port profiles assigned to logical switches, which allows a port classification to be assigned to a virtual machine template. The actual port profile used depends on the logical switch the VM is using when deployed.

Think of port classifications as being similar to storage classifications; you may create a gold storage classification that uses a top-of-the-line SAN, and a bronze storage classification that uses a much lower tier of storage. I may create a port classification of High Bandwidth and one of Low Bandwidth. Port classifications are included in-box that correlate to the included virtual port profiles. Port classifications are linked to virtual port profiles as part of the logical switch creation process. Like VM networks, port classifications are exposed to users via self-service portals and not the underlying port profiles.

Deploying Networking with SCVMM 2016

For this part of the chapter, I assume that SCVMM 2016 is up-and-running in your environment. I cover implementing SCVMM 2016 in Chapter 6, "Maintaining a Hyper-V Environment," so if you want to follow along, you may want to jump to Chapter 6 to get a basic deployment in place. The good news is that networking is one of the first components that needs to be configured with SCVMM, so once you have SCVMM deployed and you have created some host groups (which are collections of hosts), you will be ready to follow this next set of steps. Figure 3.16 provides a high-level view of the steps that will be performed.

FIGURE 3.16
The steps for SCVMM network configuration

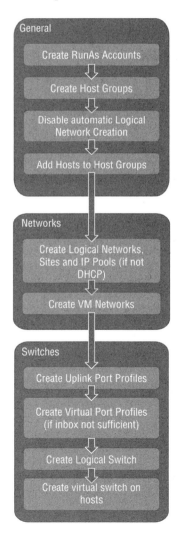

DISABLING AUTOMATIC LOGICAL NETWORK CREATION

The first action related to networking in SCVMM is to disable the automatic creation of logical networks. It may seem strange that your first configuration is to disable functionality, but it will help ensure your SCVMM modeling consistency. With automatic logical network creation enabled, when a Hyper-V host that already has a virtual switch defined is added to SCVMM, a logical network will automatically be created in SCVMM if SCVMM does not find a match for an existing logical network based on the first DNS suffix label for the network adapter network (which is the default behavior). For example, if the DNS suffix for a network connection is lab.savilltech.net, a logical network named lab will be used, and if not found, it will automatically be created.

This automatic creation of logical networks may be fine in a test environment, but in production, where you have planned for your logical networks in detail and deployed accordingly, the automatic creation of logical networks based on DNS suffix labels would likely be undesirable. Therefore, disable this automatic logical network creation as follows:

1. Open Virtual Machine Manager.

2. Open the Settings workspace.

3. Select the General navigation node.

4. Double-click Network Settings in the details pane.

5. In the Network Settings dialog box, uncheck the Create Logical Networks Automatically option, as shown in Figure 3.17, and click OK. Notice also in this dialog box that you can change the logical network matching behavior to a scheme that may better suit your naming conventions and design.

FIGURE 3.17
Disabling the automatic creation of logical networks in SCVMM 2016

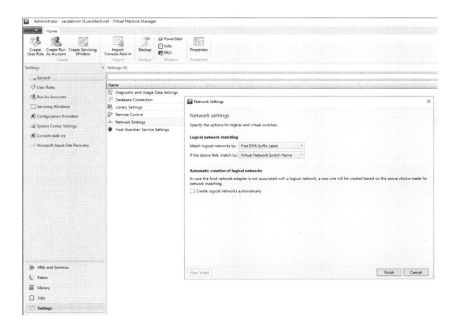

Those of you who used SCVMM 2012 SP1 will notice that the option to also automatically create virtual switches (VM networks) has been removed. The automatic creation of virtual switches, which virtual machines use to connect, caused a lot of confusion, so it was removed in R2. At this point, you can safely add Hyper-V hosts to the SCVMM environment without them automatically creating logical networks that you don't want in the environment.

CREATING LOGICAL NETWORKS

In this environment, I have three networks available that I will model as logical networks. However, they are all separate VLANs on the same physical network that will be controlled by setting the VLAN ID on the virtual network adapter. The physical ports on the switch have been configured to allow all of the various VLANs that can be configured (similar to a trunk port):

Corporate Network   The main address space used by my organization, which on my switches uses VLAN 10 in all locations.

Lab Network   The network used for numerous separate lab environments; each environment has its own IP subnet and VLAN.

Network Virtualization Network   This will be used in the future when network virtualization is explored.

The steps to create a logical network are detailed here:

1. Open Virtual Machine Manager.

2. Open the Fabric workspace.

3. Select the Networking ➤ Logical Networks navigation node.

4. Click the Create Logical Network button, which launches the Create Logical Network Wizard.

5. Enter a name and description for the logical network and click Next.

6. In the Settings tab, shown in Figure 3.18, you select a type of network. It can be a connected network that allows multiple sites to communicate with each other and use network virtualization, a VLAN-based independent network, or a PVLAN-based network. Note that when you are creating a network with the One Connected Network option, the option to create a VM network automatically to map to the logical network is available, but in this example we will manually create it. Because this is the corporate network, we won't use network virtualization. Click Next.

7. The next screen enables you to configure the sites. For corporate, you need only a single site using VLAN 10, because the switch is configured to allow VLAN 10 through to the corporate network. Click the Add button to add a site and then click Insert Row to add VLAN/IP details for the site. The IP space is configured by corporate DHCP servers in this example, so leave the IP subnet blank, which tells SCVMM to just configure the VM for DHCP.

   If the network does not use VLANs, set the VLAN ID to 0; this tells SCVMM that VLANs are not to be configured. By default, sites are given the name <Logical Network>_<number>, but you should rename this to something more useful. For example, as shown in Figure 3.19, I am renaming it *Corp Trunk*.

   For each site, select the host group that contains hosts in that site. Because this group can be used in all locations, I select the All Hosts group. Click Next.

FIGURE 3.18
Creating a logical network that represents a connected collection of sites

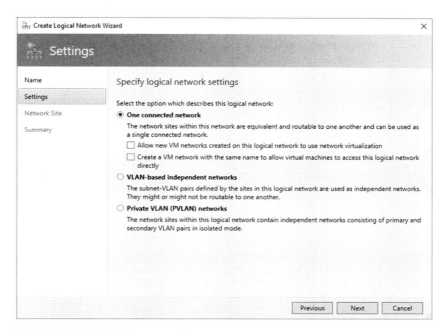

FIGURE 3.19
Adding a single site to a logical network

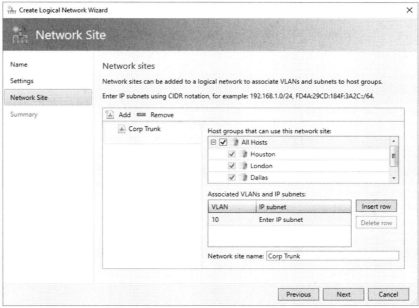

8. The Summary screen is displayed. It includes a View Script button that when clicked shows the PowerShell code that can be used to automate the creation. This can be useful when you are creating many logical networks, or more likely, many sites. Click Finish to create the logical network.

Here is the PowerShell code used to create my corporate logical network:

```
$logicalNetwork = New-SCLogicalNetwork -Name "Corp" `
-LogicalNetworkDefinitionIsolation $false `
-EnableNetworkVirtualization $false -UseGRE $false `
-IsPVLAN $false -Description "Corporate, connected network"

$allHostGroups = @()
$allHostGroups += Get-SCVMHostGroup `
-ID "0e3ba228-a059-46be-aa41-2f5cf0f4b96e"
$allSubnetVlan = @()
$allSubnetVlan += New-SCSubnetVLan -VLanID 10

New-SCLogicalNetworkDefinition -Name "Corp Trunk" `
-LogicalNetwork $logicalNetwork -VMHostGroup $allHostGroups `
-SubnetVLan $allSubnetVlan -RunAsynchronously
```

The next network for you to create is my set of lab networks. In this case, I will select the VLAN-based independent networks type, and I will create a separate site for each of the VLAN/IP subnet pairs, which represent separate lab environments, as shown in Figure 3.20. I'm creating only two of the VLANs in this example because performing this using the graphical tools is slow. My lab environments are all based in Dallas, so only the Dallas host group is selected. Because the sites in this logical network have IP subnets defined, I would also create an IP pool for each site as in the next set of steps. You will notice that most of these settings are similar to those configured for a DHCP scope, because SCVMM is performing a similar role; it just uses a different mechanism to assign the IP address. All of the details are those that will be configured on the virtual machines that get IP addresses from the IP pool.

FIGURE 3.20
Creating a VLAN-based
logical network

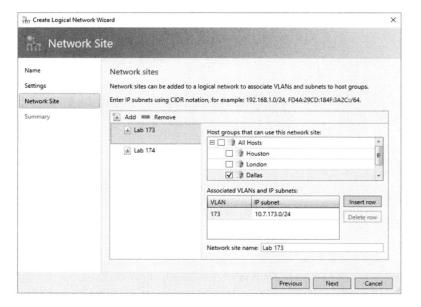

1. Click the Create IP Pool button, or right-click the logical network and select the Create IP Pool context menu action.

2. Enter a name and description. From the drop-down list, select the logical network for the IP pool.

3. The next screen, shown in Figure 3.21, allows you to use an existing network site or create a new one. Choose to use an existing one and then click Next.

FIGURE 3.21
Choose the site for a new IP pool or create a new one.

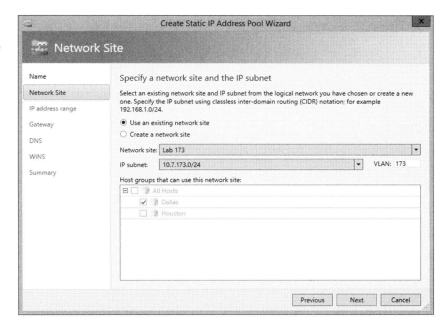

4. The IP Address Range page allows configuration of the IP address range that SCVMM will manage and allocate to resources such as virtual machines and load balancers. Within the range, you can configure specific addresses to be reserved for other purposes or for use by load-balancer virtual IPs (VIPs) that SCVMM can allocate. In Figure 3.22, you can see that I have reserved five IP addresses from the range for use by load-balancer VIPs. Fill in the fields and click Next.

5. Click the Insert button, and enter the gateway IP address. Then click Next.

6. Configure the DNS servers, DNS suffix, and additional DNS suffixes to append, and then click Next.

7. Enter the WINS server details if used, and click Next.

8. On the Summary screen, confirm the configuration, click the View Script button to see the PowerShell that will be used, and then click Finish to create the IP pool.

FIGURE 3.22
Configuring the IP
address range for
the IP pool

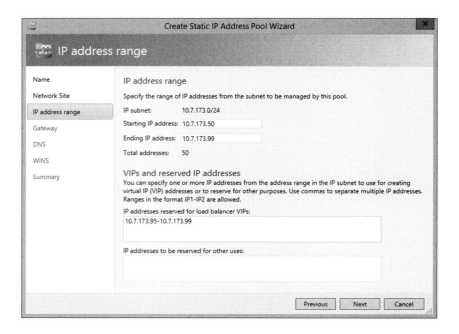

Finally, you will create my Hyper-V network virtualization logical network, which will support network virtualization and be configured with an IP pool used for the provider space for the Hyper-V hosts. This will follow the same process as the other networks, except this time you will select the One Connected Network option and the option "Allow new VM networks created on this logical network to use network virtualization." A network site is created and a VLAN is configured if needed along with an IP subnet (this must be set), and this will purely be used so that the Hyper-V hosts that are hosting virtual machines that are participating in network virtualization can be allocated their provider address (PA). An IP pool must also be created for the site for the IP address allocation for the PA. No DNS servers are required for the PA network, but if you are using multiple subnets, a gateway would need to be defined.

CREATING VM NETWORKS

With logical networks created, the next step is to create the VM networks to which virtual machines can be connected. In SCVMM 2016, within the logical networks view, there is a convenient option to create the VM network by using the Create VM Network button or by right-clicking a logical network and selecting Create VM Network. For now, you will use the old-fashioned way:

1. Open Virtual Machine Manager.

2. Open the VMs And Services workspace (not Fabric, because this is now a construct directly related to virtual machines).

3. Select the VM Networks navigation node.

4. Click the Create VM Network button.

5. Enter a name and description for the VM network, select the logical network, and click Next.

6. Depending on the logical network selected, this may be the end of the configuration. For example, a connected network without network virtualization requires no further configuration. A VLAN type network that is isolated will show an Isolation screen, which allows a specific VLAN (site) to be selected for this specific VM network, or you can select Automatic, which allows SCVMM to select a site automatically based on those available on the logical network. If a network that is enabled for network virtualization is selected, additional configuration pages must be completed to define the configuration for the IP scheme in the virtual network space (CA). I cover this in detail in the section "Network Virtualization."

Click Finish to complete the VM network creation process.

My final configuration is shown in Figure 3.23 for my logical networks and VM networks.

FIGURE 3.23
The complete logical network and VM network configuration

So far, we have done a lot of configuration but have not modeled our network to SCVMM. Consider my lab environment. I configured two of the VLANs to separate the lab environments, but suppose I have 40 or 80 or 200. This is where PowerShell is invaluable, and I created the script that follows to automate this configuration process.

This script creates a separate site for each VLAN, with the appropriate IP subnet and an IP pool (which in my case is just two addresses used for the first two machines that are domain controllers, because the rest are assigned by DHCP). In my lab, the third octet matches the VLAN ID. This script automatically creates all 40 VLAN sites, which run from 150 to 190, and the appropriate IP pools. You can customize the script to meet your own needs—including changing the name of the SCVMM server and replacing it with the logical network that all the sites should be added to (you have to create the logical network in advance, although this could also be added to this script if required). To find the GUID of your logical network, run the command Get-SCLogicalNetwork | ft Name, ID -Auto:

```
Import-Module virtualmachinemanager
Get-VMMServer -ComputerName scvmm
#Replace this with actual ID of the Logical Network.
#Get-SCLogicalNetwork | ft name, id
$logicalNetwork = Get-SCLogicalNetwork -ID "xxxxxxxx-xxxx-xxxx-xxxx-
```

```
xxxxxxxxxxxx"
$startNumber = 150
$endNumber = 190

$vlanID = $startNumber

do
{
    $allHostGroups = @()
    $allHostGroups += Get-SCVMHostGroup `
-ID "0e3ba228-a059-46be-aa41-2f5cf0f4b96e"
    $allSubnetVlan = @()
    $allSubnetVlan += New-SCSubnetVLan -Subnet "10.1.$vlanID.0/24" `
-VLanID $vlanID

    $logicalNetworkDefinition = New-SCLogicalNetworkDefinition `
-Name "VLAN_$vlanID" `
-LogicalNetwork $logicalNetwork -VMHostGroup $allHostGroups `
-SubnetVLan $allSubnetVlan -RunAsynchronously

    # Gateways
    $allGateways = @()
    $allGateways += New-SCDefaultGateway -IPAddress "10.1.$vlanID.1" `
-Automatic

    # DNS servers
    $allDnsServer = @("10.1.$vlanID.10", "10.1.$vlanID.11")

    # DNS suffixes
    $allDnsSuffixes = @()

    # WINS servers
    $allWinsServers = @()

    $NewVLANName = "VLAN_" + $vlanID + "_IP_Pool"

    New-SCStaticIPAddressPool -Name $NewVLANName `
-LogicalNetworkDefinition $logicalNetworkDefinition `
-Subnet "10.1.$vlanID.0/24" `
-IPAddressRangeStart "10.1.$vlanID.10" `
-IPAddressRangeEnd "10.1.$vlanID.11" `
-DefaultGateway $allGateways -DNSServer $allDnsServer -DNSSuffix "" `
-DNSSearchSuffix $allDnsSuffixes -RunAsynchronously

    #Now create VM Network for each

    $vmNetwork = New-SCVMNetwork -Name "Customer_VLAN_$vlanID" `
-LogicalNetwork $logicalNetwork -IsolationType "VLANNetwork" `
-Description "VM Network for Customer VLAN $vlanID"
    $logicalNetworkDefinition = Get-SCLogicalNetworkDefinition `
-Name "VLAN_$vlanID"
    $subnetVLAN = New-SCSubnetVLan -Subnet "10.7.$vlanID.0/24" `
```

```
-VLanID $vlanID
    $VMSubnetName = "Customer_VLAN_" + $vlanID + "_0"
    $vmSubnet = New-SCVMSubnet -Name $VMSubnetName `
-LogicalNetworkDefinition $logicalNetworkDefinition `
-SubnetVLan $subnetVLAN `
-VMNetwork $vmNetwork

    $vlanID += 1
}
until ($vlanID -gt $endNumber)
```

CREATING THE PORT PROFILES AND LOGICAL SWITCH

Now that the logical networks and VM networks exist, you can create my logical switch. Remember, however, that the logical switch uses the uplink port profiles to identify the connectivity available. You also use virtual port profiles and port classifications. You will use the built-in objects for those, but they are easy to create, if required, using the Fabric workspace and the Port Profiles and Port Classifications navigation areas. I recommend looking at the existing virtual port profiles and port classifications as the foundation of configuration should you need to create your own. Now is a good time to take a look at the inbox port profiles and port classifications, which you can choose to keep, delete, or even modify to meet your own needs exactly.

The first step is to create the uplink port profiles. Remember, the uplink port profile models the connectivity available for a specific connection from the host; that is, from the network adapter to the switch. If different network adapters have different connectivity to different switches, you will need multiple uplink port profiles. Here are the steps:

1. Open Virtual Machine Manager.

2. Open the Fabric workspace.

3. Select the Networking ➤ Port Profiles navigation node.

4. Click the Create button drop-down, and select Hyper-V Port Profile.

5. Enter a name and description for the new port profile, as shown in Figure 3.24. Select the Uplink Port Profile radio button. You can additionally configure a teaming mode, which is used if the port profile is used on a host where NIC Teaming is required and the settings configured in the port profile will be applied. Because I am connecting all my Hyper-V boxes to ports configured on the switch with multiple VLANs allowed, I need only one uplink port profile that can connect any of the networks. Click Next.

6. Select the network sites (which are part of your logical networks) that can be connected to via this uplink port profile (see Figure 3.25). Because all of my networks can, I select them all, as well as the check box to enable Hyper-V Network Virtualization. On Windows 2012 Hyper-V hosts, this option enables Network Virtualization in the networking stack on the network adapter, but it does nothing on Windows Server 2012 R2 and above hosts, which always have Network Virtualization enabled because they're part of the switch. Click Next.

7. Click Finish to complete the creation of the uplink port profile.

FIGURE 3.24
Setting the options
for a new uplink
port profile and NIC
Teaming options

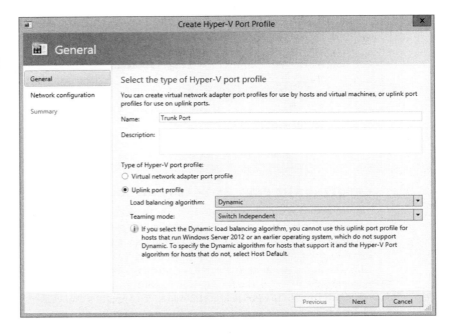

FIGURE 3.25
Selecting the net-
work sites that can
be connected to by
using the uplink port
profile

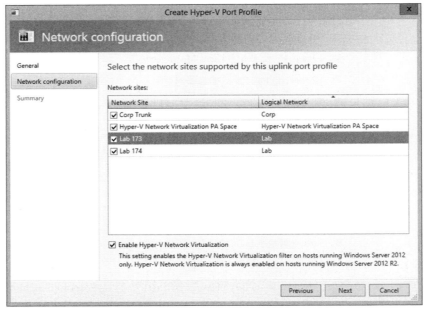

The final step of modeling is the creation of the logical switch, which will then be applied to the Hyper-V hosts. The logical switch will bring all of the components together. Follow these steps:

1. Open Virtual Machine Manager.

2. Open the Fabric workspace.

3. Select the Networking ➤ Logical Switches navigation node.

4. Click the Create Logical Switch button.

5. The Create Logical Switch Wizard launches. Read all of the text on the introduction page. It confirms all of the tasks that you should have already performed, such as creating the logical networks, installing extensions, and creating uplink port profiles (aka native port profiles). Click Next.

6. Enter a name and description for the new logical switch. Also note that you can select the uplink mode, which relates to the use of teaming, as shown in Figure 3.26. Prior to Windows Server 2016, a VM Switch was attached to a single NIC or a NIC team that comprised multiple network adapters. Windows Server 2016 introduces Switch Embedded Teaming (SET) which, as the name suggests, teams multiple adapters directly in the VM Switch instead of creating a separate NIC team by using the Load Balancing and Failover (LBFO) functionality. SET has the benefit of enabling mixed use of adapters with the VM Switch and utilizing RDMA, which I cover later in this chapter. If you select No Uplink Team, the switch can be bound to only a single NIC. If you select Team, LBFO NIC Teaming will be used to create a NIC team automatically on the host for the adapters selected when deploying the switch. If you select Embedded Team, SET is utilized with no separate NIC team created on the host. If SCVMM detects the deployment of a network controller (which I cover later), the option to use LBFO teaming is removed. I recommend using embedded teaming over LBFO, as this is definitely the future direction for teaming in Windows, and if you are using RDMA, it is a no-brainer. Click Next.

FIGURE 3.26
Selecting the type of uplink to be used in the switch

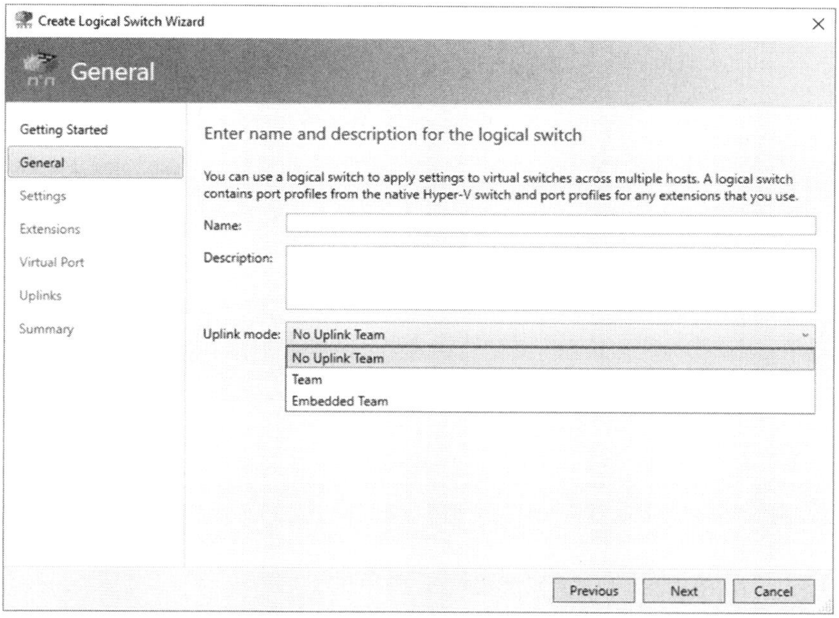

7. If you wish to use SR-IOV, you must select the Enable Single Root I/O Virtualization (SR-IOV) check box, and this cannot be changed after the switch is created. Also select the minimum bandwidth mode, which quantifies minimum bandwidth for workloads. Absolute is an actual number of bits per second, while Weight is an integer between 1 and 100 and is a relative value—the higher the weight, the greater the minimum bandwidth in times of contention. The best practice is to use Weight instead of Absolute; Absolute can cause challenges when the required value is not available.. This setting is the same as the `-MinimumBandwidthMode` switch when using `New-VMSwitch` in PowerShell. For more information, see `https://technet.microsoft.com/en-us/library/ jj735303(v=ws.11).aspx`. Click Next.

8. The list of installed virtual switch extensions is displayed and can be selected for deployment as part of the logical switch usage. This can be changed in the future if required. Click Next.

9. The virtual port profiles should now be added to the logical switch. Click the Add button, and in the dialog box that appears, click the Browse button to select the port classification. (Remember, this is the generic classification that is exposed to users of the environment.) Then select the "Include a virtual network adapter port profile in this virtual port" check box and select the virtual port profile that corresponds. For example, if you select the high-bandwidth port classification, then most likely you would select the High Bandwidth Adapter virtual port profile object. Click OK. Repeat to add classifications. Select the classification that you would like to be the default, and click the Set Default button. Click Next.

10. The uplink port profiles must be selected. Click the Add button and then select Existing Uplink Port Profile (because you've already created the profile—but note that it is also possible to create a new uplink port profile). Click OK. Multiple uplink port profiles can be added as required. Click Next.

11. Click Finish to create the logical switch.

CONFIGURING A HYPER-V HOST WITH A LOGICAL SWITCH

The final step is to configure Hyper-V hosts with the logical switch, which will trigger SCVMM to create virtual switches on the Hyper-V host that matches the configurations defined. It also sets up the environment for virtual machine and service deployments, and all of the networking elements will be configured automatically.

In my lab, my Hyper-V hosts have two 10Gbps network adapters that I wish to have teamed (using SET) to use for my Hyper-V virtual switch. I also have a separate network adapter for management actions such as RDP and file services and another network adapter for cluster and Live Migration operations. I don't use iSCSI or SMB in this environment because it uses Fibre Channel to connect to a SAN. I'm noting this so that you understand my choices in the following procedure. However, if you need the virtual switch to use all of your network adapters, including your management network adapter, SCVMM can take care of ensuring that you don't lose connectivity, which I cover in the following walk-through.

1. Open Virtual Machine Manager.

2. Open the Fabric workspace.

3. Navigate to your Hyper-V hosts under Servers ➤ <host group>.

4. Right-click a Hyper-V host and choose Properties.

5. Click the Virtual Switches tab, and click the New Virtual Switch button. The option to create a new logical switch or a new standard switch is displayed. Click the New Logical Switch option.

6. In this walk-through, only one logical switch was created, and that will be selected automatically along with one network adapter. This network adapter can be changed by using the drop-down, as can the uplink port profile it uses. Additional network adapters can be added by using the Add button if you wish to create a team.

In most environments, the uplink port profile needs to be the same for all network adapters. SCVMM will perform a check and gray out the option to change the uplink port profile for any additional network adapters, as shown in Figure 3.27. Some third-party forwarder switch extensions do allow different connectivity for different adapters in a team, which SCVMM would detect if configured for the logical switch, and the option to set different virtual port profiles was enabled.

FIGURE 3.27
Selecting the adapters to be used for the logical switch deployment

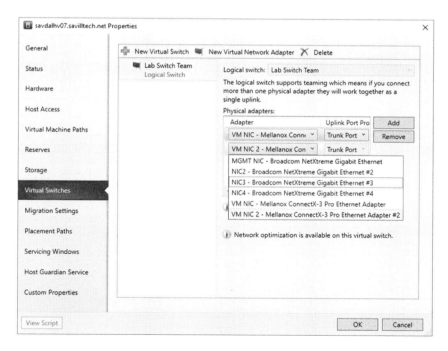

7. This step is needed only if virtual network adapters need to be created on the Hyper-V host—for example, in the scenario in which I'm using the network adapter I use for management as part of the new virtual switch. Click the New Virtual Network Adapter button. Enter a name for the new network adapter. There is a check box enabled by default, "This virtual network adapter inherits settings from the physical management adapter,"

which tells SCVMM to copy the MAC address and IP configuration from the first adapter in the team into the new virtual network adapter it is creating. This ensures continued connectivity for the host. Because the MAC address is copied, this ensures that even if DHCP is used, the same IP address will be assigned. Click the Browse button in the Connectivity section to select the connectivity for the virtual network adapter and a port profile classification. Multiple virtual network adapters can be added as required.

8. Once all configuration is complete, click OK for the configuration to be applied. A warning that connectivity may temporarily be lost during configuration is displayed. Click OK. This happens only if you are using your management network adapter in the new switch.

The progress of any action performed by SCVMM, known as a *job*, can be viewed via the Jobs workspace. Figure 3.28 shows this workspace with an old log I have from a 2012 R2 deployment. At the bottom of the workspace, you can see each step that was performed. In this example, notice that I configured the logical switch on two hosts, which are members of the same cluster. It's important to have a consistent configuration across clusters, to ensure that no problems occur with connectivity and functionality as virtual machines are moved between hosts (which is the reason I like to use this log as an example). Remember that SCVMM requires hosts to have the same logical switch available for placement during Live Migrations.

FIGURE 3.28
Viewing the status of logical switch deployment

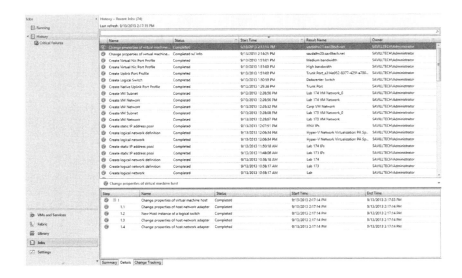

The eagle-eyed reader may notice that the logical switch creation on savdalhv20.savilltech.net (second line down from the top of Figure 3.28) shows that it completed with information, which was not the case for the savdalhv21.savilltech.net, which I configured second (the top line). The information was as follows:

```
Information (26844)
Virtual switch (Datacenter Switch) is not highly available because the switch is
not available in host (savdalhv21.savilltech.net).
```

SCVMM is telling me that I deployed a logical switch to a server that is part of a cluster, and that because the same logical switch is not available in the other node of the cluster, it is not highly available. This is why I don't get an information message when adding the logical switch to the second node, because the logical switch is available on both nodes. Figure 3.29 shows another set of logs showing that I removed a logical switch from a host, changed the logical switch to use SET instead of LBFO teaming, and then deployed the switch to the host. The upshot of these changes in SCVMM is that the VM Switch on the host is deleted, the NIC team is deleted, and a new VM Switch is deployed that now uses the NICs with SET.

FIGURE 3.29
Viewing the status of logical switch modification to SET mode

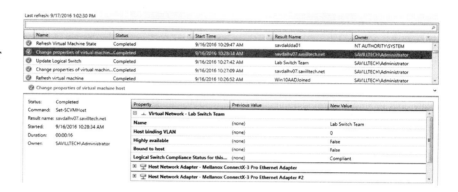

When connecting to the Hyper-V hosts where I deployed the logical switch, I now see that a new NIC team has been created and a new virtual switch in Hyper-V that matches the configurations of all of those SCVMM networking constructs that I defined.

When a virtual machine is created, the VM networks that are available will be listed to choose from, based on those available within the logical switch. The networks available depend on which were set via the uplink port profile selections.

All of this work certainly seems like far more effort than just manually creating a switch in Hyper-V Manager, which can be automated with PowerShell. However, consider having hundreds of Hyper-V hosts, and realize that now the environment has been fully modeled in SCVMM, allowing for intricate deployments without the need for users to understand the underlying network fabric or for administrators to search for which IP address and VLAN to use. With the work done up front, the ongoing management is far easier while also ensuring compliance.

Network Virtualization

Previously, I covered VLAN and PVLANs as technologies that provide some isolation between virtual machines and even abstract the connectivity from the physical network to a limited degree. However, challenges include the scalability limits of VLANs, the narrow scenarios for which PVLANs make sense, and the relative complexity and overhead of configuration required on the network equipment where VLANs are used and modified. Even with VLANs, there is not a true abstraction of the virtual network and the physical fabric.

Look at every aspect of the virtual environment. Memory, processor, and storage have all been virtualized effectively for a virtual machine but not the network. Our goal when we talk about clouds is to pool all of our resources for greater scale and flexibility, but physical networks can impede this seamless pooling. When a virtual machine is attached to a virtual switch, it needs to match the IP scheme used on the underlying network fabric to be able to communicate. A lot of time can be spent modeling the network in SCVMM, and once configured, it makes the management of the network much easier, but it also enables a far more powerful feature: network virtualization.

Network Virtualization Overview

Network virtualization separates the address space seen by the virtual machines—the customer address (CA) space—from that used to send the packets over the network—the provider address (PA) space. This separation provides abstraction of the network and complete isolation between virtual networks. This complete isolation of address space enables tenants to bring their own IP schemes and subnets to a virtual environment and enables overlapping of IP subnets among virtual networks. Additionally, because of this abstraction, it's possible for virtual machines to move between locations without requiring changes to their IP configuration.

This is important in many scenarios. Hosting companies that want to host many tenants benefit greatly from network virtualization, because each tenant is completely isolated from every other tenant with complete IP flexibility. Think about a company hosting Coke and Pepsi. It's important to be able to keep them completely isolated! Organizations that host different business units can also provide complete isolation and, again, flexible IP schemes.

Even without the need for flexible IP schemes or complete isolation, a move to network virtualization and software-defined networking (SDN) removes the complexity of managing physical network infrastructure anytime a change is required that is commonly needed when using existing technologies such as VLANs. Network virtualization also removes the scalability challenges associated with VLANs. Mega-scale public cloud services such as Azure leverage SDN to facilitate the networking in their multitenant model. Additionally, as you will explore, SDN can add many layers of security beyond the standard isolation of VLANs and perimeter firewalls. In today's world of "assume breach," it's desirable to have as many layers of protection as possible in order to help prevent lateral movement of an attacker after a network is penetrated.

Another benefit to network virtualization is that the networking visible to the virtual machines, which is now provided using software, can be managed by the virtualization administrators and even the virtualization tenants instead of having to involve the networking team, who can focus on the physical network infrastructure.

This virtual network capability is enabled through the use of two IP addresses for each virtual machine and a virtual subnet identifier that indicates the virtual network to which a particular virtual machine belongs. First, the *customer address* (CA) is the standard IP address configured within the virtual machine. Second, the *provider address* (PA) is the IP address used by the virtual machine to communicate over the physical network. The PA is invisible to the virtual machine; the Hyper-V host owns the PA.

This is best explored by an example. Say you have a single physical fabric, and running on that fabric are two separate organizations: the red and blue organizations. Each organization has its own IP scheme that can overlap, and the virtual networks can span multiple physical locations. This is shown in Figure 3.30. Each virtual machine that is part of the virtual red or blue network has its own customer address. A separate provider address is used to send the IP traffic over the physical fabric. The important part is that, as in other aspects of virtualization, the virtual machines have no knowledge that the network is virtualized. The virtual machines in a virtual network believe that they are operating on a physical network available only to them.

FIGURE 3.30
High-level over-
view of network
virtualization

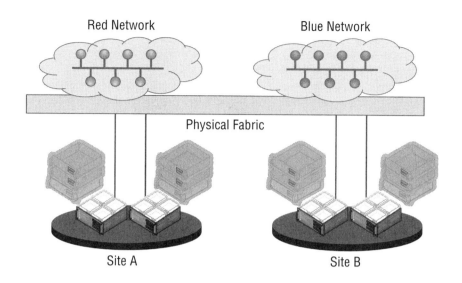

Windows Server 2012 and 2012 R2 exclusively used Network Virtualization Generic Routing Encapsulation (NVGRE) for the network virtualization implementation; it is an extension of GRE, an IETF (Internet Engineering Task Force) standard. With NVGRE, the network virtualization works by wrapping the originating packet from the VM, which uses the CAs (which are all the virtual machine is aware of), inside a packet that can be routed on the physical network using the PA IP addresses. The wrapper also includes the actual virtual subnet, which represents a specific subnet within a virtual network. Because the virtual subnet is included in the wrapper packet, each VM does not require its own PA. The receiving host can identify the targeted VM based on the CA target IP address within the original packet and the virtual subnet ID in the wrapper packet. The virtual subnet ID is stored in the GRE key, which is a 24-bit key allowing over 16 million virtual subnets, different scalability from the 4,000 limit of VLANs. The only information the Hyper-V host on the originating VM needs to know is which Hyper-V host is running the target VM, and then it can send the packet over the network.

This can be seen in Figure 3.31, where three virtual machines exist in a virtual network and are running across two separate Hyper-V servers. In the figure, CA1 is talking to CA2. However, note in the lookup table on the first Hyper-V server that the PA address for CA2 and CA3 are the same, because they run on the same Hyper-V host. The PA address is for each Hyper-V host rather than each virtual machine.

The use of a shared PA means that far fewer IP addresses from the provider IP pools are needed, which is good news for IP management and the network infrastructure. When thinking about the actual data going across the wire when using the NVGRE encapsulation, the packet structure would be composed as shown in the following list. As expected, the full Ethernet and IP header and payload from the virtual machine communication is wrapped in an Ethernet and IP header that can be used on the physical network fabric based on the Hyper-V host MAC addresses and PA IP addresses. The full specification for NVGRE can be found at:

```
http://tools.ietf.org/html/draft-sridharan-virtualization-nvgre-01
```

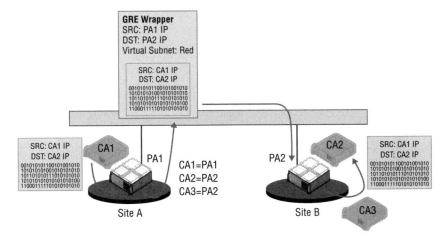

FIGURE 3.31
High-level over-
view of network
virtualization using
NVGRE

Note that VLANs can still be used on the physical fabric for the PA and would just be part of the standard packet, completely invisible to the network virtualization traffic. The packet structure for NVGRE encapsulation is as follows:

- PA Ethernet MAC source and destination addresses

- PA IP source and destination addresses

- VSID, where the isolation is enforced by NVGRE Tenant Network ID (TNI)

- VM Ethernet MAC source and destination addresses

- CA IP source and destination addresses

- Original IP payload

There is a potential downside to using NVGRE that I at least want to make you aware of. Because the original packet is being wrapped inside the NVGRE packet, any kind of NIC offloading, such as IPsec processing in the network adapter, will break, because the offloads won't understand the new packet format if it is not NVGRE aware. The good news is that many of the major hardware manufacturers have added support for NVGRE to all of their network equipment, which will once again enable offloading even when NVGRE is used. Additionally, even without offloading, typically no significant performance degradation occurs until high-bandwidth (over 5Gbps) scenarios are reached.

WHAT HAPPENED TO IP REWRITE?

If you looked at network virtualization for Windows Server 2012 early on, you would have seen two types of network virtualization technologies: NVGRE and IP rewrite. IP rewrite was originally introduced at the same time as NVGRE because there was a concern that the NVGRE encapsulation would introduce too much overhead. IP rewrite worked by rewriting the IP information of the packet as it was sent over the wire to use the PA space instead of the CA space. This meant that a regular packet was being sent over the network instead of an encapsulated packet, and therefore all existing offloads continued to function. When the packet reached the destination Hyper-V host, the IP address was rewritten again back to the CA space. There had to be a PA for every CA used, which was a lot of IP addresses from the PA space. The reality was that customers found the different technologies confusing. In addition, after testing, it was found that even without NVGRE-optimized hardware, the performance penalty expected from NVGRE did not materialize until workloads started approaching 5Gbps for a single VM, which would be a fairly isolated, extreme instance in most environments. Only at this time did NVGRE support in the networking equipment to enable offloads become a factor. For this reason, IP rewrite was deprecated in Windows Server 2012 and has been removed in SCVMM 2012 R2 and above.

Windows Server 2016 introduces an alternative encapsulation to NVGRE (which is still supported): Virtual Extensible LAN (VXLAN). VXLAN is fundamentally a tunneling protocol that wraps MAC-based layer 2 packets within UDP (layer 4) packets. Whereas NVGRE was primarily championed by Microsoft, VXLAN is an IETF standard (RFC 7348) that is supported by most vendors, which aids in compatibility across vendors and address offload support in networking equipment.

Like NVGRE, VXLAN utilizes a 24-bit segment ID known as a VXLAN network identifier (VNI), which is used to provide the isolation for the virtual subnet IDs used within the virtual networks. Only machines in the same VNI can communicate, unless other types of gateway services are deployed, creating overlay networks on the physical network topology. The hosts of the VMs act as the VXLAN tunneling end points (VTEPs), which are responsible for the construction of the UDP encapsulation packets that identify the actual VTEPs acting as the source (hosting the sending VM) and the target (hosting the destination VM). Note that because VXLAN is one layer down, encapsulating the layer 2 packet from NVGRE, which encapsulated the layer 3 IP address, the VTEPs must maintain mapping of the customer MAC address to target VTEP IP to enable the correct handling of packets on the provider network. Remember that an IP address gets resolved to a MAC, and so it is still similar in operation to NVGRE. The full details of VXLAN can be found in its RFC at `https://tools.ietf.org/html/rfc7348`.

Although VXLAN's implementation is slightly different from NVGRE in terms of the encapsulation payload, the way that it is managed and used is not different. For administrators, the information I already discussed related to NVGRE applies equally: Packets from VMs are encapsulated in wrapper packets that are routable on the physical network, which is the provider address space, and abstracted completely from the physical fabric. Hosts will have an IP address in the provider address space to enable them to communicate and transmit VM traffic. VXLAN is the default encapsulation protocol in Windows Server 2016.

Virtualization policies are used between all of the Hyper-V hosts that participate in a specific virtual network, to enable the routing of the CA across the physical fabric and to track the CA-to-PA mapping. The virtualization policies can also define which virtual networks are allowed to communicate with other virtual networks. It is at this point where the management and full sets of features in pre-Windows Server 2016 and Windows Server 2016 diverge in a major way.

Windows Server 2012 and 2012 R2 had a version 1 of Hyper-V Network Virtualization often referred to as HNVv1 or SDNv1, and those terms are used fairly interchangeably. HNVv1 is still present in Windows Server 2016. However, it has received no new functionality nor will it do so in the future. HNVv1 exclusively uses NVGRE encapsulation, and although the configuration of the virtualization policies can be accomplished via PowerShell, trying to manage network virtualization manually using PowerShell is not practical. The challenge in using the native PowerShell commands is the synchronization and orchestration of the virtual network configuration across all Hyper-V hosts that participate in a specific virtual network. The supported solution, and really the only practical way, is to use the virtualization management solution to manage the virtual networks and not to do it manually using PowerShell, which means using System Center Virtual Machine Manager.

Referring to the planes required for network virtualization to work will help you understand the criticality of SCVMM with HNVv1 and how things are changing with HNVv2 in Windows Server 2016. Whereas SCVMM can be considered "not essential" for some areas of Hyper-V where the end result could still be achieved, albeit with far more work and customization, this is not the case for network virtualization that needs SCVMM. These planes are shown in Figure 3.32.

FIGURE 3.32
The three planes that enable network virtualization for HNVv1

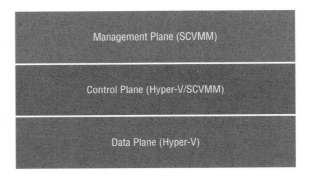

Data Plane Packets are encapsulated and decapsulated for communication over the wire on the data plane. This is implemented by the Hyper-V VM Switch and leverages NVGRE for the encapsulation.

Control Plane Controls how configuration is propagated to the networking equipment and the Hyper-V servers. This is handled efficiently by Hyper-V and SCVMM by using SCVMM as a central policy store, which is then used by the Hyper-V servers, avoiding large amounts of network "chatter" related to control traffic. This provides a scalable solution. As changes occur, such as to which host a virtual machine is hosted on, SCVMM, as that central policy store, can notify all Hyper-V hosts affected in real time.

Management Plane The network is configured and managed on the management plane. This is SCVMM using its management tool and SCVMM PowerShell cmdlets.

Windows Server 2016 still has the same three planes, but their implementation is different and is inspired by the Azure SDN implementation. *Inspired* may be too light of a word. Many components in Windows Server 2016 Hyper-V share common code with the Azure implementation, which does not use SCVMM, because, quite simply, SCVMM was never designed to handle the scale of a mega-cloud like Azure. This commonality with Azure is critical when you consider products such as Microsoft Azure Stack, which brings Azure-consistent features on premises, and that means the networking needs consistent capabilities and implementation. If you are familiar with Azure networking, many of the components I talk about for SDNv2 will be familiar, such as network security groups, software load balancer, user-defined routing, virtual appliances, and more.

The rest of this chapter focuses on the Windows Server 2016 SDNv2 implementation and not SDNv1. The only reason to use SDNv1 in Windows Server 2016 is for compatibility with Windows Server 2012 R2 environments, or if you do not have the Datacenter SKU of Windows Server 2016 (HNVv2 is not in the Standard SKU). Most Hyper-V environments, however, leverage Datacenter.

Figure 3.33 shows the three planes as they relate to the Windows Server 2016 SDN solution known as HNVv2 or SDNv2. Notice that although the data plane is still implemented by Hyper-V, which is the encapsulation using VXLAN or NVGRE, the control plane is a completely separate new component. The network controller and the management can be PowerShell, SCVMM, or Microsoft Azure Stack (MAS). For management, you need to pick one; for the most part, they cannot be used interchangeably, although there are a few exceptions. If you are using MAS, you don't have a choice: MAS will be the management plane. If you are not using MAS, you have a choice of SCVMM or PowerShell. If you are using SCVMM for other aspects of Hyper-V management (which you should be), I recommend using SCVMM; however, you could use PowerShell, which even has an express script to get the basics of SDNv2 deployed quickly. Whichever you pick, that is what you have to use going forward; you cannot start the creation with PowerShell and then switch to SCVMM, or vice versa. The exceptions I spoke of relate to SDNv2 deployments from SCVMM. Some features of SDNv2 are not manageable by SCVMM (although SCVMM is aware of them, so this will not cause problems), and in those cases PowerShell must be used for the configuration, which includes features such as user-defined routing and port mirroring. Network Security Groups (Access Control Lists, ACLs for traffic) can be configured through SCVMM PowerShell but not through its graphical interface. I don't show it in the figure, but while the majority of the data plane is implemented via the VFP in the VMSwitch (such as the actual virtual networks, ACLs, and quality of service) there are also components such as the new software load balancer (SLB) MUX (multiplexor) and gateway, which I cover later in this section.

FIGURE 3.33
The three planes that enable network virtualization for HNVv2

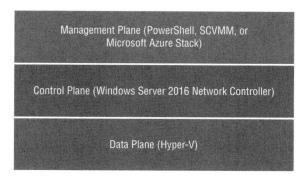

Management Plane (PowerShell, SCVMM, or Microsoft Azure Stack)

Control Plane (Windows Server 2016 Network Controller)

Data Plane (Hyper-V)

Network Controller

The *network controller* was taken directly from Azure and uses the same codebase as the Azure implementation. It is a new role in Windows Server 2016. As the brain of SDNv2, it is responsible for relaying the configuration request from the management tools to the Hyper-V hosts in addition to tracking and distributing the CA-to-PA mappings for all of the required hosts.

It has a Northbound and a Southbound API. The Northbound API, which extends upward to the management plane, is used to communicate with the management tools from which it receives the configurations, such as required virtual networks, ACLs, QoS, and so on. The Northbound API is implemented as a REST interface, which means that it can easily be communicated to any management platform that supports REST. However, the primary management tools are those already mentioned: PowerShell, Azure Stack (which uses REST), and SCVMM.

The network controller then uses its Southbound API to communicate the policies that make up the various flow tables in the VFP and more to the Hyper-V hosts, to enable network virtualization to work. The Southbound API is also used to discover information about network devices, service configurations, and other assets.

You typically have multiple Network Controllers, because of their criticality. This is enabled through a component called *Service Fabric*, a clustering technology that started life in Azure (although it is completely separate from the Failover Clustering feature in Windows Server). Service Fabric enables multiple instances of a service to operate and to synchronously exchange state information, removing the need for any shared or common storage because each instance has a complete copy of the data. This model provides great scalability and fast failover in the event of a problem. One instance is the primary controller, and one or more secondary controllers communicate and control quorum through its own consensus protocol. If the primary controller goes down, a negotiation takes place, and a secondary controller quickly takes over the role of primary with no state lost, and service is resumed. While this may sound complex, one of the key tenants for Windows Server 2016 was to simplify Network Virtualization implementation. No matter which management toolset you use, deployment of the Network Controllers is simple, as you'll see later in the chapter. Microsoft's official page on the Network Controller can be found at:

```
https://technet.microsoft.com/windows-server-docs/networking/sdn/technologies/
network-controller/network-controller
```

So far when talking about network virtualization, I have focused on the VSID, which is isolated through the NVGRE TNI (or with VXLAN, the VNI). However, strictly speaking, the VSID is not the isolation boundary. The true boundary of a virtual network is the routing domain, which has a routing domain ID (RDID), the boundary of the routing policies that control the communication and therefore the isolation boundary. Think of the routing domain as the container that then contains virtual subnets, which can all communicate with each other. You may see three names used, but they all mean a virtual network:

Virtual network: The official nomenclature

Routing domain: Name used when managing with PowerShell

VM network: Name used within SCVMM

For efficiency of communications, you may still wish to define different virtual subnets for different locations or requirements within a virtual network (even though you don't have to). A virtual subnet, like a physical subnet, acts as a broadcast boundary. Later I discuss using gateways to enable communication between virtual networks and to the Internet or physical networks.

No separate gateway technology is required for different virtual subnets within a single virtual network to communicate. The Hyper-V Network Virtualization component within the Hyper-V switch takes care of routing between virtual subnets within a virtual network. The Hyper-V Network Virtualization filter that runs within the Hyper-V virtual switch always provides a default gateway for each virtual subnet, which is always the .1 address and is commonly referred to as the *.1 gateway*. For example, if the virtual subnet is 10.1.1.0/24, the gateway address will be 10.1.1.1. The gateway routes traffic between the virtual subnets within the same virtual network, so it's acting as a router.

In addition to the network controller, two other major new components to SDNv2 fit into the category of virtual functions: the software load balancer and the gateway.

Software Load Balancer

When providing services, it's critical that those services be scalable and highly available. Although it's possible to create a single web service with a public IP address and offer that to clients, the scalability would be limited to the capacity of that single server. Furthermore, if that single server was unavailable for planned or unplanned reasons, the service offered would be unavailable. Therefore, a *load balancer* is always recommended to act as the entry point for client requests. (A *client* is something that is using the service—for example, a user on a web browser out on the Internet browsing to your site.) The load balancer can then distribute the requests to servers that are part of the load-balanced set and perform probes to check whether nodes are available and ensure that client requests are not sent to servers that are not available.

Windows Server has long had a feature called *Network Load Balancing* (NLB). NLB can be enabled on all of the servers that offer the same service (known as the *backend*, as it's behind the load balancer)—for example, a farm of IIS servers hosting the same page. The NLB instance would have its own IP address, and the virtual IP (VIP) and each machine in the NLB cluster would respond to that VIP, distributing traffic between them. Clients would access services through the NLB VIP (the *frontend*, as it's in front of the load balancer) and be serviced by one of the NLB cluster nodes. While the NLB can scale up to 32 nodes, its software runs on the actual nodes offering the backend services and therefore adds overhead to the workloads. In addition, any management requires direct communication to the nodes providing the services. In most large deployments, NLB is not used, and instead dedicated load balancer appliances are leveraged.

Azure Resource Manager has its own software load balancer (SLB) that runs as its own set of resources, can be used in a multitenant configuration, is highly scalable, and is optimized to maximum throughput. This SLB is provided as a virtual function in Windows Server 2016 as part of SDNv2 and managed through the Network Controller. However, if you have done any research, you will frequently hear of a component called the SLB MUX rather than just SLB, so what is SLB MUX? Figure 3.34 shows the SLB implementation architecture.

The SLB MUX is the SLB Multiplexer, which is implemented as its own VM. Its role is to handle the initial request from the client. Note that it is possible to have multiple SLB MUXs, which would be desirable in order to remove any single point of failure. The multiple SLB MUXs offer the same VIP, and this is possible through the use of *Borderless Gateway Protocol* (BGP). Each VIP on the SLB MUX becomes a /32 route. (/32 is the number of bits in the subnet mask, and because 32 indicates all possible bits, it means that it's a route for a specific IP address, that of the VIP.) The VIP /32 route is advertised up to the physical switches via BGP from the SLB MUXs that host the VIPs. The switches receive the advertisement of the routes and now are aware that the switch can get to the VIP through any of the MUXs. Because all the routes are equal, the switch will use a protocol called *Equal Cost Multi-Pathing* (ECMP) to distribute the requests evenly between all of the MUXs offering the same VIP. This enables scalability and the ability to easily add and remove MUXs from the deployment. BGP also has a keep-alive capability that implements constant communication between the MUX and the rest of the network infrastructure. If a MUX goes down, the physical switches will become aware that it is not available and stop sending traffic by updating its own routing tables.

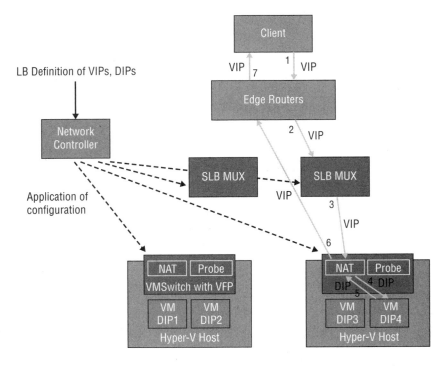

FIGURE 3.34
The SLB implemen-
tation of HNVv2

The SLB MUX accepts the incoming packet, which is addressed to the VIP. However, the actual backend VMs have dynamic IPs (also called datacenter IPs, or DIPs), which are the internal IP addresses they use to communicate on the datacenter network. On most load balancers, the packet has NAT performed to rewrite the destination of the packet from the VIP the client used, to the DIP of the backend server that will process the client request. However, this does not occur in the SLB MUX. Instead, the processing is split between the MUX and the VMSwitch, which greatly increases scale and efficiency. In Figure 3.34, I have placed numbers next to the flow of a request from a client along with the locations where the packet uses VIP or DIP. I walk through this in the following list, but please refer to the figure as well:

1. The client sends a request to the VIP of the service being offered.

2. An edge device receives the request to the VIP. Through BGP, it has a routing table and knows that VIP is available on either of the two MUXs. Using ECMP, it picks one and sends the packet to a MUX still addressed to the VIP.

3. The MUX receives the packet and picks a particular DIP to handle the request, which is part of a virtual network, so it encapsulates the packet using VXLAN and sends it to the host that is running the VM with the specific DIP.

4. The VMSwitch (and specifically the VFP) receives the packet, removes the encapsulation, and performs the NAT to rewrite the destination as the DIP instead of the VIP and forwards to the VM. Note that within the VMSwitch, the probing of the availability of VMs that are part of the backend set is performed and communicated via the SLB host agent,

which is installed on all Hyper-V hosts to the SLB MUXs. This is normally directly performed by the load balancer in most implementations, but by leveraging the VMSwitch, this removes workload from the MUX and improves the scalability.

5. The VM processes the request and sends a response. Because the packet was rewritten with its DIP as the destination, it knows nothing about the NAT, and so writes its DIP as the source of the packet.

6. Ordinarily, this response would then be sent back to the load-balancer appliance to forward on, but that is not the case with the SDNv2 SLB. The VMSwitch performs NAT to rewrite the packet so that the source is the VIP and not the DIP of the VM, and the requesting client does not see a different IP address responding from the one it sent to. Then the VMSwitch bypasses the MUX completely and sends the packet directly to the edge router over the wire. This greatly reduces the load on the MUXs, meaning fewer MUXs are required in any solution. This is known as *Direct Server Return* (*DSR*).

7. The edge device forwards the packet to the originating client.

Although this example shows the SLB being used by an external party, the SLB can also be used as an internal load balancer and works in exactly the same way. The only difference is the frontend IP configuration, with the VIP being an externally or internally facing IP address. Another optimization happens for east-west use of the SLB—that is, an internal load balancer providing services between VMs in a virtual network. In this scenario, only the first packet to an internal load balancer is sent via the MUX. After the first packet is sent and the destination Hyper-V host identified that is hosting the VM with the chosen target DIP, a redirect packet is sent from the MUX to the VMSwitch of the Hyper-V host that is hosting the source of the load-balancer usage. From that point on, all subsequent packets from the source connection to the load balancer VIP will be sent directly to the VMSwitch of the Hyper-V host that is hosting the identified target VM with the chosen VIP. This means the SLB MUX is then bypassed for the rest of the communication, which is useful for optimizing multitier services running within a network.

The SLB supports two types of load-balancing functionality:

Load-Balanced Sets   Multiple DIPs that offer the same service are placed in a load-balanced set. Through the use of probes to ensure availability of the backend servers, the incoming traffic is received on a certain port and distributed between the backend set members to a specific port. Either five, three, or two tuples can be used for the distribution of the traffic, which control the stickiness between the client and the actual backend server. Using five tuples (the default) sends the client to the same processing server only if the destination and source IP, port, and protocol are the same. Using three tuples stipulates that the destination and source IP address and protocol must be the same, but the port can change. Using two tuples simply requires the same destination and source IP address, but the port and protocol can change.

NAT Rules   Also known as *port forwarders*, NAT rules specify that traffic received on a certain port is always sent to another specific port on a specific DIP. This can be useful when you want to be able to get to a certain VM via an SLB directly; for example, perhaps a NAT rule to port 3389 on a VM to enable RDP to the VM. (Be careful, however, about ever offering RDP to services from the Internet.)

A single SLB configuration supports multiple VIPs with combinations of load-balancer sets and NAT rules.

Gateways

By default, virtual machines in a virtual network can talk to each other but not to other resources—not to services in other networks nor resources out on the Internet. To enable communication outside the virtual network, to other services in the datacenter—to services in other sites via a site-to-site tunnel or just Internet-based services—the multitenant gateway SDNv2 component is used. If you want to enable a hybrid environment, you must be able to connect virtual networks to other networks in a controlled fashion, removing the isolation. The *multitenant gateway* (also referred to as a *RAS gateway*) supports connectivity to the following:

◆ Forwarding traffic to a network acting as a simple router, for example to a VLAN, known as *L3 forwarding*. In this deployment, the gateway connects to multiple virtual networks and to trunk ports on a switch via its vNIC that maps to various VLANs. The gateway takes care of routing and encapsulating traffic as required, enabling communication.

◆ Another isolated datacenter network or MPLS using GRE tunneling. From the gateway, a GRE tunnel is established to an endpoint somewhere else in your datacenter, and a specific tenant's traffic is sent across. This is similar to L3 forwarding, whereby traffic is forwarded through a tunnel; except with GRE tunneling, separate VLANs are not required, and the GRE tunnel is established over the shared network infrastructure. Each tenant uses its own GRE tunnel instance, maintaining the tenant's isolated address space across that infrastructure. For example, you might have a red network GRE tunnel and a blue network GRE tunnel. Consider a hosting provider that currently has a tenant with dedicated hardware in a certain address space; that same tenant now wants to have resources as part of a multitenant cloud that is in the same address space and connected. If you use L3 forwarding, you'll require separate VLANs for the customers and separate routing infrastructure. With a GRE tunnel, the isolated address space is maintained between the endpoints, with no dedicated VLAN required. This same type of tunnel can also be used to connect to MPLS circuits.

◆ Another location using a site-to-site VPN tunnel that works with the SLB to frontend the gateway instances VIP. By integrating with SLB, easy scaling on the backend can be enabled without requiring any changes to the other end of the site-to-site VPN connection.

A big change from the solution in Windows Server 2012 R2 to the multitenant gateway in Windows Server 2016 is in the scaling and high availability of the gateway. In Windows Server 2012 R2, you could have an active gateway and then one passive gateway. Only one instance was performing work, while the other sat idle. If you reached the capacity of the active node, you had to add a new pair of gateways that would have their own VIP, and a tenant could use only one gateway at a time.

In Windows Server 2016, an M:N redundancy is used. M is the number of active gateways, highlighting the fact that there can be more than one. N is the number of passive gateways available in case an active gateway fails. For example, you can have four active and two passive gateways, or any other combination. Like the SLB MUX, a gateway is a VM, and multiple gateways are added to a gateway pool to provide the multitenant gateway services. A gateway pool can contain gateways of all different types or only certain types of gateways. It is really a mechanism to control resource utilization and capacity if needed. A hoster may have different pools with different levels of bandwidth, so it can charge tenants for different levels of connectivity by moving them between gateway pools. The Network Controller is responsible for checking the availability of gateway instances. If an active gateway becomes unavailable, the Network Controller can move any connections from the downed node to a passive node. There is no Failover Clustering running within the VMs; they are stand-alone instances, which makes the deployment simpler than for their 2012 R2 equivalent.

If you deployed the Windows Server 2012 R2 gateway, you will remember that the gateway VMs had to be on a separate set of Hyper-V hosts from those hosting actual VMs that participated in a virtual network. This limitation is removed in the SDNv2 multitenant gateway solution; the gateway VMs can run on the same hosts as VMs in a virtual network.

BGP and BGP transit routing are also supported. This solves the problem traditionally associated with adding new subnets to a virtual network: Other networks would not know how to get to the subnet without being manually configured. With BGP, as new subnets are added, the BGP instance (the gateway) will notify all other BGP instances of the new subnet and of the route to get to that subnet. Additionally, BGP transit routing adds the capability for BGP instances not only to notify other routes that it can be used to get to its subnets, but it can also notify routers of other networks that it can be used to access. This means that if another part of the network loses its direct connection to a network, it could use the BGP instance as an extra hop still to reach the target.

BGP Route Reflector

Ordinarily, all the BGP instances form a mesh, with every instance talking to every other to enable the full synchronization of routing. To avoid the need for this full-mesh connectivity and considerable network traffic, you can use a BGP route reflector, which is included as part of SDNv2. With a BGP route reflector, all BGP instances communicate only with the route reflector, which is responsible for the learning of all routes, calculating the best routes, and then distributing those routes to all BGP instances. The first gateway deployed for each tenant becomes the BGP route reflector.

When using BGP, you can work with several useful PowerShell cmdlets. You can use `Get-BgpRouter` to view the particular BGP router being used and its configuration, `Get-BgpPeer` to see any BGP peers, and `Get-BgpRouteInformation` to see known routes.

A single gateway instance has the following capacity:

◆ 100 tenants

◆ 200 site-to-site VPN tunnels

◆ 15,000 routes learned via BGP

◆ 8Gbps L3 forwarding throughput

◆ 2.5Gbps GRE gateway throughput

◆ 300Mbps (one core) per IPsec tunnel (site-to-site VPN)

Datacenter Firewall

Traditional network security focuses primarily on the network's perimeter. Firewall devices on the edge of the network allow certain types of traffic into a set of specific hosts in a perimeter network (the DMZ), which has another set of firewalls allowing only certain traffic to flow to the internal network. Then OS instances themselves have their own firewall, but that's about it. The reality is that once something bad makes its way onto the network, its lateral movement is fairly simple. SDNv2 adds many layers of security to help prevent this lateral movement, as shown in Figure 3.35.

FIGURE 3.35
Security layers with
SDNv2

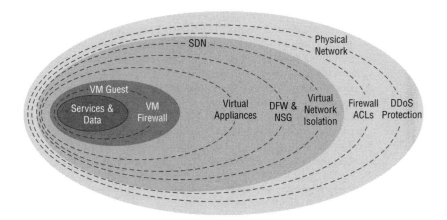

The SDNv2 adds three more layers of protection. First, using virtual networks provides isolation between networks, which itself limits the ability for malware and other types of attacks to traverse the network. Next, SDNv2 includes a datacenter firewall that, through use of policies, enables further segmentation of the virtual network by strictly controlling which traffic can flow between virtual subnets and even to specific virtual machine NIC (vmNICs). Additionally, virtual appliances can be used to supplement security through third-party technologies, such as other types of traffic inspection or filtering implementations, which are placed in the data path through the use of customized routing (user-defined routing).

The datacenter firewall is not an edge device, as its name may lead you to believe. Instead it is a set of technologies that implements a firewall enforced at the VMSwitch as traffic attempts an ingress or egress from a connected vmNIC. This firewall uses a set of policies (ACLs) distributed from a component called the *Distributed Firewall Manager*, which is part of the Network Controller. If you have used Network Security Groups in Azure, this is the SDNv2 equivalent and works in exactly the same way, with exactly the same set of properties and keywords. It is a stateful firewall: If a connection is allowed inbound, the outbound response will be allowed. Each policy consists of the following:

- A name

- Five-tuple set: destination port range, destination IP range using CIDR notation, source port range, source IP range using CIDR, and protocol (TCP, UDP or *). There are also special tags for certain types of resources.

- Type, indicating the direction (inbound or outbound)

- A priority (101–65,000 for user ranges)

- Action (allow or deny)

For example, consider the following policy:

◆ **Name:** InternetRDP

◆ **Source Address:** Internet

◆ **Source Port:** 3389

◆ **Destination Address:** 10.1.2.0/24

◆ **Destination Port:** TCP

◆ **Protocol:** 3389

◆ **Type:** Inbound

◆ **Priority:** 105

◆ **Action:** Allow

This policy allows RDP traffic inbound to subnet 10.1.2.0/24 from the Internet. (*Internet* is a special tag I cover later in this section.) You would apply this policy to the 10.1.2.0/24 virtual subnet. All other traffic inbound from the Internet would be blocked because there are default inbound and outbound rules indicating the following:

◆ Allow all inbound and outbound traffic within the virtual network (which is the known connected address space).

◆ Allow inbound communication from the SLB.

◆ Allow outbound communication to the Internet.

◆ Block all other types of inbound and outbound traffic.

These default rules all have low priorities (65,000 and above), which means that you can override them with your own policies that would have a higher priority and take precedence. Consider Figure 3.36, which shows a typical three-tier application. Here only the frontend tier should be able to communicate with the Internet, while the other tiers are blocked. The front end tier can communicate with only the middle tier and not directly to the backend tier. The backend tier can communicate only to the middle tier. By creating a set of policies and applying them to the subnets, this can be enforced. It should be noted that although I talk about applying ACLs to a subnet, it is also possible to assign a policy directly to a specific vmNIC. However, this gets complicated to manage. It is therefore a best practice to assign policies to the subnet and the Network Controller, which will then deploy the policies to the VMSwitch connected to the various vmNICs where the policies are enforced. If you apply policies to the subnet and the vmNIC, the subnet policies are applied first and then the vmNIC for inbound traffic. For outbound traffic, vmNIC policies are applied first, and then the subnet policies.

I mentioned earlier special tags that can be used in place of a source or destination IP range. These are listed next and are the same as those used with Azure Network Security Groups, which ensures consistency of application when in a hybrid environment:

VIRTUALNETWORK The virtual network's address space and all other known address spaces that are connected to via a gateway. For example, if your virtual network is connected to another location via a gateway, the IP space encompassed by VIRTUALNETWORK is that of your virtual network IP space and the entire IP space of that connected location.

FIGURE 3.36
Example use of the
datacenter firewall
restricting traffic
flow

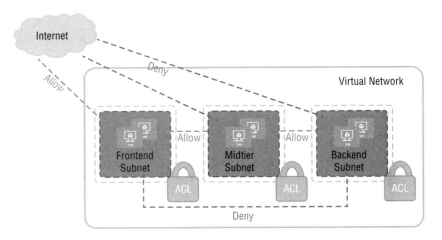

INTERNET   Every address that is *not* part of `VIRTUALNETWORK`; for example, 0.0.0.0/0—
`VIRTUALNETWORK`.

AZURELOADBALANCER   This represents the SLB health probe IP address that is implemented in the VMSwitch. This is used by a default inbound rule, and it is required to make
sure that the SLB can probe VMs to ensure that they are available. If you add any blocking
custom policies, make sure that you also add and allow for the `AZURELOADBALANCER`, or the
SLB will not function.

UDR, Port Mirroring, and Virtual Appliances

In addition to the in-box capabilities of SDNv2, many virtual appliances are available from third-
party vendors that offer network functionality. Because SDNv2 is implemented in the same manner
as the Azure SDN solution, any virtual appliance available in Azure should also work on premises
with SDNv2. These virtual appliances could perform traffic inspection, trend analysis, firewall
activities, WAN optimization, or anything else. The appliances do not need to be virtual network
aware; they simply need to be able to run on Hyper-V. They are deployed as virtual machines.

To function, however, these appliances need traffic to flow to them, which means that the
traffic routing must be changed. This is enabled through *user-defined routing (UDR)*, which
enables the default routing of a virtual network to be modified. An example is changing the
gateway for a subnet to route to the virtual appliance instead of the default gateway IP that is
part of the virtual network, by providing an alternate next-hop IP for the target address space.
Note that the VMs still route to .1 (which does not actually exist, as it's routed as part of the
VMSwitch functionality), but the switch now knows to route that traffic to the IP specified as
part of the UDR, which is to the virtual appliance.

The other way to get traffic to a virtual appliance is with port mirroring. *Port mirroring*
enables packets matching a specific set of criteria to be duplicated in their exact original form
(even the source and destination MAC addresses) and sent to a specified target, such as a traffic
analysis virtual appliance. Port mirroring works for both inbound and outbound packets and
adds no latency or additional overhead of the VMs whose traffic is being mirrored. The mirror
is not part of the primary data path; if the virtual appliance receiving the mirrored packets falls
behind, it will not impact the source VM. The mirroring is performed completely within the
SDNv2 implementation.

Implementing Network Virtualization

In my 2012 R2 version of this book, I walked step by step through deploying network virtualization and deploying a gateway. SDNv2, however, is different. There are three primary management planes, and the method of implementing the virtual network, gateway, SLB, datacenter firewall, UDR, and so on is different. It is also likely to change over time, especially with SCVMM and Microsoft Azure Stack, so any specific instructions likely would become antiquated quickly. Thus, for exact details, I recommend reviewing the Microsoft documents, which are thorough. Nonetheless, I want to cover the experience briefly when using the three management planes. Remember, after you pick one, you must continue using it—you cannot switch—with the exception of leveraging PowerShell to configure UDR and mirroring if using SCVMM.

POWERSHELL

PowerShell cmdlets are built into Windows Server 2016, and a manual deployment of every component is possible, which is documented at https://technet.microsoft.com/en-us/library/mt282165.aspx. The better option, however, is to use SDNExpress. *SDNExpress* is a script with accompanying files that is downloaded from GitHub (so it can be updated). Execute the script, and after about 30 minutes, you will have a completely deployed SDNv2 environment including the following:

◆ Distributing required certificates

◆ Multi-instance Network Controller deployment

◆ Configuration of Network Controller via REST API

◆ All Hyper-V host networking including VFP and host agents deployed

◆ Multitenant gateway deployed and configured

Information about SDNExpress can be found at https://technet.microsoft.com/en-us/library/mt427380.aspx and can be downloaded from https://github.com/Microsoft/SDN. Once deployed, the various *-NetworkController* cmdlets are used to communicate with the Network Controller and perform configuration. For example, you can use the following to connect to a network controller, get the object for a virtual network, and then view all ACLs known:

```
Import-Module networkcontroller
$URI = "https://savdalnc01.savilltech.net"

# Grab the Resource Id of the first Virtual Network
(Get-NetworkControllerVirtualNetwork -ConnectionUri $uri)[0] `
|fl ResourceId

ResourceId : 7fb0a029-136d-44cd-8697-8dbcac7a7c70

# Grab all Virtual Subnets attached to the above Virtual Network
Get-NetworkControllerVirtualSubnet -ConnectionUri $uri `
-VirtualNetworkId "7fb0a029-136d-44cd-8697-8dbcac7a7c70"

# Check for ACLs applied to a virtual subnet
Get-NetworkControllerVirtualSubnet -ConnectionUri $uri `
-VirtualNetworkId "7fb0a029-136d-44cd-8697-8dbcac7a7c70" `
```

```
| foreach { $_.Properties.AccessControlList }

Get-NetworkControllerNetworkInterface -ConnectionUri $uri `
| foreach { $_.Properties.IpConfigurations.Properties.AccessControlList }

$acl = Get-NetworkControllerAccessControlList -ConnectionUri $uri `
-ResourceId "f8b97a4c-4419-481d-b757-a58483512640"

$acl.Properties.AclRules[0].Properties
```

If you experience problems with the Network Controller, I recommend several useful PowerShell cmdlets for debugging:

- ◆ `Debug-NetworkController`: Information about the Network Controller
- ◆ `Debug-NetworkControllerConfigurationState`: Configuration state of a Network Controller
- ◆ `Debug-ServiceFabricNodeStatus`: Health of a Network Controller
- ◆ `Get-NetworkControllerDeploymentInfo`: Deployment information of a Network Controller
- ◆ `Get-NetworkControllerReplica`: Replica information for a Network Controller
- ◆ `Get-CustomerRoute`: Routing information
- ◆ `Get-PACAMapping`: Mapping between PA and CA
- ◆ `Get-ProviderAddress`: Information about provider addresses
- ◆ `Test-VirtualNetworkConnection`: Perform a test to a virtual network.

There are many others. Use `(Get-Module HNVDiagnostics).ExportedCommands` to see a full list.

System Center Virtual Machine Manager

The core logical network, logical switch, VM network, and other fabric components are all used for the SCVMM deployment of SDNv2, and they have a step-by-step guide for the following:

- ◆ Deployment of Network Controller and the basic virtual networks:
  `https://technet.microsoft.com/system-center-docs/vmm/Manage/Deploy-a-Network-Controller-using-VMM`
- ◆ Deployment of SLB:
  `https://technet.microsoft.com/en-us/system-center-docs/vmm/manage/deploy-a-software-load-balancer-using-vmm:`
- ◆ Deployment of gateway:
  `https://technet.microsoft.com/system-center-docs/vmm/Manage/Deploy-a-RAS-Gateway-using-VMM`

You need to provide a VM template, which should be Windows Server 2016 Datacenter, and can be either Server Core or Server with Desktop Experience. Where possible, I recommend using Server Core.

These deployments are all facilitated through the use of service templates, which are available for download from GitHub (`https://github.com/Microsoft/SDN/tree/master/VMM/`

`Templates/NC`) and require only minimal configuration to have multi-instance deployments of all of the services in your environment. As part of the deployment, additional logical networks are created in addition to the management logical network that exists as a foundation to provide connectivity between the hosts and the Network Controller. The additional logical networks, documented in the deployment guide, are as follows:

HNV Provider Virtual Network   Network used by hosts to communicate the encapsulated virtual traffic. This network is enabled for VM networks to be created using network virtualization. This requires an IP pool of PA addresses that will be used by the Hyper-V hosts. Once created and deployed, VM networks will be created using their own abstracted, isolated address spaces.

Transit Network   Used by the SLB deployments, and it is used for BGP peering and North/South traffic between the MUX and the upstream router (data plane). This network is documented in the SLB deployment guide. It is possible to use the management network if desired.

Private and Public VIP Networks   Used for the frontend configuration of SLB and gateways to provide the required VIPs

GRE Logical Network   Used by the gateway for GRE tunneling. Documented in the gateway documentation

Once deployed, the VM networks are created for each virtual network to which VMs are then connected, but it works the same as for any other VM network.

MICROSOFT AZURE STACK

SDNv2 is automatically deployed as part of Microsoft Azure Stack, including the Network Controller, BGP route reflector, gateways, and SLB. Deployment of configuration is consistent with Azure Resource Manager (ARM), which means deployment and configuration of networks and services can be performed using the Azure portal, AzureRM PowerShell, or JSON templates. With Azure Stack, the underlying plumbing of the SDNv2 is hidden from you, and all actions must be performed through ARM.

Summary

Some workloads do not work with network virtualization today. PXE boot, which enables booting an operating system over the network, will not function. DHCP is supported, but SCVMM has its own switch extension to intercept DHCP to allocate from IP pools, so standard DHCP in a VM would not work when you're managing your network with SCVMM.

To summarize, you can use the following types of isolation methods in your Hyper-V environment:

Physical   Use separate physical network switches and adapters to provide isolation between networks. Costly, complex, and not scalable.

External   Using virtual switch extensions, specifically the forwarding extension such as Cisco Nexus 1000V or NEC OpenFlow, can provide isolation in the switch using native technologies. This is, however, fairly opaque to SCVMM.

VLAN   Layer 2 technology provides isolation and broadcast boundary on a shared network, but the number of VLANs is limited and can become complex to manage. Does not allow IP address overlap between VLANs, nor does it allow flexibility for business units/tenants to bring their own IP scheme to the environment.

PVLAN Utilizes a pair of VLANs to provide an isolated network in different modes, but most commonly allows many virtual machines to communicate with a common set of resources/Internet while being completely isolated from each other.

Network Virtualization Abstraction of the virtual machine network from the physical network fabric provides maximum capability without the limitations and complexity of other technologies. Allows users of network virtualization to bring their own IP scheme and even IP overlap between different virtual networks. Network virtualization gateways allow virtual networks to communicate with external networks and can increase security and functionality through components such as the datacenter firewall and software load balancer.

Where possible, utilize network virtualization for its flexibility and relative ease of configuration. However, for some types of networks, such as management networks, it will still be common to use more traditional isolation methods such as VLAN technologies.

VMQ, RSS, and SR-IOV

So far, we have covered a lot of technologies related to network connectivity. The following sections cover a few technologies that can help with the performance of network communications. Although it can introduce some challenges when trying to maximize its utilization and gain the highest levels of performance and bandwidth, 40Gbps and beyond is becoming more common in many datacenters.

SR-IOV and Dynamic Virtual Machine Queue (DVMQ) are two popular networking technologies that can enhance network performance and can minimize overhead for the hypervisor. These technologies are shown in Figure 3.37.

FIGURE 3.37
Understanding the VMQ and SR-IOV network technologies compared to regular networking

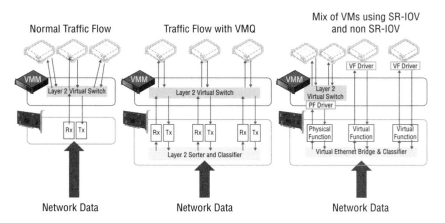

SR-IOV

Single-root I/O virtualization (*SR-IOV*) allows a single PCI Express network device to represent itself as multiple separate devices directly to virtual machines. In the case of SR-IOV and virtual machines, this means that a physical NIC can present multiple virtual NICs, which in SR-IOV terms are called *virtual functions* (*VFs*). Each VF is of the same type as the physical card and is presented directly to specific virtual machines. The communication between the virtual machine and the VF completely bypasses the Hyper-V switch because the VM uses direct memory access (DMA) to communicate with the VF. This makes for very fast and very low-latency communication between the VM and the VF, because both the VMBus and the Hyper-V switch are no longer involved in the network flow from the physical NIC to the VM. Because the Hyper-V switch is bypassed when SR-IOV is used, SR-IOV is disallowed if any ACL checking, QoS, DHCP guard, third-party extensions, network virtualization, or any other switch features are in use. SR-IOV use is permitted only when no switches' features are active.

SR-IOV does not break Live Migration, a technology not covered yet, but allows virtual machines to move between hosts with no downtime, even when you're moving a virtual machine to a host that does not support SR-IOV. Behind the scenes when SR-IOV is used, the Network Virtualization Service Client (NetVSC) creates two paths for the virtual machine network adapter inside the VM. One path is via SR-IOV, and one is via the traditional VMBus path, which uses the Hyper-V switch. When the VM is running on a host with SR-IOV, the SR-IOV path is used and the VMBus is used only for control traffic, but if the VM is moved to a host without SR-IOV, then the SR-IOV path is closed by NetVSC and the VMBus path is used for data and control traffic; this is all transparent to the virtual machine. It means that you don't lose any mobility even when using SR-IOV. To use SR-IOV, both the network adapter and the motherboard must support it. To use SR-IOV with a virtual switch, the option to use SR-IOV must be selected at the time of the virtual switch creation, as shown in Figure 3.38. If you're using the `New-VMSwitch` cmdlet to create the virtual switch, use the `-EnableIov $True` parameter to enable SR-IOV. On the Hardware Acceleration property tab of the virtual network adapter for a virtual machine that needs to use SR-IOV, make sure that the Enable SR-IOV check box is selected.

FIGURE 3.38
Enabling SR-IOV on
a virtual switch at
creation time

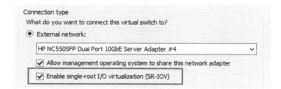

To check your server for SR-IOV support, you can run various commands. To start, run PowerShell command `Get-VMSwitch | Format-List *iov*` as shown in the following snippet.. Note that this example shows that the network adapter supports SR-IOV, but it is not supported because of limitations on the server motherboard and BIOS.

```
PS C:\> Get-VMSwitch | Format-List *iov*


IovEnabled            : True
IovSupport            : False
IovSupportReasons     : {To use SR-IOV on this system, the system BIOS
must be updated to allow Windows to control
PCI Express. Contact your system manufacturer for an update., This system
has a security
vulnerability in the system I/O remapping hardware. As a precaution, the
ability to use
```

```
SR-IOV has been disabled. You should contact your system manufacturer for
an updated BIOS
which enables Root Port Alternate Error Delivery mechanism. If all Virtual
Machines
intended to use SR-IOV run trusted workloads, SR-IOV may be enabled by
 adding a registry
key of type DWORD with value 1 named IOVEnableOverride under
HKEY_LOCAL_MACHINE\SOFTWARE\Microsoft\Windows
NT\CurrentVersion\Virtualization and changing
state of the trusted virtual machines. If the system exhibits reduced
performance or
instability after SR-IOV devices are assigned to Virtual Machines,
consider disabling the
use of SR-IOV.}
IovVirtualFunctionCount : 0
IovVirtualFunctionsInUse: 0
IovQueuePairCount       : 0
IovQueuePairsInUse      : 0
```

The following output is from another system with one adapter that does not support SR-IOV and additional adapters that do support it:

```
PS C:\> Get-VMSwitch | Format-List *iov*

IovEnabled              : False
IovSupport              : False
IovSupportReasons       : {This network adapter does not support SR-IOV.}
IovVirtualFunctionCount : 0
IovVirtualFunctionsInUse: 0
IovQueuePairCount       : 0
IovQueuePairsInUse      : 0

IovEnabled              : True
IovSupport              : True
IovSupportReasons       : {OK}IovVirtualFunctionCount : 62
IovVirtualFunctionsInUse: 10
IovQueuePairCount       : 63
IovQueuePairsInUse      : 10

IovEnabled              : True
IovSupport              : True
IovSupportReasons       : {OK}
IovVirtualFunctionCount : 6
IovVirtualFunctionsInUse: 2
IovQueuePairCount       : 7
IovQueuePairsInUse      : 2
```

You can run the PowerShell command Get-NetAdapterSriov to get SR-IOV support adapter information on a system; it also shows the number of VFs supported by the card. If a virtual machine is using SR-IOV successfully, then when you look at the Networking tab of the virtual machine in Hyper-V Manager, that status will show "OK (SR-IOV active)."

```
PS C:\> Get-NetAdapterSriov

Name               : VM NIC
InterfaceDescription: Mellanox ConnectX-3 Pro Ethernet Adapter
Enabled            : True
SriovSupport       : Supported
SwitchName         : "Default Switch"
NumVFs             : 32

Name               : VM NIC 2
InterfaceDescription: Mellanox ConnectX-3 Pro Ethernet Adapter #2
Enabled            : True
SriovSupport       : Supported
SwitchName         : "Default Switch"
NumVFs: 32
```

The reality right now is that not many systems are SR-IOV capable. SR-IOV will be used in targeted scenarios, because in most situations, the standard Hyper-V network capabilities via the virtual switch will suffice for even the most demanding workloads. SR-IOV is targeted at those very few highest networking throughput needs. The other common place where SR-IOV implementations can be found is in "cloud in a box" solutions, where a single vendor supplies the servers, the network, and the storage. The one I have seen most commonly is the Cisco UCS solution that leverages SR-IOV heavily because many network capabilities are implemented using Cisco's own technology, VM-FEX. An amazing multipart blog is available from Microsoft on SR-IOV; it will tell you everything you could ever want to know:

```
http://blogs.technet.com/b/jhoward/archive/2012/03/12/
everything-you-wanted-to-know-about-sr-iov-in-hyper-v-part-1.aspx
```

VMQ

A technology that's similar to SR-IOV is *Virtual Machine Queue* (*VMQ*). VMQ, which was introduced in Windows Server 2008 R2, allows separate queues to exist on the network adapter, with each queue being mapped to a specific virtual machine. This removes some of the switching work on the Hyper-V switch, because if the data is in this queue, the switch knows that it is meant for a specific virtual machine.

The bigger benefit is that because there are now separate queues from the network adapter, that queue can be processed by a different processor core. Typically, all the traffic from a network adapter is processed by a single processor core to ensure that packets are not processed out of sequence. For a 1Gbps network adapter, this may be fine, but a single core could not keep up with a loaded 10Gbps network connection caused by multiple virtual machines. With VMQ enabled, specific virtual machines allocate their own VMQ on the network adapter, which allows different processor cores in the Hyper-V host to process the traffic, leading to greater throughput. (However, each virtual machine would still be limited to a specific core, leading to a bandwidth cap of around 3Gbps to 4Gbps; but this is better than the combined traffic of all VMs being limited to 3Gbps to 4Gbps.)

The difference between VMQ and SR-IOV is that the traffic still passes through the Hyper-V switch with VMQ, because all VMQ presents are different queues of traffic and not entire virtual devices. In Windows Server 2008 R2, the assignment of a VMQ to a virtual machine was static; typically, first come, first served because each NIC supports a certain number of VMQs, and each VMQ was assigned (affinitized) in a round-robin manner to the logical processors available to the host, and this would never change. The assignment of VMQs is still on a first come, first served basis in Windows Server 2012, but the allocation of processor cores is now dynamic and fluid. This allows the queues to be moved between logical processors based on load. By default, all queues start on the same logical processor, the home processor, but as the load builds on a queue, Hyper-V can move the individual queues to a different logical processor to handle the load more efficiently. As the load drops, the queues can be coalesced back to a smaller number of cores and potentially all back to the home processor.

Many modern network cards support VMQ, and this is easy to check by using the PowerShell Get-NetAdapterVmq command. In the following example, you can see that VMQ is enabled on two of the network adapters because they are currently connected to a Hyper-V virtual switch and each has 125 queues. If network adapters are not connected to a virtual switch, their VMQ capabilities will not be shown.

```
PS C:\> Get-NetAdapterVmq `
|ft Name, InterfaceDescription,Enabled,NumberOfReceiveQueues -AutoSize

Name            InterfaceDescription                 Enabled
NumberOfReceiveQueues
---             -----------                          ---------------
Name                                InterfaceDescription        Enabled
BaseVmqProcessor MaxProcessors NumberOfReceiveQ

ueues
---                                 -----------                 --------------------------
NIC4                                Broadcom NetXtreme Gigabit E...#4 False
0:0               16
NIC3                                Broadcom NetXtreme Gigabit E...#3 False
0:0               16
NIC2                                Broadcom NetXtreme Gigabit E...#2 False
0:0               16
MGMT NIC                            Broadcom NetXtreme Gigabit Eth... False
0:0               16          16
VM NIC                              Mellanox ConnectX-3 Pro Ethern... True
0:0               8           125
VM NIC 2 Mellanox ConnectX-3 Pro Ethe. . .#2 True 0:0 8 125
```

By default, if a virtual network adapter is configured to be VMQ enabled, no manual action is required. Based on the availability of VMQs, a VMQ may be allocated and used by a virtual machine. Figure 3.39 shows the Hardware Acceleration setting for a virtual network adapter. Remember that just because a network adapter is configured to use VMQ does not mean that it will be allocated a VMQ. It depends on whether one is available on the network adapter when the VM is started.

FIGURE 3.39
Ensuring that VMQ is enabled for a virtual machine

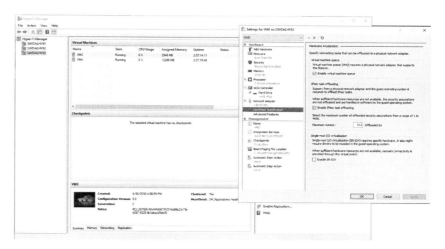

To check which virtual machines are using VMQs and which processor core is currently being used by the queue, you can use the `Get-NetAdapterVmqQueue` PowerShell command. In the following example, you can see VM1, VM2, VM3, and VM4: each has a queue and is running on a separate processor (core). The default queue (SAVDALHV07, the hostname), which is used for traffic that is not handled by a separate VMQ is running on the home processor, 0. There is no way to force a virtual machine to always be allocated a VMQ. The only way would be to make sure that those virtual machines for which you want to have a VMQ are started first when the host is started.

```
PS C:\> Get-NetAdapterVmqQueue
```

Name	QueueID	MacAddress	VlanID	Processor	VmFriendlyName
VM NIC	0			0:0	SAVDALHV07
VM NIC	1	00-15-5D-AD-15-04		0:28	VM01
VM NIC	2	00-15-5D-AD-15-03		0:30	VM2
VM NIC 2	0			0:0	SAVDALHV07
VM NIC 2	1	00-15-5D-AD-15-05		0:32	VM3
VM NIC 2	2	00-15-5D-AD-15-06		0:20	VM4

You may wonder how VMQ works if you are using NIC Teaming, and the answer is that it varies depending on the mode of NIC Teaming. Consider that it's possible to mix network adapters with different capabilities in a NIC team. For example, one NIC supports 8 VMQs and another supports 16 VMQs in a two-NIC team. Two numbers are important:

Min Queues   The lower number of queues supported by an adapter in the team. In my example, 8 is the Min Queue value.

Sum of Queues   The total number of all queues across all the adapters in the team. In my example, this is 24.

The deciding factor for the number of VMQs that are available to a NIC team depends on the teaming mode and the load-balancing algorithm used for the team. If the teaming mode is set to switch dependent, the Min Queues value is always used. If the teaming mode is switch independent and the algorithm is set to Hyper-V Port or Dynamic, then the Sum of Queues value is used; otherwise, Min Queues is used. Table 3.2 shows this in simple form.

TABLE 3.2: VMQ NIC Teaming Options

	ADDRESS HASH	HYPER-V PORT	DYNAMIC
Switch Dependent	Min Queues	Min Queues	Min Queues
Switch Independent	Min Queues	Sum of Queues	Sum of Queues

RSS and vRSS

I previously talked about a 3 to 4Gbps bandwidth limit, which was caused by the amount of traffic that could be processed by a single processor core. Even with VMQ, a virtual machine network adapter is still limited to traffic being processed by a single core. Physical servers have a solution to the single-core bottleneck for inbound traffic: Receive Side Scaling, or RSS. RSS must be supported by the physical network adapter, and the technology enables incoming traffic on a single network adapter to be processed by more than a single processor core. This is enabled by using the following flow:

1. Incoming packets are run through a four-tuple hash algorithm that uses the source and destination IP and ports to create a hash value.

2. The hash is passed through an indirection table that places all traffic with the same hash on a specific RSS queue on the network adapter. Note that there are only a small number of RSS queues. Four is a common number, so a single RSS queue will contain packets from many hash values, which is the purpose of the indirection table.

3. Each RSS queue on the network adapter is processed by a different processor core on the host operating system, distributing the incoming load over multiple cores.

Creating the hash value in order to control which RSS queue and therefore which processor core is used is important. Problems occur if packets are processed out of order, which could happen if packets were just randomly sent to any core. Creating the hash value based on the source and destination IP addresses and port ensures that specific streams of communication are processed on the same processor core and therefore are processed in order. A common question is, "What about hyperthreaded processor cores?" RSS does not use hyperthreading and skips the "extra" logical processor for each core. This can be seen if the processor array and indirection table are examined for an RSS-capable network adapter, as shown in the following output. Notice that only even-number cores are shown; 1, 3, and so on are skipped because this system has hyperthreading enabled and so the hyperthreaded cores are skipped.

```
PS C:\> Get-NetAdapterRss

Name                            : MGMT NIC
InterfaceDescription            : Broadcom BCM57800 NetXtreme II 1 GigE
(NDIS VBD Client) #131
```

```
Enabled                              : True
NumberOfReceiveQueues                : 4
Profile                              : NUMAStatic
BaseProcessor: [Group:Number]        : 0:0
MaxProcessor: [Group:Number]         : 0:30
MaxProcessors                        : 16
RssProcessorArray: [Group:Number/NUMA Distance]:
0:0/0  0:2/0  0:4/0  0:6/0  0:8/0  0:10/0  0:12/0  0:14/0
0:16/0  0:18/0  0:20/0  0:22/0  0:24/0  0:26/0  0:28/0  0:30/0

IndirectionTable: [Group:Number]:
0:4    0:20    0:6    0:22    0:4    0:20    0:6    0:22
0:4    0:20    0:6    0:22    0:4    0:20    0:6    0:22
0:4    0:20    0:6    0:22    0:4    0:20    0:6    0:22
0:4    0:20    0:6    0:22    0:4    0:20    0:6    0:22
0:4    0:20    0:6    0:22    0:4    0:20    0:6    0:22
0:4    0:20    0:6    0:22    0:4    0:20    0:6    0:22
0:4    0:20    0:6    0:22    0:4    0:20    0:6    0:22
0:4    0:20    0:6    0:22    0:4    0:20    0:6    0:22
0:4    0:20    0:6    0:22    0:4    0:20    0:6    0:22
0:4    0:20    0:6    0:22    0:4    0:20    0:6    0:22
0:4    0:20    0:6    0:22    0:4    0:20    0:6    0:22
0:4    0:20    0:6    0:22    0:4    0:20    0:6    0:22
0:4    0:20    0:6    0:22    0:4    0:20    0:6    0:22
0:4    0:20    0:6    0:22    0:4    0:20    0:6    0:22
0:4    0:20    0:6    0:22    0:4    0:20    0:6    0:22
0:4    0:20    0:6    0:22    0:4    0:20    0:6    0:22
```

It's possible to configure the processor cores to be used for an RSS adapter by modifying the `BaseProcessorNumber`, `MaxProcessorNumber`, and `MaxProcessors` values by using the `Set-NetAdapterRss` PowerShell cmdlet. This gives the administrator more-granular control of the processor resources used to process network traffic. It's also possible to enable and disable RSS for specific network adapters by using `Enable-NetAdapterRss` and `Disable-NetAdapterRss`.

RSS is a great technology, but it is disabled as soon as a network adapter is connected to a virtual switch. VMQ and RSS are mutually exclusive: You do not get the benefit of RSS for virtual network adapters connected to virtual machines. Therefore, if you have a virtual switch connected to a 10Gbps NIC, the throughput to a virtual machine is only around 3 to 4Gbps, the maximum amount a single processor core can process, and this is what was possible with Windows Server 2012. This changes with Windows Server 2012 R2 and the introduction of virtual RSS, or vRSS.

vRSS enables the RSS mechanism to split incoming packets between multiple virtual processors within the virtual machine. A virtual machine can now leverage the full bandwidth available; for example, a virtual machine can now receive 10Gbps over its virtual NIC, because the processing is no longer bottlenecked to a single virtual processor core.

For vRSS, the network adapter must support VMQ. The actual RSS work is performed on the Hyper-V host within the Hyper-V switch. Therefore, using vRSS does introduce some additional CPU load on the host, which is why, by default, vRSS is disabled in the virtual machine. It must be enabled within the virtual machine the same way regular RSS would be enabled on a physical host:

1. Use the `Enable-NetAdapterRss` PowerShell cmdlet.

2. Within the properties of the virtual network adapter inside the virtual machine, select the Advanced tab and set the Receive Side Scaling property to Enabled.

With vRSS enabled, once the processor core processing the network traffic is utilizing around 80 percent, the processing will start to be distributed among multiple vCPUs.

A great way to show and maximize the throughput of a network adapter is by using Microsoft's `ntttcp.exe` test tool, which allows multiple streams to be created as a sender and receiver, therefore maximizing the use of a network connection. The tool can be downloaded from the following location:

```
http://gallery.technet.microsoft.com/NTttcp-Version-528-Now-f8b12769
```

Once it's downloaded, copy `ntttcp.exe` into a virtual machine (with at least four vCPUs and with its firewall disabled) that is connected to a virtual switch using a 10Gbps network adapter (this will receive the traffic) and to a physical host with a 10Gbps network adapter (this will send the traffic). Within the virtual machine, run the tool as follows:

```
Ntttcp.exe -r -m 16,*,<IP address of the VM> -a 16 -t 10
```

This command puts the virtual machine in a listening mode, waiting for the traffic to arrive. On the physical host, send the traffic by using the following command:

```
Ntttcp.exe -s -m 16,*,<IP address of the VM> -a 16 -t 10
```

The virtual machine will show that traffic is being received. Open Task Manager and view the CPU in the Performance tab. Ensure that the CPU graph is set to Logical Processors (right-click the process graph, and select Change Graph To ➤ Logical Processors). Initially, without vRSS, the bandwidth will likely be around 4 to 5Gbps (depending on the speed of your processor cores, but most important, only a single vCPU will be utilized). Then turn on vRSS within the VM and run the test again. This time the bandwidth will be closer to 10Gbps, and many of the vCPUs will be utilized. This really shows the benefit of vRSS, and in Figure 3.40 and Figure 3.41, you can see my performance view without and with vRSS. Notice both the processor utilization and the network speed.

FIGURE 3.40
Network performance without vRSS enabled

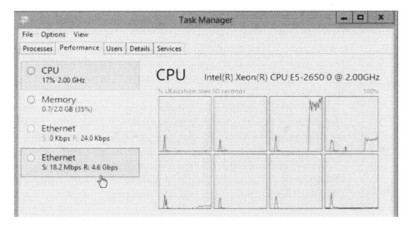

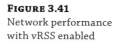

FIGURE 3.41
Network performance
with vRSS enabled

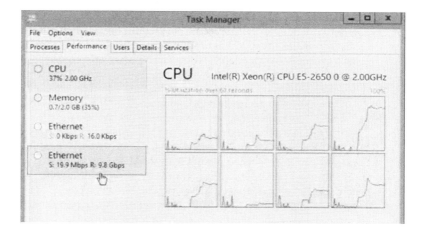

I do want to point out that there is no vRSS support in the host partition prior to Windows Server 2016, but it is introduced in Windows Server 2016. This may not seem important, because a host can normally just use RSS. It does become an issue, though, if you create multiple virtual network adapters within the host OS that is connected to a Hyper-V virtual switch. This is possible in Windows 2012 and above, and it is something I talk about later in this chapter. Prior to Windows Server 2016, virtual network adapters in the host partition would be limited in bandwidth to what is possible through a single processor core for each virtual network adapter, but this is not the case in Windows Server 2016.

Windows Server 2016 introduces another technology that builds on vRSS: *Virtual Machine Multi-Queue (VMMQ)*. With VMQ, a VM would be allocated a single queue that was affinitized to a single processor core. Modern network adapters have huge numbers of queues, typically many more than VMs running on the box. While vRSS spreads the traffic over multiple cores in the VM, that traffic still comes from a single queue for the VM and results in two interrupts: a hardware interrupt from the actual NIC queue and then a software interrupt to the VM to spread out the traffic. With VMMQ, multiple hardware queues from the NIC can be allocated to a single VM, and each queue is affinitized to a specific CPU. The default queue (used by VMs without a VMQ) also now uses a set of queues interrupting a set of CPUs. The distribution of the traffic over the multiple queues is done in the NIC hardware (using the same Toeplitz hash as RSS) instead of the VMSwitch software, which is the case with vRSS. This means that the interrupts and processing are spread over multiple CPUs, leading to better processing while minimizing the overhead on the Hyper-V switch. Note that the VMs still require multiple vCPUs to process the traffic.

To enable VMMQ for a VM (which can be executed while the VM is running), use the following:

```
Set-VMNetworkAdapter <VM Name> -VmmqEnabled $TRUE
```

NIC Teaming

As more resources are consolidated onto a smaller number of physical systems, it's critical that those consolidated systems are as reliable as possible. Previously in this chapter, we created virtual switches, some of which were external to connect to a physical network adapter.

Many virtual machines connect to a virtual switch for their network access, which means that a network adapter failure in the host would break connectivity for a large number of virtual machines and the workloads running within them. It is therefore important to provide resiliency from network adapter failure and potentially enable aggregation of bandwidth from multiple network adapters. For example, a solution would be to group four 1Gbps network adapters together for a total bandwidth of 4Gbps.

The ability to group network adapters together, made possible by a feature known as *NIC Teaming*, has been a feature of many network drivers for a long time. However, because it was a feature of the network driver, the implementation differed by vendor. It was not possible to mix network adapters from different vendors, and strictly speaking, the technology was not "supported" by Microsoft because it was not Microsoft technology.

Windows Server 2012 changed this by implementing NIC Teaming as part of the operating system itself. It allows up to 32 network adapters to be placed in a single NIC team, and the network adapters can be from many different vendors. It's important that all of the NICs are the same speed, because the Windows NIC Teaming algorithms do not consider NIC speed as part of their traffic-balancing algorithms. If you mixed 1Gbps network adapters with 10Gbps network adapters, the 1Gbps network adapters would receive the same amount of traffic as the 10Gbps network adapters, which would be far from optimal.

NIC Teaming is simple to configure via Server Manager or PowerShell. For example, the following command creates a new NIC team using Switch Independent mode, the dynamic load-balancing algorithm, and two network adapters:

```
New-NetLbfoTeam -Name "HostSwitchTeam" -TeamMembers NICTeam3,NICTeam4 `
 -TeamingMode SwitchIndependent -LoadBalancingAlgorithm Dynamic `
 -Confirm:$false
```

Additionally, as you saw earlier in the chapter, SCVMM can automatically create teams on hosts when deploying logical switches. A NIC team has two primary configurations (in addition to specifying which network adapters should be in the team): the teaming mode and the load-balancing algorithm. There are three teaming modes:

Static Teaming Configuration is required on the switches and computer to identify links that make up the team.

Switch Independent Using different switches for each NIC in the team is not required but is possible, and no configuration is performed on the switch. This is the default option.

LACP (Dynamic Teaming) The Link Aggregation Control Protocol (LACP) is used to dynamically identify links between the computer and specific switches.

For load balancing, there were two modes in Windows Server 2012 and three in Windows Server 2012 R2:

Hyper-V Port Each virtual machine NIC (vmNIC) has its own MAC address, which is used as the basis to distribute traffic between the various NICs in the team. If you have many virtual machines with similar loads, Hyper-V Port works well; but it might not be optimal with a small number of virtual machines or uneven loads. Because a specific vmNIC will always be serviced by the same NIC, it is limited to the bandwidth of a single NIC.

Address Hash   Creates a hash value based on information such as the source and destination IP and port (although the exact mode can be changed to use only IP or only MAC). The hash is then used to distribute traffic between the NICs, ensuring that packets with the same hash are sent to the same NIC to protect against out-of-sequence packet processing. This is not typically used with Hyper-V virtual machines.

Dynamic   New in Windows Server 2012 R2, and really the best parts of Hyper-V Port and Address Hash combined. Outbound traffic is based on the address hash, while inbound traffic uses the Hyper-V Port methods. Additionally, the Dynamic mode uses something called *flowlets* as the unit of distribution between NICs for outbound traffic. Without flowlets, the entire stream of communication would always be sent via the same network adapter, which may lead to an unbalanced utilization of network adapters. Consider a normal conversation: There are natural breaks between words spoken, and this is exactly the same for IP communications. When a break of sufficient length is detected, this is considered a flowlet, and a new flowlet starts, which could be balanced to a different network adapter. You will pretty much always use Dynamic mode in Windows Server 2012 R2.

Although it is possible to use the NIC Teaming feature within a virtual machine, only two vmNICs are supported (this is not a hard limit but a supportability limit), and a configuration change is required on the virtual network adapter properties of the virtual machine. This can be done in two ways:

◆   Within the properties page of the virtual machine, select Advanced Features for the network adapter and select the "Enable this network adapter to be part of a team in the guest operating system" check box.

◆   Use PowerShell and run the following command:

```
Set-VMNetworkAdapter -VMName <VM Name> -AllowTeaming On
```

Typically, you will not need to use teaming within the virtual machine. The high availability would be enabled by using NIC Teaming at the Hyper-V host level and then the created team would be bonded to the virtual switch. If, for example, you were leveraging SR-IOV, which bypasses the Hyper-V switch, you may wish to create a NIC team within the OS between two SR-IOV network adapters or one SR-IOV and one regular vmNIC.

The addition of NIC Teaming in Windows Server 2012 does not mean NIC Teaming capabilities cannot be provided by vendors, however. Because the capability is provided in the box, no network vendors have shipped their own teaming functionality in the Windows Server 2016 time frame. Historically some vendors differentiated their cards based on teaming capabilities, and customers had the choice to use teaming capabilities from the network adapter driver or use the Microsoft NIC Teaming functionality, which is fully supported by Microsoft. Nearly all customers went the Microsoft path, which is why the vendors have pulled back from providing their own.

No major changes to NIC Teaming have been made in Windows Server 2016, as a new type of teaming is introduced: *Switch Embedded Teaming* (*SET*). SET, covered in the next section, is the future direction for teaming in Windows, but this does not mean that NIC Teaming is going away anytime soon. The only change in Windows Server 2016 LBFO teaming is the ability to change the LACP timer between a slow and fast timer. This is important for people using Cisco switches.

Host Virtual Adapters and Types of Networks Needed in a Hyper-V Host

A Hyper-V host needs many types of network connectivity, especially if it's part of a cluster. It's critical that each type of traffic gets the required amount of bandwidth to ensure smooth operation. Additionally, resiliency is likely required for many types of connections to protect against a single network adapter failure. The following key types of network connectivity are required for a Hyper-V host:

Management   Communication to the host for management such as remote desktop (RDP), WS-MAN for remote PowerShell and Server Manager, and basic file copy operations. Sometimes backup operations will be performed over the management network, or a separate backup network may be required.

VM   Traffic related to virtual machines connected to a virtual switch

Live Migration   The data related to moving a virtual machine between hosts, such as the memory and even storage of a virtual machine

Cluster/CSV   Cluster communications and Cluster Shared Volumes data

SMB 3   Windows 2012 makes SMB an option for accessing storage containing virtual machines, which would require its own dedicated connection.

iSCSI   If iSCSI is used, a separate network connection would be used.

Traditionally, to ensure the required guaranteed bandwidth for each type of network communication, a separate network adapter was used for each type of traffic. However, it is possible to combine the first four types of network with either of the last two, but the use of separate network interfaces makes the implementation potentially easier to manage. Look at the preceding list again. That is a lot of network adapters—and that list is without resiliency, which may mean doubling that number, which is typically not practical. This is also outlined in the Microsoft networking guidelines at the following location:

```
http://technet.microsoft.com/en-us/library/ff428137(v=WS.10).aspx
```

Your connectivity may look like Figure 3.42. Not only does this require a lot of network adapters, but there is a huge amount of wasted bandwidth. For example, typically the Live Migration network would not be used unless a migration is occurring, and normally the Cluster network has only heartbeat and some minimal Metadata redirection for CSV, but the high bandwidth is needed for when a Live Migration does occur or when a CSV goes into redirection mode. It would be better if the network bandwidth could be used by other types of communication when the bandwidth was available.

Having this many 1Gbps network adapters may be possible, but as datacenters move to 10Gbps, another solution is needed in keeping with the converged direction in which many datacenters are focused. Some unified solutions offer the ability to carve up a single connection from the server to the backplane into virtual devices such as network adapters, which is one solution to this problem. It's also possible, however, to solve this by using the Hyper-V virtual switch, which traditionally was available only for virtual machines.

One of the properties of a virtual switch is the option to allow the management operating system to share the network adapter, which creates a virtual network adapter (vNIC) on the Hyper-V host itself that was connected to the virtual switch. This would allow the management traffic and the VM traffic to share the virtual switch. It's possible, though, to create additional vNICs on the management operating system connected to the virtual switch for other purposes by using PowerShell. QoS can then be used to ensure that sufficient bandwidth is guaranteed for each of the vNICs created so that one type of traffic would use up all of the bandwidth and stop other types of communication. To add more vNICs on the Hyper-V host connected to a virtual switch, use the following command (changing the switch name from External Switch to a valid virtual switch name in your environment):

```
Add-VMNetworkAdapter -ManagementOS -SwitchName "<External Switch>"
```

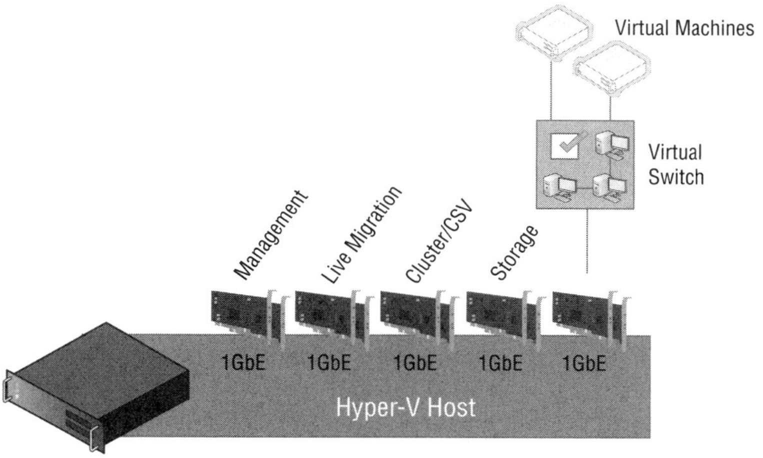

FIGURE 3.42
A nonconverged
Hyper-V host con-
figuration with separate
1Gbps NIC teams for
each type of traffic

The ability to create vNICs in the management operating system connected to a virtual switch that can in turn be connected to a native NIC team that is made up of multiple network adapters makes it possible to create a converged networking approach for the Hyper-V host. Because separate vNICs are used for each type of traffic, QoS can be used to ensure that bandwidth is available when needed, as shown in Figure 3.43. In this example, four 1Gbps NICs are used together and then used by the virtual switch, which now services virtual machines and the different vNICs in the management partition for various types of communication. However, it would also be common to now use two 10Gbps or higher NICs instead. I walk through the process in a video at www.youtube.com/watch?v=8mOuoIWzmdE, but here are some of the commands to create two vNICs in the host in a new NIC team and virtual switch. I assign a minimum bandwidth weight QoS policy. If required, each vNIC can be configured with a separate VLAN ID.

```
New-NetLbfoTeam -Name "HostSwitchTeam" -TeamMembers NICTeam3,NICTeam4 `
-TeamingMode Static -Confirm:$false
New-VMSwitch "MgmtSwitch" -MinimumBandwidthMode weight `
-NetAdapterName "HostSwitchTeam" –AllowManagement $false
Add-VMNetworkAdapter -ManagementOS -Name "LiveMigration" `
-SwitchName "MgmtSwitch"
Set-VMNetworkAdapter -ManagementOS -Name "LiveMigration" `
-MinimumBandwidthWeight 50
Add-VMNetworkAdapter -ManagementOS -Name "Cluster" -SwitchName "MgmtSwitch"
Set-VMNetworkAdapter -ManagementOS -Name "Cluster" -MinimumBandwidthWeight 50
```

FIGURE 3.43
A converged Hyper-V host configuration with a shared NIC team used

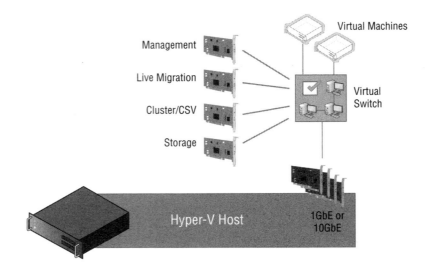

I go into detail in an article at:

http://windowsitpro.com/windows-server-2012/quality-of-service-windows-server-2012

The article is definitely worth reading if you want to understand the details of QoS and why minimum bandwidth is a better solution than the traditional maximum-bandwidth caps that always limited the available bandwidth to the cap value, even if more bandwidth was available. The exception to the use of maximum-bandwidth caps tends to be hosters that charge customers based on a certain amount of bandwidth being available and do not want to give any extra free bandwidth. No free bits! Using minimum bandwidth allows maximum utilization of all bandwidth until there is bandwidth contention between different workloads, at which time each workload is limited to its relative allocation. For example, suppose that I have the following three workloads:

Live Migration: MinumumBandwidthWeight 20

Virtual Machines: MinumumBandwidthWeight 50

Cluster: MinumumBandwidthWeight 30

Under normal circumstances, the virtual machines could use all of the available bandwidth—for example, 10Gbps if the total bandwidth available to the switch was 10Gbps. However, if a Live Migration triggered and the virtual machines were using all of the bandwidth, then the virtual machines would be throttled back to 80 percent and the Live Migration traffic would be guaranteed 20 percent, which would be 2Gbps. Notice that my weights add up to 100, which is not required but historically has been highly recommended for manageability. However, we now live in a world with VMs that are highly mobile and can move between hosts, so trying to keep totals to 100 would be impossible. What is important is to set relative values for the different tiers of comparative bandwidth required and use that scheme throughout your entire environment.

Although using this new converged methodology is highly recommended, there is one caveat: the SMB 3 usage. SMB 3 has a feature named *SMB Direct*, which uses remote direct memory access (RDMA) for the highest possible network speeds and almost no overhead on the host. Additionally, SMB 3 has a feature called *SMB Multichannel*, which allows multiple network connections between the source and target of the SMB communication to be aggregated together, providing both protection from a single network connection failure and increased bandwidth, similar to the benefits of NIC Teaming. (SMB Direct still works with NIC Teaming, because when a NIC team is detected, SMB automatically creates four separate connections by default.) The problem is that RDMA does not work with NIC Teaming. This means that if you wish to take advantage of SMB Direct (RDMA), which would be the case if you were using SMB to communicate to the storage of your virtual machines and/or if you are using SMB Direct for Live Migration (which is possible in Windows Server 2012 R2 and above), you would not want to lose the RDMA capability if it's present in your network adapters. If you wish to leverage RDMA, your converged infrastructure will look slightly different, as shown in Figure 3.44, which features an additional two NICs that are not teamed but would instead be aggregated using SMB Multichannel. Notice that Live Migration, SMB, and Cluster (CSV uses SMB for its communications) all move to the RDMA adapters, because all of those workloads benefit from RMDA. While this does mean four network adapters are required to support the various types of traffic most efficiently, all of those types of traffic are fault-tolerant and have access to increased bandwidth.

FIGURE 3.44
A converged Hyper-V host configuration with separate NICs for SMB (RDMA) traffic

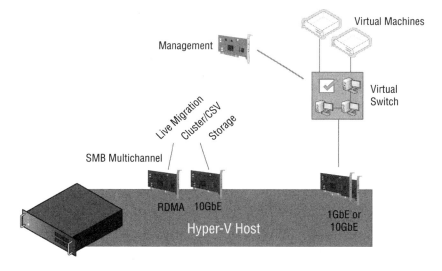

In some environments, requiring two extra RDMA network adapters and using up two extra RDMA ports on a switch for each host may be OK, but that's a pretty steep bill, just to be able to leverage RDMA because it does not work with NIC Teaming. Windows Server 2016 solves this problem with Converged NIC and Switch Embedded Teaming. With the Converged NIC, *Data Center Bridging (DCB)* is utilized to assign traffic classes to the different types of traffic traversing the NIC. For example, RDMA uses one traffic class, while regular vSwitch traffic uses another class. This enables the SDNv2 QoS still to correctly manage the bandwidth assigned to different types of traffic. However, even with the Converged NIC, you still need the ability to group multiple NICs together for scale and availability, and NIC Teaming is not compatible with the VFP extension.

Switch Embedded Teaming (SET) provides an integrated teaming solution direction in the VMSwitch, allowing up to 8 network adapters to be teamed within the switch. While 8 may seem low compared to the 32 supported by LBFO NIC Teaming, SET is focused around SDNv2 and modern network adapters that are 10Gbps, 40Gbps, and higher. It is unusual to see any server with more than 8 of those tiers of network adapters. SET requires that all adapters are identical, including the make, model, firmware, and driver. SET utilizes switch-independent teaming only with no LACP support and supports the Dynamic and Hyper-V Port modes of load distribution. Active/Passive teaming is not supported. Most important, it is RDMA/DCB aware, which enables a shared set of NICs to be utilized for RDMA capabilities and as part of the VMSwitch. This is shown in Figure 3.45.

FIGURE 3.45
A converged Hyper-V host configuration with shared NICs for SMB (RDMA) traffic

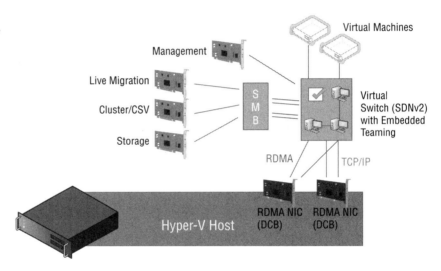

Neither Hyper-V Manager nor the LBFO management tools understand SET. To create a SET configuration, utilize SCVMM 2016 as I discussed earlier, selecting the Embedded Teaming option or PowerShell. When using PowerShell specify -EnableEmbeddedTeaming $true with New-VMSwitch, or it is implicitly implied if you pass New-VMSwitch more than one NIC. For example:

```
New-VMSwitch -Name TeamedvSwitch -NetAdapterName "NIC 1","NIC 2" `
-EnableEmbeddedTeaming $true
#Same as:
New-VMSwitch -Name TeamedvSwitch -NetAdapterName "NIC 1","NIC 2"
```

When viewing a SET VMSwitch, the multiple network adapters will appear in its properties, as shown here:

```
PS C:\> get-vmswitch -Name "Lab Switch Team" | fl

Name                              : Lab Switch Team
Id                                : e7980108-8596-4833-9283-d2622a691875
```

```
Notes                           :
Extensions                      : {Microsoft VMM DHCPv4 Server Switch
Extension, Microsoft Windows Filtering Platform, Microsoft Azure VFP
Switch Extension,
                                  Microsoft NDIS Capture}
BandwidthReservationMode        : Weight
PacketDirectEnabled             : False
EmbeddedTeamingEnabled          : True
IovEnabled                      : False
SwitchType                      : External
AllowManagementOS               : False
NetAdapterInterfaceDescription  : Teamed-Interface
NetAdapterInterfaceDescriptions : {Mellanox ConnectX-3 Pro Ethernet
Adapter, Mellanox ConnectX-3 Pro Ethernet Adapter #2}
IovSupport                      : True
IovSupportReasons               :
AvailableIPSecSA                : 0
NumberIPSecSAAllocated          : 0
AvailableVMQueues               : 250
```

FEATURE AND OFFLOAD SUPPORT

Windows Server 2016 has many features and offloads available and three types of virtual switch environments: native VMSwitch, VMSwitch with SDNv1, and VMSwitch with SDNv2 (also Microsoft Azure Stack). The exact features and offloads that work with the three types of virtualization networking are not always obvious. Microsoft has a great chart, shown in Figure 3.46, that outlines these features and offloads. I use this as a constant reference.

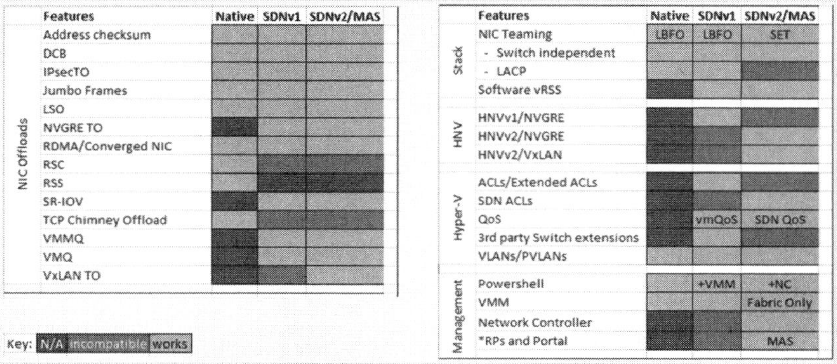

FIGURE 3.46
Breakdown of features and offloads by type of networking

Types of Guest Network Adapters

Two types of network adapters are available to a generation 1 virtual machine: legacy (emulated Intel 21140-Based PCI Fast Ethernet) and synthetic. As discussed in Chapter 2, "Virtual Machine Resource Fundamentals," emulated hardware is never desirable because of the decreased performance and higher overhead, which means that the legacy network adapter is used for only two purposes in a generation 1 virtual machine:

◆ Running an operating system that does not have Hyper-V Integration Services available and therefore cannot use the synthetic network adapter (this would mean the operating system is also unsupported on Hyper-V)

◆ Needing to boot the virtual machine over the network, known as PXE boot. If this is the reason, then initially use a legacy network adapter, but after the operating system is installed, switch to the synthetic network adapter for the improved performance.

Additionally, QoS and hardware-acceleration features are not available for legacy network adapters, making the standard network adapter your default choice. Each virtual machine can have up to eight network adapters (synthetic) and four legacy network adapters.

Many options are available for a network adapter that are configured through the virtual machine properties by selecting the network adapter (legacy network adapter or network adapter).If there are multiple network adapters for a virtual machine, each adapter has its own set of configurations. These configurations are divided into three areas: core configurations, hardware acceleration (not available for legacy network adapters), and advanced features, as shown in Figure 3.47. Figure 3.47 also shows Device Manager running in the virtual machine whose properties are being displayed, which shows the two network adapters. The Intel 21140-Based PCI Faster Ethernet Adapter (Emulate) is the legacy network adapter, and the Microsoft Virtual Machine Bus Network Adapter is the network adapter.

FIGURE 3.47
Primary properties for a network adapter

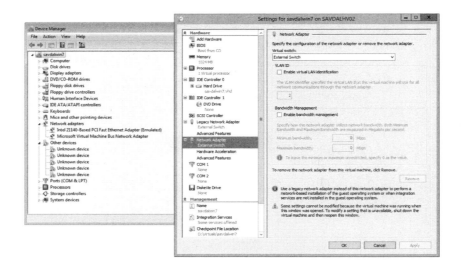

The core properties for a network adapter are as follows:

Virtual Switch   The virtual switch to which the adapter should be connected

Enable Virtual LAN Identification   If the switch port to which the virtual switch is connected is set to tagged and expects packets to be tagged with a VLAN ID, this option allows you to configure which VLAN ID packets from this network adapter will be tagged.

Enable Bandwidth Management (*not available for legacy network adapter*) Enables limits to be specified in Mbps for the bandwidth available for the network adapter. The lowest value allowed for Minimum is 10Mbps, while 0.1 is the lowest value that can be set for Maximum.

The Hardware Acceleration tab (not available to legacy network adapters) enables VMQ, IPsec, and SR-IOV by selecting the appropriate check box. Remember that even if these properties are set in a virtual machine, it does not guarantee their use. For example, if the physical network adapter does not support VMQ or has run out of VMQs, then VMQ will not be used for the vmNIC. Likewise, if SR-IOV is selected by the virtual switch, if the hardware does not support SR-IOV, or if the physical adapter has no more available virtual functions, then SR-IOV will not be used. Selecting the options simply enables the capabilities to be used if they are available, without guaranteeing their actual use.

The Advanced Features tab enables interesting options whose use will vary depending on the environment deploying the technology:

MAC Address By default, a dynamic MAC address is used, which is configured when the VM is created and should not change. However, it's also possible to select Static and configure your own preferred MAC address. The option to enable MAC address spoofing can also be set, which enables the VM to change the MAC address on packets it sends to another MAC address. This would be necessary when using network load balancing, for example, within virtual machines.

Enable DHCP Guard Network adapters configured with the DHCP Guard option will have any DHCP reply packets from the VM dropped by the Hyper-V switch. This means that if the VM is pretending to be a DHCP server when it shouldn't be, although the server still sees the DHCP request from clients and responds, those responses never get to the network. Consider a multitenant environment. It's important that one tenant not pretend that it's a DHCP server and affect the others. The best practice is to enable this feature on all virtual machine network adapters and disable it only on the virtual machines that are known DHCP servers.

Enable Router Advertisement Guard Very similar to DHCP Guard, but this will block router advertisements and redirection messages. Again, enable this by default unless a VM is acting as a router.

Protected Network This feature specifies that if the network to which the virtual machine is connected becomes disconnected, then Failover Clustering will move the virtual machine to another node in the cluster.

Port Mirroring There are three settings; None, Destination, and Source. This allows network traffic from a vmNIC set as Source to be sent to vmNICs on other virtual machines that are set as Destination. Essentially, this allows network traffic from one virtual machine to be sent to another for analysis/monitoring.

NIC Teaming This allows the network adapter to be used within a NIC team defined inside the virtual machine.

Device Naming Enables the name of the network adapter to be propagated into the guest OS. This is useful when a VM has multiple network adapters that are connected to different switches or have different configurations, and you want to be able to identify each NIC from within the guest, which normally has a generic name.

All of these options can be set with the `Set-VMNetworkAdapter` PowerShell cmdlet in addition to being set through Hyper-V Manager.

A common question arises when the network adapters inside the virtual machine are inspected, which shows an actual speed for the virtual network adapter. Prior to Windows Server 2016, this was always 10Gbps for the network adapter (synthetic) and 100Mbps for the legacy network adapter. People got confused. They would say, "But my physical network card is only 1Gbps; how can it be 20Gbps?" The fact is that this number was meaningless. Some number has to be displayed, so Hyper-V tells the virtual machine a certain number. In Windows Server 2016, the synthetic NIC now shows the actual speed of the NICs available to the switch. For example, in my deployment with two 10Gbps NICs in SET, the VM shows its NIC at 20Gbps, as shown in Figure 3.48.

FIGURE 3.48
VMSwitch network speed shown inside the guest

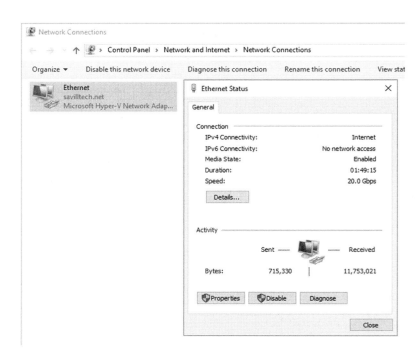

In reality, the speed achieved completely depends on a couple of factors:

◆ If the traffic is between two virtual machines on the same host, the traffic never touches a physical network adapter and will process between them as fast as the VMBus and processor can handle the traffic.

◆ If the traffic is external to the Hyper-V host, the speed is based on the speed of the network adapter (or adapters, if a team) and the processor. For example, if you have a 10Gbps network adapter, the speed will likely be determined by the processor that has to process the traffic, so you may not see 10Gbps of speed. When receiving traffic, each virtual machine NIC may be assigned a VMQ from the NIC. The VMQ is processed by a single processor core (except in Windows Server 2012 R2, which supports virtual Receive Side Scaling, or vRSS), which likely will result in speeds of between 3 and 4Gbps.

To summarize, the speed shown in the virtual machine is irrelevant in most cases, and it does not guarantee or limit the actual network speed, which is based on the physical network adapter speed and the processor capabilities.

Monitoring Virtual Traffic

Readers may be familiar with the Network Monitor (NetMon) tool that Microsoft has made available for many years as a method to monitor traffic. When it is installed on a machine, this tool can monitor the network in promiscuous mode to view all of the traffic sent over the link. This is still an option. It can even be installed inside a virtual machine, and the port-mirroring feature of the network adapter could be used to send network traffic from one virtual machine to another for monitoring.

However, Microsoft has replaced NetMon with a new tool, Message Analyzer, which is available from the following location:

```
www.microsoft.com/en-us/download/details.aspx?id=44226
```

Going into detail about Message Analyzer is beyond the scope of this book. However, I want to focus on one new powerful feature: the capability to perform remote capture of a Windows Server 2012 server or Windows client, including specific virtual machines running on a Windows Server 2012 Hyper-V host. The ability to perform remote capture is a key requirement when you consider that many production servers now run Server Core, which has no ability to run graphical management tools, such as the NetMon tool, and that would block performing network analysis.

Remote capture is made possible because the driver used by Message Analyzer, NDISCAP, is now built into the Windows 8.1 and above and the Windows Server 2012 R2 and above operating systems. It was specifically written to enable remote capture, sending packets over the network to the box that is running the Message Analyzer tool. Message Analyzer can still be used on Windows 7 (with WMI 3 installed), Windows 8, Windows 2008 R2 (with WMI 3), and Windows Server 2012, and it will install a capture driver, PEFNDIS, but it does not allow remote capturing of network data. When a remote capture is initially performed, a WMI call is made to the remote server to collect the information about what can be captured, and then RPC is used to send packets over the network to the Message Analyzer. Note that it's possible to configure only certain types of traffic to be sent to Message Analyzer, and by default, traffic is truncated to show only the first 128 bytes of each packet to minimize the amount of traffic sent over the network from the source to the analyzer machine.

Message Analyzer features a completely new interface, and I will walk through the basic steps to start a remote capture of a virtual machine on a remote Hyper-V host. Before running this process, add the remote host to the list of trusted WMI machines by running the following command from an elevated command prompt:

```
WinRM set winrm/config/client @{TrustedHosts="RemoteHostName"}
```

Now you can continue with the remote capture:

1. Launch Message Analyzer.

2. Select New Session.

3. Select Live Trace for the data source.

4. In the Live Trace tab, change the host from Localhost to the remote Hyper-V server by clicking the Edit button.

5. Enter the name of the host. Additionally, separate credentials for the remote host can be configured. Click OK.

6. The next step is to apply a scenario. Click the Select Scenario drop-down list, and select Remote Network Interfaces.

7. Click the Configure link next to the capture configuration, as shown in Figure 3.49. This allows the configuration of the exact traffic to be captured. Note that it shows the actual virtual machines that are connected to the switch. In this case, I have selected only to capture data from my VM4 virtual machine. Notice also that filters can be applied to the type of traffic to be captured (or a filter can be applied on the viewing of data post capture, but if you capture everything, then the capture file will be substantially larger). Click OK.

FIGURE 3.49
Configuring the remote traffic to capture by using Message Analyzer

8. Now click the Start button to start the capture and view the packets.

9. After the capture is finished, click the Stop button.

Figure 3.50 shows an example of my captured output from the virtual machine I selected. The ability to remotely monitor specific network adapters, specific virtual switches, and even specific virtual machines with no configuration on the source host is a huge benefit and really completes and emphasizes the capabilities available with Windows Server 2016 networking.

FIGURE 3.50
FIGURE 3.50

Example view of
captured traffic

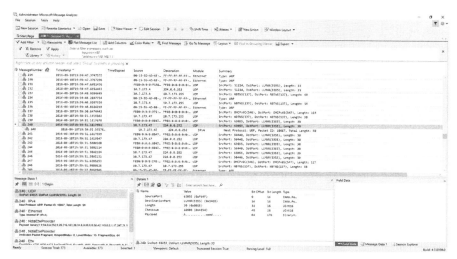

The Bottom Line

Architect the right network design for your Hyper-V hosts and virtual machines by using the options available. There are many networking traffic types related to a Hyper-V host, including management, virtual machine, cluster, Live Migration, and storage. While traditionally separate, network adapters were used with each type of traffic; a preferred approach is to create multiple vNICs in the management partition that connect to a shared virtual switch. This minimizes the number of physical NICs required while providing resiliency from a NIC failure for all workloads connected to the switch.

Master It Why are separate network adapters no longer required if SMB is leveraged and the network adapters support RDMA?

Identify when to use the types of gateways. Three types of gateways are supported by the SDNv2 multitenant gateway: basic layer 3 forwarding to connect virtual networks to other networks, GRE tunneling to other GRE endpoints or MPLS, and site-to-site VPN to connect locations. The SDNv2 multitenant gateway supports multiple active and multiple passive instances, and it is designed to support multiple tenants using shared physical infrastructure.

Leverage SCVMM for many networking tasks. While Hyper-V Manager enables many networking functions to be performed, each configuration is limited to a single host and is hard to manage at scale. SCVMM is focused on enabling the network to be modeled at a physical level, and then the types of network required by virtual environments can be separately modeled with different classifications of connectivity defined. While the initial work may seem daunting, the long-term management and flexibility of a centralized networking environment is a huge benefit.

Master It Is SCVMM required for network virtualization?

Chapter 4

Storage Configurations

In previous chapters, the compute and network resources of a virtual environment were examined, and this chapter covers the final resource building block—storage. In Windows Server 2016, many storage options and topologies are available, enabling organizations to implement various solutions to meet the many different requirements encountered.

Many organizations are familiar with using storage area networks (SANs) as the cornerstone for their storage requirements and leveraging connectivity such as Fibre Channel, and this is still a valid solution. Furthermore, in certain scenarios, this is the right architecture. However, with Windows Server 2012, the focus was on choice and offering other storage solutions that can be more cost-effective and more flexible, such as iSCSI, SMB 3, and Storage Spaces. Windows Server 2016 takes this further by offering new storage options via Storage Spaces Direct, which enables direct-attached storage for nodes in a cluster to be aggregated and used as resilient cluster storage. Also included in Windows Server 2016 is Storage Replica. This supports replication at a block level of storage in numerous scenarios. Hyper-V fully leverages these technologies in addition to supporting a new virtual hard disk format that offers the highest scalability and performance.

In this chapter, you will learn to:

♦   Explain the types of storage available to a virtual machine.

♦   Identify when to use virtual Fibre Channel vs. VHD Sets and the benefits of each.

♦   Articulate how SMB 3 can be used.

Storage Fundamentals and VHDX

Chapter 2, "Virtual Machine Resource Fundamentals," covered the basics of virtual storage, and this section quickly reviews those basics and the various limits and options provided. Nearly every virtual machine scenario requires some kind of "local" storage, such as that used to host the boot and system partitions that contain the operating system environment and locally installed applications and services. Additional storage may also be assigned to the virtual machine for data storage, although this could be accessed using other network-based methods.

Storage that is assigned to the virtual machine from the host server must first be accessible to the Hyper-V host. (Exceptions exist, but these are covered later in the book.) Examples include direct-attached storage to the host, or storage with which the host can communicate—such as on a SAN via iSCSI or Fibre Channel connectivity or even on a Windows file server or network-attached storage (NAS) device using SMB 3 with Windows Server 2012 and above, which introduced file-level access support.

It is important that any storage used by the host to store virtual machines is resilient to failure. For direct-attached storage, use technologies to enable a disk to fail without losing data (such as RAID or Storage Spaces Direct when direct-attached is leveraged across cluster nodes). For remote storage, ensure that there are multiple paths to the storage, to avoid losing storage access if a single card, cable, or switch fails. The remote storage should also be fault-tolerant. When Hyper-V hosts are clustered together, as they always should be to ensure availability of the virtual environment, it's important that storage used by virtual machines is available to all hosts in the cluster.

With storage available at the host level, it needs to be assigned to virtual machines. Although it is possible to pass a disk directly from the Hyper-V host into a virtual machine known as a *pass-through disk*, this is not something that should ever be done, for the following reasons:

◆ The disk is usable solely by the virtual machine assigned the physical disk from the host, so that not even the host can still use the disk.

◆ Virtual machine checkpoints that provide point-in-time captures of a virtual machine don't work.

◆ Migration technologies such as Live Migration do not work without an outage to availability.

◆ Replication technologies such as Hyper-V Replica do not work.

◆ Virtual machine backup at the host is not possible.

◆ Storage quality of service is not available.

With all of these problems, you may wonder why pass-through storage was even made available as an option. The answer is that sometimes virtual machines needed access to volumes and storage that was larger or faster than what was possible with the VHD format, which had a 2TB limit. Consider a large SQL database: a 2TB limit was too restrictive, and a performance hit occurred when using VHD above the bare-metal storage, especially using dynamic VHD, which grows as data is written to it. When very large volumes with the highest performance needs were required, the Windows Server 2008 VHD implementation would not suffice, and either pass-through storage had to be used or iSCSI within the VM. Windows 2008 R2 greatly improved the performance of VHD, but the 2TB limit remained. This is why pass-through was required as an option.

In Windows Server 2012, you should *never* need pass-through storage. There is no scenario that requires it, because of the new 64TB VHDX virtual hard disk format, which also features greatly improved performance, effectively matching the bare-metal storage performance. I've never seen a client with an NTFS volume that is 64TB in size. The largest I have seen is 23TB, because most organizations will limit the size of an NTFS volume in case a volume becomes corrupt and ChkDsk has to be run, although this is no longer a problem with Windows Server 2012 and above.

With the need to use pass-through storage removed, all virtual storage assigned from the Hyper-V host for normal purposes will be through the use of VHDX files. VHD files should be used only if compatibility is required for pre–Windows Server 2012 Hyper-V or Microsoft Azure. (At the time of this writing, Azure does not support VHDX, but it may by the time you read this.)

VHDX has other advantages over VHD beyond performance and scalability:

◆ Protection against corruption caused by unplanned power outages, by logging updates to the VHDX Metadata structures

◆ Alignment with physical disk structures automatically and 4KB sector support. Alignment was a big performance problem for early VHD, which was caused by the VHD file geometry, such as virtual sector size, being different from the underlying NTFS filesystem and disk. Even if the geometry was the same, an offset could exist between where the VHD started and its header, causing a VHD block not to sit within a single NTFS cluster but to span multiple NTFS clusters. This makes disk operations inefficient, because while the virtual OS may think it's fetching a single block, many clusters must be read on the physical storage. The good news is that the alignment issue is resolved in VHDX, which will always align correctly. Details can be found in the VHDX specification at the following location:

`www.microsoft.com/en-us/download/details.aspx?id=34750`

◆ Custom Metadata, allowing management applications to store information such as the OS running inside the VHDX

◆ Trim support, which enables the efficient reclaiming of blocks on SSD devices

---

WHAT IS THE CHKDSK PROBLEM?

ChkDsk is the utility that has to be run when a volume has problems. To fix the problems, the volume has to be taken offline, which means that it's unavailable while a thorough scan and fix is performed on it. The larger the number of files on a volume, the longer the scan for the problems will take and the longer the volume will be offline. For example, a 2TB volume filled with many files could be offline for hours or days, depending on the storage subsystem; this is a long time if the volume contains important data. To avoid long outages, organizations would limit the size of NTFS volumes, which reduces the number of files. Think of this scenario as a highway that is closed while a crew walks along, looking for potholes and fixing the few that it finds. This road may be closed for weeks or months while the crew is looking for the potholes.

Windows Server 2012 rearchitected ChkDsk into a two-phase process. The long process of finding problems now occurs with the volume still online. Once the problems are found, the volume is taken offline, and a spotfix of the problems is performed. In the worst-case scenario, the volume is offline for only 8 seconds and commonly for only milliseconds, which is not noticeable at all. If Cluster Shared Volumes (CSV) is used, downtime never occurs, because CSV has its own layer of indirection, resulting in just a pause in I/O. Going back to the highway analogy, in Windows Server 2012, the road stays open as the crews hop between cars, looking for the problems. Then after they find all of the potholes that are marked on a map, the road is closed for one night while all the found potholes are filled.

To perform the scan, use `chkdsk /scan <disk>:` or `Repair-Volume -Scan <disk>:` in PowerShell, and then once the search for problems is complete, perform the spotfix, which will take the volume offline for the maximum of 8 seconds to run the commands `chkdsk /spotfix <disk>:` or `Repair-Volume -SpotFix <disk>:`.

This means that NTFS volumes are no longer restricted to a certain size because of fears related to running ChkDsk.

An important point to remember about VHDX is that it is a core part of the operating system for both server and client. VHDX files can be mounted natively to the operating system, and physical machines can even boot from VHDX files, which allows great flexibility for moving an operating system instance from a virtual machine to a physical machine without any real changes being required. If you have a physical system that you would like to convert to a virtual machine, several technologies are available for this physical-to-virtual (P2V) conversion. A free tool for a small number of conversions is Disk2vhd, which is available from `https://technet`
`.microsoft.com/en-us/sysinternals/ee656415.aspx`. It takes the storage from physical machines and creates equivalent VHD and VHDX (version 2) files that can then be used with Hyper-V virtual machines.

Types of Controllers

In Chapter 2, I told you about two types of storage controllers available in a generation 1 virtual machine, IDE and SCSI, while a generation 2 virtual machine supports only the SCSI controller. In a generation 1 virtual machine, the operating system VHDX must be connected to the IDE controller because the SCSI controller does not support bootable devices. In a generation 2 virtual machine, though, the SCSI controller does support bootable devices, allowing the operating system VHDX file to be connected to the SCSI controller.

A generation 1 virtual machine has two IDE controllers, with each controller supporting up to two virtual devices, which could be VHD/VHDX files or virtual DVD drives. Both generation 1 and generation 2 virtual machines support up to four SCSI controllers, with each SCSI controller supporting up to 64 virtual hard disks. Even though the performance of the IDE controller and SCSI controller are equivalent, once the integration services are loaded, the fact that so many more disks are supported on the SCSI controller means that in most environments, the IDE controller is used solely for the operating system storage while all data disks connect to the SCSI controller.

There is one additional difference, or was, between the IDE and SCSI virtual controllers that is important to be aware of and that also makes the SCSI controller a better choice for any kind of database: caching behavior, or more specifically, how write cache is reported. For any kind of database, you typically do not want any write caching on the device. Write caching is a technology that enables storage to report that a write has been committed to disk, while it actually is cached in the controller and will be written in the most optimal way at a later time. The danger with write caching is that if an unplanned outage occurs, the data in the volatile cache is never written to the disk and is lost. This is bad for any kind of database, including Active Directory.

With Hyper-V, write caching cannot be disabled on virtual hard disks, because there is no way to ensure that there is not an always-on write cache on the underlying storage or that the VHDX may one day be moved to a disk with an always-on write cache using storage or Live Migration technologies. Additionally, because many VHDX files can reside on a single physical disk, there is no way to be sure all VHDX files on the physical disk would want the write cache disabled, and the configuration of write-cache is a physical disk setting. When the write cache is disabled on a disk that is using Device Manager and is connected to the virtual SCSI controller, an error is displayed, as shown in Figure 4.1. This is important, because applications also try to disable write caching, and the error notifying that the write cache could not be disabled allows any application that needs to ensure data write integrity to use alternative methods, specifically Force Unit Access (FUA), to ensure that data is not cached.

FIGURE 4.1
An error occurs as the administrator tries to disable write caching within a virtual machine. Applications would receive a similar error condition.

When applications try to disable write caching on a virtual disk connected to an IDE controller, no error is returned. This makes the application think that write caching has successfully been disabled, so no other actions to ensure data integrity are taken. In reality, though, write caching was not disabled. This can lead to data corruptions in the event of unplanned outages.

Windows Server 2012 R2 and above do not have this problem, and the good news for Windows Server 2012 and Windows Server 2008 R2 Hyper-V environments is that Microsoft released a fix, KB2853952. Once this fix is applied to the Hyper-V host, it will correctly return a failure error to the VM if write caching is disabled on the IDE controller, allowing the applications then to leverage FUA.

As you move forward with Windows Server 2012 R2 and generation 2 virtual machines, you don't have many choices to make: You will use a virtual SCSI controller, and you will use VHDX files for the best set of features and scalability.

Common VHDX Maintenance Actions

In Chapter 2, I covered basic commands to create VHDX files and also the basic Edit Disk actions that allow certain modifications and optimizations to be performed. I provide additional details in this section.

First, as mentioned, a VHDX file can be natively mounted in Windows Server by right-clicking it and selecting the Mount option or by double-clicking the file. To unmount, right-click the volume in File Explorer and choose Eject. This can also be performed using the various disk management tools, but for automation, scripting the mount and unmounts can be useful. PowerShell provides an easy way to mount and unmount a VHDX file:

```
Mount-VHD -Path D:\Virtuals\newdyn.vhdx
Dismount-VHD -Path D:\Virtuals\newdyn.vhdx
```

Throughout this chapter, I talk about VHDX, but many environments will have VHD files from previous deployments; you might want to convert them to VHDX to gain the new capabilities:

1. Using Hyper-V Manager, start the Edit Disk action, and select the source VHD file.

2. Under the action, select Convert, and then select the VHDX format.

This converts the VHD to a VHDX file. You also can do this via PowerShell:

```
Convert-VHD -Path d:\temp\source.vhd -DestinationPath d:\temp\destination.vhdx
```

Note that any conversion process creates a new virtual hard disk file and copies the content across, which means that you need sufficient free space to create the temporary new file until the old file is deleted. It is also possible to convert a VHDX to a VHD file by using the same process, provided the VHDX is less than 2,040GB. The `Convert-VHD` PowerShell cmdlet is also used to convert a VHD or VHDX to the new VHD Set (VHDS) type by specifying the `.vhds` extension.

Dynamic VHDX files will grow as writes are performed, but they never shrink automatically, even if large amounts of data are deleted. If you delete a large amount of data from a dynamic VHDX file and want to reclaim the space on the physical disk, you need to compact the VHDX file. This can be performed by using the Hyper-V Manager Edit Disk action and selecting the Compact action. This can also be performed using PowerShell:

```
Optimize-VHD -Path d:\temp\data1.vhdx
```

Optional parameters can be used with `Optimize-VHD` that tune the type of optimization. These are fully explained at `https://technet.microsoft.com/en-us/library/hh848458 .aspx`. However, in most cases the default optimization mode of Quick for a VHDX file will yield the desired result.

When a VHDX file is created, it can be created as a fixed or dynamic file. This can be changed through the Edit Disk action or through PowerShell `Convert-VHD`, specifying the `-VHDType` parameter as `Fixed` or `Dynamic`.

The size of a VHDX file can also be changed by using the same method, increasing the available space or even shrinking it, provided there is sufficient unallocated space on the disk inside the virtual machine. For example, if a VHDX file is 80GB but the virtual machine inside has allocated only 60GB of storage, it would leave 20GB unallocated, as shown in Listing 4.1 and Figure 4.2. This would allow the VHDX file to be shrunk by 20GB. This can be confirmed when looking at the properties of a VHDX file and inspecting the `MinimumSize` attribute. Note that when working with dynamic disks, changing the size of the file changes only its maximum size; the actual amount of space used on disk is based entirely on the data written, which is shown in the `FileSize` attribute. If you want to reduce the size of a VHDX file more than the `MinimumSize` attribute, you should connect to the virtual machine and shrink the size of the volumes inside the virtual machine by using Disk Management to increase the amount of unallocated space.

FIGURE 4.2
A virtual machine with 20GB of space unallocated

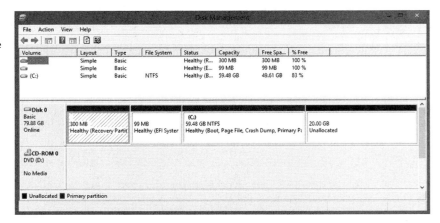

LISTING 4.1:   Setting the Size of a VHDX File

```
PS E:\ > Get-VHD .\win81nondomain.vhdx


ComputerName            : SAVDALHV01
Path                    : E:\Virtuals\win81nondomain\Virtual Hard
Disks\win81nondomain.vhdx
VhdFormat               : VHDX
VhdType                 : Dynamic
FileSize                : 11983126528
Size                    : 85899345920
MinimumSize             : 64423477760
LogicalSectorSize       : 512
PhysicalSectorSize      : 4096
BlockSize               : 33554432
ParentPath              :
DiskIdentifier          : ae420626-f01e-4dfa-a0a5-468ffdfe95ad
FragmentationPercentage : 6
Alignment               : 1
Attached                : True
DiskNumber              :
Key                     :
IsDeleted               : False
Number                  :
```

Dynamic VHDX Resize

Prior to Windows Server 2012 R2, any changes to the size of a VHDX file required the virtual machine using the VHDX file to be shut down. There was no way to resize a VHDX file dynamically while the virtual machine was still running, which some organizations found to be a pain point. Windows Server 2012 R2 introduced dynamic resize for both increasing and decreasing the size of a file. The requirements for dynamic resize are as follows:

◆   Must be a VHDX file. Dynamic resize is not supported for VHD files.

◆   Must be connected to the SCSI controller. Dynamic resize is not supported for virtual hard disks connected to the IDE controller.

Performing a dynamic resize is exactly the same as performing an offline resize operation:

1.   Within Hyper-V Manager, select the Edit Disk option.

2.   Click Next on the Edit Virtual Hard Disk Wizard introduction page.

3.   Select the VHDX file to modify (remember, the VM using it can still be running), and then click Next.

4.   Select the Expand or Shrink option, depending on your desired action, and then click Next.

5. If you selected Shrink, the minimum possible size will be shown in brackets. If you selected Expand, the maximum possible size will be shown in brackets. Enter the new size, and click Next.

6. Click Finish to perform the resize.

If you performed an expand of a virtual hard disk within the virtual machine, you need to use the newly available unallocated disk space. Either extend an existing volume or create a new volume in the unallocated space by using the Disk Management MMC snap-in or PowerShell. If a shrink was performed, no actions are required; there will simply be less or no unallocated space on the disk.

To resize using PowerShell, utilize the `Resize-VHD` cmdlet. You pass the new size by using the `-SizeBytes` parameter. (However, you do not have to type the size in bytes; you can type numbers such as 2GB or 10TB.) The new size can be less or more than the current size, as long as it is a valid size (not smaller than the `MinimumSize` attribute, and not larger than the VHDX 64TB limit or than is physically available if it is a fixed-size VHDX file). If you want to shrink the file as much as possible, instead of using `-SizeBytes`, use the `-ToMinimumSize` parameter, as in this example:

```
Resize-VHD .\win81nondomain.vhdx -ToMinimumSize
```

Storage Spaces and Windows as a Storage Solution

This section briefly covers the big shift in storage introduced with Windows Server 2012. Although it's not strictly a Hyper-V topic, I cover it because it will most likely affect the way your Hyper-V environments are architected, especially in smaller organizations and branch offices.

In the introduction, I talked about Fibre Channel and iSCSI-connected SANs, which historically have been the preferred storage choice for organizations because they provide many benefits:

◆ Storage is centralized, allowing the highest utilization of the available space as opposed to many separate instances of storage with lots of wasted space.

◆ Centralized backup is possible.

◆ They offer the highest level of performance and scalability, which is possible because the storage is all centralized, allowing higher-specification storage solutions to be purchased.

◆ Storage is accessible to all servers throughout the datacenter, provided the server has the required connectivity, such as Fibre Channel or iSCSI.

◆ Centralized storage enables easy migration of virtual machines between physical hosts, because the storage can be seen by multiple servers.

◆ They provide shared storage, which is required for many cluster scenarios.

The use of high-end, centralized storage is still a great option for many organizations and scenarios. However, another model is also being adopted by many organizations and service providers, including Microsoft Azure: just a bunch of disks (JBOD) solutions that are either local to a server or in an external enclosure connected to numerous clustered hosts. This can provide great cost efficiencies because storage subsystems based on regular disks are much cheaper than SAN solutions. It is important, though, to build in resiliency and backup solutions for what is now local storage containing critical workloads (that is, your virtual machines).

Windows Server has long had the ability to create fault-resilient storage using redundant array of independent disks (RAID) technology in one of two modes: RAID-1, which mirrored all data from one disk to another disk, and RAID-5, which used striping with parity. However, there were challenges with the software RAID implementation:

◆ It did not self-heal. If a disk was lost, another disk had to be configured manually to be the replacement.

◆ Only thick/fat provisioning was possible, which means a volume can be created only up to the physical space available. Thin provisioning, which allows volumes to be created beyond the physical space and allocated as data was written, was not possible.

◆ Management was quite painful, and RAID volumes could not be resized easily.

◆ It was not supported in a failover cluster.

Storage Space Basics

Storage Spaces was introduced in Windows Server 2012 as a completely new way to think about managing and using direct-attached storage. With Storage Spaces, the physical disks providing the underlying storage of data are completely abstracted from the process of requesting new volumes, now known as *spaces*, and any actions required to restore data redundancy in the event of a disk failure are performed automatically by the Storage Spaces technology, as long as there are sufficient physical disks available. Storage Spaces provides a software-defined storage solution that while utilizing local storage, provides highly available and scalable storage solutions.

I'm going to walk you through Storage Spaces by focusing on its incarnation in Windows Server 2012, how it changed in Windows Server 2012 R2, and then what it has become in Windows Server 2016. It's useful to explore the capabilities in each version of Windows Server and to see how Storage Spaces has evolved, in order to help better understand it.

The first step is to create a *storage pool*, which is a selection of one or more physical disks that are then pooled together and can be used by the Storage Spaces technology. Supported disk types in a storage pool are USB-, SATA-, and SAS-connected disks. These disks are just standard disks, JBOD, such as HDD, SSDs, and even NVMe for the best performance. With no hardware high availability such as RAID behind the scenes, Storage Spaces takes care of fault tolerance. The use of USB-connected drives is great on the desktop side, while servers focus on SATA- and SAS-connected drives. Additionally, shared SAS is fully supported, which means a disk enclosure could be used that is then connected to numerous hosts in a cluster, and the storage space created on those shared SAS drives is available to all nodes in the cluster and can be used as part of Cluster Shared Volumes. This allows a cluster of Hyper-V hosts to use a clustered storage space as the storage for virtual machines. If an external disk enclosure is used, Storage Spaces supports the SES protocol, which enables failure indications on the external storage if available, such as a bad disk LED in the event Storage Spaces detects a problem with a physical disk. Although many storage enclosures work with clustered storage spaces, Microsoft does have several certified enclosures for Windows Server 2012, which are documented at the Windows Server Catalog.

Other technologies, like BitLocker, can also be used with Storage Spaces. When a new storage pool is created, the disks that are added to the storage pool will disappear from the Disk Management tool because they are now virtualized and used exclusively by the Storage Spaces technology. The disks' state can be seen through the Storage Pools view within File and Storage Services in Server Manager.

Using Storage Spaces

To create a storage pool, follow these steps:

1. From the Tasks menu, choose New Storage Pool, which launches the New Storage Pool Wizard.

2. Enter a name for the new storage pool and an optional description, and then click Next.

3. On the next screen, select the physical disks that are available to be added to the new pool and their allocation. The default allocation for disks is Data Store, to be used as part of the virtual disks created, but can also be reserved for Hot Spare purposes. Click Next.

4. Once the confirmation is displayed, click Create to create the storage pool.

A storage pool is now available, and the next step is to create virtual disks within the storage pool, which can then have volumes created on them to be used by the operating system. The nomenclature is unfortunate here. While the term *virtual disk* is used by Storage Spaces, it is not a virtual hard disk of any kind and does not leverage VHD or VHDX. In this context, a virtual disk is simply an object created within a storage pool that is seen as a disk by the operating system, which writes directly to blocks within the storage pool.

Storage Spaces introduced a feature that was previously available only when using external storage solutions such as SANs and NAS devices: the capability to thin-provision storage. During the creation of a virtual disk, the option is available to create the new virtual disk as fixed (which means that all space for the size of the virtual disk is allocated at creation time) or thin (which means that space is taken from the pool only as needed). Using a thin-provisioned disk allows a virtual disk to be created far larger than the actual storage available. This allows you to create a large volume initially without having to preallocate physical storage.

Now, this does not mean that you can store more data in the thinly provisioned disk than is allocated to the pool, but that typically volumes fill up over time. I may create a 10TB thin disk that initially has only1TB of physical storage associated with it, but as the amount of data increases and approaches 1TB, I would add another 1TB of physical storage to the pool just by adding more disks. As it approaches 2TB, I add another 1TB of storage by adding more disks, and so on. As long as I add physical disks before it fills, there is no issue. Alerts will be generated, notifying me that a storage pool is reaching the threshold, giving me time to add the required storage. When you create a virtual disk, all you need to know is which storage pool you'll use to create the disk. No knowledge of physical disks is required or even openly available. The point of Storage Spaces is this abstraction to create virtual disks as needed to suit your requirements. To create a virtual disk, perform the following steps:

1. Select a storage pool in which to create a new virtual disk, and in the Virtual Disks section, select the New Virtual Disk task.

2. Confirm that the correct server and storage pool is selected in the Storage Pool selection page of the wizard, and click Next.

3. Give a name and optional description for the new virtual disk, and then click Next.

4. Select the storage layout. The options are Simple (no data redundancy and data striped over many disks), Mirrored (data duplicated to additional disks), and Parity (spreads data over multiple disks like Simple but adds parity data so that in the event of a disk loss, no data is lost). Prior to Storage Spaces, these layouts would have been referred to as RAID-0, RAID-1, and RAID-5, respectively, but that nomenclature is not used with Storage Spaces layouts because of differences in implementation.

Make the selection and click Next, as shown in Figure 4.3. A three-way mirror is possible in Windows Server 2012 and beyond, but it must be configured using PowerShell instead of the graphical interface.

FIGURE 4.3
Creating a new virtual disk within a storage space

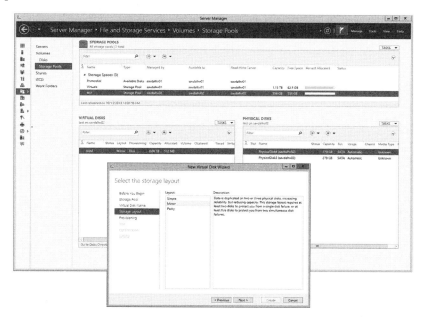

5. Choose a provisioning type of Thin or Fixed, and click Next.

6. Specify a size. Remember, if you selected Thin, you can now select a size larger than the physical free space available. Click Next.

7. A confirmation of options is displayed. Confirm them, and click Create.

Once the virtual disk is created, it will be available within Server Manager and the Disk Management MMC to create volumes and be formatted with a filesystem. The amount of space used from a pool can be seen in Server Manager or, if you're using a client, in the Storage Spaces Control Panel applet.

PERFORMANCE AND STORAGE SPACES

One concern I always had when using software RAID prior to Windows Server 2012 was performance. Any parity calculation had to use the processor, which used up processor cycles and typically was not optimal compared to a hardware RAID solution. This is still a concern with Storage Spaces.

continues

continued

Fundamentally, Storage Spaces is a software-implemented storage solution. When using any kind of parity virtual disk, it is the operating system, specifically the processor, that has to calculate the parity information. Using a parity resiliency will utilize additional processor resources. In my experience, parity utilizes only a single processor core and therefore can quickly become a bottleneck if you are performing many disk writes, making it unsuitable for some workloads. Therefore, my advice is as follows:

◆ Use mirroring for workloads requiring high performance.

◆ Use parity for archival and media-streaming purposes that don't require performance-critical write operations.

Windows Server 2012 R2 Storage Space Changes

Windows Server 2012 R2 Storage Spaces has several improvements. One is the capability to have dual-parity spaces, which allows up to two copies of parity information instead of one. That provides additional resiliency (dual parity needs to be configured using PowerShell and is not exposed in Server Manager), support for parity spaces in cluster scenarios, and much faster rebuild in the event of a failure. The missing information is rebuilt to many disks in the storage pool instead of rebuilding everything to a single disk, which would limit the speed of resolution to the IOPS possible by a single disk.

There was a bigger change in Windows Server 2012 R2 Storage Spaces that can open up new levels of performance: a differentiation between traditional spinning hard disk drives (HDDs) and solid-state drives (SSDs). In a Windows Server 2012 R2 storage space, you can create different tiers of storage, an HDD tier and an SSD tier. The Storage Spaces technology moves the most-used blocks of a file from the HDD tier into the SSD tier, giving the highest levels of performance. Additionally, the SSD tier can be leveraged for a write-back cache. As writes occur, they are written into the SSD tier initially, which is very fast, and then lazily written to the HDD tier for long-term storage. This tiering model is shown in Figure 4.4.

FIGURE 4.4
Storage Spaces architecture showing a hot block moving from the HDD tier to the SSD tier

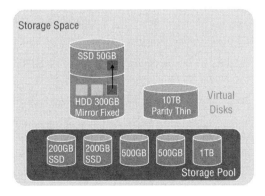

When you use tiering, you must have a sufficient number of disks from each tier to meet the data-resiliency options. For example, if mirroring is selected for a virtual disk, at least two disks need to be available with enough space in the HDD tier and in the SSD tier. The same applies for the write-back cache. Storage Spaces will not allow a drop-in resiliency.

To utilize tiering and the write-back cache, you can use PowerShell, which gives granular control (although by default a 1GB write-back cache is created on all new virtual disks if sufficient SSD space and disks are available in the pool), or Server Manager for a simpler experience but with less granularity in the configuration. In the following PowerShell commands, I create a storage space from four physical disks, two HDDs and two SSDs, and then create a virtual disk and create a volume:

```
#List all disks that can be pooled and output in table format (format-table)
Get-PhysicalDisk -CanPool $True | `
ft FriendlyName,OperationalStatus,Size,MediaType

#Store all physical disks that can be pooled into a variable, $pd
$pd = (Get-PhysicalDisk -CanPool $True | Where MediaType -NE UnSpecified)
#Create a new Storage Pool using the disks in variable $pd
#with a name of My Storage Pool
New-StoragePool -PhysicalDisks $pd `
-StorageSubSystemFriendlyName "Storage Spaces*" `
-FriendlyName "My Storage Pool"
#View the disks in the Storage Pool just created
Get-StoragePool -FriendlyName "My Storage Pool" | `
Get-PhysicalDisk | Select FriendlyName, MediaType

#Create two tiers in the Storage Pool created.
#One for SSD disks and one for HDD disks
$ssd_Tier = New-StorageTier -StoragePoolFriendlyName "My Storage Pool" `
-FriendlyName SSD_Tier -MediaType SSD
$hdd_Tier = New-StorageTier -StoragePoolFriendlyName "My Storage Pool" `
-FriendlyName HDD_Tier -MediaType HDD

#Create a new virtual disk in the pool with a name of TieredSpace
#using the SSD (50GB) and HDD (300GB) tiers
$vd1 = New-VirtualDisk -StoragePoolFriendlyName "My Storage Pool" `
-FriendlyName TieredSpace -StorageTiers @($ssd_tier, $hdd_tier) `
-StorageTierSizes @(50GB, 300GB) -ResiliencySettingName Mirror `
-WriteCacheSize 1GB
#cannot also specify -size if using tiers and also
#cannot use provisioning type, e.g. Thin
```

Normally, the hot blocks are detected over time and moved into the SSD tier as part of a nightly optimization job at 1:00 a.m. However, certain files can be pinned to the SSD tier, which will keep them there permanently. To pin a file to the SSD tier and then force a tier optimization, use the following commands:

```
Set-FileStorageTier -FilePath M:\Important\test.vhd `
-DesiredStorageTier ($vd1 | Get-StorageTier -MediaType SSD)
Optimize-Volume -DriveLetter M -TierOptimize
```

With Storage Spaces technology, you can create flexible and high-performing storage solutions using direct-attached disks, which can be useful in various scenarios and architectures. I walk through Storage Spaces in a video:

www.youtube.com/watch?v=x8KlY-aP9oE&feature=share&list=UUpIn7ox7j7bH_OFj7tYouOQ

The use of tiering is a great feature for virtualization and will help you get the highest overall performance without having to use high-end storage for the entire storage solution.

Windows Server 2016 Storage Space Changes

Windows Server 2016 continues the evolution of Storage Spaces and utilizes the technology to enable a completely new way to use direct-attached storage: as cluster storage in the form of Cluster Shared Volumes. Windows Server 2016 also differentiates between SSDs (as comparatively lower cost flash storage) and NVMe SSDs (as higher performing but higher cost). Storage Spaces utilizes the different types of flash storage automatically, in the most optimal manner, without any manual configuration of the tiers. For example, when creating a regular storage space through Server Manager in Windows Server 2016, an HDD and SSD tier are automatically created as a standard tier and faster tier, respectively. When using Storage Spaces Direct, there is even more granularity (as I cover in more detail in the following "Storage Spaces Direct" section). Additionally, in Windows Server 2016, the additional resiliency options are now part of the wizard in Server Manager, as shown in Figure 4.5.

FIGURE 4.5
Selecting the resiliency for a 2016 virtual disk

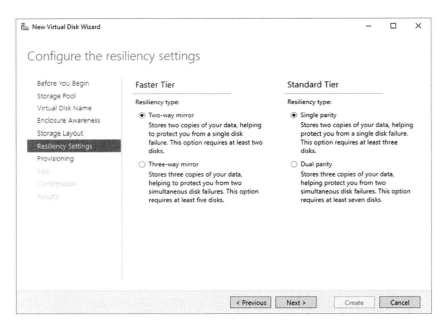

While the greatest focus for Windows Server 2016 Storage Spaces relates to Storage Spaces Direct, there are other changes outside the improved management through Server Manager:

◆ The optimization of data between the tiers runs more frequently. In Windows Server 2012 R2, the optimization runs once a day. In Windows Server 2016, it runs every four hours, which is visible via the Storage Tiers Optimization scheduled job trigger properties. This helps the optimization better keep up with workload drift. Additionally, the optimizer uses prioritization to move the most important data first (meaning biggest benefit to move between tiers), in case it cannot complete full optimization in the time allotted.

◆ A new storage health service provides a single point of monitoring for all components related to Storage Spaces that also automates the recovery processes.

Note that Storage Spaces works the same as Windows Server 2012 R2 in terms of supporting HDD and SSD as the tiers. It is possible to use NVMe with regular Storage Spaces (but not clustered Storage Spaces, since there is no way to enable shared access to the PCI Express bus outside of Storage Spaces Direct). However, the NVMe drives would be treated as one tier, and the other drives as the second tier. For example, NVMe may make up the performance tier, while SSD makes up the capacity tier. However, you can't have a third tier if you have HDDs as well, which is possible in Storage Spaces Direct; think hottest, hot, and cold data segregation with Storage Spaces Direct, but just hot and cold with regular Storage Spaces. Additionally, NTFS is still the focus filesystem for Storage Spaces in Windows Server 2016, outside of Storage Spaces Direct.

STORAGE SPACES DIRECT

I've mentioned Storage Spaces Direct (S2D) a lot so far because it's a game changer for storage with Windows Server 2016. Storage Spaces Direct builds on the idea of more efficiently using direct-attached storage and extends this to cluster scenarios with a pure software-defined storage solution. Storage Spaces Direct uses the local storage in servers, which could be internal disks or in an external storage enclosure connected via SAS HBA or SATA, and aggregates the storage to make it available as a Cluster Shared Volume providing high availability for the data and providing a scalable solution. Storage Spaces Direct uses industry-standard hardware and the existing Ethernet or RDMA network as the storage fabric for the internal replication and coordination of aggregating the local disks to a cluster volume over SMB 3. RDMA is recommended for the network connectivity because of its low server overhead and higher bandwidth connections compared to regular Ethernet, which is enabled automatically when present via SMB Direct. Figure 4.6 shows a high-level view of utilizing storage with Storage Spaces Direct.

FIGURE 4.6
High-level view of Storage Spaces Direct utilizing SMB 3 to aggregate local storage for nodes in a cluster

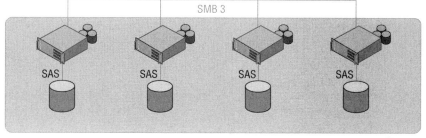

Storage Spaces Direct is used in two models: hyperconverged and converged. In a *hyperconverged model*, both the compute and storage resources are the same nodes in the same cluster; that is, the same nodes that have the local storage used by Storage Spaces Direct are also hosting the VMs that use that storage. In this model, the compute and storage scale together and are managed together. If more storage is needed, you have to add nodes, which would also increase your compute scale even if this is not required, and vice versa. Because of this tight coupling of scale, the hyperconverged deployment model tends to be used in small-to-medium sized deployments. In the *converged model*, one cluster is used for the storage services and offers the CSVs via Scale-out File Servers (SoFS), and a separate cluster is used for Hyper-V and the storage is accessed using SMB 3. This deployment model is used for larger environments, because the compute and storage can scale separately in addition to being managed separately.

Figure 4.7 shows the two deployment choices. Typically, you should have a minimum of four nodes to use parity resiliency and/or multiresiliency options. However, a three-node cluster and two-node cluster are possible with mirror resiliency providing resiliency from a single-node failure and one or two disk failures, depending on whether two-copy or three-copy mirroring is used, respectively.

FIGURE 4.7
The two types of deployment model for Storage Spaces Direct

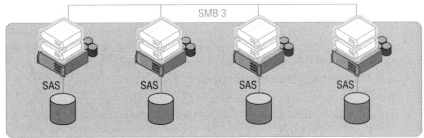

Hyperconverged

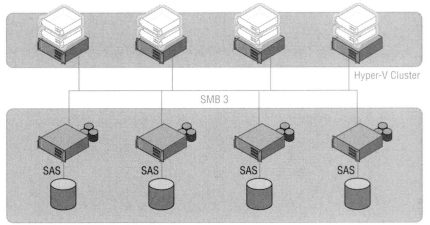

Converged

The network provides the bus over which the data is replicated to the multiple targets. The data is sent to the nodes synchronously and written to durable storage before the write is acknowledged to the application, so a high-speed and reliable network between nodes is critical. 10Gbps should be considered the minimum speed available between nodes, with preferably RDMA network connectivity. There is no hard block from a network less than 10Gbps, but performance would suffer and not be suitable for production. When thinking of latency between the nodes, you should be thinking in terms of nanoseconds, not milliseconds.

Behind the scenes, Storage Spaces Direct works via the Software Storage Bus (SSB), which brings together all of the local storage across the cluster and makes it behave as if it's attached to every node in the cluster. This is achieved through ClusPort and ClusBflt, which run on each node in the cluster. ClusBflt acts as a target that provides access to its local storage via virtual disks and virtual enclosures, while ClusPort acts as an initiator (a virtual HBA) connecting to the ClusBflt running on each node and therefore enabling the access to the storage. Through this target-initiator relationship, every node can access every disk by using SMB 3 as the storage fabric with a new block-mode transfer feature which is interesting, as SMB is normally a file-based protocol, although the *B* in *SMB* stands for *block*. Additionally, a fairness algorithm is utilized to ensure that local application I/O has priority over system requests and that all nodes receive fair access to disks. What this means in the real-world is that the VM requests to the storage take precedence over any system activities related to disk maintenance, such as replication. Note that at times when recovery is required (for example, when a disk has failed), the SSB will allocate up to 20 percent of resources to enable forward progress on restoring data resiliency if the VMs are attempting to use all of the available storage resources. If the VMs are not consuming all resources, the SSB will use as much resources as possible to restore normal levels of resiliency and performance. There is also an I/O blender that streamlines I/O streams by derandomizing random I/Os into a sequential I/O pattern when using HDDs, which normally have a seek penalty.

All of this happens underneath the existing Storage Spaces SpacePort functionality, which enables the creation of pools on which the virtual disks are created, then the filesystem, Cluster Shared Volumes, and so on. The preferred filesystem used is CSVFS (Cluster Shared Volume File System) on ReFS. It is also possible to use CSVFS on NTFS; although functionality is lost, it would enable the use of deduplication, which is not possible on ReFS. The full picture can be seen in Figure 4.8, which highlights the parts that are regular Storage Spaces and the parts that are specific to Storage Spaces Direct; they all work together to deliver the complete Storage Spaces Direct feature. Note that the virtual disk is high up in the stack, which is where resiliency is configured. Then, based on resiliency requirements, data is stored multiple times across disks in nodes via ClusPort.

FIGURE 4.8
Storage Spaces Direct workings under the hood

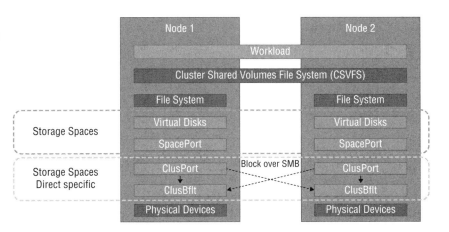

The manual configuration of tiers is not used with Storage Spaces Direct, and instead the new Software Bus Cache (SBC) that is part of the new SSB (which is the foundation of Storage Spaces Direct) performs automatic storage caching and tiering configuration. For example, if you have a storage solution with NVMe, SSDs, and HDDs, the NVMe disks will be used for caching the hottest data, the SSDs for hot data, and the HDDs for the cold data (everything else). The NVMe disks provide a read cache for the hottest data as well as providing the initial target for writes, enabling high performance; then data is destaged to SSD/HDD capacity devices as needed. By default, the cache works as follows:

- All writes up to 256KB are cached.

- Reads of 64KB or less are cached on first miss (that is, they're not in the cache already).

- Reads larger than 64KB are cached on second miss within a 10-minute interval.

- Sequential reads larger than 32KB are not cached.

- A write cache is provided only in all flash systems (since read caching with NVMe for SSDs would not provide much benefit).

Table 4.1 provides a full list of caching and capacity utilization with Storage Spaces Direct. As you can see, the highest-performance storage is used for caching, while the lower-performing storage is used for capacity. In a system with only one type of storage, the SBC is disabled. Microsoft has a great article that walks through the various combinations in detail:

```
https://blogs.technet.microsoft.com/filecab/2016/04/28/s2dtp5nvmessdhdd/
```

TABLE 4.1:   Storage Usage with Storage Spaces Direct

STORAGE CONFIGURATION	CACHING DEVICES	CAPACITY DEVICES	CACHING BEHAVIOR
SATA SSD + SATA HDD	All SATA SSD	All SATA HDD	Read + Write
NVMe SSD + SATA HDD	All NVMe SSD	All SATA HDD	Read + Write
NVMe SSD + SATA SSD	All NVMe SSD	All SATA SSD	Write only
NVMe SSD + SATA SSD + SATA HDD	All NVMe SSD	All SATA SSD and SATA HDD	Write only for SATA SSD and Read + Write for SATA HDD

```
https://technet.microsoft.com/en-us/library/mt651665.aspx
```

Behind the scenes, the disks used for the SBC have a special partition created on them that consumes all of the space except for 32GB, which is saved for storage pool and virtual disk Metadata. Also note that the SBC uses 5GB of memory per 1TB of caching devices in the node, which means that it is important to plan resource utilization accordingly, especially in hyperconverged scenarios where the storage is hosted by the same nodes hosting virtual machines. A key point is that the SBC is agnostic to storage pools and disks; it is a resource for the node and used across the various storage pools and disks present on a system and not tied to any specific pool or disk.

Resiliency of data stored in the cache is provided by virtue of the fact that the SBC is at a node level and sits below the virtual disk (see Figure 4.8), which is what defines the required resiliency. Writes are distributed based on the resiliency to the required number of nodes; for example, the write would be sent to three nodes, and then on each of those nodes, the write would be persisted to the cache and then destaged to the hot and cold tiers as required. No additional local resiliency is required on the cache storage, as the resiliency is defined at the virtual disk level and achieved through the multiple copies over multiple nodes. If a cache device has an error, the write is still available on other nodes in the cluster, which will be used to rehydrate the data on the node that experienced the problem. This is the same as for the hot and cold tiers; because the data is stored multiple times across disks in different nodes, resiliency is not at a single node level but is based on the resiliency defined for the virtual disk.

The automatic nature of using disks does not stop at the storage pool. The virtual disks created in the pool can use a mixture of resiliency types to offer a blend of best performance and capacity. Traditionally, there are two types of resiliency:

Mirror   This provides the best performance. However, it is the least efficient, as all data is duplicated multiple times (for example, a three-way mirror has three copies of the data, which means that only 33 percent of the disk footprint is usable for storage).

Parity   This provides the most capacity at the expense of performance, as computations must be performed to calculate parity values. With dual-parity, 50 percent of the disk footprint is used for data storage. (LRC erasure coding is used, which is the same scheme used for Azure Storage. Details can be found at `http://research.microsoft.com/en-us/um/people/chengh/papers/LRC12.pdf`.)

Windows Server 2016 introduces mixed-resiliency virtual disks, which as the name suggests, use a mix of mirroring and parity to provide high performance (mirroring) for the hot data, and high capacity (parity) for the cold data. Mixed-resiliency virtual disks are enabled through a combination of Storage Spaces and ReFS. To use a mixed-resiliency disk, you must create a virtual disk with storage in both a mirror tier and a parity tier. ReFS then provides the real-time tiering capability, which works as follows:

1. Data is written to the disk, and those writes always go to the mirror (performance) tier. Note that the Storage Bus Cache is used for the first write, and the source of the write is acknowledged. If the data is an update to existing data in the parity tier, the existing data in the parity tier is invalidated and the data is written to the mirror tier.

2. Data is rotated to the parity (capacity) tier as required, freeing up space in the mirror tier. (Note that this data movement bypasses the cache to avoid polluting the cache with data that does not belong.)

Using this approach provides the capacity benefits of parity while not incurring the performance penalty associated with it, since the writes are performed to the high-performance mirror tier and then moved to the parity tier in the background without impacting workload performance. This is different from the tiering that occurs in regular Storage Spaces, which is a scheduled operation to move hot and cold data. In Windows Server 2016 with mixed-resiliency disks, this is an inline tiering operation happening in real time.

REFS AND WINDOWS SERVER 2016

ReFS was introduced in Windows Server 2012 and was engineered as a new filesystem that used a completely new way of storing data on disk while exposing familiar APIs for interaction consistent with NTFS. This allowed ReFS to be used by workloads without rewriting them. Fundamentally, ReFS focused on maintaining a high level of data availability and reliability, including self-healing when used in conjunction with technologies like Storage Spaces, where alternate copies of data are

continues

continued

available and can be used to replace corrupt copies that were automatically detected. ReFS enabled online backup and repair of its critical Metadata. It was common to use ReFS for long-term archival data requiring high levels of resiliency. When using ReFS, you should use it on Storage Spaces for the best resiliency possible. However, using Storage Spaces does not imply that you need to use ReFS.

In Windows Server 2012 and Windows Server 2012 R2, ReFS was blocked as a storage media for Hyper-V because its integrity stream feature (which enabled the healing ability) caused performance problems with Hyper-V workloads. In Windows Server 2016, this block has been removed, as the integrity stream performance has been improved and is disabled by default anyway.

Why use ReFS beyond resiliency? NTFS was designed a long time ago, when disks were much smaller. It focused all of its effort on blocks on disk, which means that when you deal with large numbers of blocks, even on superfast storage, the operations still take a long time. ReFS shifts this focus to thinking about Metadata manipulation before block manipulation, where possible. For example, when a new fixed VHD file is created on NTFS, all of the blocks are zeroed on disk, requiring huge amounts of zeroing I/O. With ReFS, this zeroing I/O is completely eliminated. There is no loss of security related to reading existing data on disk. With ReFS, it is not possible to read from noninitialized clusters on disks, which means that even though the extents backing the file have been preallocated, they cannot be read from disk unless they have first been written to. The same benefit applies to extending an existing VHD. The same Metadata manipulation applies when merging differencing disks into the parent; for example, when merging a checkpoint. Instead of copying the blocks from the differencing disk into the parent, the Metadata of the parent is updated to point to the existing blocks on disk to which the differencing disk had written. Checkpoints are now used for backups with Hyper-V in Windows Server 2016, which means that backup would also benefit. These changes make the mentioned VHD operations hundreds, if not thousands, of times faster than with NTFS, meaning faster provisioning and less I/O on the underlying storage.

Does this mean that ReFS is everywhere in Windows Server 2016? At the time of this writing, the answer is no, although this could certainly change. Currently, ReFS cannot be the Windows boot volume, it does not support the deduplication feature, and its broad use has not been a focus for Microsoft. The focus for ReFS usage is with Storage Spaces Direct and where high levels of resiliency are required. Outside of those scenarios, NTFS is still the recommended filesystem. Nonetheless, when you consider the benefits it brings to Hyper-V and VHD files, it is certainly worth evaluating beyond just Storage Spaces Direct, provided you do not need data deduplication. Additionally, when ReFS is used with Cluster Shared Volumes, the CSV will run in filesystem redirected mode, which means all I/O is sent over the cluster network to the coordinator node. In NTFS, all nodes can perform Direct I/O to the shared storage. This is a big reason to carry on using NTFS for CSV, except for Storage Spaces Direct, which does not have shared storage anyway, and all access is already redirected. What Microsoft has is a maturing filesystem that is now in its third version with Windows Server 2016, and that is ready for the big time when a need requires its particular talents, such as Storage Spaces Direct.

Using Storage Spaces Direct is simple, but it must be enabled at a cluster level, and once it's enabled, you will not be able to use clustered Storage Spaces. Management is done using PowerShell or System Center Virtual Machine 2016. To enable Storage Spaces Direct, use the following command:

```
Enable-ClusterS2D [-S2DPoolFriendlyName <pool name>]
```

This command not only enables the feature but also adds all usable storage to a new Storage Spaces Direct pool with tiers based on media type, and uses the highest performing storage for the cache when more than one type of storage is present. You can specify a name for the pool if the default nomenclature of S2D on <cluster name> is not desirable.

If you have different types of SSD (as opposed to NVMe and SSD, which will automatically be used in the best way) and you want to specify the model of device that should be used for caching, you can add this to the Enable-ClusterS2D command via the –S2DCacheDeviceModel "<device model name>" parameter. By default, tiers are created with the names of Capacity and Performance, and the cache will use the highest performing storage when you have more than one type of storage available. Capacity uses parity resiliency, and Performance uses mirror resiliency. In both cases, you have two-disk redundancy. Details of the storage pool and tiers created can be seen with the following PowerShell:

```
Get-StoragePool <name, e.g. S2D* if default> | FT FriendlyName, `
FaultDomainAwarenessDefault, OperationalStatus, HealthStatus `
-autosize
Get-StorageTier | FT FriendlyName, ResiliencySettingName, MediaType, `
PhysicalDiskRedundancy -autosize[
```

Once enabled, create a volume. For example:

```
New-Volume -StoragePoolFriendlyName "<pool name>" `
-FriendlyName <VirtualDiskName> ` -FileSystem CSVFS_ReFS `
-StorageTierfriendlyNames Capacity,Performance `
-StorageTierSizes <capacity tier size, e.g. 500GB>, <performance tier
  size, e.g. 100GB>
```

Storage Spaces Direct is available only in the Datacenter SKU of Windows Server 2016, whereas regular Storage Spaces is still available in the Standard SKU.

Storage Replica

Although not a feature of Storage Spaces nor Hyper-V specific, *Storage Replica* is a Windows Server storage feature that brings great value to Hyper-V environments. Storage Spaces Direct provides resilient, highly available storage within a datacenter where the nodes have fast, low-latency connectivity.

Disk or node failure, however, is only one type of disaster. Consider the many natural disasters in recent years that have brought widespread flooding to many areas. Even organizations with well-architected datacenters with redundant generators have suffered multiday outages as a result of these natural disasters. For this reason, many organizations implement disaster-recovery facilities and plans that are used when an entire facility is compromised. If you need to fail your workloads over to another datacenter that is at least 50 miles away (likely more) to ensure that it's not impacted by the same disaster that impacted your primary datacenter, you need a way to have your workloads and data replicated.

Numerous replication solutions can operate at different levels, such as application replication (SQL Server AlwaysOn, Active Directory multimaster replication), hypervisor replication (Hyper-V Replica), in-OS replication (Azure Site Recovery for VMware or physical systems), and storage replication (traditionally provided by SAN vendors or third parties). Typically, the best solution is the one that runs at the application level; because the application is aware of the replication, the failover and can take appropriate steps. Many times, however, this is not available or practical. This is a Hyper-V book, but at times Hyper-V Replica may not meet your requirements either, because it is asynchronous and the architecture calls for a stretched cluster with automatic failover, or perhaps the 30-second minimum interval is too long. Replicating at the storage level provides a solution that works for any workload, and this is now a feature of Windows Server 2016 with Storage Replica.

Storage Replica supports both synchronous and asynchronous block-level replication. *Synchronous* means that data is written and persisted to both the source and replica before being acknowledged to the requesting application. *Asynchronous* means that writes are acknowledged to the requesting application when written to the source location, and then in the background those writes are sent to the replica, where they are persisted. With synchronous, there is no risk of data loss, but performance may be impacted, depending on the latency writing to the replica if it's in a different location. With asynchronous, there is no performance impact, but there is some risk of data loss in unplanned scenarios.

Storage Replica utilizes SMB 3.1.1 as the transport for the data being replicated. It is enabled at a volume level, and because it is block based, it does not care about the filesystem used, whether data is BitLocker protected, or whether files are locked. Storage Replica is completely agnostic to the actual storage and supports any fixed-disk storage, any storage fabric, shared cluster storage, and even Storage Spaces Direct storage, which opens up some interesting solutions that I discuss later in this chapter. Removable devices are not supported, and disks must use GPT instead of MBR. With Storage Replica, the source for the replica is fully accessible while the replica is offline and can be used only when a failover is performed, at which point the replication direction is reversed (if possible). Replication is one to one, and you cannot replicate a replica. Because SMB is used for the replication, all of the performance and scalability features of SMB are available, including SMB Multichannel, SMB Direct (RDMA), encryption, and signing.

Storage Replica can be used in various scenarios because of the replication flexibility, including replicating between floors, between buildings, between cities, and even between continents. The longer the distance and the longer the latency, the more likely you will use asynchronous replication instead of synchronous. In all of the scenarios, both asynchronous and synchronous can be used for the replication, but where possible, synchronous is preferred to remove the risk of data loss.

Figure 4.9 shows the key scenarios that leverage Storage Replica. The first is a stretch cluster with a physical separation between the two partitions of the cluster. Here Storage Replica is used to replicate the cluster storage from one partition of the cluster to cluster storage in the other partition, enabling asymmetric storage configurations. The storage could be Cluster Shared Volumes or role-assigned physical disk resources (PDRs). In this model, because it is a single cluster, automatic failover can be performed, and often synchronous is used to eliminate data risk. However, if you are willing to risk a small amount of data, asymmetric is also available. When used in this way, it helps make the cluster more disaster resilient, as the cluster can be expanded beyond a single location. This mode is primarily targeted at Hyper-V workloads and general-use file servers.

The next scenario is cluster to cluster. With cluster to cluster, you must disable automatic failover and instead fail over manually or through some kind of orchestration solution. Once again, synchronous and asynchronous are supported.

The final scenario is outside of a cluster, and simply replicating between two servers using either asynchronous or synchronous. The failover must be performed manually by using PowerShell or Remote Server Management Tools.

FIGURE 4.9
Storage Replica use
scenarios

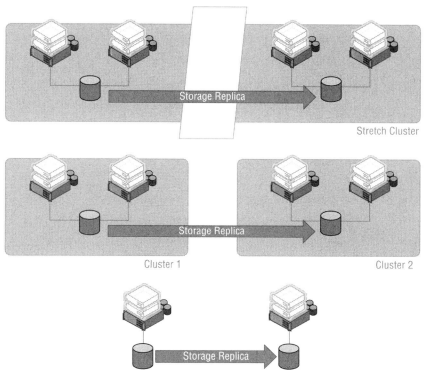

There is a fourth, unspoken scenario, discussed only in dark corners: replicating storage within the same server. However, this is not a focus for Windows Server 2016 and I won't mention it again.

Behind the scenes, Storage Replica is a brand-new technology. It is not DFSR (Distributed File System Replication) v2, and because it is replicating blocks, the filesystem could be CSVFS, NTFS, or ReFS. Storage Replica sits underneath the filesystem, as shown in Figure 4.10, which is a slightly updated version of Figure 4.8.

FIGURE 4.10
Storage Replica
placement in the
filesystem stack

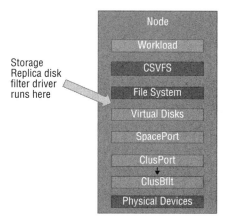

The way that Storage Replica works is through log files, and not directly to the final storage, as shown in Figure 4.11. With Storage Replica, both the source and destination have a log file that is the initial target for all writes. With synchronous replication, it works as follows:

1. The write originates from an application.

2. The write is hardened to the log file on the source and sent to the replica server.

3. The write is hardened to the log file on the destination (replica) server.

4. The write is acknowledged to the source server.

5. The write is acknowledged to the originating application now that it has been persisted to both servers.

6. At some point in the future, the write is lazily written from the log to the data disk (although this is often within milliseconds).

FIGURE 4.11
Storage Replica
synchronous replica-
tion workings

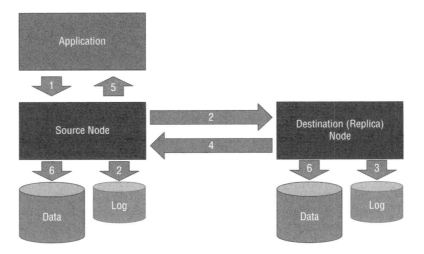

The process is basically the same for asynchronous, except that the write is acknowledged to the application as soon as it is persisted to the local source log file, and then as soon as possible the write is replicated to the destination server, where it is written to the replica log file. Then the log file data is persisted to the data disk at some point in the future. Note that even though this is asynchronous, Storage Replica does not batch up the I/Os and sends them as fast as it can, typically sub-second. Even when running in asynchronous mode, data loss would be minimal, if any, during an unplanned disaster.

Like Storage Spaces Direct, Storage Replica is easy to get up and running, whatever the method you use for management, and like Storage Spaces Direct, this feature is available only in the Datacenter SKU. To check whether a configuration is suitable for Storage Replica, run the Test-SRTopology cmdlet with the source and destination server along with the disks that will be used for both data and logs. This will check every aspect of the environment, including ports, bandwidth, and IOPS. It outputs an easy-to-read HTML report that includes how long initial synchronization will take.

To set up Storage Replica using PowerShell, use the `New-SRPartnership` cmdlet with the same parameters as `Test-SRTopology`. For example:

```
New-SRPartnership -SourceComputerName <server> -SourceRGName <name> `
-SourceVolumeName <drive>: -SourceLogVolumeName <drive>: `
-DestinationComputerName <server> -DestinationRGName <name> `
-DestinationVolumeName <drive>: -DestinationLogVolumeName <drive>: `
-LogSizeInBytes <size, 8GB by default> `
[-ReplicationMode <Asynchronous, Synchronous is the default>]
```

Storage Spaces Direct and Storage Replica Together

Storage Spaces Direct requires low latency, and it is based around nodes being in the same datacenter. However, what if you want to use direct-attached storage in a stretched cluster scenario? The solution is to combine Storage Spaces Direct and Storage Replica while utilizing new site-awareness available in the Windows Server 2016 cluster. This is shown in Figure 4.12: The cluster is divided into two sites, and in each site a site-scoped pool is created via Storage Spaces Direct; a virtual disk is created, and that virtual disk is then replicated using Storage Replica to a virtual disk created on a storage pool on the other side.

FIGURE 4.12
Storage Replica
working with Storage
Spaces Direct

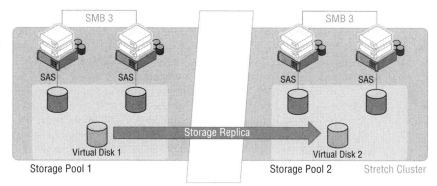

Server Message Block Usage

While Server Message Block (SMB) has been available in Windows for a long time, its usage has been limited to basic file-sharing scenarios, such as users accessing their home drives or a file share containing archived data. Hyper-V had long had the requirement of having block-level access to its storage; that is, the host mounted the volumes that contained the virtual machines, which could be direct-attached or connected via mediums such as iSCSI or Fibre Channel. However, this was a challenge for many organizations that were used to using file-level protocols with virtualization. Specifically, VMware supported NFS for virtual machine storage, which was available in many NAS solutions that typically are much cheaper than SAN solutions and are a good fit for many environments.

Windows Server 2012 invested greatly in SMB to make it an enterprise-ready solution suitable for storing virtual machines and other enterprise workloads, such as SQL Server databases. SMB 3 introduced many new features and performance improvements to make it a realistic choice for virtualization storage.

SMB Technologies

I previously talked about SMB being used to store user documents, and now with SMB 3, it will be used to store mission-critical virtual machines. This requires a big shift in resiliency and failover technologies.

When the user is editing a PowerPoint document from an SMB share, portions of the document are cached locally, and occasionally the user clicks Save. If the SMB file server experiences a problem—for example, if it reboots or if it's clustered and the file share is moved to another node in the cluster—the user would lose the handle and lock to the file, but that really does not have any impact. The next time the user clicks Save, everything is reestablished, and no harm is done.

Now consider Hyper-V storing a virtual machine on an SMB file share that experiences a problem, and the file share moves to another node in the cluster. First, the Hyper-V box will wait for the TCP time-out before realizing the original connection has gone, which can mean 30 seconds of pause to the VM, but also Hyper-V has now lost its handles and locks on the VHD, which is a major problem. Whereas user documents may be used for a few hours, enterprise services like a virtual machine or database expect handles on files to be available for months without interruption.

SMB Transparent Failover

Typically, for a clustered file service, a single node of the cluster mounts the Logical Unit Number (LUN) containing the filesystem being shared and offers the share to SMB clients. If that node fails, another node in the cluster mounts the LUN and offers the file share, but the SMB client would lose their handles and locks. SMB Transparent Failover provides protection from a node failure, enabling a share to move between nodes in a manner completely transparent to the SMB clients and maintaining any locks and handles that exist as well as the state of the SMB connection.

The state of that SMB connection is maintained over three entities: the SMB client, the SMB server, and the disk itself that holds the data. SMB Transparent Failover ensures that there is enough context to bring back the state of the SMB connection to an alternate node in the event of a node failure, which allows SMB activities to continue without the risk of error.

It's important to understand that even with SMB Transparent Failover, there can still be a pause to I/O, because the LUN still has to be mounted on a new node in the cluster. However, the Failover Clustering team has done a huge amount of work around optimizing the dismount and mount of a LUN to ensure that it never takes more than 25 seconds. This sounds like a lot of time, but realize that is the absolute worst-case scenario, with large numbers of LUNs and tens of thousands of handles. For most common scenarios, the time would be a couple of seconds, and enterprise services such as Hyper-V and SQL Server can handle an I/O operation taking up to 25 seconds without error in that worst possible case.

There is another cause of a possible interruption to I/O and that's the SMB client actually noticing that the SMB server is not available. In a typical planned scenario such as a node rebooting because it's being patched, it will notify any clients who can then take actions. If a node crashes, though, no notification to the client occurs and so the client will sit and wait for TCP time-out before it takes action to reestablish connectivity, which is a waste of resources. Although an SMB client may have no idea that the node it's talking to in the cluster has crashed, the other nodes in the cluster know within a second, thanks to the various IsAlive messages that are sent between the nodes. This knowledge is leveraged by a witness service capability that was first available in Windows Server 2012. The witness server essentially allows another node in the cluster to act as a witness for the SMB client, and if the node the client is talking to fails, the witness node notifies the SMB client straightaway, allowing the client to connect to another node, which minimizes the interruption to service to a couple of seconds. When an SMB client communicates to an SMB server that is part of a cluster, the SMB server will notify the client that other servers are available in the cluster, and the client will automatically ask one of the other servers in the cluster to act as the witness service for the connection.

No manual action is required to take advantage of SMB Transparent Failover or the witness service. When you create a new share on a Windows Server 2012 or above failover cluster, SMB Transparent Failover is enabled automatically.

SMB SCALE-OUT

In the previous section, I explained that there would be a pause in activity because the LUN had to be moved between nodes in the file server cluster, but this delay can be removed. This problem stems from the fact that NTFS is a shared-nothing filesystem and cannot be accessed by multiple operating system instances concurrently without the risk of corruption. This problem was solved with the introduction of Cluster Shared Volumes (CSV) in Windows Server 2008 R2. CSV allowed all nodes in a cluster to read and write to the same set of LUNs simultaneously by using some clever techniques, thus removing the need to dismount and mount LUNs between the nodes.

Windows Server 2012 extended the use of CSV to a specific type of file server, namely the Scale-Out File Server (SoFS) option, which was a new option available in Windows Server 2012 and is targeted for use only when sharing out application data such as SQL Server databases and Hyper-V virtual machines. The traditional style of the general-use file server is still available for nonapplication data, as shown in Figure 4.13. When selecting the option to create an SoFS, you must select a CSV as the storage when shares are subsequently created within the file server; the storage is therefore available to all nodes in the cluster. Because the storage for the share is available to all nodes in the cluster, the file share itself is also hosted by all the nodes in the cluster, which now means SMB client connections are distributed over all the nodes instead of just one. In addition, if a node fails, there is now no work involved in moving the LUNs, offering an even better experience and reducing any interruption in operations to almost zero, which is critical for the application server workloads to which this SoFS is targeted.

FIGURE 4.13
Enabling active-active through the selection of Scale-Out File Server For Application Data

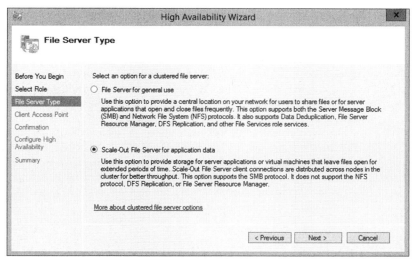

The use of SoFS offers an additional benefit. Typically, when a general-use file server is created as part of the configuration, you have to give the new cluster file server a NetBIOS name and also its own unique IP address, because that IP address has to be hosted by whichever node in the cluster is currently hosting the file server. With SoFS, all nodes in the cluster offer the file service, which means no additional IP addresses are required. The IP addresses of the nodes in the cluster are utilized via the Distributed Network Name (DNN) that is configured.

All of the nodes in the cluster are offering the same file service and therefore share with the SoFS. There is a change in functionality between Windows Server 2012 and Windows Server 2012 R2. In Windows Server 2012, a single SMB client connects to only one of the nodes in the cluster simultaneously, even if establishing multiple connections. When the SMB client initiates connections, it initially gets a list of all the IP addresses for the hosts in the cluster and picks one of them for initiating the SMB session. It then uses only that node, unless that node experiences a problem, in which case it will converse with an alternate node. The exception is that the SMB client does communicate with a second node when leveraging the witness service that I previously discussed. Windows Server 2012 R2 introduced a rebalancing feature that has two components:

◆ The CSV disk ownerships are distributed evenly between all nodes in the cluster, spreading the workload.

◆ SMB connections are rebalanced so that clients are directed to the CSV owner, giving the most optimal connection when used with clustered Storage Spaces. (This rebalancing is not required when using symmetrical storage such as Fibre Channel–connected SANs because every node has equivalent connectivity.)

This means that a single SMB client could now be connected to multiple nodes in a cluster via SMB instead of a single node.

SMB MULTICHANNEL

It is critical to avoid any single points of failure in any solution, and if SMB is being used to access the storage containing virtual machines, there must be resiliency to prevent a single network adapter, network cable, or network switch from failing. In storage fabrics, technologies such as multipath I/O (MPIO) are used to provide multiple paths to storage, and this same idea is now possible with SMB using SMB Multichannel.

SMB Multichannel allows an SMB client to establish multiple connections for a single session, providing protection from a single connection failure as well as adding performance. As with most of the SMB 3 features, no manual steps are required to utilize SMB Multichannel; it happens automatically. Once the initial SMB connection has been established, the SMB client looks for additional paths to the SMB server, and where multiple network connections are present, those additional paths are utilized. This would be apparent if you're monitoring a file-copy operation as initially only a single connection's worth of bandwidth. However, the bandwidth would double as the second connection was established, and the bandwidth aggregated, then the third connection, and so on. In the event that a connection fails, there are still other connections to continue the SMB channel without interruption.

To see whether SMB Multichannel is being utilized from your server, use the Get-SMBConnection PowerShell cmdlet, which will show the SMB connections to an SMB share. In the following example, I see that I have only two connections to my server:

```
PS C:\> get-smbconnection


ServerName        ShareName   UserName      Credential        Dialect NumOpens
----------        ---------   --------      ----------        ------- --------
savdalsofs.sav... Virtuals    NT VIRTUAL ... SAVILLTECH.N...   3.02    4
savdalsofs.sav... Virtuals    SAVILLTECH\... SAVILLTECH.N...   3.02    2
```

If I run the `Get-SmbMultiChannelConnection` cmdlet from the client, it shows me all of the possible paths over which the server can accept connections, as shown in the following output. Note that on the server side, networking uses a NIC team, which means only one IP address, but it can still leverage SMB Multichannel.

```
PS C:\> get-smbmultichannelconnection

Server Name    Selected  Client IP    Server IP    Client  Server
Client RSS     Client RDMA
                                                    Interface         Capable
                                                    Index
-----------    --------  ---------    ---------    ------- --------------
-------------- --------------
savdalsofs.... True      10.7.173.101 10.7.173.20  14      15
   True           False
savdalsofs.... True      10.7.173.23  10.7.173.20  15      15
   True           False
```

To confirm which path is being used between the client and the server, I can look at the TCP connections to the remote port 445, which is used for SMB. This confirms that I am using the two available paths with four connections for each path (which is the default number).

```
PS C:\> Get-NetTCPConnection -RemotePort 445

LocalAddress                      LocalPort RemoteAddress
         RemotePort State      AppliedSetting
------------                      --------- -------------                --
-------- -----      --------------
10.7.173.23                       56368     10.7.173.20
445        Established Datacenter
10.7.173.23                       49826     10.7.173.20
445        Established Datacenter
10.7.173.23                       49825     10.7.173.20
445        Established Datacenter
10.7.173.23                       49824     10.7.173.20
445        Established Datacenter
10.7.173.101                      49823     10.7.173.20
445        Established Datacenter
10.7.173.101                      49822     10.7.173.20
445        Established Datacenter
10.7.173.101                      49821     10.7.173.20
445        Established Datacenter
10.7.173.101                      49820     10.7.173.20
445        Established Datacenter
```

SMB DIRECT

While there are other SMB technologies, such as encryption, Receive Side Scaling, VSS for SMB File Shares, and more, the last feature I want to mention is SMB Direct, which enables the use of RDMA-capable network adapters with SMB. I discussed remote direct memory access (RDMA) in Chapter 3, "Virtual Networking" as it relates to network adapters, and it's equally important to SMB.

With SMB Direct leveraging the RDMA capability of the network adapter, there is almost no utilization of server processor resources. The network adapter is essentially pointed to a block of memory containing the data that needs to be sent to the target, and then the card takes care of sending it by using the fastest possible speed with very low latencies. Behind the scenes, the RDMA network adapter may use iWARP, RDMA over Converged Ethernet (RoCE), or InfiniBand, but that does not matter to the SMB protocol, which just benefits from the RDMA capability.

There is no special requirement to leverage SMB Direct. Like everything else with SMB, if the capability exists, it just happens. Initially, a regular SMB connection is established between the client and server. A list of all possible connections is found, which enables the use of multi-channel, and then the capabilities of the network adapters are found. If it is found that both the sender and receiver support RDMA, then an RDMA connection is established and SMB operations switch from TCP to RDMA, completely transparently.

If you used SMB Direct in Windows Server 2012, you will see a 50 percent performance improvement using the SMB Direct v2 in Windows Server 2012 R2 for small I/O workloads, specifically 8KB IOPS, which are common in virtualization scenarios.

The performance improvement is important because SMB is leveraged for more than just file operations now. SMB is also used by Live Migration in some configurations, specifically to take advantage of RDMA-capable NICs. Remember, do *not* use NIC Teaming with RDMA-capable network adapters because NIC Teaming blocks the use of RDMA.

How to Leverage SMB 3 in Your Environment

If right now your datacenter has every virtualization host connected to your top-of-the-line SAN using Fibre Channel, then most likely SMB 3 will not factor into that environment today. However, if not every server is connected to the SAN, or you have new environments such as datacenters or remote locations that don't have a SAN or that will have a SAN but you want to try to minimize the fabric costs of Fibre Channel cards and switches, SMB 3 can help.

If you already have a SAN but do not currently have the infrastructure (for example, the HBAs) to connect every host to the SAN, then a great option is shown in Figure 4.14. A Scale-Out File Server cluster is placed in front of the SAN, which provides access to the SAN storage via SMB 3. This allows the investment in the SAN and its capabilities to be leveraged by the entire datacenter without requiring all the hosts to be connected directly to the SAN. To ensure best performance, have at least as many CSV volumes as nodes in the cluster to allow the balancing to take place. Have double or triple the number of CSV volumes for even better tuning. For example, if I have four hosts in the SoFS cluster, I would want at least eight CSV volumes.

Another option if you do not have a SAN or don't want to use it for certain workloads is to leverage Storage Spaces as the backend storage. While it would be possible to have a single server using Storage Spaces and hosting storage via SMB 3 to remote hosts, this would be a poor design because it introduces a single point of failure. If the SMB 3 server was unavailable, every workload hosted on the server would be unavailable as well. Always leverage a file server cluster and use a clustered storage space, which would have the disks stored in an external enclosure and be accessible to all the nodes in the cluster that are connected. Ensure that resiliency is enabled for the virtual disks created, most likely mirroring for best performance. This would look like Figure 4.15.

FIGURE 4.14
Using a Scale-Out
File Server in front
of a SAN

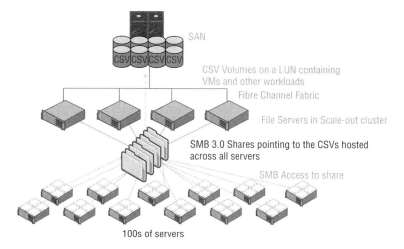

FIGURE 4.15
Using a Scale-Out File
Server and a clustered
storage space

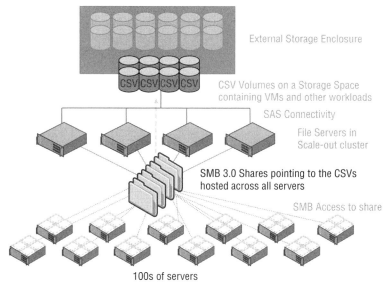

SMB for Hyper-V Storage

Using SMB 3 with Hyper-V is easy. The Hyper-V host's computer account and the cluster account (if hosts are in a cluster) requires full control at the share and NTFS filesystem level. Additionally, the administrator creating or moving the virtual machines should have full control at the share and NTFS level. The easiest way to set the correct permissions is using PowerShell, which is simple in Windows Server 2012 R2. This could also be done through Failover Cluster Manager on shares created on scale-out file servers. The following command creates a folder, and then gives the computer accounts for Hyper-V hosts HV01 and HV02 full control, and the HVCLUS account for the failover cluster they are in full control as well. Note the $ after the computer account names, which must be typed. Additionally, the administrator is given full control.

```
MD G:\VMStore
New-SmbShare -Name VMStore -Path G:\VMStore `
 -FullAccess domain\administrator, `
domain\HV01$, domain\HV02$, domain\HVCLUS$
Set-SmbPathAcl -Name VMStore
```

Note that in Windows Server 2012, the `Set-SmbPathAcl` cmdlet was not available and the NTFS permissions had to be set manually, as shown in the following command. Note this is *not* required in Windows Server 2012 R2 because the `Set-SmbPathAcl` cmdlet copied the share permissions to the NTFS filesystem.

```
ICACLS G:\VMStore /Inheritance:R
ICACLS G:\VMStore /Grant ' "domain\administrator:(CI)(OI)F"
ICACLS G:\VMStore /Grant domain\HV01$:(CI)(OI)F
ICACLS G:\VMStore /Grant domain\HV02$:(CI)(OI)F
ICACLS G:\VMStore /Grant domain\HVCLUS$:(CI)(OI)F
```

Once the permissions are correctly set, specify the SMB share as the location for VM creation or as the target of a storage migration. Figure 4.16 shows a virtual machine using the share \\savdalsofs\Virtuals for its storage. Note that not only is the disk stored on the share, but also the configuration files, checkpoint files, and smart paging files. It's possible to use different storage locations for the different assets of a virtual machine.

FIGURE 4.16
A virtual machine using SMB for its storage

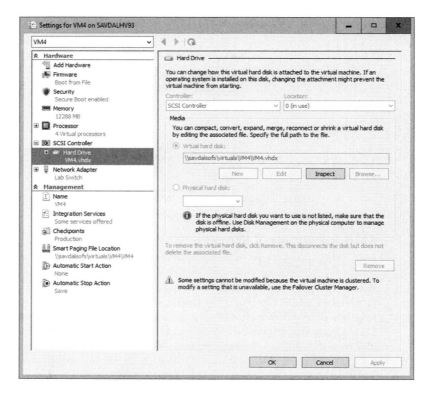

iSCSI with Hyper-V

Previously, I talked about assigning storage to the virtual machine in the form of a virtual hard disk, which required the Hyper-V host to connect to the storage and then create the VHDX files on it. There are, however, other ways to present storage to virtual machines.

iSCSI is a popular alternative to Fibre Channel connectivity that allows block-level connectivity to SAN storage using the existing network infrastructure instead of requiring a completely separate fabric (cards, cables, switches) just for storage. iSCSI works by carrying the traditional SCSI commands over IP networks. While it is possible to run iSCSI over the existing network infrastructure, if iSCSI is being used as the primary storage transport, it is common to have a dedicated network connection for iSCSI to ensure the required bandwidth or, ideally, to leverage larger network connections such as 10Gbps and use QoS to ensure that iSCSI gets the required amount of bandwidth.

In addition to using iSCSI on the Hyper-V host to access storage, it can also be leveraged within virtual machines as a means to provide storage that is accessible to the virtual machine. This includes storage that could be accessed by multiple virtual machines concurrently, known as *shared storage*, which is required in many scenarios in which clusters are implemented within virtual machines, known as *guest clustering*. If you intend to leverage iSCSI within virtual machines, it is a good idea to have dedicated networking for iSCSI. This requires creating a separate virtual switch on the Hyper-V hosts connected to the adapters allocated for iSCSI and then creating an additional network adapter in the virtual machines connected to the virtual switch. If the iSCSI communication is important to the business, you may want to implement redundant connectivity. This is accomplished by creating multiple virtual switches connected to various network adapters, creating multiple virtual network adapters in the virtual machines (connected to the virtual switches), and then using MPIO within the virtual machine. I talk more about MPIO in the section "Understanding Virtual Fibre Channel." Do *not* use NIC Teaming with iSCSI because it's not supported, except in one scenario.

If you have a shared NIC scenario (as discussed in Chapter 3), which uses separate network adapters that are teamed together via the Windows Server NIC Teaming solution (it *must* be the Windows in-box NIC Teaming solution), and the NIC team then has multiple virtual network adapters created at the host level for various purposes, one of which is for iSCSI, NIC Teaming *is* supported. But this is the only time it can be used with iSCSI. If you have dedicated network adapters for iSCSI, then use MPIO.

There are two parts to iSCSI: the iSCSI Initiator, which is the client software that allows connectivity to iSCSI storage, and the iSCSI target, which is the server software. The iSCSI Initiator has been a built-in component of Windows since Windows Server 2008/Windows Vista, and it is also available for Windows 2000 and above from the following:

    www.microsoft.com/en-us/download/details.aspx?id=18986

Windows also has a built-in iSCSI target from Windows Server 2012 and above and is available as a downloadable component for Windows Server 2008 R2:

    www.microsoft.com/en-us/download/details.aspx?id=19867

Additionally, most SAN solutions and some NAS solutions offer iSCSI as a means to connect. Other components to iSCSI are available, such as iSNS, which provides a centralized repository of iSCSI servers, making discovery simpler. A full deep dive into iSCSI is beyond the scope of this discussion. My focus is on the mandatory requirements to enable an iSCSI connection.

Using the Windows iSCSI Target

The Windows Server iSCSI target provides storage using the virtual hard disk format, which would be the equivalent of a LUN on a traditional SAN. The Windows Server 2012 iSCSI target used the VHD implementation for the storage, which limited iSCSI targets to 2TB and to the fixed type that requires all storage to be allocated at target creation time. The Windows Server 2012 R2 iSCSI target leverages VHDX instead, which allows 64TB iSCSI targets and allows the option to use the dynamic type, removing the requirement for all storage to be allocated at creation and instead allocates as data is written.

The iSCSI target is not installed by default. It must be installed using Server Manager and is available at File And Storage Services ➢ File And iSCSI Services ➢ iSCSI Target Server. A VDS and VSS iSCSI Target Storage Provider is also available (VDS and VSS hardware providers). The target can also be installed using PowerShell:

```
Install-WindowsFeature FS-iSCSITarget-Server
```

Once the iSCSI target role service is installed, it is managed through Server Manager ➢ File And Storage Services ➢ iSCSI. Use the following basic steps to enable a new iSCSI target:

1. Navigate to File And Storage Services ➢ iSCSI in Server Manager on the iSCSI target server.

2. From the Tasks menu, choose the New iSCSI Virtual Disk action.

3. Select the server to host the iSCSI target, and then select either a volume that will host the VHDX file (by default the VHDX will be created in a root folder named iSCSIVirtual-Disks on the selected volume) or a custom path. Click Next.

4. Enter a name and optional description for the VHDX file that will be created. Make the name descriptive so that its use may be ascertained by looking at the VHDX filename only. Click Next.

5. Enter the size for the new VHDX file, which will be the size available for the iSCSI target. Note, as shown in Figure 4.17, that all the types of VHDX are available for the iSCSI target, including the option to zero out the content of the disk when creating a fixed-size VHDX to ensure that no old data would be exposed. Notice also that the option to create a differencing VHDX file is available, which is useful if you have a VHDX with existing content that you wish to make available as part of the new iSCSI target without copying all the content.

   While this is not iSCSI specific, it is vital that if you use any dynamic storage, such as dynamic or differencing, you have monitoring and processes in place to ensure that the underlying storage does not run out of space, which would cause problems for any services using the target. Click Next.

6. For the iSCSI target name, which is a unique name for each target, select New iSCSI Target (or an existing target could be selected) and click Next.

7. Enter a name for the new target. While the iSCSI target name syntax is complex, you only need to enter a unique name that represents how you wish to identify the new target (for example, ProjectOne). The wizard will take care of using the name you enter within the full iSCSI target name. Enter your unique portion of the new target name and an optional description and click Next.

FIGURE 4.17
Selecting the options for the new iSCSI VHDX target

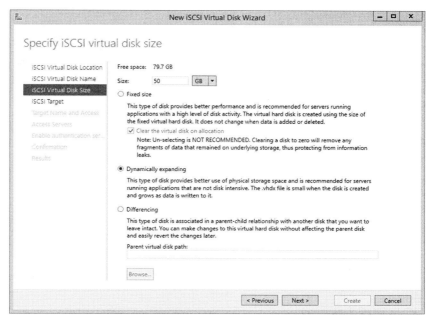

8. The next step is to grant permission to the various iSCSI Initiator names (the clients, known as the IQN) that should be allowed to connect to the new iSCSI target you are creating. Click the Add button to add each target. If you know the IQN of the iSCSI Initiator, select Enter A Value For The Selected Type, and enter the value (the IQN for a client can be viewed via the Configuration tab of the iSCSI Initiator Control Panel applet on the client).

An easier way is to select the Query Initiator Computer For ID option and enter the computer's name, which allows the wizard to scan the remote machine and find the correct IQN. That method works on Windows Server 2012 and later. Click OK. Once all the IQNs are added, click Next.

9. In the Enable Authentication section, leave all the options blank, and click Next.

10. On the confirmation screen, verify all options, and click Create. Once the target is created, click Close.

Note that the whole creation can also be automated in PowerShell using the `New-IscsiVirtualDisk` and `New-IscsiServerTarget` cmdlets. At this stage, you have a Windows-hosted iSCSI target that has been configured so that specific IQNs can access it. If the Windows iSCSI target is used to host important data, a cluster should be used to provide the iSCSI service, which is fully cluster supported.

Using the Windows iSCSI Initiator

While the iSCSI target is built into Windows Server, by default the service, called Microsoft iSCSI Initiator, is not started, and its startup is set to manual. The first time you launch the iSCSI

Initiator Control Panel applet, you will be notified that the service is not running and asked whether you wish the service to be modified so that it starts automatically. Click Yes.

The iSCSI Initiator properties are accessed through property tabs. The Configuration tab shows the IQN of the client (which can be modified) and allows CHAP and IPsec configurations. Most of the actions that you need to perform are through the Discovery and Targets tabs.

On the Discovery tab, click the Discovery Portal button, enter the DNS name or IP address of the iSCSI server, and click OK. This performs a scan of all the targets on the specified server that the initiator has permission to access. To connect to one of the targets, select the Targets tab, select a discovered target, and click Connect. This connects to the storage and adds it as a favorite by default, which means that it will automatically connect after reboots, as shown in Figure 4.18. Once connected in Disk Manager, the new disk will be shown where it should be brought online, initialized, and formatted.

FIGURE 4.18
Connecting to a new iSCSI target using the built-in iSCSI Initiator

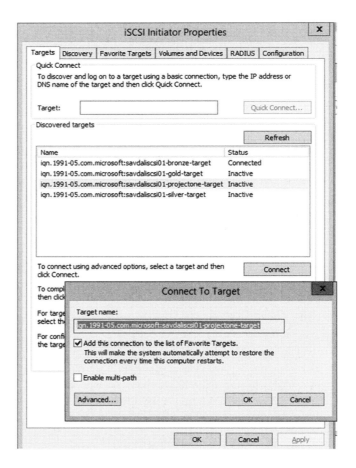

This connection could be made from a Hyper-V host to access storage or from within your virtual machine. The benefit of iSCSI is that multiple iSCSI Initiators can connect to the same iSCSI target, which would enable shared storage and numerous failover cluster scenarios within the virtual machines.

Considerations for Using iSCSI

Using iSCSI to enable shared storage between virtual machines in Windows Server 2008 R2 was the only option and was also the only way to access volumes greater than 2TB (when not connecting to a Windows iSCSI target, which still had a 2TB limit because it used VHD as the storage) without using a pass-through disk. If iSCSI is the storage standard for your organization, using it within virtual machines is still a workable solution. With Windows Server 2012 R2 and above, though, there is a better option, which I go into in the section "Leveraging Shared VHDX and VHD Sets." A benefit of iSCSI is that the Hyper-V host itself does not require any access to the storage. The virtual machine's guest OS IQN is what is given permission to the target and not the host.

There are also some challenges that you should be aware of when using iSCSI:

◆ Hyper-V has no knowledge that the virtual machine is using iSCSI-connected storage.

◆ If a backup is taken of the virtual machine at the Hyper-V host, none of the data stored in iSCSI targets would be backed up.

◆ While technologies like Live Migration and Hyper-V Replica (only if the VSS integration component is disabled for the VM) will still function, they protect and move only the VHDX/VHD content and not data stored on iSCSI targets.

◆ To use iSCSI, the guest operating system must know details of the iSCSI fabric, which may not be desirable, especially in hoster scenarios.

Understanding Virtual Fibre Channel

While iSCSI provided a method to enable shared storage within virtual machines, many organizations did not use iSCSI and instead relied on Fibre Channel to access their SAN environments. These organizations wanted to enable virtual machines to be able to access the SAN directly using the host's Fibre Channel host bus adapter (HBA, basically similar to a network card but used to connect to storage fabric with technologies to enable very fast and efficient movement of data).

Windows Server 2012 introduced virtual Fibre Channel to allow virtual machines to connect directly to storage on a Fibre Channel–connected SAN whose architecture is like that shown in Figure 4.11. The architecture is similar in structure to how networking works with Hyper-V.

Notice in Figure 4.19 that on the Hyper-V host one or more virtual SANs are created, and they connect to one or more HBAs on the Hyper-V host. The key is to not introduce a single point of failure, so multiple virtual SANs are connected to various HBAs that connect to numerous physical switches; and then within the virtual machines are multiple virtual adapters, each connecting to a different virtual SAN.

FIGURE 4.19
Using virtual Fibre
Channel with Hyper-V

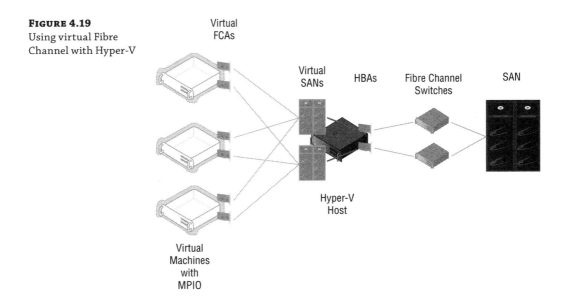

To use virtual Fibre Channel, the HBA must support and be enabled for N_Port ID Virtualization (NPIV), which allows virtual port IDs to share a single physical port. If your HBA does not support NPIV, or NPIV is not enabled, this will be shown when you are trying to create a virtual SAN, as shown in Figure 4.20.

FIGURE 4.20
Problem with the
ports that will block
using in a virtual
SAN

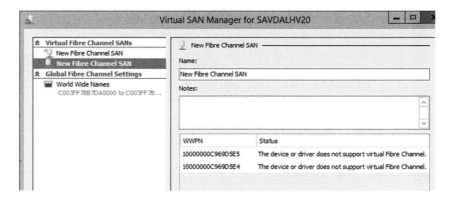

Here are some key steps to take when trying to resolve supportability with NPIV:

1. Make sure that the HBA supports NPIV. This seems obvious, but check the specifications of the HBA to ensure that it will work with NPIV.

2. Check whether NPIV is enabled. Many HBAs ship with NPIV disabled by default. Use whatever management application is available to ensure that NPIV is enabled. As shown in Figure 4.21, I used the OneCommand Manager tool to see if NPIV is enabled on my Emulex card.

FIGURE 4.21
Enabling NPIV using the OneCommand Manager tool

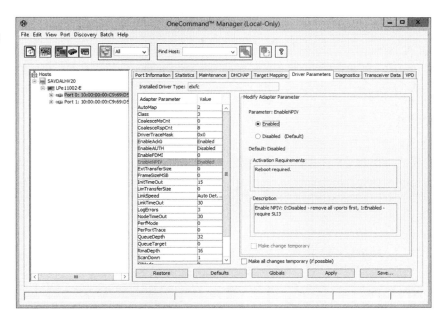

3. Update the firmware for the HBA and the driver on the Hyper-V host. Note that if you update the firmware, it may reset NPIV to be disabled again, so you will need to reenable it. In my experience, a firmware and driver update is often required to fully enable NPIV.

Assuming that I have two HBA ports in my Hyper-V host, I will create two separate virtual SANs, each connected to one of the HBA ports. This assumes that each of the HBA ports is connected to a different Fibre Channel switch to remove single points of failure. If you have four HBA ports, each virtual SAN would be configured with two of the HBA ports. A single HBA port cannot be assigned to more than one virtual SAN. My configuration is shown in Figure 4.22 with two virtual SANs, each using one of the available ports.

Once the virtual SANs are created, the next step is to add virtual Fibre Channel adapters (vFCAs) to the virtual machines that need to access the storage. Open the settings of the virtual machine, and in the Add Hardware section, select Fibre Channel Adapter and click Add. Each virtual machine should have two vFCAs, each connected to a different virtual SAN, providing the virtual machine with redundant connections and protection from a single point of failure, as highlighted in Figure 4.19 previously. The only configuration for the vFCA is to select the virtual SAN to which it will connect, and each vFCA is assigned two sets of World Wide Port Names (WWPNs), as shown in Figure 4.23, which are used to zone access to storage in the switches, effectively granting access to storage. I cover why each vFCA gets two WWPNs later. Notice the Copy button that will take the WWPN and World Wide Node Name (WWNN) information for the vFCA and copy it to the Clipboard; it can then be used in your notes or in your switch configuration tool to zone storage.

FIGURE 4.22
A virtual SAN using
one of the available
HBA ports

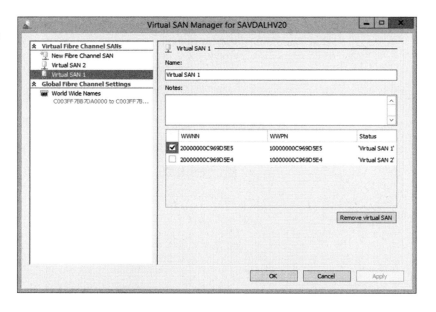

FIGURE 4.23
A virtual Fibre
Channel adapter
for a virtual
machine

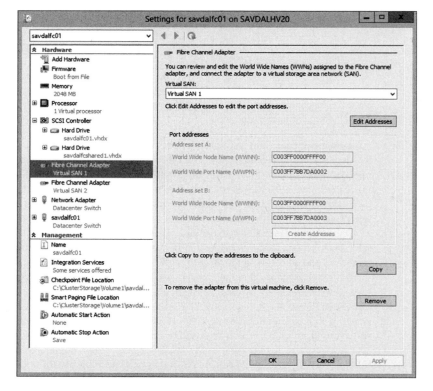

With the WWPNs available, the next step is in your switch to zone storage to the WWPNs (both of the WWPNs for each adapter) of the virtual machine and assign to LUNs on the SAN. When you start a virtual machine with vFCAs assigned but currently with no storage zoned to those vFCAs, you will notice that the virtual machine progress stays at 1 percent when starting for 90 seconds. This is because the vFCA picks an HBA from the virtual SAN to which it is connected and calls the HBA driver to create a virtual port. The vFCA then looks for at least one LUN to be accessible before it continues. If no storage is zoned to the vFCA, this LUN check will not work, and the 90-second time-out has to expire and an event log will be written:

```
Log Name:        Microsoft-Windows-Hyper-V-SynthFC-Admin
Source:          Microsoft-Windows-Hyper-V-SynthFcVdev
Date:            10/9/2013 2:13:08 PM
Event ID:        32213
Task Category:   None
Level:           Warning
Keywords:
User:            NT VIRTUAL MACHINE\1F2AA062-7677-45C0-86F6-643C33796A9D
Computer:        savdalhv20.savilltech.net
Description:
'savdalfc01': No LUNs have appeared for Synthetic Fibre Channel HBA
Fibre Channel Adapter (BB50C162-40E7-412B-AB06-B34104CF6D17). The
VM has been started after the timeout period (90 seconds). Please
review the LUN mappings for the virtual port. (Virtual machine ID
1F2AA062-7677-45C0-86F6-643C33796A9D)
```

You may need to start this way initially so that the WWPNs show on the Fibre Channel switch to allow them to be zoned. Then, after available storage is zoned, the result is another event log being written to show that storage is now available on the vFCA:

```
Log Name:        Microsoft-Windows-Hyper-V-SynthFC-Admin
Source:          Microsoft-Windows-Hyper-V-SynthFcVdev
Date:            10/9/2013 3:33:42 PM
Event ID:        32210
Task Category:   None
Level:           Information
Keywords:
User:            NT VIRTUAL MACHINE\1F2AA062-7677-45C0-86F6-643C33796A9D
Computer:        savdalhv20.savilltech.net
Description:
'savdalfc01': A new LUN '\\?\SCSI#VMLUN&Ven_NETAPP&Prod_LUN#5&12d7e3f3&0&070000#{
6f416619-
9f29-42a5-b20b-37e219ca02b0}' has been added for the Synthetic Fibre
Channel HBA Fibre Channel Adapter (BB50C162-40E7-412B-AB06-B34104CF6D17).
(Virtual machine ID 1F2AA062-7677-45C0-86F6-643C33796A9D)
```

I want to step back now and cover why each vFCA has two WWPNs. One of the most used features of Hyper-V is Live Migration, which is the capability to move a virtual machine between hosts with no downtime to the virtual machine. It was important that virtual Fibre Channel did not break the ability to live-migrate a virtual machine. However, if a vFCA had a single WWPN when a virtual machine was moved to another host as part of the migration, it would be necessary to disconnect the connection to the storage temporarily so that the WWPN could be used on the target host, which would result in storage access interruption. Therefore, each vFCA has two WWPNs, which enables the second WWPN to be used on the target of the Live Migration, enabling both the source and targets to be connected to the storage during a Live Migration and avoiding any interruption. As Live Migrations are performed, the WWPN used will switch between the A and B set with each migration. This is important because when you are zoning the storage, you must zone both the A and B WWPN, or if you live-migrate the virtual machine, it will lose access. It may be necessary to perform a Live Migration of the virtual machines to activate the second set of WWPNs to allow them to be zoned on the switches if you cannot manually specify WWPNs that are not currently visible to the switch. This means that the process may look like this:

1. Start the virtual machine.

2. Connect to the switch, and create an alias (or any other construct, depending on the switch) for the visible WWPNs.

3. Live-migrate the virtual machine to another host, which will trigger the other set of WWPNs to activate.

4. On the switch, add the newly visible WWPNs to the alias.

5. Complete zoning to storage.

Figure 4.24 shows my switch with an alias created for each of the vFCAs for each virtual machine. Notice that each alias has two WWPNs, the A and the B set, but only one is active. Figure 4.25 shows the same view after I live-migrate the two virtual machines to another host. Notice now that the second set of WWPNs is active.

FIGURE 4.24

The A set of WWPNs being used

FIGURE 4.25

The B set of WWPNs being used

A great feature here is that the Hyper-V host itself has no access to the storage. Nowhere is the WWPN of the host zoned to storage; only the virtual machines have access to the storage, which is important from a security perspective and simplifies management because there is no need to ensure that every Hyper-V host is zoned to storage, only the virtual machines' vFCAs that actually need the access.

With storage now zoned to all the WWPNs for the vFCAs used, the virtual machines can be started and the storage can be accessed as shared storage, allowing guest clustering. While this is not a Hyper-V-specific step, it is important to realize that in my architecture shown in Figure 4.19, I have redundant paths to the storage through my two vFCAs and the two virtual SANs (which can both see the storage via redundant paths), which means that for each LUN zoned, the storage will actually be seen four times, as shown in Figure 4.26. Basically, each virtual SAN sees each disk twice, once for each of its paths to the storage, and then the virtual machine has two connections to different virtual SANs, each telling it there are two disks! This would be the same experience if redundant path iSCSI was used.

FIGURE 4.26
A view of a single disk without MPIO

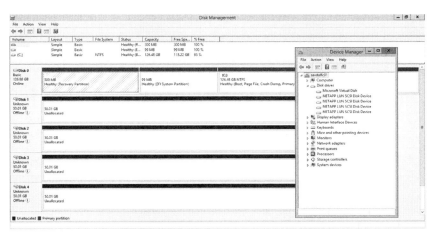

Windows has a feature called *MPIO* that solves this and adds the intelligence into Windows so that it understands that it's seeing the same storage multiple times and it has redundant paths. Install the MPIO feature and then run the MPIO tool. On the Discover Multi-Paths tab, select the SAN device and click Add, and then you will be prompted to reboot. Once the machine reboots, there will be a single instance of each disk, as shown in Figure 4.27.

The addition of virtual Fibre Channel is a great feature for organizations that have a Fibre Channel–centric storage strategy, and Microsoft made great efforts to provide a flexible while secure implementation, enabling full Live Migration compatibility without giving the Hyper-V hosts themselves access. There are still more considerations. As with iSCSI, a backup taken at the Hyper-V host will not back up any data stored on the SAN storage. To use virtual Fibre Channel, you must have a guest operating system that is Windows Server 2008 or above and the latest version of Hyper-V Integration Services must be installed. At the time of this writing, virtual Fibre Channel does not work with Linux guest operating systems. Hyper-V Replica cannot be used with a virtual machine that has vFCAs. Also, as with iSCSI, to use virtual Fibre Channel, the virtual machines need to have knowledge of the storage fabric, which is not desirable in many scenarios, especially those hoster scenarios.

FIGURE 4.27
A view of a single
disk with MPIO

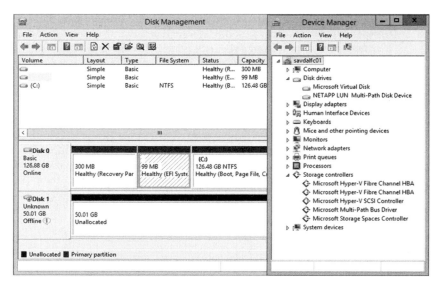

Leveraging Shared VHDX and VHD Sets

Windows Server 2012 R2 and above provides a feature that for most environments will remove the need to use iSCSI inside the virtual machine or virtual Fibre Channel and remove the need to expose the storage fabric details to the virtual machine. Shared VHDX allows a VHDX file to be connected to multiple virtual machines simultaneously, and the shared VHDX will be seen as shared storage (shared SAS) and therefore used as cluster storage within guest clusters. The requirements for shared VHDX in Windows Server 2012 R2 and above are as follows:

- Must use Windows Server 2012 R2 Hyper-V

- Guest operating systems must be Windows Server 2012 or above and must be running the Windows Server 2012 R2 Integration Services.

- The disk must be VHDX, not VHD, and must be connected to an SCSI controller, not IDE. It can be a generation 1 or generation 2 virtual machine.

- VHDX can be fixed or dynamic but not differencing.

- Can be used for data disks only. Cannot be used for operating system disks

- The storage for the VHDX file being shared must either be a CSV or be hosted from a Scale-Out File Server (SoFS) accessed using SMB 3 (the SoFS would be using CSV for its backend storage). The reason CSV must be used to store the VHDX is that the code to implement the VHDX sharing is part of CSV and not the regular NTFS code.

It is possible to force the process of loading and attaching the shared VHD filter driver to a non-CSV volume. However, this loading will survive only until the disk is offlined in some way, at which point you would have to load and attach again. Note that this is not supported or even tested by Microsoft and should be used only in basic test scenarios if a CSV is not available. Here are the steps:

1. Install the Failover Clustering feature through Server Manager or through PowerShell:

```
Install-WindowsFeature Failover-Clustering
```

2. Run the following command, specifying the volume to attach the shared VHDX filter to:

```
FLTMC.EXE attach svhdxflt <volume>:
```

Provided that a VHDX file is stored on a CSV volume or SoFS and is connected via an SCSI controller, there is only one step to make it shared: After it has been added to a virtual machine in the Advanced Features properties for the disk, select the Enable Virtual Hard Disk Sharing check box, as shown in Figure 4.28. Repeat this for the same disk on all virtual machines that need to access the shared disk.

FIGURE 4.28
Setting a VHDX file as shared

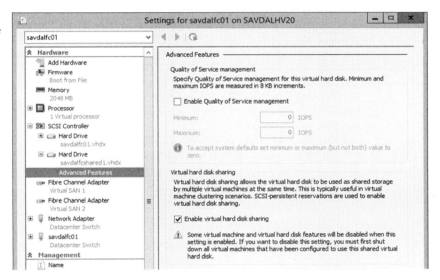

This process could also be accomplished using PowerShell. In the following example, I have two virtual machines, savdalfc01 and savdalfc02, to which I will add a shared VHDX file. Notice the use of the -ShareVirtualDisk switch when I add the VHDX file to the virtual machine.

```
New-VHD -Path C:\ClusterStorage\Volume1\SharedVHDX\Savdalfcshared1.vhdx '
-Fixed -SizeBytes 25GB
Add-VMHardDiskDrive -VMName savdalfc01 -Path '
C:\ClusterStorage\Volume1\SharedVHDX\Savdalfcshared1.vhdx -ShareVirtualDisk
Add-VMHardDiskDrive -VMName savdalfc02 -Path '
C:\ClusterStorage\Volume1\SharedVHDX\Savdalfcshared1.vhdx -ShareVirtualDisk
```

To check whether a virtual disk is using a shared VHDX, the SupportPersistentReservations property can be examined. If the property is set to True, you have a shared VHDX. For example, notice that my shared VHDX file has a value of True:

```
PS C:\> Get-VMHardDiskDrive -VMName savdalfc01 | ft vmname, path, `
controllertype, SupportPersistentReservations -auto

VMName     Path                                ControllerType  SupportPersistentReservations
------     ----                                                ------------ -- ---
------
savdalfc01 C:\ClusterSto..\savdalfc01\savdalfc01.vhdx           SCSI        False
savdalfc01 C:\ClusterSto.. \Shared VHDX\savdalfcshared1.vhdx    SCSI        True
```

Within the virtual machine, the shared VHDX would be seen as a regular shared SAS disk and used like normal shared storage. The huge benefit with shared VHDX is that the virtual machine knows nothing about the underlying storage fabric and provides complete abstraction for the storage from the physical storage fabric.

Because the VHDX file is shared between multiple virtual machines, the ability to perform a backup at the Hyper-V host or even a checkpoint is not possible. Backups would need to be taken within the guest virtual machine. Storage migration is also not supported for shared VHDX files. This also means Hyper-V Replica cannot be used for virtual machines that are connected to a shared VHDX file.

When using Shared VHDX on an SMB 3 share, an entirely new protocol called Remote Shared Virtual Hard Disk Protocol is used. This protocol leverages SMB as a transport but is not part of the SMB protocol itself.

Windows Server 2016 evolves shared VHDX to remove three key limitations of the Windows Server 2012 R2 implementation and enables:

◆ Dynamic resizing of a shared VHDX

◆ Backup of shared VHDX at the host level

◆ Replication of a shared VHDX using Hyper-V Replica

Note that live storage move and checkpointing of shared VHDX files is not possible in Windows Server 2016. To enable these new features of shared VHDX files, it has transitioned to a new feature called VHD Sets. *VHD Sets* accomplishes the same result as shared VHDX—the ability to share VHDX files between multiple hosts—but it is implemented differently.

VHD Sets uses a new type of VHD file, which signifies that it is a VHD Set. The actual VHDS file is only 260KB, and an automatically generated file (AVDHX) is created to hold the content of the VHD Set. The view of the files on disk for a VHD Set are shown in Figure 4.29. Notice the small VHDS file and the larger AVHDX containing the actual data.

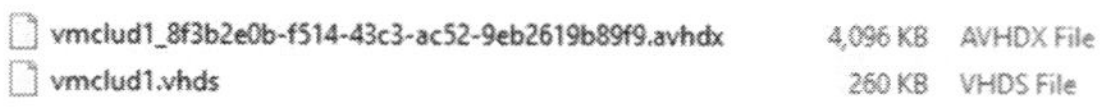

FIGURE 4.29
VHD Set files on disk

vmclud1_8f3b2e0b-f514-43c3-ac52-9eb2619b89f9.avhdx	4,096 KB	AVHDX File
vmclud1.vhds	260 KB	VHDS File

A VHD Set can be fixed or dynamic, which will impact the size and behavior of the AVHDX file. To use VHD Sets, the process is different than in Windows Server 2012 R2:

1. Create a new VHD Set file. If using Hyper-V Manager, choose New ➤ Hard Disk from the host actions menu, and for the format select VHD Set, as shown in Figure 4.30. The remaining options are the same as for a regular VHDX file creation. If using PowerShell, specify an extension type of vhds with the New-VHD cmdlet. This should be created on a Cluster Shared Volume, which is still a requirement for VHD Sets.

FIGURE 4.30
Creating a VHD Set

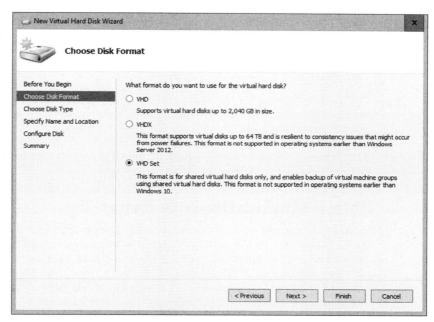

2. Attach the VHD Set to multiple VMs by selecting the option to add a Shared Drive to the SCSI Controller and then selecting a VHDS file, as shown in Figure 4.31. If using PowerShell with the Add-VMHardDiskDrive cmdlet, use the -SupportPersistentReservations parameter and specify the vhds file.

FIGURE 4.31
Adding a VHD Set to
a VM

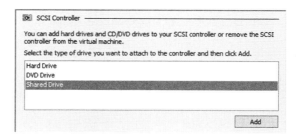

The VHD Set will be seen as shared storage in the same way as the Windows Server 2012 R2 style Shared VHDX, except the previously three mentioned restrictions that limited the use of Shared VHDX will be removed. If you upgrade Windows Server 2012 R2 hosts to Windows Server 2016, there is no automatic conversion from shared VHDX to VHD Sets, and the old restrictions will still apply. You need to convert the shared VHDX manually to a VHD Set to enable the support for dynamic resize, Hyper-V Replica, and host-level backup. The process to convert this is as follows:

1. Turn off the VMs that are connected to the Shared VHDX.

2. Remove the shared VHDX from the VMs by using `Remove-VMHardDiskDrive` or Hyper-V Manager.

3. Convert the shared VHDX into a VHD Set format by using the Edit Disk Wizard or `Convert-VHD`.

4. Add the VHD Set files back to the VM by using `Add-VMHardDiskDrive` or Hyper-V Manager.

Hopefully, you can see the large range of options for shared storage within virtual machines, including SMB 3, iSCSI, virtual Fibre Channel, and shared VHDX. Each has its own benefits and considerations, and I don't think there is a right or wrong solution as long as you take time to fully understand each technology. If possible, you should use shared VHDX first because it provides a true virtualized shared storage solution that removes the need for direct fabric knowledge and configuration from the virtual machines.

Data Deduplication and Hyper-V

So far, I have covered some of the reasons that Windows Server 2016 is a great storage platform. Storage Spaces with its thin provisioning and autorecovery, Storage Spaces Direct to use local storage in servers, Storage Replica to provide DR, improved ChkDsk error correction, iSCSI and SMB 3 and above servers, and VHDX are amazing features. There are many other features, such as the new ReFS filesystem and industry-leading NFS implementation, but I want to touch on one more feature that I would not have covered in Windows Server 2012, but is now applicable to virtualization: data deduplication.

Windows Server 2012 introduced the block-level data deduplication capability as an optional role available within the File and iSCSI Services collection of role services. In Windows Server 2012, data deduplication did not work on any file that had an exclusive lock open, which was the case for a virtual hard disk used by a virtual machine. This meant that the data deduplication feature was useful only for reducing space for archived virtual machine or libraries of content.

In Windows Server 2012 R2, the data deduplication functionality was improved to work on exclusively locked files. It can therefore deduplicate virtual hard disks used by Hyper-V virtual machines. For the Windows Server 2012 R2 release, though, deduplication is supported for only a single scenario: the deduplication of VDI deployment virtual machines, primarily personal desktop deployment that often results in a very large amount of duplicated content. When you leverage the data deduplication capability at the filesystem level, all the duplicated blocks within a virtual hard disk and between different virtual hard disks would be single-instanced, resulting in huge disk savings. Windows Server 2012 R2 also adds support for deduplication for Cluster Shared Volumes, which means that deduplication can be used on shared cluster disks and on the storage of scale-out file servers. Note that while ReFS is a possible filesystem for Hyper-V in Windows Server 2016, it does *not* support deduplication. If you need deduplication, you need to use NTFS, which is the guidance for all scenarios except Storage Spaces Direct anyway.

The way the data deduplication works is that a periodic scan of the filesystem is performed and the blocks on disk have a hash value created. If blocks are found with the same value, it means the content is the same, and the block is moved to a single instance store. The old locations now point to the single-instance store copy. The block size used is variable to achieve the greatest level of deduplication. It is common to see disk space savings of up to 95 percent in VDI environments, because most of the content of each virtual hard disk is the same as the other virtual hard disk instances. Using deduplication speeds up the performance of VDI environments because of improvements in caching instead of having a negative performance impact, which may be expected.

It should be noted that while in Windows Server 2012 R2 the data deduplication is supported for VDI deployments, the actual data deduplication is a core part of the storage stack, and so there is no block to stop data deduplication working with other virtual workloads. However, these workloads have not been tested. I would be very concerned about enabling data deduplication on some types of workloads, such as any kind of database. It is therefore important that when configuring data deduplication on a volume that has mixed workloads, you explicitly block folders containing virtual hard disks that you do not want to be deduplicated.

VDI is one of the great scenarios for using differencing disks (which, remember, are child disks of a parent disk with only differences stored in them). If data that is being read is not in the differencing disk, it is read from the parent disk. Any write actions are performed into the differencing disk. Therefore, in a pooled VDI scenario, a master VHDX file would have the core Windows client image, the gold image, and then many VDM virtual machines created with their own differencing disks that are children of the master image. Each differencing disk would still be a couple of gigabytes because of changes made during the specialization phase, but using differencing disks is still an efficient solution. The master image can be stored on a high tier of storage, such as the SSD tier if Storage Spaces is being used, and because the master would be read-only, it would also benefit from any caching. Figure 4.32 shows this architecture.

FIGURE 4.32
Using differencing disks in a VDI environment

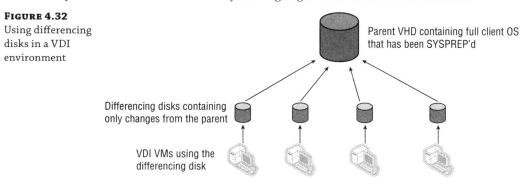

Parent VHD containing full client OS that has been SYSPREP'd

Differencing disks containing only changes from the parent

VDI VMs using the differencing disk

Windows Server 2016 continues the investment in data deduplication with the following key enhancements:

◆ Support for volumes of up to 64TB, thanks to a new data deduplication design. Instead of running the optimization as a single job with a single thread (which limited data deduplication to volumes of 10TB or less), the new deduplication process pipeline uses multiple threads running in parallel and using multiple I/O queues, resulting in improved performance and support for larger volumes.

◆ Support for files up to 1TB

◆ Support for virtualized backup applications such as System Center Data Protection Manager to include a built-in preset configuration named Virtualized Back-up Server

◆ Support for Nano Server

Storage Quality of Service

Many organizations have long focused on ensuring that virtual machines correctly get the required amounts of memory and processor resources, while network and storage controls historically have not been well implemented. Storage QoS is important to ensure that workloads receive the required amounts of IOPS and are not starved of IOPS by workloads that are of a lower priority. Windows Server 2012 R2 introduced basic IOPS-based QoS on a per-virtual hard disk level. There are two settings:

Minimum IOPS If the virtual hard disk does not receive the configured minimum number of IOPS, an event log is generated.

Maximum IOPS The virtual hard disk will be hard limited to the number of IOPS specified.

You will notice that the minimum and maximum options are implemented very differently. There is no "guaranteed" minimum number of IOPS possible for a virtual machine, because there is no way to ensure that the required number of IOPS is possible or even available. Therefore, the best solution at this time is for an event to be generated notifying that the virtual hard disk is not receiving the number of IOPS required, which will be an Event ID 32930 under `Applications and Services Logs\Microsoft\Windows\Hyper-V-VMMS\Admin`, and an Event ID 32931 when performance is back to the expected level. A WMI event is also triggered. It is simple to make sure that a virtual hard disk does not exceed a certain number of IOPS, which is why the maximum value is a hard limit and simply limits the virtual hard disk to the configured number of IOPS. To configure the storage QoS, perform the following steps:

1. Open the settings of a virtual machine.

2. Navigate to the virtual hard disk and select Quality of Service. (This was Advanced Features in Windows Server 2012 R2, as it also enabled shared VHDX configuration.)

3. Select the Enable Quality Of Service Management check box, and set the Minimum and/ or Maximum values, as shown in Figure 4.33. A value of 0 means that there is no configuration. Click OK.

FIGURE 4.33
Configuring QoS
for a disk

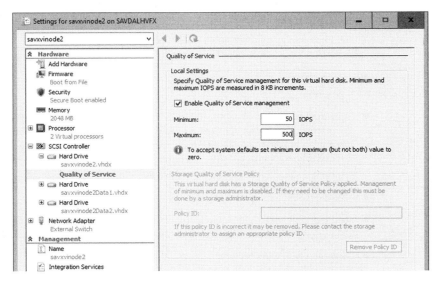

To configure storage QoS using PowerShell, use the `Set-VMHardDiskDrive` cmdlet and configure the `MaximumIOPS` and `MinimumIOPS` parameters.

In addition to enabling QoS on storage, storage details are also now reported as part of the resource metering introduced in Windows Server 2012. The storage-related data returned includes the average IOPS, average latency, and the data read and written in MB. An example of the information returned is shown in the following output:

```
PS E:\> Measure-VM -VMName savdalfs01 | fl


ComputerName                      : SAVDALHV01
VMId                              : 4c6db747-8591-4287-a8fc-ac55e37dba16
VMName                            : savdalfs01
HardDiskMetrics                   : {Microsoft.HyperV.PowerShell
.VirtualHardDiskMetrics, Microsoft.HyperV.PowerShell.VirtualHardDiskMetrics}
MeteringDuration                  :
AverageProcessorUsage             : 204
AverageMemoryUsage                : 3236
MaximumMemoryUsage                : 3236
MinimumMemoryUsage                : 3236
TotalDiskAllocation               : 260096
AggregatedAverageNormalizedIOPS   : 389
AggregatedAverageLatency          : 633
AggregatedDiskDataRead            : 103
AggregatedDiskDataWritten         : 367
NetworkMeteredTrafficReport       : {Microsoft.HyperV.PowerShell.
VMNetworkAdapterPortAclMeteringReport,
Microsoft.HyperV.PowerShell.VMNetworkAdapterPortAclMeteringReport,
Microsoft.HyperV.PowerShell.VMNetworkAdapterPortAclMeteringReport,
Microsoft.HyperV.PowerShell.VMNetworkAdapterPortAclMeteringReport}
AvgCPU                            : 204
AvgRAM                            : 3236
MinRAM                            : 3236
MaxRAM                            : 3236
TotalDisk                         : 260096
```

While the per disk QoS in Windows Server 2012 R2 is useful in certain scenarios, it fails to meet the requirements in many scenarios. I cannot actually reserve performance for storage nor can I centrally manage the policies for shared storage. Windows Server 2016 changes this with a centralized QoS implementation that is a feature of the cluster and enables actual reservation of performance. The storage must be CSV. If you are not using CSV, only the old 2012 R2 style QoS can be used. However, pretty much every Hyper-V environment uses CSV for its storage today.

Windows Server 2012 R2 implemented maximums for IOPS, which is relatively simple; however, there was no way to achieve minimum guarantees of performance as this is a far more difficult problem to solve. Windows Server 2016 tackles this in various ways; at its core is a new maximum-minimum fair-sharing technology that ensures that all targets with a minimum policy applied receive that level of performance, and then additional IOPS are distributed fairly until any maximum that may also be defined. By using a centralized policy controller, there is no need for complicated distribution solutions of the actual policies that will be enforced by the nodes in the cluster.

A key term for QoS is *normalized IOPS*, which by default is an 8KB block. Anything less than 8KB is a single, 1 normalized IOPS, while larger I/Os would be multiple normalized IOPS. For example, a 9KB I/O would be 2 normalized IOPS, a 24KB I/O would be 3 normalized IOPS, and so on. Note that this is a unit of measurement used by the various accounting methods that make up storage QoS. It is possible to reconfigure the normalized IOPS size if 8KB is not suitable for the type of workloads in your environment. Most organizations, however, should leave the default 8KB.

Three primary components make up the new storage QoS:

1. On each Hyper-V, compute node is a profiler and rate limiter that tracks utilization of storage and enforces the maximum IOPS values in the same way that it works in Windows Server 2012 R2.

2. An I/O Scheduler is distributed on the storage nodes backing the VHDs (that is, the Scale-Out File Server). This enforces the minimum IOPS allocations. Note that in a hyperconverged deployment where the storage and compute are the same nodes, the I/O Scheduler runs on those hyperconverged nodes in the same way. This also would apply when the storage is a LUN on a SAN or Storage Spaces Direct.

3. The centralized policy manager is a resource in the cluster, which means that it can move between nodes as required, and is the aggregate point for collecting and consolidating metrics about storage and driving the management of the policies. This can be seen as a cluster core resource from within Failover Cluster Manager or through PowerShell.

All these items together make up a cyclical process that enables the minimum IOPS implementation. At the compute layer, the current capacity is constantly being evaluated, as is the capacity at the storage layer. The centralized policy manager then evaluates the compute and storage capacities and adjusts limits and enforces them at the compute layer as required to meet the various minimum policies deployed. As an example, if the policy manager sees that the capacity at the compute layer is exceeding that at the storage layer and that storage resources will not get the required level of IOPS, the manager adjusts maximums for other resources to ensure that the required storage capacity is available where needed.

This functionality is enabled by default in Windows Server 2016 for any VHD on a Cluster Shared Volume. Metrics are collected at a per VHD, per VM, per host, and per storage volume level. Policies are created that define minimum and maximum IOPS and maximum bandwidth (MB/s), which while implemented at a VHD level through management tools and PowerShell, you can actually apply at various levels such as the following:

◆ Per VHD

◆ Per VM

◆ Per service

◆ Per tenant

When policies are applied to multiple VHDs, a fair-distribution algorithm is used for all of the resources within a specific policy.

Although the feature is enabled by default, you need to manage the policies. This can be done through PowerShell or System Center Virtual Machine Manager. I focus on the PowerShell approach for the management, which requires the use of GUIDs to manage policy, while System Center uses friendly names.

A default policy of all 0s specifies a minimum IOPS of 2, with no maximum, that is applied to everything; this policy therefore ensures a fair distribution of resources. The first step is to create your own policy with values to meet your requirements. The attributes of a policy are as follows:

◆ An admin-defined policy name

◆ Maximum normalized IOPS limit

◆ Maximum bandwidth (bytes per second)

◆ Minimum guaranteed normalized IOPS

◆ Policy type (dedicated—per VHD, aggregated—shared across VHDs). For example, a dedicated policy type means that every VHD gets the values defined in the policy, whereas aggregated means that every VHD shares the values (so that if the policy is applied to five VHDs, they all share the values in the policy, for example, sharing a maximum combined IOPS).

It's important to remember that policies are enacted at a per VHD level but can be applied at different levels to ease management, and so the policy type is important when applying policies to multiple VHDs, VMs, services, and so on. Use *dedicated* when you want every VHD to have its own QoS values (for example, if you want per VHD performance tiers like Silver and Gold) and use *aggregated* when you want VHDs to share the QoS values (such as across a multi-VM service). If I set a Maximum IOPS of 500 with a policy type of dedicated and apply it to five VHDs, then every VHD has a maximum of 500 IOPS. If I set the same policy as type aggregated and apply it to the same five VHDs, they would have a combined maximum of 500 IOPS—which means that if every VHD is pushing for maximum IOPS, each would max out at around 100 IOPS. Note that maximum values are not reserved for each resource, and throttling starts only when needed. For those same five VHDs sharing the 500 IOPS maximum, if only one VHD is performing work, it can use 500 IOPS; it won't be artificially limited to 100 IOPS just because it's sharing the maximum with four others. Only when others in the aggregated policy need the IOPS will it be fairly distributed. Dedicated is generally easier to manage, because every VHD gets the values defined in the policy; it gives you "one-minute management." With an aggregated policy, understanding the exact performance received per VHD is more complex, but this type may be needed when a service needs that shared QoS (for example, giving a group of resources a "bubble" of performance that they can share). I would create a separate aggregated policy for each "bubble" of resources that need to be shared. Storage QoS also works for VHD Sets (aka Shared VHDX) and in this scenario, the IOPS is shared between the nodes sharing the VHD.

You do not have to configure all the attributes of a policy. You may decide that you want to define only minimums, to ensure that VHDs are guaranteed a minimum number of IOPS in times of contention but are not limited to a maximum IOPS other than what the storage can provide. At other times, you may set only maximum values, which stop VHDs from consuming excess resources but also may artificially limit performance of VHDs when there is no contention and therefore leave storage bandwidth unused. Of course, you can configure both a minimum and maximum to ensure a certain level of performance and limit at another level. Typically, the maximum is higher than the minimum to give VHDs some fluctuation. However, it is possible to set the minimum value to be the same as the maximum, thereby setting consistent performance for the VHDs, essentially locking them to a certain IOPS. This last scenario is common for hosters where the IOPS per disk should be set; for example, in Azure, a standard disk has a 500 IOPS limit, so you could imagine the minimum and maximum set to 500 IOPS as a dedicated policy. In this way, the VHD should always get 500 when it wants it but never more than 500.

To create a new policy, use the `New-StorageQosPolicy` cmdlet, and to view existing policies, use `Get-StorageQosPolicy`. In the following example, I create a new policy with a minimum and maximum IOPS value that is of type dedicated. Notice that I save the policy to a variable so that I can then easily apply it.

```
$10to100IOPSPolicy = New-StorageQosPolicy -Name "10 to 100 IOPS" `
-MinimumIops 10 -MaximumIops 100 -PolicyType Dedicated
```

Looking at `$10to100IOPSPolicy.PolicyId` shows the GUID of the policy, which is what is required when applying the policies via PowerShell. It is possible to set the policy ID when creating a new policy via the `-PolicyId` parameter of `New-StorageQosPolicy`. The reason that you may want to set the policy ID is twofold:

◆ A policy may have been deleted that is used by VHDs, and you need to re-create it.

◆ You want to migrate VMs between clusters. The cluster is the boundary for policies. If you want consistency as you move VMs between clusters, you should create the policies on all clusters with the same policy ID. Therefore, you need to set the policy ID during creation on subsequent clusters to match the policy ID of the policy when created on the first cluster.

To apply the policy, use `Set-VMHardDiskDrive` with the `-QoSPolicyId`. For example, to set all VHDs with a policy for a particular VM, I could use the following:

```
Get-VM -Name VM1 | Get-VMHardDiskDrive |
Set-VMHardDiskDrive -QoSPolicyID $10to100IOPSPolicy.PolicyId
```

I could use any combination of PowerShell pipelining to apply policies. I could fetch every VM on a host, every VM in a cluster, or any combination. Ultimately, I am applying the policy to a VHD, and the PowerShell results in a collection of VHDs to which I apply the QoS policy. If you wish to remove the QoS policy, set the `QoSPolicyID` to `$null` for the VHD.

Existing policies can be modified using the `Set-StorageQosPolicy` cmdlet, and all attributes can be changed. Once the policy is changed, any VHD to which it has been applied will receive the updated values of the policy straightaway.

Because the policy manager receives metrics at so many levels, this also exposes new levels of monitoring of storage performance. The first command to use is `Get-StorageQosVolume`, which shows all of the CSV volumes with basic information including IOPS served, latency, and the bandwidth it can serve.

`Get-StorageQoSFlow` enables viewing of all the flows on the storage subsystem, where a flow can be thought of as a VHD used by a VM on storage managed by the policies. While `Get-StorageQoSFlow` shows only the VHDs and the VM using the VHD, it can also show a lot more data by using the following:

```
Get-StorageQoSFlow | FL *
```

Note that if you run this without creating policies, you will see that the default (all 0s) policy has been applied to all flows. This will output huge amounts of data related to each flow, including IOPS, policy applied, latency, bandwidth, and more. A slightly neater version with the most useful information is shown here:

```
Get-StorageQoSFlow | FL InitiatorName, InitiatorLatency, StorageNodeLatency,
StorageNodeBandwidth, StorageNodeIOPS, InitiatorIOPS, PolicyId, FilePath
```

An even better version can be found at https://technet.microsoft.com/en-us/library/mt126108.aspx, which shows the output in a table format. Note that all of the following output should be on a single line:

```
Get-StorageQosFlow | Sort-Object StorageNodeIOPs -Descending | ft InitiatorName,
@{Expression={$_.InitiatorNodeName.Substring(0,$_.InitiatorNodeName.IndexOf('.'))
};Label="InitiatorNodeName"}, StorageNodeIOPs, Status,
@{Expression={$_.FilePath.Substring($_.FilePath.LastIndexOf('\')+1)}};Label
="File"} -AutoSize
```

The data shown in Get-StorageQoSFlow is sampled as an average over the past 5 minutes. Although the minimum IOPS is a guarantee, meeting that value might not always be possible. If I set minimum IOPS values that are high to many VHDs, those values may exceed the capability of the underlying storage. In those cases, the configuration will be flagged as Insufficient Throughput through the monitoring. To view only flows with insufficient throughput, use this:

```
Get-StorageQoSFlow -Status InsufficientThroughput | fl
```

With the adoption of SMB 3, another type of storage QoS is applicable not only for file traffic (default), but also for hosting virtual machines and even for Live Migration. The existing QoS technologies that could control SMB allocation were not granular enough to enable different bandwidth limits for the various types of SMB traffic. Windows Server 2012 R2 added this new granularity for SMB bandwidth management: Default, LiveMigration, and VirtualMachine. This allows an amount of bandwidth to be specified for each type of SMB traffic. In most environments, this should not be required, because SMB does a good job of fair-sharing the network, but if you need to better tune the bandwidth allocation, this SMB bandwidth management will be useful.

To configure the SMB bandwidth management, perform the following steps:

1. Install the SMB Bandwidth Limit feature. This can be done through Server Manager (note that it is a feature and not a role) or using PowerShell:

```
Install-WindowsFeature FS_SMBBW
```

2. Configure the limits for each type of traffic by using the Set-SMBBandwidthLimit PowerShell cmdlet, as in this example:

```
Set-SMBBandwidthLimit -Category LiveMigration - BytesPerSecond 2GB
```

3. To view the configured SMB QoS, use the Get-SMBBandwidthLimit cmdlet. Use the Remove-SMBBandwidthLimit cmdlet to remove it.

SAN Storage and SCVMM

This chapter has shown a lot of great functionality that is enabled through the use of the Windows Server platform, but this does not mean that there are not investments related to leveraging SANs. One of the biggest features when utilizing SANs is offloaded data transfer, or ODX.

Typically, when any file move or copy operation occurs, the server becomes the bottleneck in the process, and significant resources are used on the server as the following occurs:

1. The server reads a portion of the data from the SAN.

2. The server writes that portion of the data to the SAN.

3. Both steps are repeated until all data is read and written.

This is a highly inefficient process, because the SAN is far more capable of natively moving or copying data. ODX allows the SAN to move or copy data itself through the use of a series of tokens, with each token representing a portion of the data at a point in time. The token, instead of the actual data, is passed by the host to the SAN, which then allows the SAN to natively move or copy the data.

To utilize ODX, the SAN must support it. The good news is that, by default, ODX will be utilized automatically where possible. Consider the action of deploying a virtual machine from a template. In the past, the Hyper-V host would copy the template to the new location, resulting in large amounts of processor utilization on the host and a copy operation that may take 10 minutes to perform. With ODX, the copy would use a negligible amount of processor resources and the copy operation would likely finish in about 30 seconds. File operations using Windows File Explorer, the command prompt, PowerShell, and Hyper-V will all utilize ODX where possible.

System Center Virtual Machine Manager (SCVMM) 2012 R2 also utilizes ODX when deploying a virtual machine from a template, but not in any other scenario. If ODX cannot be used, SCVMM will use a regular file copy, and if that does not work, it will resort to BITS.

While native ODX allows very fast copies of data because the SAN can natively perform the copy/move directly, it also allows SAN vendors to improve the process. For example, there is no reason the SAN actually has to copy the data. SAN ODX implementations may use native capabilities such as just creating a pointer to the original data. The NetApp implementation uses its sub-LUN cloning technology, which creates two pointers to the same block of data, so the operation finishes almost instantly because no data is actually being moved or copied. A write-forward snapshot is then leveraged so that changes to the new copy are written to a new area. Even without these additional optimizations, ODX provides a huge performance improvement during large move and copy operations.

Windows Server 2012 also introduced native support for Storage Management Initiative Specification (SMI-S). In Windows Server 2012 R2 and above, there is a built-in SMI-S provider for the inbox iSCSI solution, making it manageable from SMI-S–based management solutions without additional software required, which includes SCVMM 2012 R2.

I want to close by mentioning how SCVMM 2012 R2 can integrate with storage solutions to simplify management. The goal of SCVMM is to be the fabric management solution and not just for managing virtual machines. Storage providers can be loaded into SCVMM, which then displays the aggregates/volumes and the contained LUNs. Each aggregate/volume can be assigned a custom classification such as Gold, Silver, or Bronze. Figure 4.34 shows the Classifications And Pools view of the storage fabric. As you can see, I have three classifications of storage defined, and I have numerous storage subsystems loaded, including a Windows Server 2012 R2 iSCSI server and two NetApp SANs. Using a common classification enables SCVMM to create and allocate LUNs automatically to hosts as required, based on a storage classification in the virtual machine request.

SCVMM leverages industry standards to connect to the storage subsystems such as CIM- and WMI-based versions of SMI-S and also Windows storage APIs to manage Windows file servers, which can also be classified in SCVMM 2012 R2. I cover SCVMM in more detail later in the book, but all of the storage features related to VHDX, SMB, and virtual Fibre Channel can be managed through SCVMM 2012 R2. In addition, SCVMM 2012 R2 can deploy complete file server clusters in addition to Hyper-V hosts.

FIGURE 4.34
A view of storage managed by SCVMM 2012 R2

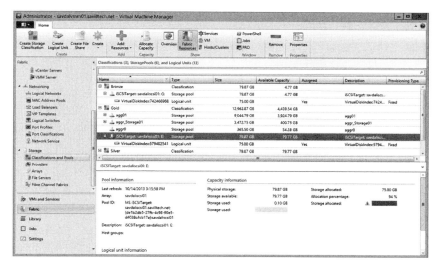

The Bottom Line

Explain the types of storage available to a virtual machine.   Windows Server provides various types of storage to a virtual machine. VHDX files provide a completely abstracted and self-contained virtual container for filesystems available to virtual machines, and 2012 R2 and above allow a VHDX file connected to the SCSI bus to be shared between multiple virtual machines, providing shared storage. Additionally, storage can be exposed to virtual machines that are hosted in SAN environments through the use of iSCSI running inside the guest operating system or through the new virtual Fibre Channel capability.

   Master It   Why is MPIO required?

Identify when to use Virtual Fibre Channel and when to use VHD Sets and the benefits of each.   Virtual Fibre Channel allows virtual machines to be directly connected to a Fibre Channel SAN without the host requiring zoning to the storage, but it requires knowledge of the storage fabric. A VHD Set provides shared storage to the virtual machine without requiring the users of the VHD Set to have knowledge of the storage fabric, which is useful in hosting the type of scenarios where all aspects of the physical fabric should be hidden from the users.

Articulate how SMB 3 can be used. SMB 3 went through a huge upgrade in Windows Server 2012, providing an enterprise-level file-based protocol that can now be used to store Hyper-V virtual machines. This includes additional storage options for Hyper-V environments, including fronting existing SANs with a Windows Server scale-out file server cluster to extend the SAN's accessibility beyond hosts with direct SAN connectivity.

Master It Which two SMB technologies enable virtual machines to move between nodes in an SoFS without any interruption to processing?

Chapter 5

Managing Hyper-V

The previous chapters explained the key building blocks of virtualization, and this chapter shows how to begin bringing together those separate blocks through consolidated management. While basic management can be performed using Hyper-V Manager, for most enterprise deployments it will be necessary to use System Center Virtual Machine Manager (SCVMM) as well as automation solutions such as PowerShell and System Center Orchestrator.

This chapter covers installing and securing Hyper-V before presenting details about virtual machine deployments and converting physical servers into a virtual machine.

In this chapter, you will learn to:

◆   Identify the ways to deploy Hyper-V.

◆   Explain why using Server Core or Nano Server is beneficial to deployments.

◆   Create and use virtual machine templates.

Installing Hyper-V

Hyper-V is a role of Windows Server 2008 and above that is enabled after the installation of the Windows Server operating system, and it's simple to enable it. Remember from Chapter 1, "Introduction to Virtualization and Microsoft Solutions," that the Hyper-V role is available in both the Standard and Datacenter SKUs of Windows Server. It's also the only role available in the free Microsoft Hyper-V Server offering that is aimed at VDI and Linux workloads that don't need the Windows Server guest licenses that are part of Standard and Datacenter licenses. The capabilities and scalability were the same for all three versions up to Windows Server 2016. However, with Windows Server 2016, the Datacenter SKU now has capabilities that the other versions do not—such as Storage Replica, Storage Spaces Direct, new network virtualization stack (HNVv2), and support for shielded VMs (which are covered later in this chapter). The scalability remains the same for all three versions in Windows Server 2016. The version you choose will depend on your exact requirements, but typically you'll choose the version based on the following:

Windows Server Datacenter   Used when you have a large number of virtual machines running Windows Server operating systems, especially when clustering hosts to provide maximum mobility for virtual machines. Datacenter also is an appropriate choice if you want to use the new network virtualization stack that has been inspired by Microsoft Azure (HNVvs) or need to use the new highly secure shielded VMs capability. While not a Hyper-V feature, many deployments today are hyperconverged, with both the compute and storage provided by the same systems, and this makes the 2016 Datacenter storage features Storage Spaces Direct and Storage Replica very useful. Datacenter allows an unlimited number of licenses for Windows Server virtual machines (known as *virtual operating environments* in Microsoft parlance).

Microsoft Hyper-V Server Used when not running Windows Server guest operating systems, which means that the virtual instance rights provided with Standard and Datacenter are not needed. Primarily aimed at environments in which VMs do not require Windows Server licenses, such as VDI environments that run Windows client operating systems in virtual machines and Linux environments. Both scenarios require their own separate licensing of the operating systems in the virtual machines.

Windows Server Standard Not typically used in virtualization environments, because Standard provides only two virtual OS instance rights running Windows Server that cannot be moved between servers. May be used in very lightly virtualized environments where clustering is typically not used.

Whether you use Standard or Datacenter, there is no difference in any operational activities; they are basically the same operating system. When you use the free Microsoft Hyper-V Server, the Hyper-V role is automatically enabled, removing the manual role additional action.

I should also note that Hyper-V is available as a feature in Windows 8 and above. It's the same Hyper-V code that is running in Windows Server; it is just missing some of the features that make no sense on a client operating system, such as virtual Fibre Channel, SR-IOV, Live Migration, and Hyper-V Replica. It's the same hypervisor using the same virtual hard disk formats, which means that you can take a virtual machine running on Windows 10 Hyper-V and run it on Windows Server 2016 Hyper-V with no changes required. You can even move in the opposite direction.

On the server side, you should make sure that servers are sized accordingly, based on the desired usage, and that they have the required network and storage connectivity. Processors are required to support hardware-assisted virtualization (Intel VT or AMD-V) and data execution prevention in the form of the Intel XD bit (execute disable bit) or AMD NX bit (no execute bit). The good news is that any server processor released since 2007 should definitely have these capabilities, and likely even older processors (the capability was added to Intel and AMD processors in 2005 and 2006, respectively).

Prior to Windows Server 2016, it was beneficial to have Second Level Address Translation (SLAT) for improved performance. It allows the processor to handle mapping of physical memory to virtual machine memory, which otherwise has to be handled by the hypervisor, increasing resource usage of the hypervisor. Intel calls this technology *Extended Page Tables (EPT)*, and AMD calls it *Rapid Virtualization Indexing (RVI)*. It was a required feature only when using RemoteFX GPU virtualization and the client versions of Hyper-V. In Windows Server 2016, this is now a requirement for base Hyper-V functionality, which means that very old servers may no longer be able to run the Hyper-V role.

To check your server processors' capabilities, download `coreinfo.exe` from:

`http://technet.microsoft.com/en-us/sysinternals/cc835722.aspx`

and execute with the -v switch, which shows virtualization-related processor features. A * means that the feature is present; a - means that it is missing.

```
PS C:\temp> .\Coreinfo.exe -v

Coreinfo v3.31 - Dump information on system CPU and memory topology
Copyright (C) 2008-2014 Mark Russinovich
Sysinternals - www.sysinternals.com
Intel(R) Xeon(R) CPU E5-2660 v3 @ 2.60GHz
Intel64 Family 6 Model 63 Stepping 2, GenuineIntel
```

```
Microcode signature: 00000036
HYPERVISOR        -       Hypervisor is present
VMX               *       Supports Intel hardware-assisted virtualization
EPT               *       Supports Intel extended page tables (SLAT)
```

Provided that you see a * for the hardware-assisted virtualization, your system is capable of running Hyper-V.

Using Configuration Levels

Before discussing enabling the Hyper-V role, this section covers configuration levels, which was a new concept in Windows Server 2012 that was built on Server Core, introduced in Windows Server 2008. Server Core was a minimal installation of the Windows Server operating system with no graphical shell, no management tools, no .NET, and no PowerShell, and it was designed to run certain Windows Server roles such as Active Directory Domain Controller, Hyper-V, and File Server. The goals behind Server Core were to have an operating system with fewer components that were not required for many server roles and therefore to cut down on patches needed, reduce possible vulnerabilities, and reduce the number of reboots associated with patches. There was also a small resource overhead reduction. This goal was a good one, but Server Core was hard to manage and could not be used with Server Manager remotely, and people largely ignored it. Windows Server 2008 R2 improved on this with remote management via Server Manager and PowerShell support, but the hard choice at installation time made using Server Core scary, and it's still avoided by most IT organizations.

Windows Server 2012 changed this inflexible choice at installation, enabling the graphic shell and management tool features to be added and removed like any other feature, which made it easy to switch a server from being in Server Core mode to being a full server with a graphical interface. Additionally, more granularity was introduced to allow different configuration levels, which are shown in Figure 5.1. Notice that with configuration levels, it is possible to remove the graphical shell but still have the management tools available locally to the server. The default installation option for Windows Server 2012 and above is now Server Core, which shows the shift to Server Core being "the norm" for a Windows server, with nearly every Windows role and feature supported on Server Core in Windows Server 2012 R2. In addition, for applications to receive Microsoft's Gold Certification, which is the highest level of application certification, the application must run without the graphical shell installed. The Windows Server 2012 R2 Server Core base footprint is about 1GB smaller than Windows Server 2012 Server Core, thanks to new optimizations and compression of optional features that are not actually installed.

FIGURE 5.1
Configuration levels available in Windows Server 2012 R2

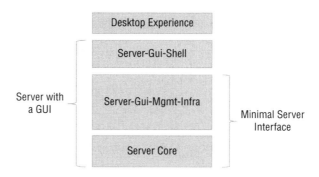

Consider a Hyper-V host. The host operating system is the management partition for the virtual machine, providing critical services and connectivity, which means that if the host operating system must be restarted, every virtual machine also has to be restarted. For this reason, it's critical that the maintenance and reboots required are as minimal as possible, and that means running all Hyper-V servers at the Server Core configuration level and managing them remotely. I should point out that in a production environment, the Hyper-V hosts should be clustered, which means that a host can be patched and rebooted with no impact to virtual machine availability, because virtual machines can be moved between hosts with no downtime. However, it is still desirable to minimize maintenance and reboots as much as possible.

SERVER CORE STILL SEEMS TO HAVE A LOT OF PATCHES IN WINDOWS SERVER 2012

In the Windows Server 2008 time frame, about 50 percent fewer patches applied to Server Core compared to a full installation (Server with a GUI), enabling servers to go many months without a reboot. For Windows Server 2012, many organizations found that many patches were required for Server Core, which meant similar reboots for Server Core and a Server with a GUI deployment.

There are a number of binaries present on Server Core that are used, but vulnerabilities that may get patched in the binary do not always apply to Server Core. The problem is that Windows Update will see the binary present and patch it and therefore require a reboot, but determining whether the patch applies to Server Core requires reading the security bulletin related to the patch. For example, in a single year about 10 critical patches with bulletins were released, but you would find that fewer than half of these were needed on Server Core if you read the bulletin. If you just ran Windows Update, though, they would have all been applied.

If you want the most optimal Server Core patching with the least possible reboots, you cannot just run Windows Update. Instead, you need to verify the security bulletins for critical updates to check whether they apply to Server Core. On the plus side, this does show that Server Core, even without the patching, is inherently less susceptible to vulnerabilities.

Although all management can be done remotely, if you ever experience a problem where the management tools would aid the resolution or even the graphical shell, simply add the components using Server Manager or PowerShell. Once the problem is resolved, remove them again. Likewise, if you have not automated the deployment of servers and like to perform initial configuration using graphical tools, you can install servers in the Server with a GUI mode, and then after the server is fully configured, the management tools and graphical shell can be removed to run in Server Core mode.

For example, to move from Server with a GUI to Server Core, I just need to remove `Server-Gui-Mgmt-Infra` (which also removes `Server-Gui-Shell`, since `Server-Gui-Shell` is dependent on `Server-Gui-Mgmt-Infra`):

```
Uninstall-WindowsFeature Server-Gui-Mgmt-Infra -Restart
```

To take Server Core and make it a full server with a GUI, use this command:

```
Install-WindowsFeature Server-Gui-Mgmt-Infra,Server-Gui-Shell -Restart
```

Windows Server 2016 and Nano Server

Windows Server 2016 has taken a giant step forward in the way Windows Server can be deployed as well as in its footprint and associated patching/reboots. However, it has also taken a little step back in the flexibility of configuration levels. Server Core is still fairly large, because it carries a lot of legacy weight from 20 years of Windows. Nano Server is a brand new deployment type in Windows Server 2016, which is not only much smaller but also represents a shift in the way we think about deploying and maintaining Windows Server deployments.

NANO SERVER OVERVIEW

Nano Server is a headless deployment of Windows Server that is managed remotely via Windows Management Instrumentation (WMI) and PowerShell. There is no local interface for Nano Server other than an emergency recovery console, which can help reset the network state and WinRM (Windows Remote Management), but that is basically it—no local GUI, no local command prompt, no local PowerShell, and no RDP. So what do you do if the server is not functioning? As I mentioned previously, there is a recovery console, shown in Figure 5.2, but unless your problem is an IP address, firewall, or WinRM issue, it won't help. Many issues can be remediated remotely using PowerShell and the management tools, which have long been a core premise of Windows Server; no local logons, however, are available, as the mentality about servers is changing.

FIGURE 5.2
Nano Server Recovery Console

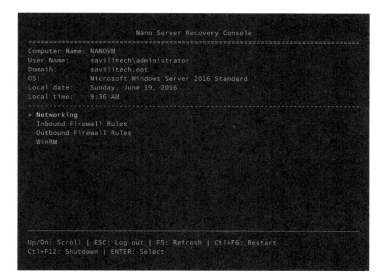

You may have heard people talk about pets vs. cattle in relation to servers, and this conversation refers to the new ways servers are deployed and managed. Traditionally, IT departments think of servers as pets. The servers are named, cared for, and healed if sick. Moreover, each server has a unique purpose that would be hard to replace. In the new world, servers are cattle. If a server is sick, it is "shot" and replaced with a new one. Effort is not wasted trying to heal servers, and all configurations can easily be deployed using declarative technologies like PowerShell DSC (Desired State Configuration), Chef, or Puppet to a standard OS image. Nano Servers are the epitome of this thinking and are designed to be created fast, deployed fast, and replaced fast as needed.

I mentioned a smaller footprint. How much smaller? The typical size for Nano Server is 500MB, but this will vary depending on the roles and features added. The first start of a Nano Server deployment is literally a couple of seconds, which includes any specialization. Reboots are equally fast when required. There was originally talk of less patching and associated reboots during early technical previews, but Microsoft has shifted to a single cumulative update (CU) once a month for Windows Server 2016. This change avoids having every organization deploy different combinations of patches, which made any comprehensive testing matrix impossible for Microsoft and was the cause of problems hitting customers in production that were not found during testing. By having a single, cumulative update that contains all updates, a singular testing platform is provided, as well as greater confidence that any problems will be discovered in testing and not in production. Because of this single CU, Nano Server will not have fewer patches; it will simply have one patch, like every other deployment type of Windows Server 2016.

One of the reasons Nano Server is so small is that unlike other deployment types of Windows Server, Nano Server has no roles of features natively included; it is a bare-bones operating system. You have to create a custom image for Nano Server and add the various roles and features that you want; alternatively, you can add them post deployment. Nano Server supports only 64-bit applications, tools, and agents. As part of making Nano Server lean, it does not support full .NET and instead supports a subset through its support of CoreCLR (`https://blogs.msdn.microsoft.com/dotnet/2015/02/03/coreclr-is-now-open-source/`) that gives access to most .NET Framework capabilities including PowerShell through a new Core PowerShell. Though initially it supports only a subset of cmdlets, this will expand over time. For the initial RTM (Release to Manufacturing) of Windows Server 2016, Nano Server is not suitable for all roles. It is not aimed at being a general application server, but this will change. Nano Server will be the foundation for Windows Server for the next 20 years. Initially, Nano Server is primarily aimed at two key scenarios:

◆ Born-in-the-cloud applications built around CoreCLR, PaaS, and ASP.NET 5

◆ Cloud platform (Hyper-V and Scale-Out File Servers)

Additional roles are supported, such as DNS and Windows Containers, and this will continue to expand in the same manner that roles were added to Server Core after initially having a limited set when it first launched in Windows Server 2008. Nano Server supports features such as clustering, shielded VMs, PowerShell DSC, Windows Defender, and the normal drivers for physical deployments and components required when running as a Hyper-V VM. Note that Nano Server is still Windows Server—it still has components such as performance counters and event logs—it has just been refactored from the ground up as "just enough OS" for the new generation of applications and services.

Nano Server Deployment

If you deploy Windows Server 2016, you will notice that there is no Nano Server option. Instead, there are two deployment options for Standard and Datacenter, as shown in Figure 5.3—Windows Server 2016 and Windows Server 2016 (Desktop Experience). In Figure 5.3, both Standard and Datacenter are shown (as no product key was entered, which normally sets the SKU).

FIGURE 5.3
Windows Server 2016
installation choices

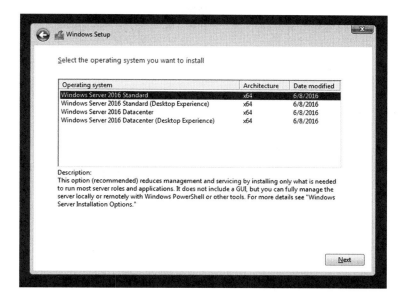

If you select the non–Desktop Experience option, you have a Server Core configuration-level deployment. Selecting the Desktop Experience option sets a Server with a GUI configuration with the Desktop Experience user interface added.

I mentioned a small step back at the start of this section. Figure 5.4 shows the new configuration levels for Windows Server 2016. Notice that unlike Windows Server 2012 R2, which had four configuration levels, Windows Server 2016 has two: Windows Server (which is Server Core) and Windows Server with Desktop Experience (everything including Desktop Experience, which is aimed for Remote Desktop Session Hosts). There is no middle ground—you either run as Server Core, which is the deployment mode of choice, or with every graphical element there is. The small step backward is that the ability to change configuration levels post deployment is no longer available. The deployment mode is set at time of installation and cannot be changed by modifying the user-interface level. No Hyper-V server should ever use Windows Server (Desktop Experience) outside of experimenting in a lab environment and should instead be running Server Core or the new Nano Server level.

So how do you deploy Nano Server if it is not an installation option from the 2016 media? On the Windows Server 2016 media is a folder named Nano Server that contains the core NanoServer.wim file, which is about only 150MB, and separate folders containing additional language-neutral packages with their associated language-specific packages that can be added to a custom Nano Server image to add functionality. Also in the folder is the PowerShell tool to create your custom Nano Server VHD or WIM file: NanoServerImageGenerator.

In addition, a graphical tool is available for download from Microsoft that is being delivered out-of-band (OOB) to enable Microsoft to continue to update and improve the tool based on feedback. This tool is the Nano Server Image Builder, a wizard-based tool that guides the user through the image creation process of both VHD and WIM images. The graphical tool is intuitive and provides the same options available through the PowerShell tool.

FIGURE 5.4
Windows Server 2016
configuration levels

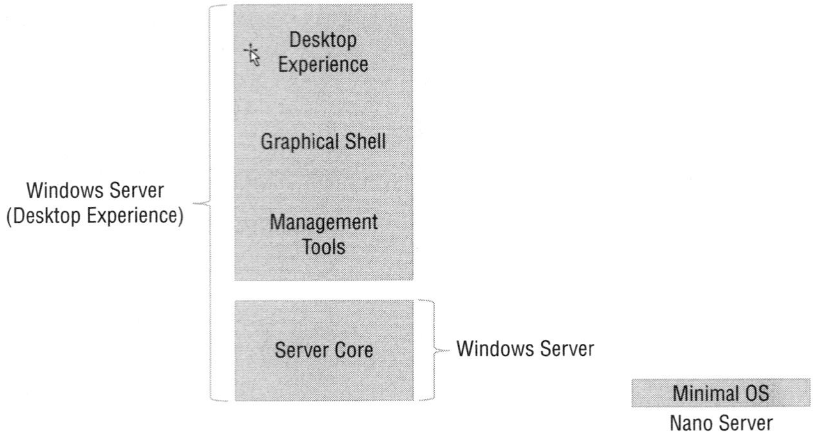

I prefer the PowerShell tool, as it enables the creation of the Nano Server instances to be automated. I use the PowerShell tool in the example in this chapter. Microsoft has a detailed document available at https://technet.microsoft.com/en-us/library/mt126167.aspx that I recommend reviewing. In this example, I create a Nano Server custom VHDX file. However, it is also possible to create custom WIM files. The VHDX files you create can be used for virtual machines and for physical deployments using the Windows Server native boot-to-VHD feature. A WIM file would be expanded out and deployed to an actual physical system where the boot-to-VHD is not desired.

Many parameters are available when using the New-NanoServerImage cmdlet to create a custom image, including naming of the OS, joining a domain, setting IP configuration, and indicating SKU version and packages. However, it is also possible to pass in an unattended answer file that enables every other aspect of the configuration in addition to configurations possible via the parameters. A good way to create the unattend.xml file is by using the Windows System Image Manager (SIM) that is part of the Windows Assessment and Deployment Kit (Windows ADK). The following XML sets the time zone of the OS to Central Time (which could also be performed using tzutil /s "Central Standard Time" remotely via Enter-PSSession post deployment):

```
<?xml version="1.0" encoding="utf-8"?>
<unattend xmlns="urn:schemas-microsoft-com:unattend">
    <settings pass="specialize">
        <component name="Microsoft-Windows-Shell-Setup"
processorArchitecture="amd64" publicKeyToken="31bf3856ad364e35"
 language="neutral" versionScope="nonSxS"
 xmlns:wcm="http://schemas.microsoft.com/WMIConfig/2002/State"
 xmlns:xsi="http://www.w3.org/2001/XMLSchema-instance">
            <TimeZone>Central Standard Time</TimeZone>
        </component>
    </settings>
</unattend>
```

You may wonder how the customization of the OS is performed when a custom unattend.xml file can be passed. The New-NanoServerImage cmdlet works by using the unattended applica-tion feature of Deployment Image Servicing and Management (DISM) that enables the offline application of an unattended answer file to an image directly, without requiring the unattend.xml to be passed during the specialization phase. If you look at the Nano Server image-generator script, you will see the DISM line that uses the /Apply-Unattend parameter, which is how the configuration is applied. The great thing about this approach is it that it allows you to add your own unattend.xml file for additional configurations required during specialization.

The following PowerShell creates a new Nano Server VHD file that can be used with VMs running on Hyper-V. The content of the NanoServer\NanoServerImageGenerator folder on the Windows Server 2016 media has been copied to the D:\NanoBuild folder in this example. In this example, the execution is performed on a member of the domain to which the Nano instance is being joined, enabling a simple join action. It is also possible, however, to join a domain when the creating environment is not part of the same domain, and this is fully documented in the Microsoft article mentioned at the start of this section (https://technet.microsoft.com/en-us/library/mt126167.aspx).

```
#Load the PowerShell module

Import-Module 'D:\NanoBuild\NanoServerImageGenerator.psm1 `

#Setup variables to store the local administrator password and location
#for target VHD to be created
$adminPass = ConvertTo-SecureString "Pa55word" -AsPlainText -Force
$NanoVHDPath = ".\NanoServerVM.vhd"

#Create the image
New-NanoServerImage -MediaPath 'S:\W2016\Expanded' `
    -BasePath .\Base -TargetPath $NanoVHDPath -ComputerName NanoVM `
    -DeploymentType Guest -Edition Standard `
    -Storage -Defender -EnableRemoteManagementPort `
    -Package Microsoft-NanoServer-DSC-Package `
    -AdministratorPassword $adminPass `

    -DomainName savilltech -ReuseDomainNode `
    -UnattendPath .\unattend.xml
```

The key components of this example are shown in Table 5.1.

TABLE 5.1:   *New-NanoServerImage* Key Parameters

PARAMETER	MEANING
-MediaPath	Location of the Windows Server 2016 media
-BasePath	Temporary folder used while creating the image
-TargetPath	Location for the created file
-ComputerName	Name of the Nano Server instance

TABLE 5.1: *New-NanoServerImage* Key Parameters *(CONTINUED)*

PARAMETER	MEANING
`-DeploymentType`	Guest for a Hyper-V VM, which adds the necessary Hyper-V guest drivers and components (`Microsoft-NanoServer-Guest-Package`), while Host adds drivers for a physical deployment (`Microsoft-NanoServer-Host-Package`)
`-Edition`	Standard or Datacenter
`-AdministratorPassword`	Password for the local Administrator account
`-DomainName`	Name of domain to join. `-ReuseDomainNode` uses an existing domain object with the same name, which is useful if replacing an existing deployment.
`-UnattendPath`	An `unattend.xml` file with additional configurations
`-Storage -Defender` `-EnableRemoteManagementPort`	Adds the file server role and other storage components, Windows Defender antimalware, and enables WinRM remote management

The output `NanoServerVM.vhd` file can be used by a VM, and it will start without further configuration. Moreover, even though it has to perform the specialization phase of the OS setup, it will still start in a couple of seconds.

If creating a Nano Server image for a physical deployment as a Hyper-V host, the `-DeploymentType Guest` would be replaced with `-DeploymentType Host`. Additionally, the `-OEMDrivers` parameter would add the standard network adapter and storage controller drivers included in Server Core, `-Compute` would add the Hyper-V role, and `-Clustering` would add the Failover Clustering feature.

NANO SERVER MANAGEMENT

The mantra of Windows Server is always to manage remotely—even *if* it has the graphical interface and management tools locally. This is accomplished by installing the Remote Server Administration Tools (RSAT) on the client-equivalent operating system; that is, Windows 10 for Windows Server 2016. The Windows 10 RSAT can be downloaded from www.microsoft.com/en-us/download/details.aspx?id=45520. Additionally, the Hyper-V Manager tool is native to Windows 8 and above (since Hyper-V is built into Windows 8 and above) via the Programs And Features Control Panel applet ➤ Turn Windows Features On Or Off ➤ Hyper-V Management Tools, as shown in Figure 5.5. The RSAT adds tools, such as Server Manager and the Microsoft Management Console (MMC) tools, which all support full remote management. Additionally, the RSAT adds the various PowerShell modules to enable remote PowerShell management.

Nano Server remote management is not just advised but necessary, because of the absence of any local console and because many Server Core users wish to use a GUI despite the presence of the local command shell, PowerShell, and SCONFIG (a text-based menu for many configurations and activities). If you want to manage machines that are in a workgroup or other domain without a trust, you need to add them as a trusted host, which removes the authentication of the remote computer. The easiest way to do this is by using PowerShell. The following code fetches the current content and then adds a new set of hosts—in this case, every machine in savilltech.net:

```
$trusthosts = (Get-Item -Path WSMan:\localhost\Client\TrustedHosts).Value
Set-Item -Path WSMan:\localhost\Client\TrustedHosts `
"$trusthosts, *.savilltech.net" -Force
```

FIGURE 5.5
Adding the Hyper-V
Management Tools to
Windows 10

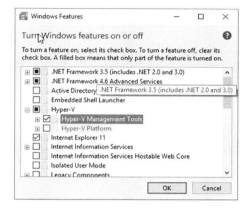

If machines are in a workgroup, you also need to configure the following:

```
reg add HKLM\SOFTWARE\Microsoft\Windows\CurrentVersion\Policies\System /v
LocalAccountTokenFilterPolicy /t REG_DWORD /d 1 /f
```

Hyper-V Manager in Windows 10/2016 enables a different credential to be specified when connecting to remote servers that are running Windows Server 2016 or Windows 10 (as does Server Manager). The use of alternate credentials is enabled by the switch to WS-MAN for remote communication, which enables the use of CredSSP, Kerberos, or NTLM for authentication. Down-level versions of Hyper-V to Windows Server 2012/Windows 8 can be managed from the Windows Server 2016 version of Hyper-V Manager. Constrained Delegation of credentials will be required in certain scenarios, and this is discussed in Chapter 7, "Failover Clustering and Migration Technologies."

Another management option that is new to Windows Server 2016 (but support for Windows Server 2012 and Windows Server 2012 R2 will be enabled through the automated deployment of Windows Management Framework 5 and a special SMT provider) is the new Server Management Tools (SMT). Hosted in Azure, these graphical tools provide most of the common configurations and actions required for Windows Server management in addition to providing a PowerShell console. While these tools are currently hosted in Azure, I would expect them also to be available in Microsoft Azure Stack at some point in the future, enabling the same capabilities without leveraging the Azure public-cloud service, which will be useful for environments that either don't have Internet connectivity or are required to not connect to the Internet.

Even though SMT is hosted in Azure, there is no requirement for the on-premises servers to connect directly to the Internet nor to have firewall ports open for inbound connections from Azure on the perimeter firewall. This is enabled through an SMT gateway that is deployed on-premises and establishes an outbound connection to Azure using HTTPS, which is then leveraged for the management activity communications. The gateway pulls requests from Azure. This can be seen in Figure 5.6. Each gateway can support connections to multiple target servers.

FIGURE 5.6
Using Server
Management Tools
with on-premises
OS instances

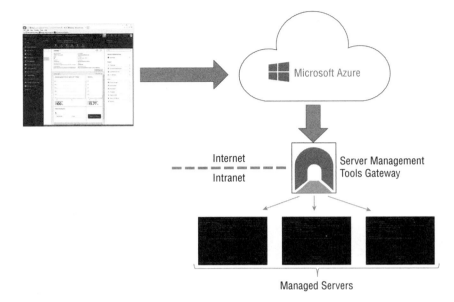

SMT instances are added via the Azure Marketplace by searching for Server Manager Tools. Once an instance is created, you will be guided through the deployment of a gateway that involves installing the generated package to an on-premises Windows Server running Windows Server 2012 R2 (with WMF 5) or above. The complete process is documented at `http://windowsitpro.com/windows-server-2016/server-management-tools-using-windows-server-2016`, but the Azure portal guides you through each step that is required, as shown in Figure 5.7.

FIGURE 5.7
Gateway deployment
guidance for Server
Management Tools

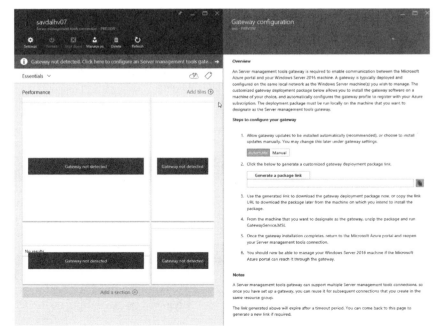

Each time an instance is connected to, you need to enter the credentials used to manage the machine, as the credentials are not stored in Azure. The credentials should be entered in the format of <domain>\<username>. Once the instance is connected, basic metrics about the management target are displayed, including CPU, memory, and network adapters. Disk metrics can also be enabled on a temporary basis, but these should not be left enabled because they have an adverse impact on performance. Actions to shut down and restart the system in addition to Settings appear on the toolbar. Clicking the Settings action opens the management options and tools available for the system, as shown in Figure 5.8. Notice the PowerShell tool item that opens a full PowerShell window enabling every aspect of configuration.

FIGURE 5.8
Server Management
Tools instance in
Azure with tools
available

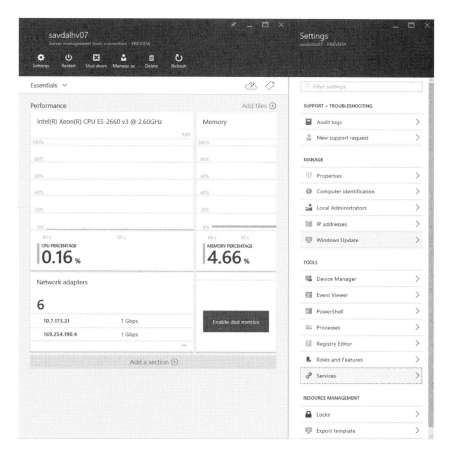

Enabling the Hyper-V Role

When the operating system has been installed on a server and has been patched, the next step is to enable the Hyper-V role. Because your server will be running at the Server Core configuration level, there is no local way graphically to install the Hyper-V role; instead, PowerShell can be leveraged:

```
Install-WindowsFeature -Name Hyper-V -Restart
```

Notice that I am not including the -IncludeManagementTools switch, because the management tools cannot install on Server Core and would require a change in the configuration level. The server will reboot, and the Hyper-V hypervisor will be loaded on the bare-metal hardware and ready for use. The next step would be to start managing through SCVMM, creating virtual switches, virtual machines, and so on.

The Hyper-V role can also be enabled using Server Manager from a remote Windows 10 machine that has the RSAT installed or from another Windows Server 2016 server that has the management tools installed. The process to enable using Server Manager is as follows:

1. Launch Server Manager.

2. From the Manage menu, choose Add Roles And Features.

3. Click Next on the wizard introduction screen.

4. For the installation type, select the Role-Based Or Feature-Based installation.

5. From the list, select the server that will have the Hyper-V role installed. If your target server is not shown, you must first add it as a managed server via the Manage ➢ Add Servers action in the main Server Manager interface.

6. In the Server Roles screen, select the Hyper-V role.

7. As shown in Figure 5.9, a dialog box appears from which you can also install the management tools and PowerShell module. Uncheck the Include Management Tools check box and click Continue (the Add Features button changes to a Continue button). Click Next on the Server Roles screen.

FIGURE 5.9
Local management tools are not wanted on a Hyper-V server that should be at the Server Core configuration level.

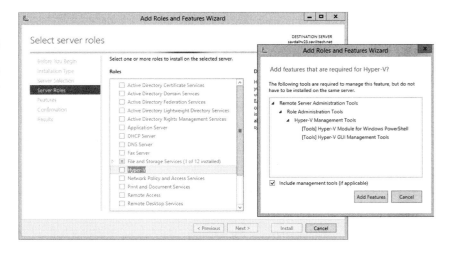

8. Click Next on the Features screen.

9. Numerous optional configurations can be performed during the Hyper-V role installation from Server Manager—specifically, creating a virtual switch, configuring migration options, and choosing the default locations for virtual machines. Click Next on the introduction screen for these options.

10. In the Create Virtual Switches page, do not select any network adapters. It is better to create the virtual switches post deployment, as discussed in Chapter 3, "Virtual Networking." Click Next.

11. On the Virtual Machine Manager screen, you can enable Live Migration and choose the authentication protocol to use. This can be changed at any time in the future, but for now, do not configure this. Just click Next again.

12. The Default Stores page allows you to specify the default location for virtual hard disks and virtual machine configuration files. These locations can be changed in the future and will be overridden by SCVMM. Click Next.

13. On the Configuration page, select the Restart The Destination Server Automatically If Required check box (click Yes when you are prompted to verify that you are sure you want the server to reboot automatically). Then click Install to complete the Hyper-V role installation. Once the reboot is complete, Hyper-V is installed.

Actions after Installation of Hyper-V

Once the Hyper-V role is enabled on a server, several important steps and processes need to be in place. Some obvious actions, such as actually creating virtual machines, are covered later in this section and throughout the book. There are other items, though, that you need to ensure are implemented or at least considered:

◆ Add the server to SCVMM. This should be the first action before you create NIC teams, configure Fibre Channel, create virtual switches, join clusters, or anything else, because all of these items can be configured and managed through SCVMM in a centralized fashion. Once the SCVMM agent is installed on the host and is being managed by SCVMM, you should add to clusters, deploy logical switches, and so on, to make the server ready to host workloads.

◆ If you are not using SCVMM, you should create NIC teams and virtual switches according to the guidelines discussed in Chapter 3. Remember to use a consistent naming scheme for your switches to ensure that there is no network connectivity interruption when you're live-migrating virtual machines between hosts.

◆ Add the server to a cluster or create a new cluster and add cluster disks to Cluster Shared Volumes to enable simultaneous access to the storage across the cluster.

◆ If you are running antivirus software on the Hyper-V hosts, ensure that you have the proper exclusions configured, or problems can arise due to locking by the malware solution. The key exclusions for files and processes, documented at `http://support .microsoft.com/kb/961804/en-us`, are essentially blocking everywhere virtual machines are stored and the `vmms.exe` and `wmwp.exe` processes. Another option is not to run malware protection, but most security departments would not be OK with this. If you consider that the Hyper-V server is running Server Core, with no one ever logging on to the box or running other applications, its vulnerability level would be very low. However, I don't advocate having no malware protection. Instead, I recommend running a supported malware solution with the exclusions just mentioned.

◆ Ensure that you have a patching strategy in place, but also remember that a reboot will bring down all virtual machines unless they are live-migrated to another server prior to reboot. Patching options range from using Microsoft Update to using Windows Server Update Services or System Center Configuration Manager, which both include a local patch repository of approved patches that can be deployed in a controlled manner, even adhering to configured maintenance windows. When you're using clusters of Hyper-V hosts, there are built-in capabilities (which are discussed in Chapter 7) that allow an entire cluster to be patched with a single click without any virtual machine downtime. The important point is to have a patching strategy that will be adhered to and that ensures that patches are tested prior to implementation in production.

◆ As workloads are running in virtual machines on the Hyper-V host, it is important that they are backed up. This backup may be performed at the Hyper-V host level or potentially from within the virtual machine. The decision will depend on the workload being protected and the desired granularity of restoration. This decision is discussed later in the book, but it's important that a backup solution is running.

◆ Virtualization is moving many operating system instances on to a reduced number of physical hosts, which means that it's critical that those physical boxes are healthy and available. Monitoring is a critical element to ensure that you have insight into the environment. Monitoring should be in place for all of the various critical components, such as the physical server, operating system, networking, storage, and services within virtual machines. Additionally, a monitoring solution that proactively notifies you of problems and nonoptimal configurations is preferred over a solution that just notifies you after something has failed. Users will notify you of failures for free.

IMPORTANCE OF A PRODUCTION-EQUIVALENT TEST ENVIRONMENT

A Hyper-V solution has many moving parts, including the servers, operating system, additional management components, drivers for hardware (such as Fibre Channel cards and network cards), firmware on servers and cards, and software versions on other components, such as storage area networks. It's important to test any changes you want to make to your production Hyper-V environment before you make them. That requires a testing/development environment that accurately reflects the production environment; otherwise, you will not have the required assurance that when you implement a change in production, it will be successful and not cause problems. This means that you need to have servers with the same hardware, the same firmware versions, the same management, and so on in your testing environment. The closer it is to the production environment, the more confidence you'll have that a successful test process will result in success in production.

I heard of a company that tested an implementation in the test environment and then moved to production, and within a few days, started suffering blue screens and huge service outages. It was caused by a mismatch of driver and firmware in production that was not present in the test environment. There are many similar stories, unfortunately.

This does not mean that the testing environment needs to be on the same scale as the production environment. I may have 200 servers in production and 2 in development, and that's generally OK (unless you are performing scalability testing). What is important is that the components are the same.

This list is not definitive, and your organization may have other processes, such as adding to change-control systems, but certainly these actions should be considered the minimum actions to take.

Deploying Hyper-V Servers with SCVMM

You already have a method to deploy operating systems to your physical servers. This could be over the network from a solution like System Center Configuration Manager or Windows Deployment Services, installation locally from a USB device or CD, or even some other process. That process may be well understood and tested and should be maintained for your Hyper-V hosts as much as possible. Minimizing the number of ways an action is performed reduces complexity and the chance of errors. If your process is not optimal, there is a solution to deploy Hyper-V hosts (and even file servers in the 2012 R2 release and above) included as part of SCVMM.

Rather than document the complete process to deploy a Hyper-V server with SCVMM, I instead refer you to the Microsoft step-by-step detailed documentation available at the following location:

```
http://technet.microsoft.com/en-us/library/gg610634.aspx
```

I do, however, want to cover the high-level process and specifically what a Hyper-V host deployed using SCVMM will look like once deployed. SCVMM uses a feature, boot-to-VHD, that allows a physical server (or desktop) to boot from a VHD file.

At a very high level, the following actions are performed:

1. Windows Deployment Services is deployed to the same subnet that the servers are being deployed to (or an IP helper-address is configured on the switch in the subnet with the servers and points to the WDS server) and is configured inside SCVMM as a PXE server (which allows SCVMM to configure and add required images to WDS).

2. You must have a sysprep'd VHDX file containing Windows Server 2012 R2. This could be the same VHDX file you use to deploy virtual machines, but it must match the type of system. For example, if the server is BIOS based, the VHDX should be from a generation 1 type VM.

3. A physical computer profile is created in SCVMM that SCVMM 2012 R2 allows you to configure if it will be used for a Hyper-V host or a Windows file server. In this profile, the VHDX file to be used is configured along with items such as domain membership, naming, product key, specific actions, and configurations. This profile will be used when deploying the physical host.

4. The physical server to be deployed is added to SCVMM via the Fabric workspace. The physical server must support one of the SCVMM-supported out-of-band management protocols such as IPMI or SMASH. You must have the address and credentials for the connection. Add the server to SCVMM (as shown in Figure 5.10), which will then deploy the new server by copying the VHDX file to the target server and configuring the host to boot from the VHDX file.

If you run into problems using the SCVMM host deployment, a troubleshooting flowchart, which is a great resource for helping to identify problems, is available at the following location:

```
http://blogs.technet.com/b/scvmm/archive/2011/04/20/
troubleshooting-os-deployment-of-hyper-v-through-sc-vmm-2012.aspx
```

FIGURE 5.10
Selecting the pro-
tocol to be used for
the new server to be
provisioned

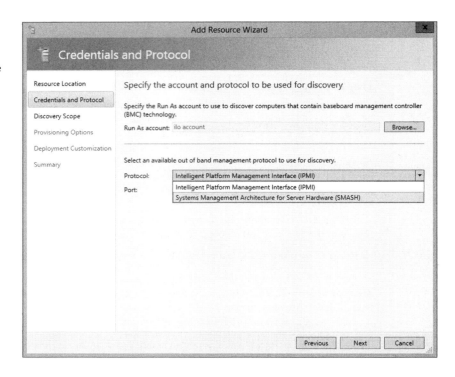

MANUALLY CONFIGURING BOOT FROM VHD

The option to use Boot from VHD simplifies the process used by SCVMM, but it can be used as part of a normal OS deployment with a few extra steps. I walk through the process at the following location (which also includes a video):

```
http://windowsitpro.com/virtualization/
q-how-can-i-install-windows-7-or-windows-server-2008-r2-virtual-hard-disk-vhd-file
```

The process is the same for Windows Server 2012, as described in the article.

Hyper-V Management Tools

Based on the assumption that your Hyper-V servers are all running Server Core, all graphical management tools will be run remotely, typically from a Windows 10 client operating
system. There are three primary Hyper-V management environments. Additionally, remember that some management functions aren't specific to Hyper-V, such as management via
Server Manager. Windows Server 2012 and above have remote management enabled by
default, which means no configurations are required to be able to manage a server instance
remotely.

The first management environment is the built-in Hyper-V Manager. Typically, for a client operating system to manage server operating systems remotely, Remote Server Administration Tools must be installed. They are available from the following location:

`www.microsoft.com/en-us/download/details.aspx?id=45520`

This would include management tools such as Server Manager, but because Hyper-V is built into Windows 10, the Hyper-V graphical management tool and the PowerShell cmdlets are also built-in and just need to be enabled, as explained previously in the Nano Server section.

The second environment is PowerShell, which contains a large number of cmdlets that are specific to Hyper-V and are available by loading the Hyper-V PowerShell module:

```
Import-Module Hyper-V
```

The preceding command manually loads the Hyper-V module, which is always the best practice. However, PowerShell version 3 and above features a module autoload capability that automatically loads modules as needed if cmdlets are used from modules not yet available.

The third environment is the SCVMM graphical tools (and strictly speaking, SCVMM also has its own PowerShell module, making it a fourth environment). The SCVMM graphical tools are covered in detail in Chapter 9, "Implementing the Private Cloud, SCVMM, and Microsoft Azure Stack," but they can easily be installed on a Windows client:

1. Launch the SCVMM setup routine.

2. Click Install.

3. On the Select Features To Install page, select the VMM Console check box, as shown in Figure 5.11.

4. Complete all of the other dialog boxes, which prompt you to accept the license agreement and configure update settings, and finally, click Install.

FIGURE 5.11
Selecting to install only the VMM console on a client operating system

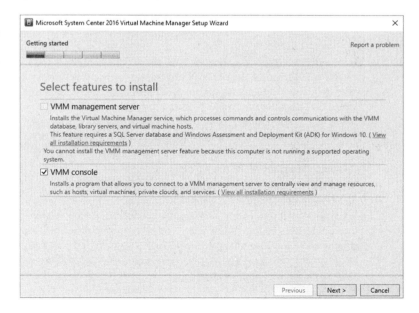

Note that additionally if you use Failover Clustering, which should always be the case for a production Hyper-V environment, many of the activities previously done with Hyper-V Manager will need to be completed using Failover Cluster Manager. If you use SCVMM, it can equally manage clustered and unclustered environments without using the native Windows Server tools. Once you decide to use SCVMM, you should *only* use SCVMM.

Figure 5.12 shows a Windows 10 client that has the Hyper-V Manager, Hyper-V PowerShell module, and SCVMM console running at the same time. The only requirement is that the user has the correct privileges on the Hyper-V hosts and SCVMM. The SCVMM 2012 R2 console is supported back to Windows 7 SP1, as documented at:

`http://technet.microsoft.com/en-us/library/gg610640.aspx`

FIGURE 5.12
All key Hyper-V management environments running on a Windows 10 client

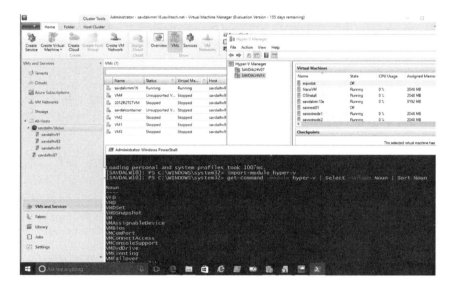

However, the Windows Server 2016 Hyper-V Manager is only part of Windows 10, and the RSAT for Windows Server 2016 will install only on Windows 10. If you really need to manage Windows 2016 servers from an older client, there are some workarounds. I walk through a solution in a video at `http://youtu.be/_dkxyr03Er4`. The solution is to configure a Remote Desktop Session Host, which has the administration tools installed, and then publish them to other client operating systems. It's not ideal, but it does work.

Using Hyper-V Manager

Many aspects of Hyper-V Manager are covered throughout this book. For example, virtual switches are covered in Chapter 3, virtual SANs are covered in Chapter 4, "Storage Configurations," and migration and replication settings are covered in future chapters. In this section, I cover the main components of Hyper-V Manager and some core configurations. If I don't cover a feature, it means that it's covered elsewhere in the book in a section that's more specific to the topic.

Figure 5.13 shows the Hyper-V Manager interface with the five main panes of information and capabilities exposed. Notice in the far-left server inventory pane that it is possible to add multiple Hyper-V servers to Hyper-V Manager. It is not possible to specify alternate credentials prior to Windows Server 2016, which means that only Hyper-V servers in trusting domains can be added where your current credentials have administrative rights. In Windows Server 2016, alternate credentials can be specified, enabling Hyper-V servers from different domains and even workgroups to be managed. To add a new Hyper-V server to Hyper-V Manager, select the Connect To Server action available on the Hyper-V Manager root navigation menu root in the navigation pane. From Windows 10 or Windows Server 2016 Hyper-V Manager, the Select Computer dialog box also has the Connect As Another User option, and the Set User button enables an alternate credential to be specified, as shown in Figure 5.14. You will need to perform this when managing from a Windows 10 client because, by default, no Hyper-V servers will be shown. In previous versions of Windows, there were various manual tasks to perform on the Hyper-V server to enable remote management, but this is no longer necessary; all configurations for remote management are enabled by default.

FIGURE 5.13
The Hyper-V Manager interface

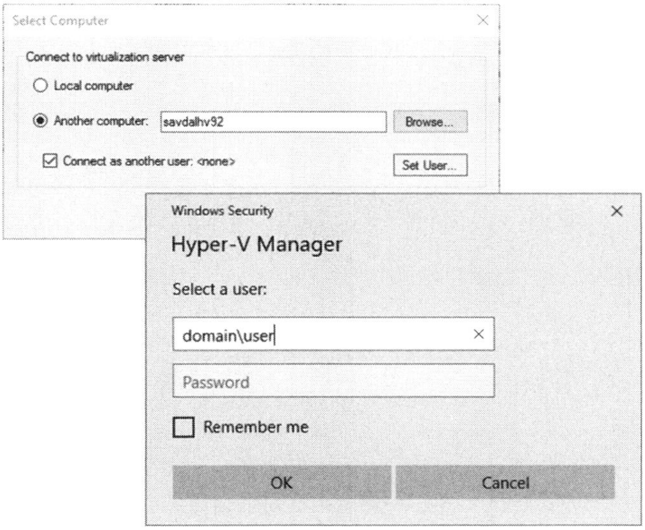

FIGURE 5.14
Specifying alternate credentials to manage a remote Hyper-V server

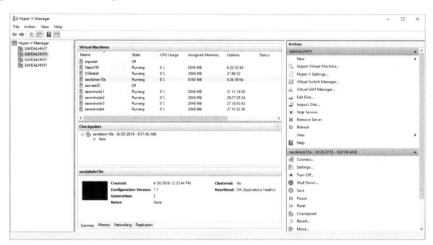

The Virtual Machines pane at the top center shows the virtual machines that are hosted by the currently selected Hyper-V server. Note that it is not possible to select multiple servers to see virtual machines from them. Only one server's virtual machine inventory can be shown. By default, several pieces of information are shown in the virtual machine's view, specifically its name, current state (such as Running, Paused, Saved, or Off), the CPU usage, assigned memory, uptime, and status. It's also possible to add a Replication Health column by right-clicking the column headings and selecting Add/Remove Columns, which also allows columns to be removed and the order rearranged. This view is useful to get a high-level view of the virtual machines on a host. If a node is clustered, only the virtual machines running on the node will be shown and not all virtual machines in the cluster.

Note that the CPU Usage value shown is the percentage of resources used of the entire Hyper-V host and not the resource usage of the virtual processors within the virtual machine. For example, a virtual machine with a single vCPU may be running at 100 percent, but if a server has 24 logical processors in total, then 100 percent would be about only 4 percent of the total system resources, which is the number that would be visible in Hyper-V Manager. This is why on large systems it is common for virtual machines to show a value of 0 for CPU usage. Figure 5.15 shows an example of this with a virtual machine running a CPU stress-test tool with its single processor running at 100 percent, while Hyper-V Manager shows it using only 3 percent. SCVMM shows the actual CPU utilization of the virtual machine's allocated resources rather than the utilization as a percentage of the entire system, which means that in my test it would have shown 100 percent processor utilization.

FIGURE 5.15
A virtual machine running at 100 percent processor utilization showing only 3 percent usage of a 24-core Hyper-V host

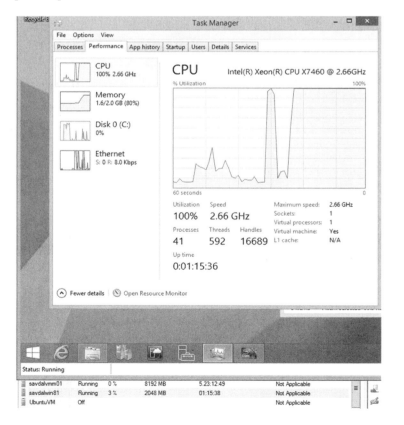

The next pane in Hyper-V Manager is Checkpoints, which is the new name for Snapshots. Checkpoints enable a point-in-time view of a virtual machine to be saved and used in the future. The view includes disk, memory, and device status. This is covered in detail later in the book.

The bottom-center pane shows detailed information about the selected virtual machine, including a thumbnail of the console and basic information such as VM version, generation, notes, and a basic health status. Additional tabs are related to memory, networking and Hyper-V Replica replication:

Memory For statically configured virtual machines, this tab offers no additional information beyond the assigned memory value shown already. For dynamically configured virtual machines, the minimum, startup, and maximum values are shown in addition to the currently assigned amount of memory, the actual memory demand of the VM, and the status of the memory, as shown in Figure 5.16. Remember that the Assigned Memory value is the actual memory currently allocated to the virtual machine from the physical memory of the host.

FIGURE 5.16
Detail tabs for a virtual machine

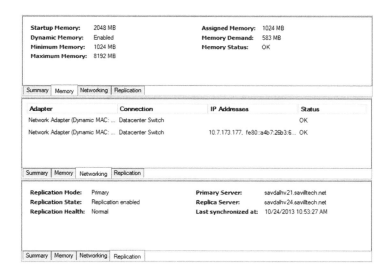

Networking Shows all adapters for a virtual machine, including IP address and status

Replication Shows the status of replication when Hyper-V Replica is used

The Actions pane shows contextual actions depending on the currently selected item. Typically, a host and virtual machine are selected, which provides host-level configurations at the top of the pane and actions specific to virtual machines in the bottom half.

While there are numerous actions for the server, such as creating new virtual machines and disks, the key configuration for the Hyper-V host is via the Hyper-V Settings action, which opens the key configurations for the server. The Server options, such as the default path for virtual hard disks, and configurations can be changed in addition to specifying which GPU can be used for RemoteFX, NUMA spanning, and other configurations (all covered throughout the book). In the User portion of the configurations, shown in Figure 5.17, I often like to change the Keyboard option to always send the special key combinations to the virtual machine, even when it's not running full screen.

FIGURE 5.17
Changing the
keyboard behavior
when the keyboard
is connected to a
virtual machine

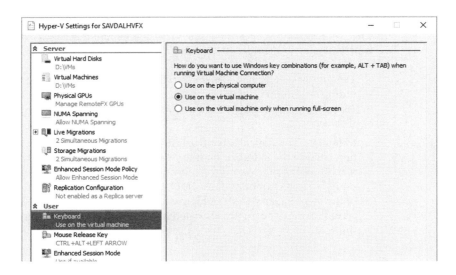

For virtual machines, the exact actions available will depend on the current state of the virtual machine. For example, the following actions are available for the Running state: Turn Off (doesn't gracefully shut down the guest operating system but is the same as just powering off a physical machine), Shut Down (sends a request to the guest operating system to perform a controlled shutdown, which is the same as selecting Shutdown within the guest operating system), Save (saves the current state, such as the memory and device state, to disk, allowing it to be resumed at a later time), Pause (suspends activity in the VM), and Reset (which is like powering off the VM and then starting it again). Options to connect to, move, export, checkpoint, rename, and enable replication are all available.

While Hyper-V Manager exposes many capabilities and configurations, it is suited only for a single host or a small number of hosts, because it doesn't allow configurations of multiple hosts in a single action. SCVMM provides the enterprise management solution, which is covered in Chapter 9.

A common question related to Hyper-V Manager is whether it gives you the ability to control management of specific activities by using role-based access control (RBAC). The original versions of Hyper-V enabled granular control of the actions available to different groups of users by utilizing the Windows Authorization Manager (AzMan) component. This authorization management approach was deprecated in Windows Server 2012 (although it still works) in favor of a new, simple authorization scheme that utilizes a new local group on each Hyper-V Server, Hyper-V Administrators. Any user who is in the Hyper-V Administrators' group on a server has complete access and management rights for the Hyper-V server and the virtual machines. If you have a group of people who should be administrators for all Hyper-V servers, the best practice is to create a group in Active Directory, add the Hyper-V administrators into that group, and then add the Active Directory group into each server's local Hyper-V Administrators' group. That way, as administrators change, only the single Active Directory group membership has to be updated. The true RBAC solution for Hyper-V is through SCVMM, which has full RBAC capabilities with granular options for assigning different rights through the use of custom user roles that can be created and assigned the required configuration targeting specific resources. Figure 5.18 shows some of the actions that can be granularly assigned within SCVMM to user roles, which users are then made part of.

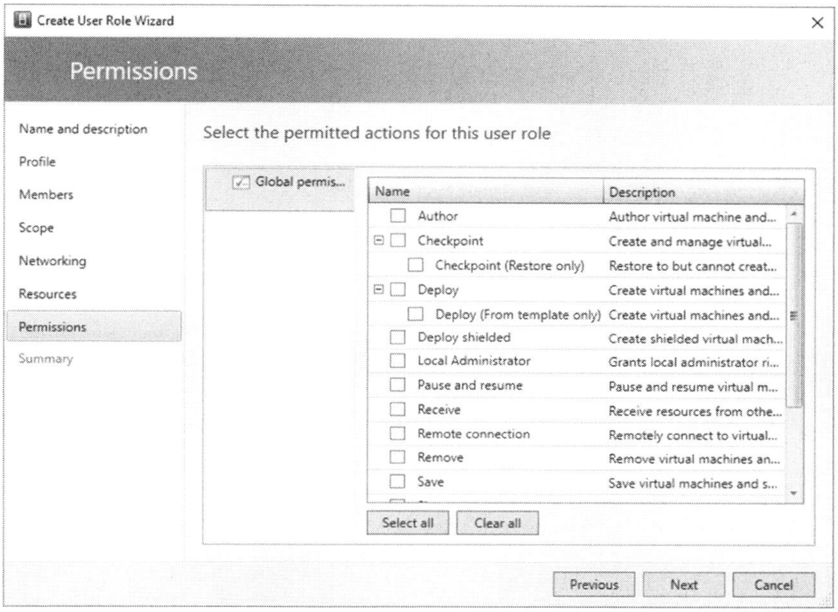

FIGURE 5.18
Configuring actions
for a specific new
user role

Core Actions Using PowerShell

The Hyper-V PowerShell module enables complete management of Hyper-V. If an action is possible in the graphical shell, that action is possible using PowerShell. If the number of cmdlets in the Hyper-V module are counted, you see that there are 232 in Windows Server 2016 (up from 178 in Windows Server 2012 R2):

```
PS C:\> (Get-Command -Module Hyper-V).Count
232
```

If you are unfamiliar with PowerShell, I cannot stress enough how important PowerShell is to any Microsoft environment. At a high level, a PowerShell cmdlet (command) takes the form of <verb>-<noun>, where the verb is a specific type of action such as new, get, or start, while the noun is a particular type of object. Many types of objects related to Hyper-V can be acted upon:

```
PS C:\> Get-Command -Module Hyper-V | Select -Unique Noun | Sort Noun

Noun
----
VFD
VHD
VHDSet
```

```
VHDSnapshot
VM
VMAssignableDevice
VMBios
VMComPort
VMConnectAccess
VMConsoleSupport
VMDvdDrive
VMEventing
VMFailover
VMFibreChannelHba
VMFile
VMFirmware
VMFloppyDiskDrive
VMGpuPartitionAdapter
VMGroup
VMGroupMember
VMHardDiskDrive
VMHost
VMHostAssignableDevice
VMHostCluster
VMHostNumaNode
VMHostNumaNodeStatus
VMHostSupportedVersion
VMIdeController
VMInitialReplication
VMIntegrationService
VMKeyProtector
VMKeyStorageDrive
VMMemory
VMMigration
VMMigrationNetwork
VMNetworkAdapter
VMNetworkAdapterAcl
VMNetworkAdapterExtendedAcl
VMNetworkAdapterFailoverConfiguration
VMNetworkAdapterIsolation
VMNetworkAdapterRdma
VMNetworkAdapterRoutingDomainMapping
VMNetworkAdapterTeamMapping
VMNetworkAdapterVlan
VMPartitionableGpu
VMProcessor
VMRemoteFx3dVideoAdapter
VMRemoteFXPhysicalVideoAdapter
VMReplication
VMReplicationAuthorizationEntry
VMReplicationConnection
```

```
VMReplicationServer
VMReplicationStatistics
VMResourceMetering
VMResourcePool
VMSan
VMSavedState
VMScsiController
VMSecurity
VMSecurityPolicy
VMSnapshot
VMStorage
VMStoragePath
VMSwitch
VMSwitchExtension
VMSwitchExtensionPortData
VMSwitchExtensionPortFeature
VMSwitchExtensionSwitchData
VMSwitchExtensionSwitchFeature
VMSwitchTeam
VMSwitchTeamMember
VMSystemSwitchExtension
VMSystemSwitchExtensionPortFeature
VMSystemSwitchExtensionSwitchFeature
VMTPM
VMTrace
VMVersion
VMVideo
```

Most of these nouns are self-explanatory. After you understand the noun you want to act on, you can see the verbs (actions) available. For example, to understand the actions available for a VM, I can use the following command:

```
PS C:\> Get-Command -Module Hyper-V -Noun VM |
        ft CommandType, Name, Version -AutoSize

CommandType Name          Version
----------- ----          -------
     Cmdlet Checkpoint-VM 2.0.0.0
     Cmdlet Compare-VM    2.0.0.0
     Cmdlet Debug-VM      2.0.0.0
     Cmdlet Export-VM     2.0.0.0
     Cmdlet Get-VM        2.0.0.0
     Cmdlet Import-VM     2.0.0.0
     Cmdlet Measure-VM    2.0.0.0
     Cmdlet Move-VM       2.0.0.0
     Cmdlet New-VM        2.0.0.0
     Cmdlet Remove-VM     2.0.0.0
     Cmdlet Rename-VM     2.0.0.0
     Cmdlet Repair-VM     2.0.0.0
```

```
Cmdlet  Restart-VM   2.0.0.0
Cmdlet  Resume-VM    2.0.0.0
Cmdlet  Save-VM      2.0.0.0
Cmdlet  Set-VM       2.0.0.0
Cmdlet  Start-VM     2.0.0.0
Cmdlet  Stop-VM      2.0.0.0
Cmdlet  Suspend-VM   2.0.0.0
Cmdlet  Wait-VM      2.0.0.0
```

I cover many of these cmdlets throughout the book, related to specific types of activity. In this section, I cover some commands that are useful for quickly getting a view of your Hyper-V environment.

To view the basic information about a Hyper-V host, use
`Get-VMHost -ComputerName server | Format-List`, and most attributes returned can be modified using the `Set-VMHost` cmdlet.

To view all virtual machines running on a Hyper-V host, use the `Get-VM` cmdlet. A key feature of PowerShell is the ability to pipe information from one cmdlet to another. This enables comprehensive feedback and intelligent, automated sets of actions, which is why PowerShell management is a much better option for performing actions across multiple servers with virtual machines. For example, I may want to export all virtual machines that are currently turned off. The first cmdlet gets all virtual machines, the second part identifies the VMs in the Off state, and then only those VMs are passed to the final cmdlet, which exports them.

```
Get-VM -ComputerName <Hyper-V host name> |
    where-object {$_.State -EQ "Off"} |
    Export-VM -Path D:\Backups
```

Likewise, I had a folder full of virtual machines I wanted to import into a Hyper-V server. This is easy with PowerShell. The following code looks for XML files (which is the format for virtual machine configurations) and then imports:

```
Get-ChildItem e:\virtuals\*.xml -recurse | Import-VM
```

In another case, I wanted to configure all virtual machines that were set to start automatically not to start if they were running when the Hyper-V server shut down. That's easy with PowerShell:

```
Get-VM | Where-Object {$_.AutomaticStartAction -eq "StartIfRunning"} |`
Set-VM -AutomaticStartAction Nothing -AutomaticStopAction ShutDown
```

SCVMM also has its own PowerShell module. Provided it's installed, it can be loaded using this command:

```
Import-Module virtualmachinemanager
```

The `virtualmachinemanager` module has 672 cmdlets with SCVMM 2016! This is where using the same commands to view all of the nouns available in the module is useful. There is, however, an even better way to learn how to use the SCVMM PowerShell cmdlets. Every action performed using the SCVMM graphical interface translates to PowerShell. As each action is performed using SCVMM, there is an option to view the PowerShell, as shown in Figure 5.19, by clicking the View Script button. You can use the PowerShell that is displayed in your own scripts.

FIGURE 5.19
Viewing the
PowerShell used
by SCVMM

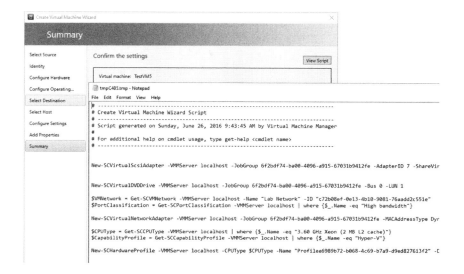

VM Groups

Using PowerShell, it is easy to perform actions on multiple VMs simultaneously by either specifying multiple VM names or sending multiple VM names through the PowerShell pipeline to another command. For example, `Get-VM VM1, VM2 | Start-VM` would send the VM objects for VM1 and VM2 to the `Start-VM` cmdlet. It would also be possible to parse a file or other input for VM names and send those objects along the pipeline. In some instances, however, the Hyper-V fabric needs to understand when certain VMs are grouped together for a common purpose or that share a common resource.

Windows Server 2016 introduces *VM Groups*, which enable exactly this type of grouping. In Windows Server 2016, VM Groups are required when using VHD Sets and performing a host-level backup of the VHD Set or replicating with Hyper-V Replica. All guest cluster member VMs are placed in a VM Group, which enables the Hyper-V environment to perform actions across all guest cluster VMs in an orchestrated manner to ensure the integrity of actions performed on VHD Sets.

There are two types of group:

◆ **VM Collection Group**　A collection of VMs

◆ **Management Collection Group**　A collection of VM Collection Groups and/or other Management Collection Groups

In addition to being required for VHD Set operations, VM Groups also provide easy management of multiple VMs when using VM Collection Groups. Some example PowerShell follows for creating and using the groups. Notice that for some actions, the VM Group is enumerated for its members that are then used for actions.

```
#Create new VM Collection Groups
New-VMGroup -Name VMCGroup1 -GroupType VMCollectionType
```

```
New-VMGroup -Name VMCGroup2 -GroupType VMCollectionType
New-VMGroup -Name VMCGroup3 -GroupType VMCollectionType

#Add VMs to the VM Collection Groups
Add-VMGroupMember -VMGroup (Get-VMGroup VMCGroup1) -VM (Get-VM VM1)
Add-VMGroupMember -VMGroup (Get-VMGroup VMCGroup2) -VM (Get-VM VM2)
Add-VMGroupMember -VMGroup (Get-VMGroup VMCGroup2) -VM (Get-VM VM3)
Add-VMGroupMember -VMGroup (Get-VMGroup VMCGroup3) -VM (Get-VM VM4)

#View the membership of the groups
Get-VM | ft Name, Groups -AutoSize
Get-VMGroup -Name VMCGroup2

#Perform actions on the group as if it were a VM
#Enable-VMReplication -VM (Get-VMGroup VMCGroup2).VMMembers ......
Start-VM -VM (Get-VMGroup VMCGroup2).VMMembers

#Create VM Management Group with VMCGroup2 and VMCGroup3 in it
New-VMGroup -Name MgmtGroup1 -GroupType ManagementCollectionType
Add-VMGroupMember -VMGroup (Get-VMGroup MgmtGroup1) `
    -VMGroupMember (Get-VMGroup VMCGroup2)
Add-VMGroupMember -VMGroup (Get-VMGroup MgmtGroup1) `
    -VMGroupMember (Get-VMGroup VMCGroup3)

#Create VM Management Group with VMCGroup1 and MgmtGroup1 to show nesting
New-VMGroup -Name MgmtGroup2 -GroupType ManagementCollectionType
Add-VMGroupMember -VMGroup (Get-VMGroup MgmtGroup2) `
    -VMGroupMember (Get-VMGroup VMCGroup1)
Add-VMGroupMember -VMGroup (Get-VMGroup MgmtGroup2) `
    -VMGroupMember (Get-VMGroup MgmtGroup1)

Get-VMGroup MgmtGroup2 | Select-Object -ExpandProperty VMGroupMembers
```

PowerShell Direct

PowerShell provides a powerful mechanism to locally manage an OS instance or remotely manage it using WinRM. At times, however, a networking issue may prevent remote PowerShell management in a way similar to how a networking issue blocks RDP access.

PowerShell Direct enables communication to a VM from its host via PowerShell, even when networking or firewall configurations would typically block communication. This communication via PowerShell Direct is enabled through the secure VMBus channel that exists between the host and each VM. A new VSP/VSC pair is part of Windows Server 2016, and the client side can be seen as a new user-mode service, vmicvmsession (Hyper-V VM Session Service), which by default is set to start when triggered; that is, PowerShell Direct is utilized. This is separate from vmicrdv, which is used to enable the rich VMConnect experience that emulates RDP experience to VMs.

Credentials are still required to use within the VM, so this is not a way to bypass security. Think of this as a way to be able to use PowerShell, even with problems such as networking misconfigurations that would typically prohibit management.

To use PowerShell Direct, leverage the new `-VMName` parameter for cmdlets such as `Invoke-Command` and `Enter-PSSession`. For example:

```
Enter-PSSession -VMName VM01
Invoke-Command -VMName VM01 -ScriptBlock {<code to run>}
```

Following is an example use that shows that the output is run on the target VM. The prompt for values is a prompt for authentication.

```
PS C:\> invoke-command -VMName savdalvmm16 -ScriptBlock { $env:COMPUTERNAME }
cmdlet Invoke-Command at command pipeline position 1
Supply values for the following parameters:
SAVDALVMM16
```

Note that it is possible to pass a credential to avoid being prompted. In the following example, I create a credential object using a text password that is used with `Invoke-Command`. Replace the password and username with one that is valid in the target VM. In most environments, you would not store passwords in plain text, and this is for demonstration purposes only. Better approaches to store passwords in scripts can be found at http://windowsitpro.com/development/save-password-securely-use-powershell.

```
$securepassword = ConvertTo-SecureString -string "Password" `
     -AsPlainText -Force
$cred = new-object System.Management.Automation.PSCredential ↵
("savilltech\administrator", $securepassword)

invoke-command -VMName savdalvmm16 -Credential $cred `
     -ScriptBlock { $env:COMPUTERNAME }
```

Securing the Hyper-V Server

Your Hyper-V servers are running the majority of your server operating system instances and potentially your desktops if you're using VDI solutions. While an administrator on a Hyper-V server cannot bypass the regular logon to an operating system in a virtual machine, if you have access to the Hyper-V server, then you have access to the virtual machine storage. The storage could then be mounted, and the content could be accessed.

The normal security best practices for servers should apply:

◆ Ensure that servers are physically secure.

◆ Ensure that the firewall is enabled.

◆ Patch servers.

◆ Run malware protection (with the required exclusions configured).

◆ Restrict who is an administrator (and by extension, domain administrators should be limited as well).

◆ Run Server Core on Hyper-V servers.

◆ Do not run other applications or browse the Web on Hyper-V servers. Running Server Core will help stop this.

◆ Use BitLocker to encrypt volumes containing virtual machines; it can also be used on Cluster Shared Volumes.

◆ Make sure administrators are well trained and understand their actions.

◆ Use Group Policy to ensure that policies are set as required.

◆ Have a monitoring solution in place, and ensure that security logs are checked to detect any attack attempts.

The best Microsoft resource to help with security is the Microsoft Security Compliance Manager, which is available at the following location:

`www.microsoft.com/en-us/download/details.aspx?id=16776`

It is a large download at over 100MB, but it provides not only documentation to help secure your entire environment but also tools and templates to ensure security.

Creating and Managing a Virtual Machine

Ultimately, you deploy Hyper-V to host virtual machines, and in this section I walk you through creating a basic virtual machine by using Hyper-V Manager and PowerShell. Once the virtual machine is created, the next step is to deploy an operating system to it. That typically means attaching to the virtual machine an ISO containing an operating system installation or even booting the virtual machine over the network by using a legacy network adapter for a generation 1 virtual machine, or booting from the synthetic network adapter for a generation 2 virtual machine. This type of virtual machine creation is manually intensive and time-consuming and is not taking advantage of the fact that the virtual machine storage is essentially a file that could just be copied, which is why using templates is a much better option and is covered in a later section.

To create a virtual machine using Hyper-V Manager, perform the following steps:

1. Select the New ➤ Virtual Machine action.

2. Click Next on the introduction wizard screen.

3. Enter a name for the new virtual machine and optionally an alternate path for the virtual machine instead of the default location configured for the host. Click Next. There is a difference in behavior if the option to store the virtual machine in a different location is selected, even if the actual path is the same as the default. When Store Virtual Machine In A Different Location is selected, a folder is created under the specified location with the name of the new virtual machine, and that's where all of its files and virtual hard disks are created. Without this setting enabled, the virtual machine configurations and disks are stored in the root of the default location in a standard structure.

4. Select the generation for the virtual machine. Remember, generation 2 virtual machines work only on Hyper-V 2012 R2 and above, and only Windows Server 2012/Windows 8 64-bit and above is supported within the virtual machine. If you need compatibility with versions of Hyper-V prior to Windows Server 2012 or, at the time of this writing, Windows Azure IaaS, you should use generation 1. You cannot change the generation of a virtual machine post creation. Click Next.

5. Select the amount of startup memory for the virtual machine. Note that the default value of 512 is insufficient for the latest generation of Windows client operating systems, which require 1GB for 32-bit versions and 2GB for 64-bit versions. Additionally, the option to use Dynamic Memory can be selected, and the values can be tweaked post creation. Click Next.

6. By default, virtual machines have a single network adapter, and the switch to connect it to should be selected. Click Next.

7. The virtual hard disk for the virtual machine is selected by default. This can be a new virtual hard disk, an existing virtual hard disk, or the option of choosing whether a disk should be added later. Click Next.

8. If the option to create a new virtual hard disk was selected, the method to install the operating system is requested, as shown in Figure 5.20. You can choose to install the operating system later, install it from a bootable ISO, or install it from a network location. Note that if the virtual machine is generation 1 and you select to install from a network location, the network adapter created for the virtual machine will be a legacy network adapter. Also a generation 1 VM has the option to install from a virtual floppy disk. Once the operating system is installed from the network, you will want to add a normal network adapter and remove the legacy network adapter to get the best performance. Click Next.

FIGURE 5.20
Selecting the method to install the operating system into the virtual machine

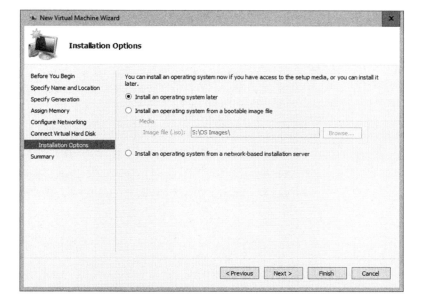

9. View the configurations in the Summary screen, and click Finish to create the virtual machine.

When the virtual machine is turned on, it will install the operating system from the ISO or over the network, and the standard operating system installation configurations will need to be performed within the guest operating system. The latest Hyper-V Integration Services will be deployed to the VM via Windows Update on first update.

To connect to a virtual machine, use the Connect action for the virtual machine within Hyper-V Manager, which launches a connection to the virtual console of the virtual machine, allowing operating system installation. Make sure that you click the mouse within the Virtual Machine Connection window when you first turn on the VM in order to be able to press a key to launch the boot from ISO or the network. The rest of the OS installation is the same as for a physical system. Note that if you are installing Windows 8/Windows Server 2012 into a generation 2 virtual machine, the physical keyboard will not work, because the keyboard driver required is not part of the Windows 8 PE environment. Either use the onscreen keyboard during OS installation, or if you really want to fix the problem, follow my instructions at the following location:

```
http://windowsitpro.com/hyper-v/
fix-vm-keyboard-problems-generation-2-virtual-machine
```

ACTIVATING THE GUEST OPERATING SYSTEM

Numerous types of product keys are available for operating systems, and your guest operating systems are still just operating systems that need to be activated. The product key specified during installation could be a Multiple Activation Key (MAK) that enables multiple activations, or you may have a Key Management Server (KMS) in your organization, which provides the ability to locally activate operating systems. Windows Server 2012 introduced a new activation option, Active Directory–Based Activation (ADBA), that automatically activates Windows Server 2012 and Windows 8 operating systems (physical or virtual) when they join the domain.

Windows Server 2012 R2 introduced a new option for Windows Server 2012 R2 virtual machines, Automatic Virtual Machine Activation (AVMA). With the AVMA technology, if the Hyper-V host is running Windows Server 2012 R2 Datacenter or above and is activated, then any virtual machine running Windows Server 2012 R2 (Essentials, Standard, or Datacenter) is automatically activated, provided that the AVMA key is used during the guest OS installation. These keys are as follows:

Server Standard: DBGBW-NPF86-BJVTX-K3WKJ-MTB6V

Server Datacenter: Y4TGP-NPTV9-HTC2H-7MGQ3-DV4TW

Server Essentials: K2XGM-NMBT3-2R6Q8-WF2FK-P36R2

They are documented at the following location:

```
http://technet.microsoft.com/en-us/library/dn303421.aspx
```

The benefit of AVMA is that the virtual machine is activated only while running on an activated Windows Server 2012 R2 Hyper-V host. If the virtual machine were given to another organization or moved, it would be unactivated unless the target host was also Windows Server 2012 R2 Datacenter and activated. The Hyper-V host must be the Datacenter SKU because only Datacenter allows an unlimited number of guest VMs running Windows Server.

The actual virtual machine connection is enabled through the vmconnect.exe image, which is automatically launched through the Connect action with the target virtual machine specified for you. Vmconnect.exe can also be manually launched, which brings up the dialog box shown in Figure 5.21, which allows a Hyper-V host to be selected and then a list of all of the virtual machines on the selected Hyper-V host to be displayed. Windows Server 2016 `vmconnect` introduces the ability to connect as another user.

Figure 5.21
Manually launching
`vmconnect.exe` allows
you to select the host
and virtual machine.

Windows Server 2012 R2 introduced a new set of capabilities related to `vmconnect`; it's known as Enhanced Session Mode (ESM). Windows 8.1 and Windows Server 2012 R2, the only operating systems that work with ESM, were enhanced so that the terminal services stack was tightly integrated with the Hyper-V VMBus.

This enables VM connections (via Hyper-V Manager or via `vmconnect.exe`) to leverage the following functionality traditionally associated with RDP connections:

◆ Rich display

◆ Audio

◆ Printers

◆ Clipboard

◆ USB devices

◆ Drives

◆ Plug and Play devices

◆ Smart cards

The requirements that need to be met are as follows:

◆ Guest OS in the VM supports Remote Desktop Services (for example, Windows 8.1/10 Pro/ Enterprise/Windows Server 2012 R2/2016).

◆ The server policy in the Hyper-V Manager server settings for ESM is enabled (the Server, Enhanced Session Mode Policy, and Allow Enhanced Session Mode check box are selected). It's disabled by default.

◆ The user policy in the Hyper-V Manager server settings is enabled (User ➤ Enhanced Session Mode ➤ Use Enhanced Session Mode).

◆ The Remote Desktop Services service is running in the guest (but the Allow remote connections to this computer in System configuration doesn't need to be enabled).

◆ User logging on is as a member of local administrators or remote desktop users groups in the guest operating system.

◆ The Out Of Box Experience (OOBE) Wizard has been completed.

When you connect to a VM that supports ESM, an initial dialog box allows the configuration of the display and local resources that are redirected in addition to letting you save the configuration, as shown in Figure 5.22. Any saved configurations are written to %APPDATA%\Roaming\ Microsoft\Windows\Hyper-V\Client\1.0 with a name format of vmconnect.rdp.<GUID of VM>.config.

FIGURE 5.22
The connection dialog box when connecting using Enhanced Session Mode

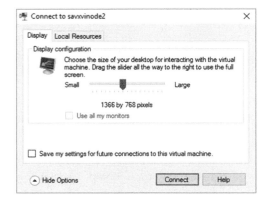

Finally, outside the Hyper-V technologies is regular Remote Desktop Protocol (RDP). Windows natively supports RDP. Provided Remote Desktop is enabled within the guest operating system (which it is not by default; only remote management is enabled by default), the guest operating system can be connected to via RDP, which would be the normal way for users of virtual machines to connect.

Shielded VMs and Host Guardian Service

A huge focus for most environments is security and providing protection from external threats. However, some threats don't originate from outside the organization. Today, in most virtual environments, many types of administrators have access to virtual machine assets such as their storage. This includes virtualization administrators, storage administrators, network administrators, and backup administrators, to name just a few. The power of administrators is not a new concept, and the normal mindset is that administrators should be trusted actors in the organization and it's OK for them to be privileged. This view is changing, however, especially in virtualization environments and even more so in virtualization environments that have VMs hosted from other organizations. For this reason, many organizations including hosting providers need a way to secure VMs even from administrators, which is exactly what shielded VMs provide. Note that this protection from administrators is needed for various reasons:

♦ Phishing attacks

♦ Stolen administrator credentials

♦ Insider attacks

Review of Shielded VMs and Host Guardian Service

Shielded VMs provide protection for the data and state of the VMs against inspection, theft, and tampering from administrator privileges. Shielded VMs work for generation 2 VMs, which provide the necessary Secure Boot, UEFI firmware, and virtual Trusted Platform Module (vTPM) 2 capabilities required to implement shielded VMs. While the Hyper-V hosts must be running Windows Server 2016 Datacenter (for the full set of capabilities), the guest operating system in the VM can be Windows Server 2012 or above.

A shielded VM provides the following benefits:

◆ BitLocker-encrypted disks (utilizing its vTPM)

◆ A hardened VM worker process (VMWP) that encrypts Live Migration/traffic in addition to its runtime state file, saved state, checkpoints, and even Hyper-V Replica files

◆ No console access in addition to blocking PowerShell Direct, Guest File Copy Integration Components, RemoteFX, and other services that provide possible paths from a user or process with administrative privileges to the VM

How is this security possible? Any kind of security is only as good as its lock and key and how they are guarded. For shielded VMs, a new Host Guardian Service (HGS) instance is deployed in the environment, which will store the keys required for an approved Hyper-V host that can prove their health to run shielded VMs.

It's important that the Hyper-V host has not been compromised before the required keys to access VM resources are released from the HGS. This attestation can happen in one of two ways. The preferred way is by using the TPM 2 that is present in the Hyper-V host. Using the TPM, the boot path of the server is assured, which guarantees that no malware or root kits are on the server that could compromise the security. The TPM is used to secure communication to and from the HGS attestation service. For hosts that do not have TPM 2, an alternate AD-based attestation is possible, but this merely checks whether the host is part of a configured AD group. Therefore, this does not provide the same levels of assurance and protection from binary meddling or host administrator privileges for a sophisticated attacker, although the same shielded VM features are available.

Once a host has gone through the attestation, it receives a health certificate from the attestation service on the HGS that authorizes the host to get keys released from the key-protection service that also runs on the HGS. The keys are encrypted during transmission and can be decrypted only within a protected enclave that is new to Windows 10 and Windows Server 2016 (more on that later). These keys can be used to decrypt the vTPM content in the VM's VMRS file, which is then used to hydrate the VM's synthetic TPM to enable the VM to access its BitLocker-protected storage and start the VM. Therefore, only if a host is authorized and noncompromised will it be able to get the required key and enable the VM's access to the encrypted storage (not the administrator, though, as the VHD still stays encrypted on disk).

At this point, it may seem like if I am an administrator on the Hyper-V, and the keys are released to the host to start the VM, then I would be able to get access to the memory of the host and get the keys, thereby defeating this security that should protect VMs from administrative privileges. Another new feature in Windows 10 and Windows Server 2016 stops this from happening. This is the protected enclave mentioned earlier, which is known as Virtual Secure Mode (VSM) and is used by various components including credential guard. VSM is a secure execution environment in which secrets and keys are maintained and critical security processes run as trustlets (small trusted processes) in a secure virtualized partition. This is not a Hyper-V VM, but rather think of it as a small, virtual safe that is protected by virtualization-based technologies such as SLAT to stop people from trying to access memory directly, IOMMU (Input-output memory management unit) to protect against DMA attacks, and so on. The Windows OS, even the kernel, has no access to VSM. Only whitelisted processes (trustlets) that are Microsoft signed are allowed to cross the "bridge" to access VSM. A vTPM trustlet is used for the vTPM of each VM, separate from the rest of the VM process, which runs in a new type of protected VM worker process. This means that there is no way to access the memory used to store these keys, even with complete kernel access. If I'm running with a debugger attached, for example, that would be flagged as part of the attestation process, and the health check would fail and the keys would not be released to the host. Remember I mentioned that the keys from the key-protection service are sent encrypted? It's the VSM where they are decrypted, always keeping the decrypted key protected from the host OS.

When you put all this together, you have the ability to create a secure VM environment that is protected from any level of administrator (when using TPM 2 in the host) and will close a security hole many environments cannot close today.

Separation of duties and sphere of influence is critical with shielded VMs and the Host Guardian Service. The HGS must not be within the influence of the virtualization administrators nor the regular Active Directory administrators. For this reason, in most environments, the HGS, which runs as its own physical cluster in its own Active Directory forest, can also then be physically separated (completely) from the rest of the servers. Think of a separate locked cage within the datacenter containing the physical HGS cluster that is accessible from only the specific HGS administrators who are completely separate from the other administrative roles. This means that to get to data, there would have to be collusion between separate roles such as the virtualization administrator and the HGS administrator. There is minimal benefit to deploying shielded VMs if the HGS runs as a VM under the management of the very people from whom it is designed to protect, unless you simply wish to encrypt the disks at rest for compliance purposes. You also can use local guardians only instead of an HGS. However, with local guardians, there is no health attestation, and only the guardian's private key is required, which can be found in the local certificate store. The benefit of local guardians is that they can work on the Standard edition, whereas guarded VMs that leverage HGS must run on hosts (known as guarded hosts) running the Datacenter SKU.

Two types of guarded VMs are running in a guarded fabric:

Shielded VMs   The full protection and restrictions discussed earlier in this section providing full protection for the VMs from the fabric administrators

Encryption Supported VMs   Supports the vTPM and uses BitLocker to encrypt the content of the storage along with the hardened VM worker process. Other restrictions such as no console access and no integration services are not enabled by default but can be configured per item.

A good way to think about which type to use is as follows: If you don't trust the fabric nor the administrators, you should use a shielded VM. If the fabric and the administrators are fully trusted in the environment, such as a corporate private cloud, and only encryption-at-rest is required for compliance reasons without impeding administration via console connections and PowerShell Direct, then use encryption-supported VMs.

Host Guardian tools are available that are installed by adding the RSAT-Shielded-VM-Tools RSAT component. One of the tools is the Shielding Data File Wizard (shieldingdatafilewizard .exe), which helps create the necessary data file that can be used to shield VMs and as part of shielded VM templates.

Deploying Shielded VMs

Microsoft has a detailed document that covers every aspect of deploying the Host Guardian Service and configuring guarded hosts. This document is available at https://gallery.technet .microsoft.com/shielded-vms-and-guarded-98d2b045, and this is the document I recommend for anyone looking to deploy. Rather than reiterating the nearly 100-page document, I instead cover at a high level the various configuration steps and what to expect, to help explain further what is going on behind the scenes. Although I am using PowerShell, the preferred approach is to use SCVMM or Windows Azure Pack. By showing PowerShell, I can explain what each step is actually doing, which is not so obvious when using the management interfaces.

HOST GUARDIAN SERVICE CONFIGURATION

The first deployment is the Host Guardian Service itself, which must be a Windows Server 2016 instance and can be the Standard or Datacenter edition. It should run on the Server Core configuration level, and at the time of this writing, it is not supported on Nano Server (but Nano Server *can* run shielded VMs). As previously mentioned, the HGS should run on a separate physical cluster of three nodes, which completely isolates it from the influence of the regular virtualization and other fabric administrators. The HGS cluster can be physically secured in the datacenter in its own locked cage. Remember that shielded VMs will be unable to start without the HGS being contactable, so it must be a highly resilient deployment having redundancy even during routine maintenance. This is why a three-node cluster is recommended, ensuring that two nodes are available even when a node is down for maintenance.

In addition to isolation from the virtualization and general fabric administrators, the HGS should be isolated from the Active Directory administrators. To facilitate this isolation, the default and recommended approach is that during the HGS provisioning, an automatically generated HGS-specific AD forest and domain is created. If the AD administrators are completely trusted, it is possible to provision HGS in an existing domain, although this is not recommended.

The first step is to install the Host Guardian Service role. PowerShell is used for all management of HGS unless you leverage SCVMM 2016 or Windows Azure Pack:

```
Install-WindowsFeature -Name HostGuardianServiceRole -Restart
```

Once the HGS node has rebooted, you must specify a safe-mode password for the new AD instance that will be created, in addition to the name for the new domain and forest that will be provisioned in which HGS will run. The HGS server will be the DC for the new domain and provide the DNS service. In this example, the new domain created will have the name savtechhgs.net:

```
$adminPassword = ConvertTo-SecureString -AsPlainText 'Pa55word!' -Force
Install-HgsServer -HgsDomainName 'savtechhgs.net' `
      -SafeModeAdministratorPassword $adminPassword -Restart
```

The HGS node will restart again, and the next step is to acquire the certificates to use for the signing and encryption actions. In this example, I use a self-signed certificate, but in production, you would use a trusted certificate authority, which the Microsoft paper walks through:

```
$certificatePassword = ConvertTo-SecureString `
    -AsPlainText 'Pa55word!' -Force
$signingCert = New-SelfSignedCertificate -DnsName "signing.savtechhgs.net"
Export-PfxCertificate -Cert $signingCert -Password $certificatePassword `
    -FilePath 'C:\signingCert.pfx'
$encryptionCert = New-SelfSignedCertificate `
    -DnsName "encryption.savtechhgs.net"
Export-PfxCertificate -Cert $encryptionCert `
    -Password $certificatePassword -FilePath 'C:\encryptionCert.pfx'
```

The next step is to initialize the HGS, which will use the generated certificates in addition to selecting the attestation method. Only one attestation method can be supported by an HGS instance: AD or TPM. When provisioning the HGS, you need to pick a service name for HGS that is not fully qualified and will be the service name used to access HGS. This is not a hostname, as you will have multiple HGS nodes providing the resilient service. Requests to the service name will be distributed to the HGS instance nodes. In this example, I name my service hgs and use TPM attestation:

```
Initialize-HGSServer -HgsServiceName 'hgs' `
            -SigningCertificatePath 'C:\signingCert.pfx' `
            -SigningCertificatePassword $certificatePassword `
            -EncryptionCertificatePath 'C:\encryptionCert.pfx' `
            -EncryptionCertificatePassword $certificatePassword `
            -TrustTPM
```

Although an HGS instance can support only one type of attestation, as previously mentioned, it is possible to change the attestation type. In the code that follows, I switch the attestation from TPM to AD:

```
Set-HGSServer -TrustActiveDirectory
```

If using AD attestation, the HGS domain must be able to resolve the primary AD DNS in the organization and trust the domain; in this example, my corporate domain is savilltech.net:

```
Add-DnsServerConditionalForwarderZone -Name "savilltech.net" `
        -ReplicationScope "Forest" -MasterServers 10.7.173.10, 10.7.173.11
netdom trust savtechhgs.net /domain:savilltech.net ↵
        /userD:savilltech.net\Administrator /passwordD:Pa55word /add
```

AD attestation is based on Hyper-V hosts being part of a global security group in the organization's AD. The SID of the group is required, which can be found running the following PowerShell in the source domain. In this example, my group is called GuardedHosts:

```
Get-ADGroup "GuardedHosts" | Select-Object SID
```

The group is added as an attestation group on the HGS server and then viewed:

```
Add-HgsAttestationHostGroup -Name "GuardedHosts" -Identifier "SID"
Get-HgsAttestationHostGroup
```

For both AD and TPM attestation, the corporate DNS has to be able to resolve names in the HGS domain for the attestation and key services. This is added through DNS Manager or PowerShell and by adding a conditional forwarder for the HGS domain and the HGS server IP address, as shown in Figure 5.23.

FIGURE 5.23
Conditional forwarder for HGS DNS zone

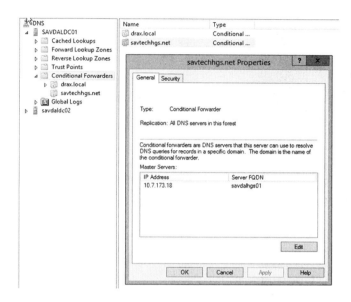

If using TPM attestation, the TPM must be activated on each host, its identifier exported, and imported to the HGS server:

```
#On a guarded host
#Initialize the TPM
Initialize-Tpm
(Get-PlatformIdentifier -Name 'savdalhv07').InnerXml |
    Out-file c:\savdalhv07.xml
#Copy the generated file to the HGS then run below on the HGS server
Add-HgsAttestationTpmHost -Path c:\savdalhv07.xml -Name 'savdalhv07' `
    -Force
```

For both AD and TPM attestation, a code integrity policy is required that controls the processes allowed to run on a host. When this is combined with Secure Boot and a TPM, it ensures that no meddling has occurred with the binaries on the Hyper-V host that could risk the integrity. Various rule levels are available. A common choice is FilePublisher, which trusts the publishers of the files instead of the more restrictive Hash option, which requires a policy update anytime a specific file changes. The code that follows should be run on a Hyper-V host that has been provisioned with the common configuration expected in the environment:

```
New-CIPolicy -Level FilePublisher -Fallback Hash `
    -FilePath 'C:\HW1CodeIntegrity.xml'
ConvertFrom-CIPolicy -XmlFilePath 'C:\HW1CodeIntegrity.xml' `
    -BinaryFilePath 'C:\HW1CodeIntegrity.p7b'
```

Copy the generated file to the HGS server and import as a policy:

```
Add-HgsAttestationCIPolicy -Path 'C:\HW1CodeIntegrity.p7b' `
   -Name 'StdGuardHost'
```

The same file should be copied to each of the Hyper-V hosts and saved as `C:\Windows\System32\CodeIntegrity\SIPolicy.p7b`, and then the hosts restarted to make the policy take effect.

If using TPM attestation, on each type of server, you need to save the TPM base policy and import to the HGS:

```
#Save the TPM base policy from the Hyper-V host
Get-HgsAttestationBaselinePolicy -Path 'C:\HWConfig1.tcglog'
#Copy the file to HGS and import
Add-HgsAttestationTpmPolicy –Path 'C:\HWConfig1.tcglog' –Name 'Dell TPM'
```

So far we have only a single HGS instance; however, because of its criticality, you should always deploy at least three HGS instances in a physical cluster. The Microsoft whitepaper walks through the details of adding HGS instances to the existing HGS instance. This process is similar to creating the initial instance, except that the new HGS instances will use the primary HGS for its DNS service, and when performing the initialization of the HGS server, the IP address of the existing instance will be specified via the `HgsServerIPAddress` parameter. Remember, if your HGS is not available, shielded VMs and encrypted VMs will be unable to start as their vTPM content cannot be accessed. Thus it's critical to make HGS highly available.

The next step is to download the script at `https://gallery.technet.microsoft.com/Script-for-Setting-Up-f8bd7f7e` and execute it on every Hyper-V host that will be part of the guarded fabric. This script takes ownership of the Device Guard registry key and configures it to leverage IOMMU, which ensures the memory protection of shielded VMs. Hosts will need to be rebooted after this script is applied.

The final step is to configure the guarded host to use the HGS instance instead of local guardians. This is done by configuring the URL for the HGS attestation service and the key-protection service:

```
Set-HgsClientConfiguration `
   -AttestationServerUrl 'http://hgs.savtechhgs.net/Attestation' `
   -KeyProtectionServerUrl 'http://hgs.savtechhgs.net/KeyProtection'
```

The configuration can be tested by performing a diagnostics test and attempting the attestation via PowerShell:

```
#Verify on the guarded host
Get-HgsTrace -RunDiagnostics

#Attempt attestation on the guarded host
Get-HgsClientConfiguration
```

The following is an example execution of the preceding commands. Note that this example runs in my lab with only a single HGS instance and is therefore a single point of failure, which is highlighted in the output.

```
PS C:\> Get-HgsTrace -RunDiagnostics
Overall Result: Warning
    savdalhv07: Warning
        Best Practices: Warning
            Resolves Service Hostname to Multiple Addresses: Warning
            >>> DNS server at 10.7.173.10 cannot resolve
"hgs.savtechhgs.net" to multiple IP addresses. The recommended
configuration is

            >>> to have multiple HGS servers available at
"hgs.savtechhgs.net" for high availability.

            >>> DNS server at 10.7.173.11 cannot resolve
"hgs.savtechhgs.net" to multiple IP addresses. The recommended
configuration is

            >>> to have multiple HGS servers available at
"hgs.savtechhgs.net" for high availability.


Traces have been stored at
 "C:\Users\administrator.SAVILLTECH\AppData\Local\Temp\HgsDiagnostics-
20160628-181852".

PS C:\> Get-HgsClientConfiguration

IsHostGuarded            : True
Mode                     : HostGuardianService
KeyProtectionServerUrl   : http://hgs.savtechhgs.net/KeyProtection
AttestationServerUrl     : http://hgs.savtechhgs.net/Attestation
AttestationOperationMode : ActiveDirectory
AttestationStatus        : Passed
AttestationSubstatus     : NoInformation
```

To switch a host back to using local mode, the PowerShell that follows can be used. If this is done, no shielded VMs or encryption-supported VMs will be able to start unless the owner key used initially to protect the VM is present on the machine. This is explained in the next section.

```
Set-HgsClientConfiguration -EnableLocalMode
```

To switch back to using HGS, the same command used to configure HGS initially is executed again.

CREATING A SHIELDED VM

There are many ways to create a shielded VM, including using Windows Azure Pack, SCVMM 2016, and PowerShell. The Microsoft deployment guide walks through the options in detail. Scenarios include instances in which the VM is created on-premises and protected using keys generated on the hosting provider's HGS, and then the VM can be exported and then imported to the tenant fabric. The aforementioned Shielding Data File Wizard helps in those scenarios.

The following example is simple, but it shows the overall process. The first step is to save the Metadata of the HGS service and use that Metadata to define a Host Guardian instance on the host, and then create a shielded VM using the keys from the HGS. The Metadata downloaded consists of the public keys of the HGS encryption and signing certificates along with other HGS instance information. The hostname of the HGS in the following example should be changed from hgs.savtechhgs.net to your HGS name. The HGS instance is now a known guardian on the machine. If the VM needs to be started in various environments using different HGS instances, a guardian for each HGS environment should be added to the local host that will be protecting the VM.

```
#Add the required information from HGS to enable key creation
Invoke-WebRequest
'http://hgs.savtechhgs.net/KeyProtection/service/metadata/2014-
07/metadata.xml' -OutFile .\SavTechGuardian.xml
Import-HgsGuardian -Path 'SavTechGuardian.xml' -Name 'SavTech' `
    -AllowUntrustedRoot

$Guardian = Get-HgsGuardian -Name 'SavTech'
```

In addition to the HGS guardians, a local guardian is used when protecting a VM. The owner's local guardian can be used to start the VM if the HGS is not available. Consider a scenario in which normally the VM runs in a hosted fabric but needs to be downloaded locally to be examined. The local guardian can be used to decrypt and leverage the vTPM of the VM. The same owner can be used with multiple VMs; in this case, I'm naming this JSavillVMs, as they are all of the VMs I protect.

```
$Owner = New-HgsGuardian -Name '<Owner name, e.g. JSavillVMs>' `
    -GenerateCertificates
```

Behind the scenes when creating a new owner (which is a local guardian), a signing and encryption certificate pair are created and stored in the Shielded VM Local Certificates store of the local machine. These can be examined:

```
PS C:\> ls 'Cert:\LocalMachine\Shielded VM Local Certificates'


    PSParentPath:
Microsoft.PowerShell.Security\Certificate::LocalMachine\Shielded VM Local
Certificates

Thumbprint                                Subject
----------                                -------
CC96FF66BB796D505EB52A0497D31BBD2603CB31  CN=Shielded VM Encryption
Certificate (JSavillVMs) (savdalhv07)
A9AF16BD57957716931AAF47C849964FFAF80FBE  CN=Shielded VM Encryption
Certificate (test123) (savdalhv07)
A8CD4EBA86F85A330BA12A5B5381C3A2993E6EE3  CN=Shielded VM Signing
Certificate (JSavillVMs) (savdalhv07)
04AC1870A1D3A3513B3C92D5828D68E648A10BC2  CN=Shielded VM Signing
Certificate (test123) (savdalhv07)
```

In this environment, I have two owners (local guardians): JSavillVMs and test123. This is why there are two sets of encryption and signing certificates. Get-HgsGuardian confirms the guardians configured on a host.

```
PS C:\> Get-HgsGuardian

Name               HasPrivateSigningKey Signing Certificate Subject
----               -------------------- --------------------------
SavTech            False                CN=signing.savtechhgs.net
test123            True                 CN=Shielded VM Signing Certificate
(test123) (savdalhv07)
JSavillVMs True                         CN=Shielded VM Signing Certificate
(JSavillVMs) (savdalhv07)
```

Three guardians are on this host: the two local guardians and my HGS instance. Note that the private keys are present on the host for the local guardians but not for the HGS guardian. It is important to back up the local guardian certificates, including the private keys, and keep them secure.

Now that a Host Guardian is available and an owner defined, a new key protector can be created that will contain the encrypted symmetric transport key that will be used to encrypt and decrypt the stored vTPM state. In this example, I apply only one guardian to the new key protector, but multiple guardians could be added if the VM needed to be moved between multiple fabrics with their own HGS instances.

```
$KP = New-HgsKeyProtector -Owner $Owner -Guardian $Guardian `
    -AllowUntrustedRoot
```

This is best understood by looking at an example key protector that has an owner (a local guardian) and two HGS guardians. In this case, they are SavTech and Azure, since I may want to run this on my fabric and in the public cloud. Table 5.2 shows the high-level content of a key protector that has this configuration. Notice that in the key protector is the transport key (TK1) that is used to encrypt the vTPM saved state and is encrypted once for each of the guardians, using the respective guardian's public encryption certificate (which means only the corresponding private key can decrypt).

TABLE 5.2: Example Key Protector Content

GUARDIAN	ENCRYPTION CERT	SIGNING CERT	TRANSPORT KEY
JSavillVMs	MyEncCert (pub)	MySignCert (pub)	TK1 encrypted with MyEncCert
SavTech	SavEncCert (pub)	SavSignCert (pub)	TK1 encrypted with SavEncCert
Azure	AzEncCert (pub)	AzSignCert (pub)	TK1 encrypted with AzEncCert

When a protected VM (shielded or encryption supported) tries to start, the saved vTPM content must be decrypted to hydrate the actual synthetic TPM for the VM. If the host running the VM is configured in local mode, it looks at the local guardians to see whether any of the rows can be decrypted and therefore access the transport key, which would enable the decryption of the encrypted vTPM state. If the host is in HGS mode, the entire key protector is sent to its configured HGS service after the host has attested to the HGS proving its health. The entire key protector, instead of just the applicable HGS row, is sent for two reasons:

1. The host does not know which row corresponds to the HGS, because the row contains only the certificates and not a friendly name for the HGS. Therefore, by sending the entire key protector, the HGS can parse the key protector, find a row it can decrypt, and then send back the transport key in an encrypted form that the virtual secure mode of the host can decrypt and use as mentioned at the start of this section.

2. Each time a VM is started, the transport key is rolled and a new transport key generated (for example, TK2), which will be used to encrypt the vTPM state on disk going forward. The HGS will encrypt the new transport key (TK2) with each of the encryption certs for each guardian (remember, the private key is needed to decrypt) and place all in a new key protector. This is sent back to the host to use going forward, along with the current TK1 needed to decrypt the current vTPM content.

Once the key protector is created, it can be assigned to a VM, and the VM can be set as shielded, and its TPM can be enabled.

```
$VMName="GuardedVM01"
Stop-VM -Name $VMName -Force

Set-VMKeyProtector -VMName $VMName -KeyProtector $KP.RawData
Set-VMSecurityPolicy -VMName $VMName -Shielded $true
Enable-VMTPM -VMName $VMName

Start-VM -Name $VMName
```

The VM is now shielded. Within the VM, the TPM would be enabled and BitLocker used to encrypt the drive. The BitLocker feature must be enabled within the server OS to use BitLocker. Once the BitLocker encryption has completed, it can be considered shielded.

```
Install-WindowsFeature BitLocker
```

If the properties of a shielded VM under Security are examined, the TPM will be enabled, state and migration traffic will be encrypted, and the VM will have shielding enabled, as shown in Figure 5.24. Because the policy is applied in a guarded fabric, the virtualization administrator cannot change any of the configuration, and the VHD(x) files are encrypted because BitLocker was used inside the VM, making them unreadable. Any attempt to use console access or PowerShell Direct will fail, as shown in Figure 5.25. If using SCVMM, a Security Summary tab can be added to the VM view that will show the VM as Shielded.

FIGURE 5.24
Properties for a
shielded VM

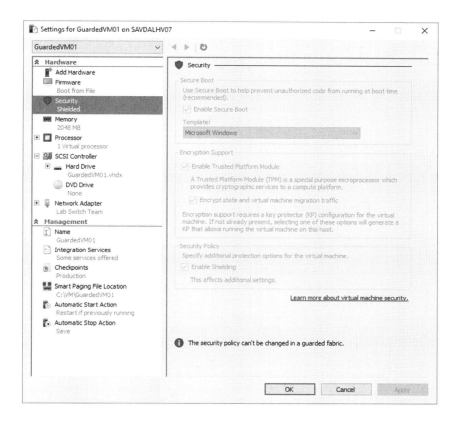

FIGURE 5.25
Console access and
PowerShell Direct
blocked for shielded
VM

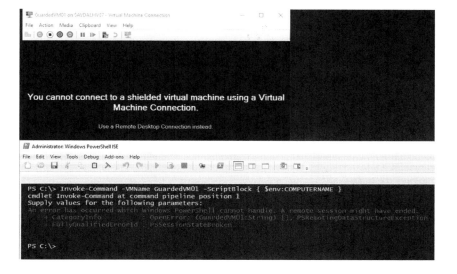

The process to create an encryption-supported VM instead of shielded is exactly the same, except `-Shielded` is set to `$false` instead of `$true` in the `Set-VMSecurityPolicy`. The VM still uses a key protector, and the process is identical. Microsoft has some great additional resources that I recommend:

◆ http://download.microsoft.com/download/1/B/C/
  1BCB8707-8D67-44BB-9317-DBA3F2D3A07F/Windows_Server_Shielded_Virtual_
  Machines_infographic.pdf

◆ https://gallery.technet.microsoft.com/Shielded-VMs-and-Guarded-b05d8078

◆ https://gallery.technet.microsoft.com/Shielded-VMs-and-Guarded-70c5b471

Creating and Using Hyper-V Templates

In the previous section, a virtual machine was manually created, and all of the attributes such as memory, CPU, network, and storage had to be configured. Then the operating system had to be manually installed. Although PowerShell can help automate this process, a much better option is to use a template, which is a virtual machine configuration and virtual hard disk with a duplication-ready operating system installed. This template can be easily deployed just by copying the VHDX file and assigning it to a new virtual machine that is created from a template VM configuration.

The first step is to create the VHDX file containing the operating system that is suitable for duplication. Any readers who have ever deployed desktops will be used to the idea of building out one "gold" desktop and then preparing it for duplication so that it could be captured and deployed to many desktops quickly. Windows has been using this method since Windows 2008, when the WIM format was introduced as the method of installing Windows. Inside the WIM file is a deployed operating system that has been prepared for duplication. All Windows installation does is to deploy the content of the WIM file, which is why installation got faster between Windows 2003 and Windows 2008. When Windows is installed, various specializations are performed, such as creating the security ID, creating the globally unique ID, and other items. Many problems arise if different systems have the same SID, GUID, and other items. For this reason, sysprep is a utility built into the operating system that removes this unique information (the process is known as *generalization*), and once it is removed, the operating system can be duplicated and started on the target. When that happens, a specialization phase creates the required unique values and runs certain critical processes to ready the copied operating system for usage. Once you have deployed the operating system to a virtual machine and tailored it, run the command at the end of this paragraph. This will generalize the operating system and shut it down. You can then copy the VHDX file to a template area and use that template for new virtual machines, essentially just copying the template to a new location for each new virtual machine that should run the same operating system. It's also possible to launch `sysprep.exe`, and a dialog box will allow you to select the same options. However, when you are using the full command line, the `/mode:VM` parameter can be specified (covered in detail in Chapter 11, "Remote Desktop Services"), but it enables sysprep to run in a mode that is optimized for virtualized hardware.

```
Sysprep.exe /generalize /oobe /shutdown /mode:VM
```

When a new virtual machine starts from a copy of your template, it will go through a basic out-of-box experience that asks minimal questions regarding country, language, keyboard layout, accepting the EULA (End User License Agreement), and a new local administrator password. Those questions can be answered through the use of an unattended installation answer file, which is how SCVMM automates deployments.

Once you have the template VHDX file, keeping it updated can be a challenge, such as having the latest patches applied. You can generalize an operating system only so many times, so it is not an option to take a template, start it with a VM, patch it, then generalize it again with sysprep, and keep repeating this process. There are several options that I think are good, and I have written instructions for the first two and even recorded a video for each:

1. Inject patches into the VHDX file directly using the DISM tool. I created a script to do this, which is available at:

    `http://windowsitpro.com/windows/add-updates-offline-vhd-or-wim-file`

    A video walk-through is available at:

    `www.youtube.com/watch?v=cOUlW2bJnK0`

2. Use a virtual machine and utilize checkpoints to create a point-in-time capture of the VM before sysprep'ing, applying updates, and sysprep'ing again, and then export the updated image and revert back to the pre-sysprep'd checkpoint ready for the next set of updates. I detail this at:

    `http://windowsitpro.com/hyper-v/easily-maintain-hyper-v-template-image`

    There is a video walk-through at:

    `www.youtube.com/watch?v=1dddszeRHpM`

3. In the past, Microsoft had the Virtual Machine Servicing Tool (VMST), which allowed the patching of Hyper-V virtual machines. However, the last supported version worked only up to SCVMM 2012. Microsoft has now released an updated solution based on Orchestrator SMA that can patch virtual machines stored in an SCVMM library from updates available in WSUS. The solution is available at:

    `http://blogs.technet.com/b/privatecloud/archive/2013/12/07/`
    `orchestrated-vm-patching.aspx`

    The solution comes in the form of the SMA runbook and instructions on its usage.

4. The Windows Server 2012 R2 and above versions of Configuration Manager support the patching of virtual hard disks. These virtual hard disks can be published into SCVMM and used as part of a template. More information on using Configuration Manager for VHD management can be found at `https://technet.microsoft.com/en-us/library/` `dn448591.aspx`.

One option with the template VHDX is to write some basic PowerShell that creates a new folder for the new VM, copies the template VHDX into that folder, creates a new VM, and attaches the copied VHDX file to the new VM. It is even possible to mount the VHDX file and inject a sysprep answer file into it to specify name, domain join instructions, and even network configuration so that when the virtual machine is turned on, it is fully configured (which is exactly what SCVMM does).

A better option is to leverage SCVMM, which has full template support and can even take an existing virtual machine and turn it into a template, including generalizing the guest operating system:

- The guest virtual machine must be a supported operating system, and the operating system in the guest must be known to SCVMM. When you are looking at the virtual machine in the VMs And Services workspace, it should show the operating system version. If it does not, right-click the VM and select Refresh while the virtual machine is running.

- The virtual machine must be shut down.

- The virtual machine must not have any checkpoints (to save the VM, create a clone of it first).

- The virtual machine administrator password does not need to be blank.

This allows you to create a virtual machine, customize it as required, shut it down, and simply right-click it in SCVMM and select the Create VM Template option. Remember that this will generalize the operating system, and so if you want to keep the state of the virtual machine, you should create a clone of it prior to using it as the source for a template creation. A warning is displayed that the template creation process will remove the state of the VM. When creating a VM template, the virtual hardware will copy the configuration of the source VM, but this can be changed in the Library post-template creation. The Operating System template properties can be modified, such as name, administrator password, time zone, and domain membership, and you can even install roles, features, and other software. An SCVMM library server must be selected as the target to store the new template along with a location within the library. Once the template is created, the original virtual machine will be deleted. You can track the status of the template creation by using the Jobs workspace in SCVMM, as shown in Figure 5.26. Note that the longest part of the process was copying the VHDX file to the library.

FIGURE 5.26
The full detail of a template creation using SCVMM

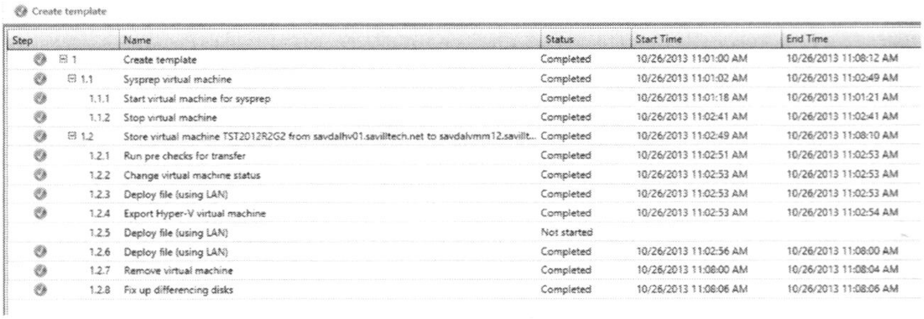

Step		Name	Status	Start Time	End Time
	⊟ 1	Create template	Completed	10/26/2013 11:01:00 AM	10/26/2013 11:08:12 AM
	⊟ 1.1	Sysprep virtual machine	Completed	10/26/2013 11:01:02 AM	10/26/2013 11:02:49 AM
	1.1.1	Start virtual machine for sysprep	Completed	10/26/2013 11:01:18 AM	10/26/2013 11:01:21 AM
	1.1.2	Stop virtual machine	Completed	10/26/2013 11:02:41 AM	10/26/2013 11:02:41 AM
	⊟ 1.2	Store virtual machine TST2012R2G2 from savdalhv01.saviltech.net to savdalvmm12.savilt...	Completed	10/26/2013 11:02:49 AM	10/26/2013 11:08:10 AM
	1.2.1	Run pre checks for transfer	Completed	10/26/2013 11:02:51 AM	10/26/2013 11:02:53 AM
	1.2.2	Change virtual machine status	Completed	10/26/2013 11:02:53 AM	10/26/2013 11:02:53 AM
	1.2.3	Deploy file (using LAN)	Completed	10/26/2013 11:02:53 AM	10/26/2013 11:02:53 AM
	1.2.4	Export Hyper-V virtual machine	Completed	10/26/2013 11:02:53 AM	10/26/2013 11:02:54 AM
	1.2.5	Deploy file (using LAN)	Not started		
	1.2.6	Deploy file (using LAN)	Completed	10/26/2013 11:02:56 AM	10/26/2013 11:08:00 AM
	1.2.7	Remove virtual machine	Completed	10/26/2013 11:08:00 AM	10/26/2013 11:08:04 AM
	1.2.8	Fix up differencing disks	Completed	10/26/2013 11:08:06 AM	10/26/2013 11:08:06 AM

SCVMM 2012 SP1 introduced the ability to create Linux-based virtual machine templates that could then be deployed. There is an additional step because Linux does not have a built-in sysprep, which means that an SCVMM agent must be installed into the Linux VM prior to using it for a template that allows SCVMM to customize the OS during deployment. The process for Linux is as follows:

1. Create a new VM and install an SCVMM-supported Linux distribution into it. At the time of this writing, this includes Red Hat Enterprise Linux (RHEL), CentOS, Ubuntu, and SUSE, with others coming in the future.

2. Install the latest version of Hyper-V Integration Services if needed (the Linux kernel 3.4 includes the Windows 2012 version of Hyper-V Integration Services).

3. Install the SCVMM Linux agent. This is found in the `C:\Program Files\Microsoft System Center 2016\Virtual Machine Manager\agents\Linux` folder on the SCVMM server. How you get the content of the folder to the Linux distribution will vary.

One option, if the Linux distribution supports SMB, is to connect to the `C$` share on the SCVMM server. Or you could create an NFS share to which Linux can connect, although I found it easier just to create an ISO with the Linux agent in it and then map the ISO to the Linux VM, which will be available as the local CD. I found the easiest way to create the ISO is to use a software package such as MagicISO. Once the files are available, you must install the Linux agent by running the install script and pick the 32-bit or 64-bit version. To run the install script, you first need to set the install script to be executable:

```
chmod +x install
```

Then execute (I use sudo because I'm not logged on as administrator): `sudo ./ install scvmmguestagent.1.0.2.1075.x64.tar.`

The agent is needed because it performs the customization of the Linux environment when a template is deployed. Once the Linux template is deployed, the SCVMM agent is automatically removed.

4. Shut down the Linux VM, and then save its VHDX file to the SCVMM library.

5. Now create a Linux template, and make sure that you set the correct operating system, which will allow you to configure automatic naming (* is a complete random name, while ### specifies an automatically incrementing number) for the hostnames along with a password for the root account, the time zone, and any scripts you want to run. Save the template.

6. You can now create new Linux VMs from the template. You will notice that when you deploy a Linux VM from the template, at one point an ISO is connected to the VM temporarily. This carries a customization file that contains the personalization data in the `linuxosconfiguration.xml` file in addition to the latest version of the SCVMM Linux agent (in case it's been updated).

Templates are visible through the Library workspace and shown in the Templates ➤ VM Templates area. Figure 5.27 shows the main configuration areas for a template. Notice that all of the virtual hardware can be changed in addition to adding new hardware to the template hardware profile. If you will be creating many types of templates rather than configuring the same hardware or operating system configurations each time, a good option is to navigate to Profiles within the Libraries workspace and create separate hardware profiles and guest OS profiles, which can then be used in templates you create, avoiding the need to perform the same configurations repeatedly. VM templates can also be exported and imported, allowing portability between SCVMM environments.

FIGURE 5.27
Modifying a template
within SCVMM

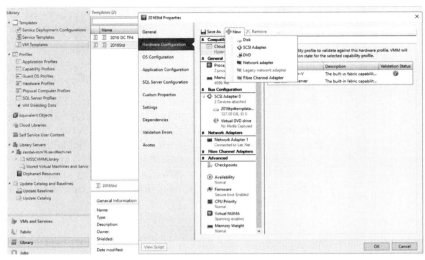

USING APPLICATION, SQL, ROLE, AND FEATURE TEMPLATE CONFIGURATIONS

You will notice that the VM templates include sections related to application configurations, SQL configuration, roles, and features. While it may seem that all of these configurations will be used when deploying the template, this is not the case. These components are used only when the VM template is deployed as part of a service template, which I cover in Chapter 9. When you're deploying a template-based virtual machine, configurations related to application, SQL, roles, and features are ignored and not available. If you require this type of deployment, either use service templates or manage these configurations by using PowerShell or System Center Orchestrator as an add-on to the VM deployment.

In most environments, you will have a limited number of template VHDX files but many templates that use the same VHDX and apply different configurations and applications. You do not want a large number of VHDX files with different configurations and applications installed. This is hard to maintain and patch. The goal is to have a plain, sometimes called *vanilla*, VHDX template with just the operating system and then deploy all other customizations using the template options and declarative technologies such as PowerShell DSC.

A Linux OS configuration has far fewer options than a Windows OS configuration, and most customizations beyond root credentials and name will need to be performed using the RunOnce Commands option.

Deploying a virtual machine using a template is simple:

1. Within the VMs And Services workspace, select the Create Virtual Machine action, which has an option to create based on an existing virtual machine, VM template, or virtual hard disk in the library, as shown in Figure 5.28. Click Next.

FIGURE 5.28
Selecting a template as the source for a new virtual machine

2. Enter a name and optional description and click Next.

3. The virtual hardware profile can be customized from the profile in the template or even a completely separate hardware profile can be loaded. If this virtual machine needs to be highly available, in the Advanced ➤ Availability section, ensure that the Make This Virtual Machine Highly Available box is checked, as shown in Figure 5.29. Click Next.

4. Customizations for the operating system can be performed, such as identity, answer file, and RunOnce commands. Notice that all of the defaults from the template are populated automatically. Click Next.

5. Select the location for the deployment. This can be to a cloud or to a host group. When you have made your selection, click Next.

6. An evaluation against all hosts is performed and each available host is given a rating based on its suitability, as shown in Figure 5.30. The rating is explained in the Details section. The first two are good matches, but the third and fourth are not, because the VM needs to be clustered, and these nodes are not clustered, which is shown in the Rating Explanation section. Select a host and click Next.

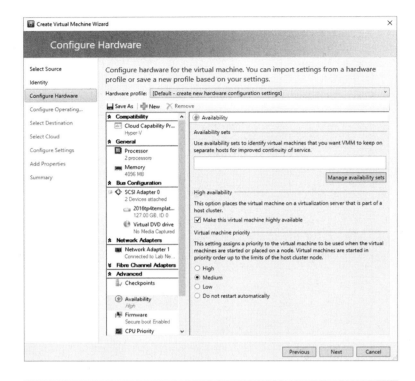

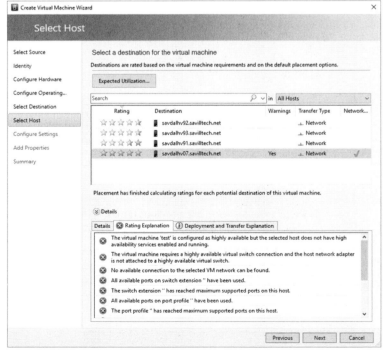

7. The Configure Settings dialog box allows changes to configurations such as the computer name and location. Make changes as required and click Next.
8. In the Select Networks dialog box, select the VM network and click Next.
9. Set the automatic actions for startup and shutdown, and choose whether the new VM should be excluded from placement optimizations. (This is covered in Chapter 7 but it's a technology that moves VMs between hosts if necessary for optimal resource utilization. This should be left enabled for most virtual machines.) Click Next.
10. A summary screen is displayed (along with the View Script button, should you wish to capture the PowerShell). Click Create to create the virtual machine.

Deploying a template is the single circumstance in which SCVMM leverages ODX if possible, which needs to be a capability of the SAN, and the LUN containing the template VHDX file must be on the same volume as the LUN that is the target for the VM deployment for most SANs. If it's not possible to leverage ODX, SCVMM will try a regular Fast File Copy, and if that fails, it will resort to using BITS. Figure 5.31 shows the complete deployment of a VM from a template. Notice the various steps. First a virtual machine is created, and then the template VHDX file is copied to the target storage. Step 1.8.2 creates a temporary ISO that contains the answer file that performs all of the configuration of the guest OS. This ISO is created in the root of the new virtual machine folder that has the name of the VM. For example, my test1 VM ISO would be called `C:\ClusterStorage\Volume1\test1\test1.iso`. This ISO is deleted after the VM is created, as are the additional virtual DVD drives that are added during deployment to attach the answer file ISO to as well as the VMM additions.

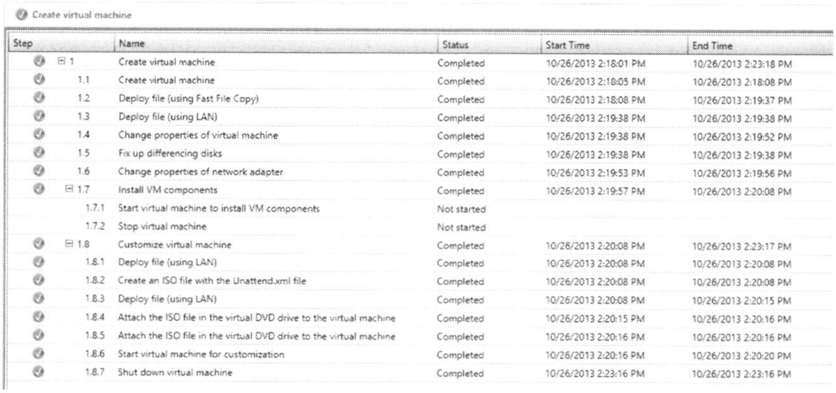
Create virtual machine

Step	Name	Status	Start Time	End Time
1	Create virtual machine	Completed	10/26/2013 2:18:01 PM	10/26/2013 2:23:18 PM
1.1	Create virtual machine	Completed	10/26/2013 2:18:05 PM	10/26/2013 2:18:08 PM
1.2	Deploy file (using Fast File Copy)	Completed	10/26/2013 2:18:08 PM	10/26/2013 2:19:37 PM
1.3	Deploy file (using LAN)	Completed	10/26/2013 2:19:38 PM	10/26/2013 2:19:38 PM
1.4	Change properties of virtual machine	Completed	10/26/2013 2:19:38 PM	10/26/2013 2:19:52 PM
1.5	Fix up differencing disks	Completed	10/26/2013 2:19:38 PM	10/26/2013 2:19:38 PM
1.6	Change properties of network adapter	Completed	10/26/2013 2:19:53 PM	10/26/2013 2:19:56 PM
1.7	Install VM components	Completed	10/26/2013 2:19:57 PM	10/26/2013 2:20:08 PM
1.7.1	Start virtual machine to install VM components	Not started		
1.7.2	Stop virtual machine	Not started		
1.8	Customize virtual machine	Completed	10/26/2013 2:20:08 PM	10/26/2013 2:23:17 PM
1.8.1	Deploy file (using LAN)	Completed	10/26/2013 2:20:08 PM	10/26/2013 2:20:08 PM
1.8.2	Create an ISO file with the Unattend.xml file	Completed	10/26/2013 2:20:08 PM	10/26/2013 2:20:08 PM
1.8.3	Deploy file (using LAN)	Completed	10/26/2013 2:20:08 PM	10/26/2013 2:20:15 PM
1.8.4	Attach the ISO file in the virtual DVD drive to the virtual machine	Completed	10/26/2013 2:20:15 PM	10/26/2013 2:20:16 PM
1.8.5	Attach the ISO file in the virtual DVD drive to the virtual machine	Completed	10/26/2013 2:20:16 PM	10/26/2013 2:20:16 PM
1.8.6	Start virtual machine for customization	Completed	10/26/2013 2:20:16 PM	10/26/2013 2:20:20 PM
1.8.7	Shut down virtual machine	Completed	10/26/2013 2:23:16 PM	10/26/2013 2:23:16 PM

FIGURE 5.31 A complete SCVMM VM deployment from a template

If you are quick enough, you can see the temporary ISO file created and could even copy it to another location. It contains a single file, `unattend.xml`, which contains all of the guest OS customizations specified in the template and the selections during VM deployment. The following code is the content of my `unattend.xml` file that SCVMM created for the deployment shown in Figure 5.31. This is useful for your own education and understanding of how your OS customizations are implemented to the virtual machine.

```
<?xml version="1.0" encoding="utf-8"?>
<unattend xmlns="urn:schemas-microsoft-com:unattend">
    <settings pass="specialize">
        <component name="Microsoft-Windows-Shell-Setup"
```

```
processorArchitecture="amd64" publicKeyToken="31bf3856ad364e35"
language="neutral" versionScope="nonSxS"
xmlns:wcm="http://schemas.microsoft.com/WMIConfig/2002/State"
xmlns:xsi="http://www.w3.org/2001/XMLSchema-instance">
            <RegisteredOwner />
            <RegisteredOrganization />
            <ComputerName>test1</ComputerName>
            <ProductKey>Y4TGP-NPTV9-HTC2H-7MGQ3-DV4TW</ProductKey>
        </component>
        <component name="Microsoft-Windows-UnattendedJoin"
processorArchitecture="amd64" publicKeyToken="31bf3856ad364e35"
language="neutral" versionScope="nonSxS"
xmlns:wcm="http://schemas.microsoft.com/WMIConfig/2002/State"
xmlns:xsi="http://www.w3.org/2001/XMLSchema-instance">
            <Identification>
                <JoinDomain>savilltech</JoinDomain>
                <Credentials>
                    <Domain>savilltech</Domain>
                    <Username>administrator</Username>
                    <Password>passwordinplaintext</Password>
                </Credentials>
            </Identification>
        </component>
        <component name="Microsoft-Windows-Deployment"
processorArchitecture="amd64" publicKeyToken="31bf3856ad364e35"
language="neutral" versionScope="nonSxS"
xmlns:wcm="http://schemas.microsoft.com/WMIConfig/2002/State"
xmlns:xsi="http://www.w3.org/2001/XMLSchema-instance">
            <RunSynchronous>
                <RunSynchronousCommand wcm:action="add">
                    <Order>1</Order>
                    <Description>Install Guest agent</Description>
                    <Path>cmd.exe /c (for %1 in
(z y x w v u t s r q p o n m l k j i h g f e d c b a) do
@(if exist %1:\VMMGuestAgent.exe (sc create scvmmadditions
binpath=%1:\VMMGuestAgent.exe type=own start=auto &amp
sc start scvmmadditions )))</Path>
                    <WillReboot>OnRequest</WillReboot>
                </RunSynchronousCommand>
            </RunSynchronous>
        </component>
    </settings>
    <settings pass="oobeSystem">
        <component name="Microsoft-Windows-Shell-Setup"
processorArchitecture="amd64" publicKeyToken="31bf3856ad364e35"
language="neutral" versionScope="nonSxS"
xmlns:wcm="http://schemas.microsoft.com/WMIConfig/2002/State"
```

```
xmlns:xsi="http://www.w3.org/2001/XMLSchema-instance">
        <UserAccounts>
            <AdministratorPassword>
                <Value>localadminpasswordplaintext</Value>
                <PlainText>true</PlainText>
            </AdministratorPassword>
        </UserAccounts>
        <TimeZone>Central Standard Time</TimeZone>
        <OOBE>
            <HideEULAPage>true</HideEULAPage>
            <SkipUserOOBE>true</SkipUserOOBE>
            <HideOEMRegistrationScreen>true</HideOEMRegistrationScreen>
            <HideOnlineAccountScreens>true</HideOnlineAccountScreens>
            <HideWirelessSetupInOOBE>true</HideWirelessSetupInOOBE>
            <NetworkLocation>Work</NetworkLocation>
            <ProtectYourPC>1</ProtectYourPC>
            <HideLocalAccountScreen>true</HideLocalAccountScreen>
        </OOBE>
    </component>
    <component name="Microsoft-Windows-International-Core"
processorArchitecture="amd64" publicKeyToken="31bf3856ad364e35"
language="neutral" versionScope="nonSxS"
xmlns:wcm="http://schemas.microsoft.com/WMIConfig/2002/State"
xmlns:xsi="http://www.w3.org/2001/XMLSchema-instance">
        <UserLocale>en-US</UserLocale>
        <SystemLocale>en-US</SystemLocale>
        <InputLocale>0409:00000409</InputLocale>
        <UILanguage>en-US</UILanguage>
    </component>
</settings>
<cpi:offlineImage cpi:source="" xmlns:cpi="urn:schemas-microsoft-com:cpi" />
</unattend>
```

Hyper-V Integration Services and Supported Operating Systems

When talking about the guest operating system running inside a virtual machine, I mentioned enlightened operating systems, which are guest operating systems that are aware that they are running in a virtual environment and can leverage specific virtual features such as synthetic hardware via the VMBus through special drivers. Additionally, numerous services between the virtual machine and the Hyper-V host are enabled when the guest has Hyper-V Integration Services installed. Hyper-V Integration Services is built into the Windows operating systems for the respective version of Hyper-V. For example, Windows Server 2012 R2 and Windows 8.1 have Hyper-V 2012 R2 Integration Services built-in, and Windows Server 2012 and Windows 8 had the Hyper-V 2012 Integration Services built-in. This means that if the guest operating system is running a version of an operating system older than the Hyper-V host, you will need to upgrade its version of Integration Services. This is the first action you should perform when deploying an operating system, and when creating a VM template, make sure that you update Integration Services prior to capturing the VHDX for use with the template.

Each Hyper-V host prior to Windows Server 2016 has the latest version of Integration Services stored at C:\Windows\System32\vmguest.iso. When vmconnect is used to connect to a virtual machine, an action, Insert Integration Services Setup Disk, is available in the Action menu that attaches vmguest.iso to the virtual DVD for the virtual machine. The vmguest.iso file will then launch within the VM and update Integration Services, which will require a reboot for the guest operating system. While the version of Integration Services always increased between Windows Server versions, it may also increment as part of the updates.

Updating Integration Services based on the version of Hyper-V host is not logical in a world where VMs may move between Hyper-V hosts that may be running different versions, which can happen in mixed clusters consisting of Windows Server 2012 R2 and Windows Server 2016 hosts. Additionally, VMs may move to a completely different fabric; for example, out to Azure. Therefore, Microsoft has shifted the delivery of Integration Services now to be delivered via Windows Update and normal support channels instead of through the Hyper-V host, which is more in line with the Linux model. This enables guest operating systems running Windows to be updated automatically to the latest version of Integration Services, which can work on the latest version of Hyper-V or earlier versions. Now there is no need to worry about Integration Service versions, for any OS that is Windows Server 2008 R2/Windows 7 or newer will automatically be updated through whatever patch solution is leveraged. The Hyper-V console no longer even shows the Integration Services version in Windows Server 2016, and the version is not shown as an attribute of a VM anymore. Integration Service updates can be downloaded for offline deployment from https://support.microsoft.com/en-us/kb/3071740.

In addition to providing the drivers and components required for the most optimal utilization of resources between the guest and the hypervisor, other integration services exist, as described in the following list. Note that each service can be disabled if required through the settings of the virtual machine in the Management ➤ Integration Services section. Unless there is a specific reason not to, you should leave Integration Services enabled.

Operating System Shutdown Enables the guest operating system to be cleanly shut down from the Hyper-V manager or the management interfaces that Hyper-V provides, such as PowerShell and WMI.

Time Synchronization Keeps the time of the guest OS synchronized with the host operating system.

Data Exchange Allows the exchange of specific Registry location values between a guest and the parent partition, known as *key-value pairs*. The Hyper-V host writes to location HKEY_LOCAL_MACHINE\SOFTWARE\Microsoft\Virtual Machine\Guest\Parameters within the VM, and the OS in the guest can then read from this location to gather information about the host. This information includes the Hyper-V hostname (which is the cluster name if it's a cluster node), version information, its fully qualified name, and the actual VM's name and ID, as shown in Figure 5.32. This can easily be read using PowerShell. For example, within a virtual machine, to find which Hyper-V host it is on, I use the following PowerShell command:

```
$regPath = "HKLM:\SOFTWARE\Microsoft\Virtual Machine\Guest\Parameters"
(Get-ItemProperty -Path $regPath).HostName
```

FIGURE 5.32
Registry within a virtual machine showing information about the host

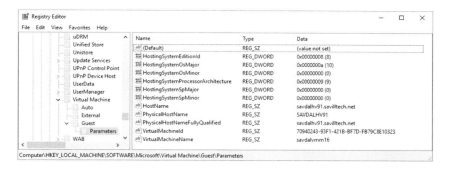

Conversely, the Hyper-V host reads information from `HKEY_LOCAL_MACHINE\SOFTWARE\ Microsoft\Virtual Machine\Auto` in the guest, which is populated by the guest OS, giving Hyper-V a lot of information about the OS, including version, naming, and IP configuration. This type of information exchange can be useful for many types of management operations, automation, and inventory. The complete list of values can be found at the following location, which documents the `Msvm_KvpExchangeDataItem` class:

`http://msdn.microsoft.com/en-us/library/cc136850(v=vs.85).aspx`

You can create your own custom values within the VM that can be read by the Hyper-V host by adding string values under `HKEY_LOCAL_MACHINE\SOFTWARE\Microsoft\Virtual Machine\ Guest`. This would be useful to, for example, populate the type of server in the guest using a custom process, such as SQLServer or IISServer, which could then be read from the host to ascertain the type of server running in the VM. There is no PowerShell cmdlet available to read values set in the guest from the Hyper-V host. Instead, you use WMI. The following PowerShell script reads the fully qualified domain name from within the guest OS from the Hyper-V host for VM savdaldc02:

```
$vmName = "savdaldc02"

$vm = Get-WmiObject -Namespace root\virtualization\v2 `
    -Class Msvm_ComputerSystem `
    -Filter "ElementName='$vmName'"

$vm.GetRelated("Msvm_KvpExchangeComponent").GuestIntrinsicExchangeItems | % {
        $GuestExchangeItemXml = ([XML]$_).SelectSingleNode(`
  "/INSTANCE/PROPERTY[@NAME='Name']/VALUE[child::text()='FullyQualifiedDomainName']")

        if ($GuestExchangeItemXml -ne $null)
        {
        $GuestExchangeItemXml.SelectSingleNode( `
        "/INSTANCE/PROPERTY[@NAME='Data']/VALUE/child::text()").Value
        }
    }
```

Heartbeat   Allows Hyper-V to check the responsiveness of the guest operating system by a heartbeat check.

Backup (Volume Snapshot)   A powerful feature that I cover in Chapter 6, "Maintaining a Hyper-V Environment;" this allows backup requests at the host level to be passed to the guest operating system, in turn allowing consistent file and application backups to be taken from the host.

Guest Services This is a new Integration Services component introduced in Windows Server 2012 R2 that is disabled by default. Guest services enables the copying of files to a virtual machine using WMI APIs or using the new `Copy-VMFile` PowerShell cmdlet.

Microsoft provides Integration Services for the supported operating systems unless it is already part of the operating system; for example, many modern Linux distributions have the Hyper-V Integration Services built-in (although Microsoft still releases updated Linux Integration Services, which are then integrated into newer distributions of Linux). The full list of the supported guest operating systems can be found at `http://technet.microsoft.com/library/hh831531` for Windows Server 2012 R2 and at `https://technet.microsoft.com/library/mt126117.aspx` for Windows Server 2016, but the primary supported operating systems for Windows Server 2016 Hyper-V are as follows:

◆ Windows Server 2016

◆ Windows Server 2012 R2

◆ Windows Server 2012

◆ Windows Server 2008 R2 SP1

◆ Windows Server 2008 SP2

◆ Windows 10

◆ Windows 8.1

◆ Windows 8

◆ Windows 7

◆ Windows Vista SP2

◆ CentOS 5.2 and above

◆ Red Hat Enterprise Linux 5.2 and above

◆ SUSE Linux Enterprise Server 11 SP2 and above

◆ FreeBSD 8.4 and above

◆ Debian 7.0 and above

◆ Ubuntu 12.04 and above

◆ Oracle Linux 6.4 and above

Most of the Linux distributions have Integration Services built-in. However, the previously mentioned article documents which ones need the Linux Integration Services downloaded and installed manually. At the time of this writing, the latest Linux Integration Services version is 4, and it is available from the following location:

`www.microsoft.com/en-us/download/details.aspx?id=46842`

This large list covers pretty much every operating system that is used in organizations today. But what if a company has another operating system? If it's not on this list of supported operating systems, will it not work? Remember that what Hyper-V provides in a generation 1 virtual machine is a virtual environment that does not require the guest operating system to be enlightened. To the guest, it appears that the virtual hardware being presented is a physical system that includes items such as the IDE controller and the emulated legacy network adapter. Even in the Windows Server 2016 version of Hyper-V, the processor compatibility for older operating systems (-CompatibilityForOlderOperatingSystemsEnabled), which was aimed at NT 4 systems, is still configurable using PowerShell. These nonenlightened systems that do not understand VMBus will have a higher overhead and see poorer performance because of the emulated nature of the storage and networking, but most likely they will work. There is a difference between what is supported and what will work. Microsoft supports only operating systems on Hyper-V that are themselves supported by the vendor. For example, Microsoft no longer supports Windows Server 2003, which means that Hyper-V can no longer support it as a guest operating system, but it will run a virtual machine. In a production environment, you typically should be running only operating systems supported by the vendor to ensure that patches are received and that in the event of a problem, you can get help from the vendor. If you have a Windows Server 2003 application, however, it most likely would run on Hyper-V just fine.

Migrating Physical Servers and Virtual Machines to Hyper-V Virtual Machines

For most organizations today, virtualization is a technology that is established in the environment, and the number of operating systems deployed to bare-metal hardware (physical servers) is decreasing. It's more likely today that you have operating systems virtualized on another hypervisor, such as VMware ESXi or Citrix XenServer. Moving from either a physical server or another hypervisor requires a migration known as physical-to-virtual (P2V) or virtual-to-virtual (V2V).

In the previous version of SCVMM, SCVMM 2012, the P2V feature was built into the product and allowed a physical server operating system to be captured and converted to a virtual machine. This worked in an online or offline mode, depending on the operating system running on the server. Online P2V is used for operating systems that support the Microsoft Volume Shadow Copy Service (VSS) and works by deploying an agent to the physical computer operating system (although this could also be an operating system running inside a VM). A capture of the hardware configuration is performed and mapped to a virtual machine configuration, and then the content of the hard drives is captured using a VSS backup, which ensures the integrity of the backup, and is written to a VHD on the Hyper-V host. It is important that the application is stopped during this process because, otherwise, once the backup is used with a virtual machine on Hyper-V, any subsequent changes on the physical host would be lost. This is not a problem if the application does not store application data or state locally. Because of the VSS requirement, the online P2V is available for Windows XP SP2 and Windows 2003 SP1 and above.

For Windows 2000 SP4 machines that don't support VSS, or for other operating systems that perhaps you don't want to use online P2V with because a VSS writer for the application is not available, an offline P2V is performed. With the offline P2V, a Windows PE OS is temporarily installed on the source server, and the computer is rebooted into the Windows PE environment through a modification to the boot record. The VMM agent in the Windows PE environment captures the disk content and streams to the Hyper-V server; and after that's complete, the machine boots back into the regular operating system, the final P2V processes are completed, and the actual VM is created on the Hyper-V host.

This feature has been removed in SCVMM 2012 R2, which does leave a gap in the ability to perform P2V with SCVMM. This gap, however, was (and still is) filled with the Microsoft Virtual Machine Converter tool, which at the time of writing is at version 3 and available from www.microsoft.com/en-us/download/details.aspx?id=42497. MVMC has the ability to perform both P2V and V2V from VMware to Hyper-V and to Azure. Recently, MVMC was retired as announced at https://blogs.technet.microsoft.com/scvmm/2016/06/04/important-update-regarding-microsoft-virtual-machine-converter-mvmc/. This is because Microsoft has another migration technology, Azure Site Recovery (ASR). Although initially positioned as a replication solution for workloads to Azure, ASR can also be used as a migration technology, because a migration is simply a replication and then a failover without ever failing back. ASR is available for free for 31 days per workload, which is generally enough time to migrate any workload. ASR is covered in more detail in Chapter 8, "Hyper-V Replica and Azure Site Recovery" but this is the migration technology of choice going forward for physical and virtual environments to Azure and Hyper-V.

One manual approach is to use the SysInternals tool Disk2Vhd from the following location:

http://technet.microsoft.com/en-us/sysinternals/ee656415.aspx

It can be run on any system supporting VSS, and it creates a VHD of the system's content. The created VHD file could then be used when creating a new virtual machine.

The other migration type, V2V, is most commonly from VMware ESX to Hyper-V, and there are numerous solutions. Many partners have V2V solutions, but Microsoft also provides options for VMware migrations to Hyper-V.

SCVMM 2016 still has built-in V2V support from VMware and can convert either a VMware virtual machine running on an ESX host or a VMware virtual machine in the library. The major conversion task for VMware is converting the virtual hard disks, because VMware uses the VMDK format, which needs to be converted to VHD. Additionally, VMware has its own version of Integration Services, called Integration Components, that is installed into guest operating systems. It must be removed from the operating system prior to starting on Hyper-V, or the OS will most likely crash. Note that this does not happen with Hyper-V Integration Services if a Hyper-V VM is started on a different hypervisor. On startup, Hyper-V Integration Services is triggered via the BIOS in the virtual machine, which controls the starting of the VMBus. If the hypervisor is not Hyper-V, the assertion to start VMBus will not occur, and Integration Services is not started or used. While SCVMM 2016 does have V2V, the focus is around ASR going forward.

When thinking about any migration, it's important to understand the workloads you have and the resources they are using. Microsoft provides a free tool, Microsoft Assessment and Planning Toolkit (MAP), which is available from http://technet.microsoft.com/en-us/library/bb977556.aspx. MAP can be used for many scenarios, such as desktop migration, Office planning, and cloud migrations. However, one key capability is that it can inventory and scan the utilization of operating systems and then create reports on the findings to help identify good virtualization and consolidation targets. It is highly recommended to run MAP for a period of time before performing any migration project to ensure that you have a good knowledge of the current systems and their real resource utilization.

In Chapter 2, "Virtual Machine Resource Fundamentals," I talked about differences in how Hyper-V handles processor allocation compared to a hypervisor such as ESX. This can make a difference in how you allocate resources. When converting from ESX, you can match the hardware exactly or you can take the migration as a chance to optimize the resource allocation or increase it if required. With Hyper-V, there is no penalty to having additional virtual processors in a virtual machine, and therefore you may choose to be more generous than with ESX. While it's important to be accurate in your planning for migrations to ensure that the right hardware is procured, quite a lot of flexibility is available, even for a running virtual machine:

Processor While processors cannot be hot-added to a virtual machine, the limits and weightings can be changed while the virtual machine is running. This is why potentially having additional virtual processors is a good idea.

Memory With Dynamic Memory, a virtual machine can have additional memory added as required, and the settings for the memory can be changed while the VM is running, allowing the maximum to be increased.

Network If bandwidth management is used, the minimum and maximum bandwidth limits can be modified, and at the host level, it's possible to add network adapters to a team to increase available bandwidth.

Storage Additional virtual hard disks can be added to the SCSI controller, and with Windows Server 2012 R2, a VHDX file attached to the SCSI controller can also be dynamically expanded.

Upgrading and Migrating from Previous Versions

For an organization that is already using Hyper-V, the adoption of Windows Server 2016 Hyper-V is a simple process. For both stand-alone and clustered hosts, Microsoft supports an n-2 upgrade support policy. This means that upgrading from Windows Server 2012 and Windows Server 2012 R2 is supported. However, when a host has a virtual switch (which every Hyper-V host will), an upgrade only from 2012 R2 to 2016 is supported. If a node is using NIC Teaming, no upgrade is possible.

It's important when upgrading your Hyper-V infrastructure that the upgrade is as transparent to the end users as possible, so minimizing downtime is important. When thinking of your upgrade, make sure you consider the following:

◆ Can your hardware run the new version of Windows Server 2016? (Likely, yes, if you are running Windows Server 2012, but remember that Windows Server 2016 now requires SLAT support in the processor, which was optional in previous versions.) Even if it can, would this be a good time for a hardware refresh? I have seen big performance differences when running Hyper-V on newer processor generations.

◆ Is your management infrastructure compatible with Windows Server 2016? Can it provide malware protection, monitoring, backup, and so on? It needs to!

◆ Have you upgraded System Center to the 2016 version for full Windows Server 2016 support?

◆ Are the administrators trained in Windows Server 2016? Ensure that administrators can properly manage Windows Server 2016, especially if they are used to Windows Server 2012. If you are moving to Server Core or Nano Server, this may be a big shift for administrators.

◆ Are administrators using Windows 10? Only Windows 10 can run the Windows Server 2016 Remote Server Administration Tools to manage Windows Server 2016 servers remotely.

Stand-Alone Hosts

For a stand-alone Hyper-V host, it is possible to perform an in-place upgrade. You launch the Windows Server 2016 setup process and select the option to perform an in-place upgrade. This maintains all of the server configurations but also means a period of unavailability to the virtual machines because the virtual machines will all be shut down during the upgrade of the host operating system. Once the upgrade is complete, the virtual machines will start, and then you can continue your management and post-upgrade actions.

Another option, if you have additional hardware available and are migrating from Windows Server 2012 R2, is to create a new Windows Server 2016 Hyper-V host and then perform a Shared Nothing Live Migration of the virtual machine from the Windows Server 2012 R2 host to the Windows Server 2016 host. For the first time, it's possible to perform a cross-version Live Migration. This allows you to move the virtual machines to Windows Server 2016 with no downtime to the virtual machine at all. Many companies use a type of rolling upgrade approach, provided that they have one spare server available to use. In this process, a new box is stood up with Windows Server 2016, and the virtual machines from a host are migrated to this new box. The host that is now emptied is then reinstalled with Windows Server 2016, and the VMs from another host are moved to this newly installed host, and the process continues. Note that while this process is targeted for Windows Server 2012 R2 to Windows Server 2016 with no downtime, you could use the same process from Windows Server 2012, except there would be some downtime as part of the virtual machine migration and a storage migration or an export/import would be performed between hosts. If the stand-alone hosts were using SAN storage, it would be possible just to unmask the LUNs used by the source host to the target host and then import the virtual machines.

Clusters

Most production Hyper-V environments will not be stand-alone hosts but rather have clusters of Hyper-V hosts.

Failover Clustering provides the ability to migrate workloads between a source and target cluster, and Hyper-V virtual machines are a supported workload that can be migrated. The way that the Cluster Migration Wizard works is that you tell the wizard that runs on the target Windows Server 2016 cluster that you wish to migrate roles and then point the wizard to the old Windows Server 2012 or Windows Server 2012 R2 cluster. The wizard then shows the roles running on specific storage volumes and disconnects the storage from the old cluster, activates on the new cluster, and migrates the roles (virtual machines) that are hosted on that storage. It's important to ensure that the switches have been zoned correctly so that the target cluster has rights to access the migrated LUNs, and the old cluster has its access removed once the storage is migrated.

The ability to move cluster resources between clusters was useful in the past when moving between OS versions, since a mixed cluster was not possible. I could not have a Windows Server 2012 cluster and replace nodes with Windows Server 2012 R2. Instead a new Windows Server 2012 R2 cluster would be created with new hardware or by removing one node at a time from the old cluster, adding to the new cluster, and gradually moving over LUNs and the contained VMs or by performing a Shared Nothing Live Migration between clusters where new storage was available (as a Live Migration was supported from Windows Server 2012 to Windows Server 2012 R2). This was a challenging experience, and is not required when moving from Windows Server 2012 R2 to Windows Server 2016.

Windows Server 2016 enables mixed-mode clusters comprising both Windows Server 2012 R2 and Windows Server 2016 nodes along with the ability to live-migrate VMs from

Windows Server 2012 R2 to Windows Server 2016 nodes and from Windows Server 2016 to Windows Server 2012 R2 nodes. This new capability provides a far more streamlined upgrade experience to Windows Server 2016, avoiding the need to create a separate target cluster and avoiding the migration of resources.

Figure 5.33 and Figure 5.34 show an example three-node cluster upgrade from Windows Server 2012 R2 to Windows Server 2016. The exact same process, however, would work in the same way from two nodes up to sixty-four nodes.

FIGURE 5.33
Windows Server 2012 R2 to Windows Server 2016 cluster rolling upgrade

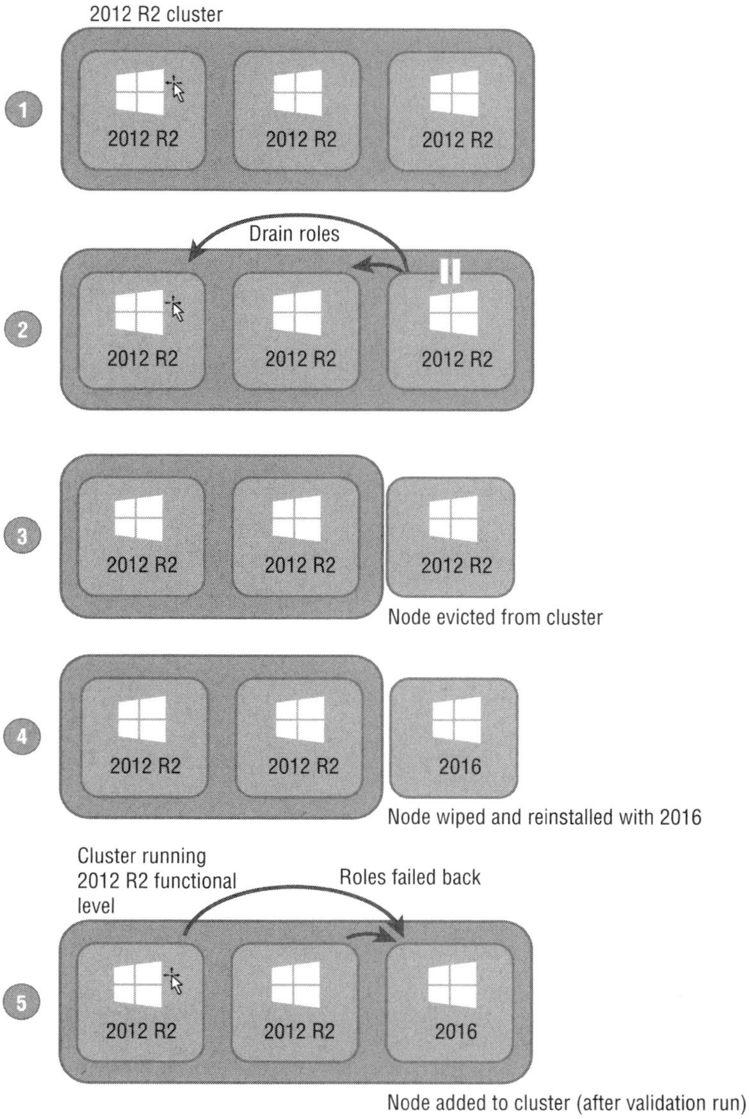

2012 R2 cluster

Drain roles

Node evicted from cluster

Node wiped and reinstalled with 2016

Cluster running 2012 R2 functional level

Roles failed back

Node added to cluster (after validation run)

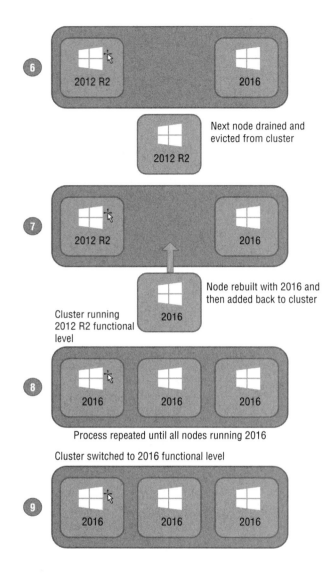

FIGURE 5.34
Continued Windows
Server 2012 R2 to
Windows Server 2016
cluster rolling upgrade

1. The starting point is the existing Windows Server 2012 R2–based cluster running various services including VMs. It also has Cluster Shared Volumes, which could be SAN based or use Clustered Storage Spaces.

2. One node at a time is moved to Windows Server 2016. The first step is to drain the node of all resources while it migrates the resources to other nodes in the cluster.

3. Once the node is drained of resources, it is evicted from the cluster.

4. The node is wiped, and a fresh install of Windows Server 2016 is performed on the box.

5. A cluster validation exercise is performed for the cluster and the newly installed node. Once validation passes, the node is added back to the cluster and acts as if it is running Windows Server 2012 R2, enabling the cluster to run in a Windows Server 2012 R2 functional level but one that is now mixed in terms of the operating systems running in the cluster. The Windows Server 2016 node can access all cluster resources, such as Cluster Shared Volumes. Roles can be moved back to the node.

6. Step 2 and step 3 are repeated on the next node, evicting it from the cluster.

7. Step 4 and step 5 are repeated, with the node being rebuilt with Windows Server 2016, a cluster validation performed, and the node added back to the cluster with resources moved back to it.

8. All nodes have gone through the process of being rebuilt with Windows Server 2016 and added to the cluster. All nodes are now running Windows Server 2016, but the cluster is still running in Windows Server 2012 R2 functional level.

9. The final step is to switch the cluster to Windows Server 2016 functional level, which will light up new Windows Server 2016 functionality. This is done by running the `Update-ClusterFunctionalLevel` cmdlet. The cluster functional level update can be seen by running `(Get-Cluster).ClusterFunctionalLevel`, which should show a value of 9. If using Clustered Storage Spaces, the storage pools should be updated by running the `Update-StoragePool` cmdlet with the friendly name of the Storage Pool as the parameter.

Additionally, after the cluster is running with all Windows Server 2016 nodes and in the Windows Server 2016 cluster functional level, the VMs can be upgraded to the Windows Server 2016 native configuration level of 8 by running the `Update-VMVersion` cmdlet. If you wanted to update every VM in the cluster, as you are sure you never need to run them on a 2012 R2 host, then you could use the following code. Note this will convert only VMs that are not running.

```
$vmgroups = Get-ClusterResource |
            Where-Object{$_.ResourceType -like "Virtual Machine"}

foreach ($vmgroup in $vmgroups)
{
    $VM = $vmgroup | Get-VM
    #If VM is off and not already version 8.0
    if($VM.State -eq "Off" -and $VM.Version -ne "8.0")
    {
        Write-Output "Updating $($VM.VMName)"
        Update-VMVersion -VM $VM -Force
    }
}
```

Your cluster is now fully upgraded and running with Windows Server 2016 features for the cluster and the VMs. Note that while a mixed-mode cluster is fully supported, it is not intended for long-term use; that is, it is a transition state. The mixed mode is to enable the migration of the cluster from Windows Server 2012 R2 to Windows Server 2016, with the goal being to get out of mixed mode as quickly as possible to leverage new Windows Server 2016 features.

The Bottom Line

Identify the ways to deploy Hyper-V.   Windows Server 2016 Hyper-V can be deployed using numerous methods. The traditional approach is to install a server from setup media, which could be a DVD, USB device, or even files obtained over the network. Enterprise systems management solutions such as System Center Configuration Manager and Windows Deployment Services can be used to customize deployments. System Center Virtual Machine Manager can also be used to deploy Hyper-V hosts using Boot to VHD technology, providing a single management solution for deployment of hosts and virtual machines. Nano Server deployments are deployed in a different manner, as custom images are created and leveraged.

    Master It   What other types of servers can SCVMM 2016 deploy?

Explain why using Server Core is beneficial to deployments.   Windows Server and Windows client operating systems share a lot of common code, and a typical Windows Server deployment has a graphical interface, Internet browser, and many graphical tools. These components all take up space, require patching, and may have vulnerabilities. For many types of server roles, these graphical elements are not required. Server Core provides a minimal server footprint that is managed remotely, which means less patching and therefore fewer reboots in addition to a smaller attack surface. Because a host reboot requires all virtual machines also to be rebooted, using Server Core is a big benefit for Hyper-V environments in order to remove as many reboots as possible. Nano Server is a completely refactored deployment of Windows Server, which is also a good choice for Hyper-V Servers but may not be compatible with an organization's management toolset.

    Master It   What was the big change to configuration levels between Windows Server 2012 R2 and Windows Server 2016?

Explain how to create and use virtual machine templates.   While it is possible to create the virtual machine environment manually and install the operating system for each new virtual machine, it's inefficient, considering the virtual machine uses a file for its virtual storage. A far more efficient and expedient approach is to create a generalized operating system template VHDX file, which can then be quickly deployed to new virtual machines. A virtual machine template allows the virtual hardware configuration of a virtual machine to be configured, including OS properties such as domain join instructions, local administrator password, and more. The configuration is then linked to a template VHDX file. When the template is deployed, minimal interaction is required by the requesting user, typically just an optional name, and within minutes, the new virtual environment with a configured guest operating system is available.

Chapter 6

Maintaining a Hyper-V Environment

Once the Hyper-V environment is deployed and virtual machines are created, it is critical to ensure that your Hyper-V environment stays healthy, optimized, and available. In future chapters, I dive into details on technologies such as clustering to provide high availability, but this chapter presents key processes and technologies that must be implemented to keep the environment running smoothly.

At some point, every environment has performance challenges, and the final part of this chapter dives into details of troubleshooting performance problems for the four key resources: computer, memory, network, and storage.

In this chapter, you will learn to:

◆ Explain how backup works in a Hyper-V environment.

◆ Identify where to use checkpoints and where not to use them.

◆ Understand the benefits of service templates.

Patch Planning and Implementation

In the previous chapter, I talked about some key processes and actions that you must take on your Windows Server 2016 Hyper-V servers. One of them was patching, and in this section, I dive into some additional detail, consider some options, and cover some other factors that need to be considered in your patch solution planning.

In a virtual environment, there are at least two workloads that you have to consider patching:

◆ The Hyper-V host itself. The hypervisor itself would be updated via updates sent to the host.

◆ The virtual machines that are running on the Hyper-V hosts, including updates to Integration Services for Hyper-V (although this should not update frequently between versions of Hyper-V). The virtual machines may be running Windows operating systems but also Linux. I focus on Windows updating in this discussion, but you would also need processes to ensure that all workloads are updated. Virtual machines that are offline for long periods of time may also need to be patched, which can be accomplished using the same processes discussed in Chapter 5, "Managing Hyper-V," related to patching templates, such as using Deployment Image Servicing and Management (DISM).

I said *at least two workloads* because you most likely will need to ensure that items such as the management infrastructure (for instance, System Center) are patched and that firmware in hardware is kept up-to-date (for example, that updated drivers from vendors are downloaded and applied). These are not considerations specific to Hyper-V. They apply to any infrastructure, but it's especially important to ensure that your Hyper-V environment is patched and stable because it's not responsible for one operating system but instead is hosting possibly hundreds of operating systems.

If you already have a patching solution for your Windows-based servers, most likely that same solution can be leveraged to patch your Hyper-V servers. What is important is that patches are tested in a test environment prior to implementation in production, and also that care be taken when applying patches that require reboots. Remember, if the Hyper-V host reboots, then all virtual machines on the host will shut down for stand-alone hosts or be moved to other hosts in a clustered environment. It's therefore important to have the ability to define specific maintenance windows for your Hyper-V hosts, delaying reboots until that maintenance window is reached. In a cluster environment, you would make sure that the maintenance windows are staggered to ensure that all hosts don't apply patches and reboot at the same time. There are better solutions for cluster environments, though, which I touch on later in this chapter.

If you have stand-alone Hyper-V hosts in Windows Server 2012 or above, it would be possible to perform a Shared Nothing Live Migration of virtual machines between hosts, or if SMB is used for the storage, then only the memory and state would need to be migrated. This would avoid any downtime to the virtual machines for planned outages; however, it would be an automated process that you would need to create leveraging PowerShell or another automation solution. Additionally, if you have virtual machines that need to be protected from unavailability (such as unscheduled outages), the hosts should really be clustered anyway. Generally, if you have virtual machines on a stand-alone host, you should expect to have some periods of unavailability.

Microsoft maintains all updates on its Microsoft Update servers, and by default computers can connect to these servers, find the list of updated patches, download them, and apply them. This process works fine for a few machines, but if you have hundreds of servers, it's inefficient to have every machine downloading the updates over the Internet connection. This process will be slow and consume your Internet connection, which likely could be used more productively for other workloads. Additionally, if machines update directly from Microsoft Update using the built-in update component of Windows, the administrator of the organization has no ability to approve patches prior to their deployment.

Leveraging WSUS

Windows Server Update Services (WSUS) is a role of Windows Server that acts as a local source for updates for machines within your organization. At a high level, the process when leveraging WSUS is as follows:

1. Enable the WSUS role on a server, and specify when synchronization with the Microsoft Update servers will occur.

2. Configure the WSUS server for the updates that should be downloaded, such as, for example, only critical and security updates and only for Windows Server 2016.

3. Create computer groups in WSUS that will be the targets for patch deployment.

4. Specify whether any types of updates should be automatically approved. Any updates that are not automatically approved need to be approved manually by a WSUS administrator before they are deployed to specified computer groups.

5. Optionally, use Group Policy to automatically configure machines to use the WSUS server and to be part of a specific computer group. I document this at the following location:

   `http://windowsitpro.com/windows-8/group-policy-settings-wsus`

Machines will now utilize the WSUS server for available patches and also download them from the WSUS server instead of the Internet (although it is also possible to configure WSUS clients to pull updates from Microsoft Update if required). In very large organizations, it's possible to chain WSUS servers so that a downstream WSUS server pulls approved updates from another WSUS server and then distributes them.

Configuring machines to pull down patches from Microsoft Update or a WSUS server via Group Policy is one option, but there are other enterprise solutions. System Center Configuration Manager, for example, leverages WSUS to ascertain that patches are available but then allows them to be packaged and targeted to different groups of servers at specific times with granular tracking and reporting.

Patching Hyper-V Clusters

The technologies I've been talking about are not specific to Hyper-V, which is logical since Hyper-V is a role within Windows Server and therefore its patch mechanisms are the same as for any other Windows Server machine. The good news is that the same patch deployment solution can be used for the Hyper-V hosts and for the virtual machines running Windows Server. There are, however, some solutions specific to Hyper-V patching and specific to patching clusters.

IF YOU CARE ABOUT VM AVAILABILITY, DON'T USE STAND-ALONE HYPER-V HOSTS

As I have already mentioned, there are not really any special solutions to patch a stand-alone Hyper-V host. If you are deploying stand-alone Hyper-V hosts, you don't really care about the availability of the virtual machines, so there are no special technologies in-box to patch stand-alone hosts and use Shared Nothing Live Migration to move VMs prior to the reboot and bring the VMs back. If you had that hardware available, you would have clustered them already, considering an SMB 3 file share can be used for the storage if a SAN is not available; you could even use a clustered external storage enclosure connected to both hosts and clustered storage spaces to provide shared access, or for Windows Server 2016, use Storage Spaces Direct to take advantage of local storage in each node. The only time you should have an unclustered Hyper-V host is if you have a location with only one Hyper-V server.

Consider a clustered Hyper-V environment with shared storage either through a SAN, SMB share, clustered Storage Spaces, or Storage Spaces Direct, and the ability to move virtual machines between hosts. In your Hyper-V environment, you are already using Server Core or maybe Nano Server to minimize the number of patches that are applicable and therefore reducing the number of reboots. However, reboots will still be required for patching and other purposes. Utilizing the ability to move virtual machines between nodes with no downtime using Live Migration prior to reboots makes the impact of a Hyper-V node reboot in a cluster zero for the virtual machines. This means no loss of availability for the virtual machines, and only some minor administrative effort. This is why, when you hear people hung up on having to patch Hyper-V, it's generally overblown as a real issue. Yes, you might need to patch, and at times you might need to reboot, but it has no impact on the availability of the virtual machines, which is what you care about in a virtual environment. The ideal process in a clustered environment is as follows:

1. The nodes in the cluster are scanned to ascertain which patches are required.

2. One node is placed in maintenance mode, drained of all virtual machines, which are Live Migrated to other hosts in the cluster.

3. The node has patches applied and rebooted.

4. The node is checked to ensure that no additional patches are needed, and if not, it is brought out of maintenance mode.

5. Virtual machines are moved back to the node, and the process is repeated for the next node, and so on.

Most administrators who manage clusters are familiar with this process and perform it manually. SCVMM 2012 introduced the ability to patch an entire Hyper-V cluster using exactly the process just described. Each node is drained, patched, and rebooted for a complete cluster patch, with no downtime to virtual machines, with a click of a button. SCVMM leverages a WSUS server in the environment for the actual patch library, which does not have to be uniquely used by SCVMM. It could be a WSUS used for other purposes, such as, for example, by SCCM. Once the WSUS server is added to the SCVMM fabric, as shown in Figure 6.1, the SCVMM instance will be aware of all of the updates known to the WSUS server. The next step is to create a baseline in the Library workspace ➢ Update Catalog And Baselines ➢ Update Baselines, which can then be assigned to specific host groups. Once a baseline is assigned, a scan can be performed on the host group via the Fabric workspace, which will show the compliance of each scanned node, and the details of the compliance can be viewed as shown in Figure 6.2. The administrator can click the Remediate button to patch the entire cluster. There's very little administrative work. It is important to note that SCVMM patches only Hyper-V hosts (even nonclustered) and *not* the actual virtual machines running on the hosts. You still require another patch strategy to patch the virtual machines.

FIGURE 6.1
Adding a WSUS
server to SCVMM

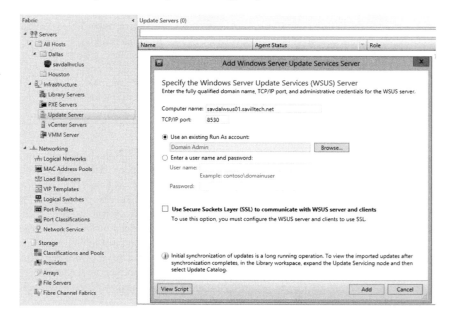

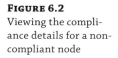

FIGURE 6.2
Viewing the compliance details for a non-compliant node

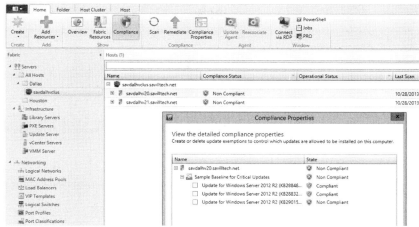

The SCVMM 2012 ability to patch an entire Hyper-V cluster with one click was a welcome feature and removed the need for many custom PowerShell and Orchestrator solutions, but Windows Server 2012 minimized the need even to use SCVMM. Windows Server 2012 introduced a native one-click patching of an entire cluster to the Failover Clustering feature. Once again, this Cluster-Aware Updating (CAU) leveraged WSUS and could patch not only Hyper-V clusters but any type of cluster with no downtime to the workloads running in the cluster. I cover this in detail in Chapter 7, "Failover Clustering and Migration Technologies."

Notice that both of these solutions used WSUS as the patch engine and not System Center Configuration Manager, which has a powerful patching solution that is utilized by many organizations. To use Configuration Manager for the patching, a custom solution using PowerShell or Orchestrator would have to be utilized; that is, until Configuration Manager 2016. Configuration Manager 2016 introduces cluster-aware settings related to updates. This new capability enables configuration that specifies not only the patches to deploy and when, but also the percentage of servers that need to remain online during the patching process, which enables the cluster to be patched must faster compared to one node at a time. With the ability to specify the percentage that must remain online, multiple nodes can be patched simultaneously, thus speeding up the overall patch process without impacting the ability to deliver services beyond your desired metrics. Additionally, the update configuration allows pre- and post-configuration tasks to be linked to the update application. Note that while this functionality works for software updates, it is not limited to software updates and applies to the various maintenance operations directed to the nodes in the cluster. This functionality is enabled as follows:

1. Add all the nodes in the cluster to a new collection.

2. Select the properties of the collection, and under the General tab, select the "All devices are part of the same server cluster" check box, which will enable its associated Settings button. Click the Settings button.

3. In the Cluster Settings dialog box, shown in Figure 6.3, you can specify the percentage of the cluster that can go offline, a specific order of sequencing for the cluster, and the optional script content for the pre- and post- actions. It is also possible to configure the script action to take should the patching require a reboot of the nodes.

FIGURE 6.3
Cluster maintenance
configuration in
Configuration Manager

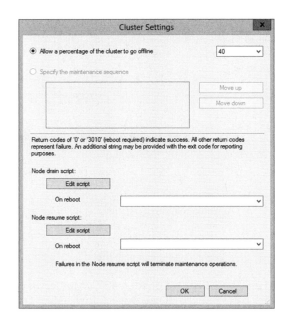

The key takeaway is that patching your Hyper-V cluster does not mean that there is any downtime to your virtual machines.

Remember that all of the previous processes relate to the Windows operating system. You still need other processes to download drivers from the hardware vendor, because even if there are drives built into Windows, for many types of hardware, it's better to use drivers directly from the vendor.

Malware Configurations

I briefly touched on antivirus recommendations in previous chapters, and there are two main schools of thought. One is that the Hyper-V server is running in Server Core configuration level, so it has no web browser, has limited vulnerabilities and a limited attack surface, is patched regularly, is never locally connected to because all management is remote, has a firewall enabled, and really does nothing but manage virtual machines. The chance of the server being infected is slight, so many people will say just don't run malware protection. Additionally, it's possible that malware protection could introduce problems because it runs at a very low level within the operating system. The Microsoft best practice is to run no additional applications on the Hyper-V host, and strictly speaking, this would include malware protection.

I personally lean a little more toward defense in depth. I prefer to have many layers of protection, which means malware support on the host. However, it's critical that any malware solution does not interfere with the Hyper-V processes or the resources of virtual machines. At the time of this writing, this means that exceptions should be configured in the malware solution not to scan the following:

◆ Default virtual machine configuration directory
(`C:\ProgramData\Microsoft\Windows\Hyper-V`)

◆ Custom virtual machine configuration directories

- Default virtual hard disk drive directory
  (`C:\Users\Public\Documents\Hyper-V\Virtual Hard Disks`)

- Custom virtual hard disk drive directories

- Custom replication data directories, if you are using Hyper-V Replica

- Checkpoint directories

- `vmms.exe` (Note that this file may have to be configured as a process exclusion within the antivirus software.)

- `vmwp.exe` (Note that this file may have to be configured as a process exclusion within the antivirus software.)

Failure to properly exclude Hyper-V resources will result in problems with virtual machines starting and functioning correctly, as documented at `http://support.microsoft.com/kb/961804/en-us`. There is a great malware exception article for more Microsoft solutions at:

```
http://social.technet.microsoft.com/wiki/contents/articles/953
.microsoft-anti-virus-exclusion-list.aspx
```

While the risk of infection is low, if an infection did hit your Hyper-V server, the impact would be large. There may also be audit problems for hosts with no malware protection. It's really an environmental choice to be made after weighing the pros and cons. If you have great processes in place to patch your systems regularly, if they are running Server Core or Nano Server, and if people don't log on locally, you would probably be fine without malware. If you don't have a good patch strategy, if you are not running Server Core or Nano Server, and if administrators do log on to the servers and browse the Web, then malware protection is probably a good idea! If you do opt to use malware protection, ensure that you have processes in place to keep its signatures updated and that it is supported to run on Hyper-V. Microsoft provides enterprise malware protection with System Center Endpoint Protection and the in-box Windows Defender in Windows Server 2016. As roles are enabled in Windows Server 2016, exceptions are automatically configured in Windows Defender, and if System Center Endpoint Protection is used, there are built-in templates for various server roles including Hyper-V.

What is important is that you still run malware protection within the virtual machines. You need malware protection running in the guest operating systems configured to whatever guidelines exist for the workload. Even if you run malware protection on the Hyper-V host, this does *not* protect the virtual machine guest operating system. Special scenarios need to be considered—for example, VDI environments with many desktops that are created and deleted very quickly and that have different malware protection requirements than regular, long-term servers. When using a solution such as Configuration Manager and Endpoint Protection, there is a built-in randomized delay when performing periodic actions to avoid the action running at the same time across many VMs on the same piece of hardware, which would cause resource peaks. Investigate the various solutions available and tailor your solution based on the services offered.

Backup Planning

When virtualization is used in an environment, there is often a decision to be made as to whether backups will be taken from the virtualization host of the virtual machines, or backup agents should still run within the virtual machines and backups will be taken from inside the virtual machines. There is no "right" answer to which is the best approach, but what is running inside the virtual machines and where you take the backup can have a big impact on the granularity of any restore operations that are performed.

Windows Server has long standardized on the Volume Shadow Copy Service (VSS), which provides facilities that allow application vendors to write special *VSS writers*. These application-specific modules, which are used to ensure that application data is ready for backup, are registered with the operating system on which the application is installed. All VSS writers registered on an operating system are called during a shadow copy backup initiated by a VSS-aware backup program. The VSS writers ensure that all data on disk for the application is in an application-consistent state and that other writers are quiesced (which means paused during the operation) while the backup is taken, maintaining the integrity of the on-disk data being backed up. An *application-consistent backup* means that the data is in a suitable state to be restored and used without corruption problems.

If a backup was taken at the Hyper-V host level of all virtual machine assets, primarily the VHD files, then ordinarily the virtual machine would know nothing of the backup being taken at the host level, so the data backed up would likely not be in an application-consistent state. Hyper-V Integration Services includes a Backup (volume snapshot) service, and this allows the Hyper-V host to notify each virtual machine when a VSS backup is taken. The process then looks like the following and ensures that backups of the virtual machines are in an application-consistent state:

1. The backup software (the VSS requestor) on the Hyper-V server makes a request for a VSS snapshot and enumerates the VSS writers (for example, the Hyper-V VSS writer) on the system to ascertain that the data that can be backed up with VSS.

2. The Hyper-V VSS writer (in conjunction with the VSS coordination service) forwards the VSS snapshot request to each guest operating system via the Backup integration service.

3. Each guest operating system thinks it is receiving a native VSS request and proceeds to notify all VSS writers on the guest to prepare for a snapshot.

4. Each VSS writer in the guest operating systems writes any information to disk that relates to its service (for example, Exchange and SQL) and notifies the VSS coordinator that it is ready for a snapshot and tells it which data to back up (although this part is ignored because we'll be backing up the entire VHD from the Hyper-V host).

5. The Backup integration service for each VM tells the Hyper-V VSS writer that it is ready for a snapshot to be taken, and the Hyper-V VSS writer notifies the backup application via the VSS coordinator that it is ready for a snapshot.

6. The backup software takes a VSS snapshot of the filesystem containing the virtual configuration files and the virtual hard disks, and all data on the virtual hard disks is consistent, thanks to the VSS request being passed into the virtual machines. Once the snapshot is taken, the VSS writer notifies the Hyper-V guests that the snapshot is complete and they continue their normal processing.

It should be noted that only VHD/VHDX content will be backed up using this method. If a virtual machine has pass-through storage, has iSCSI storage connected through the guest

OS iSCSI Initiator, is connected to storage via Fibre Channel, or, prior to Windows Server 2016, is a shared VHDX (but Windows Server 2016 adds support for host-level backup of Shared VHDX, now known as VHD Sets), then that content would not be backed up via a backup at the Hyper-V server level through the Hyper-V VSS writer and would instead need to be backed up from within the guest virtual machine. The preceding scenario describes an online backup, also known as a *child VM snapshot*, where the guest operating system meets the following requirements:

◆ The integration services are installed with the Backup integration service enabled.

◆ The operating system supports VSS.

◆ NTFS filesystems with basic disks (not dynamic) are used.

If you have guest operating systems that use dynamic disks, that use non-NTFS partitions, that don't have the integration services installed, or that don't have the Backup integration service enabled or it's just not supported (Windows 2000), then an offline backup will be taken of the virtual machine, also known as a *saved state backup*. This is because virtual machines that can't support an online backup are placed into a saved state during the VSS snapshot, which means that there is a period of downtime for the virtual machine during the backup. Operating systems that have to use saved state include Windows 2000, Windows XP, and Windows NT 4. Windows 2003, 2008, Vista, and above all support the online backup method with no virtual machine downtime.

Prior to Windows Server 2012 R2, a Linux system had to be backed up using an offline backup. Windows Server 2012 R2 introduced new features for Linux virtual machines, one of which is live backup of Linux VMs. This is achieved through a new filesystem snapshot driver that runs inside the Linux guest virtual machine. When a backup is performed on the Hyper-V host, the filesystem snapshot driver is triggered in the guest, which enables a filesystem-consistent snapshot to be taken of the VHDs that are attached to the Linux VM. It should be noted that this is a different experience from that available for Windows VMs, which provide filesystem-consistent and application-consistent backups because applications have VSS writers that ensure that application data is consistent on the disk. This is because there is not a standardized VSS infrastructure in Linux, so there's no way to ask applications to make their data ready for a backup.

If you have guest operating systems that can't use the Hyper-V pass-through VSS capability, perform backups within the virtual machine. At times, backing up within the virtual machine gives a better level of functionality, depending on the backup application. Suppose I want to use System Center Data Protection Manager (DPM), which is the Microsoft premium backup and recovery solution for Microsoft workloads. When you have the DPM agent on the virtual server in the main DPM administrator console, the level of granularity that you have for what to protect would be at a virtual machine level. You can select which virtual machines to protect, but that's all you get. You can't go into detail about what to protect within the virtual machine. During a restore operation, you would be able to restore only the entire virtual machine or files from the VM, but nothing application aware such as restoring a SQL database or Exchange mailbox.

If you deploy the agent into the guest operating systems, you will have the full granularity of knowledge that comes with DPM. For example, if the virtual machine is running SQL Server, you will be able to select the databases to protect and to capture the transaction logs, and so on. The restore granularity will be the same, enabling the restore of just a specific database. Likewise, if I backed up a SharePoint server from within the SharePoint VM, I would be able to perform item-level recovery. Figure 6.4 shows an example with two virtual machines that are protected at the host level and two other virtual machines that have the DPM agent installed locally, which allows me to protect application-aware workloads such as Exchange mailboxes and SQL databases. The same applies when using Azure Backup Server, which is essentially "DPM Lite" and is available to back up workloads to the Azure Backup service.

FIGURE 6.4
Example view of protection using DPM

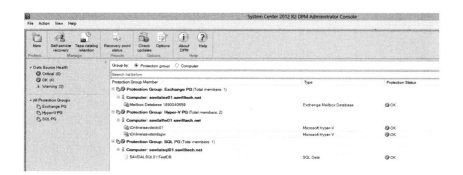

This means that for the best functionality, sometimes performing backups from within the guest OS gives the best results, especially if your backup software has application-specific modules. Make sure that you regularly test restoring the backups you take. Many times I have seen companies try to restore a backup when it's really needed, and it fails, or the right information was not being backed up.

Microsoft made big changes to how Hyper-V backups worked between Windows Server 2012 and Windows Server 2012 R2. Backups taken at the Hyper-V host call the VSS writers within the virtual machine through the Backup integration service in both scenarios, which ensures application-consistent backups even when the backup is taken at the Hyper-V host. In Windows Server 2012, there's a delay between the time the VSS snapshot is taken within the virtual machine and the time the VSS snapshot is taken at the Hyper-V host (because it takes time to pass back the various VSS communications between the guest and the host), which means that data could change in that time delta, therefore introducing the risk of data corruption.

To solve this problem, the snapshot taken of the VHD at the host is mounted as a volume on the Hyper-V host as part of the backup process; this enables the snapshot VHD to be rolled back to the state of the snapshot taken inside the virtual machine (the guest VSS snapshot) and then that state is backed up at the host. This approach creates scalability concerns, because large numbers of VHDs might need to be mounted; in addition, VHDs from virtual machines are being mounted on the Hyper-V host, which could be a security concern.

Windows Server 2012 R2 solved this problem; Hyper-V pretends that it has hardware-based snapshot support (which is typically part of high-end SANs). Therefore, when a VSS snapshot request is made inside the virtual machine, the Hyper-V VSS writer is piped directly in the host, which triggers creation of a checkpoint (which in turn creates an AVHD differencing file on the host). Then that checkpoint is used by the VSS running on the Hyper-V host, which removes the need for VHDs to be mounted in the host. However, as part of this process, an AutoRecovery VHDX has to be mounted to the virtual machine to expose the snapshot back to the virtual machine as part of the fix-up phase near the end of the backup process, and then the AutoRecovery VHDX is removed. This is invisible to the end user; however, this hot-add of a VHD is possible only on the SCSI controller, which is why the virtual machine must have an SCSI controller present in Windows Server 2012 R2 to allow host-level backups, or backup will fail and you receive an Event ID 10103.

The process to back up VMs has changed again in Windows Server 2016 in two ways; however, the end user experience for performing backups is unchanged. The first change relates to the new production checkpoint feature (covered later in this chapter), which leverages the VSS infrastructure inside the VM that is now leveraged as part of a host-level VM backup. A new Hyper-V WMI call is utilized to trigger the backup by the backup application and via the new WMI call, the Hyper-V infrastructure is responsible for getting the VMs ready for the backup, specifically creating the required AVHDX file which, at the backup application's convenience, can then be persisted to the final backup target via a separate host-level VSS snapshot. The major difference here is that in the past, every VM that was backed up resulted in a separate VSS snapshot on the underlying storage. If you backed up 100 VMs at the same time, there would be 100 hardware snapshots, resulting in backup scale challenges. With Windows Server 2016 and the decoupling between the VM snapshot and the host snapshot, all of the data from multiple VMs can be backed up by using a single hardware VSS snapshot, enabling greatly improved scale.

The second change affects the backup application vendors, and it has no direct end-user impact at all. There is no concept of "differencing" backups with Hyper-V host-level backups of VMs. Instead, a complete backup is taken. Previously, this would result in the complete VM data set being sent over the network to the backup target for every backup—meaning a huge amount of network traffic, huge amounts of backup storage, and a very inefficient backup. Each vendor had to implement their own filesystem filter that would track the blocks that changed between backups, enabling only the delta data to be sent and stored. This was a major undertaking for each backup vendor and could lead to performance degradation and even instability in the event of a bug in the third-party filter. In Windows Server 2016, Microsoft has implemented Resilient Change Tracking (RCT), which tracks the blocks changed with VHDX files as part of the VHDX file itself, meaning that the tracking moves with the VHDX in the case of VM and/or storage migrations. This removes the need for backup vendors to maintain their own filter and track the changed blocks. Now via RCT, the backup vendors can simply request which blocks have changed and back those up. RCT requires that the files are VHDX and that the VM is version 7 or above; if not, the old style differencing disks will be utilized for the backup.

No matter what other technologies are used, such as replication, multiple instances of applications, or even snapshots, none of these are replacements for backups. Backups should always be taken regularly for complete protection for all types of failure.

Defragmentation with Hyper-V

On a physical system that uses hard disk drives (HDDs), it is common to defragment the filesystem. This is required because files can become *fragmented*: instead of a file being stored contiguously on the disk, it is broken into many pieces, or fragments, over the disk. This can impair performance because when data needs to be read, many seek operations occur (moving the disk head to the data location on disk). This slows operations compared to all of the data being stored contiguously on disk, in which case the data can be read efficiently. Performing a disk defragmentation optimizes the disk by moving all the pieces of files so that they are contiguous on the disk and therefore can be accessed efficiently.

Files become fragmented for many reasons. Typically, when a file grows, if there is not empty space at the end of the file's current position, additional space must be allocated elsewhere on the disk. This would be common with a dynamic VHDX/VHD file that grows as data is written. Note that the problem with fragmentation is the seeking of the data. If you are using solid-state drives (SSDs), there is no seek time and therefore fragmentation does not incur a performance penalty. Moving data can actually decrease the life span of an SSD, so defragmentation is typically not performed or recommended. Windows 2012 and above automatically disables defragmentation on a SSD.

Consider local HDDs in a system. If you are using a fixed-size VHDX, it is likely not highly fragmented because it does not grow. Therefore, defragmentation should not often be required. If you use dynamic VHDX, the disk will most likely fragment over time, and so performing a defragmentation will improve performance. The only caveat is to remember that a VHDX file contains a filesystem that itself contains files, so even if the VHDX file is not fragmented, when the VHDX file is used by a virtual machine, the content will be randomly accessed throughout the VHDX because the OS accesses various files, but defragmenting will still make it as contiguous as possible and certainly won't do harm.

If your storage is not local HDDs but a SAN, your virtual hard disks will be split over multiple disks anyway, there will be other optimizations in place on the SAN, and typically defragmenting is not recommended. Similarly, defragmenting a tiered volume that uses different types of storage is not recommended, because this would touch different blocks of the disk and potentially interfere with the automatic tiering that optimizes performance.

The SAN recommendation of not performing defragmentation also applies when using Storage Spaces and Storage Spaces Direct. In both cases, the virtual disk created is hosted on multiple physical disks that likely again use tiering. In the case of Storage Spaces Direct, the disks are also distributed over multiple nodes. Performing defragmentation would not result in the blocks being contiguous and would taint the tiering mechanisms.

The final type of defragmentation is performing a defragmentation within the actual virtual machine for its filesystem that is contained in the virtual hard disk. There is no definite answer here. My thinking on this is that fragmentation within the virtual hard disk is another level of fragmentation, but its effect will depend on the underlying storage. If the underlying storage is SSD or a SAN, I would not defragment. If the underlying storage is local HDD, a defragmentation within the VM would optimize the data within the virtual hard disk and therefore improve storage performance, which means that I would defragment when necessary. Obviously, if you defragment within the virtual machine but not on the actual filesystem containing the virtual hard disk, you are likely not achieving any optimization, because the virtual hard disk could still be fragmented on the physical drives.

Defragmentation can be performed by using the Optimize Drives utility or the defrag.exe utility. Detailed information can be viewed about a volume by using the /a and /v switches, as shown in this example:

```
PS C:\> defrag d: /A /V
Microsoft Drive Optimizer
Copyright (c) 2013 Microsoft Corp.

Invoking analysis on Data (D:)...



The operation completed successfully.
```

```
Post Defragmentation Report:


Volume Information:
   Volume size              = 1.81 TB
   Cluster size             = 4 KB
   Used space               = 470.11 GB
   Free space               = 1.35 TB


Fragmentation:
   Total fragmented space   = 6%
   Average fragments per file  = 1.05

   Movable files and folders   = 100184
   Unmovable files and folders = 4


Files:
   Fragmented files         = 742
   Total file fragments     = 3155


Folders:
   Total folders            = 5552
   Fragmented folders       = 53
   Total folder fragments   = 248


Free space:
   Free space count         = 6505
   Average free space size  = 219.19 MB
   Largest free space size  = 604.87 GB


Master File Table (MFT):
   MFT size                 = 316.50 MB
   MFT record count         = 324095
   MFT usage                = 100%
   Total MFT fragments      = 2

Note: File fragments larger than 64MB are not included in the
fragmentation statistics.


You do not need to defragment this volume.
```

Sysinternals has a tool, Contig, that shows the fragmentation of individual files and can even defragment individual files. It is available for download, along with documentation, at the following location:

```
http://technet.microsoft.com/en-us/sysinternals/bb897428
```

Using Checkpoints

One fairly overlooked feature of Hyper-V is the *checkpoint* feature, which prior to Windows Server 2012 R2 was called *snapshots*. Checkpoints allow point-in-time views of a virtual machine to be saved. A checkpoint can be created when the virtual machine is turned off or when it's running. If a checkpoint is taken when a virtual machine is running, the current memory and device state is saved in addition to the virtual hard disk state, which is also taken when a snapshot is taken of a stopped virtual machine. When a checkpoint is taken for Windows Server 2012 R2, several files are created:

XML File   This contains the information of the files and VM configuration associated with the checkpoint.

VSV File   This contains the state of devices associated with the virtual machine. It is created only if a checkpoint is taken of a running virtual machine.

BIN File   This contains the memory content of the virtual machine. It is created only if a checkpoint is taken of a running virtual machine.

AVHDX File   To capture the state of the virtual hard disks, the differencing VHD capability is used. The current virtual hard disk state is frozen and marked read-only; this is what the checkpoint points to. A new differencing disk is created that uses the existing VHDX as the parent, and all future disk writes are written to the new differencing AVHDX file. Note that if the original file was a VHD, then a AVHD file is created.

Windows Server 2016 introduces some major changes to checkpoints. The first change is because of the move to the VMCX and VMRS files. These replace the XML, VSV, and BIN files from Windows Server 2012 R2, resulting in these files being created:

VMCX File   Contains the information of the files and VM configuration associated with the checkpoint

VMRS File   This contains the state of devices associated with the virtual machine and the memory content. If the VM is not running when the checkpoint is created, or if the checkpoint type is production, then the VMRS file is small and contains only basic information.

AVHDX File   The same as in Windows Server 2012 R2, the virtual hard disk content

In the preceding VMRS file description, I mentioned a production type of checkpoint. This is new to Windows Server 2016. Normally, a checkpoint saves the current state of the VM without any interaction with the guest OS running inside the VM, which is why their use in production environments is strongly discouraged (as covered later in this section). This is because when a checkpoint is applied, the guest is reverted back to that point in time without any knowledge that a shift in time happened, which is very different from restoring an application-consistent backup. *Production checkpoints* are a new type of checkpoint available, in addition to the existing standard checkpoint carried over from Windows Server 2012 R2.

A production checkpoint is used in the same way as a standard checkpoint, but behind the scenes it works very differently. A production checkpoint interacts with the VSS infrastructure inside the guest OS, or in the case of Linux, the filesystem freezes to create an application-consistent checkpoint that looks the same as if a backup had been taken where data is flushed to disk. Because the production checkpoint leverages VSS, there is no need to save the memory and device state of the VM, only the application-consistent disk content. For this reason, when a production checkpoint is applied, the VM will reboot from the application-consistent state in a similar manner to restoring a backup.

Windows Server 2012 R2 had a single configuration related to checkpoints: the file location for storing them. Windows Server 2016 has additional configurations that control whether checkpoints should be enabled, and if so, the type. With this new capability, you can block the action of creating checkpoints for certain VMs. These configurations are made per virtual machine. Figure 6.5 shows the configuration for a VM. Note that once checkpoints are enabled, you can choose production or standard checkpoints. If you select production checkpoints, you also configure whether a standard checkpoint should be created in the event a production checkpoint is not possible.

FIGURE 6.5
Checkpoint configuration for a VM

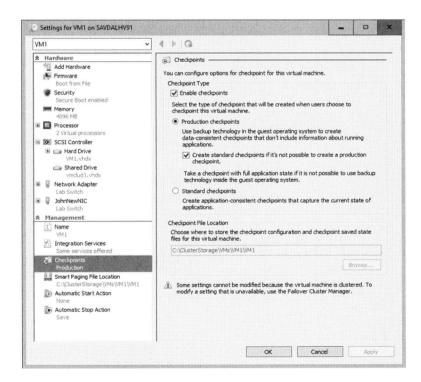

To configure the checkpoint type using PowerShell, set the `CheckpointType` attribute to one of four values:

Disabled   Checkpoints are disabled.

Standard   Use standard checkpoints.

Production Use production checkpoints if possible, and if not, use standard checkpoints.

ProductionOnly Use only production checkpoints.

For example, to configure a VM to use production checkpoints where possible, and if not, use standard checkpoints, the PowerShell would be as follows:

```
Set-VM -Name <VM> -CheckpointType Production
```

It is important to remember that although a production checkpoint is an application-consistent checkpoint that integrates with VSS and is safe for production, it does not capture the in-memory state of applications. In test and development scenarios, a standard checkpoint may be a better fit if you wish to capture the exact state, including the memory content of a system, so that it can be reverted to for troubleshooting and debugging purposes.

Entire hierarchies of checkpoints can be created, and each checkpoint can be custom named, making it easy to understand what each checkpoint represents. Checkpoints can then be applied to a virtual machine. Applying a checkpoint reverts a virtual machine back to the state that it was in when the checkpoint was created.

CHECKPOINTS WITH FIXED VIRTUAL HARD DISKS

A fixed virtual hard disk preallocates all space at creation time, but if a checkpoint is created, a differencing virtual hard disk is created for future writes. This means that a dynamic virtual hard disk is being used for writes and will therefore consume additional space that may not have been originally planned. There is also a small performance penalty as the dynamic differencing disk grows.

To create a checkpoint using Hyper-V Manager, select the virtual machine and select the Checkpoint action. This can be performed on a running virtual machine or on one that's shut down. For a running virtual machine, the creation may take a few seconds, because the contents of the memory and configuration state must be saved. By default, the checkpoint will be named <VMname>-(<date-time>), as shown in Figure 6.6, which shows a virtual machine with two checkpoints. They can be renamed simply by selecting and choosing the Rename action. Renaming the checkpoints is useful, so you'll understand at a later time what the state of the virtual machine was at the point of checkpoint. Renaming can also be performed using PowerShell with the Rename-VMSnapshot cmdlet and specifying the existing checkpoint name and the new name via the Name and NewName attributes. For example:

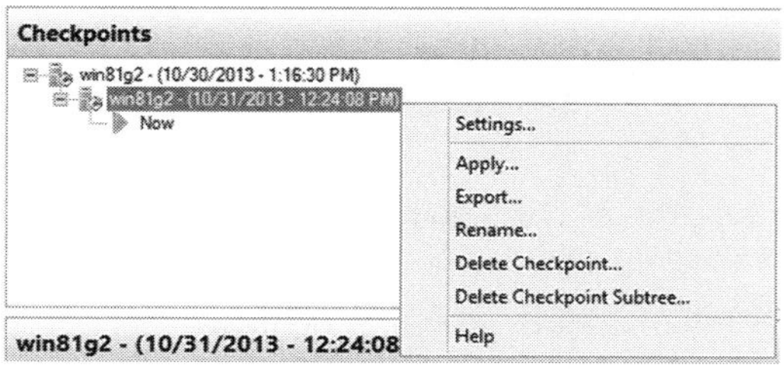

FIGURE 6.6
A VM with two checkpoints

```
Rename-VMSnapshot -VMName savdalsr02 `
-Name "savdalsr02—(5/30/2016—11:16:25 AM)" `
-NewName "Pre-Patch 5/30/2016"
```

Checkpoints can be deleted via the Delete Checkpoint action, and an entire subtree of multiple parent-child checkpoints can be deleted via the Delete Checkpoint Subtree action. What happens when you delete a checkpoint depends on where it is in the hierarchy of checkpoints and where the current Now state of the virtual machine is. If you delete a checkpoint that is on a different branch from the Now state and has no child checkpoints, its differencing virtual hard disk will be deleted along with any state and configuration files. If you delete a checkpoint that is part of the Now branch or has child checkpoints, its state files will be deleted but the contents of its differencing virtual hard disk will be merged into its child object, which could be the Now state or another checkpoint. There is an exception. If you delete a checkpoint that has multiple child snapshots, the differencing virtual hard disk is kept; to remove it would require its content to be merged into each child virtual hard disk, which would use up additional space, and that's likely not the experience administrators would expect. Although the way in which a checkpoint deletion is handled differs, what is consistent is that the checkpoint is no longer usable.

You may wonder how you get different branches of checkpoints. The key is that you can apply a specific checkpoint and then create new checkpoints from that point. This would create different branches, as shown in Figure 6.7. If you perform a Revert action on a virtual machine, you will be prompted to create a new checkpoint of the current state of the virtual machine to avoid losing its state.

FIGURE 6.7
Example of a checkpoint life cycle

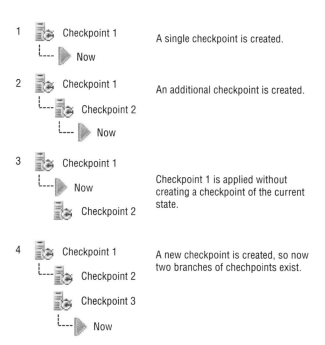

1 Checkpoint 1
   Now
   A single checkpoint is created.

2 Checkpoint 1
   Checkpoint 2
   Now
   An additional checkpoint is created.

3 Checkpoint 1
   Now
   Checkpoint 2
   Checkpoint 1 is applied without creating a checkpoint of the current state.

4 Checkpoint 1
   Checkpoint 2
   Checkpoint 3
   Now
   A new checkpoint is created, so now two branches of chechpoints exist.

Checkpoints can also be managed from PowerShell, but the naming is inconsistent. To create a checkpoint, use the `Checkpoint-VM` cmdlet as follows:

```
Checkpoint-VM -Name "TestVM10" -SnapshotName "Before change"
```

To list or apply a checkpoint, use the `Get-VMSnapshot` and `Restore-VMSnapshot` cmdlets. The following command finds the checkpoint for a VM and applies it:

```
Get-VM -Name "TestVM10" | Get-VMSnapshot | Restore-VMSnapshot
```

One great feature introduced in Windows Server 2012 was that the merging of differencing files that is required when a checkpoint is deleted was performed live, while the virtual machine was still running. Prior to Windows Server 2012, the merging of differencing files related to a checkpoint deletion did not occur until the virtual machine was stopped. Windows Server 2016 improves on the merging of the differencing files when running on ReFS, as covered in Chapter 4, "Storage Configurations," with the ability to merge files through Metadata updates only.

Windows Server 2012 R2 introduced two useful updates to checkpoints, which continue in Windows Server 2016. First, checkpoints can be exported while the virtual machine is running, which previously was not possible. Additionally, an export of the Now state of a virtual machine (that is, the running state) is possible, which effectively creates a clone of the virtual machine. This is useful in debugging situations where a problem is occurring on a virtual machine, and instead of having to debug the virtual machine, it is possible to create an export/clone of its current state and then debug that clone state. The export of the live state includes a copy of the storage, configuration, and memory dump—all without any impact to the availability of the virtual machine.

How checkpoints should be used is something often discussed. They are not replacements for backups, but rather, checkpoints that are useful for development and testing environments. Imagine in a testing or development environment the ability to save the state of an operating system, make some changes, and then revert back to a state before the changes were ever made. For a developer, the ability to freeze a system at the point of a problem and be able to keep reverting back to that problem state again and again is invaluable.

The use of checkpoints in production environments is generally discouraged because their usage can cause problems. This guidance does change in Windows Server 2016, however, when production checkpoints are utilized because of their integration with VSS and how they behave essentially like a backup. Additionally, as checkpoint hierarchies grow, some performance degradation occurs. A virtual machine can have up to 50 checkpoints. Checkpoints are specifically hazardous and known to cause problems for some types of services, such as Active Directory domain controllers. Taking a standard checkpoint of a domain controller and then reverting the domain controller back to that checkpoint can result in replication problems, duplicate security identifiers, and therefore security vulnerabilities prior to Windows Server 2012.

Windows Server 2012 introduced "virtualization safe" Active Directory when it's running on Hyper-V 2012 or above. Prior to Active Directory running on Windows Sever 2012 Hyper-V, there was a huge problem using snapshots with domain controllers. Directory services always expect time to go forward and need some way to track it, such as a logical clock, and Active Directory uses an update sequencer number (USN), which is incremented each time a new object is created along with other incremental values, such as the relative ID (RID). Look at Figure 6.8. Imagine that you have a domain controller and at USN 2 a snapshot is created, and then the DC continues using USNs up to number 6 for created users. Then an administrator applies the snapshot that was created, which puts the domain controller back to USN number 2.

The domain controller has no clue that it has been put back in time, so it carries on back at USN number 2, creating objects with the same security IDs, which causes problems with security, and the domain controller will no longer replicate correctly with the rest of the domain. We have divergence. This is a terrible problem for organizations and one of the biggest causes of Active Directory issues for Microsoft customers. Even though it's stated in many articles never to use snapshots with domain controllers, it still happens.

FIGURE 6.8
Update sequence number problems when applying a snapshot to a domain controller.

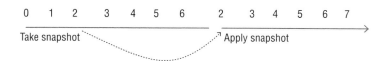

Windows Server 2012 fixed this through the use of a VM-generationID, which is provided by the Windows Server 2012 Hyper-V hypervisor. This VM-generationID is changed anytime something happens to a virtual machine that affects its point in time, such as applying a snapshot or duplicating the virtual machine. Active Directory stores the VM-generationID in the AD database, and every time an operation is performed, such as creating or changing an object, the VM-generationID stored in the AD database is compared against the VM-generationID provided by the hypervisor. If the VM-generationIDs do not match, it means that something has happened to the VM in logical time, and at this point the Active Directory service stops AD actions to protect Active Directory and performs the following:

◆ Discards the RID pool

◆ Resets the invocation ID, which is a database identifier. This is reset to ensure that no replication problems occur with other domain controllers. When the invocation ID is reset, there is no USN reuse problem, because USNs are paired with the invocation ID.

◆ Reassert the INITSYNC requirement for flexible single-master operation (FSMO) roles, which forces the domain controller to replicate with another domain controller that holds a copy of the partition in which the FSMO role is maintained.

These actions allow the domain controller to continue functioning without any risk to ongoing replication or security ID duplication. Even with this technology, there is still impact to the domain controller, because it has to take corrective actions. Therefore, do not start using checkpoints with domain controllers, but rather feel more secure that using them accidentally will not cause problems.

Using Service Templates

In previous chapters, I talked about the idea of virtual machine templates, which enable single virtual machines to be deployed. They are useful in typical deployment scenarios for individual workloads that are not dependent on other services, but few server applications work in isolation. Server applications talk to other server applications, and often multiple instances of server applications are required for availability and load-balancing needs.

Multitiered services can be deployed manually using templates by creating eight virtual machines, four for the web frontend tier, two for the middle tier, and two for the backend storage/database tier, for example. When it comes time to update a service, each virtual machine needs to be manually updated, because once a normal virtual machine is deployed, there is no ongoing relationship between the virtual machine and the template. This means that a virtual machine is not refreshed if the virtual machine template from which it was created is updated.

Service templates provide a new capability, introduced in SCVMM 2012, that allows complete services to be defined in SCVMM. The capability and service template introduced in 2012 can be one-, two-, or three-tiered applications by default, as shown in Figure 6.9, but additional tiers can be added if required. The virtual machine template for each tier can be specified in addition to which applications should be deployed, such as an IIS site using Web Deploy for the frontend, a regular application for the middle tier, and a database application using SQL DAC for the back-end tier. SCVMM 2012 introduced the concept of Server App-V, which allowed server applications to be virtualized, allowing abstraction from the underlying operating system and simple deployment and migration. This feature has been deprecated in SCVMM 2012 R2 because it was not widely adopted, and there are currently other initiatives to provide a better type of functionality, which means that it's not a technology in which to invest.

FIGURE 6.9
The default tiering options for a new service template. You'll see that a three-tier application is also available if you scroll down.

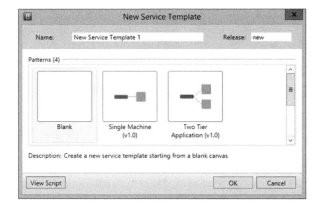

Web applications (Web Deploy) and database applications (SQL DAC) are considered first class in service templates, because service templates understand the Metadata of these types of applications and can enable parameters to perform the configuration when the application is deployed, such as by the end user. Other types of application installs are fully supported through the service template Generic Command Execution (GCE) feature because many organizations are not using SQL DAC, Server App-V, or maybe even Web Deploy yet. By using GCE, you can run both pre- and post-scripts for any type of application installation. The customization of non-first-class applications would need to be done through the application's native unattended configuration capabilities or scripting and would not integrate with the service deployment interface in the same way as first-class applications do. Standard Windows Server roles and features can also be added through standard virtual machine guest OS definitions.

A minimum, maximum, and initial number of instances of each tier are specified, which allows for easy scale out and scale in, depending on utilization. Service instances created from a service template maintain a link back to the template, and that template becomes read-only, so it becomes the source of truth for how the service looked. If an update is required, a new version of the service template is created and that updated service template is applied to deployed instances. The deployment of the new service template version will update the services while maintaining the application state through the Server App-V state backup and restore feature.

The use of services enables fewer OS images to be managed by the IT department because of the abstraction of the actual services, roles, features, and applications needed on the operating system, which traditionally may have been part of the OS image. Services also enable the related VMs to be treated as a single unit. Another nice bonus feature is that if SCVMM is integrated with Operations Manager, then Operations Manager will understand the service definition and show the VMs as part of a service.

A four-stage life cycle is the focus for service templates, to which I've previously alluded:

1. Create the service template.

2. Customize the deployment at the deployment time of the service template.

3. Deploy the service to environments.

4. Update the service template to a new version, and apply it to running instances of the service.

When an update to an existing instance of a service is made, there are three update types. The first type is a settings-only update mode, which only changes application settings but does not replace the OS image. The second update type is new, an in-place update; updates to the template settings are applied, but the actual OS images are not replaced. This would be used to update applications and modify configuration of the virtual machines in the service. The last type is the image-based update, which replaces the actual deployed instance operating system images with the new OS image and performs a reinstallation of applications but maintains the application state. If you have modified a virtual machine configuration that is part of a service, for example, and you changed the memory from 1GB to 4GB and then applied an update to the service from a new version of the service template, then any customizations you made to the configuration would be lost. Remember, with services, the service template is always the source of truth. This can be useful, for example, if your service instance has lost some VMs and you want to bring it back within the parameters of the service template. Instances can be refreshed from the service template, which will look for any missing elements of tiers that have less than the minimum number of instances and fix them by deploying additional required VMs.

In addition to allowing the definitions of virtual machine templates to use, applications to install, and various other settings, it is within a service template that you can also utilize load balancers and logical networks. By using the other fabric elements, service templates can enable rich capabilities in a completely automated fashion.

Service templates are created and maintained in the Service Template Designer, which is shown in Figure 6.10, and consists of the familiar ribbon, a designer canvas (which is the majority of the interface), and a small properties area at the bottom that shows the properties of the currently selected object. Once configurations are made, you run the Save And Validate action, which checks for any problems in the service template definition.

FIGURE 6.10
The Service
Designer

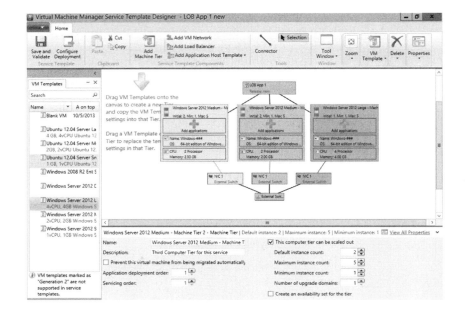

Once a service is deployed within the VMs And Services workspace in SCVMM, it is viewed as a single unit in addition to viewing the individual virtual machines that make up the service. Within the VMs And Services workspace view, you can view the application settings configured for the service, which helps to identify individual instances of deployed services.

One of the great features of using a service template is the ability to easily scale out and scale in as required. Selecting the service within the VMs And Services workspace will expose a Scale Out action that launches a wizard. You can use the wizard to select the tier to be scaled out and then specify the degree of the scale-out. Additional VMs will be created based on the scale properties. To scale in, instances of the VM in the tier are deleted.

The best way to understand the service templates is to fire up the Service Designer and start playing with the settings and looking at the options available. Even for basic services, the use of a service template is likely to make management far easier, especially when you want to make the service available for end-user deployment with some deployment time configuration options.

Performance Tuning and Monitoring with Hyper-V

When an operating system is deployed to a physical machine, it is the only operating system using that hardware. If there are performance problems, it's fairly simple to ascertain the cause by using Task Manager and Performance Monitor. When virtualization is introduced, looking at performance problems becomes more complex, because now there is the host operating system (management partition) and all the various virtual machines. Each virtual machine has its own virtual resources, which are allocated from the shared resources of the host.

It's important to be proactive and try to avoid performance problems. You can do that by being diligent in the discovery of your environment, understanding the true resource needs of the various workloads running in virtual machines, and allocating reasonable resources. Don't give every virtual machine 64 virtual processors, don't set every virtual machine's dynamic memory maximum to 1TB, and do consider using bandwidth management and storage QoS on virtual machine resources. Resource leaks can occur, bad code is written, or a user of a virtual machine may perform "tests." Any number of problems may cause guest operating systems to consume all of the available resources, so give virtual machines access only to resources that they reasonably need based on your discovery and analysis. In most cases, additional resources can be added painlessly if they are truly required fairly.

Even with all the planning in the world, performance problems will still occur that you'll need to troubleshoot. One of the first questions ever asked about using virtualization is about the "penalty;" that is, what performance drop will I see running workloads virtualized compared to running them directly on bare metal? There is no exact number. Clearly, the hypervisor and management partition consumes some resource, such as memory, processor, storage, and limited network traffic, but there is also a performance cost in certain areas caused by virtualization, such as additional storage and network latency, which although very small, does exist (although if this small additional latency is a problem for the highest-performing workloads, there are solutions such as SR-IOV to remove network latency and various options for storage, such as Direct Device Assignment).

Some people will say that for planning purposes, you should consider the worst-case scenario, and I've seen the number 10 percent used commonly (not for Hyper-V specifically, but for any virtualization solution). When planning out the available resources, remove 10 percent of the bare-metal server capability, and the 90 percent that's left is what you can expect for virtualized workloads. In reality, I've never seen anything close to this. I commonly see workloads running virtualized on Hyper-V that are on par with a nonvirtualized workload or even exceed the performance you see on the physical hardware, which at first glance seems impossible. How can virtualization improve performance above running directly on bare metal? The reason is that some workloads use only a certain amount of resources efficiently. Once you go beyond a certain number of processors and memory, the additional resources bring diminishing returns. If I have a large server with 256GB of RAM and 128 processor cores, and I install an OS directly on that box and then run an instance of a server application, it may be able to use only 64GB of memory and 32 cores efficiently. If I use virtualization on that same server and create four virtual machines with an instance of the server application in each, I'll efficiently use all of the processor cores and memory in the server, giving much better overall performance. It's the difference between scaling up (adding more resources to an instance) and scaling out (adding more instances). Remember that even if a small performance penalty exists or, more realistically, a small amount of resource is lost that is used by the management partition, the benefits of virtualization outweigh this with greater utilization, faster provisioning, easier management, and so on.

Let's recap the limits of Hyper-V in terms of what the Hyper-V host can leverage and then the limits for each virtual machine. Each Hyper-V host can address the following:

- 320 physical logical processors (If you have more than this and are using hyperthreading, turn it off so Hyper-V can access more of the real cores on the system.)

- 4TB of physical RAM

- There are no real limits that you will hit for networking or storage.

- Each host can be allocated up to 2,048 virtual processors and can run up to 1,024 virtual machines.

Each virtual machine can be allocated the following:

◆ 64 virtual processors (assuming the physical host has 64 logical processors; otherwise, the limit per VM will be the number of logical processors in the host)

◆ 1TB of RAM

◆ Up to 256 VHDX files connected via the four possible SCSI controllers, and each VHDX can be up to 64TB. In terms of storage performance, Microsoft has demonstrated IOPS in excess of one million to a VHDX file. Obviously, you need a powerful backend storage solution to get one million IOPS, but the point is that even when using virtual hard disks, you can get any level of performance that is needed without needing DirectAccess via virtual Fibre Channel, iSCSI, and so on.

◆ Eight network adapters (An additional four legacy network adapters can be added, but they should not be used because of poor performance and increased overhead.)

It's because of the huge scalability of Hyper-V with Windows Server 2012, and above that there is almost no workload that cannot be virtualized on Hyper-V. Over 99 percent of the world's SQL Server instances could now be virtualized on Hyper-V.

The key tool that you will use to troubleshoot performance problems or even just to see the utilization of a Hyper-V host is Performance Monitor. Task Manager is of limited use. It will not show processor utilization by virtual machines, because the host OS is just another operating system running on top of the hypervisor. This is also why the management OS can use only 64 processors on a system with more than 64—even the management OS is still accessing processor resources via the hypervisor. As Figure 6.11 shows, however, Task Manager does at least show the total number of processors in the Logical Processors field even though the host logical processors are limited to 64. This is not a problem, because the host OS does very little processing, while the actual hypervisor can access up to 320. Task Manager will also not show resources by virtual machine, so it's not a useful tool for troubleshooting the performance of a Hyper-V environment.

FIGURE 6.11
Only 64 processors are visible on the Hyper-V host of an 80-processor system.

Sockets:	**4**
Cores:	**40**
Logical processors:	**80**
Host logical processors:	**64**
Virtualization:	**Enabled**

Performance Monitor running on a Hyper-V host has access to detailed information on not just performance of the management OS but also on the resources used for each virtual machine. It shows information for all types of resources, including processor, memory, networking, and storage. I will cover the performance counters to use for each of these key types of resources in the following list. Remember that while most resource utilization should be consumed by virtual machines, it's always important to view the resource utilization of the host OS as well, because the host performs certain functions for the guests that can consume resources, and processes may be running on the host that are misbehaving and need to be corrected. When I refer to performance counters in the following list, I refer to the group of the counters first and then the actual counter. For example, Hyper-V Hypervisor Logical Processor is the counter group and % Total Run Time is a counter within that group.

For the processor resource, we can examine the total busy time of each logical processor in the host (used by the host or virtual machines), the processor usage by the actual host OS, and the individual virtual machines.

Hyper-V Hypervisor Logical Processor   *% Total Run Time*: The utilization of the actual logical processors as managed by the hypervisor, which is usage by the host OS and all the virtual machines.

Hyper-V Hypervisor Root Virtual Processor   *% Total Run Time*: The amount used by just the Hyper-V host OS.

Hyper-V Hypervisor Virtual Processor   *% Total Run Time*: The amount of processor used by each virtual processor for each virtual machine. There is a value for each virtual processor, which means that if a virtual machine has eight virtual processors, it will have eight values.

If you see overall that the logical processors are consistently over 90 percent busy, then this would show overall that the host is too overloaded. You can look at what is using the processor by looking at the Root Virtual Processor (if it's the Hyper-V host using it) and Virtual Processor counters for each virtual machine (if it's a specific virtual machine). If the Virtual Processor counter for each virtual processor for a specific virtual machine shows high utilization and not the overall host, then it's simply a specific virtual machine that is overloaded. In this case, the virtual machine likely needs additional virtual processors added, as opposed to the host being overcommitted in terms of resources.

For the memory resource, there are two pieces. First, has the virtual machine been allocated enough memory? That can easily be seen by Hyper-V Manager, which shows the memory status (also visible through the Hyper-V Dynamic Memory VM – Current Pressure performance counter). If the memory is too low, additional memory can be added through means such as Dynamic Memory, but this assumes that the host has enough memory to even allocate. Looking at Memory – Available MBytes shows the available memory on the host, but to check the amount of memory that can be allocated to virtual machines, look at Hyper-V Dynamic Memory Balancer – Available Memory, which shows memory available over the complete system or for each NUMA node (if NUMA spanning is disabled).

By default, Hyper-V enables NUMA spanning, which allows a virtual machine to be allocated memory across the boundary of the NUMA node of the processor cores being used. While allowing more virtual machines to run, NUMA spanning may also lead to an overall decrease in performance, because using memory outside the NUMA node of the processor is more "expensive" in performance terms. If you disable NUMA spanning (in the Hyper-V settings, select NUMA Spanning and uncheck Allow Virtual Machines To Span Physical NUMA Nodes), then a virtual machine *cannot* be allocated memory from remote NUMA nodes and would be limited to using memory on its local NUMA node.

If you disable NUMA spanning, and then if you look at the performance counter Hyper-V Dynamic Memory Balancer – Available Memory, you will see multiple values, one for each NUMA node. If you have NUMA spanning turned on, you see only a single counter, System Balancer.

Potentially, more memory may be needed in the host if the available memory is low and you are seeing high memory demand from virtual machines.

The overall number of network bytes for each network adapter can be seen by looking at Network Adapter – Bytes Total/sec, and to see how much each virtual network adapter for each virtual machine is using, look at Hyper-V Virtual Network Adapter – Bytes/sec.

Finally, for storage we typically care about the latency of reads and writes, which we can see for each physical disk (or if SMB/iSCSI, and so on, the equivalent counter) by looking at PhysicalDisk – Avg. Disk sec/Read and Avg. Disk sec/Write. This should generally be less than 50 ms. Knowing the queue length can also be useful. You can see the number of I/Os waiting to be actioned via the Physical Disk – Avg. Disk Read Queue Length and Avg. Disk Write Queue Length counters; you'll know that you have a problem if you see sustained queues.

By looking at all of these performance counters together, it should be possible to ascertain the cause of any degraded performance on your system. I create a custom MMC console, add all performance MMC snap-ins, and then add my counters and save the customized console so that all my counters are easily available, as shown in Figure 6.12.

FIGURE 6.12
A nice view of the key resources for my Hyper-V host using the report display output type

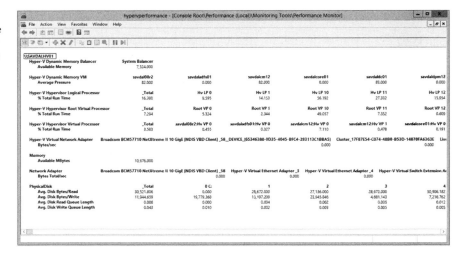

One important point is to benchmark your system. When you first deploy the server, run the counters to see how the machine runs "new" and store the results. Performance Monitor is not just for viewing live data; it can also log the data to a file so that you can save the state of a monitoring session, which is a great feature. Then after a server has been running for a while, you can run the same counters again to see how it's performing and look for any signs of performance degradation.

In Chapter 7, I talk about optimization technologies that use Live Migration to automatically move virtual machines between nodes in a cluster if the current node cannot adequately handle the requirements of its virtual machines. This provides some breathing room regarding exactly estimating the resource needs of every virtual machine, but it's still important to ensure that the overall cluster has sufficient resources and that it has sufficient resources even if a certain number of nodes fail within the cluster.

Resource Metering

Performance monitoring is useful for troubleshooting performance problems and even seeing details of virtual machines, but it's a fairly involved process. You will end up with a lot of data if you leave performance monitoring running for a long duration, and it's server specific, which means that if a virtual machine was moved between servers using Live Migration or any other migration technology, you would have to start monitoring the virtual machine on the new server and add all the counters together across multiple nodes.

Windows Server 2012 introduced a better option if you want to track the resource utilization of one or more virtual machines, typically for the purpose of billing based on the resource utilization of the virtual machine. Instead of detailed metrics of the resource usage every 5 seconds, the resource metering functionality simply tracks the total and average resource utilizations of a virtual machine, which can then be viewed at any time. The great thing about the resource metering feature is not just its simplicity, but that the metering data persists even if the virtual machine is moved between Hyper-V nodes using any of the migration technologies.

The resource metering metrics that are gathered can be accessed via PowerShell cmdlets or using WMI.

To enable resource metering for a virtual machine, use this command:

```
Enable-VMResourceMetering -VMName <VM name>
```

To view the current measurements for a virtual machine in a detailed list format, use the following command:

```
Measure-VM -VMName <VM name> | fl
```

The metrics for a virtual machine never reset unless you either disable metering or perform a manual reset. Use this command to perform a manual reset:

```
Reset-VMResourceMetering -VMName <VM name>
```

Finally, to disable the metering, use this command:

```
Disable-VMResourceMetering -VMName <VM name>
```

To check which virtual machines have metering enabled, run the following command:

```
Get-VM | Format-Table Name, ResourceMeteringEnable
```

Here is an example of the output of metering from a Hyper-V 2016 virtual machine. If you used metering in Hyper-V 2012, you will notice new metrics, specifically around storage performance, which were actually introduced in Windows Server 2012 R2.

```
PS C:\ > Measure-VM -VMName VM1 | fl


VMId                   : 6c79b7c6-13cb-4e22-b528-870f92a8d373
VMName                 : VM1
CimSession             : CimSession: .
ComputerName           : SAVDALHV91
MeteringDuration       :
AverageProcessorUsage  : 242
AverageMemoryUsage     : 2247
MaximumMemoryUsage     : 4096
MinimumMemoryUsage     : 4096
TotalDiskAllocation    : 260096
```

```
AggregatedAverageNormalizedIOPS: 5
AggregatedAverageLatency     : 1422
AggregatedDiskDataRead       : 405
AggregatedDiskDataWritten    : 77
AggregatedNormalizedIOCount  : 67933
NetworkMeteredTrafficReport  :
{Microsoft.HyperV.PowerShell.VMNetworkAdapterPortAclMeteringReport,
Microsoft.HyperV.PowerShell.VMNetworkAdapterPortAclMeteringReport,
Microsoft.HyperV.PowerShell.VMNetworkAdapterPortAclMeteringReport,
Microsoft.HyperV.PowerShell.VMNetworkAdapterPortAclMeteringReport...}
HardDiskMetrics              : {Microsoft.HyperV.PowerShell.VHDMetrics,
Microsoft.HyperV.PowerShell.VHDMetrics}
AvgCPU                       : 242
AvgRAM                       : 2247
MinRAM                       : 4096
MaxRAM                       : 4096
TotalDisk: 260096
```

Most of the values shown are fairly self-explanatory. Information is given about the average, minimum, and maximum memory usage in addition to the average processor usage, which is measured in megahertz. You may wonder why the processor is shown in megahertz instead of CPU percent. The reason is that virtual machines can move between servers, so a percentage of a CPU depends entirely on the server on which the virtual machine is running, whereas megahertz is a fairly consistent value, no matter which servers the virtual machine is moved between.

You will notice that there seem to be duplicate values related to processor, memory, and total disk allocation. AverageProcessorUsage is the same as AvgCPU, AverageMemoryUsage is the same as AvgRAM, and so on. These are in fact the same values. The reason for two different names is that the output from Measure-VM by default will be in a table format, and the regular titles such as AverageProcessorUsage would use up a lot of screen space and limit the data that's visible. Therefore, the short names are there to ensure that as much information as possible is shown when viewing in table mode, as in this example:

```
PS C:\ > Measure-VM -VMName savdalfs01

VMName     AvgCPU(MHz) AvgRAM(M) MaxRAM(M) MinRAM(M) TotalDisk(M)
NetworkIn- NetworkOut-
           bound(M)    bound(M)
---------------------------------------------------------------

savdalfs01 113         2352      2352      2352      261128      2206       3478
```

Also shown is disk information related to IOPS, latency, and read and write information, but there are also cryptic values related to HardDiskMetrics and NetworkMeteredTrafficReport, which don't actually give any useful information. Each of those entries are separate reports that have to be viewed as specific report entities. You do this by saving the metering to a variable and then inspecting the separate report elements. If you look at the storage report for Windows Server 2012 R2, you would not see the normalized I/O count, as this is new to Windows Server 2016. Also remember that when using the new Windows Server 2016 Storage QoS, additional metrics are available, as covered in Chapter 4. Here is an example of the basic metering output for networking and storage:

```
PS C:\> $report =  Measure-VM -VMName savdalfs01

PS C:\> $report.NetworkMeteredTrafficReport

LocalAddress RemoteAddress Direction TotalTraffic(M)
------------ ------------- --------- ---------------
             0.0.0.0/0     Inbound   2121
             0.0.0.0/0     Outbound  3479
             ::/0          Inbound   88
             ::/0          Outbound  2


PS C:\> $report.HardDiskMetrics

VirtualHardDisk       : HardDiskDrive (Name = 'Hard Drive on SCSI
controller number 0 at location 0', VMName =
                        'VM1') [Id = 'Microsoft:6C79B7C6-13CB-4E22-B528-
870F92A8D373\7E4A44C7-C488-4E8F-9588-8D3699
                        252C9B\0\0\D', VMId = '6c79b7c6-13cb-4e22-b528-
870f92a8d373']
AverageNormalizedIOPS: 41
AverageLatency       : 1915
DataRead             : 409
DataWritten          : 79
NormalizedIOCount    : 68626

VirtualHardDisk       : HardDiskDrive (Name = 'Hard Drive on SCSI
controller number 0 at location 1', VMName =
                        'VM1') [Id = 'Microsoft:6C79B7C6-13CB-4E22-B528-
870F92A8D373\7E4A44C7-C488-4E8F-9588-8D3699
                        252C9B\0\1\D', VMId = '6c79b7c6-13cb-4e22-b528-
870f92a8d373']
AverageNormalizedIOPS: 0
AverageLatency       : 0
DataRead             : 1
DataWritten          : 0
NormalizedIOCount: 18
```

The resource-metering functionality gives a great view into the metrics of a single virtual machine. However, if there are 10 virtual machines in a certain group—for example, all of the virtual machines for a certain client or all of the SQL servers—then to get the total resource for all of the groups' virtual machines, you would have to add all the metrics together manually or write something. This is where the concept of resource pools can be useful. CPUs, memory, storage (VHD, ISO, Fibre Channel, and virtual floppy disk), and network adapters can be added to a resource pool from a number of virtual machines. Once the resources are added to the resource pool, metering can be enabled for the resource pool and subsequently measured. The one drawback with resource pools is that they are host-specific, so if virtual machines are moved between hosts, you would need to ensure that the same resource pools are available on every node, which is why resource pools are typically not widely used.

By default, numerous resource pools, known as Primordial, exist on the system, which can be viewed as follows:

```
PS C:\> Get-VMResourcePool

Name        ResourcePoolType        ParentName ResourceMeteringEnabled
--          ---------               -----------------
Primordial FibreChannelConnection              False
Primordial VHD                                 True
Primordial FibreChannelPort                    False
Primordial VFD                                 False
Primordial ISO                                 False
Primordial Ethernet                            True
Primordial Memory                              True
Primordial Processor                           True
Primordial PciExpress                          False
```

A new resource pool is created for each type of resource, but the same resource pool name is specified, which makes it a single, reportable pool. For example, in the following code snippet, I create a resource pool for a group of virtual machines, GroupA, for the four types of resources. Then I add virtual machine CPU and memory to each created pool, in addition to virtual hard disks and the virtual switch the virtual machines use. In the following example, I add new hard disks and network adapters to a VM, but you can also use Set-<resource> -ResourcePoolName to set the pool. Notice that when the VHD resource pool is created, you must specify the path where the VHDs will be stored.

```
New-VMResourcePool -Name GroupA -ResourcePoolType Processor
New-VMResourcePool -Name GroupA -ResourcePoolType Memory
New-VMResourcePool -Name GroupA -ResourcePoolType Ethernet
New-VMResourcePool -Name GroupA -ResourcePoolType VHD `
-Paths @("\\savdalfs01\HVShare")
Add-VMSwitch -ResourcePoolName GroupA -Name "External Switch"
Set-VMProcessor -VMName savdal08R2 -ResourcePoolName GroupA
Set-VMMemory -VMName savdal08R2—ResourcePoolName Group A
Add-VMHardDiskDrive -VMName savdal08R2 -ControllerType SCSI `
-ResourcePoolName GroupA `
-Path "\\savdalfs01\HVShare\savdal08R2\data1.vhdx"
Add-VMNetworkAdapter -VMName savdal08R2 -ResourcePoolName GroupA
```

Additionally, once you create a resource pool for networking and storage, the resource pools will become visible in the Hyper-V Manager GUI (but not for processor and memory), as shown in Figure 6.13.

Once the resource pool is created, it can be enabled for metering by using the normal cmdlets, except instead of a virtual machine name (VMName), specify the name of the resource pool (ResourcePoolName), as in this example:

```
Enable-VMResourceMetering -ResourcePoolName GroupA
```

FIGURE 6.13
Viewing resource
pools in Hyper-V
Manager

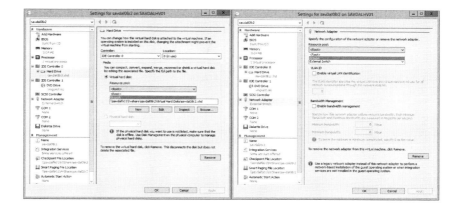

If you create a resource pool, run the `Get-VMResourcePool` cmdlet again. You will see a lot of new entries. Remember, if you use resource pools, by default, you would not be able to move a virtual machine configured in a resource pool if the target host does not have the same resource pool defined. I think resource pools are an interesting concept, but they need to be easily managed across multiple hosts to be a useful feature.

While resource pools are primarily aimed at metering, they can also be used for resource allocation. Notice in the `Add-VMNetworkAdapter` command earlier, I don't specify a switch but rather just a resource pool that has switches added to it. This allows me to easily provision virtual machines on different hosts (provided the resource pool is defined on multiple hosts) and not worry about the switch name. I don't expect many people to use resource pools in this manner. Using SCVMM to manage resource allocation is a much better and more enterprise-ready approach.

Monitoring

I want to close with the concept of monitoring your environment. When you virtualize, as I've said previously, you are putting all your eggs into a much smaller number of baskets. It's critical that those baskets are healthy and being proactively monitored, so you are not only alerted when something breaks, but also notified when something is not performing as expected, when best practices aren't used on something, and when there are signs of impending failure.

When thinking about monitoring, you have to consider not just the Hyper-V host but all of the other resources that are required for the host to run and be accessible and for the virtual machines to be able to function. At a minimum, you need to monitor the following:

◆   The Hyper-V host operating system (including the Hyper-V role-specific intelligence)

◆   Server hardware

◆   Storage subsystems (such as SANs)

◆   Networking equipment

◆   Active Directory

◆   SCVMM and its SQL database

It's also a good idea to monitor the OS within the virtual machines to get the best insight. Many monitoring solutions are available. System Center includes System Center Operations Manager, which is a powerful monitoring solution, not just for Microsoft environments, but also for the entire infrastructure. Operations Manager has management packs, which are imported and give insight into each element of the environment. Figure 6.14 is an example view from Operations Manager of the health status of a virtual machine. Operations Manager also has a great dashboard view of actual clouds that you define within SCVMM.

FIGURE 6.14
Operations Manager view of virtual machines

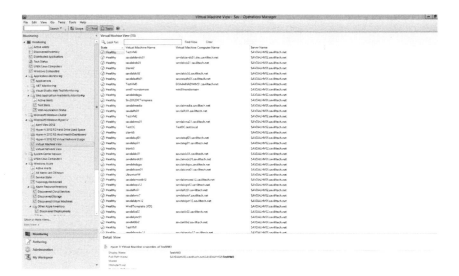

The Bottom Line

Explain how backup works in a Hyper-V environment. Windows features the VSS component that enables application-consistent backups to be taken of an operating system by calling VSS writers created by application vendors. When a backup is taken of a virtual machine at the Hyper-V host level, the VSS request is passed to the guest operating system via the backup guest service, which allows the guest OS to ensure that the disk is in a backup-ready state, allowing the virtual hard disk to be backed up at the host and be application consistent.

Master It Is shared VHDX backed up when you perform a VM backup at the host level?

Understand how to best use checkpoints and where not to use them. Checkpoints, previously known as snapshots, allow a point-in-time view of a virtual machine to be captured and then applied at a later time to revert the virtual machine back to the state it was in at the time the snapshot was taken. Windows Server 2016 introduced a new type of checkpoint, the production checkpoint. Production checkpoints interact with the VSS infrastructure inside the guest OS that provides an application-consistent checkpoint. Production checkpoints can be used in production environments. Standard checkpoints that do not interact with VSS and save the complete state of a VM, including memory, are useful in testing scenarios but should not be used in production because the effect of moving a virtual machine back in time without the OS knowledge can cause problems for many services. It can even cause domain membership problems if the computer's AD account password changes after the checkpoint creation.

Understand the benefits of service templates. Typically, a virtual machine is created from a virtual machine template, which allows a single virtual machine to be deployed. A service template allows a complete, multitiered service to be designed and then deployed through a single action. Additionally, each tier can be configured to scale up and down as workloads vary, which enables additional instances of the virtual machine for a tier to be created and deleted as necessary. Deployed instances of a service template retain their relationship to the original service template, which means that if the original service template is updated, the deployed instances can be refreshed and updated with the service template changes without losing application state.

Chapter 7

Failover Clustering and Migration Technologies

As previously discussed, when implementing virtualization, you consolidate your operating systems onto fewer pieces of hardware, effectively putting your eggs in a smaller number of baskets. It's therefore important that those baskets are as secure as possible and, in the event a basket breaks, there is another basket underneath to catch the eggs that fall.

Failover Clustering provides resiliency for Windows services such as SQL, Exchange, file, and print—and now for Hyper-V. By leveraging the failover cluster feature, Hyper-V servers can share storage resources such as LUNs on a SAN or, with Windows Server 2016, local storage in each node through Storage Spaces Direct. More important, however, clustering provides high availability from a node failure by moving virtual machines to another node, plus it enables highly efficient migrations of virtual machines between nodes in planned scenarios such as hardware maintenance. Clustering also ensures that if a break occurs between nodes in a cluster, only one part of that cluster will offer services, to avoid any chances of corruption. Windows Server 2012 introduced new types of mobility, both within a cluster and outside a cluster, providing even more flexibility for Hyper-V environments, which has seen continued investment in Windows Server 2012 R2 and Windows Server 2016.

In this chapter, you will learn to:

◆ Understand the quorum model used in Windows Server 2012 and above.

◆ Identify the types of mobility available with Hyper-V.

◆ Understand the best way to patch a cluster with minimal impact to workloads.

Failover Clustering Basics

Failover Clustering was first introduced in Windows NT 4, known then as Microsoft Cluster Services, and it was developed under the very cool code name of Wolfpack. Prior to Windows Server 2012, the clustering feature was available only in the Enterprise and above SKUs of Windows Server. However, with the standardization of features and scalability in Windows Server 2012 editions, the Failover Clustering feature is now available in the Standard SKU in addition to Datacenter. Even with the divergence of feature equality in Windows Server 2016 between Standard and Datacenter, Failover Clustering is still present in the Standard edition and has all the same features as its Datacenter bigger brother.

Failover Clustering is a feature and not a role in Windows Server, because clustering just helps make another role more available. The difference between roles and features is that a *role*, such as Hyper-V or File Services, designates the primary purpose of a server. A *feature*, such as backup, BitLocker, and clustering, helps a server perform its primary purpose.

Failover Clustering can be installed through Server Manager or through PowerShell as follows:

```
Install-WindowsFeature Failover-Clustering
```

A cluster consists of two or more nodes that offer services to the network, as shown in Figure 7.1. While the cluster itself has a name, IP address, configuration, and, optionally, storage available to all nodes in the cluster, the actual services offered by the cluster have their own resources, such as an IP address, network name, and disks from those available to the cluster. The types of service offered by a cluster include file servers, print servers, DHCP servers, Hyper-V virtual machines, or any other application that has been written to be cluster aware, such as Exchange and SQL Server.

FIGURE 7.1
The components of a failover cluster

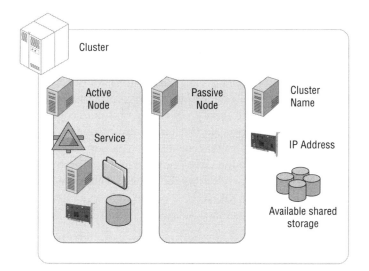

A ONE-NODE CLUSTER?

I stated that a cluster consists of two or more nodes, but strictly speaking, that is not accurate. A cluster can consist of a single node, and many times you may start with a one-node cluster. Remember, the point of a cluster is to provide high availability of services by enabling services to move between servers if a server fails. With a single-node cluster, if the node fails, there is nowhere for the services to move to. Therefore, you always want at least two nodes in a cluster to provide high-availability services.

However, some features of Failover Clustering apply even to single-node environments, such as the ability to monitor services that run inside virtual machines and restart the virtual machine if a service fails three times.

Figure 7.1 shows an active node and a passive node. In the example, a single service is configured in the cluster. The node the service is running on is the active node. The node not running the service is the passive node, but it would become the active node if the service moved to it as part of a planned move or if the existing active node failed.

While we will talk about active and passive nodes, in reality we can configure multiple services and applications within a cluster that can be hosted on different nodes in the cluster, and so at any time every node may be running a specific server or application. You just need to ensure that the resources in the cluster nodes are sufficient to run the services and applications from other nodes in the cluster in the event of planned failover of services or server failure, or if applications are stopped for maintenance purposes.

The cluster consists of numerous nodes that can be active or passive. An *active node* is simply a node that currently owns a service or application. Windows Server 2012 and above allow up to 64 nodes in a cluster, up from the 16 nodes in previous versions of Windows Server.

A cluster can contain multiple services and applications, and these can be spread among all of the nodes in the cluster. A service or application consists of various resources that enable the service or application to function, such as a disk resource, a share, a name, and an IP address. Different types of services and applications use different resources.

Any resource that is cluster aware and hosted in a cluster can move between nodes in the cluster to increase its availability. In an unplanned failure, such as a node failing, a small period of service interruption may occur, because the node failure must be detected and then the service's resources moved to another node and restarted. In most planned scenarios, such as moving resources from one node to another to enable maintenance on the source node, any outage can be avoided, such as using Live Migration when a Hyper-V virtual machine moves between nodes in a cluster.

If you used clustering prior to Windows Server 2008, then you will have experienced an extremely long and painful cluster creation process that required pages of configuration information, was hard to troubleshoot, and required special hardware from a cluster-specific hardware compatibility list. This completely changed with Windows Server 2008. Windows Server 2008 introduced a greatly simplified cluster creation process that required you to specify only the nodes to be added to the cluster and to provide a name for the cluster and an IP address if DHCP was not used. All the other details are automatically configured by the cluster setup wizard. Additionally, the separate cluster hardware compatibility list was removed, replaced with a new cluster validation process that is run on the desired nodes prior to cluster creation. If the cluster validation passes, the cluster will be supported by Microsoft.

Understanding Quorum and Why It's Important

With a cluster, multiple nodes share a common cluster database in which services are defined that can run on any node in the cluster. The goal of the cluster is to provide high availability so that if something bad happens on a node, the services move to another node. It's important to note that in some scenarios, a network problem may stop different parts of a cluster from being able to communicate, rather than actual node problems. In the case of a communication problem between different parts (partitions) of the cluster, only one part of the cluster should run services, to avoid the same service starting on different parts of the cluster, which could then cause corruption.

The detection of "something bad" happening within a cluster is facilitated by cluster heartbeat communications. The nodes in the cluster communicate constantly via a heartbeat to ensure that they are available. In the event of a change of cluster status, such as a node becoming unavailable or network problems stopping the cluster nodes from communicating, the cluster goes into arbitration: The remaining nodes basically fight it out to decide who should be hosting which services and applications, to avoid split-brain. In a *split-brain* situation, multiple nodes in a cluster try to bring online the same service or application, which causes the nodes to try to bring online the same resources.

Quorum Basics

Quorum is the mechanism used to ensure that in the event of a break in communication between parts of the cluster or the loss of parts of the cluster, you always have a majority of cluster resources for the cluster to function. Quorum is the reason it is common to have a shared disk or file share that can be used in arbitration when an even number of nodes exists in different parts of the cluster.

Imagine that you have a cluster of four nodes without any shared disk or file share used for quorum and arbitration. A split occurs, and for some reason each node can contact only the node next to it. Then, each half of the cluster has two nodes, which is a disaster because both halves may think that they should own all of the services and applications. That is why the quorum model is based on a majority—that is, *more* than half is needed for the cluster to function. In our example of two nodes on each side, neither side has a majority (half is not a majority), so no cluster resources would be serviced. This is far better than multiple nodes trying to service the same resources.

The behavior in this scenario, with exactly half the nodes in each partition of the cluster, changed in Windows Server 2012 R2, so that services would be offered by one of the partitions. Each node can be seen as having a vote. By adding an extra vote with a file share, disk, or cloud storage account in Windows Server 2016, you can ensure that one part of the cluster can always get more than 50 percent by claiming the file share, disk, or cloud storage account vote.

Let's look in detail at quorum. Prior to Windows Server 2012, various quorum models were available, and even with Windows Server 2012, there was specific guidance about when to use a file share witness or disk witness. In Windows Server 2012 R2, this all changed.

Prior to Windows Server 2012, various cluster models existed, but Windows Server 2012 simplified this to a single model. Within a cluster, by default, each node has a vote. These votes are used in times of arbitration to decide which partition of a cluster can make quorum—that is, has more than half the number of votes. When creating a cluster, you also define either a disk witness or a file share witness, which also has a vote.

Prior to Windows Server 2012 R2, a file share witness or disk witness was configured only if you had an even number of nodes. An even number of nodes would equal an even number of votes, and therefore, in the event of partitioning of the cluster, neither partition would have more votes than the other side. When you configure the file share witness or disk witness, the extra vote ensures that one partition of the cluster could claim that vote and therefore have more than 50 percent of the votes and make quorum. Only when the witness is required to make quorum is it locked by one partition of the cluster. For a file share witness, the lock is performed by locking the witness.log file on the share by one of the cluster partitions. To lock a disk witness, the disk has a SCSI persistent reservation made by one of the partitions. Both types of locks stop another partition of the cluster from being able to take ownership of the witness and try to use its vote to make quorum. This is shown in Figure 7.2, along with an odd number of vote scenarios showing why the witness is not required.

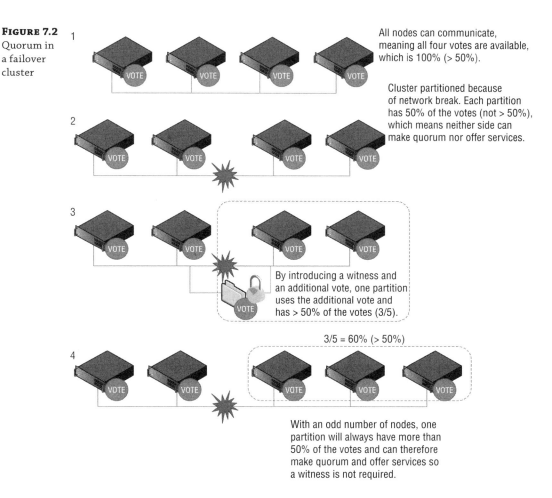

FIGURE 7.2
Quorum in
a failover
cluster

Windows Server 2012 R2 changed the recommendation always to configure the disk witness or file share witness. It enhances the dynamic quorum feature introduced in Windows Server 2012 to extend to the additional witness to give it a vote only *if* there are an even number of nodes. If there are an odd number of nodes, the witness does not get a vote and is not used.

A *file share witness* is simply a share on an SMB file server that is running Windows Server 2003 or above and is on a node that is in the same forest as the cluster. The file share should not be hosted on the actual cluster. If you have a multisite cluster, host the file share witness on a server in a third site to avoid any dependence on one of the two sites used by the cluster. A single file server can host file shares for different clusters. The cluster object in Active Directory (cluster name object, or CNO) must have full control on both the file share and the folder that the file share is sharing. A good naming convention to use to avoid confusion for the share is FSW_<Cluster Name>. It's possible to have the file share witness for a cluster hosted on a different cluster to provide additional resiliency to the file share. Note that the clustered file share can be hosted on a traditional file server or a Scale-out File Server. Both will work well.

A *disk witness* can be any cluster disk, which means that it's accessible from all nodes in a cluster that is NTFS or Resilient File System (ReFS) formatted and is at least 512MB in size. You may wonder why the cluster disk needs to be 512MB. The cluster disk stores a copy of the cluster database, hence the size requirement. By default, when you're creating a cluster, the smallest cluster disk that is over 512MB is automatically made the disk witness, although this can be changed. The disk witness is exclusively used for witness purposes and does not require a drive letter.

Windows Server 2016 introduces a third type of witness resource, a cloud witness. A *cloud witness* utilizes an Azure storage account, which can utilize any of the Azure regions. A cloud witness has the following benefits:

◆ It uses Azure as a third site, which solves a challenge for many multisite deployments today that need the witness in a separate location that they don't actually have.

◆ There is no maintenance for the witness, since it's just using an Azure storage account accessed over the Internet via HTTPS.

◆ It is ideal when other types of witnesses are not available or not easily available (for example, creating a guest cluster in Azure or other private cloud).

◆ It's cheap—very cheap—maybe even free, but more on this in a second.

The cloud witness works by creating a 0-byte block blob for each cluster in an automatically created container named `msft-cloud-witness` in the specified Azure storage account. Azure charges based on consumption. While not guaranteed, the price for a 0-byte file will likely be 0 but may cost you a cent eventually. Multiple clusters can use the same storage account; a new block blob is created using the GUID of the cluster. Figure 7.3 shows an example storage account that is being used by two separate clusters; hence the two separate block blobs, one per cluster. Note that the file is not empty; it contains a sequence number, but it's so small that Azure rounds it down to 0. Note that when using a cloud witness, the access key for the storage account is not stored in the cluster; instead, a shared access signature (SAS) token is generated, stored, and used. Details on SAS can be found at `https://azure.microsoft.com/en-us/documentation/articles/storage-dotnet-shared-access-signature-part-1/`.

To modify the witness configuration for a cluster, perform the following steps:

1. In Failover Cluster Manager, select the main cluster object in the navigation pane.

2. From More Actions, select Configure Cluster Quorum Settings.

3. Click Next on the introduction page of the wizard.

4. Select the Select The Quorum Witness option and click Next. Note also the option Use Default Quorum Configuration, which allows the cluster to configure witness configuration automatically, as it would during the initial cluster creation process.

5. Select the option to use a disk witness, file share witness, cloud witness, or no witness (never recommended) and then click Next.

6. Depending on the option selected, you now must select the disk witness, file share, or if using a cloud witness, the Azure storage account name and the primary or secondary storage account access key and then click Next.

7. Click Next on the remaining pages to complete the quorum configuration.

FIGURE 7.3
Viewing the block blobs used in an Azure storage account for the cloud witness

This can also be configured using PowerShell with one of the following commands, depending on your desired quorum configuration:

◆ Set-ClusterQuorum -NoWitness (Don't do this.)

◆ Set-ClusterQuorum -DiskWitness "<disk resource name>"

◆ Set-ClusterQuorum -FileShareWitness "<file share name>"

◆ Set-ClusterQuorum -CloudWitness -AccountName <storage account name> -AccessKey <access key>

◆ Set-ClusterQuorum -DiskOnly "<disk resource name>" (Don't do this either.)

WHICH ONE: FILE SHARE WITNESS, CLOUD WITNESS, OR DISK WITNESS?

You never want two or even three additional votes. The entire point of the witness vote is to provide an additional vote if you have an even number of votes caused by an even number of nodes.

You can decide whether it is better to have a disk witness, cloud witness, or a file share witness. If you have a multisite cluster, you most likely will have to use a file share witness or a cloud witness because there would not be shared storage between the two sites. The decision to use a cloud witness or file share witness will likely depend on whether you already have a third location to host the file share. If you have a third site, you can leverage a file share witness; however, if a third site is not available or you simply don't want to use or manage a file share, then use the cloud witness. Either way, it provides protection from a site failure.

In a cluster where shared storage is available, always use a disk witness over a file share cluster, and there is a good reason for this. When you use a file share witness, a folder is created on the file share named with the GUID of the cluster, and within that folder a file is created that is used in times of arbitration so that only one partition of a cluster can lock the file. Also, the file shows a timestamp of the last time a change was made to the main cluster database, although the file share does not have a copy of the cluster database. Every time a change is made to the cluster database, the timestamp on the file share witness is updated but the data is not stored on the file share witness, making the amount of network traffic very light.

Consider a scenario of a two-node cluster, node A and node B. If node A goes down, node B keeps running and makes updates to the cluster database, such as adding new resources, and it also updates the timestamp of witness.log on the file share witness. Then node B goes down, and

continues

continued

node A tries to start. Node A sees that the timestamp on the file share witness is in advance of its own database and realizes that its cluster database is stale, and so it will not start the cluster service. This prevents partition-in-time from occurring because node A is out-of-date (which is a good thing, because you don't want the cluster to start out-of-date) and you would have different cluster states on different nodes, but you can't start the cluster without node B coming back or forcing quorum on node A.

Now consider a disk witness that stores a complete copy of the cluster database. Every time a change is made to the cluster database, that change is also made to the copy of the cluster database on the disk witness.

Now in the same two-node cluster scenario, when node A tries to start and sees that its database is out-of-date, it can just copy the cluster database from the disk witness, which is kept up-to-date, so while a file share witness prevents partition-in-time from occurring, a disk witness solves partition-in-time.

For this reason, always use a disk witness over a file share witness or cloud witness if possible.

As you can see, the number of votes is key for a cluster quorum (specifically having more than 50 percent of the total number of votes), but the total number of votes can be a problem. Traditionally, the number of votes is set when the cluster is created, when the quorum mode is changed, or when nodes are added or removed from the cluster. For any cluster, the total number of votes is a hard number that can be changed only through one of the actions previously mentioned. Problems can occur, though. Consider a five-node cluster with no witness configured, which means that there are five possible votes and three votes must be available for the cluster to make quorum. Consider the following sequence of actions:

1. An administrator performs patching on a node, which requires reboots. The node is unavailable for a period of time, and therefore its vote is not available. This leaves four out of the five possible votes available, which is greater than 50 percent, so the cluster keeps quorum.

2. The administrator starts to perform maintenance on another node, which again requires reboots, losing the vote of the additional node and leaving three out of the five possible votes available. That is still greater than 50 percent, which keeps quorum and the node stays functional.

3. A failure in a node occurs, or the administrator is an overachiever and performs maintenance on another node, losing its vote. Now there are only two votes out of the five possible votes, which is less than 50 percent. The cluster loses quorum, the cluster services stop on the remaining two nodes, and all services in the cluster are no longer offered.

In this scenario, even though planned maintenance is going on and even though there are still two healthy nodes available, the cluster can no longer make quorum because less than 50 percent of the votes are available. The goal of clustering is to increase availability of services, but in this case it caused services to become unavailable.

Windows Server 2012 changed how the vote allocation works and cures the scenario just described with a feature called *dynamic quorum*. With dynamic quorum, the total number of votes available in the cluster changes as node states change; for example, if a node is taken down as part of maintenance, the node removes its vote from the cluster, reducing the total number of votes in the cluster. When the node comes out of maintenance, it adds its vote back, restoring the total number of possible votes to the original value. This means that the cluster has greater resiliency when it comes to problems caused by a lack of votes. Consider the preceding scenario in Windows Server 2012 with dynamic quorum:

1. An administrator performs patching on a node, which requires reboots, so the node is unavailable for a period of time. As the node goes into maintenance mode, it removes its vote from the cluster, reducing the total number of votes from five to four.

2. The administrator starts to perform maintenance on another node, which again requires reboots. The node removes its vote, reducing the total number of votes in the cluster to three.

3. A failure in a node occurs, or the administrator is an overachiever and performs maintenance on another node, losing its vote. Now only two votes are left, out of the three total votes, which is greater than 50 percent, so the cluster stays running! In fact, that node that is now unavailable will have its vote removed from the cluster by the remaining nodes.

The dynamic quorum feature may seem to introduce a possible problem to clustering, considering that the whole point of the votes and quorum is to protect the cluster from becoming split-brain, with multiple partitions offering services at the same time. With dynamic quorum in place and votes being removed from the cluster when nodes go into maintenance or fail, you may think, "Couldn't the cluster split and both parts make quorum?" The answer is no. There are still rules for how dynamic quorum can remove votes and keep quorum.

To be able to deterministically remove the vote of a cluster node, the remaining nodes must have quorum majority. For example, if I had a three-node cluster and one of the nodes fails, the remaining two nodes have quorum majority, two out of three votes, and therefore are able to remove the vote of the failed node, which means that the cluster now has two votes. Let's go back to our five-node cluster, which experiences a network failure. One partition has three nodes, and the other partition has two nodes. The partition with three nodes has quorum majority, which means that it keeps offering services and can therefore remove the votes of the other two nodes. The partition with two nodes does not have quorum majority, so the cluster service will shut down. The partition with three nodes now has a total vote count of three, which means that partition can now survive one of the three nodes failing, whereas without dynamic quorum, another node failure would have caused the cluster to shut down. This is shown in Figure 7.4.

With the ability to remove votes from the cluster as nodes fail or are shut down in a planned manner, it is now possible to go from a 64-node cluster all the way down to a single node, known as *last man standing*, provided the node shutdowns are sequential and a majority quorum is maintained with simultaneous node removals. It is important to note that if you remove a large number of nodes from a cluster, it is unlikely the remaining nodes would be able to run all of the services present in the cluster unless you had a highly underutilized cluster. Dynamic quorum is enabled by default, and the recommendation is to leave it enabled. Dynamic quorum is a cluster property, and if you want to disable it, this is done through PowerShell by setting the cluster `DynamicQuorum` property to 0 instead of the default 1, as in (`Get-Cluster`)

`.DynamicQuorum = 0`. Note that as nodes are resumed/fixed and communication is restored, the nodes votes are restored to the cluster. To summarize the dynamic quorum scenarios:

◆ When a node shuts down in a planned manner (an administrator shutdown or automated shutdown such as cluster-aware updating), the node removes its own vote.

◆ When a node crashes, the remaining active nodes remove the vote of the downed node.

◆ When a node joins the cluster, it gets its vote back.

FIGURE 7.4
Dynamic quorum in action

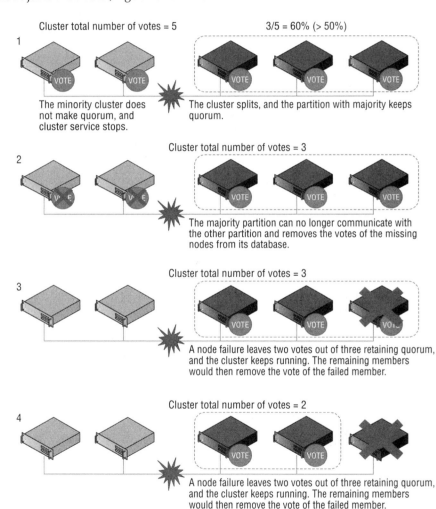

A feature called Node Vote Weights enables certain nodes to be specified as not participating in quorum calculations by removing the vote of the node. The node still fully participates in the cluster, it still has a copy of the cluster database, and it still runs cluster services and can host applications, but it no longer affects quorum calculations. There is only one scenario for which you would want to make this type of change, and that is for multisite clusters where failover must be manually performed, such as with a SQL Always On High Availability configuration using asynchronous replication that requires manual interaction to failover. In this scenario, the nodes in the remote site would have their votes removed so that they cannot affect quorum in the primary site.

Modifying Cluster Vote Configuration

Modification of votes can be performed using the Failover Cluster Manager graphical interface and PowerShell. To modify votes using the graphical tools, perform the following steps (note that the same process can be used to revert the cluster back to the default configuration of all nodes having votes):

1. In Failover Cluster Manager, select the main cluster object in the navigation pane.

2. From More Actions, select Configuration Cluster Quorum Settings.

3. Click Next on the introduction screen of the wizard.

4. Select the Advanced Quorum Configuration option, and click Next.

5. On the Select Voting Configuration page, choose the Select Nodes option, and then uncheck the nodes that should not have a vote, and click Next (see Figure 7.5). Note that on this screen, the default is All Nodes, meaning that all nodes should have a vote, but also that there is an option that no nodes have a vote, which means that only the disk witness has a vote. This is the original cluster quorum model and, frankly, it should never be used today because it introduces a single point of failure. It is there for historical reasons only.

FIGURE 7.5
Changing the votes for nodes in a cluster

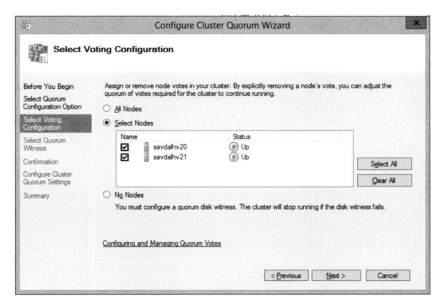

6. Click Next to all remaining screens. The witness configuration will be changed, and the modification will then be made to the cluster.

To make the change using PowerShell, set the vote of the node to 0 (instead of the default value of 1), as in this example:

```
(Get-ClusterNode <name>).NodeWeight=0
```

To view the current voting state of nodes in a cluster, use the Nodes view within Failover Cluster Manager, as shown in Figure 7.6. Note that two values are shown. The administrator-configured node weight is shown in the Assigned Vote column, while the cluster-assigned dynamic vote weight as controlled by dynamic quorum is shown in the Current Vote column. If you run a cluster validation, the generated report also shows the vote status of the nodes in the cluster. Remember, use the node vote weighting only in the specific geo-cluster scenarios requiring manual failover. In most scenarios, you should not manually change the node weights.

FIGURE 7.6

Viewing the current voting state of a cluster

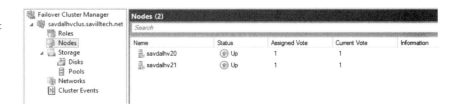

Earlier in this chapter, I explained that in Windows Server 2012 R2 and above, the guidance is always to configure a witness for the cluster. This is because the dynamic quorum technology has been extended to the witness in Windows Server 2012 R2; this technology is known as *dynamic witness*. Failover Clustering is now smart enough to decide whether the witness should have a vote or not:

◆ If an even number of nodes have a vote (dynamic weight = 1), the witness dynamic vote = 1.

◆ If an odd number of nodes have a vote (dynamic weight = 1), the witness dynamic vote = 0.

This is logical because the witness is needed only when there is an even number of nodes, which ordinarily would not be able to make quorum in the event of a split. If the witness goes offline or fails, its witness dynamic vote value will be set to 0 in the same manner a failed nodes vote is removed. To check whether the witness currently has a vote, run the following PowerShell command:

```
(Get-Cluster).WitnessDynamicWeight
```

A return value of 1 means that the witness has a vote; a return value of 0 means that the witness does not have a vote. If you look at the nodes in the cluster, the witness vote weight should correlate to the dynamic votes of the cluster nodes. To check the dynamic votes of the cluster nodes from PowerShell, use the following:

```
PS C:\> Get-ClusterNode | ft Name, DynamicWeight -AutoSize

Name          DynamicWeight
----          -------------
savdalhv20                1
savdalhv21                1
```

Advanced Quorum Options and Forcing Quorums

In all of the quorum explanations so far, the critical factor is that a majority of votes must be available for the cluster to keep running; that is, greater than 50 percent. At times an even number of votes will be in the cluster due to other failures (although dynamic witness should help avoid ever having an even number of votes unless it's the witness that has failed) or misconfiguration. Windows Server 2012 R2 and above provide tie-breaker code so that the cluster can now survive a simultaneous loss of 50 percent of the votes while ensuring that only one partition keeps running and the other partition shuts down. In the event of the loss of 50 percent of the votes, clustering will automatically select one of the partitions to "win" by using a specific algorithm.

The way the winning partition is selected is as follows: If an even number of node votes are in the cluster, the clustering service randomly selects a node and removes its vote. That changes the number of votes in the cluster to odd again, giving one of the sites a majority vote and therefore making it capable of surviving a break in communication. If you want to control which site should win if a break in communication occurs, you can set the cluster attribute `LowerQuorumPriorityNodeId` to the ID of the node that should lose its vote when you have an even number of nodes and no witness available. Remember, provided you have configured a witness, this functionality should not be required.

Even in single-site configurations, the same last-man-standing code will be implemented. If I have a single site with only two nodes left in the cluster and no witness, one of the nodes would lose its vote. Let's look in more detail at this "last two votes standing" scenario. as shown in Figure 7.7, which continues with the scenario we looked at in Figure 7.4. Note that in this example, there is no witness, which would not be best practice.

♦ If node B now has a failure, the cluster continues running on node A, because node A has the last remaining vote and has quorum majority (it has the single vote, so it has 100 percent of the vote and therefore > 50 percent).

♦ If node A has a failure and shuts down, then node B's cluster service will stop, because node A had the only vote and therefore node B has no vote and cannot make quorum.

♦ If a communication failure happens between node A and node B, then node A will keep running with quorum majority while node B's cluster service will stop.

♦ If node A shuts down cleanly, then before it shuts down it will transfer its vote to node B, which means that the cluster will continue running on node B.

FIGURE 7.7
Two remaining nodes in a cluster

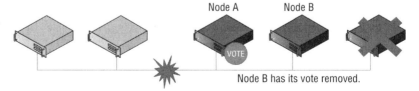

Node A   Node B

Node B has its vote removed.

With all of these new technologies, it's hard for the cluster to lose quorum. To lose quorum, the cluster would have to simultaneously lose more than half the number of votes, in which case you should shut down the cluster to protect the integrity of the services.

This brings us to forcing quorum. Consider a remote site that has a minority number of votes but in a disaster the cluster service must be started. Even in normal circumstances, at times nodes could be lost and the cluster service must be started even without quorum majority. This is known as *Forced Quorum*, and it allows the cluster to start without a majority of votes. When a cluster is started in Forced Quorum mode, it stays in that mode until a majority of nodes is available as they come online again, at which point the cluster automatically switches from Forced Quorum mode to the normal mode. To start the cluster in Forced Quorum mode, perform one of the following on *one* node that will be part of the Forced Quorum partition:

◆ Run the command `Start-ClusterNode -ForceQuorum`.

◆ Run the command `Net start clussvc /ForceQuorum`.

◆ Perform a forced start in Failover Cluster Manager.

All other nodes that will be part of the Forced Quorum should be started in Prevent Quorum mode, which tells the nodes that it must join an existing cluster, preventing different nodes from creating their own partitions by using one of the following methods:

◆ Run the command `Start-ClusterNode -PreventQuorum`.

◆ Run the command `Net start clussvc /PQ`.

◆ If you used Failover Cluster Manager to perform a force start, no action is required on other nodes. When you Force Quorum through the management tool, one node is picked to start with Force Quorum and then all other nodes that can be communicated with will be started with Prevent Quorum.

Windows Server 2012 R2 introduces Force Quorum resiliency, which is important when Force Quorum is used. Consider Figure 7.8, which shows how the cluster works when Forced Quorum is used. Step 1 shows that the partition with two nodes is started with Force Quorum. In step 2, the other partition starts and makes quorum because it has three out of five votes, so it has majority but no communication to the partition that started with Force Quorum. In step 3, the communication is restored and the partition with three nodes detects a partition that was started with Force Quorum. At this point, the three-node partition restarts the cluster service in Prevent Quorum mode on all nodes, which forces them to join the Force Quorum partition. In step 4, the merged cluster now has quorum majority and exits Force Quorum mode.

Care should be taken when using Force Quorum because it would potentially be possible to start the cluster service on multiple cluster partitions, which could cause big problems. Make sure that you understand what is happening within the cluster that has caused the cluster to lose quorum and be 100 percent certain that the cluster is not running in another location before performing Force Quorum.

FIGURE 7.8
Force Quorum resiliency in action

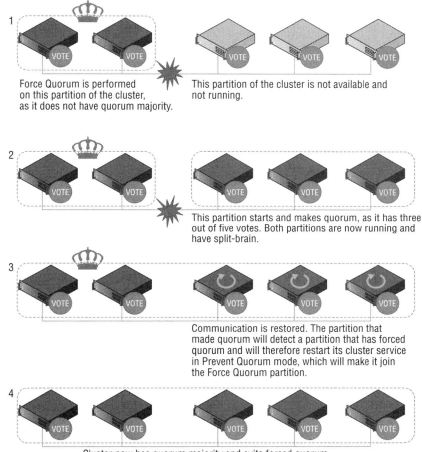

1 Force Quorum is performed on this partition of the cluster, as it does not have quorum majority.

This partition of the cluster is not available and not running.

2 This partition starts and makes quorum, as it has three out of five votes. Both partitions are now running and have split-brain.

3 Communication is restored. The partition that made quorum will detect a partition that has forced quorum and will therefore restart its cluster service in Prevent Quorum mode, which will make it join the Force Quorum partition.

4 Cluster now has quorum majority and exits forced quorum.

Geographically Distributed Clusters

With enhancements to networking, storage, and particularly Failover Clustering in Windows Server, it is much easier to have multisite clusters, and many of the quorum features discussed previously can be very useful. The first decision that must be made when dealing with a multi-site environment is how the switch of services between sites should be performed.

If the failover between sites is automatic, the sites can be considered equal. In that case, it's important to use a file share witness in a third location to ensure that if one site fails, the other site can use the witness vote and make quorum and offer services. If you have a synchronous storage replication solution that supports arbitration of storage, a disk witness could be used, but this is rare, which is why in most cases a file share witness would be used. It is important that both sites have an equal number of nodes. You would need to leverage a technology to replicate the storage used by Hyper-V virtual machines to the other location. If this type of SAN replication of storage is not available, the Hyper-V Replica technology can be leveraged. However, this would require separate clusters between locations and would not be an automated failover. The good news is that Windows Server 2016 has a native Storage Replica capability, and a stretched cluster is a specific scenario that Storage Replica has been designed to support and solve, providing automatic failover between sites.

Can I Host My File Share Witness in Microsoft Azure IaaS?

Microsoft Azure IaaS enables virtual machines to run in the Microsoft Azure cloud service, which can include a file server offering a file share that can be domain joined, making it seem a plausible option to host the witness for a cluster.

Technically, the answer is that the file share for a cluster could be hosted in a Microsoft Azure IaaS VM, and the Microsoft Azure virtual network can be connected to your on-premises infrastructure using its site-to-site gateway functionality or ExpressRoute. Both of these solutions can connect to multiple on-premises locations. However, while the use of a file share in Azure may be required for Windows Server 2012 R2 clusters, it is unnecessary in a Windows Server 2016 cluster since an Azure storage account can be directly used as the witness resource. Therefore, if you have a multisite cluster, the use of the cloud witness is likely the best solution.

The other option is a manual failover in which services are manually activated on the disaster-recovery site. In this scenario, it would be common to remove votes from the disaster-recovery site so that it does not affect quorum on the primary location. In the event of a failover to the disaster-recovery location, the disaster-recovery site would be started in a Force Quorum mode.

Both with Hyper-V and for other services hosted in a multisite cluster, there is often the concept of a primary site and a secondary or DR site. If a split occurs in the cluster communications, the requirement is to control which of the partitions keeps running (that is, the primary site). One option is the `LowerQuorumPriorityNodeID` property I referred to earlier, which is configured on the cluster to indicate a specific node that in the event of a 50-50 vote split would lose its vote, thereby causing its partition to lose quorum and keep the other partition running. You would configure this node as one in the secondary location.

The challenge is that `LowerQuorumPriorityNodeID` applies in only a 50-50 split, which often will not be the case, as in Windows Server 2012 R2 you should always configure a witness resource that dynamically has its vote status changed depending on the number of nodes and ensures that there is always an odd number of votes. What actually happens is that the core cluster group is owned by a node in the cluster, and that core cluster group includes the witness resource. In the event of a cluster split, the partition that already owns the core cluster group and therefore the witness will typically keep it and therefore maintain quorum. This means that you can proactively move the core cluster group to a node in your preferred site to help ensure that site would stay active. It can be moved by using the following:

```
Move-ClusterGroup "cluster group" -Node <target node>
```

It can also be moved through Failover Cluster Manager via the More Actions ➤ Move Core Cluster Resources context menu for the cluster.

Therefore, make sure that the core cluster group is running on your preferred site *and* set `LowerQuorumPriorityNodeID` to a node in the secondary site to try to ensure that your primary site will win in the event of a split. This is not very pretty, and it gets much better with Windows Server 2016, as will be explored shortly.

In reality, it was not that common to see stretched clusters for Hyper-V virtual machines because of the historical difficulty and high expense of replicating the storage prior to Windows Server 2016. Additionally, if virtual machines moved between locations, most likely their IP configuration would require reconfiguration unless network virtualization was being used or VLANs were stretched between locations, which again is rare and can be expensive. In the next chapter, I cover Hyper-V Replica as a solution for disaster recovery, which solves the problems of moving virtual machines between sites. Multisite clusters are commonly used for application workloads, such as SQL and Exchange, instead of for Hyper-V virtual machines.

As mentioned, Windows Server 2016 changes multisite cluster practicality in numerous ways, and not just with the introduction of Storage Replica to enable storage replication between locations. Clustering has become site aware in Windows Server 2016, providing enhanced multisite cluster capabilities. Site awareness enables nodes to be grouped based on their physical location. This knowledge of physical location is used in various ways by clustering:

◆ When a node fails or needs to be drained, the resources are moved to nodes in the same site if possible.

◆ VMs follow the site owning the CSV, so if a CSV moves to a new site, the VMs will follow within a minute via Live Migration.

◆ A primary site can be defined that in the event of a split and all other things being equal will maintain quorum and offer services, as dynamic quorum prunes nodes from the nonpreferred site first. The preferred site is also used at startup; VMs will start in the preferred site first.

◆ Heartbeats behave differently within a site and between sites instead of being based on IP subnets (which still exist and are explored later in this chapter). The cluster has two additional properties in Windows Server 2016 to support the new site awareness: CrossSiteDelay and CrossSiteThreshold. These properties define the time between heartbeats in milliseconds (1,000 by default) and the number of missed heartbeats before the connection is considered down (20 by default), respectively. These can be modified by using the following:

```
(Get-Cluster).CrossSiteDelay = <value>
(Get-Cluster).CrossSiteThreshold = <value>
```

There are two modes for site awareness: automatic and manual. To enable automatic site-awareness based on Active Directory sites for the cluster, use this:

```
(Get-Cluster).AutoAssignNodeSite = 1
```

To manually define, you must first create the sites and then assign the site to nodes. For example:

```
#Create Sites
New-ClusterFaultDomain -Name Dallas -Type Site -Description "Primary" -Location
"Dallas DC"
New-ClusterFaultDomain -Name Houston -Type Site -Description "Secondary" -
Location "Houston DC"
#Set site membership for nodes
Set-ClusterFaultDomain -Name Node1 -Parent Dallas
```

```
Set-ClusterFaultDomain -Name Node2 -Parent Dallas
Set-ClusterFaultDomain -Name Node3 -Parent Houston
Set-ClusterFaultDomain -Name Node4 -Parent Houston
```

Once you set the preferred site for a 2016 cluster that has sites defined, use this:

```
(Get-Cluster).PreferredSite = <site name, e.g. Dallas>
```

If you have the situation with multiactive datacenters, you can define different preferred sites for different cluster groups that will be used to govern where VMs start initially:

```
(Get-ClusterGroup <group>).PreferredSite = <site name>
```

Note that because of the various levels of preference, it may be confusing which one wins. The order of priority for placement is as follows:

1. Storage affinity

2. Group preferred site

3. Cluster preferred site

Why Use Clustering with Hyper-V?

In the previous sections, I went into a lot of detail about quorum and how clusters work. The key point is this: Clusters help keep the workloads available with a minimal amount of downtime, even in unplanned outages. For Hyper-V servers that are running many virtual machines, keeping the virtual machines as available as possible is critical.

When looking at high availability, there are two types of outage: planned and unplanned. A *planned outage* is a known and controlled outage—for example, when you are rebooting a host to apply patches or performing hardware maintenance or even powering down a complete datacenter. In a planned outage scenario, it is possible to avoid any downtime to the virtual machines by performing a Live Migration of the virtual machines on one node to another node. When Live Migration is used, the virtual machine is always available to clients.

An *unplanned outage* is not foreseen or planned, such as in the case of a server crash or hardware failure. In an unplanned outage, there is no opportunity to perform Live Migration of virtual machines between nodes, which means that there will be a period of unavailability for the virtual machines. In an unplanned outage scenario, the cluster will detect that a node has failed and the resources that were running on the failed node will be redistributed among the remaining nodes in the cluster and then started. Because the virtual machines were effectively just powered off without a clean shutdown of the guest OS inside the virtual machines, the guest OS will start in what is known as a *crash-consistent state*, which means that when the guest OS starts and applications in the guest OS start, there may be some consistency and repair actions required.

In Windows Server 2008 R2, the Live Migration feature for moving virtual machines with no downtime between servers was available only between nodes in a cluster, because the storage had to be available to both the source and target node. In Windows Server 2012, the ability to live-migrate between any two Hyper-V 2012 hosts was introduced. It's known as *Shared Nothing Live Migration*, and it migrates the storage in addition to the memory and state of the virtual machine.

One traditional feature of clustering was the ability to move storage smoothly between nodes in a cluster. It was enhanced greatly with Windows Server 2008 R2 to allow storage to be shared between the nodes in a cluster simultaneously; it's known as *Cluster Shared Volumes (CSV)*. With CSV, an NTFS volume can be accessed by all of the nodes at the same time, allowing virtual machines to be stored on a single NTFS-formatted LUN and run on different nodes in the cluster. The sharing of storage is a huge feature of clusters, and it makes the migration of virtual machines between nodes a much more efficient process because only the memory and state of the virtual machine needs to be migrated and not the actual storage. Of course, in Windows Server 2012, nodes not in a cluster can share storage by accessing a common SMB 3 file share, but many environments do not have the infrastructure to utilize SMB 3 at a datacenter level or already have large SAN investments.

As you can see, some of the features of clustering for Hyper-V are now available outside of a cluster at some level, but not with the same level of efficiency and typically only in planned scenarios. Additionally, a cluster provides a boundary of host membership, which can be used for other purposes, such as virtual machine rebalancing, placement optimization, and even automation processes such as cluster patching. I cover migration, CSV, and the other technologies briefly mentioned in detail later in this chapter.

Clustering brings high availability solutions to unplanned scenarios, but it also brings some other features to virtual machine workloads. It is because of some of these features that occasionally you will see a single-node cluster of virtual machines. Hyper-V has great availability features, but they are no substitute for clustering to maintain availability during unplanned outages and to simplify maintenance options, so don't overlook clustering.

Service Monitoring

Failover Clustering provides high availability to the virtual machine in the event of a host failure, but it does not provide protection or assistance if a service within the virtual machine fails. Clustering is strictly making sure that the virtual machine is running; it offers no assistance to the operating system running within the virtual machine.

Windows Server 2012 clustering changed this by introducing a new clustering feature, *service monitoring*, which allows clustering to communicate to the guest OS running within the virtual machine and to check for service failures. If you examine the properties of a service within Windows, actions are available if the service fails, as shown in Figure 7.9. Note that in the Recovery tab, Windows allows actions to be taken on the first failure, the second failure, and then subsequent failures. These actions are as follows:

◆ Take No Action

◆ Restart The Service

◆ Run A Program

◆ Restart The Computer

Consider that if a service fails three times consecutively, it's unlikely that restarting it a third time would result in a different outcome. Clustering can be configured to perform the action that is known to fix any problem and reboot the virtual machine on the existing host. If the virtual machine is rebooted by clustering and the service fails a subsequent time inside the virtual machine, then clustering will move the virtual machine to another host in the cluster and reboot it.

FIGURE 7.9
Service retry actions

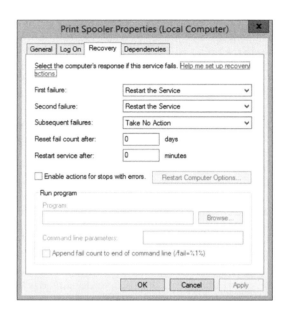

For this feature to work, the following must be configured:

◆ Both the Hyper-V servers must be Windows Server 2012 or above, and the guest OS running in the VM must be Windows Server 2012 or above.

◆ The host and guest OSs are in the same or at least trusting domains.

◆ The failover cluster administrator must be a member of the local administrator's group inside the VM.

◆ The service being monitored must be set to Take No Action (see Figure 7.9) within the guest VM for subsequent failures (which is used after the first and second failures), and it is set via the Recovery tab of the service properties within the Services application (services.msc).

◆ Within the guest VM, the Virtual Machine Monitoring firewall exception must be enabled for the Domain network by using the Windows Firewall with Advanced Security application or by using the following Windows PowerShell command:

```
Set-NetFirewallRule -DisplayGroup "Virtual Machine Monitoring" -Enabled True
```

After everything in the preceding list is configured, enabling the monitoring is a simple process:

1. Launch the Failover Cluster Manager tool.

2. Navigate to the cluster and select Roles.

3. Right-click the virtual machine role for which you wish to enable monitoring, and under More Actions, select Configure Monitoring.

4. The services running inside the VM will be gathered by the cluster service communicating to the guest OS inside the virtual machine. Select the check box for the services that should be monitored, as shown in Figure 7.10, and click OK.

FIGURE 7.10
Enabling monitoring
of a service

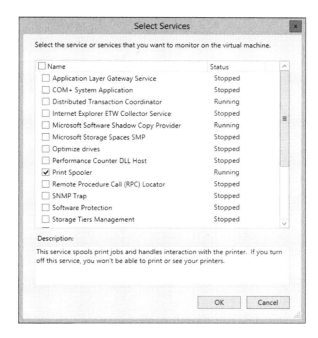

Monitoring can also be enabled using the `Add-ClusterVMMonitoredItem` cmdlet and `-VirtualMachine`, with the `-Service` parameters, as in this example:

```
PS C:\ > Add-ClusterVMMonitoredItem -VirtualMachine savdaltst01 -Service spooler
```

After two service failures, an event ID 1250 is logged in the system log. At this point, the VM will be restarted, initially on the same host. On subsequent failures, however, it will restart on another node in the cluster. This process can be seen in a video located at `http://youtu.be/H1EghdniZ1I`.

This is a rudimentary capability, but it may help in some scenarios. As mentioned in the previous chapter, for a complete monitoring solution, leverage System Center Operations Manager, which can run monitoring with deep OS and application knowledge that can be used to generate alerts. Those alerts can be used to trigger automated actions for remediation or simply to generate incidents in a ticketing system.

Protected Network

While the operating system and applications within virtual machines perform certain tasks, the usefulness of those tasks is generally being able to communicate with services via the network. If the network is unavailable on the Hyper-V host that the virtual machine uses, traditionally clustering would take no action, which has been a huge weakness. As far as clustering is aware, the virtual machine is still fine; it's running with no problems. Windows Server 2012 R2 introduced the concept of a protected network to solve this final gap in high availability of virtual machines and their connectivity.

The Protected Network setting allows specific virtual network adapters to be configured as protected, as shown in Figure 7.11, via the Settings option of a virtual machine and the Advanced Features options of the specific network adapter. If the Hyper-V host loses network connectivity that the virtual machine network adapters configured as a protected network are using, the virtual machines will be live-migrated to another host in the cluster that does have network connectivity for that network. This does require that the Hyper-V host still have network connectivity between the Hyper-V hosts to allow Live Migration, but typically clusters will use different networks for virtual machine connectivity than those used for Live Migration purposes, which means Live Migration should still be possible.

FIGURE 7.11
Configuring a protected network on a virtual machine network adapter

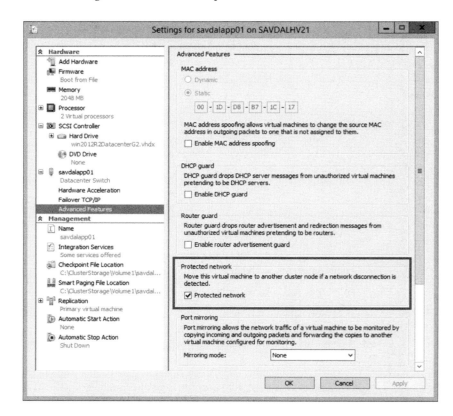

It is important to try to provide as much resiliency as possible for network communications, which means using NIC Teaming on the hosts as described in Chapter 3, "Virtual Networking," but the protected network features provide an additional layer of resiliency to network failures.

Cluster-Aware Updating

Windows Server 2012 placed a huge focus on running the Server Core configuration level, which reduced the amount of patching and therefore reboots required for a system. There will still be patches that need to be installed and therefore reboots, but the key point is to reduce (or ideally, eliminate) any impact to the virtual machines when hosts have to be rebooted.

In a typical cluster, any impact to virtual machines is removed by live-migrating virtual machines off of a node, patching and rebooting that node, moving the virtual machines back, and repeating for the other nodes in the cluster. This sounds simple, but for a 64-node cluster, this is a lot of work.

SCVMM 2012 introduced the ability to automate the entire cluster patching process with a single click, and this capability was made a core part of Failover Clustering in Windows Server 2012. It's called *Cluster-Aware Updating* (CAU). With CAU, updates are obtained from Microsoft Update or an on-premises Windows Server Update Services (WSUS) implementation, and the entire cluster is patched with no impact on the availability of virtual machines.

I walk through the entire Cluster-Aware Updating configuration and usage at the following location:

```
http://windowsitpro.com/windows-server-2012/
cluster-aware-updating-windows-server-2012
```

Both SCVMM cluster patching and the native Windows Server Cluster-Aware Updating can leverage WSUS or Windows Update, but they cannot use System Center Configuration Manager, which many organizations use as their patch solution. System Center Configuration Manager 2016 has its own cluster awareness now, which enables a rolling cluster patch process. Additionally, Configuration Manager includes the ability to specify what percentage of the cluster may stay online during the operation and additionally pre- and post-scripts can be set as each node has actions performed. The only requirement is that all the nodes in the cluster may be in their own Configuration Manager collection, as this is where the configuration is applied. A change is made to the collection, specifically selecting the All Devices Are Part Of The Same Server Cluster check box, which will enable the Settings button as part of the collection properties. Under the Settings, there are a number of options, as shown in Figure 7.12. Patching when applied will respect these configurations as will other maintenance operations, giving easy ability to patch clusters.

FIGURE 7.12
Cluster operations settings in Configuration Manager 2016

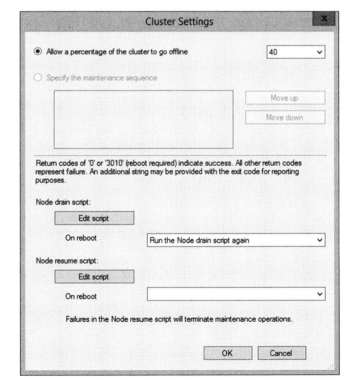

Where to Implement High Availability

With the great features available with Hyper-V clustering, it can be easy to think that clustering the Hyper-V hosts and therefore providing high availability for all of the virtual machines is the only solution you need. Clustering the Hyper-V hosts definitely provides great mobility, storage sharing, and high availability services for virtual machines, but that doesn't mean it's always the best solution.

Consider an application such as SQL Server or Exchange. If clustering is performed only at the Hyper-V host level, then if the Hyper-V host fails, the virtual machine resource is moved to another host and then started in a crash-consistent state; the service would be unavailable for a period of time, and likely an amount of consistency checking and repair would be required. Additionally, the host-level clustering will not protect from a crash within the virtual machine where the actual service is no longer running but the guest OS is still functioning, and therefore no action is needed at the host level. If instead guest clustering was leveraged, which means a cluster is created within the guest operating systems running in the virtual machines, the full cluster-aware application capabilities will be available—for example, detecting that the application service is not responding on one guest OS, allowing another instance of the application to take over. Guest clustering is fully supported in Hyper-V virtual machines, and as covered in Chapter 4, "Storage Configurations," numerous options provide shared storage to guest clusters, such as iSCSI, virtual Fibre Channel, and shared VHDX.

The guidance I give is as follows:

◆ If the application running inside the virtual machine is cluster aware, then create multiple virtual machines, each with the application installed, and create a guest cluster between them. This will likely mean enabling some kind of shared storage for those virtual machines.

◆ If the application is not cluster aware but works with technologies such as Network Load Balancing (NLB)—for example, IIS—then deploy multiple virtual machines, each running the service, and then use NLB to load-balance between the instances.

◆ If the application running inside the virtual machine is not cluster aware or NLB supported, but multiple instances of the application are supported and the application has its own methods of distributing load and HA (for example, Active Directory Domain Services), then deploy multiple instances over multiple virtual machines.

◆ Finally, if there is no application-native high-availability option, rely on the Hyper-V cluster, which is better than nothing.

It is important to check whether applications support not only running inside a virtual machine (nearly all applications do today) but also running on a Hyper-V cluster, and extending that, whether they support being live-migrated between hosts. Some applications initially did not support being live-migrated for technical reasons, or they were licensed by physical processors, which meant that moving the virtual machine between hosts was expensive because all processors on all possible hosts would have to be licensed. Most applications have now moved beyond restrictions of physical processor instance licensing, but still check!

You should perform another configuration on your Hyper-V cluster for virtual machines that contain multiple instances of an application (for example, multiple SQL Server VMs, multiple IIS VMs, multiple domain controllers, and so on). The goal of using multiple instances of applications is to provide protection from the VM failing or the host that is running the virtual machines from failing. Having multiple instances of an application across multiple virtual machines is not useful if all of the virtual machines are running on the same host. Fortunately, Failover Clustering has an anti-affinity capability, which ensures where possible that virtual machines in the same anti-affinity group are not placed on the same Hyper-V host. To set the anti-affinity group for a virtual machine, use `cluster.exe` or PowerShell:

◆ `(Get-ClusterGroup "<VM>").AntiAffinityClassNames = "<AntiAffinityGroupName>"`

◆ `cluster.exe group "<VM>" /prop AntiAffinityClassNames="<AntiAffinityGroupName>"`

The cluster affinity can be set graphically by using SCVMM, as shown in Figure 7.13. SCVMM uses *availability set* as the nomenclature instead of *anti-affinity group*. Open the properties of the virtual machine in SCVMM, navigate to the Hardware Configuration tab, and select Availability under the Advanced section. Use the Manage Availability Sets button to create new sets and then add them to the virtual machine. A single virtual machine can be a member of multiple availability sets.

FIGURE 7.13
Setting affinity by using SCVMM

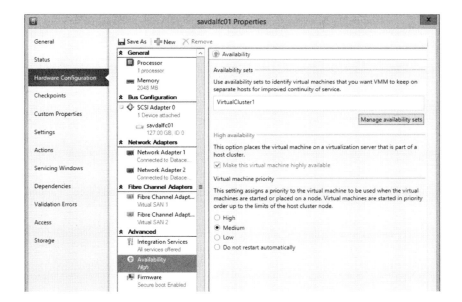

By default, this anti-affinity solution is a soft enforcement: Clustering will do its best to keep virtual machines in the same anti-affinity group on separate hosts, but if it has no choice, it will place instances on the same host. This enforcement can be set to hard by setting the cluster `ClusterEnforcedAntiAffinity` attribute to 1, but this may mean that virtual machines may not be able to be started.

For virtual machines that are clustered, it is possible to set the preferred owners for each virtual machine and set the order of their preference. However, it's important to realize that just because a host is not set as a preferred owner for a resource (virtual machine), that doesn't mean that the host can't still run that resource if none of the preferred owners are available. To set the preferred owners, right-click a VM resource and select Properties, and in the General tab, set the preferred owners and the order as required.

If you want to ensure that a resource never runs on specific hosts, you can set the possible owners. When a resource is restricted to possible owners, it cannot run on hosts that are not possible owners. This should be used with care, because if no possible owners are available that are configured, the resource cannot start, which may be worse than it just not running on a nonoptimal host. To set the possible owners, you need to modify the cluster group of the virtual machine, which is in the bottom pane of Failover Cluster Manager. Right-click the virtual machine resource group and select Properties. Under the Advanced Policies tab, the possible owners are shown. If you unselect servers, that specific virtual machine cannot run on the unselected servers.

The same PowerShell cmdlet is used, Set-ClusterOwnerNode, to set both the preferred and possible owners. If the cmdlet is used against a cluster resource (that is, a virtual machine), it sets the preferred owners. If it is used against a cluster group, it sets the possible owners.

It's common where possible to cluster the Hyper-V hosts to provide mobility and high availability for the virtual machines and create guest clusters where applications running within the virtual machines are cluster aware. This can be seen in Figure 7.14.

FIGURE 7.14
Guest cluster running within a Hyper-V host cluster

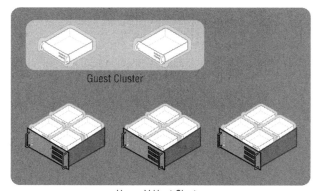

Guest Cluster

Hyper-V Host Cluster

Configuring a Hyper-V Cluster

Creating a Hyper-V cluster is essentially the same process as creating any cluster running on Windows Server 2012 or above. You need to follow some general guidelines:

- Ensure that the nodes in the cluster are running the same hardware, especially for the processor. If different generations of processor are used, it may be required to configure the processor compatibility attribute on virtual machines to enable migration between hosts without downtime.

- Ensure access to shared storage to enable virtual machines to be stored on Cluster Shared Volumes.

◆   Network connectivity is required, such as for virtual machines and management but also for cluster communications and Live Migration. I went over the network requirements in detail in Chapter 3, but I review them in the next section. It is important that all nodes in the cluster have connectivity to the same networks to avoid loss of connectivity if VMs move between different servers.

◆   Each node must be running the same version of Windows and should be at the same patch/service pack level.

The good news is that the process to create a cluster actually checks your potential environment through a validation process, and then only if everything passes validation do you proceed and create the cluster. The validation process gives a lot of information and performs in-depth checks and should be used anytime you wish to make a change to the cluster, such as when adding another node. It's also possible to run the validation without any changes because it can be a great troubleshooting tool. If you experience problems or errors, run the cluster validation, which may give you some ideas of the problems. The validation process also has some checks specific to Hyper-V.

Cluster Network Requirements and Configurations

Before I go into detail on validating and creating a cluster, this section touches on the networking requirements for a Hyper-V cluster and, specifically, requirements related to the cluster network.

The cluster network is critical to enable hosts in a cluster to communicate with each other. This is important for health monitoring, to ensure that hosts are still running and responsive. If a server becomes unresponsive, the cluster takes remedial actions. This is done via a heartbeat that is sent by default every second over port 3343 (both UDP and TCP). This heartbeat is not a basic "ping" but rather a request-reply type of process for the highest level of reliability and security that is implemented as part of the cluster NetFT kernel driver, which I talk more about in the next section "Cluster Virtual Network Adapter." By default, if a node does not respond to five consecutive heartbeats, it is considered down, and the recovery actions are performed.

If the cluster network fails, clustering will use another network that has been configured to allow cluster communications if needed. It is important always to have at least two networks configured to allow cluster communications.

The requirements of the cluster network have changed since early versions of clustering because the cluster network is not just used for heartbeat communications, but it is also used for Cluster Shared Volumes communications, which now leverage SMB. The use of SMB means that the cluster network adapter must have both the Client For Microsoft Networks and File And Printer Sharing For Microsoft Networks bound, as shown in Figure 7.15. Note that you can disable the Link-Layer services because they are not required for the cluster communications.

It's also important that the Server and Workstation Services are running on the hosts and NTLM is used for authentication, so they must be enabled. Both IPv4 and IPv6 are supported for cluster communications, and although Microsoft performs most testing with IPv6 enabled, if it's disabled, clustering will still work fine. However, where possible leave IPv6 enabled. If both IPv4 and IPv6 are enabled, clustering will use IPv6. Disabling NetBIOS, as shown in Figure 7.16, has been shown to increase performance, and while enabling jumbo frames will not hurt, it has not been found to make any significant performance difference.

FIGURE 7.15
Binding for network adapters used for cluster communications

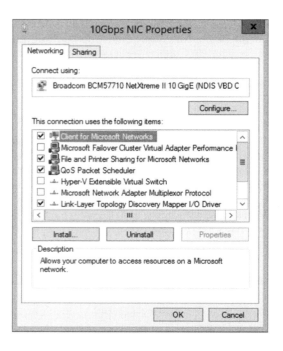

FIGURE 7.16
Disabling NetBIOS for the IPv4 protocol

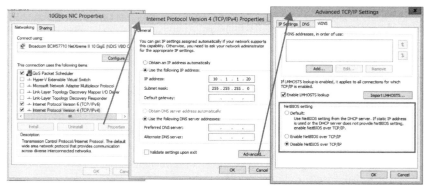

The binding order for the network adapters in a multinetwork adapter system is important. It tells Windows which network adapter to use for different types of communication. For example, you would not want normal management traffic trying to use the Live Migration or the cluster network. You can change the binding order for network adapters by using the following steps:

1. Open the Network And Sharing Center Control Panel applet.

2. Select the Change Adapter Settings action.

3. In Network Connections, press the Alt key to see the menu and select Advanced ➤ Advanced Settings.

4. The binding order is displayed. Make sure that your management network/ public network is at the top of the binding order. Your cluster networks should be at the bottom, as shown in Figure 7.17.

FIGURE 7.17
Setting the network adapter binding order

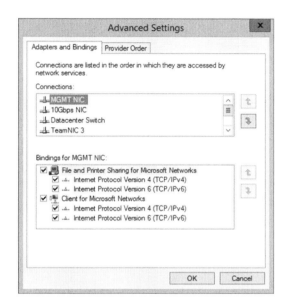

5. Click OK to close the dialog box.

A network topology generator is used to build the various cluster networks that are available to clustering. If multiple network adapters exist that are on the same IP subnet, they will automatically be grouped into the same cluster network. This is important to understand from a resiliency perspective. Imagine that you place two NICs in a node, both on the same subnet, that you wish clustering to use for high availability. What will happen is that both NICs will be placed in the same cluster network and only one of them will be used, removing any redundancy. The correct way to achieve redundancy in this situation is to use NIC Teaming to join the two NICs. When you have NICs on different subnets, they will be seen as different cluster networks, and then clustering can utilize them for high availability across the different network routes. If you were looking to leverage SMB multichannel, you would need to place each NIC on a different subnet, which is a cluster-specific requirement, because normally SMB multichannel will work with NICs on the same subnet.

By default, the cluster creation process will use the network topology generator, and the most appropriate network to be used for clustering will be automatically selected based on connectivity. However, this can be changed after the cluster is created. Automatic metrics are used to determine the network used for clustering and other services based on the automatic configurations made by the cluster wizard and your customizations post creation. Figure 7.18 shows the properties available for each network available to Failover Clustering. Note that the network adapters used by Hyper-V virtual switches are not shown because they effectively offer no services to the Hyper-V host itself.

FIGURE 7.18
Cluster network
properties

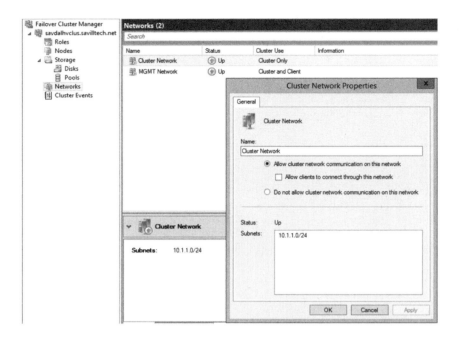

Notice that for each network, the following options are available, which are initially configured during clustering setup based on the IP configuration of the network adapter and whether
a gateway was configured. These configure the role of the networks in relation to cluster activities, and they also have a numeric value, shown in square brackets:

Allow Cluster Network Communication On This Network [1] This is set automatically
for any IP-enabled network adapter, and it allows the cluster to use this network if necessary unless the iSCSI Software Initiator is bound to the IP address, in which case this is not
configured.

Allow Clients To Connect Through This Network [3] This is set automatically if the IP
configuration for the network adapter has a gateway defined, which suggests external communication and therefore client communication.

Do Not Allow Cluster Network Communication On This Network [0] The cluster cannot
use this network. This would be configured on something like an iSCSI network, which is
automatically set if the iSCSI Software Initiator is bound to the IP address.

These roles can also be configured by using this PowerShell command:

```
(Get-ClusterNetwork "<network name>").Role=<new role number>
```

These three settings are used by clustering to create an automatic metric for each network
adapter, which sets the priority for the preferred network to be used for cluster communications
from all those available. You can see the metrics by using the following PowerShell:

```
PS C:\> Get-ClusterNetwork | ft Name, Role, AutoMetric, Metric -AutoSize

Name              Role AutoMetric Metric
__                _____
```

```
Cluster Network    1        True   30240
MGMT Network       3        True   70384
```

The lower the metric value, the cheaper it is considered to be and therefore a greater preference to be used for cluster communications. The way these values are calculated is primarily on the role of the cluster, which sets a starting value for the metric:

◆ Role of 1: Starting metric 40000

◆ Role of 3: Starting metric of 80000

Then the metric is reduced for each NIC, based on its link speed and whether it's RDMA capable and has RSS capabilities. The higher the performance and feature set of the NIC, the greater the metric reduction, making it cheaper and therefore more appealing to be used for cluster communications. It is possible to change these metric values by disabling AutoMetric on the cluster network and then manually setting a metric value, but generally this should not be performed. Note that this prioritization of networks for cluster communications does not apply to SMB-based communications; SMB uses its own selection mechanism. If you did need to modify the metric, use the following:

```
(Get-ClusterNetwork "<cluster network>".AutoMetric = $false
(Get-ClusterNetwork "<cluster network>".Metric = 42
```

When considering network capacity planning for network traffic, it's important to realize that in addition to network health monitoring (heartbeats) traffic, the cluster network is used for intra-cluster communications such as cluster database updates and CSV I/O redirection.

The heartbeat communications are lightweight (134 bytes, to be exact) in Windows Server 2012 R2 and Windows Server 2016, and they are sent by default once a second. You don't require a big network pipe (that is, bandwidth), but the heartbeats are sensitive to latency (the lag between a request and response), because if too many heartbeats are not acknowledged in a period of time, the host is considered unavailable.

Intra-cluster communication traffic related to cluster database changes and state changes is light but does vary slightly, depending on the type of workload. Our focus is Hyper-V, which has light intra-cluster communications, but a SQL or Exchange cluster tends to have a higher amount of traffic. Once again, though, the size of the pipe is not as important as the latency. This is because in the event of a cluster state change, such as a node being removed from the cluster, the state change is synchronous among all nodes in the cluster. This means before the state change completes, it must have been synchronously applied to every node in the cluster, potentially 64 nodes. A high-latency network would slow state changes in the cluster and therefore affect how fast services could be moved in the event of a failure.

The final type of communication over the cluster network is CSV I/O redirection. There are two types of CSV communication, which I cover in detail later in this chapter, but both use SMB for communication. *Metadata updates*, such as file extend operations and file open/close operations, are lightweight and fairly infrequent, but they are sensitive to latency because latency will slow I/O performance. In *asymmetric storage access*, all I/O is performed over the network instead of just the Metadata. This asymmetric access, or redirected mode, is not the normal storage mode for the cluster and typically happens in certain failure scenarios such as a node losing Direct Access to the storage and requiring its storage access to be fulfilled by another node. If asymmetric access is used, the bandwidth of the network is important to handle the I/O.

The takeaway from the preceding explanation is that typically the bandwidth is not important; the latency is the critical factor, which is why traditionally the cluster had a dedicated network. As described in Chapter 3, it is now possible to use a converged network, but you should leverage quality of service (QoS) to ensure that the cluster network gets the required bandwidth and, more important, priority for its traffic because a high priority will ensure as low a latency level as possible. In Chapter 3, I focused on the bandwidth aspect of QoS because for most workloads that is most critical. However, you can also use QoS to prioritize certain types of traffic, which we want to do for cluster traffic when using converged fabric. The code that follows is PowerShell for Windows Server 2016 (and it also works on Windows Server 2012 R2) that sets prioritization of traffic types. Note that the priority values range from 0 to 6, with 6 being the highest priority.

Once created, the policies can be applied using the `Set-NetQoSPolicy` cmdlet:

```
New-NetQoSPolicy "Cluster" -Cluster -Priority 6
New-NetQoSPolicy "Live Migration" -LiveMigration -Priority 4
```

You can find details on `New-NetQoSPolicy` and the types of built-in filters available here:

```
http://technet.microsoft.com/en-us/library/hh967468.aspx
```

With QoS correctly configured, you no longer have to use a dedicated network just for clustering and can take advantage of converged environments without sacrificing performance.

I've mentioned several times the heartbeat frequency of once a second and that if five consecutive heartbeats are missed, then a node is considered unavailable and removed from the cluster and any resources it owns are moved to other nodes in the cluster. Remember that the goal of clustering is to make services as available as possible; a failed node needs to be detected as quickly as possible so that its resources and therefore its workloads are restarted on another node as quickly as possible. The challenge here, though, is that if the networking is not as well architected as you would like, 5 seconds could be just a network hiccup and not a host failure (which with today's server hardware is far less common, as most components are redundant in a server and motherboards don't catch fire frequently). The outage caused by moving virtual machines to other nodes and then booting them (because remember, the cluster considered the unresponsive node gone and so it could not live-migrate the VMs) is far bigger than the few seconds of network hiccup. This is seen commonly in Hyper-V environments, where networking is not always given the consideration it deserves, which makes 5 seconds very aggressive.

The frequency of the heartbeat and the threshold for missed heartbeats is configurable:

- ◆ `SameSubnetDelay`: Frequency of heartbeats, 1 second by default and maximum of 2
- ◆ `SameSubnetThreshold`: Number of heartbeats that can be missed consecutively, 5 by default with maximum of 120

You should be careful when modifying the values. Generally, don't change the delay of the heartbeat. Only the threshold value should be modified, but realize that the greater the threshold, the greater the tolerance to network hiccups but the longer it will take to react to an actual problem. A good compromise threshold value is 10, which happens automatically for a Hyper-V cluster. As soon as a virtual machine role is created on a cluster in Windows Server 2012 R2 or above, the cluster goes into a relaxed threshold mode (instead of the normal Fast Failover); a node is considered unavailable after 10 missed heartbeats instead of 5. The value can be viewed using PowerShell:

```
(Get-Cluster).SameSubnetThreshold
10
```

Without any configuration, the Hyper-V cluster in Windows Server 2012 R2 will automatically use the relaxed threshold mode, allowing greater tolerance to network hiccups. If you have cluster nodes in different locations, and therefore different subnets, there is a separate value for the heartbeat delay, CrossSubnetDelay (new maximum is 4), and the threshold, CrossSubnetThreshold (same maximum of 120). Once again, for Hyper-V, the CrossSubnetThreshold value is automatically tuned to 20 instead of the default 5. Note that the automatic relaxed threshold is only for Hyper-V clusters and not for any other type of workload. Remember also that Windows Server 2016 has site awareness and will utilize the site thresholds instead of subnet thresholds, but by default the values are the same.

Windows Server 2016 introduces additional resiliency options to solve many of the causes of service interruption today that are related to the factors previously mentioned (suboptimal cluster configurations). A transient failure in network or storage connectivity would cause VMs to be moved or crash, resulting in outages far longer than the actual transient network or storage issue.

Compute resiliency is enabled by default and changes the behavior of nodes when they lose connectivity to the rest of the cluster. Prior to Windows Server 2016, if a node lost connectivity to other nodes in the cluster, it would become partitioned, lose quorum, and no longer be able to host services. This would result in any VMs currently running on the node to be restarted on other nodes in the cluster, resulting in an outage for many minutes, whereas the actual network interruption may have been over in 15 seconds. In this scenario, clustering is causing a greater outage than the underlying network issue. Compute resiliency enables the node to behave differently when it loses connectivity to other nodes in the cluster that could be caused by networking issues or even a crash of the cluster service.

Compute resiliency introduces two new cluster node states and a new VM state. The new cluster node states are Isolated and Quarantined. *Isolated* reflects that the node is no longer communicating with other nodes in the cluster and is no longer an active member of the cluster; however, it can continue to host VM roles (this is the important part). I cover Quarantine later in this section. The new VM state corresponds to the Isolated node state on which the VM runs and is *Unmonitored*, which reflects that the VM is no longer being monitored by the cluster service.

While in the Isolated state, a cluster node will continue to run its virtual machines, with the idea being that within a short time any transient problems such as a network blip or cluster service crash will be resolved and the cluster node can rejoin the cluster, all without any interruption to the running of the VM. By default, a node can stay in the Isolated state for 4 minutes, after which time the VMs would be failed over to another node, as the node itself would go to a down state and no longer be able to host any cluster services.

The following two configurations are applicable to compute resiliency:

ResiliencyLevel   Defines whether compute resiliency is always used (which is the default, and denotes a value of 2) or is used only when the reason for failure is known (for example, if the cluster service crashes, which is configured by setting the value to 1). This is configured at the cluster level by using (Get-Cluster).ResiliencyLevel = <value>.

ResiliencyPeriod   The number of seconds, that a node can stay in Isolated mode. A value of 0 configures the pre-2016 behavior of not going into Isolated state. The default value is 240 (4 minutes), which is just less than the average time for a network switch to reset. This is configured at the cluster level by using (Get-Cluster).ResiliencyDefaultPeriod = <value>. Additionally, cluster resources can have their own value set that overrides the cluster default value: (Get-ClusterGroup "VM Name").ResiliencyPeriod= <value>. If you set an override value for a cluster resource and wish to revert to using the cluster default, simply set the cluster resource's ResiliencyPeriod to -1.

The compute resiliency may sound perfect, but there is a challenge related to the storage of the VMs, as a VM cannot run without its storage. If the VM is using SMB storage, which has been possible since Windows Server 2012, then that storage can still be accessed even when the hosting node is in isolated mode and the VM can continue to run. If, however, the VM is using cluster storage, such as a block-backed Cluster Shared Volume, then that storage will not be available because the node can no longer coordinate with the coordinator node and reliably interact with the storage. In Windows Server 2012 R2, if a VM loses its storage, then the OS inside the VM would crash. In Windows Server 2016, however, there is a second kind of resiliency: storage resiliency.

Transitory storage problems have long been a pain point for Hyper-V environments. A small blip in storage connectivity will result in widespread crashes of the virtual machines and significant downtime as VMs restart. *Storage resiliency* changes the behavior when a node loses connectivity to the storage for a VM. In Windows Server 2012 R2, the VM simply crashes, as previously stated. In Windows Server 2016, Hyper-V will detect the failure to read or write to the VHD/VHDX file, provided it is stored on a Cluster Shared Volume, and freeze the VM. This results in the VM going into a Paused-Critical state. This state protects the OS inside the VM from crashing, as it stays frozen until connectivity to the storage is reestablished, at which time the VM is thawed and resumes running from its exact state before it was frozen. This minimizes the downtime to that of the actual storage interruption duration. By default, a VM can stay in Paused-Critical state for up to 30 minutes; however, this can be changed per VM.

To configure a VM to use or not use storage resiliency, use the following:

```
Set-VM -AutomaticCriticalErrorAction <None or Pause>
```

If enabled to set the time, a VM can start in Paused-Critical state use (24 hours is the maximum possible value, and a value of 0 would power off the VM immediately):

```
Set-VM -AutomaticCriticalErrorActionTimeout <value in minutes>
```

When you put compute resiliency and storage resiliency together for VMs that use cluster storage, the behavior will be as follows. If a node becomes Isolated because of a break in communication with the rest of the cluster, the VMs will stay on that node (for up to 4 minutes) but will go into a Paused-Critical state. Figure 7.19 shows a node, savdalhv93, whose cluster service has been crashed, which results in its Isolated status. Note that both the VMs on the node change to Unmonitored, and that VM3 is in Paused-Critical state, while VM4 continues to run. This is because VM3 is stored on a CSV and therefore loses its storage, while VM4 uses SMB storage, which enables it to continue running as its storage is still accessible.

Storage resiliency is also utilized in full-disk scenarios. In Windows Server 2012 R2, when a volume has less than 200MB of free space, Hyper-V will pause any VMs with dynamic/differencing disks, while VMs using fixed-size VHDs are not affected. In Windows Server 2016 that uses storage resiliency, a VM is paused only when performing an I/O that will fail due to the VHD being unable to grow. Once a VM is paused in Windows Server 2016, you will need to resume it manually after you have made additional disk space available.

Shared VHDX behavior is slightly different, because multiple VMs are using the same VHD spread over multiple nodes in the cluster. With Shared VHDX files, if a VM loses connectivity to the Shared VHDX, instead of the VM being paused, the Shared VHDX is removed from the VM. This allows the VM to notice that the disk is missing and take appropriate action through the cluster capabilities; for example, moving the resource using the disk to another node in the cluster that does have access. Any VM that loses connectivity will check every 10 minutes for the storage to be re-attached (when the Hyper-V host regains access to the underlying storage).

FIGURE 7.19

Cluster network
properties

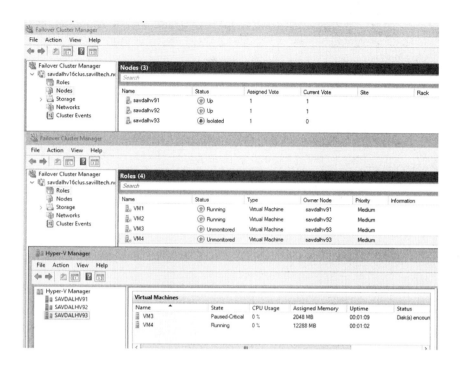

Storage resiliency works for pretty much every deployment combination that utilizes CSV (either directly or through a Scale-out File Server), whether it's a generation 1 or generation 2 VM and whether the disk is VHD or VHDX. Only VMs using local storage or pass-through disks will not benefit from storage resiliency.

There is another feature that was mentioned previously in the new node states: *Quarantine*. It is not desirable to have a node constantly falling in and out of cluster membership, which is likely caused by some underlying configuration or hardware issues. This "flapping" of membership can cause resources to move constantly between nodes, resulting in service interruption. Thus Windows Server 2016 introduces the Quarantine logic to stop this from happening. Quarantine is triggered for a node if the node ungracefully leaves the cluster three times within an hour. By default, that node will stay in Quarantine state for 2 hours, during which time it is not allowed to rejoin the cluster nor host cluster resources. Once the 2 hours has passed, the node can rejoin, as it is assumed during that 2-hour window that actions would be taken to resolve the underlying cause of the flapping. Clustering will not allow more than 25 percent of nodes to go into a quarantine state at any one time. When a node is quarantined, any VMs are gracefully drained to other nodes without interrupting the actual workloads. It is possible to customize the quarantine behavior through settings that are configured at a cluster level; that is, with (Get-Cluster).<setting> = <value>:

QuarantineThreshold   The number of failures within the hour before quarantine (3 by default).

QuarantineDuration   The number of seconds a node stays in quarantine (7,200 by default, which is 2 hours). Note that if you set the value to 0xFFFFFFFF, the node will never automatically leave quarantine and will stay in that state until manually brought online.

To force a node that is currently quarantined to rejoin the cluster, use the `Start-ClusterNode` cmdlet with the `-ClearQuarantine` flag; for example:

```
Start-ClusterNode -Name Node3 -ClearQuarantine
```

Cluster Virtual Network Adapter

When talking about the cluster network, it's interesting to look at how the cluster network functions. Behind the scenes, a Failover Cluster Virtual Adapter is implemented by a `NetFT.sys` driver, which is why it's common to see the cluster virtual adapter referred to as NetFT. The role of the NetFT is to build fault-tolerant TCP connections across all available interfaces between nodes in the cluster, almost like a mini NIC Teaming implementation. This enables seamless transitions between physical adapters in the event of a network adapter or network failure.

The NetFT virtual adapter is a visible virtual device. In Device Manager, the adapter can be seen if you enable viewing of hidden devices. You also can use the `ipconfig /all` command, as shown here:

```
Tunnel adapter Local Area Connection* 11:

    Connection-specific DNS Suffix  .:
    Description . . . . . . . . . .: Microsoft Failover Cluster Virtual Adapter
    Physical Address.. . . . . . .: 02-77-1B-62-73-A9
    DHCP Enabled.. . . . . . . . .: No
    Autoconfiguration Enabled .. ..: Yes
    Link-local IPv6 Address .. . . .: fe80::80fc:e6ea:e9a4:a940%21(Preferred)
    IPv4 Address.. . . . . . . . .: 169.254.2.5(Preferred)
    Subnet Mask .. . . . . . . . .: 255.255.0.0
    Default Gateway . . . . . . . .:
    DHCPv6 IAID .. . . . . . . . .: 688049663
    DHCPv6 Client DUID.. . . . . .: 00-01-00-01-19-B8-19-EC-00-26-B9-43-DA-12
    NetBIOS over Tcpip.. . . . . .: Enabled
```

Remember, this is not a physical network adapter but rather a virtual device that is using whatever network has the lowest cluster metric; the adapter can move between physical networks as required. The MAC address of the NetFT adapter is generated by a hash function based on the MAC address of the local network interface. A nice change in Windows Server 2012 was that it is now supported to sysprep a cluster member because during the specialized phase, a new NetFT MAC address will be generated based on the new environment's local network adapters. Previously, the NetFT MAC was set at cluster membership and could not be changed or regenerated.

The user of the NetFT adapter is the cluster service. It communicates using TCP 3343 to the NetFT, which then tunnels over the physical network adapters with the fault-tolerant routes using UDP 3343. Figure 7.20 shows this. Notice that there are two physical network adapter paths because two network adapters in this example are enabled for cluster communications and the NetFT has built the fault-tolerant path.

What is interesting here is that the cluster service traffic essentially flows through the networking stack twice, once through the NetFT bound stack and then through the stack bound to the network adapter being used. In Windows Server 2012, a new component was introduced, the NetFT Virtual Adapter Performance Filter that was automatically bound to physical network adapters. When it sees any cluster traffic on the physical network adapter, it sends it to the NetFT adapter directly, bypassing the redirection through the physical network stack. This sounds good, but if you also have a guest cluster running on virtual machines within the Hyper-V host cluster and guest VMs are running on different nodes in the cluster, the performance filter would grab not only the host cluster communications but also the guest cluster communications, which means that the communication would never reach the virtual machines and therefore break clustering. To resolve this problem, the Microsoft Failover Cluster Virtual Adapter Performance Filter would need to be disabled in Windows Server 2012, which is why it's disabled by default in Windows Server 2012 R2 and above.

FIGURE 7.20
Cluster network
properties

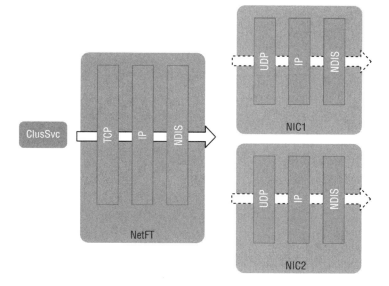

No manual firewall configurations are required when using clustering. When the Failover Clustering feature is installed, built-in inbound and outbound rules are automatically enabled for the inbox Windows Firewall. If you are using a third-party firewall solution, however, it's important that you enable the required firewall exceptions. The best way to do this is to look at all of the Failover Cluster firewall exceptions and emulate them in whatever firewall product you are using.

Performing Cluster Validation

Now that you understand the importance of the cluster network and communications, it's time to get a cluster up-and-running, which is a simple process. The cluster validation process performs detailed tests of all the major areas related to the cluster configuration, such as network, storage, OS tests, and tests specific to Hyper-V in order to ensure that the cluster will be workable and supported by Microsoft.

As previously mentioned, the cluster validation should be performed prior to creating a cluster and anytime you make a major change to the cluster, such as adding a new node to the cluster, adding a new network, or adding new types of storage. Additionally, the cluster validation tool is useful to run if you are experiencing problems with the cluster; it allows specific groups of tests to be run instead of all tests.

Provided the Failover Clustering feature is installed on the cluster nodes to perform a validation, follow these steps:

1. Start Failover Cluster Manager.

2. The root Failover Cluster Manager navigation node will be selected, which in the Management section has a Validate Configuration action, as shown in Figure 7.21, that you should click. If you wish to validate an existing cluster, select the cluster in Failover Cluster Manager and then click its Validate Cluster action.

FIGURE 7.21
The empty Failover Cluster Manager interface

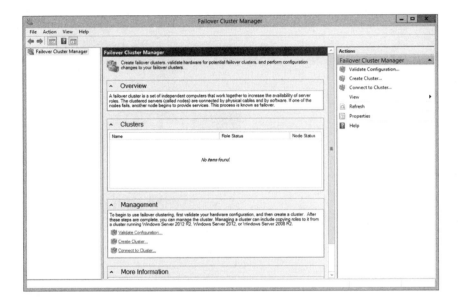

3. Click Next on the introduction screen of the Validate a Configuration Wizard.

4. If this is a validation for what will be a new cluster, you must add all the servers that will become members of the new cluster by entering their names or by clicking Browse and selecting them. Remember that all members of a cluster must be part of the same domain. As each name is entered, a check will be performed on the node. Once all machines are added to the server list, click Next.

5. The tests to be performed can be selected. For a new cluster, you should always leave the default of Run All Tests selected. Even for a validation of an existing cluster, it's a good idea to run all tests. However, you can select the Run Only Tests I Select option to expose an additional configuration page that allows you to select the specific tests that you wish to run (shown in Figure 7.22, which I've edited to show all the Hyper-V options in detail). If the Hyper-V role is not installed, then the Hyper-V tests are not run. Notice the level of depth the cluster tests perform on Hyper-V. Click Next.

FIGURE 7.22
Cluster tests available

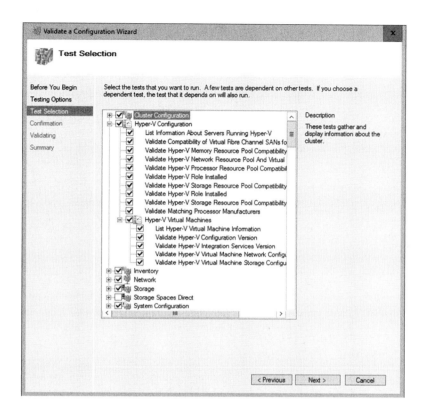

6. If you selected to perform storage checks on an existing cluster, you can select which storage will be validated. Storage validation involves testing arbitration and moving tested storage units, which would shut down any roles using the storage, so do not test any storage that is running roles, such as virtual machines. I like to have a small LUN that I don't use that I keep for storage validations. If this is a validation for what will be a new cluster, then you are not prompted for which storage to validate. Click Next.

7. A confirmation is shown of the tests that will be performed. Click Next to start the validation.

8. The validation can take some time, especially if a large amount of storage is attached, but the progress of the test and its success/failure is shown (see Figure 7.23).

9. Once the validation is complete, a summary is displayed, showing the success/failure of each test. You can click a View Report button to see the report results and details of each test in a web browser. If the validation is for servers not yet in a cluster, a check box is automatically selected (Create The Cluster Now Using The Validated Nodes), which means that when you click Finish, the Create Cluster Wizard will launch with the servers automatically populated. Click Finish to exit the validation wizard.

FIGURE 7.23
Cluster validation
in progress

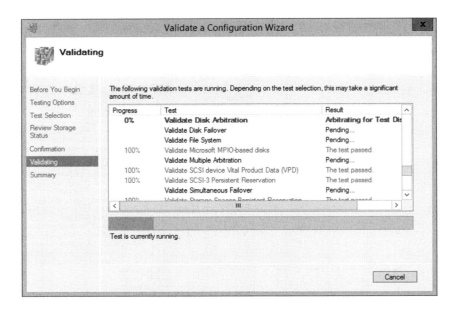

The validation reports are also saved to the folder C:\Windows\Cluster\Reports, which can be viewed at any time. The report name contains the date and time of execution. Open a report and look at the huge amount of detail. These reports can be useful to keep as a record of the server configuration.

Validation can also be performed using PowerShell with the Test-Cluster cmdlet. This can be used to validate an existing cluster by passing a cluster name (or no cluster name, and it will be performed on the local cluster) or used to validate nodes that will join a cluster by passing the server names of the future cluster members, as shown in these examples:

◆ Use Test-Cluster to validate the local cluster.

◆ Use Test-Cluster -Node node1,node2 to validate node1 and node2 for a potential new cluster.

For more examples of Test-Cluster, view the Microsoft documentation at the following location:

http://technet.microsoft.com/en-us/library/ee461026.aspx

One useful tip is to select a specific disk for the purpose of storage testing. The disk can be passed using the -Disk parameter. For example, this just runs the storage test on a specific disk:

```
Test-Cluster -Cluster <cluster> -Disk "<disk, for example Cluster Disk 5>" `
-Include Storage
```

Creating a Cluster

Once the validation process has been run, the next step is to create the cluster, which is simple. At the end of the validation, there was a check box option, Create The Cluster Now Using The Validated Nodes. Keep that selected, and when you click Finish, the Create Cluster Wizard will launch. If you did not select the Create Cluster option, simply run the Create Cluster action, and the only additional step that you will need to perform is to specify the servers that will be joining the cluster. The only information that you need to create the cluster is a name for the cluster and an IP address if you don't wish to use DHCP. Perform the following steps to complete the cluster process:

1. Click Next on the introduction page of the Create Cluster Wizard.

2. Enter the NetBIOS name that will be used to manage/access the cluster. If DHCP is used for the network adapters in the cluster servers, DHCP will automatically be used. If DHCP is not used, an IP address should be configured. Click Next.

3. The confirmation screen is displayed. Leave the Add All Eligible Storage To The Cluster check box selected, because this will automatically add all storage that is accessible to all nodes in the cluster and that supports being clustered. Click Next.

4. The cluster is created and a summary displayed. When the report is visible, review it and click Finish.

A computer object would have been created in Active Directory automatically and named the same as the cluster name specified during cluster creation. By default, it will be created in the Computers container.

Note that, by default, the Create Cluster process selected the smallest cluster disk that was 512MB or greater, and initialized and formatted for the disk witness, whether there was an even or odd number of nodes. If you wish to change the witness, use the More Actions ➤ Configure Cluster Quorum Settings and change it as previously described in this chapter.

Creating Clusters with SCVMM

SCVMM can also help with clustering your Hyper-V hosts (and with Windows Server 2012 R2 and above, your Scale-Out File Server clusters). SCVMM can be used to deploy Hyper-V hosts initially as part of a cluster or to take existing Hyper-V hosts and join them to a cluster. To use SCVMM to create and manage the cluster, it's important that SCVMM also fully manages the storage it uses. There are other requirements for using SCVMM to create and manage clusters:

◆ The cluster should meet the normal cluster requirements (part of Active Directory domain, same OS, and configuration level) and pass validation.

◆ The domain of the Hyper-V hosts must be trusted by the domain of the SCVMM management server.

◆ The Hyper-V hosts must be in the same host group in SCVMM.

◆ Hyper-V hosts must be on the same IP subnet.

Microsoft has detailed documentation on the requirements at:

`http://technet.microsoft.com/en-us/library/gg610630.aspx`

The actual cluster creation is a wizard-driven process that validates the requirements of the cluster, enables the failover cluster feature on the hosts if it's not already installed, ensures that all storage is correctly unmasked to the hosts (remember, SCVMM must be managing the storage that is presented to the cluster and for Windows Server 2016, it can also use Storage Spaces Direct), and makes each disk a Cluster Shared Volume. Follow these steps to create a cluster:

1. Open the SCVMM console, and open the Fabric workspace.

2. Select Servers in the navigation pane.

3. From the Home tab, select Create ➤ Hyper-V Cluster.

4. Enter a name for the new cluster, and select the Run As account to use to perform the configurations on each host. Click Next.

5. On the Nodes page, add the nodes that will be part of the cluster by selecting the servers and clicking the Add button. Then click Next.

6. If any of the nodes are using static IP configuration, you will be prompted for the IP configuration, which can be either an IP pool or a specific IP address to use. Enter the IP configuration, and click Next.

7. Storage that can be clustered (that is, storage that is available to all the nodes) will be displayed. Select the storage to be used for the cluster, and then select the classification, partition style, filesystem, format instructions, and whether to make the disk a CSV. By default, a format is performed, so all data would be lost, although you can select Do Not Format in the File System area. Click Next.

8. Configure the virtual networks that will be available for all cluster nodes. Click Next.

9. On the Summary page, click Finish, and the cluster will be created. Once the creation process is complete, the cluster will be shown in the Servers view of SCVMM.

Once the cluster is created, it can be fully managed with SCVMM, and you may want to customize some attributes. Right-click the cluster, and select Properties. On the General page of the properties is a cluster reserve value that by default is set to 1. This defines the number of nodes in this cluster that you want to be tolerant of failure. For example, a value of 1 means that you want the cluster to be able to tolerate the failure of one node. This is used when deploying resources; SCVMM will ensure that the cluster is not overutilized so that it can't run all deployed virtual machines in the event of a node failure. If you had a four-node cluster and had the reserve set to 1, SCVMM would allow the deployment of only virtual machines that could be run on three nodes. If this was a lab environment and you wanted to fill every node, then you could set the cluster reserve to 0. Alternatively, in a larger cluster, such as a 64-node cluster, you may want to increase the reserve value to 2 or 4 to support more nodes being unavailable. This value is important not just for node failures but also for maintenance, where a node is drained of all virtual machines so that it can be patched and rebooted. This means that it's important in a production environment always to have the reserve set to at least 1 so that maintenance can be performed without having to shut down virtual machines.

The other tabs of the cluster properties show information about the status, storage, and networks. Figure 7.24 shows the view of the current shared volumes, giving easy insight into the utilization.

FIGURE 7.24
Shared volumes

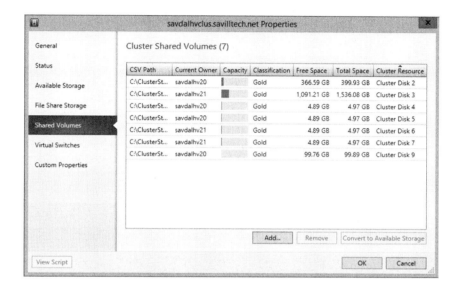

Another nice feature for the cluster is the ability to view the networking details via the View Networking action, as shown in Figure 7.25. This shows the cluster, the nodes in the cluster, and the networks that are connected to from each node.

FIGURE 7.25
Viewing the networking available for a cluster

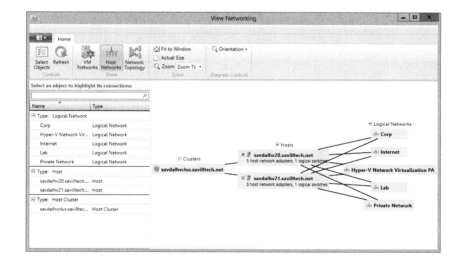

As with networking guidance, the best practice when using SCVMM to manage Hyper-V is to perform all actions from SCVMM, including creating clusters. If you do create clusters outside of SCVMM, then SCVMM will still detect them and allow them to be configured.

Using Cluster Shared Volumes

Traditionally, with a cluster that has shared storage (which means that the storage is accessible to all nodes in the cluster), only one node in the cluster would actually mount a specific LUN that is NTFS formatted. The basic problem is that NTFS is a Shared Nothing filesystem. It does not support multiple operating system instances connecting concurrently to it, which is the limitation. More specifically, Metadata updates such as file open/close of extension operations cannot be performed by multiple operating system instances; the actual SAN holding the LUNs supports multiple concurrent connections with no problem.

One solution would have been to create a new cluster-aware filesystem that could be mounted on multiple nodes in the cluster at the same time, which would remove the LUN failover requirement. However, this would have been a huge undertaking both from a development perspective and from a testing perspective when you consider how many services, applications, and tools are based around features of NTFS.

With this in mind, Microsoft looked at ways to make NTFS-formatted LUNs available to multiple nodes in a cluster concurrently, enabling all the nodes to read and write at the same time, and came up with Cluster Shared Volumes (CSV). In Windows Server 2012, when you're viewing a CSV in Disk Manager, the filesystem type shows as CSVFS instead of NTFS. Under the covers, CSVFS is still NTFS, but the CSVFS adds its own mini filesystem, which is leveraged to enable many of the capabilities that I cover in this section. For the most part, though, it just acts as a pass-through to NTFS (or ReFS in Windows Server 2012 R2, although NTFS should still be used in nearly all cases).

Prior to Windows Server 2012, to use CSV, the feature had to be enabled manually. CSV is now available by default, and to make a cluster disk a CSV, you select the disk in the Storage ➤ Disks view of Failover Cluster Manager and use the Add To Cluster Shared Volumes action, shown in Figure 7.26. This can also be performed using the `Add-ClusterSharedVolume` cmdlet and passing the clustered disk name, as in the following example:

```
Add-ClusterSharedVolume –Name "Cluster Disk 1"
```

FIGURE 7.26
Making a cluster
disk a CSV

When a disk is enabled for CSV, any previous mounts or drive letters are removed and the disk is made available as a child folder of the `%systemroot%\ClusterStorage` folder as `Volume<n>`—for example, `C:\ClusterStorage\Volume1` for the first volume, `C:\ClusterStorage\Volume2`

for the next, and so on. The content of the disk will be visible as content within that disk's `Volume` folder. Place each virtual machine in its own folder as a best practice, as shown in Figure 7.27.

FIGURE 7.27
Viewing cluster shared volumes in Explorer

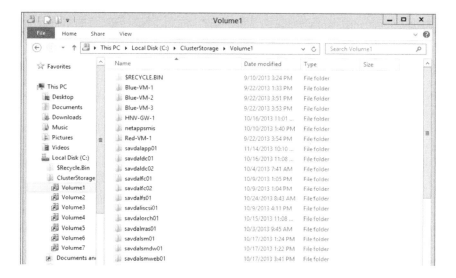

The `ClusterStorage` structure is shared, providing a single consistent filename space to all nodes in the cluster so that every node has the same view. Once a disk is added to CSV, it is accessible to all nodes at the same time. All nodes can read and write concurrently to storage that is part of `ClusterStorage`. Remember that when using Storage Spaces Direct, any disks created are automatically added as CSVs.

The problem with NTFS being used concurrently by multiple operating system instances is related to Metadata changes and the chance of corruptions if multiple operating systems make Metadata changes at the same time. CSV fixes this by having one node assigned to act as the coordinator node for each specific CSV. This is the node that has the disk online locally and has complete access to the disk as a locally mounted device. All of the other nodes do not have the disk mounted but instead receive a raw sector map of the files of interest to them on each LUN that is part of CSV, which enables the noncoordinator nodes to perform read and write operations directly to the disk without actually mounting the NTFS volume. This is known as *Direct I/O*.

The mechanism that allowed this Direct I/O in Windows Server 2008 R2 was the CSV filter (CsvFlt) that was injected into the filesystem stack in all nodes in the cluster that received the sector map from the coordinator node of each CSV disk and then used that information to capture operations to the ClusterStorage namespace and perform the Direct I/O as required. In Windows Server 2012, this changed to the CSVFS mini filesystem. The CSV technology allows the noncoordinator nodes to perform I/O to the disk directly, which is the most common activity when dealing with virtual hard disks. However, no namespace/Metadata changes can be made by noncoordinator nodes; for example, when creating, deleting, resizing, and opening files. These operations require management of the NTFS filesystem structure, which is carefully controlled by the coordinator node to avoid corruption. Fortunately, these types of actions are relatively rare, and when a noncoordinator node needs to perform such an action, it forwards the action via SMB to the coordinator node that then makes the namespace changes on its behalf, since the coordinator has the NTFS locally mounted and thus has full Metadata access. This is shown in action in Figure 7.28, where a single node is acting coordinator for both disks.

FIGURE 7.28
Cluster Shared
Volume normal
operation

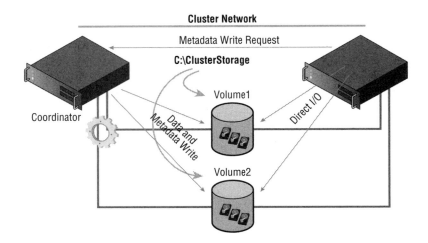

The CSV technology provides another useful feature. If a noncoordinator node loses Direct Access to the LUN—for example, its iSCSI network connection fails—all of its I/O can be performed over SMB via the coordinator node using the cluster network. This is known as *redirected I/O*, and it is shown in Figure 7.29.

FIGURE 7.29
Cluster Shared
Volume in redi-
rected mode

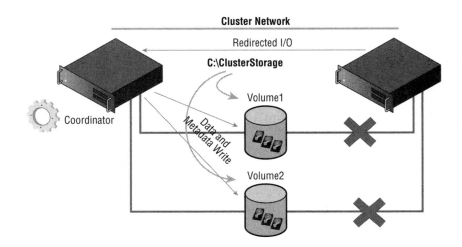

The coordinator node can be changed with minimal impact. A slight pause in I/O occurs if you move the coordinator to another node, because the I/O is queued at each node. However, the pause is unlikely to be noticed, which is critical given how important the coordinator node is to CSV. Windows Server 2012 R2 introduced an automatic rebalancing of coordinator roles for CSV volumes, which is why typically you will see each node in the cluster having an equal number of disks for which it is coordinator.

There are some considerations when you have multiple nodes directly writing to blocks on the disk in some operations—for example, in disk maintenance such as defragmentation or performing a backup. In Windows Server 2008 R2, manual actions were required before performing these maintenance actions in addition to ensuring that actions were taking on the coordinator node for the disk. Windows Server 2012 optimized this process to place the CSV automatically in maintenance mode when required, and it also moves the coordinator of the CSV between nodes as required. In Windows Server 2012, the backup applications are all CSV aware to ensure proper actions. In Windows Server 2012 R2, VSS got more intelligent; it understands when the VSS snapshot is performed, even when running on a noncoordinator node. The ChkDsk process was completely rewritten in Windows Server 2012 to reduce the amount of volume offline time, from potentially hours to at most 8 seconds, and on CSV there is no offline time at all because of the additional redirection introduced by CSV. Behind the scenes, if ChkDsk needs to run against a CSV volume, the handles between the physical disk and CSV are released, but CSV maintains the handles that applications have to CSV. This means that once ChkDsk has completed, within a few seconds the handles are restored between the disk and CSV. CSV can then map the restored handles back to the original and persisted handles of the applications to CSV, which means no break in access—only a slight pause in I/O.

Cluster Shared Volumes in Windows Server 2008 R2 supported only Hyper-V virtual machine workloads. In Windows Server 2012, CSV was also supported for a special type of cluster file share, a Scale-out File Server, which leveraged CSV as the storage for a file share that could be shared by multiple nodes in the cluster simultaneously. This was targeted to provide SMB 3 services for enterprise workloads such as Hyper-V virtual machines running over SMB 3, but it also allowed SQL Server databases to run over SMB 3. Windows Server 2012 R2 further adds to CSV-supported workloads, including SQL Server databases, without connecting to storage via SMB 3.

With CSV, all nodes in the cluster can access the same storage at the same time. This makes moving virtual machines between nodes simple, because no dismount/mount is required of LUNs. However, it also means that you can reduce the number of LUNs required in the environment, since virtual machines can now run across different servers, even when stored on the same LUN.

Windows Server 2012 introduced additional features to CSV, specifically around performance, with CSV Cache. CSV uses unbuffered I/O for read and write operations, which means no caching is ever used. Windows Server 2012 introduced the ability to use a portion of the system memory as a read cache for CSV on each node in the cluster, which improves read performance. There are two steps to enable CSV Cache in Windows Server 2012 and only one step to enable it in Windows Server 2012 R2.

First, the amount of memory that can be used by the host for CSV Cache must be configured. In the following examples, I set a value of 4GB.

Windows Server 2012:

```
(Get-Cluster).SharedVolumeBlockCacheSizeInMB = 4096
```

Windows Server 2012 R2:

```
(Get-Cluster).BlockCacheSize = 4096
```

For Windows Server 2012, the CSV Cache must be enabled per disk. For Windows Server 2012 R2, the CSV Cache is enabled by default. To enable a disk for CSV Cache with Windows Server 2012, use the following command:

```
Get-ClusterSharedVolume "Cluster Disk 1" | `
Set-ClusterParameter CsvEnableBlockCache 1
```

The property is renamed EnableBlockCache in Windows Server 2012 R2 if you ever want to disable CSV Cache for a specific disk. No reboot is required when changing the CSV cache configuration.

In Windows Server 2012, the CSV Cache could be set to up to 20 percent of the system memory only. In Windows Server 2012 R2, it can be set to up to 80 percent of the system memory. The ability to set such a large cache is aimed at Scale-out File Servers, where committing more memory to cache will result in great performance gains. For Hyper-V clusters, typically it's better to have memory available to virtual machines, while some CSV cache will help overall performance.

Windows Server 2012 R2 adds support for ReFS with CSV. However, Hyper-V virtual machines are not supported on ReFS, which means that you will still use NTFS to store your active virtual machines. Windows Server 2012 R2 also adds extended clustered storage space support, including support for storage spaces that use tiering, write-back cache, and parity. Data deduplication is also supported with CSV in Windows Server 2012 R2. While Windows Server 2016 adds Hyper-V support with ReFS, this is only for Storage Spaces Direct deployments. Normal non–Storage Spaces Direct CSV should use NTFS. A big reason for this is that ReFS does not handle Direct I/O, and all I/O is therefore redirected at the filesystem to the coordinator node of the CSV over the cluster network. This is why RDMA networking is recommended for Storage Spaces Direct, and with Storage Spaces Direct everything is redirected anyway since there is no shared storage. Ultimately, use NTFS.

A nice addition in Windows Server 2012 R2 is increased diagnostic capabilities for CSV. You can see the reason a CSV is in redirected mode, which previously was hard to ascertain. Using the Get-ClusterSharedVolumeState PowerShell cmdlet shows the CSV state and the reason for the state. In the following example, all my CSVs are not block redirected, but you can see where the reason for redirection would be displayed. My disks are in filesystem redirected mode because I'm using ReFS and not NTFS to show a type of redirection. However, typically you should always be using NTFS for CSV unless you are using Storage Spaces Direct, as previously mentioned:

```
PS C:\> Get-ClusterSharedVolumeState


BlockRedirectedIOReason       : NotBlockRedirected
FileSystemRedirectedIOReason: FileSystemReFs
Name                          : Cluster Disk 2
Node                          : savdalhv93
StateInfo                     : FileSystemRedirected
VolumeFriendlyName            : VMs
VolumeName                    : \\?\Volume{772694a4-985d-48ee-9902-104be6c64181}\
```

```
BlockRedirectedIOReason     : NotBlockRedirected
FileSystemRedirectedIOReason: FileSystemReFs
Name                        : Cluster Disk 2
Node                        : savdalhv92
StateInfo                   : FileSystemRedirected
VolumeFriendlyName          : VMs
VolumeName                  : \\?\Volume{772694a4-985d-48ee-9902-104be6c64181}\
BlockRedirectedIOReason     : NotBlockRedirected
FileSystemRedirectedIOReason: FileSystemReFs
Name                        : Cluster Disk 2
Node                        : savdalhv91
StateInfo                   : FileSystemRedirected
VolumeFriendlyName          : VMs
VolumeName                  : \\?\Volume{772694a4-985d-48ee-9902-104be6c64181}\
```

In a Hyper-V environment, I recommend making every cluster disk used for storing virtual machines a CSV. There is no downside, and it enables the efficient mobility of virtual machines and limits the number of LUNs required.

Making a Virtual Machine a Clustered Virtual Machine

To create a new clustered virtual machine using Failover Cluster Manager, select the Virtual Machines ➤ New Virtual Machine action from the Roles navigation node, as shown in Figure 7.30. This prompts for the node on which to initially create the virtual machine. Then the normal New Virtual Machine Wizard as seen in Hyper-V Manager launches and allows all the attributes of the virtual machine to be specified.

FIGURE 7.30
Creating a new clustered virtual machine using Failover Cluster Manager

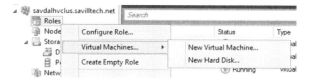

If you have existing virtual machines that are hosted on cluster nodes but are not actually cluster resources, it is easy to make a virtual machine a clustered resource:

1. Within Failover Cluster Manager, select the Configure Role action from the Roles navigation node.

2. Click Next on the wizard introduction screen.

3. From the list of available role types, scroll down, and select Virtual Machine, and then click Next.

4. You'll see a list of all virtual machines that are running on the cluster hosts but are not clustered. Select the check boxes for the virtual machines you wish to cluster, as shown in Figure 7.31, and click Next.

FIGURE 7.31
Selecting the virtual machines to be made clustered resources

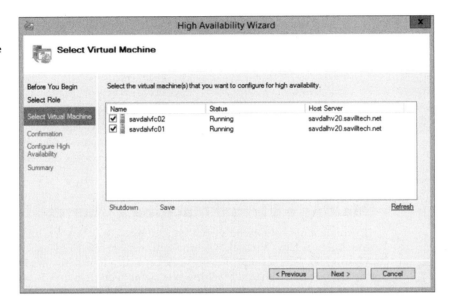

5. Click Next on the configuration screen.

6. Once complete, click Finish.

If you have virtual machines that are cluster resources but you wish to make them nonclustered, select the resource in Failover Cluster Manager, and select the Remove action. This has no impact on the availability of the virtual machine and does not require the virtual machine to be stopped.

To create a clustered virtual machine in SCVMM, the process is exactly the same as creating a regular virtual machine. There is only one change to the virtual machine configuration. On the Configure Hardware page of the Create Virtual Machine Wizard, look at the Advanced options and select the Availability section. Select the Make This Virtual Machine Highly Available check box, as shown in Figure 7.32. This tells SCVMM to deploy this virtual machine to a cluster and make the virtual machine highly available.

Once a virtual machine is clustered, you can configure a priority for the virtual machine via the virtual machine's properties within Failover Cluster Manager. The property can be set to Low, Medium, or High and is used when virtual machines need to be started, ensuring that the high-priority virtual machines start first and so on. This is also used when there are not enough resources to start all virtual machines, and lower-priority virtual machines can be stopped to allow higher-priority virtual machines to start.

FIGURE 7.32
Setting the high availability option for a virtual machine

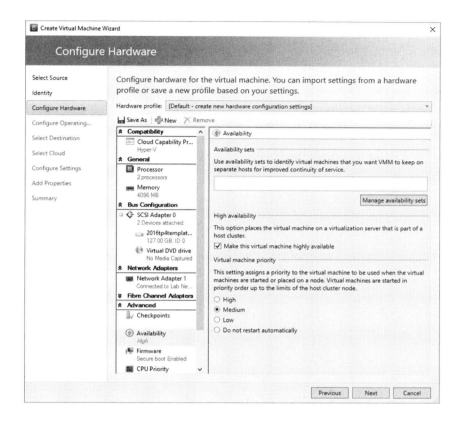

Live Migration

Live Migration is the Hyper-V technology that enables a virtual machine to be moved between Hyper-V hosts. In Windows Server 2008 R2, Live Migration provided the functionality to migrate the memory and state of a virtual machine between hosts in a cluster while the virtual machine was still running. The storage of the virtual machine was available to both hosts in the cluster simultaneously through the use of Cluster Shared Volumes.

There are six key stages to the original Live Migration process in Windows Server 2008 R2, and they remain today when using shared storage:

1. A Live Migration connection is made between the source and target Hyper-V hosts.

2. The virtual machine configuration and device information is transferred, and a container virtual machine is created on the target Hyper-V host.

3. The memory of the virtual machine is transferred.

4. The source virtual machine is suspended, and the state and remaining memory pages are transferred.

5. The virtual machine is resumed on the target Hyper-V host.

6. A reverse ARP is sent over the network to enable network traffic to find the virtual machine on the new host.

The transfer of the memory is the most interesting aspect of Live Migration. It's not possible just to copy the memory of a virtual machine to another node. As the memory is being copied, the VM is still running, which means parts of the memory being copied are changing, and although the copy is from memory to memory over very fast networks, it still takes a finite amount of time, and pausing the VM while the memory is copied would be an outage. The solution is to take an iterative approach that does not result in a perceived period of unavailability by any clients of the virtual machine and ensures that any TCP/IP connections do not timeout.

An initial transfer of the VM memory is performed, which involves the bulk of the information and the bulk of the time taken during a Live Migration. Remember that the virtual machine is still running, and so we need a way to track pages of memory that change while we are copying. To this end, the worker process on the current node creates a "dirty bitmap" of memory pages used by the virtual machine and registers for modify notifications on the pages of memory used by the VM. When a memory page is modified, the bitmap of memory is updated to show that a page has been modified. Once the first pass of the memory copy is complete, all of the pages of memory that have been marked dirty in the memory map are recopied to the target. This time, only the changed pages are copied, so there will be far fewer pages to copy and the operation should be much faster. Once again, though, while we are copying these pages, other memory pages may change, and so this memory copy process repeats itself.

In an ideal world, with each iteration of memory copy, the amount of data to copy will shrink as the time to copy decreases. We reach a point where all of the memory has been copied and we can perform a switch. However, this may not always be the case, which is why there is a limit to the number of memory copy passes that are performed; otherwise, the memory copy may just repeat forever.

Once the memory pages have all been copied or we have reached our maximum number of copy passes (five with Windows Server 2012 R2 and above), it comes time to switch the virtual machine to execute on the target node. To make this switch, the virtual machine is suspended on the source node, and any final memory pages that could not be copied as part of the memory transfer phase are transferred along with the state of the VM to the target; this state of the VM that is transferred includes items such as device and processor state. The virtual machine is then resumed on the target node and an unsolicited ARP reply is sent, notifying that the IP address used by the VM has moved to a new location, which enables routing devices to update their tables. It is at this moment that clients connect to the target node. Yes, there is a slight suspend of the VM, which is required to copy the state information, but this suspend is milliseconds and below the TCP connection time-out threshold, which is the goal because clients will not disconnect during the Live Migration process and users are unlikely to notice anything. Once the migration to the new target is complete, a message is sent to the previous host, notifying it that it can clean up the VM environment. This whole process is shown in Figure 7.33 to help clarify the sequence of steps.

A Live Migration operation uses a large amount of network bandwidth, which in the Windows Server 2008 R2 time frame meant a dedicated 1Gbps network was advised for Live Migration. That then changed in the Windows Server 2012 time frame to leverage converged networking and to use QoS to ensure that Live Migration received sufficient bandwidth.

FIGURE 7.33

The complete Live Migration process

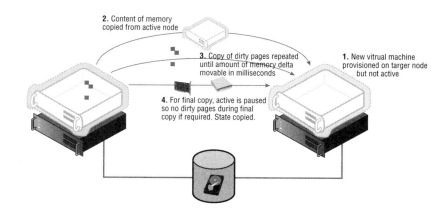

Previously, I mentioned that a metric is used to prioritize the cluster networks to be used for cluster communications and that the cluster network would use the lowest-cost network. The same prioritization is used for Live Migration, but to avoid conflicting with cluster traffic, Live Migration will automatically select the second-least-cost network. If you want to use the same network for Live Migration as for cluster communications, you can override this by using the graphical interface and PowerShell.

In Windows Server 2008 R2, the network used for Live Migration was set on the virtual machine group properties via the Network For Live Migration tab. I have a write-up on the Windows Server 2008 R2 method at the following location:

`http://windowsitpro.com/windows/q-which-network-does-live-migration-traffic-use`

This was changed in Windows Server 2012 to be a property of the cluster networks for the cluster. This can be set as follows:

1. Launch Failover Cluster Manager.

2. Right-click Networks and select Live Migration Settings.

3. A list of all cluster networks is displayed. Check the networks that should be used for Live Migration and move them up or down to set their priority. As shown in Figure 7.34, I used the cluster network, which is a 10Gbps network, and I leveraged QoS to ensure that Live Migration gets sufficient bandwidth. Click OK.

The Live Migration network can be changed using PowerShell, but it's the configuration to actually specify the name of the networks that should *not* be used for Live Migration. Therefore, if you have a specific network to be used for Live Migration, it should be placed in the following PowerShell command (in the example, my Live Migration network is named Migration Network):

```
Get-ClusterResourceType -Name "Virtual Machine" | Set-ClusterParameter `
-Name MigrationExcludeNetworks -Value ([String]::Join(";",(Get-ClusterNetwork `
| Where-Object {$_.Name -ne "Migration Network"}).ID))
```

FIGURE 7.34
Setting the Live
Migration network
for a cluster

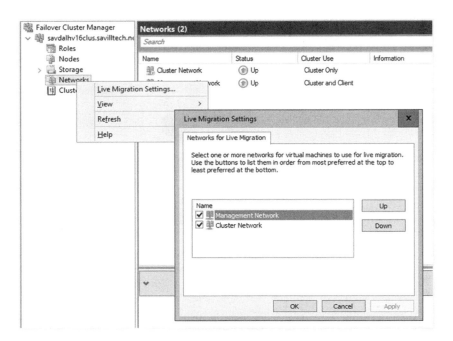

In Windows Server 2008 R2, only one concurrent Live Migration could be performed between any two nodes in a cluster. For example, a Live Migration could be performed between node A and node B, and a separate Live Migration could be performed between node C and node D, but it would not be possible to have two Live Migrations between A and B, nor would it be possible to have a Live Migration between node A and node B and between node A and node C. Failover Cluster Manager would also not allow the queuing of Live Migrations (although SCVMM did). The logic was that a single Live Migration would saturate a 1Gbps network link and most data-centers were 1Gbps. This has changed in Windows Server 2012 to allow multiple concurrent Live Migrations between hosts up to the limit you specify as part of the Live Migration configuration, which I cover later in this chapter. Windows Server 2012 Failover Cluster Manager also introduces the concept of queuing Live Migrations that cannot be actioned immediately.

In Windows Server 2012 and above failover clusters, the Live Migration process remains the same. Virtual machines are always created on shared storage. However, instead of the virtual machines having to be stored on cluster storage, they can be stored on an SMB 3 file share that has been configured so that each node in the cluster and the cluster account have full permissions. Note that if you are storing virtual machines in a cluster on an SMB 3 file share, it's important that the file share is not a single point of failure; it should be a Scale-out File Server, which itself is using Cluster Shared Volumes for the shared storage. This also allows the use of Shared VHDX.

Windows Server 2012 Live Migration Enhancements

One of the key reasons that Live Migration was restricted to within a cluster in Windows Server 2008 R2 was that the storage between the source and the target must be available, which meant that Cluster Shared Volumes had to be used. Windows Server 2012 introduced the ability to use an SMB file share to store virtual machines, enabling hosts outside of a cluster to view the same storage, provided they had the right permissions. This enabled a new type of Live Migration in Windows Server 2012: SMB is leveraged to store the virtual machine, and then the Live Migration technology is leveraged to move the virtual machine state and memory before the handle of the virtual machine's resources on the SMB share switches to the target node.

In a cluster environment, the network used for Live Migration is configured as part of the cluster network configuration. For nonclustered hosts, Live Migration must be configured and enabled if it was not enabled when you enabled the Hyper-V role on the server. The configuration for Live Migration is part of the Hyper-V host's core configuration, which is as follows:

1. Launch Hyper-V Manager (this can also be configured using SCVMM in the Migration Settings area of the server's properties).

2. Select the Hyper-V host, and select the Hyper-V Settings action.

3. Select the Live Migrations area.

4. Select the Enable Incoming And Outgoing Live Migrations check box, as shown in Figure 7.35.

FIGURE 7.35
Enabling Live Migration for a stand-alone Hyper-V host

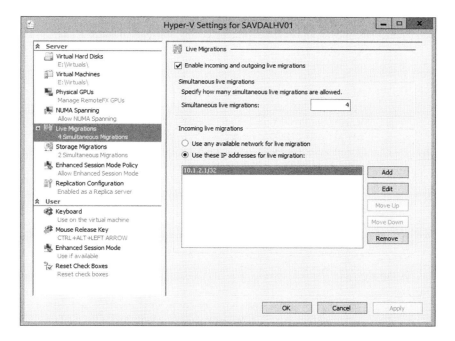

5. Note that the number of simultaneous Live Migrations allowed can be configured, and this number is the maximum allowed and not necessarily the number of simultaneous Live Migrations that will always be performed. The migration module examines the amount of available bandwidth and dynamically ascertains whether an additional Live Migration could be supported by the amount of bandwidth available on the migration network. If not, the migration is queued.

6. The configuration allows any network that is available to be used for Live Migration. Or you can select a specific network or networks by selecting the Use These IP Addresses For Live Migration check box and then adding and ordering IP networks that should be used in CIDR notation—for example, *xxx.xxx.xxx.xxx/n*, where the *n* is the number of bits to use for the subnet mask, so 10.1.2.0/24 is the same as 10.1.2.0 with a subnet mask of 255.255.255.0. This would allow any IP address in the 10.1.2.0 network to be used for Live Migration.

   To set this using PowerShell, use the `Add-VMMigrationNetwork` and `Set-VMMigrationNetwork` cmdlets. Note that this setting is for the networks that can be used to receive incoming Live Migration. When a host is the source of a Live Migration, it will use whatever network it has available that can communicate with the Live Migration network configured to receive on the Live Migration target.

7. Click OK.

By default, CredSSP is used for the security between the source and target Hyper-V host, but there is another configuration option, known as constrained delegation, which I cover later.

Live Storage Move

Windows Server 2012 introduced the ability to move the storage of a virtual machine without having to shut down the virtual machine first, sometimes call Live Storage Move or Storage Migration.

Windows Server 2012 supports three main types of storage for virtual machines: direct attached; SAN based, such as storage connected via Fibre Channel or iSCSI; and new to Windows Server 2012 was support for SMB 3 file shares such as those hosted on a Windows Server 2012 file server or any NAS/SAN that has SMB 3 support. Windows Server 2012 Storage Migration allows the storage used by a virtual machine, which includes its configuration and virtual hard disks, to be moved between any supported storage with zero downtime to the virtual machine. This could be migration just to a different folder on the same disk, between LUNs on the same SAN, from direct attached to a SAN, from a SAN to a SMB file share—it doesn't matter. If the storage is supported by Hyper-V, virtual machines can be moved with no downtime. It should be noted that storage migration cannot move nonvirtualized storage, which means if a virtual machine is using pass-through storage, that cannot be moved. The good news is that with the new VHDX format, which allows 64TB virtual disks, there really is no reason to use pass-through storage anymore from a size or performance perspective. It is also not possible to perform a storage migration for a Shared VHDX.

The ability to move the storage of a virtual machine at any time without impacting the availability of the virtual machine is vital in two key scenarios:

◆ The organization acquires new storage, such as a new SAN, or is migrating to a new SMB 3.–based appliance and needs to move virtual machines with no downtime as part of a planned migration effort.

◆ The storage in the environment was not planned out as well as hoped and now has either run out of space or can't keep up with the IOPS requirements. Virtual machines need to be moved as a matter of urgency. In my experience, this is the most common scenario. It is important to realize that performing a storage migration puts a large additional load on the storage, because every block has to be read and written to. Therefore, if you are having a storage performance problem, the problem will be worse during a storage migration.

The mechanics behind the Windows Server 2012 storage migration are simple, but they provide the most optimal migration process. Remember that the virtual machine is not moving between hosts; it's only the storage moving from a source location to a target location.

Storage migration uses a one-pass copy of virtual hard drives that works as follows:

1. The storage migration is initiated from the GUI or PowerShell.

2. The copy of the source virtual hard disks, smart paging file, snapshots, and configuration files to the target location is initiated.

3. At the same time as the copy initiates, all writes are performed on the source and target virtual hard disks through a mirroring process in the virtual storage stack.

4. Once the copy of the virtual hard disks is complete, the virtual machine is switched to use the virtual hard disks on the target location (the target is up-to-date because all writes have been mirrored to it while the copy was in progress).

5. The virtual hard disks and configuration files are deleted from the source.

The storage migration process is managed by the VMMS process in the parent partition, but the heavy lifting of the actual storage migration is performed by the virtual machine's worker process and the storage virtualization service provider (VSP) in the parent partition. The mechanism for the copy of the storage is just a regular, unbuffered copy operation plus the additional I/O on the target for the mirroring of writes occurring during the copy. However, in reality the additional I/O for the ongoing writes is negligible compared to the main unbuffered file copy. The path used is whatever path exists to the target, which means that if it's SAN, it will use iSCSI/Fibre Channel, and if it's SMB, it will use whichever network adapter or network adapters have a path to the share. Any underlying storage technologies that optimize performance are fully utilized. This means that if you are copying over SMB (from or to) and you are using NIC Teaming, SMB direct, or SMB Multichannel, then those technologies will be used. If you are using a SAN and that SAN supports offloaded data transfer (ODX) and a virtual machine is being moved within a single LUN or between LUNs, ODX will be utilized, which will mean that the move uses almost no load on the host and will complete very quickly.

The SAN ODX scenario is the best case. For all of the other cases, it is important to realize exactly what an unbuffered copy means to your system. The unbuffered copy is used because during the storage migration it would not be desirable on a virtualization host to use a large amount of system memory for caching data. Performing a copy can cause a significant amount of I/O load on your system, for both reading the source and writing to the target.

To get an idea, try a manual unbuffered copy on your system by using the xcopy command with the /J switch (which sets the copy to unbuffered). That is similar to the load a storage migration would inflict on your system (once again considering the ongoing mirrored writes as fairly negligible). Consider, therefore, moving a virtual machine between folders on a local disk, likely a worst-case scenario. The data would be read from and written to the same disk, causing a huge amount of disk thrashing. It would likely take a long time and would adversely affect any other virtual machines that use that disk. That is a worst-case scenario, though. If the source and target were different storage devices, the additional load would not be as severe as a local move but would still need to be considered.

There is nothing Hyper-V specific about the disk I/O caused by moving a VM. It would be the same for any data migration technology (except that other technologies may not have capabilities like ODX if a SAN is involved); ultimately, the data has to be read and has to be written.

This does not mean that you should not use storage migration, but it does mean that you should plan carefully when you use it. It's not something you would likely want to perform during normal working hours because of the possible adverse effect on other loads, and I suspect that's why at this time there is no automated storage migration process as part of the Dynamic Optimization in System Center Virtual Machine Manager that rebalances virtual machines within a cluster. If you detected a large I/O load on a storage subsystem in the middle of the day, the last thing you would want to do is to add a huge extra load on it by trying to move things around. The best option is to track I/O over time and then at a quiet time move the virtual machines' storage, which would be easy to script with PowerShell or automate with technologies like System Center Orchestrator.

There is no specific configuration to enable storage migration. As previously stated, storage migration uses whatever path exists to communicate with the source and target storage and is enabled by default (in fact, you can't disable it). The only configuration is setting how many simultaneous storage migrations are allowed, and this is configured via the Hyper-V Settings action in the Storage Migrations area.

This can also be configured using PowerShell:

```
Set-VMHost -MaximumStorageMigrations <number to allow>
```

Extra configuration is required in only one scenario, and that is if you are using SMB storage for the target of a storage migration and are initiating the migration remotely, either through Hyper-V Manager or PowerShell; that is, you are not running the tools on the actual Hyper-V host, which is the preferred management approach for Windows Server 2012 because all management should be done remotely using PowerShell or from a Windows 8/8/1 machine. When you configure SMB storage for use with Hyper-V, you set numerous specific permissions, including giving the administrators full control as the person creating a VM on SMB or moving to SMB as part of a storage migration as their credentials are used. To enable the credential to be used on a remote SMB file server, constrained delegation must be used, which I mentioned earlier related to Live Migrations in nonclustered environments. I cover constrained delegation in detail later.

Storage migrations can be triggered through Hyper-V Manager or through PowerShell, and there are two options when performing a storage migration. You can move everything to a single location or select different locations for each item stored as part of a virtual machine; that is, one location for the configuration file, one for the snapshots, one for smart paging, one for virtual hard disk 1, one for virtual hard disk 2, and so on, as shown in Figure 7.36.

Start with performing the move using Hyper-V Manager, which will help you understand the options that are possible:

1. Launch Hyper-V Manager.

2. Select the virtual machine whose storage needs to be moved, and select the Move action.

3. Click Next on the Before You Begin page of the wizard.

4. Since we are moving only the storage, select the Move The Virtual Machine's Storage option.

5. You can now choose to move all of the virtual machine's data to a single location, which is the default, or you can select to move the virtual machine's data to a different location or move only the virtual hard disks for the virtual machine but none of its other data. Make your selection and click Next.

6. If you selected the default to move everything to a single location, you will be prompted for the new storage location. Just click Next. If you selected either of the other two options, you will have a separate page to select the target location for each element of the virtual machine's data, so set the location for each item, and click Next.

7. Review your options, and click Finish to initiate the storage migration.

FIGURE 7.36
The different storage objects for a virtual machine

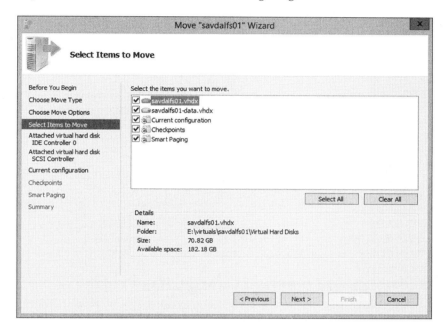

To perform the storage migration from PowerShell, use the Move-VMStorage cmdlet. If you're moving everything to a single location, it's easy; you just pass the virtual machine name and the new target location with the DestinationStoragePath parameter (note that a subfolder with the VM name is not created automatically, so if you want the VM in its own subfolder, you need to specify that as part of the target path). Here's an example:

```
Move-VMStorage -DestinationStoragePath <target path> -VMName <vmname>
```

If, however, you want to move the parts to different locations, it's more complicated. Instead of DestinationStoragePath, the SmartPagingFilePath, SnapshotFilePath, and VirtualMachinePath parameters are used to pass the location for the smart paging file, snapshots, and virtual machine configuration, respectively, but this still leaves the virtual hard disks. For the VHDs, the Vhds parameter is used. You could have more than one VHD for a single virtual machine (in fact you could have hundreds), and PowerShell does not really like an arbitrary number of parameters. Therefore, to pass the virtual hard disk's new location, you have to create a hash value for SourceFilePath and DestinationFilePath for each virtual hard disk and then place those into an array that is passed to the –Vhds parameter. Pleasant!

In the following example, a virtual machine is being moved with three hard disks and its smart paging file, configuration, and snapshots. You don't have to move all of the elements of a virtual machine; you need to specify only the pieces you wish to move. Other elements not specified would just stay in their current location. Note that in the following command, curly brackets {} are used for the hash values (value pairs), while parentheses() are used for the array.

```
Move-VMStorage -VMName <vmname> -SmartPagingFilePath d<smart paging file path> `
-SnapshotFilePath <snapshot path> -VirtualMachinePath <vm configuration path> `
-Vhds @(@{ "SourceFilePath " = "C:\vm\vhd1.vhdx "; `
"DestinationFilePath " = "D:\VHDs\vhd1.vhdx "}, `
 @{ "SourceFilePath " = "C:\vm\vhd2.vhdx ";`
 "DestinationFilePath " = "E:\VHDs\vhd2..vhdx "}, `
@{ "SourceFilePath " = "C:\vm\vhd3.vhdx ";`
 "DestinationFilePath " = "F:\VHDs\vhd3.vhdx "})
```

Once the storage migration is initiated, it will run until it's finished; it will never give up, no matter how long it may take. As the administrator, you can cancel the storage migration manually through the Cancel move storage action. Rebooting the Hyper-V host would also cause all storage migrations to be cancelled. You can see the progress of storage migrations in the Hyper-V Manager tool or you can query them through WMI, as shown here:

```
PS C:\ > Get-WmiObject -Namespace root\virtualization\v2 `
 -Class Msvm_MigrationJob |
 ft Name, JobStatus, PercentComplete, VirtualSystemName

Name            JobStatus      PercentComplete VirtualSystemName
__              _____-        _____-
Moving Storage  Job is running              14 6A7C0DEF-9805-...
```

Shared Nothing Live Migration

With the existing Live Migration technology and the new ability to move the storage of a virtual machine with no downtime, Windows Server 2012 introduced *Shared Nothing Live Migration*. This feature allows you to move virtual machines between any two Windows Server 2012 Hyper-V hosts with no downtime and no shared resource. This means no shared storage, no shared cluster membership; all that is needed is a gigabit network connection between the Windows Server 2012 Hyper-V hosts. With this network connection, a virtual machine can be moved between Hyper-V hosts, which includes moving the virtual machine's virtual hard disks, the virtual machine's memory content, and then the processor and device state with no downtime to the virtual machine. Do not think that the Shared Nothing Live Migration capability means Failover Clustering is no longer needed. Failover Clustering provides a high availability solution, while Shared Nothing Live Migration is a mobility solution but does give new flexibility in the planned movement of virtual machines between all Hyper-V hosts in your environment without downtime. It can supplement Failover Cluster usage. Think of now being able to move virtual machines into a cluster, out of a cluster, and between clusters with no downtime to the virtual machine in addition to moving them between stand-alone hosts. Any storage dependencies are removed with Shared Nothing Live Migration.

Failover Clustering provides some assurance that the hosts in a failover cluster have a similar configuration as long as it passed validation. This provides a confident migration of virtual machines between hosts without the fear of misconfigurations and therefore problems with virtual machines functioning if migrated. When Shared Nothing Live Migration is used to migrate virtual machines between unclustered Hyper-V hosts, there is no guarantee of common configuration, and therefore you need to ensure that the requirements for Shared Nothing Live Migration are met:

◆ At a minimum, there must be two Windows Server 2012 or above installations with the Hyper-V role enabled or the free Microsoft Hyper-V Server OS.

◆ Each server must have access to its own location to store virtual machines, which could be local storage, SAN attached, or an SMB share.

◆ Servers must have the same type of processor or at least the same family of processor (that is, Intel or AMD) if the Processor Compatibility feature of the virtual machine is used.

◆ Servers must be part of the same Active Directory domain.

◆ Hosts must be connected by at least a 1Gbps connection (although a separate private network for the Live Migration traffic is recommended but not necessary), over which the two servers can communicate. The network adapter used must have both the Client For Microsoft Networks and File And Printer Sharing For Microsoft Networks enabled, because these services are used for any storage migrations.

◆ Each Hyper-V server should have the same virtual switches defined with the same name to avoid errors and manual steps when performing the migration. If a virtual switch has the same name as that used by a virtual machine being migrated, an error will be displayed, and the administrator performing the migration will need to select to which switch on the target Hyper-V server the VM's network adapter should connect.

◆ Virtual machines being migrated must not use pass-through storage or shared VHDX (with Windows Server 2012 R2 and Windows Server 2016).

Earlier, in the section "Windows Server 2012 Live Migration Enhancements," I described how to enable and configure Live Migration in the scenario of using Live Migration with SMB as the storage. It is the same for Shared Nothing Live Migration; no additional configuration is required.

To perform a Shared Nothing Live Migration, select the Move action for a virtual machine, and for the move type, select the Move The Virtual Machine option, type the name of the destination Hyper-V server, and finally choose how the virtual machine should be moved. For a Shared Nothing Live Migration, you need to select one of the first two options available: Move the virtual machine's data to a single location, or move the virtual machine's data by selecting where to move the items. The first option allows you to specify a single location where you want to store the virtual machine's configuration, hard disks, and snapshots on the target. The second option allows you to select a specific location for each of the virtual machine's items in addition to selecting which items should be moved. Make your choice, and select the folder on the destination server. The move operation will start and will take a varying amount of time, based on the size of the virtual hard disks and memory to move as well as the rate of change. The move will be completed without any downtime or loss of connectivity to the virtual machine. This can be seen in a video at the following location:

www.savilltech.com/videos/sharednothinglivemigration/sharednothinglivemigration.wmv

The move can also be initiated using the Move-VM PowerShell cmdlet.

In my experience, the Shared Nothing Live Migration can be one of the most troublesome migrations to get working, so here are my top troubleshooting tips:

◆ First, make sure that you have adhered to the requirements I listed previously.

◆ Check the Event Viewer for detailed messages. The location to check is Applications and Services Logs ➤ Microsoft ➤ Windows ➤ Hyper-V-VMMW ➤ Admin.

◆ Make sure that the IP configuration is correct between the source and target. The servers must be able to communicate. Try pinging the target Live Migration IP address from the source server.

◆ Run the following PowerShell command in an elevated session to show the IP addresses being used for a server and the order in which they will be used:

```
gwmi -n root\virtualization\v2 Msvm_VirtualSystemMigrationService |`
  select MigrationServiceListenerIPAddressList
```

◆ Make sure that the Hyper-V (MIG-TCP-In) firewall exception is enabled on the target.

◆ The target server must be resolvable by DNS. Try an nslookup of the target server. On the target server, run the command ipconfig /registerdns, and then run ipconfig / flushdns on the source server.

◆ On the source server, flush the Address Resolution Protocol (ARP) cache with the command arp -d *.

◆ To test connectivity, try a remote WMI command to the target (the Windows Management Instrumentation, WMI-In, firewall exception must be enabled on the target), such as the following:

```
gwmi -computer <DestinationComputerName> -n root\virtualization\v2 Msvm_
VirtualSystemMigrationService
```

◆ Try changing the IP address used for Live Migration; for example, if you're currently using 10.1.2.0/24, try changing to the specific IP address (for example, 10.1.2.1/32). Also check any IPsec configurations or firewalls between the sources and target. Check for multiple NICs on the same subnet that could be causing problems, and if you find any, try disabling one of them.

◆ Try setting authentication to CredSSP, and initiate locally from a Hyper-V server. If this works, the problem is the Kerberos delegation.

The most common problems I have seen are a misconfiguration of Kerberos and the IP configuration, but failing to resolve the target server via DNS will also cause problems.

Configuring Constrained Delegation

Performing a Live Migration within a cluster removed the need for any special security considerations when moving virtual machines, because the cluster account was used throughout migration operations. However, Shared Nothing Live Migration, Live Migration using SMB, and the ability to move storage to SMB shares introduce some additional security (specifically, credential) considerations.

Outside of a cluster, each Hyper-V host has its own computer account without a shared credential, and when operations are performed, the user account of the user performing the action is normally used. With a Live Migration, actions are being taken on the source and target Hyper-V servers (and file servers if the VM is stored on an SMB share, but more on that later), which both require that the actions be authenticated. If the administrator performing the Live Migration is logged on to the source or the target Hyper-V server and initiates Shared Nothing Live Migration using the local Hyper-V Manager, then the administrator's credentials can be used both locally and to run commands on the other Hyper-V server. In this scenario, CredSSP works fine and allows the user's credentials to be used on the remote server from the client—basically, a single authentication hop from the local machine of the user performing the action (which happens to be one of the Hyper-V servers) to a remote server.

Remember, however, the whole goal for Windows Server 2012 (and above) and management in general: remote management and automation. Having to log on to the source or target Hyper-V server every time a Live Migration outside of a cluster is required is a huge inconvenience for remote management. If a user was logged on to their local computer running Hyper-V Manager and tried to initiate a Live Migration between Hyper-V host A and B, it would fail. The user's credential would be used on Hyper-V host A (which is one hop from the client machine to Hyper-V host A), but Hyper-V host A would not be able to use that credential on host B to complete the Live Migration, because CredSSP does not allow a credential to be passed on to another system (more than one hop).

This is where the option to use Kerberos enables full remote management. Kerberos supports constrained delegation of authentication: When a user on their local machine performs an action on a remote server, that remote server can use that user's credentials for authentication on another remote server. This initially seems to be a troubling concept, that a server I remotely connect to can just take my credentials and use them on another server, potentially without my knowing. The constrained part of *constrained delegation* comes into play and requires some setup before Kerberos can be used as the authentication protocol for Live Migration. To avoid exactly the problem I just described, where a server could use a remote user's credentials on another server, delegation has to be configured for each computer account that is allowed to perform actions on another server on behalf of another user. This delegation is configured using the Active Directory Users and Computer management tool and the computer account properties of the server that will be allowed to delegate. Additionally, when leveraging SMB file shares for Shared Nothing Live Migration or part of a storage migration, constrained delegation must be configured for the cifs service to each SMB file server. Follow these steps:

1. Launch Active Directory Users and Computers.

2. Navigate to your Hyper-V servers, right-click one, and select Properties.

3. Select the Delegation tab.

4. Make sure that Trust This Computer For Delegation To Specified Services Only is selected and that Use Kerberos Only is selected.

5. Click Add.

6. Click Users or Computers, and select your other Hyper-V servers or SMB file servers. Click OK.

7. In the list of available services, select Microsoft Virtual System Migration Service or cifs for each server, depending on whether it's a Hyper-V host (Microsoft Virtual System Migration Service) or SMB file server (cifs). Click OK.

8. Repeat the steps for all of the Hyper-V hosts or SMB file shares with which it will communicate that need constrained delegation, as shown in Figure 7.37.

FIGURE 7.37
The storage objects for
a virtual machine

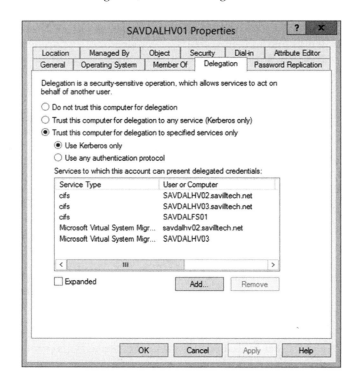

9. Repeat the whole process for every other Hyper-V so that every Hyper-V host has constrained delegation configured to the other Hyper-V hosts and SMB file shares.

You *must* set authentication to Use Kerberos Only. It will not work if you select Use Any Authentication Protocol. It also won't work if you use the Trust This Computer For Delegation To Any Service (Kerberos Only) option. In my example configuration, I have numerous Hyper-V hosts, and in Figure 7.37, the configuration for savdalhv01 is shown. It has been configured for constrained delegation to the Hyper-V hosts savdalhv02 and savldalhv03 for cifs and migration, in addition to the file server savdalfs01 for cifs only. I would repeat this configuration on savdalhv02 and savdalhv03 computer accounts, allowing delegation to the other hosts. I have cifs enabled in addition to Microsoft Virtual System Migration Service for each Hyper-V host in case virtual machines are using SMB storage that is being migrated, in which case cifs is required.

Once the Kerberos delegation is configured, the Live Migration will be able to be initiated from any remote Hyper-V Manager instance between trusted hosts. Remember also that all hosts that are participating in the Live Migration must have the same authentication configuration. While there is more work involved in the use of Kerberos authentication, the additional flexibility makes the additional work worthwhile and definitely recommended. To configure the authentication type to use from PowerShell, use the `Set-VMHost` cmdlet and set `VirtualMachineMigrationAuthenticationType` to either CredSSP or Kerberos.

Initiating Simultaneous Migrations Using PowerShell

The `Move-VM` PowerShell cmdlet can be used to trigger Live Migrations. To trigger multiple Live Migrations, the following can be used:

```
Get-VM blank1,blank2,blank3 | Move-VM -DestinationHost savdalhv02
```

The problem is that this would live-migrate `blank1`, and once that is finished, it would live-migrate `blank2`, then `blank3`, and so on. It is not performing a simultaneous Live Migration, which is possible in Windows Server 2012 and above.

One solution is to use the `-parallel` option available in PowerShell v3 workflows to trigger the Live Migrations to occur in parallel, as in this example:

```
Workflow Invoke-ParallelLiveMigrate
{
    $VMLIST = get-vm blank1,blank2,blank3
    ForEach -Parallel ($VM in $VMLIST)
    {
        Move-VM -Name $VM.Name -DestinationHost savdalhv02
    }
}

Invoke-ParallelLiveMigrate
```

The Live Migrations will now occur in parallel. Make sure that your Hyper-V hosts are configured with the needed setting for the number of concurrent Live Migrations you wish to perform on both the source and destination Hyper-V hosts.

Windows Server 2012 R2 Live Migration Enhancements

Windows Server 2012 R2 introduced performance improvements to Live Migration by allowing the memory transferred between hosts to be compressed or sent using SMB. The option to use compression means less network bandwidth and therefore faster Live Migrations, but additional processor resources are used to compress and decompress the memory. The option to use SMB is targeted to environments that have network adapters that support remote direct memory access (RDMA), which gives the fastest possible transfer of data with almost no server resource usage (compression is not used; it's not needed). By selecting SMB when network adapters support RDMA, you leverage the SMB Direct capability, which gives the best possible performance. Do *not* select SMB if your network adapters do not support RDMA.

By default, the compression option is selected for Live Migration, but it can be changed as follows:

1. Launch Hyper-V Manager (this can also be configured in SCVMM via the Migration Settings area of the server's properties).

2. Select the Hyper-V host and select the Hyper-V Settings action.

3. Select the Live Migrations area.

4. Click the plus sign next to Live Migrations to enable access to the Advanced Features configuration area.

5. Select the desired Performance Options setting, as shown in Figure 7.38. Notice also that the authentication protocol (CredSSP or Kerberos) is also selected in this area.

FIGURE 7.38
Setting the advanced configurations for Live Migration

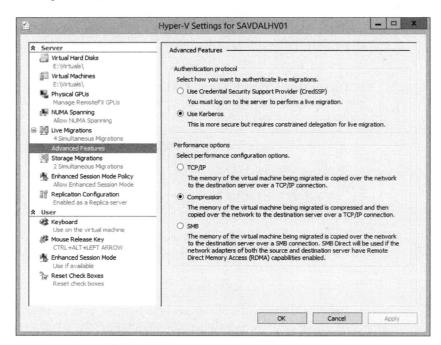

6. Click OK.

Windows Server 2012 R2 also enables cross-version Live Migration. This allows a Live Migration from Windows Server 2012 to Windows Server 2012 R2 (but not the other way). This Live Migration enables an upgrade from Windows Server 2012 to Windows Server 2012 R2 Hyper-V hosts without requiring any downtime of the virtual machines. With Windows Server 2016, it is possible to perform cross-version Live Migration from Windows Server 2012 R2 to Windows Server 2016 and back to Windows Server 2012 R2 until the VM is upgraded to version 8. This ability to move back and forth is key to the Windows Server 2016 capability to have mixed-mode clusters containing Windows Server 2012 R2 and Windows Server 2016 nodes (as covered in Chapter 5, "Managing Hyper-V").

Dynamic Optimization and Resource Balancing

When a virtual machine is created with SCVMM to a cluster, each node is given a star rating based on its suitability to host the new virtual machine, and one of the criteria is the host's current utilization. Over time, as new virtual machines are created, your cluster may become uneven, with some hosts running many more virtual machines than others.

Dynamic Optimization (DO) was a new feature in SCVMM 2012 that was designed to ensure that the hosts within a cluster (Hyper-V, ESX, or XenServer) were spreading the virtual machine load as evenly as possible, avoiding certain hosts being heavily loaded (potentially affecting the performance of virtual machines) while other hosts were fairly lightly loaded. Dynamic Optimization is one of the most used features in almost all virtualized environments because of the dynamic balancing of virtual machines and because it removes a lot of the manual activities required of administrators around the placement of virtual machines. It is important to note that no amount of dynamic balancing can compensate for a poorly architected or overloaded environment, and it's still critical to perform accurate discovery and design of virtual environments.

DO is not considered a replacement for Performance Resource Optimization (PRO), which was present in SCVMM 2008 and leveraged System Center Operations Manager for detail on utilization of the environment. Instead, DO is considered a complementary technology that does not rely on Operations Manager and is seen very much as a reactive technology. DO works by periodically looking at the resource utilization of each host in a cluster, and if the utilization drops below defined levels, a rebalancing of the virtual machines is performed to better equalize host utilization throughout the cluster. As Figure 7.39 shows, thresholds for CPU, memory, disk, and network can be defined in addition to how aggressive the rebalancing will be. The more aggressive it is, the quicker DO will be to move virtual machines for even a small gain in performance, which means more Live Migrations.

FIGURE 7.39
Dynamic Optimization options for a host group

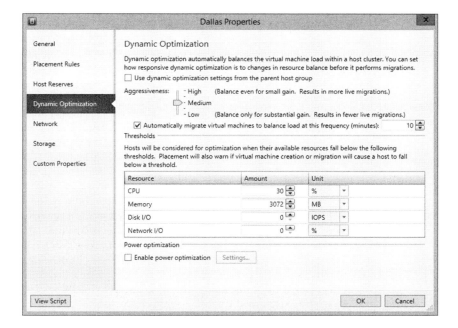

While any host group can have the DO configurations set, the optimizations will be applied only to hosts that are in a cluster. In addition, that cluster must support zero-downtime VM migrations such as Live Migration on Hyper-V, XenMotion, and vMotion on ESX. A manual DO can be initiated at any time by selecting a host cluster and running the Optimize Hosts action, which will display a list of recommended migrations. The great part is that this manual DO can be used even if DO is not configured on the actual host group, allowing one-off optimizations to be performed.

PRO is still present in SCVMM 2012. It leverages Operations Manager and is used as a more long-term placement technology, and it's also the only extensible placement technology. Third-party PRO packs can be installed to extend the placement logic.

Also shown in Figure 7.39 is an option to enable Power Optimization (PO, but I'm not going to refer to it as that). While Dynamic Optimization tries to spread load across all the hosts in a cluster evenly, Power Optimization aims to condense the number of hosts that need to be running in a cluster in order to handle the virtual machine workload without negatively affecting the performance of the virtual machines and without powering down those not required. Consider a typical IT infrastructure that during the workday is busy servicing employees and customers but during nonwork hours is fairly idle. Power Optimization allows thresholds to be set to ensure that VMs can be consolidated and that evacuated hosts can be powered down, provided the remaining running hosts don't have any CPU, memory, disk, or network resources drop below the configured thresholds.

This is similar to the configuration options we set for DO, but this time it's controlling how much consolidation can occur. Your Power Optimization thresholds should be set higher than those for Dynamic Optimization. The goal of Power Optimization is to consolidate in quiet times, and if the Power Optimization thresholds were lower than the Dynamic Optimization thresholds, then hosts would be powered off and lots of Live Migrations would occur. VMs would be moved around, and the hosts that were just powered off would be powered on again. The Power Optimization thresholds also need to be generous, leaving plenty of spare resources because resource utilization fluctuates even in quiet times and eventually will pick up again during busy times. It will take time to power on and boot the servers that were powered down during Power Optimization times, so plenty of buffer capability is required to ensure no resource shortage.

Additionally, as Figure 7.40 shows, you can set the times Power Optimization can occur. In this example, I don't want Power Optimization to occur during business hours except for a few exceptions. However, there is no reason to stop Power Optimization during working hours, provided you set well-defined thresholds to ensure that hosts have sufficient spare resources and won't suddenly be overtaxed during the time it takes to power back on servers that were powered down.

Waking servers is important, because we don't want to power down servers that are not needed at a certain time and then be unable to start them up when they are needed again. A powered-down host is started using the host's baseboard management controller (BMC), which needs to be configured per host. If the BMC is not present in a host or not configured, the host will not be able to be powered off as part of the Power Optimization process.

In partnership with the SCVMM placement logic and Dynamic Optimization is the ability to create placement rules that can guide where virtual machines are placed. SCVMM contains 10 custom properties named Custom1 through Custom10. You can also create additional custom properties for the various types of SCVMM objects, such as a virtual machine (VM), a virtual machine template, hosts, host groups, clouds, and more.

You might create a custom property to store information, such as a VM's cost center, primary application function, desired physical location, or a contact email address—anything you can think of. These properties can then be used for administrators and business users to understand more easily information about assets in SCVMM and for reporting. The real power is realized when your custom properties are combined with custom placement rules that can utilize the custom properties to help control where VMs are placed.

FIGURE 7.40
Power Optimization options for a host group

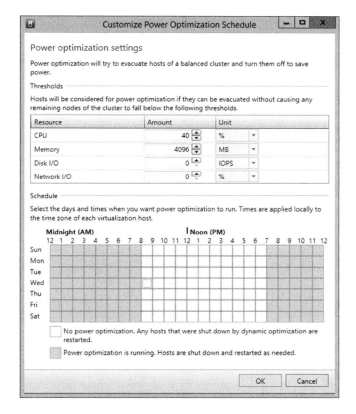

For example, consider the scenario in which each business unit group has its own set of hosts. You could create a cost center property for VMs and hosts and then create a custom placement rule that says the cost center of the VM must match that of the host for placement.

These rules are used both for initial placement and as part of Dynamic Optimization. It's important to note that when you create your custom placement rules, you have options that the rule *should*, *must*, or *not* match. *Should* means the placement will try to match but doesn't have to; if placement violates the rule, a warning is generated. If *must* is used, placement isn't possible if the rule is violated. To create a custom property, use the following procedure:

1. Start the Virtual Machine Manager console.

2. Navigate to the VMs And Services workspace, select the VM for which you want to set a custom property, and open its properties.

3. Select the Custom Properties area, and click the Manage Custom Properties button.

4. In the Manage Custom Properties dialog box, click the Create button.

5. Enter a name and description for the custom property and click OK.

6. The new custom property is available in the list of available properties. Select it, and click the Add button so it becomes an assigned property, and then click OK. Note that the View Script button is available to show Windows PowerShell script to perform the action you just performed in the GUI; for example:

```
New-SCCustomProperty -Name "Cost Center" `
-Description "Cost Center of the object" -AddMember @("VM")
```

7. You can now set a value for the custom property, and again the View Script button will show you the PowerShell script to perform the action.

8. Now select the properties of a host group, select the Custom Properties area, and click Manage Custom Properties. The custom property you already created is available. Add it to the assigned properties and enter a value.

9. In the same host group properties dialog box is the Placement Rules page, which allows you to select custom properties. It also shows you how the custom property must/should relate to the host, as shown in Figure 7.41.

10. Click OK to all dialog boxes.

FIGURE 7.41
Setting a placement rule for a host group

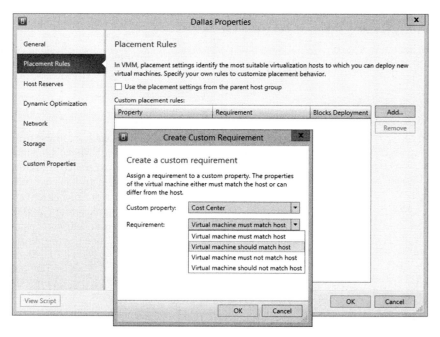

Windows Server 2016 introduces some new native capabilities: Node Fairness and VM Start Ordering. Node Fairness provides a native, basic version of Dynamic Optimization in Failover Clustering.

Node fairness is enabled by default, and based on memory and CPU utilization, it will automatically live-migrate VMs between cluster nodes to rebalance utilization. Any rules around possible owners, fault domains, and anti-affinity are honored as part of the rebalancing. There are some configurations as to how aggressive the balancing should be, based on the host being 60 percent, 70 percent or 80 percent utilized. The exact options are shown in Table 7.1.

TABLE 7.1:   *AutoBalancerLevel* Options

AUTOBALANCERLEVEL	AGGRESSIVENESS	HOST LOAD PERCENTAGE
1 (default)	Low	80%
2	Medium	70%
3	High	60%

This is configured via the AutoBalancerLevel property of the cluster; for example:

```
(Get-Cluster).AutoBalancerLevel = 2
```

Additionally, when the autobalancing is performed, it can be configured as shown in Table 7.2. The options show that node fairness can be disabled, can be performed only when a node joins, or can be performed only when a node joins and every 30 minutes. This can also be configured viaFailover Cluster Manager through the Balancer tab of the cluster properties, as shown in Figure 7.42.

TABLE 7.2:   Node Fairness Configuration

AUTOBALANCERMODE	BEHAVIOR
0	Disabled
1	Load balance on node join
2	Load balance on node join and every 30 minutes

When using SCVMM with Windows Server 2016, the native Node Fairness is automatically disabled. To view the current configuration for Node Fairness, examine the cluster AutoBalancer properties. For example:

```
PS C:\> Get-Cluster | fl AutoBalancer*

AutoBalancerMode : 2
AutoBalancerLevel: 1
```

FIGURE 7.42
Configuring node fairness using Failover Cluster Manager

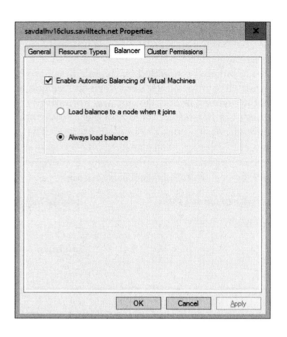

The other nice feature related to VM placement is Start Ordering. As the name suggests, this capability enables VMs to be placed into sets and then dependencies to be defined between sets of VMs. While my focus is on VMs, Start Ordering works with any cluster resource group—for example, a SQL database. Once the dependencies are defined, it allows an order to be determined for VMs. Consider a three-tiered application with a web frontend, a middle layer, and then a database backend. The database needs to start first, then the middle layer, and finally the web frontend. The web frontend set would depend on the middle layer set, and the middle layer set would depend on the database set. The database may also require AD, so the database set would have a dependency on the domain controllers set. No special action is needed when starting VMs. If you attempt to start a VM that is part of a dependency, then the VMs upon which it is dependent (and those other dependent VMs required by the dependent VMs, and so on) will all be started in the required order before the VM you selected to start will actually attempt to start.

The first step is to create the sets:

```
New-ClusterGroupSet -Name <set name, e.g. WebServers>
```

Next add cluster resources (VMs in our case) to the set:

```
Add-ClusterGroupToSet -Name <set name, e.g. WebServers> -Group <name of
group, e.g. IISVM01>
```

Once all the sets are defined and resources added to the set, the dependencies are defined. To make one set dependent on another set use the following:

```
Add-ClusterGroupSetDependency -Name <set name, e.g. WebServers> `
        -Provider <set name, e.g. MiddleLayer>
```

To view the configuration of the sets and the dependencies, use the following PowerShell:

```
Get-ClusterGroupSetDependency | ft Name, GroupNames, ProviderNames -AutoSize
```

You also can customize the delay between sets starting (which by default is 20 seconds) via the -StartDelay parameter and the Set-ClusterGroupSet cmdlet. It is also possible to create a set as global, which means every other set is dependent upon it without having to manually set a dependency. For example, consider your domain controllers; these need to be started before any other set. The following code is an example of setting a utility set as global. Note only VMs in a set will cause sets defined as global to be started, and not VMs that are not in a set.

```
New-ClusterGroupSet -Name UtilitySet
Add-ClusterGroupToSet -Name UtilitySet -Group savdaldc01
Set-ClusterGroupSet -Name UtilitySet -IsGlobal 1
```

If you have multiple sets defined as global, then all global sets will start at the same time if another set is started. Note that you can create dependencies between the global sets themselves to give them a start order! For example, the global set UtilitySet2 will be started before the global set UtilitySet:

```
New-ClusterGroupSet -Name UtilitySet2
Add-ClusterGroupToSet -Name UtilitySet2 -Group savdalnwgw
Set-ClusterGroupSet -Name UtilitySet2 -IsGlobal 1
Add-ClusterGroupSetDependency -Name UtilitySet -Provider UtilitySet2
```

Start Ordering is respected when you start VMs through Failover Cluster Manager, the Start-ClusterGroupSet PowerShell cmdlet, and System Center Virtual Machine Manager. If you start a VM using Hyper-V Manager or the Hyper-V PowerShell, Start Ordering is not enforced, allowing the VM to start straightaway. However, once the VM is started, clustering will detect that the VM has started, and the first in the set dependency chain will be started, and then the rest of the chain in the normal order, based on the dependencies defined.

The Bottom Line

Understand the quorum model used in Windows Server 2012 R12 and above. Windows Server 2012 R2 removed all of the previous models that were based on the way votes were allocated and the type of quorum resource. In Windows Server 2012 R2, each node has a vote and a witness is always configured, but it's used only when required. Windows Server 2012 introduced dynamic quorum, which helps ensure that clusters stay running for as long as possible as nodes' votes are removed from quorum because the nodes are unavailable. Windows Server 2012 R2 added dynamic witness to change the vote of the witness resource based on whether there are an odd or even number of nodes in the cluster.

Identify the types of mobility available with Hyper-V. Mobility focuses on the ability to move virtual machines between Hyper-V hosts. Virtual machines within a cluster can be live-migrated between any node efficiently, since all nodes have access to the same storage, allowing only the memory and state to be copied between the nodes. Windows Server 2012 introduced the ability to move the storage of a virtual machine with no downtime, which when combined with Live Migration enables a Shared Nothing Live Migration capability that means a virtual machine can be moved between any two Hyper-V hosts without the need for shared storage or a cluster, with no downtime to the virtual machine.

Shared Nothing Live Migration does not remove the need for Failover Clustering but provides the maximum flexibility possible, enabling virtual machines to be moved between stand-alone hosts, between clusters, and between stand-alone hosts and clusters.

Master It   Why is constrained delegation needed when using Shared Nothing Live Migration with remote management?

Understand the best way to patch a cluster with minimal impact to workloads.   All virtual machines in a cluster can run on any of the member nodes. That means before you patch and reboot a node, all virtual machines should be moved to other nodes by using Live Migration, which removes any impact on the availability of the virtual machines. While the migration of virtual machines between nodes can be performed manually, Windows Server 2012 Failover Clustering provides Cluster-Aware Updating, giving you a single-click ability to patch the entire cluster without any impact to virtual machines' availability. For pre-Windows Server 2012 clusters, SCVMM 2012 also provides an automated patching capability. Configuration Manager 2016 provides a cluster-aware patching capability for organizations that leverage Configuration Manager for patching.

Chapter 8

Hyper-V Replica and Cloud Orchestration

High availability is essential for providing the most resilient infrastructure possible for a Hyper-V environment in order to ensure the availability of virtual machines. However, the ability to provide disaster-recovery services to protect against the loss of an entire site is becoming a high priority for many organizations. Windows Server 2012 introduced a capability to Hyper-V that provides replication from one Hyper-V server to another, independent of any cluster or storage replication capabilities, and this has continued to evolve with each new version and can also integrate with Azure.

This chapter covers the options for providing disaster recovery for services in an organization, and it explains how Hyper-V Replica fits into a complete disaster-recovery solution. The chapter also presents the options for providing orchestration of disaster-recovery failover.

In this chapter, you will learn to:

- Identify the best options for providing disaster recovery for the various services in your organization.

- Describe the types of failover for Hyper-V Replica.

- Explain the automated options for Hyper-V Replica failover.

The Need for Disaster Recovery and DR Basics

Modern organizations have various applications that are used internally by partners and by customers. These applications range from ones that are "nice to have" but not essential to doing business to those that would shut down the company if not available. Even the briefest outage of these business-critical applications can cause organizations harm in multiple ways, including the following:

- Financial loss through not being able to perform normal business functions

- Damage to reputation through publicly visible outages that erode confidence in the organization for external parties

- Potential compliance gaps to regulatory requirements

It is therefore important to ensure that business-critical applications are always available, both within the primary datacenter through high-availability technologies and in alternate locations through disaster-recovery technologies. (Often a single technology can be leveraged for both high availability and disaster recovery.) To provide disaster recovery, the data related to an application must be available in the alternate location, which means data replication. There must be a means to run the application and connect to it, so compute and network resources are required.

It is important to understand which applications are critical to the organization, and that can be ascertained only with the involvement of the business groups. Once the business-critical applications are identified, you must understand the dependent applications and services of those applications, because protecting the business-critical applications without their dependencies would result in a nonfunctional solution in the event of a system outage or disaster scenario.

As an example, consider a typical line-of-business application that may run on one or more application servers. That application may leverage a SQL database that runs on a separate infrastructure, it may publish services through a corporate reverse proxy that is Internet facing, and it may require Active Directory for authentication. For the line-of-business application to be functional, all of those dependent services must be available. In fact, when planning for high availability and disaster recovery, it's necessary to protect the applications and services that the target application depends on at the same or higher protection level.

There are many ways to provide resiliency and availability to services locally, within a location and between locations, and there is no single "best" technology; rather, it is important to utilize the best availability technology for specific applications and services. Many availability solutions leverage the Failover Clustering feature that was covered in the previous chapter. A cluster-enabled application is protected from the failure of a node and will either seamlessly transition to another node or restart on another node without any administrator intervention.

Traditionally, a physical location was the boundary for a cluster for the following reasons:

◆ Cluster applications historically required access to shared storage that was facilitated via SAN storage and connected using technologies such as iSCSI and Fibre Channel. Making shared storage available to a remote SAN was typically not possible because of the latencies introduced with remotely accessing storage, and having a remote site dependent on storage in another remote site defeated the point of having a multisite cluster, which was to protect from a site failure. The solution was to have SAN-level replication, which historically was not available or was prohibitively expensive. However, Windows Server 2016 does offer an in-box Storage Replica capability in the Datacenter SKU that can help offset this limitation.

◆ Nodes in a cluster required a high-quality connection between nodes that was not tolerant to latency. This network was used for heartbeats between nodes to ensure that all nodes were healthy and available. Cluster resources required an IP address that could not be changed between locations. Most multisite environments use different IP networks at the different locations, which meant that using clustering in a multisite environment, complex VLAN configurations, and geo-networks were required.

◆ Clusters used a special quorum disk that provided the foundation for partitioning protection. This quorum disk always had to be available, which typically meant that it was located in one physical location.

Windows Server 2008 and a new shift in many datacenter applications removed these barriers for enabling multisite clusters. Key datacenter applications, such as SQL Server and Exchange, introduced options that did not require shared storage and instead leveraged their own data-replication technologies. Failover Clustering introduced changes that enabled multiple

IP addresses to be allocated to a resource, and whichever IP address was required for the site in which the resource was active was used. Failover Clustering also enabled more-flexible heartbeat configurations, which tolerated higher-latency networks; in addition, the reliance on a quorum disk was removed, offering additional quorum models based on the number of nodes and even a file share located at a third site. Being able to run clusters over multiple locations without shared storage enables certain disaster-recovery options that will be discussed.

When designing a disaster-recovery solution, many options typically are available that offer different levels of recoverability. The *recovery point objective (RPO)* is the point to which you want to recover in the event of a disaster. For example, only 30 minutes of data should be lost. The *recovery time objective (RTO)* is how quickly you need to be up-and-running in the event of a disaster. For example, the systems should be available within four hours in the event of a disaster. It's important to understand the RPO and RTO requirements for your systems when designing your disaster-recovery solution. Also, different systems will likely have different requirements.

It is important to be realistic about the capabilities of your organization. An alternative to implementing new disaster-recovery solutions for services may be to host the service in a public cloud infrastructure that provides site resiliency as part of the service. Using the public cloud as the disaster-recovery location can also be an option.

Create detailed processes that will be used in the event of a disaster to facilitate the failover. These processes should be updated anytime a system changes or a new system is added. Disaster-recovery tests should be performed at least every six months. Make sure that the disaster-recovery plans do not assume any amount of knowledge, because the regular IT personnel may not be available in the event of a disaster.

Asynchronous vs. Synchronous Replication

As discussed, disaster recovery requires having the application data available in the disaster-recovery location. This either requires the data to be stored somewhere that is available to both locations, such as in the public cloud, or more commonly, it requires the data to be stored in both locations and replication technologies to be used to keep the replica copy of the data synchronized with the primary (live) copy of the data.

The mode of the replication can be either asynchronous or synchronous:

Asynchronous Mode   This mode allows transactions to be committed on the primary source before the transaction has been sent to the replicas or has been acknowledged. The exact mechanism for asynchronous replication differs, but the key point is that the primary source can continue working independently of the replica receiving and acknowledging the data. This gives the best performance on the primary replica (although there is always a slight risk of data loss in a failure situation because data is committed on the primary before it's committed or potentially even sent to the replica).

Synchronous Mode   This mode ensures that no transactions are committed on the primary source until they are acknowledged on the replica. This ensures that there is no risk of data loss, but this will incur some performance impact because of the additional delay while waiting for the acknowledgments from the replica. The higher the latency between the primary and the replica, the greater the performance impact.

Nearly every type of cross-site replication leverages asynchronous as the replication type because of the typical high latency between different locations and the performance impact that synchronous replication across high-latency links imposes. Synchronous replication is typically reserved within a datacenter for highly critical data that cannot risk any kind of data loss.

SQL Server is a good example of a workload that leverages both asynchronous and synchronous replication with its Always On technology. Always On provides the replication of SQL databases between a primary replica and one or more secondary replicas. Within a datacenter, synchronous Always On replication may be used; between locations, the asynchronous Always On replication is typically used. SQL Always On allows switching between replication types, which opens up some interesting failover solutions such as running in asynchronous normally but switching to synchronous prior to failover to ensure no data loss.

Many storage solutions, such as SANs, offer replication at a storage level from one SAN to another, and very high-end SANs can offer a synchronous replication capability. This is typically expensive and is specific to the type of SAN used. The benefit of using SAN-level replication where available is that a cluster can then use the SAN storage in multiple locations as a single logical storage device, enabling clusters to span multiple locations with "shared" storage. Some large organizations leverage this type of SAN replication for their tier 1 workloads.

Windows Server 2016 features native block-level replication using the Storage Replica feature that supports both synchronous and asynchronous replication, which is completely agnostic of the storage subsystem used. This also integrates tightly with Failover Clustering to offer cluster storage across geographies.

Introduction to Hyper-V Replica

The news over the past few years has been filled with natural disasters, such as Hurricane Sandy, which have caused a loss of life and huge damage to the infrastructure of entire cities. Even if the possibility of this type of disaster is recognized weeks in advance, many organizations lack the technologies to enable disaster recovery to alternate locations. In the previous section, I talked about SAN-level replication, which is expensive and has requirements that are not available to many organizations. Some applications such as SQL, Exchange, and Active Directory have their own replication technologies to enable disaster-recovery protection, but many other applications do not have any kind of replication capability. As more and more of the datacenter is using virtualization, organizations are looking for a solution at the virtualization layer to help in disaster-recovery planning.

Windows Server 2012 was an enormous release, particularly with regard to virtualization and enabling cloud services. One of the biggest new features was the introduction of Hyper-V Replica. Hyper-V Replica introduces the ability to replicate a virtual machine asynchronously to a second Hyper-V host. The target Hyper-V server, the *replica*, does not have to be part of a cluster with the primary Hyper-V host (in fact, the replica cannot be in the same cluster as the primary), does not need any shared storage, and does not even require dedicated network infrastructure for the replication. The goal of Hyper-V Replica is to enable disaster-recovery capabilities for any Hyper-V environment without steep requirements, and this is achieved through its use of asynchronous replication.

Hyper-V Replica uses asynchronous replication efficiently and at a high level works as follows:

1. When a virtual machine is enabled for replication, a new virtual machine is created on the Hyper-V replica host that matches the configuration of the primary virtual machine, and the replica virtual machine is turned off.

2. The storage of the primary virtual machine is replicated to the replica virtual machine, and a log is started on the primary virtual machine for the VHDs being replicated that stores the writes to the VHDs. The log file is stored in the same location as the source VHD.

3. Once the initial replication of the storage is complete, the log file is closed. A new log file is started to track ongoing changes, and the closed log file is sent to the replica Hyper-V host and merged with the VHDs for the replica VM. The replica VM remains turned off.

4. At a defined time interval, the log file is closed, a new one is created, and the closed log file is sent to the replica and merged.

Note that the only replication is of the virtual hard disks of the virtual machine, not the ongoing configuration of the virtual machine and not the memory. This is why you cannot enable Hyper-V Replica for virtual machines that leverage virtual Fibre Channel, iSCSI, or pass-through storage. The virtual machine must use virtual hard disks for all storage because it is through the VHD implementation that replication is enabled. If you use virtual Fibre Channel or iSCSI, the assumption would be that the SAN is performing some level of replication between the primary and replica locations, which means that it would make more sense for that SAN replication to replicate the VHDs of the virtual machine as well as the LUNs attached to the VM using virtual Fibre Channel/iSCSI. You would not want two replication technologies used that would be out of sync with each other.

Because Hyper-V Replica uses asynchronous replication, there is a period where the replica is missing some of the data from the primary source. Potentially, in an unplanned failure, a certain amount of data may be lost. The exact amount of loss depends on how frequently the replica is updated. In Windows Server 2012, this was every 5 minutes, but in Windows Server 2012 R2 and above, it can be every 30 seconds, every 5 minutes, or every 15 minutes. This possible data loss needs to be compared against the RPO of the application. If the application has an RPO of 5 minutes, you can replicate at a 5-minute or 30-second interval. If the RPO is 1 minute, you must replicate at the 30-second interval and also ensure that there is sufficient bandwidth to handle the transmission of logs from the source to the replica. The good news is that because the replication is asynchronous, the introduction of the replica does not lead to any performance degradation on the source virtual machine and does not require very fast, low-latency network connections between the source host and the replica host.

The use of asynchronous replication by Hyper-V Replica opens up the use of replication for disaster-recovery scenarios to many more scenarios and types of companies. These are some key ones that are often considered:

◆ Datacenter-to-datacenter replication for tier 1 applications for organizations without SAN-level replication such as small and medium-sized organizations

◆ Datacenter-to-datacenter replication for tier 2 applications for organizations with SAN-level replication but that don't want to use the SAN-level replication for applications that are not tier 1

◆ Replication from branch office to head office to protect applications hosted at the branch location

◆ Replication from hoster location 1 to hoster location 2 for hosting companies

Small organizations that do not have a second datacenter can replicate to a hoster as the secondary datacenter for DR needs or even to a consulting organization's datacenter for their clients.

Many more scenarios exist, including anything that is enabled through the asynchronous replication of a virtual machine. The key point is that with Hyper-V Replica, the ability to replicate virtual machines is now an option for any organization with two locations. As I cover later in the chapter, it's an option even if an organization has only one location. It is also important to note that Hyper-V Replica is completely agnostic of the underlying storage technology used.

Enabling Hyper-V Replica

Hyper-V Replica is simple to configure, and the easiest way to understand how it works is to walk through its setup options and enable replication for a virtual machine. The first step in using Hyper-V Replica is to configure the replica Hyper-V server to accept requests for it to host a replica. This is performed using Hyper-V Manager. Select Hyper-V Settings from the server's list of actions, and in Hyper-V Settings, select the Replication Configuration list of configurations, as shown in Figure 8.1. Select the Enable This Computer As A Replica Server check box. Then you have a couple of choices to make.

FIGURE 8.1
Enabling inbound replication for a Hyper-V server

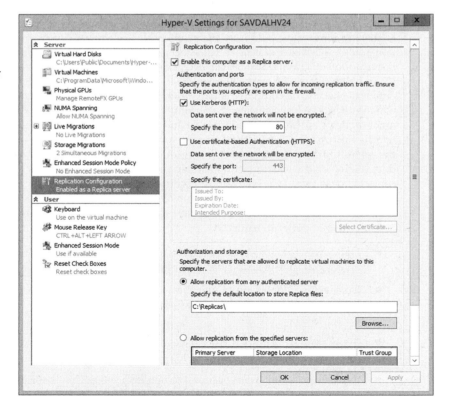

The first choice is to enable the use of Kerberos (which uses HTTP) or certificate-based authentication (which uses HTTPS). Kerberos is the simpler option to configure, but it requires that the primary and replica Hyper-V servers use Kerberos authentication and therefore are part of the same Active Directory forest or trusted domain. When using Kerberos, the replication of data between the primary and replica is not encrypted and is sent over the standard HTTP port 80. If encryption is required, the Windows IPsec implementation could be used. The other option is to use certificate-based authentication, which enables the primary and replica *not* to be part of the same Active Directory forest or even organization and requires a certificate to be specified for use with an added benefit of using HTTPS, meaning that all data transferred is now encrypted. Both Kerberos and certificate-based authentication can be enabled; in that case, when a new replication relationship is established, the administrator configuring the replication will be given a choice to use either Kerberos or certificate-based authentication. The option to use certificate-based authentication would be useful if you wanted to replicate to a Hyper-V server that's not part of your organization, such as a host offered by a hosting company as part of an external disaster-recovery solution.

The only other configuration choice is to specify which servers the replica server will accept replication requests from and where those replicas will be stored. One option is to allow replication from any authenticated server, in which case a single location is selected where all replicas will be stored. The other option is to indicate specific servers that can replicate to the server; in this case, each server can have a different storage location. When specifying servers, it is possible to use the wildcard character within the server name (but only one wildcard is supported in the server name); this allows the enablement of a group of servers such as `*.savilltech.net` for all servers whose fully qualified domain name ends in `savilltech.net`. The Trust Group setting is simply a tag to allow VMs to move between Hyper-V hosts with the same trust group and continue replicating without issue. With Shared Nothing Live Migration, virtual machines can be moved between Hyper-V hosts that are not clustered with no downtime. With this new mobility capability, you need to ensure that groups of servers have the same trust group tag to enable replication to be unaffected if virtual machines are moved between servers within a trust group.

You can also perform this configuration using PowerShell via the `Set-VMReplicationServer` cmdlet. For example, to enable replication with the default settings (allow replication from any server and use Kerberos), I use the following:

```
Set-VMReplicationServer -ReplicationEnabled 1 -ComputerName savdalhv24
```

Further configuration can be performed using `Set-VMReplicationServer`. The easiest way to see the options is to view the output of `Get-VMReplicationServer`, as shown here:

```
PS C:\> get-vmreplicationserver -computername savdalhv24 | fl


ComputerName                      : savdalhv24
ReplicationEnabled                : True
ReplicationAllowedFromAnyServer   : True
AllowedAuthenticationType         : Kerberos
CertificateThumbprint             :
KerberosAuthenticationPort        : 80
CertificateAuthenticationPort     : 443
KerberosAuthenticationPortMapping :
```

```
CertificateAuthenticationPortMapping:
MonitoringInterval              : 12:00:00
MonitoringStartTime             : 15:00:00
DefaultStorageLocation          : C:\Replicas\
OperationalStatus               : {Ok}
StatusDescriptions              : {The Replication Service is fully
operational.}
AuthorizationEntries            : {*}
Key                             :
IsDeleted                       : False
RepEnabled                      : True
KerbAuthPort                    : 80
CertAuthPort                    : 443
AllowAnyServer                  : True
AuthType                        : Kerb
```

Additionally, replication entries from specific hosts can be added by using the
-New-VMReplicationAuthorizationEntry cmdlet. Here's an example:

```
New-VMReplicationAuthorizationEntry -AllowedPrimaryServer <primary server>
  -ReplicaStorageLocation <location> -TrustGroup <tag if needed>
```

The final step to complete in order to have a server accept replication is to enable the required firewall exception for the port used: 80 for HTTP and 443 for HTTPS. The firewall exceptions are built into Windows Server but are not enabled even after replication configuration is complete. Thus you will need to start the Windows Firewall with the Advanced Security administrative tool, select Inbound Rules, and enable either (depending on your authentication methods) Hyper-V Replica HTTP Listener (TCP-In) or Hyper-V Replica HTTPS Listener (TCP-In), or both.

Once the replica server has been enabled for replication, it is important also to enable the primary Hyper-V server as a replica. This allows the reversal of replication in the event that the virtual machine is activated on the replica server and now needs to start replicating to the server that was previously the primary but would now be considered the replica.

One item that you do not need to configure as part of the replication configuration is the network to use for the replication traffic. The assumption is that this technology is used between datacenters and that there would be only one valid path between them; therefore, Hyper-V Replica will automatically choose the correct network to use for the replication traffic.

If you have existing Windows Server 2012 Hyper-V Replica environments to upgrade to Windows Server 2012 R2, you must upgrade the replica Hyper-V server first. The same logic applies when upgrading to Windows Server 2016; the replica server must be updated to the 2016 version before the source.

Configuring Hyper-V Replica

Once the Hyper-V hosts are configured to enable the Hyper-V Replica capability, the next step is enabling virtual machines to be replicated. To show how to enable replication, I will initially use Hyper-V Manager, although PowerShell can also be used and would be used in any kind of automated bulk configuration. You select the virtual machine on which you want to enable replication and select the Enable Replication action. The Replication Configuration Wizard then launches. Then follow these steps:

1. Specify the replica server that will host the replica and be sure that the authentication type to use is selected. A check is performed against the replica server to check the types of authentication that are supported. If both Kerberos and certificate-based authentication are supported on the target replica server and are usable, you will need to select the authentication method to use, typically Kerberos. Additionally, you can select whether the data sent over the network should be compressed, which will save network bandwidth but will also use additional CPU cycles both on the primary and replica Hyper-V servers. The option to use compression is enabled by default.

2. Select the virtual hard disks that should be replicated. If a virtual machine has multiple virtual hard disks, the hard disks to be replicated can be selected to ensure that only the required ones are replicated. For example, you could do this in order not to replicate VHDs containing just a pagefile, although this does cause more management overhead and, given the churn of pagefiles, is typically quite light; so, this is not a mandatory step. Be aware that only VHDs can be replicated; if a virtual machine uses pass-through disks, they cannot be replicated with Hyper-V Replica (another reason to avoid pass-through disks).

3. Identify the frequency of replication, which can be 30 seconds, 5 minutes, or 15 minutes. This step was not present in Windows Server 2012, which supported a 5-minute replication frequency only.

4. Configure the recovery history. By default, the replica will have a single recovery point: the latest replication state. For an extended recovery history, set optional additional hourly recovery points, as shown in Figure 8.2. The additional recovery points are manifested as snapshots on the virtual machine that is created on the replica server; you can choose a specific recovery point by selecting the desired snapshot. Windows Server 2012 R2 increased the number of hourly recovery points from 16 to 24, which provides the ability to have a full day of incremental protection. Windows Server 2012 R2 also improves the mechanics of how the replica works, which now behaves more like a copy-on-write backup because writes written to the replica VHD have the replaced blocks now written to undo logs. This provides performance improvements and continues in Windows Server 2016.

An additional option to create an incremental VSS copy at a configurable number of hours is also available. This gives an additional level of assurance in the integrity of the replica at that point in time. The normal log files sent at the replication interval provide the latest storage content, but at that point the disk may have been in an inconsistent state on the source virtual machine. Therefore, when the replica was started, the replica VHD might not have been in a consistent state. The incremental VSS option, when enabled, triggers a VSS snapshot on the source prior to that cycle's replication, which forces the source virtual machine to ensure that the disk content is in an application-consistent state (in the same manner as if a backup were taken, the log file was closed and sent to the replica, and then that state was saved as the application-consistent recovery point on the target). If the virtual machine contains an application that has VSS writers, I suggest using the option to create an application-consistent recovery point. The default of 4 hours is a good balance between integrity and the additional work caused by creating a VSS recovery point on the source virtual machine.

FIGURE 8.2
Recovery-point
configuration

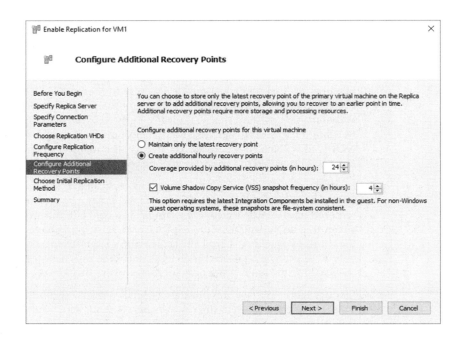

Once the recovery-point configuration is complete, you need to choose the method to replicate the storage initially. It can be accomplished by any of the following:

- Sending the VHD content over the network

- Sending the VHD content via external media and specifying a location to export the content

- Using an existing virtual machine on the replica server as the initial copy. This can be used if you already restored the virtual machine to the target Hyper-V server, or perhaps if you previously had replication enabled and broke the replica but now want to enable it again. An efficient bit-by-bit comparison will be performed between the primary and replica to ensure consistency.

The initial replication can be configured to begin immediately or at a later time, such as outside normal business hours when contention on the network resources would be less. Depending on the choices made, the virtual machine would be created on the replica Hyper-V server in the off state, and the initial replication would begin. Once complete, at the replica time interval, the Hyper-V Replica log (HRL) file is closed, sent to the replica, and merged into the replica VHD. The entire time the replica virtual machine is turned off. No memory, processor, or device state is replicated to the replica virtual machine; only disk content is replicated. In the event that the replica is activated, it will be turned on and booted, similar to a crash-consistent state as if it previously had just been powered down without a clean shutdown. This is one of the reasons that performing the periodic VSS snapshot recovery point is useful to ensure disk integrity.

To view the exact replication configuration of a virtual machine once the configuration has been performed, view the settings of the virtual machine. The Replication tab shows all of the details of the Hyper-V Replica configuration, including the replica interval and authentication and recovery-point configuration.

You can also enable replication using PowerShell with the `Enable-VMReplication` cmdlet. The only parameters to enable replication are to specify `VMName` for the virtual machine to be replicated, to specify the replica server using `ReplicaServerName` and `ReplicaServerPort`, and to specify the authentication type using `AuthenticationType`. Once replication is enabled, you need to start the initial replication using `Start-VMInitialReplication`.

Once the replica virtual machine is created, it is now a separate virtual machine from the primary virtual machine. Any changes in configuration to the primary virtual machine are not reflected in the replica virtual machine. This allows changes to be made on either side, and the replication of the VHD content will continue. Still, if changes are made to the primary source, such as increasing resources like memory or processor, you will need to reflect that change manually on the replica.

The fact that the virtual machine on the primary and on the replica are separate virtual machines in terms of configuration enables some nice functionality. In most environments, the primary and secondary datacenters use different IP networks, which means that when a virtual machine is started in the disaster-recovery site, it needs a new IP address. As part of the Hyper-V Replica functionality, an additional configuration is available on the virtual machine once replication has been enabled, namely, a failover TCP/IP configuration (found under the Network Adapter configuration of the virtual machine). This allows an alternate IPv4 and IPv6 configuration to be specified on each virtual network adapter for the replica virtual machine, which is injected into the virtual machine in the event of a failover, as shown in Figure 8.3.

FIGURE 8.3
Configuring an alternate IP configuration to be used during failover

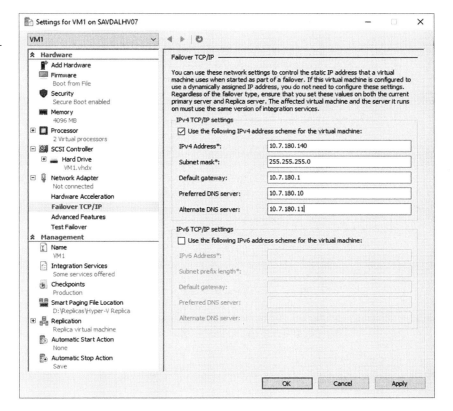

It is important to understand that this process works by Hyper-V updating the virtual machine through the Windows Server Hyper-V Integration Services running on the virtual machine. This works only on synthetic network adapters, not legacy network adapters, and it requires Windows XP SP2/Windows Server 2003 SP2 and newer to be running on the virtual machine to work. This also works with Linux virtual machines that are running the latest Linux distributions. A good practice is to complete the failover TCP/IP configuration on the primary virtual machine with its normal IP configuration. That way, if the replica is ever activated, replication is reversed, and the virtual machine is then failed back to what was the primary, and the correct IP address for the primary location can automatically be put back.

INJECT IP CONFIGURATION OUTSIDE HYPER-V REPLICA BY USING POWERSHELL

Hyper-V Replica offers the ability to inject an IP address into a virtual machine; you can also use this functionality outside Hyper-V Replica.

To perform the injection with PowerShell, use the following code, which leverages the `Msvm_GuestNetworkAdapterConfiguration` class [http://msdn.microsoft.com/en-us/library/hh850156(v=vs.85).aspx]. Replace the name of the VM and the IP configuration as needed.

```
$vmName = "win81g2"

$Msvm_VirtualSystemManagementService = Get-WmiObject `
    -Namespace root\virtualization\v2 `
    -Class Msvm_VirtualSystemManagementService

$Msvm_ComputerSystem = Get-WmiObject -Namespace root\virtualization\v2 `
    -Class Msvm_ComputerSystem -Filter "ElementName='$vmName'"

$Msvm_VirtualSystemSettingData =
($Msvm_ComputerSystem.GetRelated(«Msvm_VirtualSystemSettingData», `
    "Msvm_SettingsDefineState", $null, $null, "SettingData", `
   «ManagedElement», $false, $null) | % {$_})

$Msvm_SyntheticEthernetPortSettingData = $Msvm_VirtualSystemSettingData
.GetRelated(«Msvm_SyntheticEthernetPortSettingData»)

$Msvm_GuestNetworkAdapterConfiguration = ($Msvm_SyntheticEthernetPortSettingData
.GetRelated( `
    "Msvm_GuestNetworkAdapterConfiguration", "Msvm_SettingDataComponent", `
    $null, $null, "PartComponent", "GroupComponent", $false, $null) | % {$_})

$Msvm_GuestNetworkAdapterConfiguration.DHCPEnabled = $false
$Msvm_GuestNetworkAdapterConfiguration.IPAddresses = @("192.168.1.207")
```

```
$Msvm_GuestNetworkAdapterConfiguration.Subnets = @("255.255.255.0")
$Msvm_GuestNetworkAdapterConfiguration.DefaultGateways = @("192.168.1.1")
$Msvm_GuestNetworkAdapterConfiguration.DNSServers = @("192.168.1.10",
«192.168.1.11»)

$Msvm_VirtualSystemManagementService.SetGuestNetworkAdapterConfiguration( `
$Msvm_ComputerSystem.Path, $Msvm_GuestNetworkAdapterConfiguration.GetText(1))
```

Separating the virtual machine between the primary and the replica carries a disadvantage. If additional virtual hard disks are added to the primary virtual machine, those virtual hard disks will not automatically start replicating to the replica. The only way to add the new virtual hard disks for the virtual machine to those being replicated is to break the replication between the primary and the replica and then reestablish replication by selecting the new virtual hard disks as part of the replication set. When reestablishing replication, you can specify to use the existing virtual machine for the initial data, which will optimize the amount of data required to seed the replica. Additionally, enterprise virtualization management solutions like SCVMM will handle this scenario automatically and add new disks as part of the replica configuration. Windows Server 2016 improves on this situation by allowing new disks to be attached to a VM without causing any errors and then allowing disks to be added or removed to the VM's replication set without requiring the entire replication relationship to be re-created. Instead, the Set-VMReplication cmdlet is used with the -ReplicatedDisks argument, which can specify the disks that should be replicated. For example, to add all disks to the replication set, you could use the following:

```
Set-VMReplication -VMName <vm name> `
-ReplicatedDisks (Get-VMHardDiskDrive -VMName <vm name>)
```

One key point of Hyper-V Replica is that a virtual machine can have only one replica. Additionally, in Windows Server 2012 and above, you cannot create a replica of a replica VM, known as *extended replication*. This is not a problem if you consider the original goal of Hyper-V Replica, which is having a replica of a virtual machine in a disaster-recovery location. This is also why the fixed interval of 5 minutes was a good default value.

But some organizations used Hyper-V Replica differently. They used Hyper-V Replica within a single datacenter where they could not use clustering or did not want to use it. This is also the reason the 5-minute replication frequency was too restrictive and organizations wanted to replicate more frequently. These same organizations still wanted to be able to have a replica to an alternate site, which required extending replication. As mentioned, the ability to add a replica to the existing replica virtual machine was added in Windows Server 2012 R2. Note you still cannot have more than one replica for a single VM; so, with Windows Server 2012 R2 and above, the primary virtual machine can still have only one replica, but that replica can now have its own replica, as shown in Figure 8.4.

Note that an extended replica can be used in any situation, not just if you have the main replication within a datacenter. If you have two DR locations, the Hyper-V extended replica can be beneficial. I've also seen it when in the primary datacenter the standard Hyper-V

Replica feature is used to replicate a virtual machine from one cluster to another cluster and then the extended replica is used to replicate to the DR datacenter. The extended replica has its own replication interval that is independent of the primary replica, but its interval cannot be less than that of the primary replica. For example, if the primary replica replicates every 5 minutes, then the extended replica can replicate every 5 minutes or 15 minutes but not at the 30-second interval.

FIGURE 8.4
Windows Server 2012
R2 Hyper-V extended
replication

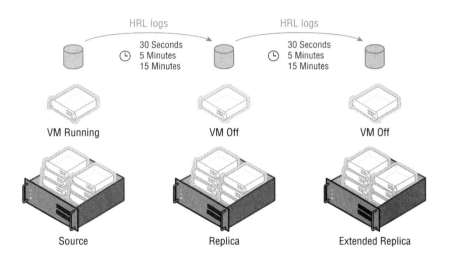

To enable the extended replication, perform the following steps:

1. Open Hyper-V Manager, and select the Hyper-V host that hosts the replica virtual machine (note the replica and not the source virtual machine).

2. Right-click the replica virtual machine, and select the Extend Replication action from the Replication menu.

3. Click Next on the introduction screen of the Extend Replication Wizard.

4. Select the server that will host the extended replica, and click Next.

5. The rest of the configuration is the same as enabling a normal replica: Select the authentication type, the frequency of replication, the additional recovery points, and the initial method of replication.

There is no separate PowerShell cmdlet to enable extended replication. The same `Enable-VMReplication` cmdlet is used for extended replication by specifying the replica VM. For `ReplicaServerName`, specify the extended replica Hyper-V server.

Replication can be removed for a virtual machine by using the Replication – Remove Replication action or using the `Remove-VMReplication` PowerShell cmdlet.

Prior to Windows Server 2016, it was not possible to enable replication for a shared VHDX file, which is a VHDX connected to multiple virtual machines. Windows Server 2016 removes this limitation when using VHD Sets (which is the 2016 version of Shared VHDX) and fully supports Hyper-V Replica.

Using Hyper-V Replica Broker

If you use Failover Clustering, there is an additional requirement since a failover cluster consists of multiple Hyper-V hosts. If a failover cluster is the target for Hyper-V Replica, it's important that the whole cluster can host the replicated virtual machine and not just a single host. This means that the storage of the replica must be on an SMB share or cluster-shared volume. Hyper-V Replica support in a failover cluster is enabled by adding the Hyper-V Replica Broker role to the failover cluster. This will require a name and IP address for the Hyper-V Replica Broker role, which serves as the client access point (CAP) for Hyper-V Replica and will be the name used when selecting the cluster as a target for a replica.

When enabling replication within a cluster, once the Hyper-V Replica Broker role is added, the replication configuration is performed within the Failover Cluster Manager tool. Once the configurations for replication are completed (which are the same as for a stand-alone Hyper-V host), all hosts in the cluster will automatically be configured, unless certificate-based authentication was selected, in which case each host needs its own certificate configured.

You must configure the Hyper-V Replica Broker role in the cluster even if the cluster is not a replica target (although this is highly unlikely, since in the event of a failover, replication is typically reversed). This means that you always need the Hyper-V Replica Broker role for a cluster that is participating in Hyper-V Replica in any way. If the cluster is the replica target, the broker redirects the replication traffic because the VM may move between hosts in the cluster. If the cluster is the source of the replica, the broker enables authorization of the primary hosts at a cluster level, and of course the replica is needed if the replication is reversed.

Once the Hyper-V Replica Broker role is created, you should modify its configuration by selecting the Replication Settings action for the broker. Then enable the cluster as a replica server and choose the various configurations, which are the same as for a normal replica server, as shown in Figure 8.5. Once replication is enabled, you will need to enable the required firewall exceptions on each host manually as this is not performed by the broker configuration; an example is the Hyper-V Replica HTTP Listener (TCP-In) firewall exception.

To enable the firewall rule on every node in a cluster with PowerShell quickly, use the following. Change the cluster name to that of your cluster.

```
$clusname = "savdalhv16clus"
$servers = Get-ClusterNode -Cluster $clusname
foreach ($server in $servers)
{
    Invoke-Command -ComputerName $server.Name -ScriptBlock `
        {Enable-Netfirewallrule -DisplayName `
        "Hyper-V Replica HTTP Listener (TCP-In)"}
}
```

FIGURE 8.5
Enabling inbound
replication for the
Hyper-V Replica
Broker role

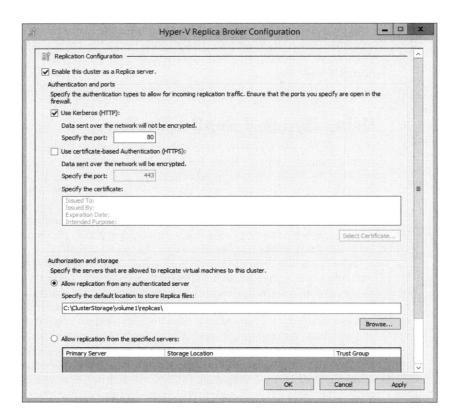

Performing Hyper-V Replica Failover

Once replication is configured, the next step is to perform failovers. But before failing over,
it's important to ensure the ongoing health of the replication. In Hyper-V Manager, each virtual machine has a Replication tab as part of its high-level status. This tab shows the mode
of replication, the health of the replication, and the time of last synchronization. This same
information is available in Failover Cluster Manager for the virtual machine, and you can
view more-detailed health of the replication state by using the Replication – View Replication
Health action, as shown in Figure 8.6. The replication health view shows the same basic overview information but also details of the average and maximum size of the transferred data,
the average latency, any errors, and the number of replication cycles. It also shows pending
replication data.

It may be confusing because there is a Replication State entry and a Replication Health
entry, but Replication State shows the current state of replication, and Replication Health factors in events over a period of time, which helps identify whether there has been a problem
at some point in that evaluation time period. You can find a full list of possible values for
Replication State and Replication Health at http://blogs.technet.com/b/virtualization/
archive/2012/06/15/interpreting-replication-health-part-1.aspx.

FIGURE 8.6

Viewing the health of replication

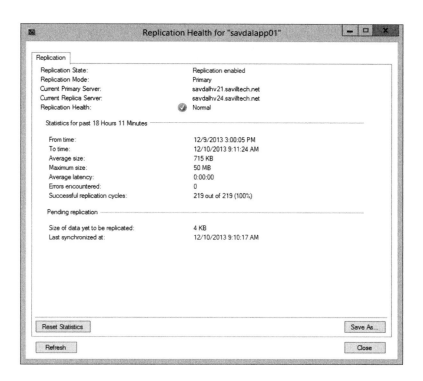

You can also see this health information with PowerShell by using `Measure_VMReplication`. As shown here, the output contains the same basic information as in the replication health graphical interface. If you need a detailed level of monitoring for Hyper-V Replica, one option is to use System Center Operations Manager and the Hyper-V Management Pack, which monitors the health of Hyper-V Replica and many other Hyper-V aspects.

```
PS C:\> Measure-VMReplication -ComputerName savdalhv21 -VMName savdalapp01 | fl


VMName                      : savdalapp01
ReplicationState            : Replicating
ReplicationHealth           : Normal
LastReplicationTime         : 12/10

/2013 9:30:17 AM
PendingReplicationSize      : 4096
AverageReplicationLatency   : 00:00:00
SuccessfulReplicationCount: 223
MissedReplicationCount      : 0
```

If a virtual machine is the replica virtual machine and also has its own extended replica, Measure-VMReplication will return information about its relationship with the primary and extended replica. If you want to view information about only one of the relationships, add -ReplicationRelationshipType and specify either Simple (to view the primary relationship) or Extended (to see the extended relationship).

You can see the HRL files used by Hyper-V Replica if you look at the folder containing the VHD files being replicated. It is possible to pause and resume replication, but be careful to not pause replication for too long because this will cause the log files to build up. You can also pause and resume the replication by using the Suspend-VMReplication and Resume-VMReplication cmdlets. Once again, you can specify ReplicationRelationshipType for a virtual machine that is the replica of the primary and the source for the extended replica (in other words, the one in the middle).

This can also happen if a network break occurs between the primary and replica that stops transmission of the log files. If the size of the log files is greater than 50 percent of the size of the VHD file, a resynchronization is required. Resynchronization performs a block-by-block comparison of the source of the replica, with only different blocks being sent over the network. This is deemed more efficient than sending over the accumulated log files, although there is a performance impact during a resynchronization. Other scenarios can force a resynchronization, but they are rare. See http://blogs.technet.com/b/virtualization/archive/2013/05/10/ resynchronization-of-virtual-machines-in-hyper-v-replica.aspx, which is a great blog post and worth reading for more information on the exact resynchronization process.

Now that you understand how to view the ongoing health of your Hyper-V Replica environment, you can look at the types of failover that you want to perform with Hyper-V Replica. Three types of failover are used with Hyper-V Replica, as detailed here. Depending on its type, the failover is triggered from either the primary or replica Hyper-V host by selecting one of the failover actions from the Replication action menu.

Test Failover This is triggered on the replica virtual machine, which allows the replica VM to be started on the replica Hyper-V host by creating a temporary virtual machine based on the recovery point selected. Testing is performed to ensure that replication is working as planned and as part of a larger site failover test process. During the test failover, the primary VM continues to send log updates to the replica VM, which are merged into the replica VHDs, ensuring that replication continues. Once testing is complete, the temporary virtual machine is deleted. When triggering the test failover, you have the option to select the point in time to use for the failover if the virtual machine was enabled to store multiple points in time when replication was enabled, as shown in Figure 8.7. The test failover virtual machine is not connected to the regular network to avoid interfering with normal network communications.

FIGURE 8.7
Selecting the point in
time for the test failover

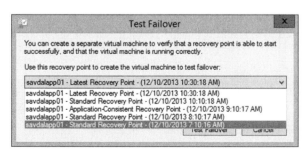

Planned Failover This is triggered on the primary virtual machine and is the preferred failover type. This process shuts down the primary VM, replicates any pending changes to ensure no data loss, fails over to the replica VM, reverses the replication (if the option is selected) so that changes flow in the reverse direction, and then starts the replica VM, which becomes the primary (while the old primary becomes the replica). Figure 8.8 shows the options for the planned failover that include whether replication should be reversed and whether the virtual machine should be started on the replica side. You should enable the reversal of replication unless there is a specific reason not to do so, such as if you are using extended replication (this will be discussed later in this section). Note that even though this is a planned failover, the virtual machine is still shut down during the failover, which is different from a Live Migration operation.

FIGURE 8.8
Performing a
planned failover

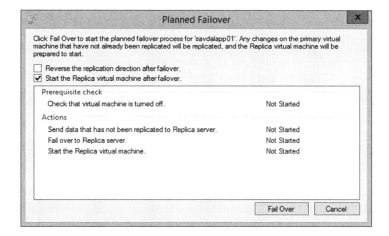

Unplanned Failover (Failover) This is triggered on the replica virtual machine because the assumption is that the failover was not planned, and the primary is not available because a disaster has occurred. When this is performed, a replication of pending changes is not possible, and reverse replication has to be manually enabled with a resynchronization required because there is no way to know where the primary and the replica stopped replicating. When starting the reverse replication, choose Do Not Copy The Initial Replication on the Initial Replication page. The VM on the original primary VM can be used, and a block-by-block comparison will be performed to synchronize between the replica VM and the original primary VM. Only the delta content needs to be sent over the network. When performing an unplanned failover, an option to select the point in time is available in the same way as for the test failover.

In Windows Server 2012, if the option to maintain periodic snapshots of the primary virtual machine was enabled with Hyper-V Replica, then the replica virtual machine would show those point-in-time snapshots in the Snapshots view. This is no longer the case in Windows Server 2012 R2 and above Hyper-V, which may initially lead you to believe that the snapshots are not being maintained for the replica, which is not the case. The various points in time are available and listed when performing a failover with Hyper-V Replica, as previously discussed. You can also see this using PowerShell, as shown here:

```
PS C:\> Get-VMSnapshot savdalapp01

VMName        Name              SnapshotType
CreationTime
___    __       _____                       _____
savdalapp01 savdalapp01—Standard Replica-(12/2/2015—7:08:59 AM) Replica
12/2/2015 7...
savdalapp01 savdalapp01—Standard Replica-(12/2/2015—8:09:00 AM) Replica
12/2/2015 8...
savdalapp01 savdalapp01—Application-consistent Replica-(12/2/2013—9:09:00
AM) AppConsistentReplica 12/2/2013 9...
savdalapp01 savdalapp01—Standard Replica-(12/2/2015—10:09:01 AM) Replica
12/2/2015 1...
```

To perform a failover using PowerShell, you use the `Start-VMFailover` cmdlet with different switches, depending on the type of failover. Windows Server 2012 R2 and above utilizes a new technology to maintain the recovery points instead of regular Hyper-V snapshots, which is why you will see HRU files if you look on the filesystem. Each HRU file represents a recovery point through use of undo logs that utilize the change tracking that is leveraged by Hyper-V Replica. By using the HRU files instead of snapshots, the VM's VHD file is always in the most current state. Only if a historical recovery point is selected are the HRU files used to roll back the state. This approach uses less IOPS and reduces any chance of corruption.

For a test failover, typically you need to list all of the snapshots and save to an array, so a specific snapshot can be selected to be used for the test. Next, one of the snapshots in the array is used as part of the test failover. Zero would be the first item in the array, so take care to look at the snapshots to ensure that the correct one is selected. This is performed on the replica virtual machine.

```
$VMSnapshots = Get-VMSnapshot -VMName <vm> -SnapshotType Replica
Start-VMFailover -Confirm:$false -VMRecoverySnapshot $VMSnapshots[0] -AsTest
```

A planned failover is a bit more involved and includes running commands against the primary VM to prepare it for failover and then activating on the replica VM. On the primary VM, the following commands are run:

```
Stop-VM <VM>
Start-VMFailover -VMName <VM> –prepare
```

Next, on the replica VM, the following commands are run to perform the actual failover, reverse the replication, and then start the replica VM:

```
Start-VMFailover -VMName <VM>
Set-VMReplication -reverse -VMName <VM>
Start-VM <VM>
```

An unplanned failover is used when the primary has been lost and you need to force the replica to start. If multiple points in time are available, one of those times can be selected in a similar fashion to the test failover, with the major difference that the `-AsTest` switch is not used.

Remember to select the right snapshot or don't use a snapshot at all, and use -VMName instead of the -VMRecoverySnapshot parameter.

```
$VMSnapshots = Get-VMSnapshot -VMName <vm> -SnapshotType Replica
Start-VMFailover -Confirm:$false -VMRecoverySnapshot $VMSnapshots[0]
```

At this point, you would check that the virtual machine is in the desired state and then complete the failover by using this command:

```
Complete-VMFailover -VMName <VM> -Confirm:$false
```

The failover is invisible to the virtual machine guest operating system. The operating system is aware only of a reboot and likely its IP address change, which is performed by Hyper-V if alternate IP configuration was configured as part of the network adapter configuration. If you performed a planned failover, the replication is reversed, provided you selected that option. To fail back so that the virtual machine is running in the main datacenter, you perform another failover, which will move the virtual machine back to the main datacenter and then reverse the replication to resume the normal operation. This is why even on the primary virtual machine, you typically set its IP configuration in the failover IP section so that when you use Hyper-V Replica to fail back, the correct IP configuration will be injected back into the virtual machine.

A complication arises for the failback scenario if you are using extended replication (you have a replica of the replica). The reason for the complication is that if your configuration indicates that A is replicating to B and then the replication is extended from B to C (where A, B, and C are Hyper-V hosts), you cannot reverse replication if you fail over from A to B (so that B would now be replicating to A). This is because B is already replicating to C, and a single virtual machine cannot have more than one replica. When performing the initial failover from A to B, you should *not* select the option to reverse replication. Once you have performed the failover from A to B, you do have a choice on server B. You can choose to continue the replication from B to C, or you can select to replicate from B to A, which will halt the replication to C. In many instances, you will select the option to continue replication to C, since A is likely not available. To perform the continued replication, select the Resume Extended Replication action. You can also use Resume-VMReplication -VMName <name> -Continue to continue using PowerShell. If you do want to replicate to A, you select the option Reverse Replication, which will break the Hyper-V Replica extended relationship. The virtual machine on C has now become orphaned. With PowerShell, you first need to remove the extended replica and then reverse the replication.

```
Remove-VMReplication -VMName <name> -ReplicationRelationshipType Extended
Set-VMReplication -VMName <name> -Reverse
```

Assuming that the option to continue replication from B to C was selected, this makes the failover of the virtual machine to run on server A a more complex operation because the virtual machine on server A is no longer receiving updates. The process involves manually performing the following steps:

1. Break the replication relationship between B and C.

2. Set up replication from B to A, which can use the existing virtual machine on server A, and the resynchronization process will be used to minimize data sent over the network.

3. Perform a failover from B to A and reverse the replication, which means that A is now replicating to B.

   4. Reestablish the extended replica from B to C. Once again the existing virtual machine on server C can be used as the base, and resynchronization is used to minimize data sent over the network.

Sizing a Hyper-V Replica Solution

After understanding the capability of Hyper-V Replica, the first question from my clients is, "What is the impact on my storage and network, and what are the requirements?" This is a valid question and is fairly complex. The answer ultimately boils down to the rate of change on the storage of the virtual machines that need to be replicated, because Hyper-V Replica works by replicating the changes. The higher the rate of change to the storage of the virtual machine, the greater the size of the Hyper-V Replica log (HRL) files and the more data that needs to be sent over the network from the primary to the replica.

You also need to consider the impact on storage, both on the primary storage hosting the primary VM VHDs, which also store the HRL files, and on the replica storage hosting the replica VM that receives the update files and then has to merge them into the replica VHDs as well as maintain snapshots if configured. It is not possible to configure the HRL files to be written to different storage than the actual VHD files, which means that the storage containing the VHD will incur whatever storage I/O is associated with the log files.

There is a negligible impact for processor and memory, but it is generally not considered as part of your Hyper-V Replica planning, which is focused on the network and storage. The network is fairly simple, and the amount of network bandwidth relates directly to the rate of change of the virtual machine. While compression does decrease the amount of network traffic (and incur some processor overhead) by compressing all of the zeros in the data, there aren't really any additional considerations. The amount of network traffic relates directly to the rate of change. If you need a higher rate of network compression, one option is to leverage WAN optimizers such as those from Riverbed, which will provide greater network bandwidth savings.

If you need to throttle the amount of bandwidth used for Hyper-V Replica, you should use network quality of service (QoS). QoS could be based on the target subnet (assuming that the only traffic to the target subnet is Hyper-V Replica traffic), or you can throttle based on the destination port, which is possible because Hyper-V Replica uses port 8080 for the transmission of the log data. For example, here I limit the replica traffic to 200Kb:

```
New-NetQoSPolicy "Replication Traffic to 8080" -DestinationPort 8080 `
     -ThrottleRateActionBitsPerSecond 200000
```

The storage consideration is more complex, specifically on the replica side, where the changes have to be merged into the replica VHDs. On the primary side, the additional storage required to host the log files is equal to the rate of change, and the additional I/O impact is less than 1.5 times than that of the IOPS of the workload, so less than 50 percent additional I/O. This is achieved by the use of a 32MB memory buffer to track writes to optimize the actual writes to the log files.

On the replica side, a major change has occurred between Windows Server 2012 and Windows Server 2012 R2, related to both the amount of storage and the IOPS. In Windows Server 2012, the IOPS requirement on the replica storage was between one and five times that of the workload, a big range. Windows Server 2012 R2 changes this to between one and two times that of the workload, which is a huge improvement and is enabled by the new mechanism to manage changes to the storage. The modification in applying the changes also reduces the storage required if recovery points are used. In Windows Server 2012, each recovery point would be around 10 percent of the size of the base VHD, which could be very large. In Windows Server 2012 R2 and above, each recovery point is equal to the actual change between the recovery points, which is a huge improvement.

Ascertaining the rate of change for each virtual machine is the key factor for all of these estimates. To help with this, Microsoft has created a capacity planner available at www.microsoft .com/en-us/download/details.aspx?id=39057. Once the capacity planner is downloaded and installed, the application should be executed.

The tool asks for the primary Hyper-V server or the broker if it's a cluster, and the replica Hyper-V server or the broker of the replica cluster. It will also ask for the estimated WAN bandwidth and a duration for collecting data. Next the tool will display a list of virtual machines running on supported storage such as local and CSV and allow you to select the specific VHDs on which you want to gather information on the change, as shown in Figure 8.9. The tool will then monitor those VHDs for the period of time you specify. Once collection is complete, it will know the rate of change of the VHD and ascertain the actual processor, memory, network, and storage impact for using Hyper-V Replica with those VHDs. A full report is generated that shows the before and after impact to help you plan for the Hyper-V Replica implementation; I definitely recommend using it.

FIGURE 8.9
Selecting the VHDs to use for the planner

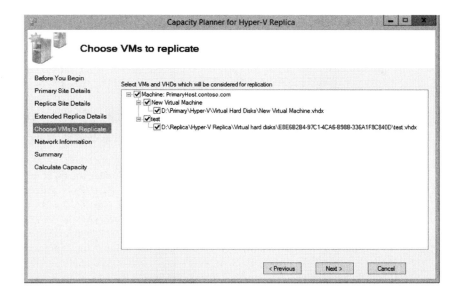

Figure 8.10 shows an example of the process in action. The information from the tool can be used with the Azure Site Recovery Capacity Planner tool, which is documented at https://azure.microsoft.com/en-us/documentation/articles/ site-recovery-capacity-planner/ to estimate more-detailed metrics around longer-term bandwidth and disk-space requirements based on user-defined retention criteria.

FIGURE 8.10
Example of the
capacity planner
tool in action

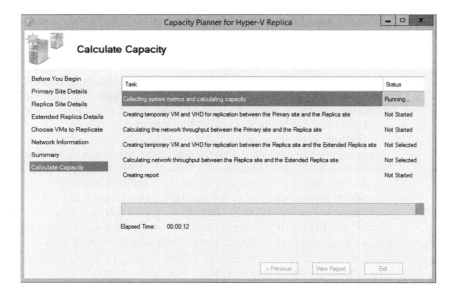

Microsoft also has a performance optimization document at http://support.microsoft.com/kb/2767928 that discusses registry changes that you can apply. One key setting is MaximumActiveTransfers, which may be of interest if you are replicating a large number of virtual machines. The default number of active transfers in Windows Server 2012 R2 and Windows Server 2016 is six (up from three in Windows Server 2012); however, you may need to increase this per the article instructions if you have many replicated virtual machines.

Using Hyper-V Replica Cloud Orchestration for Automated Failover with Azure Site Recovery

Hyper-V Replica is a great technology, but as you have seen, it's very manual. You trigger the failover for each virtual machine. There is no automated or bulk failover capability. Most organizations don't want an automated DR failover because there are too many false positives that could trigger a DR failover. What organizations do want is the ability to perform an orchestrated disaster-recovery failover, allowing scripts to be run, VMs to be failed over in a specific order, and all of this performed from a single interface using predefined failover plans.

Like all of Windows Server, PowerShell can be used for every aspect of Hyper-V Replica. You can use it to craft your own solution to perform your Hyper-V Replica DR failover, but that would be a lot of work, and each time you added new virtual machines, you would have to update your process.

Microsoft released some Hyper-V Replica runbooks that leverage System Center Orchestrator to enable an orchestrated failover process. They are available from http://blogs.technet.com/b/privatecloud/archive/2013/02/11/automation-orchestrating-hyper-v-replica-with-system-center-for-planned-failover.aspx. While a nice solution, System Center Orchestrator is really focused on Windows Server 2012 and has not been updated for Windows Server 2012 R2 and beyond; still, it's a great starting point.

A better solution is provided by the Microsoft Azure Site Recovery (ASR) solution. You can find details at https://azure.microsoft.com/en-us/services/site-recovery/. In the following section, I will walk you through its main capabilities, its integration with Hyper-V Replica, and SCVMM, as well as how to get started.

Overview of Hyper-V Protection with Azure Site Recovery

Figure 8.11 shows the main architectural view of an ASR-based solution when using Hyper-V Replica between on-premises locations. First notice that ASR is a service provided by Microsoft Azure, and it acts as a cloud-based broker and orchestration engine for Hyper-V Replica activities and failovers. The replication of the virtual machines is still from the Hyper-V servers in datacenter 1 to the Hyper-V servers in datacenter 2. No virtual machine storage replication happens to Microsoft Azure, at least not in this scenario, and instead only Metadata of the Hyper-V configuration is sent to Microsoft Azure to enable management.

FIGURE 8.11
ASR architectural overview for Hyper-V to Hyper-V replication

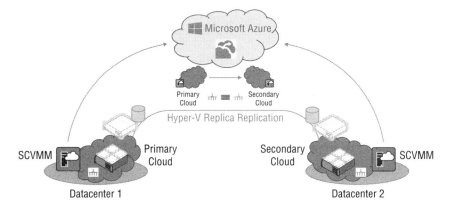

The communication to ASR is via an SCVMM instance at each datacenter; you enable this by downloading an ASR provider that installs into SCVMM and enables SCVMM to communicate to ASR using HTTPS. A certificate is used for the secure communications that you configure in ASR and in the SCVMM ASR provider, which gives a mutually trusted certificate. A proxy can be configured for the communication from SCVMM to ASR, and the only configuration is outbound HTTPS. ASR never contacts SCVMM; all communication is initiated from SCVMM outbound to ASR.

ASR works at a cloud level. Specifically, in SCVMM at each datacenter, you need to create one or more clouds that contain the Hyper-V host groups that will be participating in Hyper-V Replica replication. The clouds within SCVMM are then enabled to send information to ASR by checking the Send Configuration Data About This Cloud To The Windows Azure Hyper-V Recovery Manager option on the General tab of the cloud properties.

Once the clouds are known to ASR, a relationship is created between two clouds. This is a *pairing*, which tells the primary cloud it has a replication relationship to a target cloud. As part of the pairing of clouds, ASR will trigger workflows on SCVMM that automatically configure the Hyper-V hosts for Hyper-V Replica replication using certificate-based authentication. There is no manual configuration for Hyper-V Replica required on the hosts. Once the cloud relationship is established, a relationship between networks on the primary and replica cloud are configured in ASR. This enables virtual machines to be updated with the correct connectivity when established on the replica Hyper-V server, and a new IP address is injected into the virtual machine from the IP pool of the new network, ensuring continued connectivity.

A recovery plan is then created in ASR that defines groups of virtual machines to be failed over from all of the types supported by ASR (which includes VMware and physical hosts), defines the ordering of failover, and even defines optional scripts to be executed that need to be present on the SCVMM servers in addition to triggering runbooks stored in Azure Automation and even manual actions that should be acknowledged as part of a runbook execution. The final step is to enable virtual machines for protection using ASR via SCVMM, which behind the scenes configures the virtual machine to use Hyper-V Replica and makes the replication known to ASR. The option to use ASR can also be made part of a virtual machine template in SCVMM. This makes it easy to let the user deploy virtual machines that will be protected with Hyper-V Replica.

In the event a failover is required, one of the defined recovery plans can be initiated that triggers workflows on the SCVMM servers to perform the orchestrator Hyper-V Replica failovers and reverse replication as required.

As this high-level overview shows, no virtual machine or data ever goes to Microsoft Azure. All replication is directly between Hyper-V hosts in the organization's datacenters. The ASR service in Windows Azure is simply communicating with the SCVMM instances at each location to help orchestrate the initial configuration of Hyper-V Replica between the hosts, enabling replication for virtual machines and then triggering workflows to perform failovers, all from a separate cloud-based location.

Maintaining an entire second datacenter just for the purposes of disaster recovery is an expensive proposition for any organization, and ASR offers an alternate option for Hyper-V virtual machines—which is replicating to Azure, as shown in Figure 8.12. In this deployment mode, which can work through SCVMM or direct from Hyper-V hosts without SCVMM management, the Hyper-V Replica replication is to Azure, where the virtual hard disks are stored in an Azure Storage account. A mapping is still created between the on-premises network; however, its target is now a virtual subnet in an Azure virtual network. In the figure, I show a virtual machine. This does not exist, however, during normal replication. The virtual machine is only created in the event of a failover, and at that time it is connected to the replicated VHD file, and any pending HRL files are merged into the VHD in the Azure storage account. This approach of creating the VM only when needed optimizes Azure spend, since compute charges will be more than storage. If you view the storage account, a VM is replicated into in Azure. You will see both a VHD container (the Azure storage equivalent of a folder) and an HRL container, which contains the Hyper-V Replica log files that have not yet been merged into the target VHD.

You may notice a large number of files, as shown in Figure 8.13. Don't panic; this is normal. Rather than merge HRL files as they arrive, a process runs periodically to merge in HRL files, or it is triggered if a failover is performed.

While the focus of this book is Hyper-V, Azure Site Recovery also has a guest-based agent replication. (Hyper-V is a host agent since the replication is at the host level with no action from the guest OS other than calling VSS during an application-consistent recovery-point creation.) The guest-based replication uses an in-guest agent (known as the Mobility Service) that utilizes a disk driver that sits under the filesystem but above the volume manager, and it fractures any writes that pass through so that the write continues down to the volume manager but also is sent to a process server that collects the writes and sends them to a master target (which is a service in Azure), which then sends those writes to an attached VHD for each protected disk. As with Hyper-V protection to ASR, when using the guest-based agent, there is no VM running in Azure until you perform a failover. The guest agent is used when protecting VMs running on ESX and for physical machines. (However, physical machines failed over to Azure can fail back only to ESX VMs and not back to a physical machine.) There is an in-guest agent for Windows and Linux. There is no schedule for the replication; instead it sends as quickly as possible, meaning generally that the replica is within a second or two of the source.

FIGURE 8.12

ASR architectural overview for replication from Hyper-V to Azure

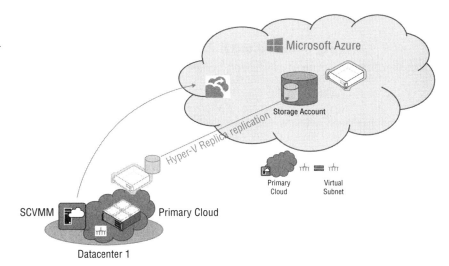

FIGURE 8.13

View of Azure storage account containing Hyper-V Replica target VM

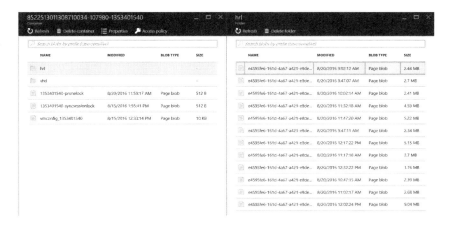

ASR also integrates and manages SQL Server Always On replication in addition to SAN replication when replicating between on-premises locations. For a full list of workloads that can be protected with ASR, see `https://azure.microsoft.com/en-us/documentation/articles/site-recovery-workload/`. Remember that ASR also integrates with Azure Automation, which is essentially PowerShell. This means that any type of failover that is possible through PowerShell can also integrate with an ASR recovery plan.

ASR is licensed through the Operations Management Suite or as a separate license. Note that ASR provides the replication technology, and the only additional cost is the storage used in Azure Storage and the compute charges in the event of a failover. The ASR license for on-premises to on-premises replication is cheaper than on-premises to Azure replication. Remember that use of ASR is free for the first 31 days for any protected workload, which enables it to be used as a migration solution without charge. Beyond 31 days, it is a metered service, and you will be charged accordingly.

Getting Started with ASR

Microsoft has great documentation for Microsoft Azure that details the steps to implementing ASR for each of the scenarios. This section walks you through the basics of getting started using ASR.

The first step is to create a Recovery Services vault that houses the replication and backup services. In the Azure portal, select New, and in the Marketplace, search for Backup and Site Recovery. Select the Backup And Site Recovery (OMS) result and click Create. Enter a name for the vault and a location, as shown in Figure 8.14. Note that the location should be where you wish to create the VMs in Azure in the event of a disaster.

FIGURE 8.14
Creating a new Recovery
Services vault

Once created, the vaults can be viewed by browsing the Recovery Services vaults from the list of services, which will bring up its dashboard, as shown in Figure 8.15. The Settings section has Getting Started options for backup and site recovery. As shown in the figure, you select the scenario for the replication, including whether the replication is to on-premises or Azure and then whether the source is Hyper-V or ESX/physical. Getting Started then provides the exact steps to perform to complete the full implementation of the replication.

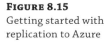

FIGURE 8.15
Getting started with
replication to Azure

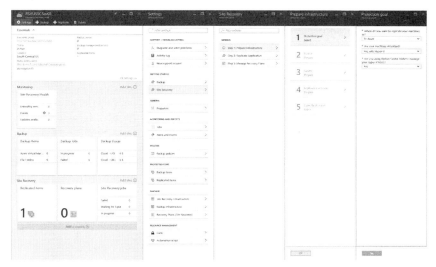

Following are the high-level steps required to set up replication from Hyper-V to Azure by using SCVMM:

1. A new source for replication is added to the recovery vault by adding the VMM server. On the VMM server, you run the ASR setup and provide the credential file generated by the ASR portal. In VMM under Settings, it will now show you as registered to an ASR instance, and clouds can be configured to show in ASR.

2. A target for the replication is selected, which will be Azure, and a check performed to ensure that there is at least one compatible storage account and virtual network.

3. A policy is associated with the VMM server that set the replication details, such as frequency of replication and number of recovery points to keep.

4. The VM(s) to be replicated are selected from those in ASR-enabled SCVMM clouds.

5. The initial replication will be triggered, and then the VM will be replicated per the policy.

The process to protect ESX and physical machines is similar, except you also require a separate OS instance that will provide the process server/configuration on-premises component to receive the writes from the Mobility Service running inside the guests.

Architecting the Right Disaster-Recovery Solution

After reading this chapter, you may think that you will just use Hyper-V Replica for all of your disaster-recovery needs. The reality is that should not be the case. It's a good technology, but better options may be available for specific workloads and applications.

Your first preference should be to use an application's replication and disaster-recovery capabilities if it has them, because it's always better for the application to be aware of a failover and manage its own data if possible. For example, SQL has its Always On replication and failover technology, which means that if I had data in SQL Server, I would always use Always On first.

Likewise, Exchange has database availability groups and replicates mailboxes. In that case, I would use that technology. Active Directory has multimaster replication, which means that I would simply have domain controllers running in my DR location that would replicate from my primary location for normal operation.

If the application is not stateful, such as a website, then I could have instances of the application running in the primary and DR locations and use network load balancing to spread the load. Another option is to update DNS to point to DR instead of primary. Although there are some considerations around caching of DNS records, solutions exist.

If the storage has some kind of synchronous replication capability that could be used as if it were a single logical piece of storage that would allow a cluster to be used, my next preference would be to treat the replicated SAN as shared storage and enable any cluster-aware application to leverage the SAN. This could include virtual machines running on the replicated SAN. This could also include Storage Replica's synchronous option that integrates with clustering.

If none of those other options were available, I would use Hyper-V Replica. That is not to say that it's not a great solution, but a hypervisor-level asynchronous replication solution that is not application aware is simply not as rich in its functionality as one that is part of an application. Most organizations have a lot of applications that don't have their own replication technology and can't run on a replication SAN, so a huge number of virtual workloads can benefit greatly from Hyper-V Replica.

The Bottom Line

Identify the best options to provide disaster recovery for the various services in your organization. When planning disaster recovery, application-aware disaster recovery should be used first where possible, such as SQL Always On, Exchange DAG, Active Directory multimaster replication, and so on. If no application-aware replication and DR capability is available, another option is to look at the replication capabilities of the SAN, such as synchronous replication. Additionally, replicating at the virtual machine disk level, such as with Hyper-V Replica, provides a replication solution that has no requirements on the guest operating system or the application.

Master It Why is Azure Site Recovery useful?

Describe the types of failover for Hyper-V Replica. There are three types of Hyper-V Replica failover. A test failover is performed on the replica server, and it creates a clone of the replica virtual machine that is disconnected from the network and allows testing of the failover process without any impact to the ongoing protection of the primary workload as replication continues. A planned failover is triggered on the primary Hyper-V host and stops the virtual machine, ensures that any pending changes are replicated, starts the replica virtual machine, and reverses the replication. An unplanned failover is triggered on the replica Hyper-V host and is used when an unforeseen disaster occurs and the primary datacenter is lost. This means that some loss of state may occur from the primary virtual machine. When possible, a planned failover should always be used.

Master It In an unplanned failover, how much data could be lost?

Explain the automated options for Hyper-V Replica failover. Hyper-V Replica has no automated failover capability. To automate the failover steps, PowerShell could be used, System Center Orchestrator could be used, or, for a complete solution, Azure Site Recovery could be used. The key point is that the decision to use failover should not be automatic, because many conditions (such as a break in network connectivity) could trigger a false failover. The automation required should be the orchestration of the failover after a manual action is taken to decide whether a failover should occur.

Chapter 9

Implementing the Private Cloud, SCVMM, and Microsoft Azure Stack

So far this book has covered aspects of Hyper-V, such as types of resources, high availability, and management. This chapter takes the capabilities enabled through Hyper-V and shows you how to build on them by using the System Center management stack and the virtual infrastructure.

Microsoft Azure Stack builds on Hyper-V to bring Azure-consistent services to on-premises and hosting environments utilizing the same code that runs the Azure public cloud.

In this chapter, you will learn to:

◆ Explain the differences between virtualization and the private cloud.

◆ Describe the must-have components to create a Microsoft private cloud.

The Benefits of the Private Cloud

What is the private cloud? Understanding this is the hardest part of implementing it. One of my customers once said the following, and it's 100 percent accurate:

> *If you ask five people for a definition of the private cloud, you will get seven different answers.*
>
> —*Very smart customer in 2011*

I like to think of the private cloud as having the following attributes:

◆ Scalable and elastic, meaning that it can grow and shrink as the load on the application changes

◆ Better utilization of resources

◆ Agnostic of the underlying fabric

◆ Accountable, which can also mean chargeable

◆ Self-service capable

◆ All about the application

Let me explain this list in more detail. First, the *all about the application* attribute. In a physical setup, each server has a single operating system instance, which, as I've explored, means lots of wasted resources and money. The shift to virtualization takes these operating system instances and consolidates them to a smaller number of physical servers by running each operating system instance in a virtual machine. Virtualization saves hardware and money, but it doesn't change the way IT is managed. Administrators still log on to the operating system instances at the console and still manage the same number of operating system instances. In fact, now administrators also have to manage the virtualization solution. Although you may not log on to the console of a server, you are still remotely connecting directly into the operating system to perform management, and this is basically managing at the console level. The private cloud shifts the focus to the service being delivered and the applications used in that service offering. The private cloud infrastructure is responsible for creating the virtual machines and operating system instances that are required to deploy a service, removing that burden from the administrator.

Think back to the service templates covered in Chapter 6, "Maintaining a Hyper-V Environment." Service templates in System Center Virtual Machine Manager allow the design of multitiered services, with each tier having the ability to use different virtual machine templates and different applications and configurations. Service templates allow administrators (and users, as you will explore later) to easily deploy complete instances of services without any concern for the virtual machine configuration or placement. Those service templates also integrate with network hardware such as load balancers, enabling automatic configuration of the network hardware when services are deployed that require hardware load balancing.

Initial deployment is fine, but what about maintenance, patching, and scaling? I'll cover other components of System Center 2016 (such as Configuration Manager, which can simplify automated patching of both server and desktop operating systems), but you can still use service templates. Unlike a normal virtual machine template, which loses any relationship with a virtual machine deployed from the template, any instances of a service deployed from a service template maintain the relationship to the template.

Think about being scalable and elastic. Those same service templates allow a minimum, maximum, and initial instance count of each tier of service. Let's look at the web tier as an example. I could configure the tier to have a minimum instance count of 2, a maximum of 20, and an initial of 4. When load increases, the user can access the tool and scale out the tier to a higher number, such as 10, and the backend infrastructure automatically takes care of creating the new virtual machines, setting up any configuration, and adding the new instances to the load balancer and any other associated actions. When the load dies down, the user can scale in that service, and once again the backend infrastructure will automatically delete some virtual machines that make up that tier to the new target number and update the hardware load balancer. I'm focusing on the user performing the scale-out and scale-in, but that same private cloud could have monitoring in place, such as with System Center Operations Manager; when load hits a certain point, it runs an automated process using System Center Orchestrator that talks to System Center Virtual Machine Manager to perform the scaling. That's why when I talk about the private cloud and focus on the application, it's not just about System Center Virtual Machine Manager; the entire System Center product plays a part in the complete private cloud solution. This scalability and elasticity—meaning having access to resources when needed but not using them, and allowing other services to leverage them when not needed— are key traits of the private cloud. Many organizations charge business units for the amount of computer resources that are used by their applications, which is why the ability to scale is important. By running many services on a single infrastructure, you will see high utilization of available resources, getting more bang for the infrastructure buck.

AGNOSTIC OF THE UNDERLYING FABRIC

"Agnostic of the Underlying Fabric" can be confusing. For example, say I want to offer services to my customers, which could be my IT department, business units in the organization, or individual users. To those customers, I want to provide a menu of offerings, known as a *service catalog* in ITIL terms. When those customers deploy a virtual machine or service, they should not need to know which IP address needs to be given to the virtual machine or virtual machines if deploying a single or multitiered service. The customer should not have to say which storage area network to use and which LUN to use.

Imagine that I have multiple datacenters and multiple types of network and multiple hypervisors. If I want to allow non-IT people to deploy virtual machines and services, I need to abstract all that underlying fabric infrastructure from them. The user needs to be able to say (or request through a self-service interface), "I want an instance of this service in Datacenter A and B, and it should connect to the development and backup networks on a silver tier of storage." Behind the scenes, the private cloud infrastructure works out that for the development network in Datacenter A, the network adapter needs an IP address in a certain subnet connected to a specific VLAN and some other subnet and VLAN in Datacenter B. The infrastructure works out that silver-tier storage in Datacenter A means using the NetApp SAN and only certain LUNs, while in Datacenter B the EMC SAN is used with other specific LUNs. The user gets the service and connectivity needed with zero knowledge of the infrastructure, which is exactly as it should be.

Self-service by the user for the provisioning of these services is a great way to think of the difference between virtualization and the private cloud. Let me walk you through the most basic case: creating a new virtual machine for a user. Provisioning virtual machines in a virtual world goes like this (see Figure 9.1):

1. The user makes a request to the IT department. This could be a phone call, an email, or a help-desk request.

2. The IT department gets the request and may perform some validation, such as checking with a manager to ensure that the request is approved.

3. IT launches their virtualization management tool and creates a virtual machine from a template.

4. IT contacts the user and provides the IP address of the VM.

This process sounds fast, but in reality it ranges from a few days to six weeks in some companies for which I've worked. It's a manual process, IT teams are busy, they just don't like the particular business user, or there could be "solar activity disrupting electronics" (which is the same as not liking the user). Whatever the case, because it's a manual process, it takes time and is often fairly low on the priority list.

It can also be fairly hard to track the allocation of virtual machines, which often means that there is no ability to charge business units for the requested virtual machines. This can lead to virtual machine sprawl, because to the business the virtual machines are free.

FIGURE 9.1
Traditional process for requesting virtual machines that is hands-on for the administrator

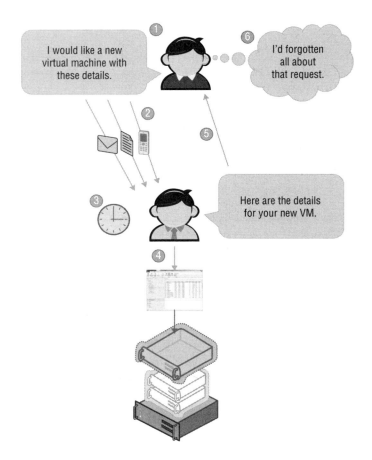

In the private cloud, this changes to the process shown in Figure 9.2.

The resources used are the same, but the order of the steps and method has changed:

1. The IT team uses their management tool to carve out clouds of resources, which include compute, storage, and network resources, and it assigns clouds to users or groups of users with certain quotas. This is all done before any users request resources, and it is the only time that the IT team has to do any work in this process, freeing them up to spend their time on more forward-looking endeavors.

2. The user accesses a self-service portal and fills out a basic request, selecting the type of VM or application and the cloud in which to create it based on IT's allocations and quotas.

3. The private cloud infrastructure takes the request and automatically provisions the VM, which could include workflows to request authorization from management if required. The user can see the details of this new VM in the self-service portal and can even get an automated email providing details.

4. The user is happy. If the user had a red button that said "That was easy," they would be pressing it.

FIGURE 9.2

Provisioning process when using private cloud

The number one fear of many IT departments I talk to about the private cloud is that enabling users and business units to help themselves to virtual machines via this self-service will result in millions of virtual machines being created for no good reason, plunging the IT infrastructure into a dark age of VM sprawl beyond any previously envisioned nightmare scenario. But that is simply not the case.

Remember what you are doing. First, you are creating clouds of resources. You are defining what these clouds can access in terms of particular virtualization hosts and, on those virtualization hosts, the amount of memory, virtual CPU, and disk IOPS that can be consumed. You are setting which tiers of storage that cloud can access and the amount of space. You are setting which networks that cloud can connect to. You are setting which VM templates can be used by the users to create the virtual machines. For each user or group of users, you set the quotas indicating the number of virtual machines they can create or the amount of memory and virtual CPUs they can use in each cloud. You can even set what the virtual machines can look like in terms of CPU and memory allocations. With a private cloud solution, you can set charge-back and show-back capabilities, so if a business unit creates a large amount of virtual resource, it gets charged accordingly, so the solution is fully accountable. You can set expiry of virtual machines so that they are automatically deleted after a period of time. Users can create only on the resources that you have defined and within the limits you have configured. If they have a limit of five virtual machines and want to create a sixth, they would either have to delete a virtual machine, export a virtual machine to a library that you have granted them, or request an extension of their quota and go through an approval process.

I think you will find that this is more controlled and enforceable than any manual process you may have today. Users request a VM today, and you give it to them; it just takes you weeks, which may discourage business units from asking for virtual resources unless they really need them. That's a terrible way to control resources—by making it painful. Business users might go elsewhere for their services, such as setting up their own infrastructures or using public cloud services, which I've seen happen at a lot of organizations. It's far better to put good processes in place and enable the business so that users can function in the most optimal way and use internal services where it makes sense. Remember, with the private cloud, you can configure costs for virtual resources and charge the business, so if more virtual resources are required because the business units can now provision resources more easily, the IT department has the ability to gain the funding to procure more IT infrastructure as needed.

You can start slow. Maybe you use the private cloud for development and test environments first, get used to the idea, and get the users used to working within quotas. The private cloud infrastructure can be used in production, but perhaps it's the IT department using the private cloud and maybe even the self-service portal initially, and then over time you turn it over to end users.

Private Cloud Components

The difference between virtualization and the private cloud is in the management infrastructure. The same compute, network, and storage resources used for a virtualization infrastructure can be used for a private cloud. To turn virtualization into a private cloud solution, you need the right management stack. For a Microsoft private cloud, this is System Center 2016 added to the virtualization foundation provided by Hyper-V 2016. Additionally, Windows Azure Pack is deployed on top of System Center 2016 to provide the complete user experience. Another option to implement a private cloud is Microsoft Azure Stack, which is covered later in this chapter. I provided a brief overview of System Center in Chapter 1, "Introduction to Virtualization and Microsoft Solutions." Here I cover the components that are critical for a private cloud and the reasons they are critical.

Many of the benefits of virtualization are related to the abstraction of resources, scalability, and controlled self-service. All of these benefits primarily come through SCVMM, so in this section I cover some of these.

Consider a typical virtualization administrator who has full administrative rights over the virtualization hosts and the compute resource but no insight into the storage and network. This leads to many problems and challenges for the virtualization administrators:

◆ "I have no visibility into what is going on at a storage level. I would like to have insight into the storage area networks that store my virtual machines from SCVMM."

◆ "Deploying server applications requires following a 100+ page procedure, which has human-error possibilities and differences in implementation between the development, testing, and production phases. I want to be able to install the server application once, and then just move it between environments, modifying only changes in configuration."

◆ "My organization has many datacenters with different network details, but I don't want to have to change the way I deploy virtual machines based on where they are being deployed. The management tool should understand my different networks, such as production, backup, and DMZ, and set the correct IP details and use the right NICs in the hosts as needed."

◆ "I need to save power, so in quiet times I want to consolidate my virtual machines on a smaller number of hosts and power down unnecessary servers."

Although the name System Center Virtual Machine Manager might make it seem like it's focused on virtual machine management, some of its most powerful features relate not to virtualization but to the storage and network fabric, as discussed in this book. SCVMM integrates with the storage in your environment by using SMI-S to give insight into the storage, but it also classifies and assigns storage to hosts as required. SCVMM allows the network to be designed in SCVMM, providing easy network assignment for the virtual workloads, including providing network virtualization with connectivity to nonvirtualized networks with 2016. All of this insight into the compute, storage, and network resources is completely abstracted for the end user, enabling simple provisioning. Because all of the resources are exposed and managed centrally, this leads to a greater utilization of resources, which is a key goal of the private cloud.

Once all of the types of resources are centrally managed and abstracted, a key piece to the private cloud is creating the clouds that can be consumed by various groups within an organization. These could be business units, teams of developers, or parts of IT, or they could even be used by the same group of administrators for provisioning. But using separate clouds for different users/groups provides a simpler tracking of resources. A cloud typically consists of key resources and configurations that include the following:

◆ The capacity of the cloud, such as the amount of memory, processor, and storage resources that can be used by the cloud and the hosts that are used

◆ The classifications of storage exposed to the cloud

◆ The networks that can be used by the cloud

◆ The capabilities exposed to the cloud, such as the maximum number of vCPUs per VM

◆ Library assets available to the cloud, such as templates

◆ Writeable libraries for the purpose of storing virtual machines by cloud users

Notice that the cloud has a specific capacity assigned rather than exposing the full capacity of the underlying resources. This means that a single set of hosts and storage could be used by many different clouds. Once clouds are created, the cloud is assigned to groups of users, or *tenants*, and those specific tenants have their own quotas within the capacity of the cloud. Individual users in the tenant group have their own subset of quotas if required, giving very high levels of granularity and control over the consumption of resources in the cloud. Like clouds and underlying resources, many tenants can be created for a single cloud. Clouds and tenants are defined and enabled through SCVMM. SCVMM also enables visibility into the usage of current cloud capacity and features role-based access control, which means that end users could be given the SCVMM console to use for the creation of virtual machines because they would see only options related to their assigned actions; however, this is not a good interface for end users to consume.

To provide the self-service capability commonly associated with the private cloud, System Center 2016 offers an interesting choice. In the 2012 wave of System Center, the obvious choice for an end-user interface to provision and manage services in the private cloud was the System Center App Controller, which not only exposed clouds in SCVMM but also integrated with Microsoft Azure–based clouds and even hosting partners that leverage the Service Provider Framework (SPF). This provided a single portal for users to provision, view, and control their services across clouds. Unfortunately, App Controller has been removed in System Center 2016, leaving an apparent gap, as SCVMM has no native portal. However, all is not as it seems. Although App Controller exposed the clouds defined in SCVMM to the end user and allowed self-service within the quotas defined as part of the cloud capacity and the tenant quotas, there was no concept of a provisioning workflow nor approval of requests. SCVMM and App Controller also lacked detailed reporting on resource usage and the ability to charge business units based on resource consumption. To achieve this requirement, you would (and still could) leverage the Orchestrator and Service Manager components, as I explain later in this chapter.

This was the challenge: two separate portals. App Controller provided a nice control portal to stop, start, and view services provisioned in clouds. To enable a workflow-based provisioning process, however, the Service Manager self-service portal would be leveraged, utilizing runbooks defined in Orchestrator to publish request offerings to the end user. The solution in System Center 2012 R2 for a single portal, and the only real control solution for System Center 2016, is to leverage Windows Azure Pack with System Center 2016, which exposes clouds defined in SCVMM but can also publish request and service offerings defined in Service Manager through the third-party GridPro solution, enabling workflow-based provisioning and then full control of the created resources. Another option is not to use SCVMM for the clouds and instead use Microsoft Azure Stack, but that is covered later in this chapter.

SCVMM Fundamentals

Two common sayings that can be adapted to Hyper-V and SCVMM are "A poor workman blames his tools" and "Behind every great man is a great woman" (maybe that's a song lyric). The tools that are used to manage and interact with Hyper-V are critical to a successful virtualization endeavor. I would not blame an administrator for blaming an inefficiently run Hyper-V implementation on his tools if all the administrator had access to was the Hyper-V management tool supplied in the box; thus, "A poor Hyper-V admin blames Hyper-V Manager, and so he should." For effective and comprehensive management of a Hyper-V environment and a heterogeneous virtualization environment including ESXi, System Center Virtual Machine Manager is a necessity. Thus "Behind every great Hyper-V implementation is a great SCVMM."

Major New Capabilities in SCVMM 2016

The new capabilities of SCVMM 2016 tightly align to the investment areas in Windows Server 2016 and can be broken down into four key areas: Compute, Storage, Networking, and Security.

COMPUTE

◆ Full lifecycle management of Nano Server-based hosts and virtual machines (VMs), including initial deployment of Nano to VMs and physical hosts and managing Nano deployments.

◆ Rolling Upgrade of a Windows Server 2012 R2 host cluster to Windows Server 2016 with no downtime for the hosted workloads

◆ Configure bare metal machines as a Hyper-V host cluster in one step instead of two.

◆ Configure bare metal machines as additional nodes of an existing Scale-Out File Server (SOFS) cluster without leaving VMM console.

◆ Increase/decrease memory and add/remove virtual network adapter for a running VM.

◆ Take production checkpoints.

◆ Note that Server App-V has been deprecated in SCVMM 2016 and is only available for existing Service Templates upgraded from 2012 R2.

STORAGE

◆ Deploy and manage storage clusters with Storage Spaces Direct (S2D) in dis-aggregated or hyper-converged topology.

◆ Synchronously replicate storage volumes using Storage Replica (SR) instead of expensive storage-based replication.

◆ Set quality of service (QoS) for VM storage to avoid noisy neighbor problem.

NETWORKING

◆ Template-based deployment for Software Defined Networking (SDN) components, such as the Network Controller, Gateway, and Software Load Balancer

◆ Isolation and filtering of network traffic flowing in and out of a VM vNIC by defining port access control lists (ACLs), which is managed through SCVMM PowerShell cmdlets

◆ Consistent naming of virtual network adapters, as seen by the guest operating system

◆ Self-service capability for Network Controller managed fabric through Windows Azure Pack (WAP)

◆ Reliable and atomic Logical Switch deployment across hosts, which means if there is a failure the entire set of actions are rolled back restoring the host to its original state

SECURITY

◆ Full lifecycle management of newly introduced guarded hosts and shielded VMs, including the management of pre-existing Host Guardian Service (HGS) servers and the creation and management of shielded VMs

◆ Convert a non-shielded VM to a shielded VM.

Installation

SCVMM 2016, supports installation only on Windows Server 2016, which requires a 64-bit server. Additionally, it must be installed on a Windows Server 2016 with Desktop Experience or the GUI-less Server Core preferred install. Nano Server is also not supported to host SCVMM but can be a managed Host OS or a SCVMM library server. The other software requirements are fairly minimal. The only requirement that you will have to install manually is the latest Windows Assessment and Deployment Kit (WADK), which includes components to create and manage operating system images that are required for SCVMM's bare-metal deployment features. You can download the correct WADK version from https://developer.microsoft.com/en-us/windows/hardware/windows-assessment-deployment-kit. SQL Server Feature Pack (both the 2012 and 2014 versions) must also be installed. The other requirements are part of the Windows Server operating system, such as Microsoft .NET Framework 4.5 and 4.6, and are automatically installed by the SCVMM installation process. SCVMM must be installed on a server that is part of an Active Directory domain but does not have any strict requirements, such as a Windows Server 2008 domain or forest-level mode.

SQL Server 2012 SP2 or above is preferred for SCVMM 2016 to store its configuration and data, but this does not need to be installed on the SCVMM server. It is possible to use any currently supported version of SQL Server if required, however the newer the better. I recommend having a separate SQL server used for SCVMM and leveraging an existing SQL server farm in your organization that is highly available and maintained by SQL administrators. If you are testing SCVMM in a lab with a small number of hosts, installing SQL on the SCVMM server is fine. Where possible, however, you should leverage an external, dedicated SQL environment.

If you are running an older version of SCVMM 2012, specific operating system and SQL server requirements are documented at the following locations:

◆ Operating system requirements:
http://technet.microsoft.com/en-us/library/gg610562.aspx

◆ SQL Server requirements:
http://technet.microsoft.com/en-us/library/gg610574.aspx

The hardware specifications required will vary based on the number of virtualization hosts being managed by SCVMM. A single SCVMM 2016 server can manage up to 1,000 hosts containing up to 25,000 virtual machines. The Microsoft recommendations state that when you have fewer than 150 hosts per SCVMM, you can run SQL Server on the SCVMM instance. I still prefer to limit the number of SQL instances in my environment, and it's better to invest in that well-architected and maintained highly available SQL farm rather than a local SQL installation. Also, if you are planning on implementing a highly available SCVMM installation, you need SQL Server separate from your SCVMM server. Virtualizing SCVMM 2016 is fully supported and indeed recommended. All of the clients I work with virtualize SCVMM.

As with any virtualized service, it is important to ensure that the necessary resources are available to meet your virtualized loads and that you don't overcommit resources beyond acceptable performance. Because SCVMM is so important to the management of your virtual environment, I like to set the reserve on the vCPUs for my SCVMM to 50 percent to ensure that it can always get CPU resources in times of contention. Of course, as you will see, SCVMM should be doing a great job of constantly tweaking your virtual environment to ensure the most optimal performance and to ensure that all the virtual machines get the resources they need, moving the virtual machines between hosts if necessary. If you have severely overcommitted your environment by putting too many virtual machines on the available resources, performance will suffer, which is why proper discovery and planning are vital to a successful virtual environment.

Dynamic Memory is fully supported by SCVMM. For production environments, I recommend setting the startup memory to 4,096 and the maximum to 16,384 (the Microsoft minimum and recommended values). SCVMM 2012 R2 had two sets of guidance for sizing: environments of 150 managed hosts or fewer (which could use smaller amounts of memory) and environments of 151 managed hosts or more. This no longer applies, and SCVMM lists only its minimum and recommended values regardless of the number of managed hosts. You can certainly exceed these maximums if you find that memory is low (though that should be unlikely), but I don't recommend that you go below the minimum supported for the startup unless perhaps you have a small lab environment with only a couple of hosts and you are short on memory.

You must specify an account to be used to run the SCVMM service during the installation of SCVMM. During installation, you are given the option either to specify a domain account or to use Local System. Don't use Local System; although it may seem like the easy option, it limits some capabilities of SCVMM (such as using shared ISO images with Hyper-V virtual machines) and can make troubleshooting difficult because all of the logs will show Local System instead of an account dedicated to SCVMM. On the flip side, don't use your domain Administrator account, which has too much power and would have the same problem troubleshooting because you would just see Administrator everywhere. Create a dedicated domain user account just for SCVMM that meets your organization's naming convention, such as svcSCVMM or VMMService. Make that account a local administrator on the SCVMM server by adding the account to the local Administrators group. You can do this with the following command, or you can use the Server Manager tool to navigate to Configuration ➢ Local Users And Groups ➢ Groups and add the account to the Administrators group.

```
C:\ >net localgroup Administrators /add savilltech\svcSCVMM
The command completed successfully.
```

Do not use a generic domain service account for different applications. This can cause unexpected results and once again makes troubleshooting hard. Use a separate account for each of your services—one for SCVMM, one for System Center Operations Manager (in fact, you need more than one for Operations Manager), another for System Center Configuration Manager, and so on. What do I mean by *unexpected results*? When SCVMM manages a host, it adds its management account to the local Administrators group of that host—in my case, svcSCVMM. If that host is removed from SCVMM management, that account is removed from the local Administrators group of that host. Now imagine you use a shared service account between SCVMM and another application that also needs its service account to be part of the local Administrators group. When you remove the host from SCVMM management, that shared service account is removed from the local Administrators group on that host, so you just broke that other application.

If you have multiple SCVMM servers in a high-availability configuration, the same domain account is used on all servers. It's a requirement to use a domain account in a SCVMM high-availability scenario or if you have a disjointed namespace in your domain. For information on disjointed namespaces, see http://support.microsoft.com/kb/909264. Ideally, this is not something you have in your environment because it can be a huge pain for many applications.

During the installation of SCVMM, there is an option to specify the storage of the distributed keys that are used for the encryption of data in the SCVMM database. Normally, these keys are stored on the local SCVMM computer, but if you are implementing a highly available SCVMM installation, the keys need to be stored centrally. For SCVMM, this means storing in Active Directory. For details on creating the necessary container in Active Directory for the distributed key management, refer to http://technet.microsoft.com/en-us/library/gg697604.aspx.

The installation process for SCVMM 2016 is a simple, wizard-driven affair that will guide you through all of the required configuration steps, so I don't go into the details here. Just remember to specify your domain account for the service.

SCVMM 2016 supports being installed on a failover cluster now, which means that the SCVMM service becomes highly available and can be moved in planned and unplanned scenarios using Failover Clustering technologies. An external SQL Server should be used to host the SCVMM database, and the installation of SCVMM to a highly available configuration is simple. Start the SCVMM 2016 installation to an operating system instance that is part of a failover cluster, and the SCVMM installation process will detect the presence of the Failover Clustering feature and ask whether the SCVMM installation should be made highly available. If you answer yes, you will be prompted for an additional IP address and a name to be used for the cluster SCVMM service, and that is really the only change in the installation process. You need to specify a domain account for running the VMM service, and Active Directory will be used for storing the encryption keys. You also need to install SCVMM on all of the other nodes in the failover cluster so that the SCVMM service can run on all nodes.

If you are upgrading from SCVMM 2012 R2 to 2016, the process is similar; however, a regular in-place upgrade is not supported. Instead, the sequence of activities is as follows:

1. Perform a backup of the SCVMM database and server.

2. Uninstall SCVMM 2012 R2, and select the option to retain the database.

3. On a clean Windows Server 2016 server install SCVMM 2016.

4. When prompted, elect to use an existing database, and confirm that the database will be upgraded.

5. All configuration will be maintained, and you will need to update the SCVMM agents on all hosts. If you had the ASR agent of other software installed, ensure that this is also installed on the server.

6. You may need to copy over library content if you have custom assets in the library that was on the SCVMM host previously and you have installed SCVMM 2016 on a fresh host.

SCVMM Management Console

The SCVMM management console looks different from consoles that you may be used to, because System Center has moved away from the Microsoft Management Console (MMC) standard in favor of a new workspace-based layout. This does not have an official name, but I like *System Center Console Framework*. The SCVMM 2016 console can be installed on Windows 8, Windows Server 2008 R2 SP1, and above. Figure 9.3 shows the console for SCVMM.

The console is divided into five main elements (also known as *panes*):

Ribbon   The ribbon has become a standard in most Microsoft applications. You will quickly come to appreciate this dynamically changing ribbon, which shows the actions available for the selected object and highlights the most popular actions based on a lot of research by the SCVMM team.

Workspaces   The entire console is workspace based, and in the Workspaces pane you select the workspace in which you wish to work, which is reflected in all other areas of the console. The Workspaces pane shows the five available standard workspaces: VMs And Services,

Fabric, Library, Jobs, and Settings. You will also hear workspaces unofficially referred to as *wunderbars*. After the initial configuration of SCVMM, you will not use Settings much, but you will use the other workspaces as you enhance your environment.

FIGURE 9.3
All elements of the SCVMM console change based on the current workspace and selected element of the workspace.

Navigation   This shows the areas of management available in the current workspace.

Results   Based on the current navigation node selected, this area shows all of the results for that area. Note the Results pane is affected by elements selected in the ribbon; these elements can control what is shown in the Results pane based on the current workspace and Navigation pane.

Details   The Details pane is not always shown, but when available, it shows detailed information on the currently selected object in the Results pane.

The best way to learn the SCVMM console is to fire it up and look around. Explore all of the workspaces, select the various nodes in the Navigation pane, and pay attention to the ribbon, which will change and show some interesting options that you will want to play with.

The MMC was great for its original concept of a standardized interface that could allow various snap-ins to be placed and organized in a single console. However, restrictions existed, particularly around role-based access control (RBAC), which is a key tenant of System Center 2016 (and the older 2012/2012 R2 wave). I'm talking about System Center here instead of SCVMM because the focus on RBAC is common for all of System Center and not just SCVMM. As System Center is used more broadly across an organization, it's likely that different groups of users will be given access to only certain functionality areas of System Center 2016 components, and within those functionality areas be able to perform actions on only a subset of all the objects. In the past, although delegating different permissions was possible, the people delegating rights would still see all of the elements of the administrative console and would get Access Denied messages. With the new System Center model and RBAC, delegated users see only the areas of the console to which they have rights and only the objects with which they are allowed to work. A great example in SCVMM is granting delegated rights to a group of users for only a specific collection of virtualization hosts. As Figure 9.4 shows, full administrators see the entire host hierarchy and all of the available clouds on the left side, while a tenant administrator (a user with limited access and capabilities) for the Replicated Cloud cannot see any of the clouds nor do they have any knowledge of host groups. By showing application administrators only console elements and objects to which they have rights, it makes the console easier to use, makes it more intuitive, avoids the "Why don't I have access to *x*, *y*, and *z*?" questions, and makes the administrative tool usable by standard users such as self-service users. Notice that the delegated user also has no view of the Fabric workspace at all, and the other workspaces have information limited to their specific cloud.

FIGURE 9.4
On the left is the view for a normal SCVMM administrator, while on the right is the view for a Replicated Cloud tenant administrator.

SCVMM user roles are created and assigned in the Settings workspace in the User Roles navigation area. By default, user role profiles exist for fabric administrators, self-service users, read-only administrators, and tenant administrators. In addition, an Administrator's user role contains the administrators of SCVMM who have full permissions to all aspects of SCVMM; this role should contain only the most trusted administrators. The user role profiles are used to assign user roles to users or groups of users that can be modified, such as limiting the scope of resource access and assigning only a subset of available actions. The capabilities of each type of user role profile are as follows:

Fabric Administrator (Delegated Administrator)   Can perform all tasks related to their delegated host groups, clouds, and library servers. Fabric Administrators cannot modify core VMM settings nor add or remove members of the Administrator's user role.

Read-Only Administrator   Can view all properties, status, and job objects within their assigned host groups, clouds, and library servers but cannot modify objects. Can also view Run As accounts that have been assigned to the role.

Tenant Administrator   Can manage self-service users and VM networks for their delegated clouds. Tenant Administrators can also create and manage their own VMs and services but cannot view other resources in the cloud not owned by them.

Application Administrator (Self-Service User)   Can perform the actions assigned to them on the assigned clouds. This commonly includes the ability to create and control VMs and services.

By installing the SCVMM 2016 console on machines, you can remotely manage SCVMM and avoid having to log on to the SCVMM server. I like to install all of the various management consoles from Windows and System Center on a remote desktop session host and then publish the administrator tools by using RDP. I can then get to the admin tools from any device and operating system. I walk through the process in a video at `http://youtu.be/ _dkxyr03Er4`.

Once you start using SCVMM for managing your Hyper-V environments, you should not use Hyper-V Manager or the Failover Cluster Management tool for normal virtualization resource management. If you do make changes using Hyper-V Manager directly, SCVMM may not be aware of the change and may need some time to detect it, giving inconsistent views between Hyper-V Manager and SCVMM. For best results, after SCVMM is implemented and managing virtualization resources, don't use other management tools to manage the same resources.

UNLOCKING ALL POSSIBILITIES WITH POWERSHELL

When you look at any resource on System Center 2012 and newer, or on Windows Server 2012 and newer, one common theme is the prevalence of PowerShell. Everything that is done in the System Center consoles is performed by an underlying PowerShell cmdlet. As you make a selection in a console and click an action, the console composes the correct PowerShell command and executes it behind the scenes. There are many actions that you can take only with PowerShell, and as you become more acquainted with System Center, you will start to use PowerShell more and more. I'm not talking about manually running actions, but when you consider that you can perform every management action for the entire System Center 2012 and System Center 2016 product by using PowerShell, the automation possibilities can truly be realized, and you will start to automate more and more processes.

A great way to get started with PowerShell is to use the graphical interface to perform an action, such as creating a new virtual machine. In the Summary stage of the wizard, you will see a View Script button at the bottom-right corner. Click this button, and you will be shown all of the PowerShell commands that the console is going to run to perform the actions selected. You can now take all of these commands and add them into your own scripts or automation processes.

Libraries

Throughout this book, I talk about many aspects of SCVMM, and in this section I want to spend some time on the libraries in SCVMM because they are critical to many activities. Although it would be possible to store all of the SCVMM resources in various locations, the best way is to utilize the SCVMM library feature, which allows one or more file shares to be used by SCVMM as a central repository for assets that can be used in the virtualization management. Typical assets placed in the library include the following:

◆ Virtual machine templates, which include the virtual machine hardware configuration as well as OS configuration information such as domain membership, the product key, and other configuration options for enabling the fast creation of new virtual machines

◆ Virtual hard disks, which will primarily be VHD for Hyper-V virtual machines but can also store VMDK for ESX. VHD files can also be used to deploy physical Hyper-V servers.

◆ Virtual machines that are not in use. This allows you to save disk space on the virtualization hosts or shared storage by storing unused machines in the SCVMM library. You can then deploy them again if needed. For end users, this saves their VM quota!

◆ ISO files, which are images of CDs and DVDs that can be attached to virtual machines to install operating systems or applications

◆ Drivers

◆ Service templates, which describe multitiered services

◆ Various types of profiles, such as hardware profiles and guest OS profiles, which are used as building blocks for creating templates; host profiles (for physical deployments of Hyper-V servers); capability profiles that describe the capabilities of different hypervisors or environments; SQL Server profiles when installing SQL Server; and application profiles for application deployment. Think of profiles as building blocks for use in other activities within SCVMM.

◆ Updated baselines and catalogs

◆ Scripts and commands used for management, which can be grouped into packages called *custom resources* (which as previously mentioned are just folders with a `.cr` extension)

I should be clear that although libraries do have a physical manifestation by storing content on the file shares that you specify when you add new library servers, not everything in the library is saved as a file. You will not find virtual machine templates or profiles as files on the filesystem; instead, templates and profiles are stored as Metadata in the SCVMM SQL database.

The filesystem that corresponds to a location in the library can be accessed by right-clicking a library branch and selecting Explore or by selecting Explore from the ribbon. To add content not related to virtual machines,, such as drivers and ISO files, you use the Explore feature and then copy content onto the filesystem via Windows Explorer. When the library content is refreshed, the new content is displayed; you can force this to occur by selecting the library server and then selecting the Refresh action on the Library Server ribbon tab. By default, library content is automatically refreshed once an hour, but you can change this in the Settings workspace and in the General navigation area by selecting Library Settings and changing the refresh interval per your organization's requirements.

I previously covered the creation of templates, so I'm going to move on to using other types of resources. Templates are one of the primary reasons to use SCVMM. Although a single SCVMM library server is added during the installation of SCVMM, additional library servers can be added. It's common to add multiple library servers, particularly so that you have a library server in each datacenter that has virtualization hosts; this ensures that content that may need to be accessed by the hosts is locally available and prevents you from having to traverse a WAN connection. When you add a library server when the share is selected, select the Add Default Resources check box for all of the SCVMM default library content to be copied to the share. SCVMM fully supports hosting the file share that stores the library content on a highly available file server, which means that it's part of a failover cluster and helps ensure that the content is available even if a node fails.

To ensure that hosts use a library server that is closest to them, you can assign library servers to host groups by selecting the properties of the library server and setting up the host group, as shown in Figure 9.5. The recommendation is that virtualization hosts should be connected by at least a 100Mbps link to the library server they use, but ideally 1Gbps.

FIGURE 9.5
Specifying the library server for a specific host group

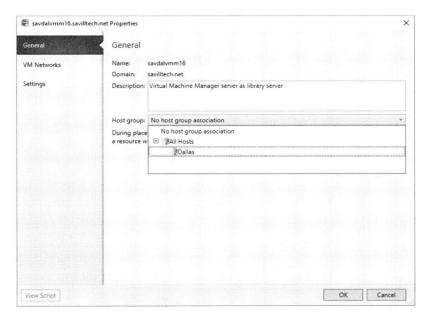

REPLICATING LIBRARY CONTENT BETWEEN MULTIPLE LIBRARY SERVERS

SCVMM has no capability to replicate the content of the library servers. If your organization has 20 SCVMM library servers, you have 20 file shares, all with their own content that you need to keep maintained. If you add a VHD to one library, you need to manually add it to the other 19 file shares.

Numerous solutions can keep the content replicated, but all involve initially having a single *master* library—to which you add new content, and from which you update/remove existing content. You then use a technology to synchronize this master copy to all of the other library servers. One way to replicate the content is to use the Microsoft Robust File Copy tool (Robocopy), which copies the

continues

continued

content from the master to all of the other libraries in the organization. Once the copy is complete, a manual refresh of the library is performed in SCVMM to load the new content, which can be performed in PowerShell by using the `Read-SCLibraryShare` cmdlet. Another option is to use Distributed File System Replication (DFSR). This allows master-slave relationships to be created and automatically replicates changes from the master to the slave library shares, but the new content won't show until a library refresh is performed. You *cannot* use Distributed File System Namespaces (DFSN) as a location for libraries, only the DFSR replication component.

If you have other replication technologies in your organization, that is fine. The two technologies mentioned here are free, Microsoft-provided technologies.

If you have multiple libraries, you will end up with the same content on many library servers, and your templates will refer to the content on a specific library server. For instance, a template might indicate a server in London, such as `\\londonlib\SCVMM\VHDs\2008R2.vhd`. But you are actually deploying to a server in New York, and there is a library server in New York, `\\newyorklib\SCVMM`, that has exactly the same file, which you would rather use than copying the content over the North Atlantic. SCVMM allows equivalencies to be created in the library, which as the name suggests enables you to specify that various content from all of the libraries are the same object. This means that even though a template may say to deploy `\\londonlib\SCVMM\VHDs\2012R2.vhd`, because you created an equivalency between the `\\londonlib\SCVMM\VHDs\2012R2.vhd` and `\\newyorklib\SCVMM\VHDs\2012R2.vhd` files, if you deployed the template in New York, it would use the VHD from the New York share. This also provides redundancy because if the New York library is not available, the London library can be used.

To create an equivalency, you select the root Library Servers node in the Navigation pane in the Library workspace. You can then add a filter in the Results pane to show the objects of interest. Select the objects that are the same and then select the Mark Equivalent action; a dialog box opens that asks for a family for the objects and then a release. Both of these values are text values used to help find other objects that match the family and release, so be consistent in your naming. As you type in the values, autocomplete shows existing values, or you can select from the drop-down.

One of the interesting ways that library content is used is via ISO files, which are files that contain the content of a CD or DVD. To inject a CD/DVD into a virtual machine, you access the properties of a virtual machine by selecting the VM in the Results pane of the VMs And Services workspace and selecting the Properties action. Within the properties of the virtual machine, you select the Hardware Configuration tab, and then under Bus Configuration you select Virtual DVD Drive. Notice the option for No Media, which means that the drive is empty. Physical CD or DVD Drive links the virtual drive to the physical optical drive in the virtualization host, and Existing ISO Image File allows you to select an ISO file from the library.

Notice an interesting option in Figure 9.6: Share File Instead Of Copying It. A CD/DVD image is usually used to install software onto an operating system. If the VM accesses an ISO file over the network and that connectivity is lost, unexpected results may occur, because it would appear that the media was suddenly ripped out. To avoid this from happening by default, when an ISO is attached to a VM drive, the ISO is first copied using BITS over HTTPS to the Hyper-V host in the virtual machine's folder, and then the VM attaches to the local copied ISO file. Any network interruption would not stop the access to the ISO. When the ISO is ejected from the VM, the copied ISO file is deleted from the local host. Although this does use disk space while the ISO is being used, it provides the safest approach. This same copy approach is used for ESX, but it uses a different file copy technology specific to the virtualization platform. For Hyper-V, only SCVMM gives the option of not copying the ISO to the virtualization host and attaches the virtual drive to the ISO on the SCVMM library file share, which is the Share File Instead Of Copying It option. Some specific configurations are required to enable sharing; see http://technet.microsoft.com/en-us/library/ee340124.aspx.

FIGURE 9.6
Attaching an ISO by using SCVMM from the library

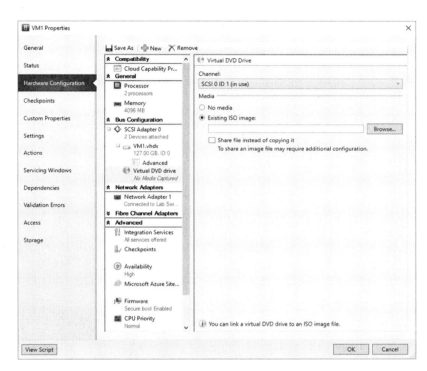

The library is one of the key capabilities of SCVMM. All types of resources can be stored in the library, even entire virtual machines, so it's important to architect the right number of library servers, ensuring proximity of a library server to your hosts in all of your datacenters.

Creating a Private Cloud by Using System Center Virtual Machine Manager

In this section, I assume that System Center Virtual Machine Manager is fully configured with all of your hypervisor compute resources, such as all the Hyper-V servers that have been placed into failover clusters that have been dynamically and power-optimized to get the best-performing and highly available solution that minimizes power waste by turning off hosts when not needed. SCVMM has been connected to your hardware load balancers, all of the storage area networks have their SMI-S providers in SCVMM, and the storage has been classified as gold, silver, or bronze for all locations. Logical networks and sites have been defined. Virtual machine templates for all common configurations have been created, and common services have been modeled as a service template. System Center Operations Manager is monitoring the environment, System Center Data Protection Manager is backing up and protecting the environment, and System Center Configuration Manager is providing patching, desired configuration, and inventory information. Everything is well configured and healthy, so you are ready to create a cloud.

To truly understand what goes into creating a cloud in System Center Virtual Machine Manager and all of the options, I will walk you through creating a cloud and granting users access to it. This will show all of the capabilities and the delegation options for various groups of users.

You use the Virtual Machine Manager Console to create a new cloud, which is achieved through the VMs And Services workspace by selecting the Create Cloud action from the ribbon. The first step is to specify a name and description for the cloud. A good example may be Development for the name, and then for the comment specify development purposes, with access to the development network only and silver tier storage. Make the name and description something useful.

The next step sets the resources to be included in the cloud, as shown in Figure 9.7. The host groups will govern the computer resources (virtualization hosts) that will be included in the created cloud in addition to the various storage and networks that are available in those host groups. Remember that just because a host group is specified does not mean the entire capability or connectivity of that host group is exposed to the cloud. You can specify exactly what you want to give access to later in the wizard. The same host groups can be included in multiple clouds. Also note in the dialog box that a VMware resource pool can be selected directly.

FIGURE 9.7
Selecting the host group that is available for utilization by the cloud

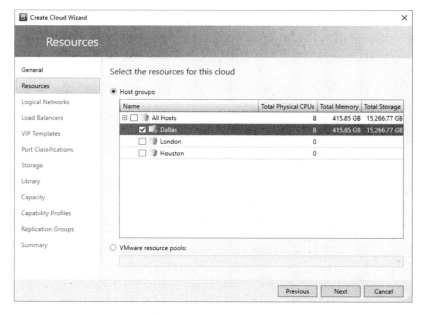

The next stage of the wizard enables you to select the logical networks available to the cloud. The logical networks displayed will vary depending on the connectivity available to the hosts in the host groups specified in the previous screen. Select the logical networks to which this cloud should have access, as shown in Figure 9.8, and click Next to continue with the wizard.

FIGURE 9.8
Selecting the logical networks available to the cloud

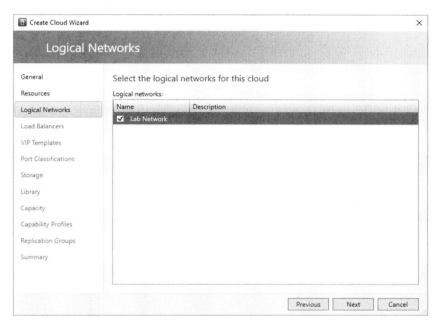

The hardware load balancers that can be used can be selected on this screen. The hardware load balancers displayed will depend on the host groups selected and the logical networks selected, because a hardware load balancer is tied to host groups and logical networks. Once again, click Next to continue; now you can select the virtual IP profiles to make available to the cloud; these are tied to the load balancers selected on the previous screen (do you see the pattern now?). Make the selections and click Next. The various types of port classifications for the cloud are displayed; you should select the ones desired for the cloud and click Next.

The Storage stage of the wizard displays all tiers of storage that are available within the selected host groups. Select the tiers of storage that should be available to the cloud, as shown in Figure 9.9. For a development cloud, as an example, I would select lower tiers of storage such as bronze. Only storage tiers that are available to the selected host groups will be displayed. Click Next.

The next step is selecting a library configuration. There are two parts to this. First, you select the read-only library shares, which are standard SCVMM libraries in the environment to which you want to grant this cloud access and the contained resources that can be used to create virtual machines and services. You could create libraries with a subset of ISO images to limit what can be created in the clouds. The read-only library needs to be unique and not used as part of a standard library. Second, you specify a stored VM path, which is an area in which the users of the cloud can store content. Why do you want to give the cloud users a writeable library area? Consider that users of the cloud will have a certain quota that limits the number of virtual machines they can create. It is possible that they may exceed this quota and need to create another VM, or maybe they don't need a VM right now but don't want to lose its configuration. When you give users a place to store VMs, the users can save a VM to storage, which removes it from the virtualization host and thus frees up their quota. In the future, the VM could be deployed from the library back to a virtualization host and once again count against the quota. Note that the path specified for the storage of VMs cannot be part of a library location specified as a read-only library. An easy solution is to create a new share on a file server, add it to SCVMM as a library, and then use it as the writeable area for a cloud. Once everything has been configured, click Next.

FIGURE 9.9
Selecting the storage classifications available to the cloud

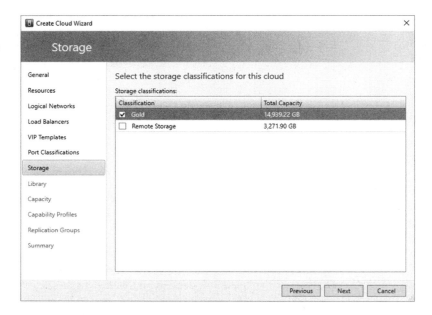

The next stage is configuring the capacity for the cloud (see Figure 9.10), and this gets interesting because an organization can take various approaches to managing capacity for the cloud. By default, the capacity is unlimited, but you can change any of the dimensions of capacity, such as virtual CPUs, memory, storage, custom quota (which is carried over for compatibility with SCVMM 2008 R2), and virtual machines. You can set the values to use the maximum, a smaller amount, or a higher amount. In my example, I set all to the maximum as shown in Figure 9.10. Remember, this is the capacity available to this cloud, so you don't have to expose the full capabilities of the underlying host groups; you may have 10 clouds on a single set of host groups and want to divide the resources between clouds. But wait a minute; I just set the memory to *higher* than I have available in the underlying hosts in the selected host groups. How does this work? It's quite acceptable to set the capacity of a cloud to exceed that of the current underlying resources of the cloud. It is just as important that the proper resource utilization mechanisms and processes are in place so that as a cloud starts to approach the capacity of the underlying resources, additional resources are added to the host groups. This is where System Center Operations Manager is great for monitoring the usage of resources and can then work with

System Center Virtual Machine Manager and System Center Orchestrator to add new Hyper-V hosts and place them into host groups. The same could be done for storage by adding new LUNs to the required storage tiers. Scalability is a key attribute of the private cloud. Set the capacity for the cloud and click Next.

FIGURE 9.10
Configuring the capacity for the cloud

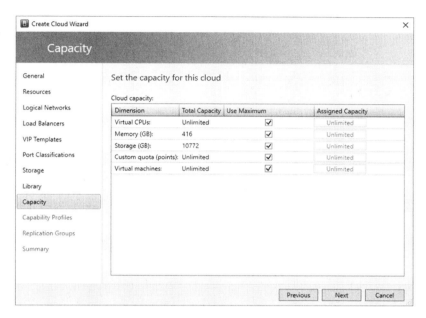

The next stage, capability profiles, is an interesting concept. This is different from capacity. *Capacity* is the limit of what can be stored in the cloud, whereas *capability* defines what the virtual machines created in the cloud are, well, capable of. For example, what is the maximum number of virtual CPUs that can be assigned to a virtual machine, and what is the maximum amount of memory for a VM? By default, two capability profiles exist—one for Hyper-V and one for ESX—which indicate the maximum capabilities for each hypervisor platform. For example, the Hyper-V capability profile sets the processor range from 1 to 64 and sets the memory from 8MB to 1TB, which are the limits for Hyper-V 2012 and Hyper-V 2012 R2. I expect this will be revised in an update with the new Windows Server 2016 maximums of 240 vCPUs and 16TB of memory. The ESX capability profile sets the processor range from 1 to 64 and the memory from 4MB to 255GB. Again I expect to see this updated with the more recent maximums. By default, you can select any combination of the two built-in, locked capability profiles for your cloud based on the hypervisors used in the cloud, but you don't have to.

Imagine that you are creating a development cloud today. Windows Server 2016 Hyper-V is available with its support for virtual machines that have 240 virtual CPUs and 16TB of RAM. I may give a user a quota of 100 virtual CPUs and 4TB of memory, so do I want that user consuming their whole quota with a single VM? Not likely. Instead, I could create a custom capability profile in the Library workspace and under Profiles ➤ Capability Profiles create a new profile to meet the capabilities that I want in a specific cloud. In Figure 9.11, I have created a custom capability profile that limits virtual CPUs and indicates a memory range from 512MB to 4GB. I could also mandate the use of Dynamic Memory. Note that I can also set the number of DVD drives allowed; if shared images are used, I could set the number of hard disks allowed and their type and size, number of network adapters, and even whether high availability is available or required.

FIGURE 9.11
Custom capability profile

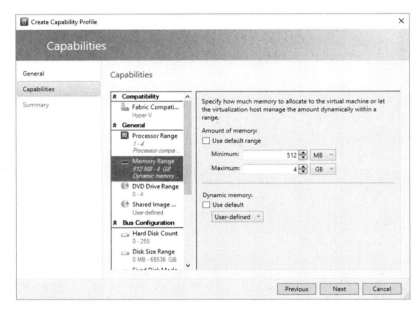

A potential pitfall exists when creating customer capability profiles if you don't plan well. Many resources, such as virtual machine templates, have a configuration that sets the required capability profile. If you don't update the resources with your custom capability profile, you won't be able to assign any resources to your new cloud. This is configured through the Hardware Configuration area of the VM template; select the Compatibility option, and ensure that the new capability profile is selected.

Once you've created your custom capability profiles, you can elect to use them for your cloud. The custom capability profiles created can be used in addition to, or instead of, the built-in capability profiles. Click Next.

A summary of all your choices is displayed in a confirmation screen along with the magic View Script button that will show the PowerShell code to create a complete new cloud. This is a basic example without hardware load balancers or virtual IP templates, but it gives you an idea of what is going on. Now that you have the PowerShell code, you could use this in other components such as System Center Orchestrator to automate the creation of clouds based on requests from Service Manager.

```
Set-SCCloudCapacity -JobGroup "XXXXXX" -UseCustomQuotaCountMaximum $true `
-UseMemoryMBMaximum $false -UseCPUCountMaximum $false `
-UseStorageGBMaximum $false -UseVMCountMaximum $true -MemoryMB 36864 `
-CPUCount 40 -StorageGB 1024

$resources = @()
$resources += Get-SCLogicalNetwork `
-Name "Hyper-V Network Virtualization PA" `
-ID "c75b66eb-c844-49a2-8bbd-83198fc8ccc0"
$resources += Get-SCLogicalNetwork -Name "Lab" -ID " XXXXXX "



$resources += Get-SCStorageClassification -Name "Gold" -ID " XXXXXX "


$addCapabilityProfiles = @()
$addCapabilityProfiles += Get-SCCapabilityProfile -Name "Hyper-V"

Set-SCCloud -JobGroup " XXXXXX" -RunAsynchronously `
-AddCloudResource $resources `
-AddCapabilityProfile $addCapabilityProfiles

$hostGroups = @()
$hostGroups += Get-SCVMHostGroup -ID " XXXXXX "
New-SCCloud -JobGroup " XXXXXX " -VMHostGroup $hostGroups `
-Name "Test Cloud" -Description "" -RunAsynchronously `
-DisasterRecoverySupported $false
```

You now have a cloud that no one can use, so the next step is to assign the cloud to users and groups. To assign access to clouds, you use user roles. These can be either a Delegated Administrator who can do anything to the objects within their scope, a Read-Only Administrator who can view information about everything but can see nothing that is useful for auditors and interns, or a Self-Service user. Each user role has a scope that defines the clouds to which it applies and the capabilities and the users/groups within that user role. It is common, therefore, that you will create a new Self-Service user role and possibly a Delegated Administrator user role for every cloud you create to enable granularity in assigning cloud access.

Open the Settings workspace, navigate to User Roles, and select the Create User Role action on the ribbon. The Create User Role Wizard opens, requesting a name and description for the object being created. If the user role is cloud specific, include the name of the cloud in the role name. Click Next, and the wizard requests the type of user role; select Self-Service User, and click Next.

The next stage prompts for the users and groups that are part of this role. Normally, my recommendation is to always use Active Directory groups and add users to the AD group that need access to the user role, so that it's unnecessary to keep modifying the user role. When a user is added to the AD group, the user automatically gets the cloud rights that the AD group has. This works great if you are creating a cloud for a certain business unit and that business unit already has an AD group. Just grant that business unit's AD group access to the cloud-specific Self-Service user role, and then as users join the business unit, they get access to the cloud. Even if the cloud is not business-unit specific, but you have good processes in place to add users to groups, you could use an AD group. For example, developers could have access to a development cloud. My guidance changes when good processes are not in place to add users to groups, and it's beyond the control of the team implementing the private cloud to fix it or effect change. In those cases, I may lean toward adding users directly into user roles within SCVMM, which can be automated through PowerShell and can cut out potentially large delays associated with adding the user to an AD group. Add the users and/or groups and click Next.

On the next page, you select the clouds to which the user roles apply. Note there are no host groups shown, only clouds. With System Center Virtual Machine Manager self-service access is via clouds or nothing. Select the clouds and click Next.

Next you set the quotas for the user role. Remember, when creating the actual cloud, you set the capacity. Now you are setting the quotas for this specific user role in the cloud as well as the quotas of each user within the user role. Note that you may have multiple Self-Service user roles for a single cloud with different quotas and different actions available. In Figure 9.12, I have set an unlimited quota for the role, giving it full access to the cloud, but each user has far smaller limits. Make your configurations, and click Next.

FIGURE 9.12
Setting the quotas for a specific tenant

The next step is adding the resources that should be available to the role, such as virtual machine templates, hardware profiles, service templates, and so on. These resources are what will be available when the users of this role create virtual machines, so make sure that the right templates are available for them. Additionally, you can specify a location for user role data that is shared between all members of the role. Click Next to continue.

You can now configure permitted actions for the user role, which are fairly granular and fully documented at http://technet.microsoft.com/en-us/library/gg610613.aspx. Once the actions have been configured, the next step allows any specific Run As accounts to be made available to the user role. Be careful as to which Run As accounts are made available, because you don't want to give basic users access to highly privileged Run As accounts. Click Next, and a summary is shown; then the role is created. Once again, you can export the PowerShell code used.

Granting Users Access to the Private Cloud

I've talked about installing the SCVMM management console for end-user access, but this is really not practical. Although it has full role-based access control, it requires a client to be deployed on every machine. Instead, the preferred interface for users is via a web browser that enables users to provision, manage, and control their resources.

System Center 2012 R2 had a component called App Controller, as noted previously in this chapter. This was Silverlight based, very thin, and simply deployed, and provided a web interface for users to interact with the following:

◆ Clouds defined in SCVMM

◆ Clouds in Azure

◆ Clouds at hosting partners who leverage Service Provider Foundation

It was an intuitive interface, and it made basic provisioning and management across clouds simple. However, it had no ability to integrate with workflow engines to enable provisioning as part of any approval or larger process. In System Center 2016, App Controller has been removed, which leaves many wondering how to expose clouds to end users.

Enabling Workflows and Advanced Private Cloud Concepts by Using Service Manager and Orchestrator

System Center Orchestrator provides two primary great capabilities. It can communicate with many systems and automate defined series of activities that can span many systems through runbooks. These two capabilities can be highly beneficial to your private cloud implementation.

At the most basic level, Orchestrator can be leveraged to create virtual machines, deploy service templates, and even create entire clouds through runbooks. In Figure 9.13, I show a basic runbook that receives initialization data, makes a call to SCVMM to create a VM, and then runs PowerShell to configure ownership of the VM.

FIGURE 9.13
A basic Orchestrator runbook

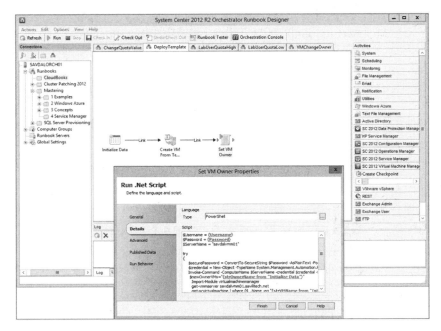

This is just the tip of the iceberg. Running PowerShell scripts to perform actions through Orchestrator is great, and error checking and updating of other applications such as Service Manager are benefits. But you can run PowerShell without Orchestrator. If you look again at Figure 9.13, you will see on the right side a list of activity groups, known as *integration packs*, including System Center Virtual Machine Manager, System Center Configuration Manager, and VMWare vSphere. Each integration pack contains activities specific to the target. For vSphere, there are activities for virtual machine creation and management; the same types of activities are available for SCVMM and for Configuration Manager, including deploying software. Using integration packs for systems, the built-in Orchestrator activities, and most commonly PowerShell, it is possible to automate any action related to the private cloud (and anything else) and to customize those actions based on exactly how your organization functions. The general direction for automation is PowerShell over using the integration packs in Orchestrator, so by all means use Orchestrator, but my guidance is to focus most of the functionality of the runbook as PowerShell called through .Net Script activities rather than utilizing the integration pack activities, which are not being maintained anymore. Once you create the runbooks, they can then be called by the rest of System Center or triggered automatically. Here are some great scenarios for using Orchestrator:

◆ Creating a new cloud based on an IT request though a service catalog that calls a created Orchestrator runbook

◆ Deploying a new virtual machine or service instance

◆ Offering a runbook that automatically patches and reboots all virtual machines for a particular user or business group

♦ Automatically scaling up and down deployed services by triggering runbooks that perform scaling based on performance alerts from Operations Manager

♦ Deprovisioning virtual machines or services that have passed a given length of time or date for development purposes

Remember that the point of the private cloud is its automation, and you can't automate by using graphic consoles. Therefore, as you learn System Center and Virtual Machine Manager in particular, look at the series of actions you perform, look at PowerShell, look at the activities in integration packs, and start creating runbooks in Orchestrator that can be used. Once the runbooks are created, they can be manually triggered by using the Silverlight web-based Orchestrator interface or triggered from other systems such as an item in Service Manager's service catalog. With Orchestrator being able to connect to almost any system, with a little bit of work, any manual process you perform should be able to be automated—and more important, orchestrated—with System Center Orchestrator.

I've talked about System Center Service Manager repeatedly in this chapter. Service Manager is the configuration management database (CMDB) of your organization. It has feeds and connections to all of the other System Center components. Service Manager offers various services, including basic ticketing activities, such as incidents (things not doing what they should), problems (something is broken), and change requests (I want something). When problems occur in the environment, you can look at a computer in Service Manager; because it connects to all the systems, information from all of those systems is visible, so you have a single point of truth about the asset as well as solutions. In Service Manager, you can see all of the hardware, software, and patch status gathered from Configuration Manager. You can see AD information that was pulled from AD. You can see any alerts that were generated by Operations Manager plus any more complex service dependencies, such as all the systems that are responsible, from providing messaging services to the organization.

Because of all these connections to systems, Service Manager can provide a great service for your private cloud. So far I've talked about creating clouds, virtual machines, and services with the SCVMM console, App Controller, PowerShell, and Orchestrator. There are problems, though, when you think of end users for all these approaches. Users typically don't want a separate interface just for requesting a virtual machine. Users are not going to run PowerShell scripts you give them, and giving them a list of runbooks they can run through a web interface is likely to baffle them.

So Service Manager 2012 introduced a new feature called a *service catalog*. The service catalog is a single source that can contain all of the types of services offered by the organization. This could include creating a new user, requesting the installation of a software package through SCCM, asking for a new keyboard, or anything that Service Manager has the ability to enable through its connections to other systems. The service catalog is primarily available to end users through a SharePoint site that uses Service Manager Silverlight web parts. Users can browse the service catalog as a single go-to place for all of their needs, which makes it a perfect place to offer virtual services on the private cloud. How do you offer the private cloud services in the service catalog? You add the runbooks from Orchestrator, and then when a user makes a request from the service catalog, the standard Service Manager workflows can be used such as request authorization. Then the workflow calls the runbook in Orchestrator to perform the actions. Service Manager and Orchestrator have great bidirectional communications in System Center, allowing the status of the runbook execution to be visible within Service Manager, as shown in Figure 9.14. Once the process is complete, the service request is marked as completed, and the user can even be sent an email. I walk through creating this type of service by using Service Manager in a video at http://youtu.be/T1jTX9xE66A.

FIGURE 9.14

Service catalog view in Service Manager of request offerings that call Orchestrator runbooks

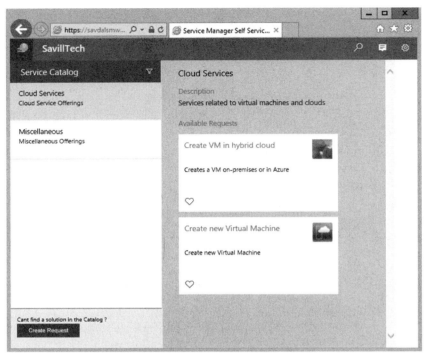

Service Manager also has the ability to create charge-back price sheets that allow prices to be assigned to various aspects of the virtual environment—such as price per day for the VM; price per core, memory, and storage per day; and then additional items such as a price for a highly available VM or static IP address. These price sheets can then be used within Service Manager to allow charge-back to business units based on their utilization.

Utilizing Windows Azure Pack

The integration of Service Manager and Orchestrator provides a great self-service catalog for users; services can be requested and utilize a rich workflow system that can include authorization activities. However, it does not provide an interface to view and manage provisioned services such as a VM in a SCVMM-hosted private cloud. This is where Windows Azure Pack is utilized—the ultimate end-user experience for architectures built on System Center.

With the word *Azure* being a key part of the name *Windows Azure Pack*, it would be natural to think of Windows Azure Pack as a solution that provides an Azure-like experience on premises. This is not the case, however. That is not to say that it's not a good solution; it just isn't Azure running on premises. Instead, Windows Azure Pack provides services on premises (and for hosting partners) that utilize numerous components of System Center and expose those through a web-based interface that looks a lot like the classic Azure portal. Behind the scenes, it's a completely different solution than the public cloud Azure, and it is not Azure consistent in that you cannot write an application using Azure Resource Manager and run it on premises with

Windows Azure Pack. You cannot write a JSON template that works in Azure and deploy it on premises by using Windows Azure Pack. Instead, what you do get is a highly extensible REST-based solution that enables many services to be offered to end users and has a large partner ecosystem extending its capabilities. Out-of-the-box through Microsoft-provided extensions, this includes capabilities such as deploying virtual machines, websites, and even databases. Figure 9.15 shows the basic experience of creating a new VM by using Windows Azure Pack's web interface.

FIGURE 9.15
Creating a new VM by using Windows Azure Pack's web interface

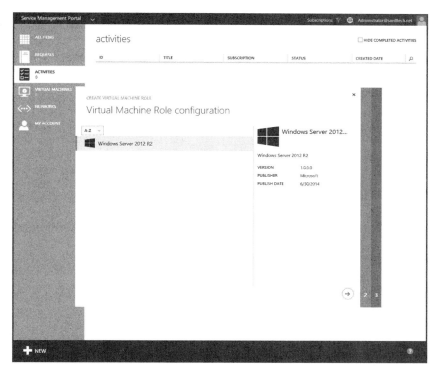

Windows Azure Pack is not the simplest installation; it utilizes other System Center components including the Service Provider Foundation, which acts as the interface layer to communicate to other System Center components such as Virtual Machine Manager. Most organizations that are deploying Windows Azure Pack in production utilize a partner who can deploy it quickly and fairly cheaply. If you wish to deploy it yourself, you can reference the many articles out there. Here are links to two that I have written that will get you up-and-running with Windows Azure Pack and deploying VMs, plus a Microsoft article that walks through the gallery items:

◆ Installing Windows Azure Pack—http://windowsitpro.com/private-cloud/
requirements-install-windows-azure-pack-v1

◆ Enabling IaaS in Windows Azure Pack—http://windowsitpro.com/private-cloud/
enable-iaas-windows-azure-pack

◆ Deploying Gallery items to Windows Azure Pack to offer additional services and template types—http://social.technet.microsoft.com/wiki/contents/articles/20194.downloading-and-installing-windows-azure-pack-gallery-resource.aspx#Download_Windows_Azure_Pack_Gallery_Resources

Once deployed, Windows Azure Pack provides a single interface to meet all of the user requirements. Users can perform basic provisioning, and see and manage their VMs, but they also can expose more-advanced provisioning through integration with the Service Manager service catalog through the third-party GridPro solution, which is detailed at www.gridprosoftware.com/products/requestmanagement/. Windows Azure Pack can also integrate with the public Azure cloud by using the Azure Pack Connector. Available from www.microsoft.com/en-us/download/details.aspx?id=51203, the Azure Pack Connector enables resources both on premises and in the public Azure cloud to be managed and utilized by users through Windows Azure Pack.

How the Rest of System Center Fits into Your Private Cloud Architecture

In this chapter, I've touched on several components of System Center 2016, such as Virtual Machine Manager, Orchestrator, and Service Manager. Other components, although not key private-cloud building blocks, are still important to a complete infrastructure.

Fabric management and deployment of services are critical. However, to ensure the ongoing health of the fabric, the Hyper-V hypervisor, the virtual machines, and the applications running inside the virtual machines, monitoring is necessary to safeguard the long-term availability and health of the environment.

System Center Operations Manager (SCOM) provides a rich monitoring solution for Microsoft and non-Microsoft operating systems, applications, and hardware. Any monitoring solution can tell you when something is broken. SCOM does that, but its real power is in its proactive nature and best-practice adherence functionality. SCOM management packs are units of knowledge about a specific application or component. For example, there is an Exchange Management Pack, and there is a Domain Name System (DNS) for the Windows Server management pack. The Microsoft mandate is that any Microsoft product should have a management pack that is written by the product team responsible for the application or operating system component. All the knowledge of those developers, the people who create best-practice documents, is used to create these management packs that you can then just deploy to your environment. Operations Manager then raises alerts of potential problems or when best practices are not being followed. Customers often raise objections that when Operations Manager is first implemented, it floods them with alerts. Well, this could be for several reasons; perhaps the environment has a lot of problems that should be fixed, but often Operations Manager will be tuned to ignore configurations that, while perhaps not best practice, are accepted by the organization.

Many third parties provide management packs for their applications and hardware devices. When I think of *all about the application* as a key tenant of the private cloud, the ability for Operations Manager to monitor from the hardware, storage, network, and everything all the way through the OS to the application is huge, but it goes even further in Operations Manager 2012 and beyond.

System Center Operations Manager 2012 introduced changes, and two huge ones focus on network monitoring and custom application monitoring. First, Microsoft licensed technology from EMC called Smarts that enables a rich discovery and monitoring of network devices. With this network discovery and monitoring functionality, Operations Manager can identify the relationship between network devices and services to understand, for instance, that port 3 on this switch connects to server A; then if a switch problem occurs, Operations Manager will know the affected servers. Information such as CPU and memory information (among other information) is available for supported network devices.

The other big change was the acquisition of AVIcode by Microsoft, which is now Application Performance Monitoring (APM) in Operations Manager 2012. APM provides monitoring of custom applications without any changes needed by the application. APM currently supports .NET applications and Java Enterprise Edition (JEE). A great example to help you understand this is to look at a custom web application in your environment today without APM when performance problems occur.

> *User phones IT: "Application X is running slow and sucks."*

> *IT phones the app developer: "Users say Application X is running really slow and really sucks."*

> *App developer to self: "I suck and have no clue how to start troubleshooting this. I will leave the industry in disgrace."*

With System Center Operations Manager's APM configured to monitor this custom application, the scenario changes.

> *User phones IT: "Application X is running slow and sucks."*

> *IT phones the app developer: "Users say Application X is running really slow. I see in Operations Manager the APM shows that in function X of module Y this SQL query 'select blah from blah blah' to SQL database Z is taking 3.5 seconds."*

> *App developer to self: "It must be an indexing problem on the SQL server, and the index needs to be rebuilt on database Z. I'll give the SQL DBA the details to fix."*

> *App developer to SQL DBA: "Your SQL database sucks."*

Operations Manager can be used in many aspects of the private cloud. Although it's great that it monitors the entire infrastructure to keep it healthy, the Operations Manager's ability to monitor resource usage and trending also helps plan growth and can trigger automatic scaling of services if resources hit certain defined thresholds. Figure 9.16 shows an example view through Operations Manager of a complete distributed service comprising many elements. To prove the flexibility of Operations Manager in this example, I'm monitoring an ESX host through information gained through SCVMM and also my NetApp SAN, some processes running on Linux, and a SQL database. All of those elements make up my complete application to show an overall health roll-up, but I can drill down into the details as needed.

Operations Manager 2012 R2 also understands clouds and has a cloud view capability. Once the SCVMM MP has been imported into Operations Manager, and the SCVMM connector to Operations Manager has been configured, you will be able to navigate to Microsoft System Center Virtual Machine Manager ➢ Cloud Health Dashboard ➢ Cloud Health within the Monitoring workspace. This lists all of the clouds. Select a cloud and in the Tasks pane select the Fabric Health Dashboard, which, as shown in Figure 9.17, provides insight into all of the fabric elements that relate to the cloud.

FIGURE 9.16
A view of a distributed service and its various services visible through Operations Manager

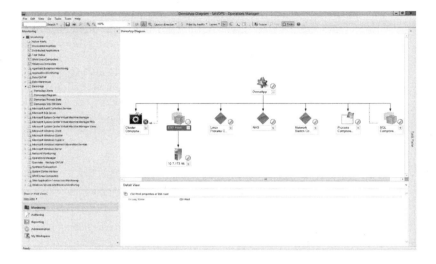

FIGURE 9.17
The Fabric Health dashboard for a SCVMM cloud

With the environment being monitored, a key aspect is the backup that I talked about in Chapter 6, namely, Data Protection Manager. As discussed previously, DPM is a powerful solution for the backup and restore of not just Hyper-V but also key Microsoft applications such as Exchange, SQL, and SharePoint. Although it has limited Linux VM backup on Windows Server 2012 R2 Hyper-V, DPM is still very much a Microsoft-focused protection solution.

The final component of System Center is Configuration Manager. SCCM provides capabilities to deploy operating systems, applications, and OS/software updates to servers and desktops. Detailed hardware and software inventory and asset intelligence features are key aspects of SCCM, enabling great insight into the entire organization's IT infrastructure. SCCM 2012 introduced management of mobile devices such as iOS and Android through ActiveSync integration with Exchange and a user-focused management model. However, with System Center 2012 R2, Configuration Manager shifted to manage mobile devices through integration with the Microsoft Intune cloud management service, and this investment has continued to the 2016 version. In Configuration Manager 2016, organizations also have the ability to manage mobile devices directly without leveraging Intune for mobile devices that do not connect to the Internet, such as devices on a shop floor. For most regular mobile devices, the management should still be performed via Intune. Now, however, organizations have a choice.

One key feature of SCCM for servers is settings management, which allows a desired configuration to be defined, such as OS and application settings, and then applied to a group of servers (or desktops). This can be useful for compliance requirements. The challenge I face in recommending SCCM for servers today is that SCCM's focus seems to be shifting to the desktop. The benefits that SCCM can bring to servers, such as patching, host deployment, and desired configuration, are better handled through other mechanisms. For patch management, both SCVMM and Failover Clustering one-click patching leverage WSUS and not SCCM. For host deployment, SCVMM has the ability to deploy physical servers for Hyper-V and for file servers and automatically manage cluster membership and more. Desired configuration is possible through PowerShell v4's Desired State Configuration feature. Therefore, if you are already using SCCM, you can take advantage of some of those capabilities in your environment. I would not implement SCCM for the sole purpose of server management; there are better options, in my opinion, in the other components and base operating systems. I also expect more and more features to be added to the cloud Operations Management Suite (OMS), which will render Configuration Manager redundant for server management tasks.

Understanding Microsoft Azure Stack

I previously said that Windows Azure Pack was not really Azure. It had a portal that looked like the Azure classic portal, but its plumbing was completely different and did not offer services in a consistent manner with Azure. *Microsoft Azure Stack* is something completely different. This brand-new product brings Azure-consistent services on premises by using Azure code. This means that for the services available in Azure Stack (because not every Azure service is available in Azure Stack), they will be usable in a consistent manner:

◆ If a JSON template is created to deploy services in Azure, it will also work on premises against Azure Stack.

◆ If an application is written on ARM, it will work in Azure and in Azure Stack.

◆ Applications using Azure Storage APIs will function the same way.

◆ AzureRM PowerShell will work with on-premises subscriptions through Azure Stack and subscriptions in the public Azure cloud.

Microsoft Azure Stack does not utilize System Center because Azure does not use System Center. Instead, Azure has its own fabric management around storage, networking, and compute that is being translated to function on premises at a much smaller scale with Azure Stack. Consider that Azure operates millions of nodes with storage accounts spanning a thousand nodes across thousands of disks. This is very different from what will be available on premises with Azure Stack in even the largest enterprises. Therefore, the fabric implementation will be different in some ways between Azure Stack and Azure, especially in the way that storage works. The key point, however, is that the management framework that interfaces with the fabric elements and the services built on that framework will operate and be managed in the same way, giving a consistent end-user experience.

Many of the new technologies in Windows Server 2016 were inspired by Azure and utilized much of the engineering work already performed in Azure that was built on Windows Server 2012 R2 Hyper-V. Key new technologies include the following:

◆ Software Defined Networking v2 with the Network Controller and various Network Functions, such as the Software Load Balancer and Multi-Tenant Gateway

◆ Storage Spaces Direct, which enables disks local to the nodes in a cluster to be aggregated and utilized as clustered storage that is resilient to disk or node failure

◆ Service Fabric that enables multiple instances of services to replicate synchronously to offer a highly available and scalable service

◆ Hyper-V advances such as Discrete Device Assignment and Shielded VMs

◆ Nano Server, which has a small footprint, provisions fast, and uses the Current Branch for Business (CBB) servicing model, enabling feature updates throughout its deployment life cycle

As Azure adopts Windows Server 2016, it will be able to utilize more of the in-box functionality instead of having custom fabric elements to achieve the required functionality, and Azure Stack will utilize this from its initial release as the backbone of the core compute, storage, and network resource providers. Azure Stack is built on Windows Server 2016 Hyper-V, and will provide a fast update cadence to Azure Stack; like Azure, it will constantly be evolving with new features being made available in Preview (think Beta) and then through General Availability, or GA (think Release).

Initially, Azure Stack will support only a small number of Azure services, which will include the following but could change as Azure Stack gets closer to release. Again, this list will change over time as more and more services are added:

◆ Blob storage (required to store IaaS VHDs)

◆ Virtual network

◆ Load balancer

◆ VPN gateway

◆ Virtual machine

◆ Containers

◆ Portal

◆ Key vault

◆   VM Image Gallery and VM Depot

◆   Azure SDK

◆   Tables

◆   Queues

Based on these services, it is easy to realize that the initial workload is essentially IaaS, which requires compute, storage, networking, and management—all of the main services that will be available at GA. Additionally, various services will be available in Azure Stack in Preview mode; for example, Azure Web Apps, Service Fabric, and Premium Storage. Over time, however, expect more services to be added to Azure Stack.

Architecture

As previously mentioned, Azure Stack is built on Windows Server 2016 Hyper-V Server. There is a core cloud infrastructure layer on which an extensible service framework is utilized to enable both Microsoft Azure services and third-party services to operate providing foundational services, additional services, and core services.

A *foundational service* can be considered out-of-the-box for Azure Stack; for example, IaaS with its VMs, images, networks, and storage. These foundational services are used to enable higher-order PaaS services. A *core service* is something common across all types of IaaS and PaaS resources (for example, a subscription or role-based access control), and these are provided by ARM. An *additional service*, as the name indicates, is an extra service utilizing the other types of services as a building block, such as PaaS Web Apps.

On top of this is a unified application model on which end-user experiences are offered such as virtual machines, virtual networks, and more. If you understand ARM, you will understand the key constructs for Azure Stack, including subscriptions, resource groups, resource providers, resources, and more.

Behind the scenes, most Azure Stack deployments consist of a Windows Server 2016 Hyper-V environment and numerous virtual machines, as shown in Figure 9.18 which shows the state for TP1 at the top and TP2 at the bottom. This shows the changes between releases, and I expect it to continue to change as it releases and evolves, but this gives some idea to the scope of the core Azure Stack services.

These virtual machines provide the base services for Azure Stack at TP2. You will see this does not exactly match the TP1 screen shot:

ACS VM   Provides the Azure-Consistent Storage services

AD/DC VM   A local Active Directory instance used by Azure Stack for its internal purposes. This VM also provides DNS and DHCP services.

ADFS VM   Hosts the ADFS services

BGP/NAT VM   Border Gateway Protocol instance, which in Windows Server 2016 is a separate, independent service and infrastructure component acting as a BGP route reflector. This enables better separation and scaling of connections. It also provides Network Address Translation gateway and VPN services from the Azure Stack virtual networks outbound to other networks.

Certificate Authority VM   Provides CA services for Azure Stack

FIGURE 9.18
The core VMs used by Azure Stack in a single-box deployment with TP1 at top and TP2 at bottom

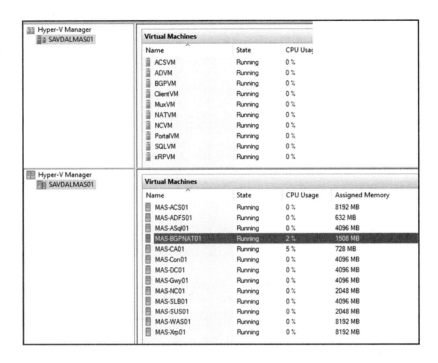

Client Connection VM   A VM to which users can connect for easy testing and interaction with the Azure Stack instance without requiring separate network connectivity.

Gateway VM   Provides the multi-tenant gateway services for edge services

SLB MUX VM   Provides the Software Load Balancer Multiplexer (MUX) part of the load balancer in Windows Server 2016. Incoming requests are received by a MUX instance that selects a backend DIP (Dynamic/Datacenter IP), encapsulates the packet, and forwards to the host that is hosting the DIP. The Hyper-V switch removes the encapsulation, rewrites the packet, and forwards to the DIP. The VM with the DIP can then respond directly to the source, bypassing the MUX and increasing the scalability of the load balancer.

NC VM   Network Controller instance for the software-defined network

Portal/WAS VM   Hosts the Azure Resource Manager Control Plane and Azure portal services (plus some additional services that enable admin and tenant usage)

SQL VM   SQL Server instance used by various fabric services

SUS VM   Provides Windows Service Update Services to the Azure Stack fabric

xRP VM   Hosts the Compute, Storage, and Network resource providers

Additionally, on the physical host are storage services that utilize technologies such as Storage Spaces Direct, ReFS, and Scale-Out File Services to provide the Azure Consistent Blob Services (ACS Blob Service). This may seem like a lot of virtual machines that require a lot of resources, which is why the single-box deployment needs at least 96GB of memory (although

128GB is recommended) and 12 cores (16 recommended) along with 4 local data disks (which are used with Storage Spaces Direct to provide the base storage). You should realize, however, that this is just a basic, single-box deployment meant for nothing more than testing and POCs. In a production deployment, there would be multiple physical boxes (at least four) and many of the preceding VMs would have multiple instances, some that leverage the Service Fabric to replicate state and provide a highly available, highly scalable service, such as the Azure Consistent Storage and Network Controller services, while others have their own multi-instance support, such as the MUX and gateway VMs. Additionally, in production, Storage Spaces Direct would spread the data over multiple hosts to increase resiliency.

Microsoft has full documentation on the deployment at https://azure.microsoft.com/en-us/documentation/articles/azure-stack-poc/. The good news is that although this may seem intimidating, the deployment consists of running a script that creates all of the VMs for you. Your only obligation is to follow the requirements and prerequisites to the letter and, after a few hours, you will have an Azure Stack deployment that you can start playing with. Note that at time of this writing, Azure Stack is in its infancy at Technical Preview 1; I expect many things to change as Azure Stack evolves to its GA state in 2017.

Additional management actions are required with Azure Stack, since it does run on premises and no separate vendor is looking after the fabric. This is part of the administration experience and a core part of the Azure Stack solution and doesn't require additional add-ons for management. In fact, I expect Azure Stack to be locked down specifically to block adding software to its core fabric.

What does Azure Stack look like? See Figure 9.19. It looks like the modern Azure portal. You authenticate with an Azure AD or AD credential (via federation), depending on your deployment. As a service administrator, you will craft various offers and plans that contain sets of services and quotas that are then purchased by tenants to use in their subscriptions.

FIGURE 9.19
The Azure Stack portal experience

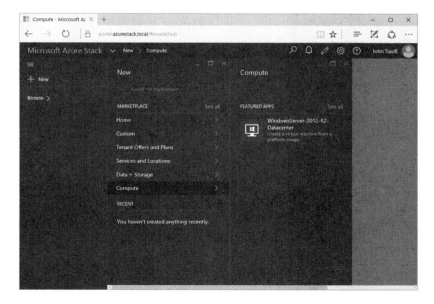

Types of Deployment

The previous section described a single-box deployment of Azure Stack: All of the VMs and the services that are created run on a single node. This is one of the two deployment types of Azure Stack. In this section, let's explore the two types in more detail, because critical differences exist. You can review the official Microsoft explanation at https://azure.microsoft.com/en-us/blog/growing-the-azure-ecosystem-with-microsoft-azure-stack/. The two deployment types are as follows:

Single-Box Self-Install Deployment This option is available for customers who have a piece of hardware that meets the requirements to perform a self-installation of Azure Stack. These installations cannot span multiple physical boxes nor have highly available instances of the Azure core and foundational services. These deployments are not supported for production workloads and are designed only for testing and proof-of-concept scenarios.

Turnkey Integrated Systems This is the production-supported deployment of Azure Stack. Customers purchase a complete, preinstalled, configured Azure Stack from one of the key partners that consists of a minimum of four boxes, providing a highly available Azure Stack environment that can be expanded to additional nodes.

Initially, although this could change in the future, there is no option for customers to self-install Azure Stack by using their own existing hardware in a multinode, production manner. The reasoning for this has come from Microsoft's early testing with customers; the reality has been that customers are not equipped to deploy and manage a highly complex infrastructure with software-defined networking and software-defined storage. How many organizations build their own storage area networks (SANs)? Hardly any. The complexities and intricacies of architecting, testing, and maintaining the exact combinations of controller, disk, firmware, driver, software, and more makes it unrealistic for a customer—and that's just one component of Azure Stack. For this reason, Microsoft has focused on providing Azure Stack through the turn-key partners so that every element of the solution can be prescriptively controlled and tested.

At the time of this writing, the exact licensing has not been shared. However, I expect it to be something similar to Azure's, where customers pay based on the type and amount of services utilized.

What Does Azure Stack Mean?

The key point of Azure Stack is that it brings choice and consistency for customers. A customer can create a JSON template that deploys services and deploy it to Azure, to Azure Stack on premises, or to a hosting partner that uses Azure Stack. An application can be written with ARM and deployed anywhere. Services will be able to easily burst from on premises to Azure or a hoster with no rewrites or modifications required, and it will be easy to move between clouds as required. Customers may test applications in Azure and then deploy to production on premises by using Azure Stack, or vice versa.

A common question is, "Will feature x be available in Azure Stack because it's running on premises?" For example, Windows Server 2016 supports Shielded VMs and VHDX. No features will be available in Azure Stack that are not available in Azure, as it is a joint engineering effort. This does mean that sometimes the base hypervisor has capabilities that will not initially be available for Azure Stack deployments, but they should be added over time as Azure enables them.

Where Does System Center and Operations Management Suite Fit with Azure Stack?

Azure Stack does not utilize System Center as part of its architecture, but this does not mean that System Center has no place. Consider services running in Azure IaaS today. You may deploy Operations Manager agents to monitor services or utilize Operations Management Suite (a set of cloud services that complements System Center). You may patch using Configuration Manager. You may deploy configuration through PowerShell DSC with Azure Automation/OMS. Automation through Azure Automation enables activities such as deployment, scale operations, and really any other type of action for workloads. The same applies with Azure Stack. System Center and OMS may be utilized to provide services to the workloads running on Azure Stack, especially IaaS VMs.

For most organizations, I expect Azure Stack to be a new deployment sitting next to their existing virtualization solution that will continue to house the standard infrastructure workloads. The Azure Stack instances will be utilized for the true cloud service requirements for scenarios in which Azure consistency is key.

The Bottom Line

Explain the differences between virtualization and the private cloud. Virtualization enables multiple operating system instances to run on a single physical piece of hardware by creating multiple virtual machines that can share the resources of the physical server. This enables greater utilization of a server's resources, reduction in server hardware, and potential improvements to provisioning processes. The private cloud is fundamentally a management solution that builds on virtualization but brings additional capabilities by interfacing with the entire fabric, including network and storage, to provide a complete abstraction and therefore management of the entire infrastructure. This allows a greater utilization of all available resources, which leads to greater scalability. Because of the abstraction of the actual fabric, it is possible to enable user self-service based on their assignment to various clouds.

Master It Do you need to change your fabric to implement the private cloud?

Describe the must-have components to create a Microsoft private cloud. The foundation of a Microsoft private cloud solution comprises virtualization hosts using Hyper-V and then SCVMM and Windows Azure Pack to provide the core fabric management, abstraction, cloud creation, and end-user self-service functionality. Orchestrator and Service Manager can be utilized to build on this core set of private cloud functionality to bring more-advanced workflows, authorization of requests, and charge-back functionality.

Chapter 10

Containers and Docker

Containers have existed in the Linux world for a long time and have gained industry acceptance through the Docker standard and repository. Containers have finally come to Windows with Windows Server 2016, along with compatibility with Docker management.

In this chapter, you will learn to:

◆   Articulate the reasons to use containers.

◆   Explain the difference between Windows Containers and Hyper-V Containers.

◆   Manage containers.

Challenge of Application Deployment

Organizations today have numerous challenges with traditional application deployment. Let's explore some of those challenges through a simple example of a common custom application deployment.

Say that an application developer has completed work on a masterpiece that has taken six months to write. The application now needs to be deployed to production. The developer uploads the compiled application to a folder, along with vague instructions that the application needs Windows Server 2016, Internet Information Services (IIS), and some other components. The IT administrator gets the request and needs to find the spare resources to create a new Windows Server 2016 instance. After those resources are found, the admin creates the VM, which takes about 30 minutes as the IT shop has a pretty good provisioning system utilizing a well-maintained gold Windows Server 2012 R2 image. A few hours later, the administrator checks back, logs on to the OS instance, and reviews the email from the developer about the requirements for the app. After meeting the requirements by adding the various roles, features, and extra software (and a few reboots), the admin then installs the custom application and tries to start it. The application does not start. After rechecking the vague instructions from the developer, the admin still cannot make the application start. The administrator contacts the developer for help. The developer logs on to the server, installs some of the organization's troubleshooting tools, and gets the application to start because the application had requirements on items that were installed on the developer's machine but these were not understood as requirements and therefore not previously installed.

This common scenario highlights some of the key challenges of deploying custom applications and even commercial software. To summarize, here are the common causes of failed application deployment:

◆   Difficulty modeling application deployments and dependencies

◆   Inconsistent library and sharing for custom and commercial applications

◆   Lack of portability of applications

◆   Low density, as each application runs in its own OS instance to achieve basic levels of isolation

◆   Slow provisioning of environments

While virtualization helps with many aspects of IT operations, it does not solve this set of challenges. Instead, another technology that belongs to the virtualization family saves the day: containers.

Hyper-V Nested Virtualization

Before covering containers, let's look at a long-requested feature that is finally available in Windows Server 2016 and Windows 10 Hyper-V: *nested virtualization*. This capability enables you to run a hypervisor inside a virtual machine.

Hyper-V requires certain capabilities from the processor to enable virtualization, primarily hardware-assisted virtualization (Intel VT and AMD-V). While the Hyper-V hypervisor exposes most capabilities of the underlying physical processor to virtual machines, it has not until Windows Server 2016 been able to expose the hardware-assisted virtualization capability that makes Hyper-V virtualization possible. Prior to Windows Server 2016, this meant that within a Hyper-V VM, it was not possible to install the Hyper-V role and run a VM within the VM (although the role could be installed, a VM would not be able to start). Historically, there has not been a serious need to run VMs in VMs (outside of test environments on a developer's laptop). This changed, however, with Windows Server 2016 containers, as you will see later in this chapter, and there is now a very real requirement to be able to create Hyper-V VMs inside other Hyper-V VMs.

Enabling a VM to support nested virtualization requires the following:

◆   The VM must be turned off.

◆   Any saved state must be deleted.

◆   Dynamic Memory must be disabled, and the VM must have at least 4GB of memory. It might need significantly more, depending on the memory requirements of the VMs that will run nested inside. Nested VMs running inside the VM can use Dynamic Memory.

◆   MAC address spoofing must be enabled on the VM's NIC if the VMs running inside the VM need network connectivity.
    ```
    Set-VMNetworkAdapter -VMName <VM Name> -MacAddressSpoofing On
    ```

◆   Virtualization extensions must be exposed to the virtual CPU inside the VM. To do this, the following PowerShell is executed:
    ```
    Set-VMProcessor -VMName <VM Name> -ExposeVirtualizationExtensions $true
    ```

Microsoft has a script available at `https://raw.githubusercontent.com/Microsoft/Virtualization-Documentation/master/hyperv-tools/Nested/Enable-NestedVm.ps1` that performs all of the configurations previously mentioned. It can be downloaded to a local file by using the following PowerShell and then executed on a VM:

```
Invoke-WebRequest https://raw.githubusercontent.com/Microsoft/Virtualization-
Documentation/master/hyperv-tools/Nested/Enable-NestedVm.ps1 `
    -OutFile ~/Enable-NestedVm.ps1
~/Enable-NestedVm.ps1 -VmName "<VM Name>"
```

Within the VM, the Hyper-V role can now be installed and VMs created. Only one level of nesting is supported. However, additional levels of nesting are possible, and in my testing this worked just fine.

Windows Container Fundamentals

Consider the challenges highlighted at the start of this chapter: the amount of time for provisioning environments, wasted resources (as every application has its own OS instance in order to attain a basic level of isolation from other applications), and the problems associated with the deployment of applications and their dependencies. *Containers* solve these challenges by enabling multiple applications to share a single OS instance while providing isolation between them. Furthermore, containers utilize a model that enables applications to be encapsulated and dependencies to other containers containing various libraries and binaries to be documented as part of the container Metadata.

For any readers who may have dabbled in the desktop space, some of these features may sound like App-V. This technology enabled desktop applications to run in their own bubbles, with their own virtual view of the filesystem completely isolated from other App-V virtualized applications. As you will see, similarities exist between containers and App-V, especially related to the isolation capabilities, but containers go a lot further.

Containers can be thought of as another type of virtualization, because they enable any application running inside the container to perceive that it has its own isolated operating system view that is separate from any other application that happens to be running in a different container on the same OS instance, known as a *sandbox*. This isolation is at a user-mode level. Each container has its own isolated namespace, which provides the following to the application:

◆ Its own view of the filesystem, which consists of its own virtual filesystem content that is unioned with the underlying pristine OS filesystem content and any container filesystem content upon which it is dependent. This requires updates to NTFS. For example, I may have a web application in a container that depends on another container that contains IIS, which depends on the Nano Server container that contains the OS image. Inside the container instance, I would see the union of my application container filesystem, the IIS container filesystem (containing the IIS binaries), and the underlying container OS image (containing the OS), enabling the application to function. Any writes from the application are made to its virtual filesystem overlay (the sandbox), avoiding any cross-pollination to other containers, and any other images in the dependency chain are read-only.

◆ Its own view of the registry, and just like the filesystem, the registry layers are unioned through a new vreg capability

◆ Its own view of processes, hiding processes from other containers

◆ Its own networking configuration that leverages virtual switches on the container host (the OS instance that hosts the container instances)

Figure 10.1 shows a graphical, high-level representation of containers compared to traditional virtualization. Notice that with traditional OS virtualization, each application runs in its own VM with its own OS instance and all the associated overhead. However, the application enjoys total isolation from other applications, and the resources available can be controlled through configuration of the virtual CPU, memory, and network resources assigned to the VM. With containers, each application runs in its own container that is isolated at a user-mode level and can have dependencies on other containers that may contain libraries that are then dependent on a host OS image (which needs to match the container host OS). Notice that different containerized applications can be dependent on the same containers or different containers. This is useful, as some applications may require the same version of libraries, while other applications may need different versions of libraries, something that is difficult to achieve traditionally on a shared OS. Control groups (known as *job objects* in Windows) enable the grouping of processes. The access to resources they are allowed to have is a key point of the isolation.

FIGURE 10.1

Traditional virtualization-hosting applications vs. applications running in containers

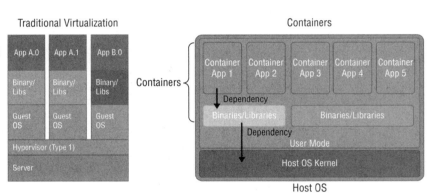

The dependencies between containers are prescribed by the application developer at the time of the application creation, and the container technology is leveraged throughout the application's life cycle. This is achieved by creating a *composition file* that specifies the images used and any actions required. (In Docker, this is called a *Docker file,* and it is different from a Docker Compose file, as explained at `https://docs.docker.com/compose/compose-file/`.) The container images are stored in a central repository, and when you combine a composition file by using a shared set of images, the result is immutable. It will always provision and perform the same, ensuring consistency as it is deployed between environments. This is not the case when developers normally install "stuff" on their machines, write the code, and then try to describe the same "stuff" to be installed in QA, then live, and so on. But as an application developer writes an application to be run in a container, the developer presses F5 to debug; the container is created, the application is instantiated into it, and testing is performed. Once development is complete, the application developer publishes the containerized application either to a public or private repository, which includes the dependency information related to other containers. The IT operations team performs a pull from the repository for the application, which also pulls down any containers on which the application's container depends, and deploys the application to a container host. No complicated deployment instructions are required, as the deployment is essentially self-contained. This is a completely immutable operation that ensures that the containerized application will always run the same way. The operations team then monitors the application, provides feedback to the developers in the form of insights and metrics that may lead to updated versions of the application, and the entire life cycle begins again. The containerization of the application also helps if a rollback of an application update is required. If version 2.5 has a problem, for instance, version 2.4 of the container can be quickly pulled and deployed.

The deployment is also fast. There is no creation of a new OS instance and no finding of resources. The container is deployed to an existing container host, which could be physical or virtual, and it happens quickly, potentially in subseconds, which opens up new ways to run applications.

In the new "cloud era," we see more microservices; an application is broken into its component processes, and each process runs as its own microservice. Containers embrace the microservice philosophy and enable it, which is best understood with an example. Consider a stock application. The stock application's web frontend runs in a container, and a request is made for information about five stocks. A container instance is created for each request, thus five containers, and the application in the container performs the research into its delegated stock, responds with the required information, and then the container is deleted. This approach not only is efficient with resources, but also scales the application, with the only limit being the resources available in the farm of container hosts.

Because each container shares a common container host instance, a greater density of workloads is realized when compared to traditional machine virtualization, in which every virtual machine requires its own complete OS instance.

Using a separate virtual machine for each application provides another benefit beyond isolation: control of resource consumption. Containers provide resource controls (for example, quality of service, or QoS) to ensure that one container does not consume more than its fair share of resources, which would negatively impact other containers on the same container host—the "noisy neighbor" problem. The container QoS allows each container to have specific amounts of resources, such as processor, memory, and network bandwidth to be assigned. This is covered later in this chapter, but it ensures that a container does not consume more than its allotted amount of resources.

Containers rely on container images, which are analogous to a VHD with Hyper-V. A container image is read-only (although layers can be added on top of images to create new images, as you will explore later in this chapter). A container image is utilized by container instances, and it is the container image that depends on other container images. A container image consists of its Metadata, which includes items such as its name, commands to execute when using it to start a container instance, its dependencies, and its payload, which comprises the files and folders that make up its virtual filesystem layer. Multiple container instances created from the same container image are guaranteed to start and behave in the same way.

I've been talking about containers so far; I've not said *Windows containers*. Containers have been around for a long time on Linux, and the features I have described are a core part of its container feature set and philosophy. Windows Server 2016 brings those same features to Windows applications with Windows containers, which is a different implementation of the technology to enable containers, but the management is performed in a consistent manner through Docker, which is covered later in this chapter.

The official Microsoft container resources are a great asset and are available at the following locations:

◆ **Forum**—http://aka.ms/containers/forum

◆ **Videos**—http://aka.ms/containers/videos

◆ **Documentation**—http://aka.ms/containers

LINUX APPS ON WINDOWS?

People often ask whether the introduction of containers on Windows means that Linux applications will run on Windows Server. The answer is no. Linux containers will not run on a Windows container host, and Windows containers will not run on a Linux container host. If you look again at Figure 10.1, this makes sense. The application container depends on a library container that depends on an OS version that has to match the container host OS. The application is still running on the underlying container host OS; it's just isolated from other applications. Linux applications don't run on Windows, and vice versa. If you want to run Linux applications on a Windows OS, you need virtualization and to create a VM running Linux. Maybe one day when containers utilize VMs in some way, it may be possible, but not today. Keep reading . . .

Windows Server Containers vs. Hyper-V Containers

Windows Server containers provide user-mode isolation for applications in different container instances. All the container instances on the same container host share common host operating system instances and a common kernel. In a trusted environment such as within a private cloud, or when the applications being deployed are from a well-managed and audited library, user-mode-only isolation may meet the required levels of security. In a public cloud, the environment utilized by different tenants sharing a common kernel may not be desirable, as each application may not be trusted, and a tenant running a container on the same container host could possibly try to use the shared kernel to attack other containers.

Another challenge of regular containers is the dependency on the container host OS version, which is specified as part of the dependency chain from the application, through its binary and library containers, and through to the host OS specified in those dependent libraries. If the OS changes on the container host, it may break the containers running on it.

To address these concerns, Windows Server 2016 has an additional type of container: Hyper-V containers. As the name suggests, a *Hyper-V container* leverages the Hyper-V role of Windows Server 2016 to automatically create and manage (and eventually delete) a virtual machine into which the containerized application is instantiated, along with the other containers upon which it depends and its own base OS image. This approach gives the Hyper-V container standard user-mode isolation but also kernel-mode isolation. This is shown in Figure 10.2, where both types of containers are running on a single container host.

FIGURE 10.2
Windows Server containers vs. Hyper-V containers

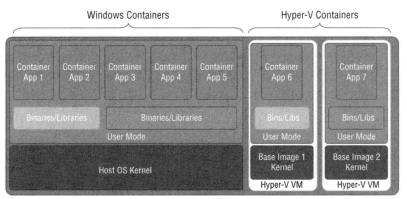

The virtual machine created for a Hyper-V container is automatically managed and is not visible in standard Hyper-V management tools, such as Hyper-V Manager. However, if the list of processes for a container host is examined, a VM worker process (vmwp.exe) will be present for each Hyper-V container. This is a special type of Hyper-V VM specifically created just to launch a container: a utility VM. Because a Hyper-V container requires a VM to be created and a separate OS instance to be built, it will provision slower than a regular Windows container, which typically deploys fast because the container instance is created on an existing container host. Additionally, having a separate base image for a Hyper-V container will make it "heavier" from a resource perspective, since it needs its own instance-specific OS disk storage along with additional memory and processor resources to run a complete Windows Server instance. However, Hyper-V containers use the Nano Server deployment mode for Hyper-V containers, which provides the lightest possible Windows Server deployment along with fast provisioning times that enable even Hyper-V containers to be provisioned in seconds. Additionally, because this Hyper-V VM is being used for a known reason (that is, to run containers), special steps are taken to accelerate the provisioning of the Hyper-V container VMs. This includes creating a single VM, making it read-only, and then cloning it for future containers, greatly accelerating the provisioning times. If a regular container deploys in subseconds, a Hyper-V container based on Nano Server will deploy in around 5 seconds and even less once the cloning is utilized, which demonstrates that these are still fast deployments.

A container host can run any of the Windows Server 2016 deployment modes/configuration levels: Server with Desktop Experience (aka Server with a GUI), Server Core, and Nano Server. The deployment mode of the container host impacts the server image used by containers running on that host, as shown in Table 10.1. This is known as the container OS image (aka base image), which forms the foundation of any container instance.

TABLE 10.1:   OS Image Used Based on Container Host OS

CONTAINER HOST OPERATING SYSTEM	WINDOWS SERVER CONTAINER	HYPER-V CONTAINER
Windows Server with Desktop Experience	Server Core image or Nano Server image	Server Core image or Nano Server image
Windows Server Core	Server Core image or Nano Server image	Server Core image or Nano Server image
Windows Nano Server	Nano Server image	Server Core image or Nano Server image
Windows 10	Not available	Server Core image or Nano Server image

Source: https://msdn.microsoft.com/en-us/virtualization/windowscontainers/deployment/system_requirements

This table shows that Hyper-V containers can run either base OS image, since the container is being created in a VM that has no dependence on the container host OS. For a Windows container that is using the container host OS, the base OS image has to be based on the same image as the container host or a lower deployment mode image. For example, Windows Server with Desktop Experience is a superset of Server Core, which is a superset of Nano Server, so it can therefore use Server Core or Nano Server base OS images. Server Core has all of the APIs in Nano Server, so a Server Core container host can run either type of base OS image; however, Nano Server does not contain all of the APIs of Server Core and can therefore run only base OS images that are Nano Server. Microsoft provides these two container base OS images (Windows Server Core and Nano Server), which can be obtained via PowerShell or through the Docker Hub.

It is because of Hyper-V containers that Microsoft added nested virtualization in Windows Server 2016. Nested virtualization enables a container host to be a virtual machine and still support the VM-dependent Hyper-V containers.

An important point to understand is that within a Hyper-V container is a regular Windows container along with any containers it depends on and the base OS image. The application container is not a different type of container for Hyper-V containers. The choice to use a Windows container vs. a Hyper-V container is a deployment time decision, depending on whether user-level or kernel-level isolation is required. This is no major difference in the creation of the container. The only difference is that at deployment time you would specify `--isolation=hyperv` to create a Hyper-V container instead of a Windows container. If using containers in Windows 10, Hyper-V isolation is the default and only option, which means the `--isolation=hyperv` is not explicitly required.

For the maximum density, you would use Windows containers; for the maximum isolation, you would use Hyper-V containers.

DRIVERS AND CONTAINERS

It is not possible to install drivers in a container image. Container instances can utilize drivers in the base OS image, but no other container images can include drivers.

Docker

A container solution has various requirements—such as the isolation technology itself to enable containerized applications to run in their own isolated namespace, which is known as the *container runtime* and is provided by Windows Server. Another requirement is the ability to communicate over the network, which is enabled through virtual switches. You also need an entire toolset to develop and manage containers. Initially, during the technical preview stages of Windows Server 2016, Microsoft had two management approaches: its own native PowerShell-based management fabric and Docker. This scenario, however, was complicated for users, as it led to two container implementations with no real cross-management set interaction or visibility. Thus Microsoft removed the native PowerShell management version of containers and instead embraced Docker management fabric.

Docker is the de facto industry standard for container development and management in the Linux world. Microsoft worked closely with Docker and the open-source community to bring Docker to Windows in order to enable a consistent toolset and management fabric across Windows and Linux. As you will see when the installation of a container host is covered later in this chapter, Docker is a required component for containers to exist on Windows. In fact, I believe that it's the first time an in-box feature has required external software to function.

At the foundation of Docker is the Docker Engine, a lightweight runtime and set of tools for building and executing Docker containers. It has been updated to enable execution on both Windows and Linux. Several components run on top of the Docker Engine, including these:

◆ *Docker client* to perform actions against the Docker Engine

◆ *Docker PowerShell*, which executes against the REST API provided by the Docker Engine

◆ *Docker Compose*, a tool to enable the definition and running of multicontainer applications

◆ *Docker Registry*, which enables the storage and distribution of Docker images

◆ *Docker Swarm*, which provides clustering capabilities to groups of Docker hosts, enabling a single virtual Docker host that provides greater scale and resiliency

◆ *Docker Universal Control Plane (UCP)*, which enables a single management pane of glass to manage thousands of nodes (container hosts managed by Docker) as if they were one

Figure 10.3 provides a high-level overview of the way the various components fit together to provide a complete container solution.

FIGURE 10.3
Windows Server 2016 container architecture with Docker

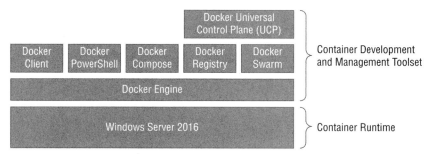

Other technologies, such as Mesosphere and Kubernetes, offer management solutions that run on top of the Docker Engine and other components. The Microsoft public cloud Operations Management Suite also provides container management. Through these various components, Docker enables the complete life cycle of services, from the initial build using the Docker client and Docker Compose, the shipping of containers with Docker Hub (cloud-hosted public and private container image repository), and the Docker Trusted Registry (on-premises image storage solution), through to the actual execution using Docker Cloud (which hooks into Azure) and the Docker UCP. It's also possible to create and run containers directly on premises without any external service connectivity, as you will explore in this chapter. It's important to realize, however, that higher levels of service are available for more enterprise scenarios.

Developers who use Visual Studio can also download Docker Tools for Visual Studio 2015, which will enable Docker features to be accessed as part of the development experience. These tools can be downloaded from `https://aka.ms/DockerToolsForVS`.

For more information on Docker, I recommend the following resources (as in this chapter I focus more on the Windows container functionality and its primitives rather than on the full set of Docker functionality):

- `www.docker.com/what-docker`

- `https://docs.docker.com/`

- `https://blog.docker.com/`

Installing the Container Feature

As previously mentioned, the container feature is the first feature that is not complete natively in Windows. Because the container feature relies on the open source Docker, which is not part of Windows Server and is updated so frequently, it does not make sense to try to include this feature with Windows. Therefore, to enable containers, I walk through multiple steps in this section. Over time, however, this process could change, so if you experience problems, review the Microsoft installation document at `https://msdn.microsoft.com/en-us/virtualization/windowscontainers/deployment/deployment`. If your container host is a virtual machine and you want to use Hyper-V containers, you need to ensure that you have enabled nested virtualization for the VM, as outlined at the start of this chapter.

The first step is to enable the container feature, which can be accomplished via Server Manager or through PowerShell. This enabling of container functionality provides the sandboxes that container instances will run in, the *container runtime*. After the installation, you need to restart the computer. If you wish to run Hyper-V containers, you also need to install the Hyper-V role.

```
Install-WindowsFeature containers
Install-WindowsFeature hyper-v
Restart-Computer -Force
```

Once the reboot is complete, the next step is to download and install the Docker client (`docker.exe`) and the Docker daemon (`dockerd.exe`), which is the service that other tools interact with as the management fabric (the Docker Engine). Microsoft maintains a zip file of both the Docker client and Docker daemon along with `docker-proxy.exe`, which provides a caching proxy that is completely transparent to the Docker containers but will speed up the fetching of any dependencies. The following code downloads and installs the Docker components:

```
Invoke-WebRequest "https://get.docker.com/builds/Windows/x86_64/docker-
1.12.0.zip" -OutFile "$env:TEMP\docker-1.12.0.zip" -UseBasicParsing
Expand-Archive -Path "$env:TEMP\docker-1.12.0.zip" `
-DestinationPath $env:ProgramFiles
[Environment]::SetEnvironmentVariable("Path", $env:Path + ";C:\Program
Files\Docker", [EnvironmentVariableTarget]::Machine)
& $env:ProgramFiles\docker\dockerd.exe --register-service
Start-Service Docker
```

Note that the preceding code snippet is downloading a specific version, which will change over time. Thus be sure to refer to the aforementioned Microsoft article to check for newer versions. It is also possible to pull down each executable directly:

```
Invoke-WebRequest
https://master.dockerproject.org/windows/amd64/dockerd.exe -OutFile
$env:ProgramFiles\docker\dockerd.exe
Invoke-WebRequest
https://master.dockerproject.org/windows/amd64/docker.exe -OutFile
$env:ProgramFiles\docker\docker.exe
Invoke-WebRequest https://master.dockerproject.org/windows/amd64/docker-
proxy.exe -OutFile $env:ProgramFiles\docker\docker-proxy.exe
```

If you ever need to update Docker to a new version, you will need to remove the old one first. This can be accomplished with the following:

```
Stop-Service Docker
Remove-Item "C:\Program Files\Docker\docker.exe"
Remove-Item "C:\Program Files\Docker\dockerd.exe"
```

The next step is to pull down the base OS images, both Server Core and Nano Server. In this example, `docker.exe` is used, which was added to the system path. You will need to exit and restart your PowerShell window so that the Docker folder is now part of the path and `docker.exe` found. (`docker.exe` will work in a PowerShell window because it's an executable, but you could also use `cmd.exe`.)

```
docker pull microsoft/windowsservercore
docker pull microsoft/nanoserver
```

This can also be done with PowerShell, which requires the `ContainerImage` OneGet PowerShell module to be installed from GitHub:

```
Install-PackageProvider ContainerImage -Force
Find-ContainerImage
Install-ContainerImage -Name NanoServer
Install-ContainerImage -Name WindowsServerCore
```

You will notice in the PowerShell example that `Find-ContainerImage` was used to find the base OS images that could be used with a Windows container host. To search for base images using `docker.exe`, you can use `docker search`—for example:

```
docker search windowsserver
```

To find only official builds, you can add the `is-official` filter, for example. (I use CentOS in the example, as at the time of writing there were no official builds for Windows images.)

```
docker search centos --filter is-official=true
```

You can also search for all the published images via the Docker Hub website at `https://hub.docker.com/search/` after you have created a free account.

Once the base OS images are installed, they can be viewed using `docker images` or `Get-ContainerImage` (after the full PowerShell module has been installed, which is covered later in the chapter). The following is an example view of images after both Windows Server images have been pulled from the Docker Hub.

```
PS C:\> docker images
REPOSITORY                       TAG             IMAGE ID
CREATED             SIZE
microsoft/windowsservercore    latest          02cb7f65d61b         7
weeks ago           7.764 GB
microsoft/nanoserver           latest          3a703c6e97a2         7
weeks ago           969.8 MB


PS C:\> Get-ContainerImage

RepoTags                              ID                    Created
Size(MB)
--------                              --                    -------
--------
microsoft/windowsservercore:latest    sha256:02cb7f65d6... 6/16/2016
4:29:45 PM          7,404.57
microsoft/nanoserver:latest           sha256:3a703c6e97... 6/16/2016
3:57:35 PM          924.92
```

Notice that the same images are shown when using docker.exe or the PowerShell interface, proving that a single management interface is used. This is the case for all Docker configurations. Where are the actual images stored on the container host? The default location is under C:\ProgramData\docker, but do not manually modify anything in this folder structure. Always manage via the Docker management interface.

Also note that each image has the tag of latest that enables the image to be used without having to specify an explicit version. If a certain image version is downloaded but does not have the latest tag, you may need to add the tag manually. This can be done by finding the ID of the image through the docker images command and then adding the latest tag (to remove a tag, use docker rmi); for example:

```
docker images microsoft/nanoserver
docker tag <image ID from previous output> nanoserver:latest
```

Creating and Managing Containers

Now that the containers feature and Docker are installed, the next step is to create container instances in your environment. Before a useful container can be created to perform a function, it's important to understand and set up the desired network connectivity, to enable communication to and from container instances.

Configuring Networking

To enable the connectivity from the Docker Engine and its libnetwork plug-in, Windows Server 2016 (and Windows 10) implements the Host Network Service (HNS) as part of its servicing layer to communicate with the underlying OS networking components and create the required objects (for example, a network compartment that I'll cover shortly). The libnetwork plug-in is an extensible model to implement their own networking stack to work with the underlying container host OS while providing a consistent management interface to the higher Docker management services, allowing them to work consistently across platforms. The Microsoft official container networking information is located at https://msdn.microsoft.com/en-us/virtualization/windowscontainers/management/container_networking.

MODES OF NETWORK CONNECTIVITY

Containers are used in many scenarios. These range from single-node developer environments requiring only simple network configurations (such as using NAT with port mappings or transparent connectivity directly to a network), through to multinode and cloud environments that require far more complex networking configurations. These configurations may leverage virtual networks overlaying a physical network fabric and network policies, such as access control lists (ACLs) and QoS which will be required along with load-balancing capabilities between container instances.

To enable the different levels of network configuration along with the different requirements for Windows containers and Hyper-V containers, a network stack is implemented. This stack is based on the Hyper-V virtual switch for all of its connectivity to the outside world, along with other technologies such as WinNAT and network compartments, depending on the network mode utilized. Network compartments are not container specific, but rather are a TCP/IP construct (which will extend to other components such as NDIS and even Windows Firewall over time) that isolates the contained processes within their own namespace, and containers takes advantage of this by placing each Windows container in its own network compartment. A host vNIC (a virtual NIC visible on the host) is added to the network compartment that is then connected to the virtual switch providing connectivity. In the case of a Hyper-V container, a regular synthetic vmNIC (a virtual machine NIC) is used that is then connected to the virtual switch. The virtual switch can be either internal or external, depending on the networking mode. However, all of the virtual switches and other components are automatically configured via the Docker network configurations performed. If you have a Linux background, the management actions are the same—it is the underlying implementation that is different. Linux enables network connectivity through a Linux bridge device that is really just a connection from a physical NIC to a virtual Ethernet pair, which is not as feature rich as the Hyper-V virtual switch. For isolation, Linux has namespaces, which is not a universal feature in Windows, so instead each component in Windows implements its own isolation feature, which in the case of networking is the network compartment.

Three modes are available for container networking:

NAT This is the simplest option, and it is the default. It is aimed at developers and smaller deployments utilizing the IP address of the container host OS and then using Network Address Translation to enable the private IP range used for the container instances to communicate to the external network. Port forwarding rules can be used to enable ports on the container host to map to ports on specific containers. If NAT is utilized, the virtual switch is an internal type, and it then connects via another host vNIC that is assigned the IP address selected as the gateway IP for the private network, which then utilizes WinNAT to provide the address translation and connectivity via the TCP/IP stack in the container host that has external connectivity. This is shown in Figure 10.4, where both Windows containers and Hyper-V containers share networking, with the only difference being that a Hyper-V container uses a vmNIC instead of a host vNIC, and it does not require a network compartment because the container is already isolated in its own network stack, since it runs inside its own VM.

FIGURE 10.4
Container networking with NAT mode

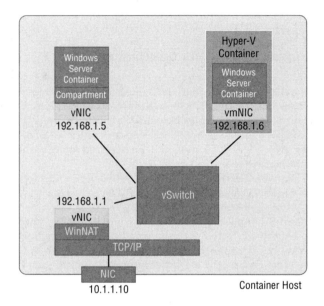

Transparent This is the most familiar mode to Hyper-V users, and it works in the same way as regular VMs, using a VM switch to connect containers to the network connected by the switch. In this mode, the Hyper-V switch is of type external in order to enable connectivity beyond the container host. This is shown in Figure 10.5. The vNIC or vmNIC has raw traffic frames sent to the NIC via the switch, and it can be assigned IP addresses via DHCP (Dynamic Host Configuration Protocol) or statically. While Transparent is the most familiar mode to Hyper-V administrators and works well for virtual machines, it is may cause problems for containers because the life cycle of a VM is different from that of a container. VMs are created and run for a long time before being deleted. When a vmNIC is introduced to an external switch, it has its MAC address that is learned by the upstream network switch ports in the infrastructure to enable traffic to be forwarded as required, but these introductions with virtual machines are infrequent and therefore not a problem. Containers may have short life cycles, especially when using the microservices model, as containers are created, run a task, and then are deleted. Constant creation of NICs with MAC address learning will negatively impact the network infrastructure, as the CAM tables on the switch will fill up. Therefore, although this mode is a simple solution, it is likely not a good fit for many implementations.

FIGURE 10.5
Container networking
with Transparent mode

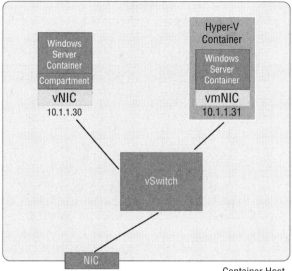

Connected to 10.1.1.0/24 network

L2 Bridge/Tunnel This is also known as *SDN mode*. Either l2bridge or l2tunnel drivers can be used to connect container endpoints to an overlay virtual network in Microsoft cloud-based deployments. In this case, the container host will be a guest VM. The only difference between the two modes is that l2tunnel forwards all container network traffic to the physical Hyper-V host (regardless of subnet), while the l2bridge driver forwards only cross-subnet (or cross-host) traffic to the physical Hyper-V host. Network traffic between container endpoints attached to the same subnet on the same host will be bridged directly in the container host VM. These modes utilize the Windows Server 2016 software-defined networking stack including the Network Controller role, NC Host Agent, and virtual filtering platform (VFP) vSwitch extension to enforce network policy, and they provide connectivity to a virtual network by encapsulating the container traffic. Dynamic IP address assignment is handled through the Host Network Service (HNS) in the Container Host VM, and static IP assignment is not possible. For more information on using these types of networks with containers, see https://technet.microsoft.com/en-us/windows-server-docs/networking/sdn/manage/connect-container-endpoints-to-a-tenant-virtual-network. For the networking configuration, either the Docker client (docker.exe) or the PowerShell module can be used today. However, PowerShell-based networking management may change in its entirety, so for the most part I focus on the Docker client for network management. All of the standard Docker network commands will work for a Windows container host through the Docker network plug-in for Windows component. Microsoft's official Docker networking page is at https://msdn.microsoft.com/en-us/virtualization/windowscontainers/management/container_networking, and I recommend reviewing this for the latest updates, as one of the challenges with open source is that it updates so frequently. Documentation can become out-of-date, but the key concepts covered here will remain valid even though some details could change.

OBTAINING THE DOCKER POWERSHELL MODULE

The PowerShell module for Docker is an ongoing open source project still under development that utilizes the Docker REST API and not the separate management stack, which was present in early technical previews of Windows Server 2016. This means that images, containers, and every element managed through docker.exe are the same, which you will see when leveraging the PowerShell module. The decision of whether to use docker.exe or PowerShell comes down to which technology you are most comfortable with. In both cases, because the tools are running on the core Docker fabric, they can be used to manage both Windows and Linux Docker instances. Help on the PowerShell module can be found at `https://github.com/Microsoft/Docker-PowerShell/tree/master/src/Docker.PowerShell/Help`.

To obtain the module, navigate to `https://github.com/Microsoft/Docker-PowerShell` and follow the instructions to download and install on the site.

DEPLOYING A NAT NETWORK

To create a new NAT network, you must identify a subnet for the internal network from which containers will be assigned IP addresses automatically, along with the vNIC on the container host, to enable the vNIC to act as the gateway and use the NAT of the container host. I'm going to walk through how to create these, but do not try this exercise in the RTM of Windows Server 2016, as you can have only one NAT network per host, and one is created by default. This is for informational uses only at this time. However, I will cover some additional options.

DOCKER.EXE IS CASE SENSITIVE

Windows administrators rarely pay any attention to case, because Windows is case insensitive. Linux, on the other hand, is case sensitive, and because Docker started out in Linux, it is case sensitive also. Therefore, you should be careful about the case of objects, resource types, and parameters when using docker.exe. The wrong case will not work, and errors will not be obvious.

The Docker client command to create a new NAT network follows. In this example, the subnet used for the NAT is 172.16.1.0/24 with a name of NatNetwork1:

```
docker network create -d nat --subnet=172.16.1.0/24 NatNetwork1
```

Once the network is created, look at the network adapters on the container host and you will notice that an HNS internal NIC has been added. If you install the Hyper-V Manager, you will see that a new internal network has been added that matches the name of the network specified.

To view available networks, use either docket network ls or Get-ContainerNetwork. You will notice that an existing NAT network is already present. This is created for Docker when starting the service. If you do not want the default NAT network to be created, use the `"bridge":"none"` option in `C:\programdata\docker\config\daemon.json`, as I cover later in this section. To get more detail about a network, use the `inspect` parameter. For example:

```
PS C:\> docker network inspect NatNetwork1
[
    {
        "Name": "NatNetwork1",
        "Id": "66662a657b107a275cf0be76c4824f5a2ac0d0d7ff4aefe89ac34979e6a2e0e6",
        "Scope": "local",
        "Driver": "nat",
        "EnableIPv6": false,
        "IPAM": {
            "Driver": "default",
            "Options": {},
            "Config": [
                {
                    "Subnet": "172.16.1.0/24"
                }
            ]
        },
        "Internal": false,
        "Containers": {},
        "Options": {
            "com.docker.network.windowsshim.hnsid": "a34a64a6-a0af-4d46-
b536-feeb611098b7"
        },
        "Labels": {}
    }
]
```

I previously mentioned that a default NAT network exists that is created automatically when the Docker daemon starts, which uses the single instance of WinNAT supported on Windows Server 2016. You can see this with `docker network ls` and `Get-NetNat`:

```
PS C:\> docker network ls
NETWORK ID          NAME                DRIVER              SCOPE
8ad4b336d4d4        nat                 nat                 local
d784acd605cd        none                null                local

PS C:\> Get-NetNat


Name                             : H7bef00fb-b7bc-4fa3-930b-69f0f8d0d23f
ExternalIPInterfaceAddressPrefix :
InternalIPInterfaceAddressPrefix : 192.168.1.1/24
IcmpQueryTimeout                 : 30
TcpEstablishedConnectionTimeout  : 1800
TcpTransientConnectionTimeout    : 120
```

```
TcpFilteringBehavior          : AddressDependentFiltering
UdpFilteringBehavior          : AddressDependentFiltering
UdpIdleSessionTimeout         : 120
UdpInboundRefresh             : False
Store                         : Local
Active                        : True
```

By default, the IP space used by the automatically created NAT network is 172.16.0.1/12, but in my example it is 192.168.1.1/24. How did this happen? There are two ways to use your own custom IP space for the NAT network if the default IP range does not meet your needs.

The first way is to change the IP configuration of the default NAT network. To do this, perform the following:

1. Stop the Docker daemon:
   ```
   stop-service docker
   ```

2. Remove the default network:
   ```
   Get-ContainerNetwork | Remove-ContainerNetwork
   ```

3. Ensure that the default switch and WinNAT instance are gone by running `Get-VMSwitch` and `Get-NetNat`.

4. Edit the `daemon.json` file in folder `C:\ProgramData\docker\config`, or if it does not exist, create the file. For more information on Docker configuration, see `https://msdn.microsoft.com/en-us/virtualization/windowscontainers/docker/configure_docker_daemon`.

5. In the file, add the following JSON, but change it to match the IP range you wish to use:

   ```
   {
     "fixed-cidr": "192.168.1.0/24"
   }
   ```

6. Restart Docker.
   ```
   start-service docker
   ```

The default WinNAT instance will now be using your custom IP range as will the created NAT network.

The other option is to suppress the automatic creation of the default NAT network and then create your own NAT network by using the commands covered at the start of this section. To suppress the automatic creation of the default NAT network, perform the same steps, but replace the code to be added in step 4 with the following:

```
{
  "bridge": "none"
}
```

Note that if you create a user-defined network, you will have to specify which network the container endpoint should attach to by using the `--network=<network name>` with the `docker run` command.

The key point here is that in most environments, the default NAT network is all you need, and no manual actions should be required. Only if you need to use a different IP space should you perform one of the preceding actions, but in no circumstances should you try to add additional NAT networks to the default. There is a pull request (PR) in GitHub related to enabling multiple NAT networks, provided they are a subset of the default WinNAT IP range (`172.16.0.0/12`). This will likely be available by the time you read this, and I expect in future branches of Windows Server there to be support for multiple WinNAT instances, but that would not be until 2017 at the earliest.

If you want the container to offer services when using NAT, it needs to do this by using port-forwarding rules on the IP address of the container host. These are known as *endpoints*. I cover adding endpoints when creating container instances later in this chapter, but it essentially consists of adding a port mapping as part of the Docker run command by using `-p <port on container IP>:<port in container>`, so using `-p 8080:80` would map port 8080 on the container IP to port 80 on the container.

If you find that you have gotten yourself into a strange situation, to reset your networking for containers and wipe any containers, use the following:

```
Get-Container | Stop-Container
Get-Container | Remove-Container -Force
Get-ContainerNetwork | Remove-ContainerNetwork -Force
Stop-Service docker
```

DEPLOYING A TRANSPARENT NETWORK

Deploying a transparent network is simple, as it consists of adding a new external vSwitch and creating the network so that it's available to containers. To create a transparent network, use the following:

```
docker network create -d transparent TransparentNetwork1
```

It's also required to add a gateway if you plan to use statically assigned IP addresses for containers (for dynamic IP addresses with DHCP, the gateway will be sent as part of the DHCP offer and therefore does not need to be configured on the network). The gateway should be the gateway IP for the network to which the physical NIC is connected and the one that containers need to use based on the statically assigned IPs.

```
docker network create -d transparent --gateway=10.7.173.1
"TransparentNetwork1"
```

If the container host has only a single NIC, it will be used for the newly created external vSwitch. If the container host has multiple NICs, one will be randomly chosen. Alternatively, you can set a specific NIC to be used by adding `-o com.docker.network.windowsshim .interface="<Ethernet X>"` to the network create command.

If the container host is a VM and you are using DHCP for IP assignment to the containers on a transparent network, you will need to enable MAC spoofing for the container host VM.

```
Get-VMNetworkAdapter -VMName savdalcontainer | Set-VMNetworkAdapter `
-MacAddressSpoofing On
```

DEPLOYING A LAYER 2 BRIDGE

Much like a transparent network, a Layer 2 Bridge network creates an external vSwitch and uses similar options. You must also specify the subnet for an L2 Bridge network.

```
docker network create -d l2bridge --subnet=192.168.1.0/24
--gateway=192.168.1.1 BridgeNetwork1
```

Creating and Interacting with Containers

A deep dive into the intricacies of using containers and Docker is beyond the scope of this chapter. However, I want to walk you through a few examples to help reinforce how containers work and the basics of using them.

As a quick refresher, remember that containers are all about layers. The actual container host OS kernel that is shared between the containers appears at the bottom of Figure 10.6. (If using Hyper-V containers, it just so happens that only one container exists on that kernel.) On the kernel is the base OS image that marks the start of the container environment which has no parent image. On top of the base image are various images that include middleware, runtimes, and other content upon which the final application depends. At the top is the container instance that is writeable: the sandbox. The processes running in the sandbox see the unioned filesystem and registries down through the layers.

FIGURE 10.6
Container layers

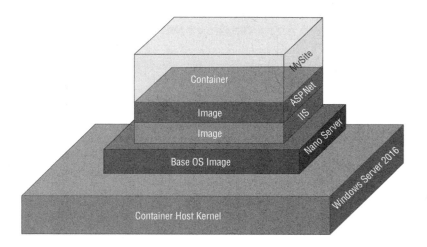

A container can be created easily and used in an interactive fashion. In the first example, I will create a new container based on the `windowsservercore` base OS image, run it interactively, and tell it to run `cmd.exe`. I am not specifying a network, which means that it will connect to the default NAT network:

```
docker run -it --name demo1 microsoft/windowsservercore cmd.exe
```

To run the container as a Hyper-V container, the only change is to add `--isolation=hyperv`:

```
docker run -it --isolation=hyperv --name demo1 microsoft/windowsservercore cmd.exe
```

Once the container instance is created, it will open cmd.exe, which is now running inside the container. The -it switch used with docker run tells Docker to run the container interactively (-i) with a pseudo text-terminal (-t).

Commands can be entered inside the cmd.exe window—for example, ipconfig. To exit, simply type **exit**. The container will change to a stopped state because it was started in an interactive mode. To view container processes, use docker ps -a:

```
C:\>docker ps -a
CONTAINER ID        IMAGE                          COMMAND
CREATED             STATUS                      PORTS           NAMES
9f5c5054438e        microsoft/windowsservercore    "cmd.exe"        3
minutes ago         Exited (0) 2 seconds ago                     demo1
```

To restart the container and attach again, use the following:

```
docker start demo1
docker attach demo1
```

To delete a container, use the following:

```
docker rm demo1
```

Although in this example I am only running the container interactively, I can enable roles and features, change files, and configure my application. Once I delete the container, all of the changes I made would be lost. If you create a configuration inside a container and wish to save it as a new image that can then be used by other future containers, use the docker commit <container name> <new image name> command. There is a better way, however.

Remember that one of the major pain points with traditional deployment was a lack of consistency in deployment. Using images provides the immutability that if the same layer of images is used, the output will be the same. However, if manual steps are then performed in the container instance, some of the benefit is lost. Instead, a better option is to use a Dockerfile, which is a prescriptive list of actions to perform to build a new image that contains all of the configuration. This continues the immutability of the deployment between environments and provides a much cleaner experience.

A Dockerfile is a simple text file, but many actions are available. The following are useful links to enable you to continue your learning about Dockerfiles:

◆ Microsoft Dockerfile page—https://msdn.microsoft.com/en-us/virtualization/windowscontainers/docker/manage_windows_dockerfile

◆ Docker Dockerfile documentation—https://docs.docker.com/engine/reference/builder/

In my modest example, I'm going to create a simple web server. I will base this on the microsoft/windowsservercore base OS image. Although I could manually install IIS and then add my custom site, instead Microsoft has an IIS image available in Docker Hub that I will pull down to run on the windowsservercore base OS. I will then add my custom site on top of the IIS image and save it as a new image, which I can use to run a container instance.

First, I search for an IIS image and then download the IIS image from Docker Hub:

```
PS C:\> docker search iis
NAME                                    DESCRIPTION
        STARS     OFFICIAL   AUTOMATED
microsoft/iis                           Internet Information Services (IIS)
instal...   26
friism/mono
        3                   [OK]
shawnyhw6n9/centos                      IISI Security Server Environments
        2                   [OK]
xluiisx/odoo-ubuntu                     odoo instance for ubuntu 14.04
        0                   [OK]
jacekkow/bamboo-agent-rich-iisg         Customization of bamboo-agent-rich
        0                   [OK]

PS C:\> docker pull microsoft/iis
Using default tag: latest
latest: Pulling from microsoft/iis
1239394e5a8a: Already exists
847199668046: Pulling fs layer
4b1361d2706f: Pulling fs layer
847199668046: Verifying Checksum
847199668046: Download complete
847199668046: Pull complete
4b1361d2706f: Verifying Checksum
4b1361d2706f: Download complete
4b1361d2706f: Pull complete
Digest: sha256:1d64cc22fbc56abc96e4b7df1b51e6f91b0da1941aa155f545f14dd76ac522fc
Status: Downloaded newer image for microsoft/iis:latest

PS C:\> docker images
REPOSITORY                    TAG          IMAGE ID
CREATED            SIZE
microsoft/iis                 latest       accd044753c1      6
days ago           7.907 GB
microsoft/windowsservercore   latest       02cb7f65d61b      8
weeks ago          7.764 GB
microsoft/nanoserver          latest       3a703c6e97a2      8
weeks ago          969.8 MB
```

Something may look strange about the output of docker images. The size of the IIS image is larger than the windowsservercore image, and the whole point of containers and images is that they build on each other and contain only the deltas. That is exactly what is happening; however, the size shows the total size of the image and the images it depends upon. If you dig around C:\programdata\docker\ on the filesystem, you would find that only one folder under windowsfilter is close to the actual size: that of the windowsservercore base OS image.

The following is a basic Dockerfile that I would save as a `Dockerfile` on the filesystem (with no extension). It specifies to use the `iis` image that is built on `windowsservercore`, delete the `iisstart.htm` file (which will not actually delete from the `iis` image since it's read-only, but it will make that change in my sandbox space), and then copy the contents of a local folder named `website` on my machine into the `/inetpub/wwwroot` folder insider the container:

```
FROM microsoft/iis
RUN del C:\inetpub\wwwroot\iisstart.htm
COPY /website /inetpub/wwwroot
```

I build a custom image from this Dockerfile (in the same folder, I also have a folder named `website` containing my new website content). Then I create a container instance from my custom image, mapping port 8080 of the container host IP (because I'm using a NAT network) to port 80 on the actual container:

```
C:\dockerdemo>docker build -t demosite .
Sending build context to Docker daemon   234 kB
Step 1 : FROM microsoft/iis
 ---> accd044753c1
Step 2 : RUN del C:\inetpub\wwwroot\iisstart.htm
 ---> Running in efc2aeaa17df
 ---> 96dac595afcf
Removing intermediate container efc2aeaa17df
Step 3 : COPY /website /inetpub/wwwroot
 ---> 34ddc45b3c32
Removing intermediate container 73bd44d5e240
Successfully built 34ddc45b3c32

C:\dockerdemo>docker run --name demo1 -d -p 8080:80 demosite ping -t localhost
d7a14c74cf9349526707546959597928c7695958e769f6ac98f970edb560018
```

Make sure that you also have the 8080 firewall exception opened on the container host. Currently to test, you must access from another box, as the connection will not work on the actual container host OS to a port forward to a container.

To stop the container, delete the container, and remove my custom image, I can use the following:

```
C:\dockerdemo>docker stop demo1
demo1

C:\dockerdemo>docker rm demo1
demo1

C:\dockerdemo>docker rmi demosite
Untagged: demosite:latest
Deleted: sha256:34ddc45b3c32c3be572038e1ca28062fb7229cbdb110ec8e406acb3700ac7d68
Deleted: sha256:faa5ae99b967cb4b68bac48f98eba30d3bbe375483abb7a8a8abe93b367d88cc
Deleted: sha256:96dac595afcf0752cc8335e3f683511506980b33f522264f692bf9c6451248b8
Deleted: sha256:48815155808f823d2e53af41232d578b48e88e243d0d662078bbc4edf4ce4ad4
```

When you start a container and wish to stipulate a specific network, add the
`--net parameter=<network name>` ; for example:

```
Docker run -itd --name=Container1 --net=NATNetwork1 windowsservercore
cmd.exe
```

You can also connect a container to a network post start by using the
`docker network connect <options> <network name> <container name>`
command. A static IP can be assigned using `--ip=<ip address>` if required,
but to set this, the container must be in a stopped state.

Another way to map ports is as part of the Dockerfile by using EXPOSE. I add the line at the
end of my Dockerfile to expose port 80:

```
EXPOSE 80
```

After building the new image when running, `-P` must be added (instead of the
`-p <host port>:<container port>`). The port assigned on the container IP is ephemeral
and can be viewed using `docker ps -a`. In the example, it shows that port 3232 was assigned
on the container host IP.

```
C:\dockerdemo>docker run --name demo1 -d -P demosite ping -t localhost
a5c6e7afe7725d504555d425a6a010371747001a2ea7422a54f4ec183034dc55


C:\dockerdemo>docker ps -a
CONTAINER ID       IMAGE           COMMAND              CREATED
       STATUS              PORTS                NAMES
a5c6e7afe772       demosite        "ping -t localhost"  8 seconds
ago      Up 4 seconds        0.0.0.0:3232->80/tcp  demo1
```

To view dependencies between images, use the `docker history` command. It uses the image
ID that is shown in the `docker images` command. The following is an example that shows that
my `demosite` depends on the IIS image, which depends on the `windowsservercore` image.

```
C:\dockerdemo>docker history demosite
IMAGE              CREATED           CREATED BY
            SIZE              COMMENT
ab15060e024b       11 minutes ago    cmd /S /C #(nop) COPY
dir:290b95092f931d49670   4.805 MB
4232b44c1241       11 minutes ago    cmd /S /C del
C:\inetpub\wwwroot\iisstart.htm    142.3 MB
accd044753c1       7 days ago        cmd /S /C powershell -
executionpolicy bypass    43.08 kB
<missing>          7 days ago        cmd /S /C #(nop) ADD
file:43092a194a8c2ebb991    7.764 GB


C:\dockerdemo>docker images
REPOSITORY                    TAG             IMAGE ID
CREATED            SIZE
<none>                        <none>          85e4f2ebd154       11
minutes ago    7.912 GB
demosite                      latest          ab15060e024b       11
```

```
minutes ago         7.912 GB
microsoft/iis                   latest              accd044753c1         7
days ago            7.907 GB
microsoft/windowsservercore     latest              02cb7f65d61b         8
weeks ago           7.764 GB
microsoft/nanoserver            latest              3a703c6e97a2         8
weeks ago           969.8 MB
```

You can upload your images either to Docker Hub or to an on-premises Docker Trusted Repository via docker login and docker push, but take care not publish images that are not suitable for public consumption.

In my examples, I have created container instances that have access to all available resources on the system. It's also possible, however, to control the resources available for a container. Docker supports a large range of resource management tools; however, at the time of this writing, only CPU shares can be configured, and this applies to Windows containers and not Hyper-V containers. A container instance can be configured with a CPU share, which is a value relative to other containers. By default, a container receives a cpu-share value of 500, but it can be anything from 1 to 10,000. A container with a cpu-share of 1,000 would get twice the CPU resources of a container with a cpu-share of 500. To use this, I would add the --cpu-shares <value> as part of the docker run command. For the full list of possible constraints that will likely be implemented in Windows containers over time, see https://docs.docker.com/engine/reference/run/#/runtime-constraints-on-resources.

Understanding Storage for Containers

Container instances should be considered stateless, with any data within an instance considered transient and not stored in a persistent manner. Every time a container is deleted and re-created, any data that is not part of the image will be lost as each instance gets a new, clean scratch space.

Often we talk about storage as pets or cattle. We say that traditional servers are like pets that we name, care for, and heal if they are sick. Storage in the new cloud service model is like cattle; if cattle are sick, they are shot and new cattle are stood up in their place—something for which Nano Server is specifically designed. Well, in that analogy a container is a chicken, and you don't even bother to brand it—the chickens just run around, and you don't give them any thought at all. Therefore, the container is not a good fit for persistent storage unless a container instance is committed to create a new image, which is uncommon. What if persistent storage is required?

Volume mappings allow a volume on the host to be connected to a container instance when it starts in either a read-only or read-write mode. Multiple container instances can connect to the same container host volume.

This use of volume mappings is achieved by using the -v parameter and specifying the folder location to which it will be mapped in the container instance and the target location on the contain host filesystem. For example, the following line maps a folder in the container instance named c:\data to the contents in the d:\ContainerData folder on the host. Inside the container instance, it would be able to interact with c:\data as if it was local content. Any data written is written directly to the folder on the container host filesystem and is therefore persisted.

```
docker run -v d:\ContainerData:c:\data
```

By default, the volume mapping is read-write. However, if read-only mode is required, append `:ro` to the end; for example:

```
docker run -v d:\ContainerData:c:\data:ro
```

A full example using the earlier demosite container image and enabling interaction would be the following. Once inside the container, I would be able to navigate to `c:\data`, which would show the data storage in the `c:\containerdata` folder on my actual container host.

```
docker run --name demo1 -it -v C:\containerdata:c:\data demosite cmd.exe
```

Another option is to use traditional network-based storage, such as an SMB share that will be accessed via the container's network stack.

Integrating Active Directory

In a normal environment consisting of server OS instances, it is common to join those instances to Active Directory. This introduces a small amount of overhead during the provisioning process and creates objects in the Active Directory. Because containers can be created and torn down frequently, it does not make sense to join instances to the Active Directory. The ability to authenticate securely, however, is still critical for container instances.

The solution works by utilizing default accounts within the container image for services and tasks (for example, the LocalSystem, Network Service account). A credential specification is then created that contains the domain account to be used as the default service account and used when starting the container. Now in the container instance when the service starts and tries to access remote services, it will use the credential specification instead of the local account used by the service within the container instance.

The credentials are not stored in the image itself. Therefore, the container can be moved between environments without having to rebuild, since the environment-specific credentials are external to the container instance and are bound at runtime.

Working with Image Registries

A registry provides capabilities around the discovery of images, their storage, and the ability to distribute them. There are two types of registries, as mentioned earlier in this chapter.

The first type of registry is Docker Hub, which is a cloud-hosted service provided by Docker, Inc. that can contain both public and private content in addition to supporting automated build support. To use Docker Hub, you sign up for an account and it is then possible to publish things publicly and privately.

The second type of registry is the Docker Trusted Registry, which runs on-premises (or in a cloud instance private to your organization) and is utilized only by your organization. This registry is not available through the general Internet and thus does not require Internet connectivity. It is managed through a web-based management console and can integrate with Active Directory and LDAP to enable granular control of who can access the registry. When using a trusted registry, the registry name or IP is specified as part of the pull request (for example, `docker pull 10.7.173.56/iis` will pull the IIS image from my trusted repository at 10.7.173.56).

When a Docker pull is performed, it will first check local repositories. If an image cannot be found and if the client has access, it will try to check for the image in a public repository.

Patching and Updating

You can manage updates and patches in various ways. This applies to base OS images, dependency images such as those containing binaries and libraries, and the application images themselves.

In the first approach, when an update or patch is available, a new base OS image or container image is created with the update/patch applied and uploaded to the repository. The Dockerfile is updated to use the new version number (if a version number is used as opposed to specifying to use the latest), and the container instances are rebuilt, which will pull the updated images. You must rebuild any containers that need to use an updated version of an image/base OS image, as every image stores Metadata about the layers on which it depends with a strong identifier in the form of a file hash. It is possible to configure autobuild for images by also uploading the corresponding Dockerfile that created the image, and then, when a dependent layer is updated, the image will automatically be rebuilt.

The second approach is just to apply the updates to the container instance, which will create a new layer containing the updates. Remember that any writes to a container are applied to the top layer, as all other container/base OS images it depends on are read-only. Therefore, any updates/patches to dependency images will have the filesystem/registry updates written to a new layer above the application. The updates will then be unioned with the underlying layers (with the highest layer taking precedence if a conflict occurs because updates are applied but the original version of the file/registry is still present in the lower-level base/container image). This is shown in Figure 10.7. Where possible, the first approach is preferred.

FIGURE 10.7
Two options for
updating images

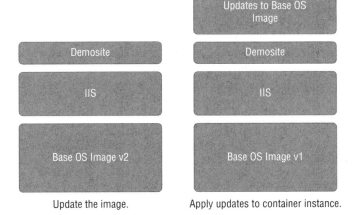

Update the image.   Apply updates to container instance.

Using Containers in Your Organization

This chapter has dived into some of the key characteristics and capabilities of containers. Their immutable and prescriptive nature is unique in the IT world in terms of really embracing the devops mentality and enabling it within an organization. While some IT pros may use containers in isolation, this is for a minority of scenarios. The real power of containers is achieved when developers embrace containers and use them throughout the entire life cycle of application development and deployment. Certainly consider using a Docker Trusted Repository instance on-premises for your custom applications if you are not comfortable saving content even to a private repository on Docker Hub.

Many developers understand Linux containers but don't know that Windows now supports containers. Therefore, developers need to be educated about this capability and learn how containers can integrate with developer tools such as Visual Studio.

The next question may be whether to use Windows or Linux containers. Remember that the management fabric is the same: Docker. The difference between containers on Windows vs. Linux boils down to two main factors:

◆ The underlying capabilities of Windows vs. Linux will likely be the biggest factor in determining the platform for an application. Now that Windows has containers, it removes that as a potential block for organizations that have bought into containers.

◆ Levels of isolation required. Containers on Windows enable the use of Hyper-V containers and kernel mode isolation as a deployment mode choice.

Nano Server and containers are like peanut butter and jelly, and most organizations looking at Nano Server today are also looking at using it closely with containers, as they complement each other so well in terms of small footprint, fast provisioning, and the "cattle" mentality.

The Bottom Line

Articulate the reasons to use containers. Containers provide many benefits including fast provisioning, high density and a prescriptive method to deploy applications in different environments leading to consistent and repeatable deployments. Containers also leverage repositories providing a simple way to obtain images and share images to be used during implementations.

Explain the differences between Windows containers and Hyper-V containers. Windows containers provide a user-mode level of isolation from other containers. Hyper-V containers run the Windows container in a dedicated, utility VM that is automatically managed and provides kernel-mode-level isolation from other containers.

Master It When would Hyper-V containers be used over Windows containers?

Manage Containers. Containers are managed using the docker CLI. While a PowerShell module is available this module utilizes the Docker REST API and the same management structure as the docker CLI. This means management performed either with the docker CLI or PowerShell is working on a single management platform.

Master It Can Linux applications run on Windows containers?

Master It Can the Docker client on Windows manage Linux containers

Chapter 11

Remote Desktop Services

Up to this point in the book, I have focused on the core technologies of virtualization, and I have primarily used server operating system workloads for examples. Historically, this has been the principal usage for machine virtualization. You can, however, use virtualization with a client operating system to offer virtualized desktops.

This chapter presents Windows Server Remote Desktop Services (RDS), which enables remote access to operating systems, both server and desktop, with the primary goal of providing users with a desktop experience. As I will explain, you can achieve this in various ways, and this chapter focuses on where Hyper-V is critical.

In this chapter, you will learn to:

◆ Explain the types of desktop virtualization provided by RDS.

◆ Describe the benefits of RemoteFX and its requirements.

◆ Articulate the other technologies required for a complete virtualized desktop solution.

Remote Desktop Services and Bring Your Own Device

Remote Desktop Services is a core role of Windows Server; it was called Terminal Services before Windows Server 2008 R2, but it was renamed to better reflect the range of its functionality. If you are familiar with Terminal Services, you know that it was focused on providing a complete desktop to remote users that was hosted on a server operating system. Each connected user had their own Windows session on the server operating system, which provided them with a level of isolation from other users connected to the same server operating system. The remote connection was enabled through the Remote Desktop Protocol (RDP). RDP is a core part of all Windows operating systems, and it is also what enables the ability to Remote Desktop to a desktop operating system remotely. A Terminal Server, or Remote Desktop Session Host (RDSH) as it is now known, provides a desktop to the remote user—including the Start menu, desktop icons, Internet Explorer/Microsoft Edge, and the various applications installed on the server operating system, which could include Microsoft Office and line-of-business (LOB) applications. To the end user, the experience is no different than that of a desktop operating system; however, actions that affect all users, such as reboots and application installations, are blocked in a session virtualization environment.

Figure 11.1 shows a typical session virtualization solution with RDSH. In this example, the session host is running as a virtual machine on a Hyper-V server, but it could also be running on a physical host directly. As you can see, many different users connect for their own desktop. As I cover later in this chapter, while RDSH provides a desktop environment, other technologies are required to give users a full experience such as profile, applications, and their data.

FIGURE 11.1
Session virtualization using Remote Desktop Session Host

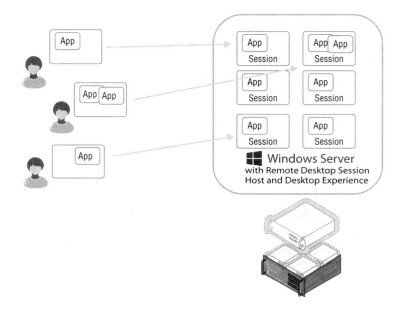

ENABLING A RICH DESKTOP EXPERIENCE USING RDSH

I've talked about configuration levels for the operating system, which should be Server Core for most server uses, and Nano Server for some fabric components or modern applications. For a session host that is providing an environment for a user, the full graphical experience is required. In Windows Server 2012 R2, that required the Server Graphical Shell configuration level, which provides the graphical shell, Windows File Explorer, Internet Explorer, and more. For the complete desktop experience of a client operating system, you would also enable the Desktop Experience configuration level, which adds features such as themes, Windows Media Player, Windows Store, and photo tools. It was really the only time you should have enabled the Desktop Experience configuration level, because it consumes more resources on the server operating system. However, some applications require Desktop Experience, specifically for the graphical codecs it includes.

In Windows Server 2016, the *only* way to get the graphic shell is with Desktop Experience, and it must be set at installation time. Therefore, for the Remote Desktop Session Hosts in your environment, make sure that Windows Server (Desktop Experience) is the configuration level selected during the operating system installation, as shown in the following image. Remember that in Windows Server 2016, the configuration level cannot be changed post deployment.

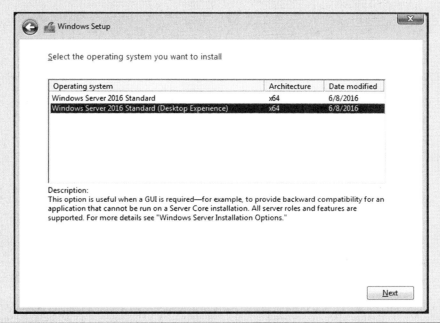

While Remote Desktop Services provides a complete desktop with the Start menu, sometimes end users don't want a complete desktop. Instead, they want a specific application displayed on their device, such as a line-of-business application or an office application. This is especially true when using a smaller device such as a phone or tablet. Imagine trying to interact with the complete Windows desktop on a 4-inch iPhone screen compared to just launching a specific Windows application. Or say that a user is already running a Windows desktop but has to run a specific application remotely. In these cases, the users just want the application's window to be displayed on their existing desktop or device, without a completely separate desktop, in order to launch applications from a website or some kind of local application catalog. Windows Server 2008 introduced the ability to publish applications in addition to a full desktop, which allowed just the application window to be sent to the user's local device.

For a long time, this type of session virtualization was the most popular way to provide a virtualized desktop. Recently, Virtual Desktop Infrastructure (VDI) has been getting a lot of attention and is being touted as the best solution by many vendors. A VDI solution differs from session virtualization in that each end user connects to a separate client operating system running in a virtual machine, as shown in Figure 11.2. This gives a greater level of isolation for each user, since the users are now running in their own isolated operating system; therefore, it is a good fit for power users and developers who need to customize the operating system or reboot it. The downside is that a VDI solution uses up far more resources, because each VDI desktop is a complete desktop environment including memory, processor, and desk utilization.

FIGURE 11.2
VDI solution
in action

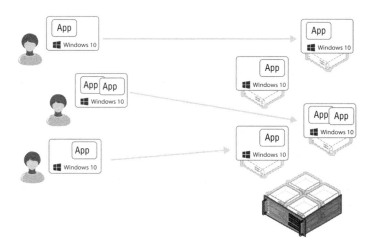

A VDI deployment has two modes: pooled and personal desktops. Most VDI deployments will leverage a pooled deployment for the majority of VDI users. In a *pooled VDI* configuration, numerous virtual machines running the client OS are grouped into a pool. As a user connects, the user is automatically assigned one of the VMs not currently in use. Once the user has logged off, the VM is placed back into the pool. Because a user potentially (and probably) gets a different VM each time they connect, it is essential that you have solutions to maintain the user's profile and data between logons. After a user logs out, the VM in the pool is reset to a clean state in case anything was changed by the previous user.

Pooled desktops should be the default for all users, but certain users might need the same client OS instance every time they connect. Maybe they are modifying the OS in some way, or perhaps they have an application that needs to be installed because it can't be virtualized. Whatever the reason, you have the capability to statically assign a VM to a particular user so that they always get the same client OS. This is known as a *personal desktop*.

A pooled desktop environment allows a gold image to be used as the template for all VMs in the pool. Because no user state is stored in the VMs in the pool, there is no need to patch or maintain those VMs. The only maintenance required is to patch and manage the gold image, which will then refresh all VMs in the pool. This is not possible for a personal desktop, because the VM is maintained for the specific user between logons and therefore must be patched just like a regular desktop. It also may lay dormant if not used by the user but will still consume resources. It is therefore far more preferable to use pooled VMs over personal VMs when you use VDI.

Windows Server 2016 introduces a new type of VDI deployment: *Personal Session Desktops*. Personal Session Desktops behave in a similar fashion to personal VDI desktops except that the operating system running in the VM assigned to a user is Windows Server 2016 configured as a session host and the user optionally has administrative rights. The use of a server OS is beneficial primarily when a VDI level of isolation is required but the licensing restrictions of Windows clients prohibit a typical VDI deployment, such as running in a public cloud (where Windows client operating systems cannot be licensed), or when an agent cannot be deployed on the virtualization hosts (which is required for VDI and not possible in a public cloud). At times, a server OS might be a better fit for user scenarios, such as for certain developers.

It won't come as any surprise to you that the vendors who push VDI as the best solution for every scenario are those who don't have a session virtualization solution, so VDI is their only way to expand into the desktop market. Vendors who have both VDI and session virtualization, such as Microsoft and Citrix, take a more balanced approach. I give more guidance later in this chapter on when to use each type of desktop virtualization, because most organizations need some of each.

Whether session virtualization or VDI is used, the end result is virtualization of the desktop, or simply virtual desktops. So why do people even want these virtual desktop solutions? The following are some of the most common reasons:

- Disaster-recovery situations in which the normal work office for users is not available because of a disaster or for some other reason. Say a huge blizzard prevents workers from leaving their homes. With a virtual desktop environment available, users can connect to the virtual desktop, and their complete desktop environment is available.

- Contract users with their own computers who need a corporate desktop environment. Rather than rebuild their computers, just give them access to a desktop in the corporate virtual desktop environment.

- Users who need to use many devices and require a consistent desktop experience. This could include users who use shared devices such as in hospital environments.

- High-security situations in which data cannot leave the datacenter and the user's desktop must also be housed in the datacenter. It's not practical to sit users in the actual datacenter, so remotely accessing the desktop that is colocated in the datacenter is the best of both worlds.

- Certain applications that access huge amounts of data that is stored in the datacenter. Sending the data over the network may be impractical or give poor performance, so hosting the desktop in the datacenter with the application effectively running on the same local network gives great performance.

- Critical desktops that need high resilience. Consider that with virtual desktops, the desktop operating system is running on server hardware, which means server-class performance and server-class high availability and redundancy including RAID-based storage.

- ◆ Remote developers who need to be able to customize their operating system environment and reboot

- ◆ CEOs who need to bring in their iPad and access Windows applications

- ◆ Bring Your Own Device (BYOD), whereby organizations allow users to bring their own computers into the office (and may even give them money each year to buy a device). Installing the corporate image on these devices does not make sense, so a virtual desktop can give the users a desktop.

BYOD has become the driving force behind the huge interest in desktop virtualization, because many organizations are looking at ways to enable their users to work from any device and from anywhere. Microsoft has made huge strides in its Remote Desktop Services solution that minimize the need to leverage third-party solutions, such as those from Citrix and Quest, although they still have a place in certain scenarios.

In the rest of this chapter, you will look at the key components of Microsoft Remote Desktop Services and how it's used to deliver a virtual desktop solution.

Microsoft Desktop and Session Virtualization Technologies

To offer a virtual desktop solution, whether session virtualization or VDI, various components are required to complete the solution and enable connectivity from end users:

- ◆ Machine virtualization to host the virtual machines (for example, Hyper-V)

- ◆ Virtualization management to enable the creation of virtual machines and stopping/ starting them as needed in addition to passing information back to the VDI components

- ◆ Client platform to run inside the virtual machines, meaning Windows 10

- ◆ Access protocol to communicate with the virtual desktop OS, which is Remote Desktop Protocol for native Windows

- ◆ Connection Broker to decide which virtual desktop a user should be connected to, which could be via session virtualization or VDI, and to remember which desktop a disconnected user was last using for reconnections

- ◆ Gateway capability for users connecting from outside of the corporate network and avoiding the need for VPN connections or technologies like DirectAccess

- ◆ Licensing

In this section, I walk you through the typical process of connecting to a hosted desktop in a Microsoft VDI implementation and demonstrate the Microsoft role services used and how they interact. Figure 11.3 depicts the major steps required for VDI functionality, from the initial user contact all the way to a usable VDI session with an empty Windows 10 operating system. If using session virtualization, the flow is similar, except that the endpoint for the virtual desktop is a session host instead of a virtual machine; in addition, step 6 in the flow is not performed.

FIGURE 11.3
The full VDI implementation has many components to give a rich capability set while being invisible to the end user.

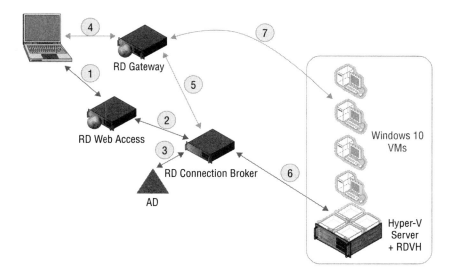

The steps are as follows:

1. Users need to find the remote desktops to which they can connect, which can be desktop virtualization sessions (RDSH), published applications, and the VDI sessions. While an RDP file can be created and deployed to users using various methods, a more dynamic approach is to use the Remote Desktop Web Access role service, which presents a browser-based list of available connections from which the user can choose.

2. To create the list of published applications and connections that are presented to the user, the Remote Desktop Web Access server communicates with the Remote Desktop Connection Broker, which has knowledge of the VDI pools, personal desktops, and other published connections and applications through its own communications with configured RemoteApp sources.

3. To ascertain the exact access a user has, the Connection Broker communicates with Active Directory, which also provides any personal desktop configurations.

4. No matter what the exact method, be it Remote Desktop Web Access, RemoteApp, and Desktop Connections, or a deployed RDP file, the users now have an RDP file that can be used to initiate the connection. If the user is outside the corporate network, a direct RDP connection would be blocked by most organizations' firewalls. So, traditionally, the user would need to initiate a virtual private network (VPN) secure connection or use DirectAccess. But you have an alternate solution that does not require any end-user action or additional client-side software. Windows Server 2008 introduced TS Gateway, which allows the RDP traffic to be encapsulated in HTTPS (port 443) packets, which is the RD Gateway component.

5. The user needs an initial RDP connection point, since their VDI client VM destination will not be known yet unless the user has a personal desktop configured. The RD Connection Broker acts as the connection point for the user's RDP connection and then redirects the client to the true endpoint, the VDI session. The RD Connection Broker knows what the RDP target should be for the requesting client.

6. The RD Connection Broker communicates with the Remote Desktop Virtualization Host role service that is enabled on the Hyper-V boxes to check the state of the VMs, start the VM if required, and gather any needed information such as IP address of the client VM OS. This information is then passed back to the RD Connection Broker, to the RD Session Host in redirection mode, and then back to the client.

7. The client now makes an RDP connection to the destination client VM via the RD Gateway (if connecting from outside the corporate network), and the connection is complete. The logon process for the user would now be complete.

One part I haven't mentioned is the role of System Center Virtual Machine Manager, which while not a requirement, definitely helps in the management of the virtual machines and helps automate the bulk creation and updating of virtual machines. Next you'll spend a little time looking at each component in a bit more detail. It should go without saying, but all of the roles can be virtualized on Hyper-V, and it is common practice to do so.

RD Web Access

The RD Web Access role provides the initial entry point for users; it provides a web-based interface to select the desired VDI or published desktop/application target. While not absolutely required, this helps give a simple-to-use portal that supports form-based authentication, provides single sign-on, and differentiates between public and private computers for credential caching. The Web Access portal utilizes HTTPS to protect the credentials that are passed and could be made available to the Internet through publishing enabled by gateway services such as Microsoft User Access Gateway.

Although not directly part of RD Web Access, Windows 7 introduced RemoteApp and Desktop Connections, which allows a feed from RD Web Access to populate the same content shown in the website directly into the Start menu, avoiding the need to use the website. The standard URL is `https://<RD Web Access server>/RDWeb/Feed/webfeed.aspx`.

This was continued in Windows 8 and beyond as a Control Panel applet and extended with the new Remote Desktop windows application available from the Windows Store. The Remote Desktop application enables easy access to the feeds provided by RD Web Access. The Manage RemoteApp and Desktop Connections setting in the application enable a new connection to be added, as shown in Figure 11.4. Previously, either a web feed URL or the user's email address could be specified. Behind the scenes, when an email address is entered, the domain part of the email address is extracted and then used to perform a DNS lookup for `_msradc.<domain from email>`. The record in DNS is a TXT record that must be created by administrators, and the value of the DNS record is the URL of the RD Web Access feed. In the current version, the ability to use an email address has been removed and a URL must be specified. The email address, however, still works with the RemoteApp and Desktop Connections Control Panel applet and the iOS and Android applications.

RD Connection Broker

The updated Connection Broker in Windows Server 2008 R2 was one of the major components that allowed an all-Microsoft VDI solution and gave Remote Desktop Services the ability to balance and track connections to nonsession hosts, specifically the ability to manage connections to client operating systems. It's important to note that the Connection Broker still helps balance connections to session hosts as well. Additionally, Windows 2008 R2 introduced the ability for the Connection Broker to balance RemoteApps and support servers with different published applications, allowing a sum view of all the applications gathered from all servers in the farm to be displayed to the user. This removes the need for all servers to have the same applications. The Connection Broker is the brains of the virtual desktop environment and communicates and controls the other components; it works particularly closely with the RD Session Host in redirection mode that is required pre–Windows Server 2012, which is why they are frequently placed on the same OS instance. However, when you start having more than 250 simultaneous connections, you may need to consider breaking the roles onto separate servers.

Windows Server 2012 also enabled the Connection Broker to act as the initial entry point for the incoming RDP connection, which previously required a dedicated RD Session Host in redirection mode. This has removed the need to ever have an RD Session Host in a redirection mode. Prior to Windows Server 2012, the RD Session Host in redirection mode was required because when you have a large session host server farm, to avoid users having to connect to different session hosts, the initial entry point is always a designated session host that does nothing more than talk to the broker and then redirect the RDP connection to the right RDP endpoint. This is the same concept in a VDI environment; you still need an initial RDP connection point for the RDP clients, which is exactly what the RDSH in redirection mode provides. It then redirects the RDP client to the right client OS VM that will be providing their desktop OS. By moving the functionality into the Connection Broker, you have one less component to deploy.

The Connection Broker is also in charge of cleaning up the VDI instance after the user logs off. This is achieved by the creation of a checkpoint, RDV_Rollback, when the VM instance is created from the template, which is in a clean state before a user logs on. Once a user logs off, the RDV_Rollback checkpoint is applied to the VM instance, reverting the VM to the pre-user logon state and making it ready for the next logon. In Windows Server 2008 R2, the RDV_ Rollback checkpoint had to be manually created, but this is done automatically in Windows Server 2012 and newer.

Typically, the Connection Broker uses a SQL Server cluster when deployed in a high-availability configuration. However, Windows Server 2016 also adds support for using Azure SQL Database, which reduces the number of roles and VMs required when deploying an RDS solution in Azure. It's also possible to use Azure AD Domain Services for RDS in Windows Server 2016, which further reduces infrastructure requirements as domain controllers are no longer required. Windows Server 2016 has scale improvements for the Connection Broker, with tests up to 10,000 connections, including burst storms that would have a significant percentage fail on Windows Server 2012 R2 but now are all successful with Windows Server 2016.

RD Virtualization Host

The RD Virtualization Host role service is installed on any Hyper-V host that will be participating in a VDI pool. It enables the Connection Broker to communicate with the Hyper-V hosts, start/stop VMs, and gather information from within to enable client connections. The RD Virtualization Host role also enables the use of RemoteFX GPU virtualization.

RD Gateway

The RD Gateway allows RDP traffic to be encapsulated in HTTPS packets, allowing secure RDP connection through corporate firewalls without having to open up firewall ports or use additional VPN solutions. Figure 11.5 shows a high-level overview.

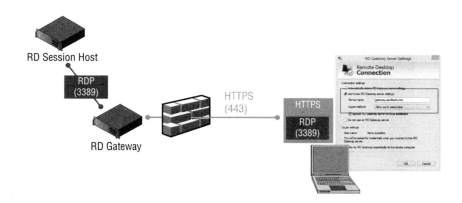

FIGURE 11.5
How RD Gateway works

The RD Gateway is placed in the DMZ (or, more securely, behind some kind of firewall/ proxy). The clients connect to the RDP destination via the RD Gateway, which is accomplished by adding the RD Gateway server as part of the RDP file configuration that is given to the client. The client encapsulates the RDP traffic in HTTPS and sends it to the RD Gateway, which extracts the RDP and forwards it to the RDP destination. When traffic comes back from the

RDP destination bound for the client, the RD Gateway encapsulates it in HTTPS and sends it to the client. With this technology, users outside the corporate network can still access all RDP resources without additional steps or software. Users who are on the corporate network would bypass the RD Gateway and communicate directly with the RDP destination.

Using RD Gateway, you can configure who can connect through the RD Gateway service, what they can connect to, the supported RDP settings such as device redirection, and so on. This allows access from outside the organization without the use of a separate VPN-type technology while still maintaining control of the levels of access. RD Gateway can be used with any RDP connection, which means that it can be used with session virtualization, VDI, and application publishing.

Requirements for a Complete Desktop Virtualization Solution

Everything I have discussed so far is about providing an operating system environment for the end users, but what the users actually care about is accessing applications and the related data in a familiar environment. This requires much more than just an operating system. Additionally, you must provide the following:

◆ Access to a user's data

◆ A consistent set of user customizations; that is, their profile

◆ Access to a user's applications

Many organizations already have solutions to protect and provide access to user data. The most important data resides in collaboration solutions such as SharePoint, and with features like OneDrive for Business, it's possible to have a local cache on a user's machine that is a local copy of the data stored in the user's SharePoint area. For unstructured data, such as that stored on a user's home drive, it is possible to use work folders (introduced in Windows Server 2012 R2) and the more traditional offline files with folder redirection.

Folder redirection allows well-known folders such as Documents to be redirected to a corporate file server but also to be cached locally using offline files/client-side caching to make the data available even when the machine is not connected to the corporate network. These technologies are mature and should be used at a minimum for the Documents and Desktop user folders. By redirecting these locations to a central file server, the user's data is always available, no matter which device a user is connected to. Granular controls are available to manage which data is redirected to a corporate file server and which data stays local to a machine and therefore will not roam with the user.

While providing access to data is a no-brainer for most organizations, providing a consistent user experience by making the user's profile move between different machines, known as *roaming profiles*, is a different story. While roaming profiles have existed in Windows for many versions, they have a history of problems. Roaming profiles in Windows 7 and newer are a fairly solid solution, but they have numerous limitations. For instance, you cannot use a single roaming profile between Windows XP and Windows 7 machines. You won't use a single profile between client and server operating systems. In addition, application settings don't work well between locally installed applications and those that are virtualized with solutions such as App-V. The root problem is that roaming profiles work by synchronizing predominantly a single file, `ntuser.dat`, which contains the registry of the user, and this synchronization occurs at logon and logoff with some limited synchronization periodically. This means that for many settings to synchronize, the user must log off, which is a problem if the user is utilizing many devices simultaneously or needs to use various types of devices or connections that differ for certain parts of the profile.

Microsoft provides an alternate solution for roaming the user's settings, called User Experience Virtualization (UE-V), which is available as part of the Microsoft Desktop Optimization Pack (MDOP). UE-V is enabled per application in addition to basic desktop settings. The locations in the registry and the filesystem for the user settings for each application are defined and therefore should be captured and virtualized by UE-V. This allows granularity in which application settings should be roamed between user environments, and each application has its own setting store, enabling much more flexible synchronization of settings. Let's imagine that a user has two logon sessions, their local Windows 10 PC and a Windows 2016 Remote Desktop Services session, and walk through the experience of using roaming profiles. I should point out that sharing a profile between a Windows 10 desktop and a 2016 RDS server is not recommended, but it helps you to see the problem.

1. In the Windows 10 session, the user launches PowerPoint, customizes the environment, and then closes PowerPoint.

2. In the 2016 session, the user launches PowerPoint, and none of the customizations made on the Windows 10 session are available. The user sets different customizations and then logs out of the 2016 session, at which point roaming profiles replicate the new profile.

3. The user logs out of the Windows 10 session, and the profile overwrites that of the 2016 session.

With UE-V, which has been configured to virtualize settings for Microsoft Office, this is what happens:

1. In the Windows 10 session, the user launches PowerPoint. As the application launches, the UE-V service hooks into the application, pausing the start, and checks for any updates to the settings package for PowerPoint from the UE-V remote repository, which is just a file share. If there is an updated settings package, the UE-V service synchronizes the application by using offline files to a local cache, and the application starts using the settings in the settings package exposed by the UE-V service. The UE-V service provides the technology to inject the user's application settings that are stored in the registry and filesystem onto their current OS as the application starts and then saves them back to the UE-V settings package when the application closes. This allows the abstraction of the application settings from the OS without any changes being needed by the application. The user now customizes the environment and then closes PowerPoint. As the application is closed, UE-V saves the updated settings to the settings package for the application and writes to the remote repository.

2. In the 2016 session, the user launches PowerPoint, and once again UE-V hooks into the application and pulls down and presents the user's customizations. Now the user sees the changes made in the Windows 10 session for PowerPoint and can get on with their work. If they make changes to the application settings, then upon application close, those changes would be saved to the remote repository.

This demonstrates how UE-V changes the user experience. Roaming profiles replicate changes only at logon and logoff. UE-V replicates application settings when the application launches and is closed. For desktop settings such as the theme (desktop background, sounds, and so on) and accessibility configurations, the changes are replicated at logon, logoff, lock, unlock, connect, and disconnect. Internet Explorer 8 (and newer) is supported and is treated like any other application; settings are replicated as the application is opened and closed. UE-V also works seamlessly with a mix of locally installed applications and virtualized applications with App-V, giving a single configuration for an application, no matter how it is implemented for users. For power users, a PowerShell cmdlet can enable an individual's application settings to be rolled back to the default configuration. This is useful if a user has completely corrupted their settings for an application. The default configuration is created the first time an application is launched for a user and stored away in case a settings rollback is required.

From a platform perspective, UE-V 2.1 SP1 is supported on Windows 7, Windows 8, Windows 8.1, Windows 10, Windows Server 2008 R2, Windows Server 2012, and Windows Server 2012 R2, which means a single application configuration for any session on any supported platform. While Windows Server 2016 is not supported at the time of this writing, I would expect an update to UE-V to add this support shortly after release. As long as the UE-V agent is installed and has the template registered for the applications and desktop, then the user will have a consistent experience.

There is no server infrastructure for UE-V other than a file share to store the settings packages for each user (who would have their own subfolder), or the user's settings packages could be part of their standard Active Directory–specified home drive. The templates that detail what applications should have settings virtualized and that document the various registry and file-system locations that make up those settings and need to be intercepted can be registered at the time of the UE-V agent installation. The templates also can be stored on a file share, where the UE-V agent can be configured to check for updates every 24 hours. This makes UE-V easy to deploy, because most of the work will be just deploying the agent, which can be done manually, through an enterprise software deployment (ESD) solution such as System Center Configuration Manager or even through Group Policy.

The final component is to provide the applications. One option is to install the applications into the operating system such as the RD Session Host or client OS in the VM for VDI; however, this is a lot of overhead and hard to maintain. Another option is to run applications separately on specific farms of session hosts that publish just the applications to the virtual desktop. Another option is to leverage App-V, which like UE-V is part of MDOP and is a great solution not just for virtual desktops but for physical desktops as well.

App-V virtualizes the application separately from the operating system, with each application running in its own virtual environment, or bubble. This bubble contains a virtual filesystem, registry, and many other system resources that sit on top of the operating system resource. These virtual layers contain the resources specific to the application. This allows the application to run on the operating system without having any footprint on the local resource, such as writing to the filesystem or changing the registry. A single cache on each machine holds the virtualized streams for each App-V application along with application icons and file type associates. The experience to the end user is completely seamless. App-V also streams applications to machines on first use where required; however, for session virtualization and VDI, that is typically not used, and instead a central cache can be shared that is prepopulated with all of the virtualized applications.

Figure 11.6 shows a Microsoft technology-complete solution with session virtualization or VDI providing the operating system and other technologies providing the data, profile, and applications. This is not the only possible solution; rather, it's an example of how different technologies work together to create the complete end-user experience. The key point is that these technologies can all be used on physical desktops and also enable a single set of technologies to provide a consistent and manageable experience for all the types of desktops in your organization.

FIGURE 11.6
Providing the complete user experience

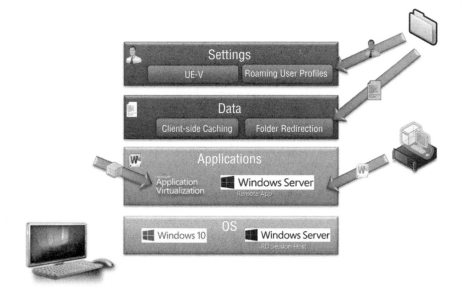

Another RDS-specific solution for the user profile and parts of the data is called *user profile disks*. The option to use a user profile disk is available when creating the VDI or session-based pools, also known as *collections*. This solution creates a VHDX file for each user that uses the pooled virtual desktops. The first time a user connects to the pool, a new VHDX file is created and attached to the virtual machine (if VDI) or the RD Session Host that is hosting the user's session (if session-based). The entire user's profile is stored on the attached user profile disk by default. All of the user's data and settings are stored on the user profile disk, since Documents is part of the user profile area. On subsequent logons by the user, the user profile disk VHDX is attached to the required VM image or RD Session Host, providing the same user profile area and therefore the same user experience and data access. Within the virtual desktop that is using the user profile disk, the VHDX is seen as mounted for the location of the user's profile using the MOUNTVOL command.

User profile disks can be enabled when creating a VDI or session-based pool or after the creation of the pool. Granular control of the data stored on the user profile disk is possible, as shown in Figure 11.7; a maximum size for the data stored on the VHDX is also shown.

Using user profile disks has some advantages and disadvantages. The big advantage is that they are easy to use and provide users with a consistent profile and data experience without having to use roaming profiles, UE-V, folder redirection, or any other technology. The disadvantage is that the user profile disks are specific only to the RDS environment, and the profile/data will not be available to other environments such as a physical desktop. In fact, it's more restrictive than that. When VDI or session-based deployments are created with RDS, specific servers are selected to be part of the deployment, which makes up a specific collection. An environment may have many collections, which could be VDI or session-based for different types of users. The user profile disks are specific to a particular collection defined in RDS, which means that they cannot be shared between RDS collections. Therefore, if users leverage virtual desktops from different collections, they would have a different user profile disk and therefore a different profile for each collection, which would not be a good end-user experience.

FIGURE 11.7
User profile disk configuration options

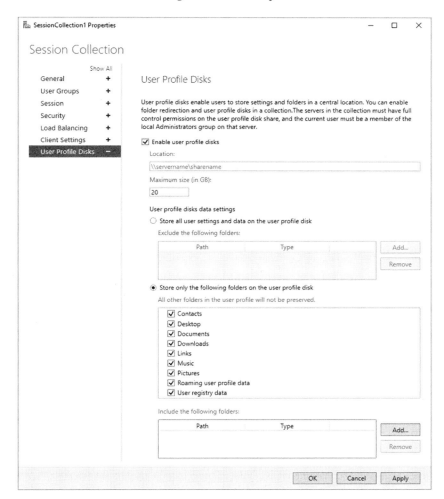

I think of user profile disks as a great solution for pilot environments in which integration with a normal desktop environment is not required or for production environments that have a set of users who will leverage only a specific RDS collection or who do not need access to their normal profile or data. Outside of that, I think it is better to leverage user state virtualization technologies that are usable across all desktop environments such as the aforementioned roaming profiles, UE-V, and folder redirection.

Creating the VDI Template

One of the most important decisions when using VDI is which operating system you will use in the image. Where possible, a consistent operating system between your physical desktops and the virtual desktops is advantageous because it will avoid additional application testing and different OS configuration and validation exercises. This may not be practical, however. One reason VDI may be attractive is that the physical desktops are all running Windows XP, and you need a more modern operating system for some users or applications.

A Windows Server 2016 VDI deployment has various client operating system options:

- Windows 7 Enterprise
- Windows 8/8.1 Pro
- Windows 8/8.1 Enterprise
- Windows 10 Pro
- Windows 10 Enterprise

Where possible, Windows 10 Enterprise is the best option because it gives the richest client experience and highest set of functionality. Also, while the Pro versions may work, Enterprise is the supported SKU by Microsoft. Compared to Windows 10 Pro, the Enterprise edition has the following additional capabilities:

RemoteApp   This offers application publishing and enables specific applications running on the operating system to be published and used by users instead of a complete desktop. RemoteApp provides a far more seamless experience in addition to being more accessible and usable on smaller form-factor devices where a full desktop is not optimal. The Pro edition does not enable RemoteApp.

RemoteFX Device Redirection   RemoteFX has several technologies, one of which enables the redirection of almost any USB device at a port level. Only Enterprise has this feature.

RemoteFX vGPU   The feature of RemoteFX most people think of is the virtual GPU capability, which enables a physical GPU in a server to be virtualized and made available to virtual machines. Even if a server does not have a GPU or a certain level of graphical capability, it can still be exposed to the virtual machine through a software rasterizer. This enables the virtual machine to see a vGPU and perform local graphics rendering, such as with DirectX, enabling advanced graphics applications to be executed in the VDI environment. This is enabled only on the Enterprise edition.

User Profile Disk   This enables a VHD to be attached to the virtual machine and used for profile and data storage so that a user's experience is consistent even when connecting to different VDI VM instances. This is available only on the Enterprise edition.

For the 32-bit vs. 64-bit decision, I generally recommend using whatever version you use on your physical desktops in the organization to avoid a large amount of additional software testing. Obviously, if you have 64-bit desktop applications and if you need more than 4GB of memory, you will need to use the 64-bit version of Windows. The one downside of 64-bit Windows is that it uses around 2GB of additional disk space per virtual machine, but that is really the only difference in overhead. Memory and processor are about equal.

Once you decide on the operating system version, there are many steps to optimize the image that will be the gold image and template for all the VM instances that will be created for the VDI collection. You will likely be running hundreds of instances of this VM template, so you want to optimize it as much as possible. Microsoft has great resources to help with this. I recommend the following:

◆ `http://download.microsoft.com/download/6/0/1/601D7797-A063-4FA7-A2E5-74519B57C2B4/Windows_8_VDI_Image_Client_Tuning_Guide.pdf`. This is a great tuning guide that talks about OS considerations and customizations, services to disable, and software such as malware usage. This is a mandatory read.

◆ `http://blogs.technet.com/b/jeff_stokes/archive/2013/04/09/hot-off-the-presses-get-it-now-the-windows-8-vdi-optimization-script-courtesy-of-pfe.aspx`. This is a great script to automate most of what is discussed in the previous reference. It also has some guidance at the start of the script for actions to be performed on the image. Although it is for Windows 8, it works for Windows 10 as well.

You may also choose to install certain applications into the image. Generally, I recommend keeping the image as light as possible; don't install many applications into the image because each application update will require an update to the image. Instead, use technologies such as App-V and RemoteApp to deliver the applications. At times you may still have to install applications into the image, but try to keep these to a minimum. You must not install modern applications into the reference image, because you have to run Sysprep at the end of the image creation process and modern applications are currently not understood by Sysprep, which means that the applications will have to reinstall anyway during the template's deployment in the VDI collection.

On this same theme, don't use a Microsoft account when creating the reference image. Use a local account, because you also don't want to join the reference image to the domain, which would be removed during the Sysprep process and can confuse things.

Once the image is the way you want it, the next step is to prepare it to be used by an RDS collection. This involves generalizing it, which is achieved by running Sysprep. On Windows 10 Enterprise, prior to running Sysprep, I had to uninstall the Candy Crush Saga and Twitter Windows applications. This was because I was running the 1511 branch, which included the new Consumer Experiences feature that adds certain applications if the machine is connected to the Internet. This can be disabled through the following policy: Computer Configuration ➤ Administrative Templates ➤ Windows Components ➤ Cloud Content. Then turn off Microsoft Consumer Experiences and set to Enabled. Microsoft has a full article on the Consumer Experiences at `https://blogs.technet.microsoft.com/mniehaus/2015/11/23/seeing-extra-apps-turn-them-off/`. The command to be used in the OS is as follows:

```
C:\windows\system32\sysprep\Sysprep /generalize /oobe /shutdown /mode:vm
```

Windows 8 introduced the /mode:vm switch, which should be used when preparing a Windows 8 VM that is being used as part of a VDI deployment. When Sysprep runs, it performs several actions, including removing unique information such as the SID and GUID; but it also resets the hardware information. In a VDI environment where all of the duplicates are running on the same hypervisor as the source VM, there's no need to reset the hardware information. Not resetting the hardware is what the /mode:vm switch enables. This speeds up the startup of the duplicates on first boot.

I recommend an extra step before running Sysprep. Over time, you will want to update the template, including adding patches. There are ways to patch the virtual machine without starting it, and I walked through some options in Chapter 5, "Managing Hyper-V." Still, it's useful to be able to start the virtual machine, but remember that it is not possible to run Sysprep continually on an operating system. Instead, I recommend doing the following:

1. Complete the customization of your reference image and shut down the virtual machine.

2. Create a checkpoint and label it **Reference Pre-Sysprep**.

3. Start the virtual machine and run Sysprep, which will then shut down the virtual machine so it will be ready for duplication.

If at any point in the future you need to boot the image to modify it, you apply the pre-Sysprep checkpoint, make the changes needed, shut down the VM, delete the original checkpoint, and create a new pre-Sysprep checkpoint. (You want to save this state because it has the updates applied, but is pre-Sysprep allowing this to be used for future changes) You then boot the virtual machine and run Sysprep again. The important part is that the checkpoint is updated with the updates, but this is always before the Sysprep action. Don't worry about having the checkpoint; when a virtual machine is used by the VDI collection creation, the virtual machine is exported to the target collection, the latest state is used, and the checkpoints are ignored. What is important is that the virtual machine should have no checkpoints that were taken while the virtual machine was running; otherwise, the detection will show the virtual machine as running, even though it isn't.

You will now have a virtual machine template that will be referenced when creating a VDI collection. Don't forget to use Dynamic Memory for the virtual machine, because this will give the most efficient use of memory and the greatest density of virtual machines on the server. Make sure that the virtual machines have at least 1024MB of memory.

One great feature in Windows Server 2012 R2 and above Hyper-V and the file services is that data deduplication is supported for virtual machines that are used in a VDI scenario. Remember that the free Microsoft Hyper-V Server is a great solution in VDI scenarios, because the included Windows Server guest OS licenses with Windows Server Standard and Datacenter are not required, so using the free Microsoft Hyper-V Server makes great sense.

Even though the VDI collection automatically uses differencing disks for each VM instance in the collection to save space, the use of data deduplication will further save disk space. Some guidelines will say not to use differencing disks at all and instead rely entirely on data deduplication. Note that while data duplication is supported for VDI environments only, it is not blocked for other purposes. You should be careful if you decide to use data deduplication for other workloads because some workloads may not behave as expected if deduplicated.

Deploying a New VDI Collection Using Scenario-Based Deployment

I focus on a pooled scenario in this walk-through because it's by far the most common VDI deployment. The process is intuitive, with minimal changes required. If you do need some personal VDI images, the personal VDI assignment is configured through the Active Directory

Users and Computers MMC snap-in via the Personal Virtual Desktop tab. A user can be assigned only one personal desktop, and a VM can be assigned to one user as a personal desktop. A personal desktop must not be in a VDI pool. Make sure that the personal desktop name exactly matches the name of the VM. The name needs to be the fully qualified domain name (FQDN), which means that you need to give the VMs the name of the FQDN of the client OS. When using personal virtual desktops, you need to ensure that the name of the virtual machine in Hyper-V matches the FQDN of the OS within the virtual machine.

If I had walked through deploying VDI in Windows Server 2008 R2, this would be a different section. I would direct you to the 50-page Microsoft Quick Start Guides that require huge amounts of complicated configuration. Windows Server 2012 completely changed this with the new scenario-based deployments available in Server Manager. Remote Desktop Services deployment is now performed through Server Manager; all of the servers that will participate in the scenario are deployed through a single wizard to a best-practices configuration. While it is still possible to deploy and configure each server role manually, it's strongly discouraged and offers no advantage. The management of Remote Desktop Services is also through Server Manager for nearly all actions (except for licensing management and troubleshooting).

Server Manager supports deployment for all of the major scenarios, including session virtualization with application publishing, VDI with pooled desktops, and VDI with personal desktops. The scenario deployment also features two types of deployment. The quick-start installs all of the required components on a single server and is designed to be used in a test or pilot-type scenario or small environment. The standard deployment option allows multiple servers to be selected for a more production-ready deployment. The easiest way to understand the scenario-based deployment is to walk through a deployment. For a session virtualization deployment, the entire process can be performed through Server Manager, but VDI requires extra steps because of the additional configurations required. The basic process to use RDS scenario deployments is as follows:

1. Launch Server Manager.

2. From the Manage menu, select the Add Roles And Features action.

3. Click Next on the introduction page of the Add Roles And Features Wizard.

4. The installation type must be selected. Select the Remote Desktop Services installation option, which performs the scenario-based deployment instead of the standard role or feature-based installation. Click Next.

5. The type of deployment must be selected: Standard deployment or Quick Start. In this example, I use a Standard deployment so that multiple servers can be selected. Click Next.

6. The next step is to select the type of deployment. In this case, I select a virtual machine–based desktop deployment.

7. Complete the remaining configurations by selecting the servers to be used for the required RDS roles, which are RD Connection Broker, RD Web Access, and RD Virtualization Host. You can find the full walk-through at http://technet.microsoft.com/en-us/library/hh831541.aspx.

After RDS is deployed on the various required servers, the next step to complete the environment is to deploy the actual VDI collection. This is all performed through Server Manager:

1. In Server Manager, navigate to Remote Desktop Services ➢ Collections.

2. From the Tasks menu, select Create Virtual Desktop Collection, which launches the Create Collection Wizard.

3. Click Next on the introduction screen.

4. Enter a name for the collection and an optional description, and click Next.

5. Select the Pooled Virtual Desktop Collection option and leave the Automatically Create And Manage Virtual Desktops option selected. Click Next.

6. Select the virtual machine that will act as the gold image for the VDI collection. Remember, this virtual machine must be shut down and has been sysprep'd, as shown in Figure 11.8.

FIGURE 11.8
Selecting the virtual machine to be the reference image for the VDI collection

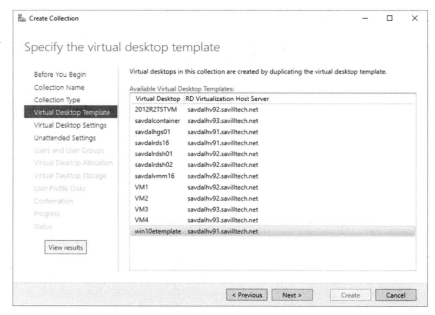

7. When the virtual machine template is deployed to the many VM instances in the collection, the VM instances are customized. You can specify an unattended answer file that exists or complete settings through the wizard by leaving the default Provide Unattended Installation Settings option selected. Click Next.

8. Select the time zone, domain, and organizational unit the VMs in the VDI collection should use, and click Next.

9. The next screen, as shown in Figure 11.9, specifies the users who can use the collection, the number of virtual desktops to be created in the collection, and a prefix and suffix for the VM instances. Configure the options you require, and click Next.

FIGURE 11.9
Configuring the options for the VDI VM instances

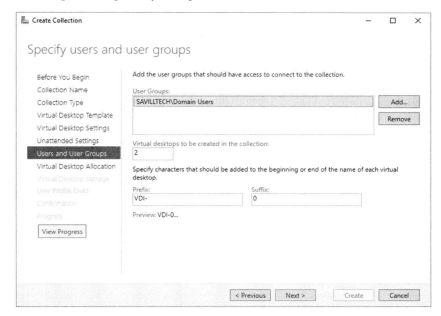

10. The next step allows the Hyper-V hosts to be selected that will host the VDI VM instances by checking the Hyper-V hosts to use. Once selected, click Next.

11. Select the storage location to be used for the VM instances, which can be a local location on the Hyper-V hosts, a SMB file share, or a cluster shared volume. Note that even if you have an alternate storage location configured for virtual machines on the Hyper-V host, this location is not used unless you specify a location explicitly in this wizard. By default, the VDI collection VMs will be created in the location `C:\ProgramData\Microsoft\Windows\RDVirtualizationHost\<collection name>`. By default, the option to roll back the virtual desktop automatically when the user logs off will be selected, which creates the RDV_Rollback checkpoint that is applied when users log off; this checkpoint reverts the VM to a clean state. Click Next.

12. Select the option to use user profile disks, and specify the share (ensuring that the computer accounts of the servers in the collection have full control for the share).

13. A summary of the configurations selected are shown. Click Create.

14. The progress is displayed, which includes creating the virtual desktop template image, importing on the target, and then creating the new virtual machines that are part of the VDI collection. The exact duration will depend on the size of the image and your storage subsystem.

After the deployment is complete, the collection will show in Server Manager and the virtual machines will display in Hyper-V Manager, as shown in Figure 11.10. Note that for the VDI virtual machines, the RDV_Rollback checkpoint was automatically created. What is more interesting is to look at the filesystem on the Hyper-V host to understand exactly what happened.

FIGURE 11.10

The deployed VDI collection

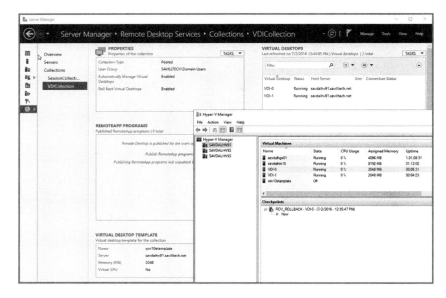

Figure 11.11 shows the filesystem objects related to my collection. You can see the copy of the actual reference virtual machine and its storage and then folders for each of the virtual machines. Notice the size of the VHDX files. The VHDX file in the IMGS subfolder is the original VHDX file that was exported from the reference virtual machine, so it has the same original size, 12GB. For each of the virtual machines, VDI-0 and VDI-1, there are two virtual hard disk files. The first is the VDI-n.VHDX file, which is the original virtual machine checkpoint state, RDV_Rollback, and then there is an AVHDX file, which is the current state of the virtual machine that has the differences from the checkpoint state. (This is normal.)

FIGURE 11.11

The deployed VDI collection filesystem content for the virtual hard disks

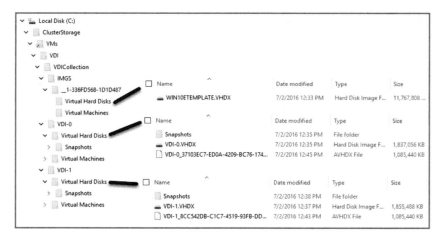

But why is the main VHDX file for each virtual machine only just under 2GB in size compared to the 12GB of the main image? The answer is that the RDS VDI collection is being efficient with storage and creates differencing disks for each virtual machine in the VDI collection instead of a complete copy of the original image. This can be seen using the Get-VHD PowerShell cmdlet on one of the VM instance VHDX files, as shown here:

```
PS C:\> Get-VHD .\VDI-0.VHDX


ComputerName            : SAVDALHV91
Path                    : c:\clusterstorage\vms\vdi\vdicollection\vdi-
0\virtual hard disks\vdi-0.vhdx
VhdFormat               : VHDX
VhdType                 : Differencing
FileSize                : 1881145344
Size                    : 64424509440
MinimumSize             : 64423477760
LogicalSectorSize       : 512
PhysicalSectorSize      : 4096
BlockSize               : 2097152
ParentPath              : C:\ClusterStorage\VMs\VDI\VDICollection\IMGS\__1-
336FD568-1D1D487\VIRTUAL HARD DISKS\WIN10ETEMPLATE.VHDX
DiskIdentifier          : 9356349E-BB7B-41A0-A53C-57A1538E4954
FragmentationPercentage:
Alignment               : 1
Attached                : True
DiskNumber              :
Number                  :
```

Notice that the VHDX is a type of differencing and that its parent is the VHDX file in the IMGS subfolder. Each VM still has around 2GB of customizations, which if you have 100 VM instances adds up to a lot of storage. This is where using data duplication will help reduce disk overhead.

The VDI collection will be available through RD Web Access, as shown in Figure 11.12; so will the other published desktops and applications. This gives a consistent experience for end users.

If you ever update the template virtual machine, you can refresh the deployment VM instances by selecting the Recreate All Virtual Desktops task for the collection and selecting the updated reference VM. This can also be done using the Update-RDVirtualDesktopCollection PowerShell cmdlet. Microsoft has a good blog on this at https://blogs.technet.microsoft.com/enterprisemobility/2012/10/29/single-image-management-for-virtual-desktop-collections-in-windows-server-2012/.

As you can see, it's simple to deploy VDI with Remote Desktop Services. Deploying session virtualization uses the same process, except that no virtual machines are required. The same wizard is used to deploy, and the same Connection Broker can be used for multiple session virtualization collections and VDI collections. I walk through a session host deployment in a video at http://youtu.be/_dkxyr03Er4.

FIGURE 11.12
Seeing the VDI
collection in RD
Web Access

FIGURE 11.12
Seeing the VDI
collection in RD
Web Access

Personal Session Desktops

Also notice in Figure 11.12 a Personal Session Desktop environment, which at the time of writing is managed with PowerShell. For Personal Session Desktops, you must pre-create the Remote Desktop Session Host instances, which are then mapped 1:1 to a user. Personal Session Desktops cannot be pooled. To enable a pool of RDSH VMs for users to connect to 1:1, simply deploy a number of RDSH servers in a standard RDSH session collection and then configure the session limit to 1 on each RDSH server. There is no rollback with Personal Session Desktops, as Personal Session Desktops utilizes the session host deployment model, plus rollback/checkpoints are not supported in public clouds like Azure anyway.

As previously mentioned, a benefit of the Personal Session Desktops feature over traditional VDI is that it uses a server OS instead of a client OS, and the RD Virtualization Host component is not required on the virtualization hosts. This makes Personal Session Desktops a good solution for public cloud scenarios where components cannot be installed on the fabric.

The following PowerShell creates an example Personal Session Desktop deployment consisting of two RDSH instances that are then each mapped to a user. In my environment, both the RDSH instances are VMs running Windows Server 2016. However, technically this example should work with physical and virtual instances and even pre-Windows Server 2016 RDSH instances.

```
#Define the RDSH instances that will be targets within the Personal
#Session Host collection
$RDSH1 = "savdalrdsh01.savilltech.net"
$RDSH2 = "savdalrdsh02.savilltech.net"

#Define the users that will be mapped to desktops
$User1 = "savilltech\john"
$User2 = "savilltech\bond"

#Set the target connection broker (that already exists) and collection name
$CollectionName = "PDSCollection"
$ConnectionBroker = "savdalrds16.savilltech.net"

#Add the RDSH instances to the connection broker
Add-RDServer -Server $RDSH1 -Role "RDS-RD-Server" `
-ConnectionBroker $ConnectionBroker
Add-RDServer -Server $RDSH2 -Role "RDS-RD-Server" `
-ConnectionBroker $ConnectionBroker

#Create the new collection granting users local admin privileges
New-RDSessionCollection -CollectionName $CollectionName `
-ConnectionBroker $ConnectionBroker `
-SessionHost $RDSH1,$RDSH2 `
-PersonalUnmanaged -GrantAdministrativePrivilege

#Map the users to RDSH instances
Set-RDPersonalSessionDesktopAssignment -CollectionName $CollectionName `
    -ConnectionBroker $ConnectionBroker -User $User1 -Name $RDSH1
Set-RDPersonalSessionDesktopAssignment -CollectionName $CollectionName `
    -ConnectionBroker $ConnectionBroker -User $User2 -Name $RDSH2

Get-RDPersonalSessionDesktopAssignment -CollectionName $CollectionName
```

Following is an example execution.

```
PS C:\ > Add-RDServer -Server $RDSH1 -Role "RDS-RD-Server"
-ConnectionBroker $ConnectionBroker
PS C:\ > Add-RDServer -Server $RDSH2 -Role "RDS-RD-Server"
-ConnectionBroker $ConnectionBroker

Server                                  Roles
___                                     __-

savdalrdsh01.savilltech.net             {RDS-RD-Server}
savdalrdsh02.savilltech.net             {RDS-RD-Server}


PS C:\> New-RDSessionCollection -CollectionName $CollectionName
-ConnectionBroker $ConnectionBroker -SessionHost $RDSH1,$RDSH2
```

```
-PersonalUnmanaged  -GrantAdministrativePrivilege

CollectionName                   Size  ResourceType     CollectionType
CollectionDescription
-------                          -------  -------  -----------
PDSCollection                    2       Remote  Desktop   PersonalUnmanaged


PS C:\> Set-RDPersonalSessionDesktopAssignment
-CollectionName $CollectionName `
    -ConnectionBroker $ConnectionBroker -User $User1 -Name $RDSH1
PS C:\> Set-RDPersonalSessionDesktopAssignment
-CollectionName $CollectionName `
    -ConnectionBroker $ConnectionBroker -User $User2 -Name $RDSH2

PS C:\> Get-RDPersonalSessionDesktopAssignment -CollectionName $CollectionName

CollectionName      DesktopName                         User
-------             ------                              --
PDSCollection       SAVDALRDSH01.SAVILLTECH.NET         SAVILLTECH\john
PDSCollection       SAVDALRDSH02.SAVILLTECH.NET         SAVILLTECH\bond
```

Using RemoteFX

Windows 2008 R2 Service Pack 1 introduced two huge technologies. The first was Dynamic Memory, and the second was RemoteFX, which was aimed squarely at VDI environments. The goal of RemoteFX was to provide a consistent experience to end-user devices no matter what the capabilities of that device actually were.

Normally, the Remote Desktop Protocol leverages client-side capabilities for Windows Media playback, such as WMV files, and for desktop composition, such as Aero Glass and Flip 3D (which are now gone from Windows 8 and beyond). If the client device does not support media redirection, the user experience is very basic. Additionally, because the remote operating system is in a virtual machine with no graphical hardware, many types of application technologies cannot run or run as a software-based emulator, such as DirectX, Silverlight, Flash, and so on. This also limited the use of many types of business applications such as videoconferencing.

RemoteFX originally consisted of three technologies: GPU virtualization, enhanced codec, and USB port-level redirection. The technologies associated with RemoteFX have grown since Windows Server 2008 R2, but together they give a great desktop experience remotely. In Windows Server 2008 R2 SP1, the RemoteFX technology was supported only in LAN environments, but this has been extended to WAN scenarios in Windows Server 2012. (There are obvious limitations to graphical fidelity if the connection is too slow.) RemoteFX has been enhanced over new versions to include capabilities such as Multi-Touch, Adaptive Graphics, WAN support, and Media Redirection. I will focus on the original core capabilities, however, especially as they relate to GPU virtualization.

The virtualization of the GPU (known as *para-virtualization*) in the server allows virtual GPUs to be made available to the virtual machines running on the Hyper-V server. The virtual GPUs can be leveraged by Windows 7 SP1 Enterprise/Ultimate, Windows 8/8.1 Enterprise, and Windows 10 Enterprise guest operating systems running in those virtual machines. Windows Server 2016 can also leverage virtual GPUs, which is a new capability for server operating systems when running on Windows Server 2016 Hyper-V hosts. Windows 7 SP1 and beyond included the updated integration services, which allows the guest OS to see the virtualized GPU and use it without additional software installation. The virtual client operating system guest now sees a fully featured GPU, which allows advanced graphics to be rendered on the server side. Then the screen output is sent to the RDP client for display, which includes server-side rendering of rich graphical interface effects, multimedia, and other types of media and applications not previously possible, such as Flash, Silverlight, DirectX applications, and with Windows Server 2016 and Windows 10, Open GL and Open CL applications as well as enhanced capabilities in applications such as PowerPoint and Internet Explorer. Because all of the rendering is performed on the Hyper-V server within the VM, the client capabilities do not matter anymore. You can connect from a full, rich client or a basic, thin client; the experience and graphical fidelity will be the same because all of the graphical processing can be done on the server side. The only requirement is that the end client must support RDP 10 for the best experience with Windows Server 2016.

Once a client VM is RemoteFX enabled and is connected to a RemoteFX-capable client, it will appear as if the VM actually has a GPU and an amount of graphical memory based on the RemoteFX configuration for the VM. Running DXDiag on the client will show the presence of a WDDM graphics driver and the Microsoft RemoteFX Graphics Device along with support for DirectDraw, Direct3D, and AGP Texture acceleration, as shown in Figure 11.13. The version of DirectX 3D supported is 11.1 for Windows Server 2012 R2. Prior to Windows Server 2016, there was OpenGL support in RemoteFX. However, the version of OpenGL supported was very old and was essentially limited to the OpenGL provided out-of-the-box in Windows, version 1.1. This OpenGL did not leverage the GPU but rather the CPU only, making its usage very restricted. Windows Server 2016 changes this and introduces support for Open GL 4.4 and Open CL 1.1, which leverage the GPU in addition to supporting this in generation 2 virtual machines, whereas previously RemoteFX worked in only generation 1 virtual machines. Only Windows Server 2016 and Windows 10 guests can leverage the OpenGL and OpenCL features of RemoteFX. Windows 7 and Windows 8.1 guests can still leverage the DirectX capabilities.

FIGURE 11.13
A RemoteFX vGPU-enabled virtual machine

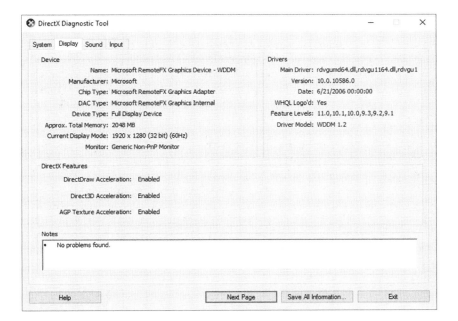

Because the GPU is virtualized, you don't need a discrete GPU for every VM that will be RemoteFX enabled. Just as with CPU virtualization that enables a single logical CPU (such as a core) to be mapped to many virtual CPUs, as the GPU resource is shared among all of the VMs, there will be a limit in terms of the performance improvements that are seen, based on the type of workload and the characteristics of the card. One key consideration when you virtualize the GPU is the amount of graphical memory each VM will need. You can't overcommit GPU memory to achieve the 12:1 ratio. You would need to ensure that the graphics card has sufficient video RAM for all of the VMs. Windows Server 2016 RemoteFX enables a specific amount of VRAM to be assigned to virtual machines up to 1GB, which is a fourfold increase from the 256MB maximum that was dynamically set based on the resolution and number of displays configured in Windows Server 2012 R2. The amount of memory can be configured from the RemoteFX 3D Video Adapter configuration under the Settings of the VM or using the Set-VMRemoteFx3dVideoAdapter cmdlet with the -VRAMSizeBytes parameter. Windows Server 2016 also allows you to set the number of monitors and the resolution independent of the VRAM.

The requirement of a GPU in the Hyper-V server in the Windows 2008 R2 SP1 implementation of RemoteFX was a challenge for many environments that traditionally did not have powerful GPUs in their servers. Windows Server 2012 introduced a basic software rasterizer that allows RemoteFX capabilities in VDI and session-based environments that do not have physical GPUs for some types of graphical capability; however, for rich graphics rendering, you will still require a physical GPU to virtualize.

To use RemoteFX vGPU, the graphics card must support DirectX 11.0 or newer, OpenGL 4 or newer, and it must have a WDDM 1.2 driver or newer. Microsoft has a good blog at http://blogs.msdn.com/b/rds/archive/2013/11/05/ gpu-requirements-for-remotefx-on-windows-server-2012-r2.aspx that walks through some of the GPUs it has tested and recommends.

Once all of the requirements are met, the GPU is enabled for RemoteFX use through the Hyper-V settings in the Physical GPUs section. Figure 11.14 shows my environment that leverages an AMD FirePro V5900 card.

Virtual machines can then have a RemoteFX 3D video adapter added to it via the Add Hardware option in the virtual machine's settings. Note that prior to Windows Server 2016, a RemoteFX 3D video adapter was compatible only with generation 1 virtual machines; it will not be listed as available for a generation 2 virtual machine. When adding the RemoteFX 3D video adapter, you will be prompted to select the maximum number of monitors that may be connected, the maximum resolution for the monitors connected, and the amount of dedicated video memory to assign, which is new to Windows Server 2016, as shown in Figure 11.15. This configuration controls the display settings when connecting and the graphic memory allocated to the virtual machine.

Windows Server 2016 introduces an alternative to RemoteFX for the rich graphical capabilities discussed in Chapter 2, "Virtual Machine Resource Fundamentals." Discrete Device Assignment (DDA) provides the ability to map PCI-Express devices directly to specific virtual machines (pass-through). I mention it again here because DDA is primarily aimed at two types of PCI-Express devices: NVMe storage devices and graphics cards, of which the latter is of interest here. The graphics card vendor has to support DDA through its graphics driver, so not all graphics cards work with DDA. Which should be used, DDA or RemoteFX?

FIGURE 11.14
Enabling a GPU
for use with
RemoteFX

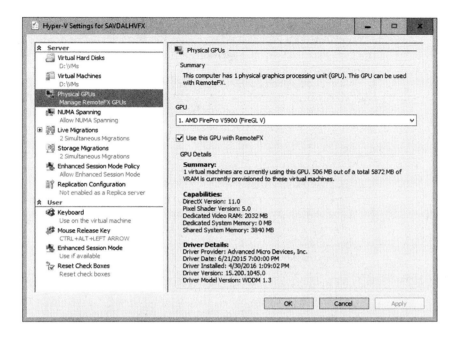

FIGURE 11.15
RemoteFX 3D
video adapter
options for a
virtual machine

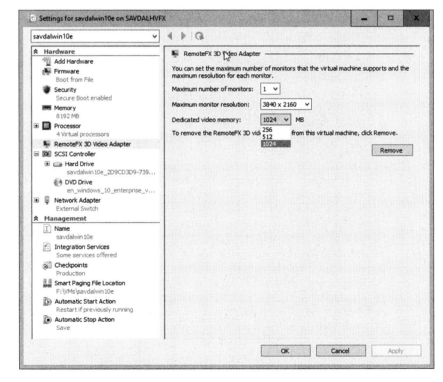

Remember that with Windows Server 2016 DirectX 11.1, OpenGL 4.4 and OpenCL 1.1 are all supported by RemoteFX for use within the VM. Additionally, up to 1GB of VRAM can be applied per VM with support for guests running Windows 7 and above or Windows Server 2012 R2 and above.

With DDA passing a GPU to a VM, it enables the native GPU driver to be used within the VM and all capabilities such as DirectX 12, CUDA, and so on. With DDA, you cannot share the GPU between VMs; it is assigned directly to a specific VM. Additionally, the guest must be Windows 10, Windows Server 2012 R2, Windows Server 2016, or Linux. The Azure N-Series VMs will use the 2016 DDA functionality to enable CUDA as well as to provide graphics acceleration within the VMs.

Generally, use RemoteFX for scale where RemoteFX projects the GPU features required to the VM and can be shared between multiple VMs. Use DDA when you need the full capacity and performance of the graphics card and its native drivers; for example, when using CUDA cards for computational purposes or you need DirectX 12. With DDA, you sacrifice density for application compatibility. Additionally, if you want a Linux VM to have access to a GPU, DDA is the only option.

When you have a GPU-less environment, the WARP capability is used. This software emulation of a GPU using a CPU is what we commonly see in most virtualization environments. With the WARP driver, the graphical performance is low, but there is basic DirectX support.

At the time of this writing, GPU partitioning is not supported by Hyper-V. GPU partitioning works in a similar fashion to SR-IOV; a network adapter supplies multiple "virtual functions" that act like network adapters that are then assigned to VMs, with each VM getting a portion of the adapter's resources. NVIDIA, AMD, and Intel are all working on GPU partitioning technologies to expose their own versions of graphic virtual functions, and I expect at some point in the future Hyper-V will support this.

The new graphical capabilities mean a lot more screen update data and therefore bandwidth. The second original part of the RemoteFX technology package was a new codec that was designed to efficiently encode and decode the display updates associated with the more intensive RemoteFX-enabled workloads. This was the only part of RemoteFX that was available to Remote Desktop Session Hosts in Windows Server 2008 R2 before RemoteFX was more widely available in Windows Server 8. The RemoteFX codec has been greatly enhanced since its original version. Consider a typical highly graphically intense workload. In Windows 7, this workload may have resulted in around 50Mbps of network traffic. With the Windows 8 changes, this same workload resulted in around 5Mbps of traffic, which was reduced a further 50 percent in Windows 8.1 to around 3Mbps of traffic. RDP 10 with Windows 10 and Windows Server 2016 continues this evolution, as once again graphical remoting requirements have changed, with 4K displays becoming far more common. RDP 10 introduces H.264/AVC 4:4:4 mode support that results in less blurry text and better utilization of hardware resources to improve the graphical fidelity and frame rates. This is required because H.264 codecs are typically utilized, which are good for streaming video (such as Netflix), and most graphics cards enable offloading of the processing; but this results in the blurry text, which the AVC 4:4:4 mode codec fixes while still being able to use hardware offloading. This is examined in detail at https://blogs.technet .microsoft.com/enterprisemobility/2016/01/11/remote-desktop-protocol-rdp- 10-avch-264-improvements-in-windows-10-and-windows-server-2016-technical- preview/. The 4:4:4 is enabled by default for RemoteFX vGPU sessions but has to be enabled via policy for all other sessions (DDA and WARP), and once enabled, all content uses 4:4:4 instead of the default Calista codec.

The final piece of the original RemoteFX technology is often overlooked; however, it really completes the ability to have a fully featured remote desktop experience by enabling the redirection of basically any USB device from the local client to the remote session. Prior to the RemoteFX USB redirection feature, there have been advancements in the types of devices that could be redirected to a remote session. We have keyboard, mouse, microphone, smartcard, disk, imaging devices with in-box functionality, and a few others that can be redirected; however, they are all redirected by abstracting the device into one of the supported high-level RDP redirection device types, which means that you can access these devices on the remote session without needing any drivers on the remote OS installed. This also means that you may miss device-specific functionality, and many types of USB devices cannot be redirected that don't fall into these high-level types such as multifunction printers, advanced communication devices, scanners, and barcode readers.

The RemoteFX USB redirection solves this by redirecting at the USB port level in a similar way to how RDP handles the redirection of serial and parallel ports. With the RemoteFX USB redirection, the actual USB request blocks (URBs) are intercepted from the client and sent to the remote session, which means basically that any type of USB device can be redirected using the RemoteFX USB redirection feature. But this does not mean that you no longer want to use the RDP high-level device redirection for devices supported by the RDP high-level redirection. The RemoteFX USB redirection is designed to supplement the RDP high-level device redirection to add support for devices that don't work with the standard RDP redirections, and there are some good reasons for that.

For the RDP high-level supported device redirections, such as input (keyboard/mouse), audio, drive, smartcard, port, printer (Easy Print), and Plug and Play, optimized protocols are used for each of the redirection types to minimize bandwidth usage and ensure the best responsiveness and experience for that type of device. Additionally, the RDP high-level device redirections don't require extra drivers in the remote sessions, and multiple remote sessions can access the same local device simultaneously. Because of these optimizations, the RDP high-level device redirections can be used in both LAN and WAN environments.

Now consider the RemoteFX USB redirection, where you are redirecting at the USB port level to the remote session. Because the port is being redirected, no device/load-specific optimizations can be made. The device driver must be installed in the remote session, since on the remote session it will look like the device has been plugged into a virtual USB port, so it needs the driver to use the device. Also, because you are redirecting at a port level, only one session can access a device at a time, and that includes the local client. If you redirect a device using RemoteFX USB redirection from your local client, no other session can see the device, nor can your local client. Make sure that you don't try to use RemoteFX USB to redirect your keyboard. RemoteFX USB redirection is also optimized for LAN environments and cannot be used on WAN connections like the rest of RemoteFX.

Although the RemoteFX USB redirection is not using any GPU resources, it was tied to the RemoteFX experience in Windows Server 2008 R2 SP1, and the RemoteFX USB redirection could not be used with RDSH or a non-RemoteFX-enabled Windows VDI virtual machine. In Windows Server 2012, this restriction was removed, enabling the RemoteFX USB redirection to be used even when RemoteFX GPU virtualization was not used, such as in session host scenarios.

Remote Desktop Protocol Capabilities

A protocol must be used between the client and the server for the Remote Desktop connection. That server could be an RD Session Host, a client OS running inside a virtual machine that is part of a VDI collection, or even just a regular desktop that someone wants to remotely connect to. Windows uses the Remote Desktop Protocol (RDP) that with Windows Server 2016 and Windows 10 is currently at version 10. As RDP is updated, so too is the Remote Desktop Client (RDC) that is provided as part of Windows.

RDP has improved greatly with each new version, which typically corresponds to new versions of the Windows operating system. For the best experience, the client should support the same version as the server; otherwise, the only features available will be those of the lowest common version. For example, if a Windows 8.1 box running RDP 8.1 connects to a Windows Server 2016 session host that supports RDP 10, the usable features will be limited to those supported by RDP 8.1. Therefore, it is a good idea always to update the RDP client to the latest possible version on your clients. To verify the RDP version supported by your Remote Desktop Client, start the client (`mstsc.exe`) and click About, as shown in Figure 11.16.

FIGURE 11.16
Showing the
supported version
of RDP

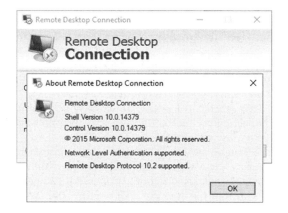

Initially, RDP just had to handle the sending of changes to the display as bitmap updates and passing the keyboard and mouse input. Today, the reality is that a remote desktop could be a user's primary workspace, so RDP has had to evolve to offer a lot more. As RDP has evolved, so too has the built-in RDC, which provides the remote connections over RDP. As enhancements to RDP are made, the RDC is updated to take advantage of the new capabilities. Often the RDC will be updated for the version of Windows that offers the new RDP features, but sometimes a new version of the RDC is created for older versions of the operating system, allowing the older operating systems to be able to connect to newer operating systems and take advantage of new features.

RDP supports virtual channels, which allows different types of traffic and use scenarios for RDP to be enabled, including third parties creating additional capabilities on top of RDP. Up to

64,000 separate virtual channels are available for an RDP connection. The new RemoteFX technology takes advantage of RDP virtual channels to offer its functionality.

Looking at the RDP capabilities today, it quickly becomes apparent that a full desktop experience is possible using an entirely remote session while still accessing local devices including printers. Key capabilities include the following:

◆ Full keyboard, mouse, and touch redirection including keyboard hooking, allowing special Windows key combinations to be redirected to a remote session

◆ Support for 32-bit color and desktop composition, enabling a full Aero Glass experience (no Aero Glass for Windows 8 and newer)

◆ True multimonitor support, enabling discrete displays to be selected for use in a remote session. Prior to RDP 7, while multiple monitors could be used, they were treated as a single display with a combined dimension, which meant dialog boxes would be displayed in the center of a dual display environment. Treating each display separately resolves this.

◆ Multimedia redirection, enabling certain types of media, such as those that typically would be played in Windows Media Player, to be redirected and played natively on the client device if the client device has the capability. This gives cleaner media playback and saves bandwidth. For example, if I played a WMV file in a remote session, the actual WMV primitive is sent over RDP to the local client and rendered locally.

◆ Progressive rendering of images, enabling a lower-quality version of the image to display initially and then increasing in quality as bandwidth allows. Other items on the screen such as text would still be rendered with full fidelity including font smoothing.

◆ Bidirectional audio, enabling sounds to be sent to the local client and from the local client. This enables capabilities such as Voice over IP applications.

◆ Print redirection. The RD EasyPrint functionality driverless printing is available in remote sessions (this also works for Windows 7 target machines and newer).

◆ Reduction of bandwidth and fully configurable experience settings to optimize the experience based on the type of connection, including a great WAN experience

◆ Full encryption where required, using 56- or 128-bit keys, enabling FIPS compliance where needed and Network Level Authentication (NLA) to ensure authenticity of both the server and the client

◆ Clipboard, drive, port, device, and smartcard redirection. Certain types of devices can be redirected to a remote session in an abstracted fashion, which avoids a driver having to be installed for the specific hardware on the remote server. Devices with in-boxes such as cameras are great examples.

◆ Port-level USB redirection with RemoteFX, enabling any USB device to be redirected to a remote session. However, because the redirection is at a port level, the driver for the USB device must be present on the remote server, and the device is available only to one remote session at a time and is no longer available to the local client.

- RDP 8 added automatic network detect, removing the need to select the type of network manually in the Remote Desktop Client.

- RDP 8 added UDP and TCP support to provide the best possible experience over different types of networks.

- RDP 8 added multitouch support with up to 256 touch points (and of course RemoteFX Multi-Touch offers a richer experience where available).

- RDP 8 adds the ability to have nested RDP sessions.

- RDP 8.1 provides dynamic monitor and resolution changes, which supports automatic changing of the display in the remote session as the display of the local client changes; for example, rotating a table or adding a second display.

- RDP 8.1 improved transparent windows and moves/resizes of RemoteApps on the local device.

- RDP 10 adds support for AutoSize zoom. When connecting to older operating systems from a HiDPI client, the remote session would look very small; the Zoom option is available through the RDP icon of your connection.

- RDP 10 adds pen remoting, which enables native pen functionality in the remote session instead of the pen being projected to the remote session as mouse actions.

- RDP 10 adds the aforementioned 4:4:4 codec support.

- RDP 10 adds Remote Credential Guard (often called Remote Guard), which as the name suggests helps protect credentials from attack on a remote system. It does this by keeping the credential locally on your box and not sending it to the remote system. If you try to access another system from the remote session, your local box will request the required tickets for access.

To summarize, as you look at RDP, it is not a basic protocol anymore. It has a huge array of features, it works well over WAN connections, and, even better, Microsoft now provides RDP clients not just for Windows (including the nice-to-use modern Remote Desktop application). Microsoft also provides RDP clients for Mac, iOS, and Android. These clients all support RD Gateway and application publishing.

- iOS: https://itunes.apple.com/us/app/microsoft-remote-desktop/id714464092

- Android: https://play.google.com/store/apps/details?id=com.microsoft.rdc.android

- Mac: https://itunes.apple.com/us/app/microsoft-remote-desktop/id715768417?mt=12

Figure 11.17 shows the published applications from an iOS device on my network. Note that the applications are the same as those that you saw in the RD Web Access site earlier in this chapter and the same ones you would see on a Windows client.

FIGURE 11.17
A view of published
applications on an
iOS device using the
Microsoft client

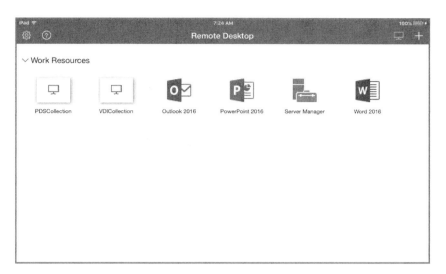

FIGURE 11.17
A view of published
applications on an
iOS device using the
Microsoft client

Using Multipoint Services

Multipoint Services is a new role in Windows Server 2016, which is part of Remote Desktop
Services as a new deployment type, as shown in Figure 11.18. The Multipoint Services role
contains the functionality that was previously in the Windows MultiPoint Server (WMS) 2012
separate product along with some enhancements.

FIGURE 11.18
MultiPoint Services
RDS deployment
type

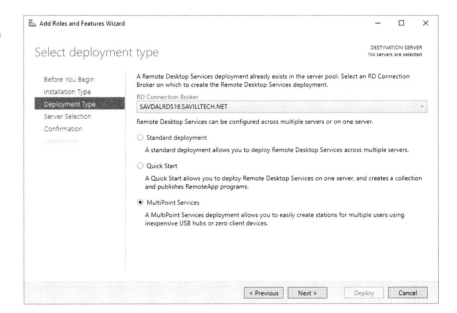

WMS was aimed primarily at educational institutions for use in labs and classrooms. WMS enables multiple users to share a single host computer by connecting multiple keyboards, mice, and monitors to a single machine. Each user has their own Windows 10 experience, which should sound familiar to Remote Desktop Services users. WMS, however, does not require connection brokers or gateways. It is a simpler deployment and a simpler management experience with a great console, the MultiPoint Dashboard, that enables the lab leader to easily see the screen output of everyone connected and even orchestrate actions across them by launching (or even closing) applications. WMS also typically costs less per user than an equivalent RDSH full deployment because the clients can use the zero client hubs, which are between $20 and $50 as compared to more expensive RDP thin clients and desktops. WMS also has disk protection that restores the server to a known good state every time the machine is rebooted, which is useful in classroom environments. The goal is for the users to be in close proximity to the WMS instance. WMS can run as a server-shared OS mode, like RDSH, or it can provide a VDI-in-a-box solution once the customer provides the Windows 10 (or older) media.

A variety of client options are available that are detailed at `https://technet.microsoft` `.com/en-us/library/jj916411.aspx`. However, they primarily fall into three categories:

Direct-Video-Connected Stations   A machine can have multiple graphical outputs that enable multiple monitors to connect to a machine, and each user has their own USB-connected mouse and keyboard via a USB hub to the machine, which is mapped to a specific physically connected display. WMS provides each display/keyboard/mouse set their own Windows 10-like experience.

USB-Zero-Client-Connected Stations   This is similar to the previous type of connection, except in this case a special type of USB zero client is used that connects to the host machine via a single USB connection and then the user's monitor, keyboard, and mouse connect to the USB zero client. This has the benefit of not requiring the machine to have multiple video outputs, but it does require the special USB zero client. Note that a variation exists that is USB-over-Ethernet, where the zero clients connect over the LAN, removing limitations of USB cable length.

Remote Desktop Protocol Clients   This uses the familiar RDP protocol over the network, enabling the use of LAN thin clients and existing machines with an RDP client. Some functionality is lost, such as split-screen, which enables a single display to be split in half to be used by two separate users.

WMS is designed for small-scale deployments. While the 20-user limit has been removed with Windows Server 2016 and there have been substantial scale and performance improvements, it is still not targeted at large-scale deployments, which is where traditional RDSH should be leveraged. With WMS now a core part of Windows Server 2016, its can be expanded beyond educational use to any use case requiring a simple sharing environment (for example, in retail locations), and the MultiPoint Dashboard is useful where the supervisor could see and help the users and remove the need for expensive point-of-sale devices in favor of the cheap zero clients.

Choosing the Right Desktop Virtualization Technology

Earlier in this chapter I talked about how VDI was pushed by some vendors and is the "in thing" right now, but often using session-based desktops is a better solution. How do you decide where to use each type of technology? There is no right answer, and every environment is different.

In this section, I share my insights about where VDI and session virtualization work best, but there are always different opinions. In reality, most companies I work with have a mix of session virtualization and VDI. The key is no matter what approach, or combination of approaches, is used, the same user state, data, and application virtualization can be used for all of them, and the physical desktops in the organization give the user a consistent experience across every device they will ever use—physical, session, or virtual.

I'll quickly recap the key difference between session virtualization and VDI. Figure 11.19 shows session virtualization on the left and VDI on the right. With session virtualization, each user connects to their own session on a shared server operating system such as Windows Server 2016. With VDI, each user connects to their own desktop operating system, such as Windows 10 running inside a virtual machine running on a machine virtualization platform such as Microsoft Hyper-V. As the figure shows, to the end user it looks exactly the same.

FIGURE 11.19
Session-based virtualization and VDI high-level overview

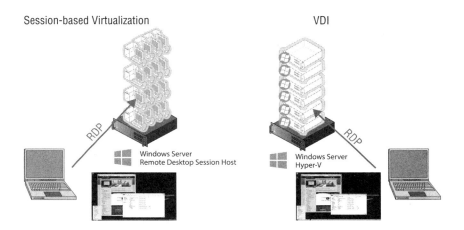

To help you make the right decision, I will cover what is the same and then what is different about using session virtualization and VDI. I explore both from the user's experience and from the infrastructure/management perspective. Both factors must be evaluated to help guide organizations the right way.

What is the same is the desktop environment. With session virtualization, the user is connecting to a server operating system; and with VDI, the user connects to a client operating system. But under the covers, both the server and the client OS share a huge amount of code, so the actual desktop experience will look and feel the same. The users have the same Start screen, same capabilities, and same ability to run the same applications, and each user can still have a unique IP address (a feature of RDS that enables IP virtualization, giving each session or a specific application within the session a unique IP address, required for some applications). The same RDP protocol is used to connect to both environments, which means the same client devices can be used. User settings and data virtualization plus application virtualization can and should be used with both session virtualization and VDI.

The key difference is that with session virtualization, each user has their own session on a shared operating system, while with VDI each user has their own operating system instance. Fundamentally, the difference is in the level of isolation users have from other users. I think of session virtualization as being many people sharing an office, each having their own cubicle, but because they share a room, they have to behave, can't sing loudly, or run about changing the office because it would affect the other users sharing that office. They can do their work in the cubicle and customize their cubicle with pictures on the cubicle walls. I think of VDI as each user having their own heavily padded office; the users can run around, bouncing off the walls screaming, and they won't affect users in other offices.

Session virtualization is a good fit for task-based workers who run things like Internet Explorer, Office, and line-of-business applications but who don't need to customize the operating system. They can still perform customizations of their desktop wallpaper, shortcuts, and applications. A user in session virtualization needs to be locked down so they can't install and uninstall applications or reboot the operating system, which would affect everyone else on the server.

VDI is a good fit for power users, for developers, or for users who run applications that will not run on a server operating system. Basically, if the user needs to modify the operating system or reboot the operating system, then VDI must be used. If you ever hear someone talking about using VDI but needing to heavily lock down the environment because it's being used for task workers who shouldn't change the OS, then they should probably be using session virtualization instead. If there are applications that run only on a client operating system, which is rare, then VDI would also have to be used.

This is why often you will see a mix of session virtualization and VDI being used—specifically, session virtualization for most of the user population and VDI for those power users. The next question is, "Well, wouldn't VDI work for everyone? Why use two solutions if VDI works for all?" That brings us to the other differences between session virtualization and VDI.

Session virtualization uses a server operating system that hosts large numbers of sessions for many concurrent users. This could be hundreds of users on each session host, depending on the applications being run and the amount of memory needed. Each session may use a couple of hundred megabytes of memory, assuming a fairly heavy application workload for each user. If I have a server with 64GB of RAM, I can probably get around 300 users on that box. That's one operating system instance with 300 users.

With VDI, I take the same piece of hardware. I run a hypervisor on it and then create lots of virtual machines, and each virtual machine runs a full client operating system (which has CPU and memory requirements). Then I run the applications on that client OS. Hypervisors have some great memory technologies to get the most from the box, assigning memory only as the OS needs it. Typically, a client OS will need around 700MB of memory just to log on, and then additional memory as applications run, so let's say a very low 1GB of memory per virtual machine. Remember that realistically the actual memory needed could rise to 2GB. On that same server, removing memory for the OS, that may be 62 virtual machines.

On the same server, with session virtualization, I get five times more users than with VDI, and in some environments I see ten times more users on a session-based environment than the same VDI environment. That's a huge difference in bang for the buck for the same hardware. There are other differences that also make VDI more expensive.

The licensing is also different because with session virtualization, an RDS Client Access License is required, but with VDI numerous licenses are needed, depending on the exact solution.

So the issue is not that session virtualization has capabilities beyond VDI, but rather that VDI is more expensive, requires more hardware, and needs more management than session virtualization. This means, where possible, use more session virtualization and save VDI for where it's actually needed.

I've heard of organizations talking about moving to VDI to save money. I've never found this to be the case. If an organization has a poorly managed desktop environment, moving it to the datacenter with VDI will mean a poorly managed VDI and a bigger mess. The move to VDI normally introduces a whole new infrastructure that makes the environment more managed, which in reality could have been used to clean up the physical desktop environment without purchasing all of the hardware for the VDI servers.

What is interesting is when I talk to clients who need to enable BYOD scenarios or overseas contractors, they always talk VDI; they never think of session virtualization. The reason is simply that there are some companies that have only VDI solutions and don't have a session virtualization solution. Therefore, VDI is the solution for everything. If you sell only hammers, then a hammer is the right tool for everything. Take time to understand your requirements and identify the right solution based on the factors I've discussed. To summarize, start with a normal desktop operating system that is well managed. If that is not an option, think session virtualization. If session virtualization is not an option because the users are power users, the users are developers, or the applications will not run on a server OS or run multiple instances on one OS, then use VDI. Remember, you don't have to pick one solution. Use a well-managed desktop environment for corporate assets that can run a modern desktop OS, and use session virtualization and VDI where it fits best. You will likely have all three.

Notice that many times I talk about a well-managed desktop environment. Most companies have good desktops and laptops that can run Windows 10, so just adopting session virtualization or VDI to cut down on the management of the machine is a huge waste of all the resources available on those desktops and laptops. Get the right management infrastructure in place to patch the client operating systems, set up good processes to deploy new operating systems, and use the user settings and data/application virtualization to simplify the environment, and the desktops in your environment will become far less of a help-desk headache.

This does not mean that you should never consider using session virtualization or VDI for your desktops in the organization. What if your organization has not done a desktop refresh for six years and the machines are running Windows XP but on 128MB of memory with a Pentium II processor? That hardware will not run Windows 7; in fact, it's probably barely running Windows XP. I had an experience with a company in just this position that wanted to move to a modern OS but had nowhere near enough budget to refresh 5,000 desktop machines. They set up a farm of remote desktop session hosts and replaced Windows XP with Windows Fundamentals for Legacy PCs, which allows the machine basically to act as an RDP client, and configured the OSs to connect to the new farm of remote desktop session hosts. Each desktop got a new widescreen monitor, keyboard, and mouse, and now when the users logged on, they got a Windows 7 desktop experience (even though it was actually Windows Server 2008 R2; they couldn't tell) and thought they had new PCs. They had no idea they were using session virtualization and RDP. This is one scenario where session virtualization can really save on hardware budget.

I should once again stress that whenever I talk about session virtualization, VDI, and RDP, there are great partners such as Citrix and Quest that build on the Microsoft solutions by offering their own session virtualization and VDI solutions. Look at what Microsoft provides in the box with Windows Server 2016, and if that does not meet your needs, then look at their partner offerings.

I also have not touched on the public cloud, since this is a book on Hyper-V. Nevertheless, when considering your complete solution, leveraging the public cloud may be the right choice. The public cloud can be leveraged in different ways, such as using IaaS to host Remote Desktop

Service–based solutions running in the public cloud. The use of public cloud VMs is a prime reason that Personal Session Desktops was added to Windows Server 2016, but it's also possible to deploy regular Remote Desktop Session Hosts. Additionally, there are actual offerings such as Azure RemoteApp, which through a special client enables users to access published applications directly from the Azure service. These applications can be from Microsoft-provided templates, such as Office, or an organization's own applications enabled through a custom template uploaded to Azure. An organization that has a geographically distributed workforce using Azure may make a lot of sense, or a scenario where organizations are leveraging RDS in DR situations where it will not be required under normal circumstances may also experience the benefits. The consumption-based billing of the public cloud means that you would pay for services only when they were actually required.

The Bottom Line

Explain the types of desktop virtualization provided by RDS.   Windows Server 2016 provides two main types of desktop virtualization: session-based desktops and VDI-based desktops. There are two types of VDI deployments: pooled and personal.

Master It   When should VDI be used over session-based virtualization?

Describe the benefits of RemoteFX and its requirements.   RemoteFX brings various technologies such as USB port-level redirection and improved codecs that with Windows Server 2012 and above are available separately from GPU virtualization, which is the other primary RemoteFX technology that allows a physical GPU to be virtualized and assigned to VDI virtual machines running client operating systems. Using RemoteFX vGPU enables virtual machines to have local graphical resources, which enables the ability to run rich graphical applications, specifically those that leverage DirectX. To use RemoteFX vGPU, the graphics card must support DirectX 11 or newer and have a WDDM 1.2 driver or newer. The processor must also support SLAT.

Master It   Is RemoteFX vGPU a good solution for OpenGL applications?

Articulate the other technologies required for a complete virtualized desktop solution.   The complete user experience comprises numerous layers. The operating system provided by VDI or session virtualization is just the foundation for the user experience. The users need access to their profiles, their data, and their applications. To provide data access, the most common technology is folder redirection. For a user's profile, while historically roaming profiles were used, a better and more granular solution is UE-V, which provides application-level setting replication. For the applications, technologies such as App-V and RemoteApp can be leveraged, while specific core applications could be installed on the RD Session Host or VDI virtual machine template.

Master It   Why is it best to minimize the number of applications installed in the VM VDI template image?

Chapter 12

Microsoft Azure IaaS, Storage, and Networking

Microsoft has long provided solutions that an organization can run in its own datacenters, such as Windows Server, Exchange, SQL Server, and more. Microsoft has also long provided public solutions such as Outlook.com (formerly Hotmail), Windows Update, MSN, Xbox Live, Bing, and Office 365. These services are all software-as-a service (SaaS) solutions, which means that they offer a complete service online. Just as the private cloud gained momentum, so too did the public cloud; that is, the idea of services and applications being available over the Internet. Organizations could bring their own services or entire virtual machines. Microsoft's offering in this space is Microsoft Azure, which has constantly been evolving, with new capabilities added regularly.

This chapter focuses on the Microsoft Azure infrastructure as a service (IaaS) offering, which allows customers' virtual machines to be hosted on Microsoft infrastructure in Microsoft datacenters in a shared, multitenant environment. Additionally, we'll explore Microsoft Azure Storage and networking and how they can benefit organizations in different ways.

In this chapter, you will learn to:

◆ Explain the difference between platform as a service and infrastructure as a service.

◆ Connect Microsoft Azure to your on-premises network.

◆ Move data between on-premises and Microsoft Azure.

Understanding Public Cloud "as a Service"

I briefly introduced the core types of cloud services in Chapter 1, "Introduction to Virtualization and Microsoft Solutions." Figure 12.1 shows the key types of cloud services again so that we can review them as they relate to Microsoft Azure. The image shows the main elements of a service and the boundaries of responsibility for the different cloud service options.

FIGURE 12.1
The key types
of public cloud
services

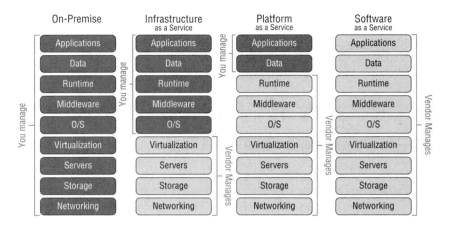

As you move from on-premises to infrastructure as a service (IaaS) to platform as a service (PaaS) and finally to software as a service (SaaS), the elements of the solution that you as an organization are responsible for decrease, until with SaaS there is no infrastructure management at all. Instead, only basic administration may be required, such as deciding which accounts should have which capabilities in the service.

IaaS can be thought of as a virtual machine in the cloud. The provider has a virtual environment, and you purchase virtual machine instances. You then manage the operating system, the patching, the malware definition updates, the backups, the data, and the applications within them. Microsoft introduced an IaaS component to Microsoft Azure in 2012.

PaaS provides a framework in which custom applications can run. Organizations need to focus only on writing the very best application within the guidelines of the platform capabilities, and everything else is taken care of. There are no worries about patching operating systems, updating frameworks, backing up SQL databases, or configuring high availability. The organization just writes the application and pays for the resources used. Microsoft Azure is the classic example of a PaaS, and it was the original focal point for Microsoft Azure.

SaaS is the ultimate in low maintenance. The complete solution is provided by the vendor. There is nothing to write or maintain by the organization other than configuring who in the organization should be allowed to use the software. A commercial example of SaaS is Outlook.com, which is a messaging service on the Internet. An enterprise example is Office 365, which provides a cloud-hosted Exchange, SharePoint, and Lync service, all accessed over the Internet with no application or operating system management for the organization.

The first type of cloud solution, infrastructure as a service, differs from an on-premises solution (where you are responsible for everything) because IaaS enables your focus to shift to the components within a virtual machine. This is because IaaS basically provides the ability to host virtual machines. You can see in Figure 12.1 that the IaaS provider is responsible for the networking, storage, server, and virtualization layer, and then you are responsible for all aspects of the operating system within the VM, the middleware, the runtime, data, and of course the application. While it may seem like IaaS gives the most flexibility, the trade-off is that the amount of management required is still high. Many organizations, however, may first dip their toe into the cloud by using IaaS and then move on to the other types to cut down on management and gain benefits offered with PaaS and SaaS.

Platform as a service drastically changes the amount of management for your organization. With PaaS, you have to worry only about the application you manage and the data, leaving everything else to the PaaS provider. I should point out that although you manage the data, the provider likely still provides services to replicate and protect the data.

Finally, with software as a service, you are responsible for nothing. You just use the cloud-based software. Not every system can be SaaS, because some organizations have their own custom code, but the goal for many organizations is a combination of PaaS and IaaS, and there will always be some systems on premises.

Unless your organization enjoys IT infrastructure management, the end goal is SaaS for everything. With SaaS, the complete service is provided, backed up, updated, and maintained completely for you. Your only work is basic administration. However, only certain types of solutions are available as SaaS. Popular examples include messaging, collaboration, and customer relationship management. Even when a SaaS solution is available, its flexibility may be limited because, remember, the vendor is providing this service for thousands of customers on a shared infrastructure, which limits the amount of customization possible. Therefore, even if a solution is available as SaaS, it may not be a good fit for some organizations.

If a SaaS solution is not available, the next best choice is PaaS. With PaaS, you can focus on just your application, provided you write the application in a language supported by the PaaS offering and stay within its guidelines. The challenge for many organizations is that they have legacy applications that don't fit within the guidelines and the developers have long since left the company, leaving no documentation and no hope of making the application work in a PaaS environment. Additionally, many organizations run applications by third parties who don't follow the guidelines for the application to run in PaaS. Although PaaS is a great solution, many applications are therefore simply not a fit.

Then you get to IaaS, which is essentially just a VM in the sky. Provided that the operating system you wish to use is supported by the IaaS supplier, your application should be able to be moved up to the IaaS environment without modification. This is why IaaS is a big focus for public cloud computing right now. It enables pretty much anything to run, although some restrictions remain that may mean some services stay on premises. These restrictions could be technical, such as scalability or the type of functionality needed, or they could be legal, such as restrictions on certain types of data leaving the company's premises or leaving the country. (IaaS vendors don't have datacenters in every country, which means outside primary locations, a company's hosting may be provided in a datacenter geographically located in another country. Microsoft Azure, however, has a large global footprint.) Restrictions could even simply be a matter of trust. Many organizations are not comfortable with hosting some types of workloads and data off premises because of concerns that initially may be labelled as "security" issues. Realistically, they boil down to a matter of trust, as providers such as Microsoft with Azure maintain levels of certification and pass audits way beyond those as compared to other companies.

I think of IaaS as a great "on-ramp" to the public cloud. If your organization wants to start with public cloud services, start with IaaS. Test specific workloads and then work from there, such as using other types of services and more important workloads.

When Are Public Cloud Services the Best Solution?

I don't think there is a right or wrong answer for this. I know some companies want to move their entire infrastructure to public cloud services and get out of the infrastructure business completely. Other companies want to use the public cloud for disaster-recovery purposes.

Others want to use it for test/dev scenarios. Still others want to use it for specific projects. And some don't want to get anywhere near it!

Each company has specific drivers and factors that guide their public cloud strategy, and once again, they could be based on technical considerations. They can also be based on personal preference, which may not be grounded in fact but is still a real factor in the decision-making process to leverage the public cloud.

At this point, I want to take a step back and talk about a key advantage of the public cloud over on-premises solutions: You pay for what you use. The public cloud operates on consumption-based pricing. Various units are used for pricing with Microsoft Azure, such as computer minutes (a change from the per hour billing Azure used to use), which vary in price depending on the size of the virtual machine that is running and various other configurations. The key point is that if I run 10 four-vCPU virtual machines in Microsoft Azure for 4 hours a month, I pay for only those 4 hours instead of having the cost of running servers all month, which would be the case if they were run on premises.

You also pay for storage, for SQL Server storage, and for bandwidth used out of the Microsoft Azure datacenters. Notice that you don't pay for inbound (ingress) traffic into Microsoft Azure. On the compute side, you are paying for the time that the virtual machine is deployed. Whether the VM is idle or running at full capacity, you pay the same (unless you completely deprovision it, which I cover in more detail later). That is why it's important that you don't create instances and forget to deprovision them.

Many organizations may have certain tasks that run perhaps only once a month but require huge amounts of compute or storage when they run. It is a waste to have all that computer and storage fabric idle for most of the month. This would be a great type of application to run on Microsoft Azure, because you would deploy only the application and scale to many instances during those critical few days each month. Other types of businesses may get really busy on a particular day of the year, and only on that day require thousands of instances of their website VMs and application VMs, while the rest of the year they may need only a hundredth of those instances or perhaps run on premises during that time. The sidebar "Super Bowl Sunday and the American Love of Pizza" takes a look at a great use of Microsoft Azure.

SUPER BOWL SUNDAY AND THE AMERICAN LOVE OF PIZZA

I'll be up front; I'm English, and I don't understand the American football game. I've tried to watch it a couple of times. I even watched the 2006 Super Bowl—it seemed like it took 5 hours for 2 minutes of action, then a 5-minute commercial break, and then a different set of players coming out and moving the ball a couple of yards. It would be hard to get me to watch it again, but nonetheless, it's popular in the United States.

As Americans watch the Super Bowl, they like to eat pizza, and the Super Bowl represents a perfect storm for pizza-ordering peaks. During the Super Bowl, people throughout the entire United States—across all four time zones—are in sync and ordering at the same times, during breaks between the first and second quarters, at halftime, and between the third and fourth quarters. These three spikes require 50 percent more compute power to handle the ordering and processing than a typical Friday dinner time, which is the high point for pizza ordering.

Normally systems have to be built to handle the busiest time, so our pizza company would have to provision a capacity of 50 percent more than would ever be needed just for that one day. Remember also that it's 50 percent more than is needed for dinner time on Friday, which itself is much more than is needed any other time of the week. This would be a hugely expensive and wasteful exercise. Instead, Microsoft Azure is used.

During normal times, there could be 10 web instances and 10 application instances handling the website and processing. On Friday between 2 p.m. and midnight, this increases to 20 instances of each role, and then on Super Bowl Sunday between 12 p.m. and 5 p.m., this increases to 30 instances of each role. I'm making up the numbers of instances, but the key here is that the additional instances exist only when needed, and therefore the customer is charged extra only when additional resources are needed and not at other times. This elasticity is key to public cloud services.

To be clear, I totally understand the eating pizza part!

The pizza scenario is a case of *Predictable Bursting*, which is a known period of increased utilization and one of the scenarios that is perfect for cloud computing. Figure 12.2 shows the four main scenarios in which cloud computing is clearly the right choice. Many other scenarios work great in the cloud as well, but these four are uniquely suited because there are periods of utilization, and with the public cloud, you pay only for what you use.

FIGURE 12.2
The key types of highly variable workloads that are a great fit for consumption-based pricing

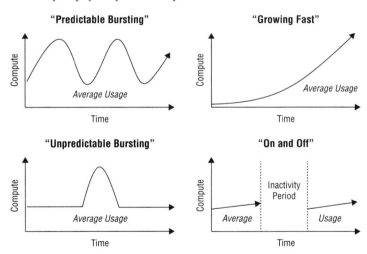

In the Growing Fast scenario, a particular service's utilization is growing rapidly and a traditional on-premises infrastructure may not be able to scale fast enough to keep up with demand. Leveraging the "infinite" scale of the public cloud removes the danger of not being able to keep up with demand.

With Unpredictable Bursting, there may be big bursts in utilization, but the exact timing cannot be planned. With the On and Off scenario, services are needed at certain times but completely turned off at other times. This could be in the form of monthly batch processes that run for only 8 hours a month, or it could be used by a company such as a tax return accounting service that runs for three months out of the year.

Although the use of the public cloud is a no-brainer in these four cases, a public cloud solution is also a good option for many other scenarios (some I hinted at in the beginning of this section). Additionally, while these four scenarios are great for the public cloud, some are also a good fit for hybrid solutions with a mix of on-premises and public cloud services. Consider the various bursting scenarios like our pizza example. The normal baseline could be handled on premises, but the bursts could be expanded out to use public cloud capacity.

For startup organizations, there is a saying, "Fail fast." This does not mean that the goal of the startup is to fail; rather, if it is going to fail, it's better to fail fast because less money is wasted than would be in a long drawn-out failure. The public cloud is a great option for startups because very little up-front capital expenditure is needed to buy servers and datacenter space. Instead, the startup has just operating expenses, paying for the amount of service it actually uses. This is why startups like services such as Office 365 for their messaging and collaboration. They not only don't not need infrastructure, but also don't need messaging administrators to maintain it. Public cloud IaaS is a great solution for virtual machines because, once again, no up-front infrastructure is required and companies pay for what they use. As the company grows, its utilization goes up and so does its operating expenditure, but it's proportional to the business. This type of pay-as-you-go model is also attractive to potential financers because it requires less initial outlay and therefore reduced risk.

If your organization needs a highly available application but you don't have the infrastructure to support the level of availability required, Microsoft Azure is a great fit. This can similarly apply to disaster recovery, and I've seen a lot of organizations interested. Some organizations have a main datacenter but not a second datacenter that can be used for disaster recovery. In this case, leveraging a public cloud IaaS can be a good option for a disaster-recovery plan. There are a lot of considerations. First, for the smoothest failover, the hypervisor used on premises should match that in the public cloud, which for Microsoft Azure would be Hyper-V. Otherwise, messy conversions are required when moving between the hypervisors. The good news when using Azure Site Recovery, however, is that even if VMware is used on premises, there is still seamless replication and failover to Azure and even failback. You also need to consider the best way to keep the virtual machines and templates in Microsoft Azure IaaS current, which definitely is simpler when the same hypervisor is used on premises and in the cloud.

If you have an application that has a fairly short lifetime (maybe related to a specific promotion or advertising campaign), Microsoft Azure is a great fit. The resources are spun up in Microsoft Azure for the duration of the workload and then deleted.

Another popular type of workload is development and test workloads, which are lower priority workloads but also tend to be constantly provisioned and deprovisioned, resulting in a lot of churn and overhead for the on-premises infrastructure and IT team. By moving these workloads to the public cloud, you remove that overhead, and if the organization does not currently have private cloud solutions, then the end-user experience will also be simpler, which will result in faster provisioning times. I urge caution here, though, because the point of testing is to ensure that an application works as anticipated. The operating system, application, and data would look the same running on premises or in a public cloud IaaS, and if the same hypervisor is used, the hardware would also look the same. However, the actual underlying networking and the underlying storage is different, and so while initial development and testing can be performed in a nonproduction-like environment, the final user acceptance testing should be performed on premises to ensure that there is no difference in storage or networking or even the compute that will affect the functionality of the application.

Microsoft Azure has some technical limitations that relate to elements of compute, network, and storage (and I cover them later in this chapter). However, outside of those, there is no workload that couldn't run in Microsoft Azure IaaS.

The decision about whether a workload is a better fit for on premises or the public cloud comes down to how well architected and managed an organization's on-premises resources are and what workloads they've been architected to support. If an organization has implemented an on-premises private cloud, helping to maximize resource utilization, pool all resources, ease the ongoing management, and give fast provisioning capabilities, then many scenarios will be able to be handled efficiently using the on-premises private cloud solution, but for specific scenarios the public cloud might be a better fit. If, on the other hand, an organization has not implemented a good management infrastructure, has not pooled resources, and has many siloed resource islands, which has led to limited scalability and slow provisioning, then the public cloud will be a great fit for many more workloads and scenarios. In Chapter 13, "Bringing It All Together with a Best-of-Breed Cloud Solution," I talk in more detail about architecting the right solution.

Microsoft Azure 101

The focus of this chapter is on Microsoft Azure IaaS and storage, but Microsoft Azure does have other capabilities. This section covers the major ones briefly so that you have at least some basic knowledge of the breadth of Microsoft Azure functionality.

Figure 12.3 shows the four main building blocks of the Microsoft Azure platform. I have concentrated on the Infrastructure services that have compute, storage, and networking, which are the focus of this chapter. Security and Management include services such as the Azure portal, Azure Active Directory, multifactor authentication, automation, and the Marketplace. Hybrid Operations include services such as backup, Site Recovery, and privileged identity management. Platform Services is a small box in the picture, but in reality it is a huge part of what Azure delivers, including the Service Fabric, Cloud Services, Web Apps, SQL Database, Tables, HDinsight, Data Factory, Machine Learning, Media Services, Content Delivery Network, and the list goes on. Azure has about 200 offerings at the time of this writing, and the list is constantly growing.

FIGURE 12.3
The four main building blocks of the Microsoft Azure platform

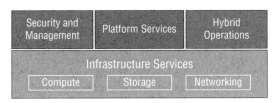

In the next sections, I cover compute, storage, networking, load balancing, and all of the goodness needed to run applications for all of these components. There are Azure regions throughout the world, with each region having multiple datacenters. Regions exist in the United States, Europe, Asia, Japan, China, Australia, India, Canada, and Brazil, with more being added each year. The full list can be found at https://azure.microsoft.com/en-us/regions/. When an application is deployed to Microsoft Azure, the customer can select where the application should be deployed. All regions in Microsoft Azure are paired to protect the data replicated between them in the event of a site failure.

In the following sections, I cover the main services available in Microsoft Azure, but keep in mind that Azure is constantly changing. For the most up-to-date list of available services and more details, I recommend viewing www.windowsazure.com/en-us/services/.

Microsoft Azure Compute

The main building block of the Microsoft Azure platform is Microsoft Azure infrastructure services, which provides key capabilities to enable cloud-based hosting of applications and data. Microsoft Azure has evolved, and so have the names of the types of services and where they sit in the hierarchy. If you looked at Microsoft Azure a year ago, the components would have seemed different from those I describe today.

The fundamental building block of everything is the virtual machine. This is the part that runs the applications, which could be a website, custom middleware code, or a legacy application. All of the compute capabilities are enabled through virtual machines that vary in size. While virtual machines are directly accessible and used with Microsoft Azure IaaS, other services such as PaaS, websites, networking, and so on are also built using virtual machines, although they may not be visible to you. The IaaS virtual machines are something I focus on in this chapter.

Many platform services have the benefit of enabling the user to step up a level and no longer worry about virtual machines and rather focus on their application and service. Examples include Web Apps and the Service Fabric in addition to Analytics services like Machine Learning and Data Lake. As mentioned previously, a huge number of services are offered under the Platform Services umbrella, and while the focus of this chapter is IaaS, this should not be the first choice unless as an organization maintaining virtual machines is appealing!

Microsoft Azure does not automatically scale instances of most IaaS roles, unlike many PaaS solutions. For example, if you had five IaaS VMs and the instances were running at full capacity, it would not add two more automatically. Instead, through the Microsoft Azure website, it is easy to request additional instances of a role, which are instantly deployed, or you can leverage Windows Azure Pack on premises, or you can programmatically request new instances, allowing you to write your own autoscaling functionality. If scaling is required for VMs, VM Scale Sets enable the automatic creation of VMs, provided they are all identical, based on a single template. Then there is the Fabric Controller itself. Microsoft Azure seems like magic. As a customer, I deploy my application and Microsoft Azure spins up as many instances as I tell it to. I can scale up or scale down at any time. My service is always available per the Microsoft Azure 99.95 percent monthly service-level agreement (SLA), and the operating systems and dependent services are constantly patched and tuned. This magic is enabled by the Microsoft Azure Fabric Controller, which itself is a distributed application running on Microsoft Azure that has a fabric agent running on all of the virtual machines (except for those that are IaaS VMs) and hosts that make up the Microsoft Azure Compute fabric. The Fabric Controller constantly monitors, and if it sees a problem, it can spin up new instances of a role. If a request is made for more instances of a role, the Fabric Controller creates the new instances and adds them to the load balancer configuration. The Fabric Controller handles all patching and updates (again, apart from those VMs that are IaaS VMs), and this is a key reason that to be covered by the 99.95 percent SLA, you must deploy at least two instances of any role placed in an availability set. The Fabric Controller will take down one instance to patch, and then once it's running again, it will take down the other. As you have more and more instances, more instances can be patched simultaneously based on groupings of role instances called *upgrade domains*. When patching occurs, all instances within an upgrade domain are brought down and updated at the same time, and then when the update is complete, the next upgrade domain is updated, and so on. Availability sets also distribute instances between fault domains, which can be thought of as racks in an Azure datacenter to ensure that if there is a rack-level problem, the entire service is not taken down.

Previously Azure leveraged the Azure Service Manager (ASM) to manage resources that Azure IaaS was built on, which is why VMs were created in Cloud Services. However, many limitations existed, such as a lack of parallel action execution, which limited the ability to provision services quickly, no role-based action control to finely assign permissions, and limited ability to deploy services in an idempotent fashion. Today Azure has moved to Azure Resource Manager (ARM), which has been redesigned to address the previous limitations of ASM and enhance its capabilities. Key features of ARM are as follows:

- ◆ IaaS no longer utilizes cloud services.

- ◆ Massive parallelism enables hundreds of resources to be created in the same time as one with ASM.

- ◆ Resources live in a Resource Group.

- ◆ Role-based access control is available at a resource and Resource Group level.

- ◆ Perform JSON-based deployment of workloads.

While a resource must exist in one and only one Resource Group, this does not stop resources in different Resource Groups from working together. For example, a VM in one Resource Group can use a virtual network that is in a different Resource Group. Resource Groups can be heterogeneous or homogeneous. In a heterogeneous example, you would place all resources that share a common life cycle—such as a storage account, NIC, virtual machine, Azure SQL Database, and a web app—that offer a particular service in a common Resource Group to enable easy visibility, billing, and management. A homogeneous example is a Resource Group for all storage accounts, another for virtual networks, and so on. There is no right or wrong approach. If your organization separates management into different groups for storage, networking, and computing, then having separate Resource Groups for each type of resource would aid in the delegation of management. If instead each project has its own resources that share a common life cycle, using a heterogeneous approach will fit closest with how you actually leverage Azure.

Capabilities of Azure IaaS and How It Is Purchased

Let's start with a completely strange example of Microsoft Azure IaaS in action. My goal is to stress an important point that will aid in your understanding of exactly what IaaS is: IaaS simply provides virtual machines in the cloud. What you do with those virtual machines is pretty much up to you, provided that the usage is within the capabilities exposed by the IaaS provider. Remember, in our private cloud it was possible to create capability profiles that defined which features were available and what a virtual machine could look like, such as, for example, how many vCPUs it could have, how much memory, how many disks. Just as with a private cloud, you can choose what storage to expose and what the networking will look like. This is exactly the same with Microsoft Azure IaaS, and as with any IaaS solution, you create virtual machines within the capabilities allowed, and then within the virtual machines you install operating systems that are supported by Microsoft Azure IaaS or use some of the provided templates in Microsoft Azure IaaS or even use your own. Behind the scenes, at the time of this writing,

Microsoft Azure runs on Windows Server 2012 R2 Hyper-V and will move to Windows Server 2016, but it is not a special version. It's the same Hyper-V that you and I run.

To stress this, one of the first projects I ask people to perform is to spin up a Minecraft server in Microsoft Azure IaaS. If you don't know what Minecraft is, go ask some kids. They'll tell you it's a popular building game. A Minecraft server allows multiple people to play together to build worlds. It's a Java application that was never designed to run in a public cloud service, so it's a great example to show that you can run almost anything in an IaaS solution and, specifically, in Microsoft Azure IaaS. It also helps demonstrate some of the key concepts that I describe in more detail throughout the rest of this chapter.

Before you get started, you will need a Microsoft Azure account. Your organization may already have Microsoft Azure but may not want you to create a Minecraft server using the corporate account. There are various ways to get Azure services:

◆ If you have an MSDN subscription, depending on the subscription level, you have a quota for Microsoft Azure included. Activate this subscription via the MSDN subscription site, and under your My Account details, you will see the subscription benefits. One of these is Microsoft Azure, and there is a link to activate it. Once it's activated, you will have a certain amount of Microsoft Azure credit each month. For example, MSDN Visual Studio Ultimate subscriptions receive $150 of Microsoft Azure credit each month and reduced prices for the consumption of resources, as detailed at www.windowsazure.com/en-us/offers/ms-azr-0049p.

To put this into perspective, at the time of this writing, it costs around $45 to run a single vCPU VM in Microsoft Azure for an entire month. This means that I could run three small virtual machines all month in Microsoft Azure with the Ultimate MSDN subscription.

◆ Sign up for a one-month free trial with $200 of credit (the cost at the time I was writing this) at https://azure.microsoft.com/en-us/free/. This is a great way to learn Microsoft Azure for free.

◆ As an organization, pre-buy a certain amount of Azure spending as part of an Enterprise Agreement, which provides a discount for Azure services in addition to access to the Enterprise Portal that enables departments and accounts to be created in a delegated model and also provides great insight into the billing of services.

◆ Pay as you go for services by using a credit card or other agreement.

Once you have a subscription, you manage Microsoft Azure via https://portal.azure.com. Through this portal, you can perform nearly every aspect of Microsoft Azure management. Previously, you had to supply a credit card number even if you had included Microsoft Azure credit, but Microsoft removed this requirement and instead will now simply shut down your services if you run out of credit. If you want to remove the spending limit, this can be done via the account page by using a credit card, but it does mean you could be billed if you go over the included credit amount.

When you first connect to the portal, you will be presented with the dashboard that shows basic information about the health of the various Azure regions, which can be selected for more information. From the navigation menu on the left of the portal, you can view existing resources and create new ones. The portal is highly configurable, enabling tiles to be added to the dashboard and tiles resized as required. To see basic information about the subscription, choose Browse ➢ Subscriptions from the navigation menu. Select your subscription, and a new blade (a vertical pane made up of lenses with specific aspects of information) will be displayed with information about the subscription, including how Azure spending has been consumed, estimated future spending, and the amount left, as shown in Figure 12.4.

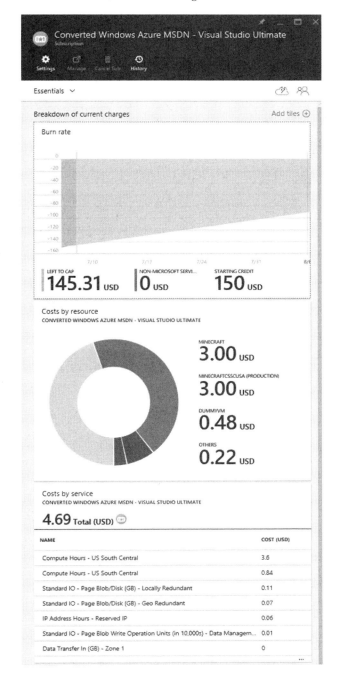

Now that you have a Microsoft Azure subscription, follow the step-by-step tutorial I have uploaded at `https://youtu.be/YuMXm7owGEw`. This walks you through every step of creating a new virtual machine in Microsoft Azure, adding a data disk, installing Minecraft, enabling access from the Internet, and then connecting. It will probably take about 45 minutes, but I recommend that you stop and do this now. Even if you don't want to play Minecraft (your kids will think you are a hero if you do this for them), the video walks you through key elements of using Microsoft Azure IaaS. In the next section, I explain the details of creating virtual machines. But for now, I want to stress some key points to keep in mind:

◆ An extra-small Azure virtual machine would be fine for fewer than 10 users; however, consider a small VM for more than that, and unless you are very short on credit, I recommend using a small VM for even fewer than 10 users.

◆ Use the Windows Server 2012 R2 Datacenter gallery image. Use the version with the latest release date, which is just a patch level.

◆ Create a separate data disk to store the Minecraft server executable and its data files. You will need to initialize and format this disk by using Disk Management (`diskmgmt.msc`).

◆ Install the 64-bit version of Java. At the time of this writing, the Java Runtime Environments were available from the following location: `http://java.com/en/download/`.

◆ Download the latest version of the Minecraft server from `https://minecraft.net/download`, and save to the Minecraft folder you create on your data drive.

◆ Create a firewall exception for TCP port 25565 within the guest OS, which is what Minecraft listens on.

◆ Create an exception for the Network Security Group (NSG) used by the VM in the Azure portal for public and private port 25565 to enable external communication to the port on the VM.

◆ Add your Minecraft account name to the `ops.json` file to make yourself an operator on the server. I cover this in more detail at `http://savilltech.com/blog/creating-a-minecraft-server-using-the-new-azure-portal/`.

◆ To run the Minecraft server, I use the following command, which gives Minecraft 1GB of memory instead of 100MB. Save this to a `start.bat` file and use it to initialize.

```
"C:\Program Files (x86)\Java\jre1.8.0_91\bin\java " -Xms1024m -
Xmx1024m -jar Minecraft_Server.jar
```

You now have an up-and-running Minecraft server that you can access by using the name that you specified during the VM instance creation, as shown in Figure 12.5. There was nothing special that was Microsoft Azure IaaS-specific except creating the endpoint to allow connectivity over the Internet. (And thanks to my son for creating the likeness of me on his Microsoft Azure Minecraft server.) Notice also in the figure that through the Microsoft Azure portal, I can see the various resource usage states of the virtual machine. This helps me check whether my son is playing when he should be doing his homework. Notice that you have full console access to this virtual machine and can do anything you want within the capabilities of Microsoft Azure IaaS.

FIGURE 12.5
A connection to my Minecraft server running in Microsoft Azure

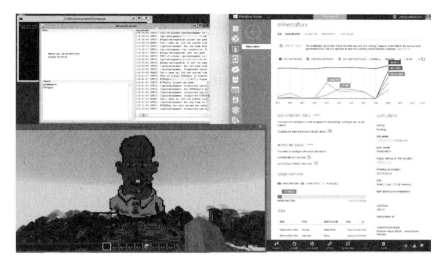

It should be noted that the Microsoft Azure IaaS virtual machine is not the same as the previously available VM role that was part of PaaS; that was a stateless virtual machine that had no persistent state. The Microsoft Azure IaaS virtual machine is a fully persistent solution.

Let's look at the capabilities of Microsoft Azure IaaS in more detail, starting with the list of supported operating systems. Microsoft Azure IaaS supports only 64-bit operating systems, specifically these:

◆ Windows Server 2008 R2 SP1

◆ Windows Server 2012

◆ Windows Server 2012 R2

◆ Windows Server 2016

◆ A number of Linux distributions, which is constantly expanding but includes Oracle Linux, openSUSE, SUSE Linux Enterprise Server, Red Hat Enterprise Linux (RHEL), Ubuntu Server, and OpenLogic (CentOS). The full list can be found at `https://azure.microsoft.com/en-us/documentation/articles/virtual-machines-linux-endorsed-distros/`.

One easy way to check supported operating systems is to look at the templates provided in Microsoft Azure itself through its Marketplace. However, just because an image is not provided in the Marketplace does not mean that it is not supported in Azure. Figure 12.6 shows the Marketplace search results screen that you see when creating a new virtual machine; in this example, I have searched for *Linux*. The Marketplace contains not only OS templates but templates containing applications and virtual appliances. You do not have to use these templates. You can create your own sysprep'd images, but do *not* put an `unattend.xml` answer file in the image (Microsoft Azure needs to create that when deploying) and do not install the Microsoft Azure integration components. Once your image is ready, you upload the templates to Microsoft Azure and use them. The included Microsoft Azure templates are just there to help you get started. Microsoft has a step-by-step guide on uploading your own VHD to Microsoft Azure at the following location:

www.windowsazure.com/en-us/manage/windows/common-tasks/upload-a-vhd/

FIGURE 12.6
The template selection output in Microsoft Azure when searching for Linux

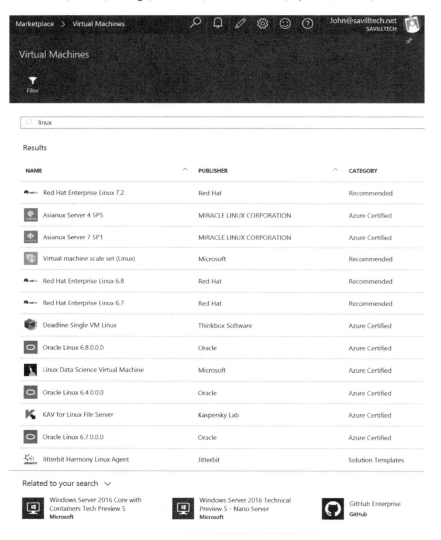

Regarding what can run in the Microsoft Azure IaaS virtual machine, remember that it is just a virtual machine. However, this does not mean that vendors support their applications running in Microsoft Azure IaaS. Notice that Microsoft has templates in Microsoft Azure IaaS for SharePoint, SQL Server, Visual Studio, and BizTalk, but that's not the only Microsoft software that is supported. Microsoft has a full list at `http://support.microsoft.com/kb/2721672/en-us`, which also shows which components of System Center can run in Microsoft Azure IaaS and which roles of Windows Server run in Microsoft Azure. Remember, there is a difference between what is supported and what works, but do you really want to run something for production purposes that is not supported by the vendor of the application?

By default, an agent is installed in all Azure IaaS VMs. This agent is for your benefit as a customer and lights up certain capabilities. For example, the VM agent enables local passwords to be reset and remote desktop connectivity to be enabled within the VM by the VM owner through the portal and through PowerShell. Additionally, the VM agent can be used to allow the Azure fabric to use declarative technologies such as PowerShell DSC, Chef, and Puppet to perform configuration in addition to other types of services, such as malware definition updates and more.

The virtual machines created can be one of a set of defined series and sizes. You cannot create custom combinations of vCPUs and memory. At the time of this writing, various series of Azure VMs have their own memory, CPU, storage, and networking capabilities. The key VM series available are as follows:

A Series The original Azure VM series that has a wide range of CPU and memory combinations. The temporary storage for these VMs is HDD based.

D Series Similar combinations for CPU and memory to the A series, but the temporary storage for the VM is SSD based

F Series High memory sizes—each CPU core has 2GB of memory and 16GB of SSD-based temporary storage. For example, an F2 has two vCPUs, 4GB of memory, and 32TB of temporary storage.

G Series G is for Godzilla. Very large sizes all the way up to a G5, which has 32 cores, 448GB of memory, and 6TB of SSD-based temporary storage

N Series Provides nVidia CUDA cards available to the VM using Discrete Device Assignment (DDA) in various combinations for compute and graphical purposes

Servers are deployed around 1,000 at a time in Azure, and a deployment unit is called a *stamp* (also known as a *scale unit* or *cluster*). All servers in the stamp are the same. Over time, hardware changes so that new generations of stamp are deployed with new capabilities and faster processors. There are also v2 versions of some series, which have faster processors but cost the same as the v1. The reason that they are differentiated as a series is to ensure performance consistency to the customer, as opposed to on one day, a VM created on one stamp in Azure gets an old processor, and then on the next day the VM is created on a new stamp and the VM runs 30 percent faster because it is on newer processors. Customers can choose whether they want the v1 or v2 levels of performance. Azure measures CPU performance using Azure Compute Units (ACU), which are documented at `https://azure.microsoft.com/en-us/documentation/articles/virtual-machines-windows-sizes/#performance-considerations`.

The aforementioned article lists all sizes for all available series. Table 12.1 contains a subset of the sizes available for the A series to demonstrate some of the combinations of CPU and memory, in addition to temporary storage and network resource differences.

TABLE 12.1: Subset of Microsoft Azure IaaS Virtual Machine Sizes for A Series

SIZE	CPU CORES	MEMORY	TEMPORARY STORAGE (GB)	MAXIMUM NUMBER OF DATA DISKS	MAXIMUM NUMBER OF NETWORK ADAPTERS
Extra Small (A0)	Shared	768MB	20	1	1
Small (A1)	1	1.75GB	70	2	1
Medium (A2)	2	3.5GB	135	4	1
Large (A3)	4	7GB	285	8	2
Extra Large (A4)	8	14GB	605	16	4
A5	2	14GB	135	4	1
A6	4	28GB	285	8	2
A7	8	56GB	605	16	4
A8	8	56GB	382	16	2
A9	16	112GB	382	16	4
A10	8	56GB	382	16	2
A11	16	112GB	382	16	4

Source: https://azure.microsoft.com/en-us/documentation/articles/
virtual-machines-windows-sizes/

The sizes also refer to the number of data disks that can be connected, which can be up to 1TB each and have a 500 IOPs limit (for a standard pricing tier VM. For the A series, a Basic pricing tier also has a 300 IOPS per disk limit and restricted set of features, which are designed for test/dev scenarios where the cheapest possible cost is desired). You can view the exact type of processor that your VM is using by looking in Task Manager at the processor details. The exact cores will vary based on the VM series, datacenter, and generation of the servers being used; my current virtual machine is using Intel Xeon CPU E5-2673 v3 (Haswell) cores.

Notice that the different-sized virtual machines have different sizes for the temporary storage disk, which can be used for any temporary data (think scratch space) that does not need to be persisted (that is, sustained).

The Windows pagefile is also stored on this temporary storage. Anytime the VM is moved, such as for patching, upgrades, or simply because of a node problem, the contents of the temporary disk will be lost. Figure 12.7 shows the view of my Minecraft Azure IaaS virtual machine, which has the standard 127GB operating system disk, the 70GB temporary disk, and a 100GB data disk that I added.

FIGURE 12.7
Disk view within
a Microsoft Azure
IaaS virtual
machine

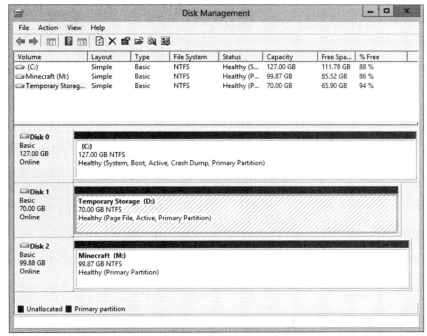

Notice that the A8 is the same as the A10, and A9 is the same as A11. The difference is that the A8 and A9 also have RDMA network adapters providing 40Gbps of bandwidth between them, making them useful for high-performance computing solutions that need massive pipes between the instances. The A10 and A11 don't have the RDMA network adapters. More information on these RDMA adapters can be found at https://azure.microsoft.com/en-us/documentation/articles/virtual-machines-windows-a8-a9-a10-a11-specs/.

If you walked through the Minecraft tutorial, you will have noticed that you did not specify an IP address or a number of network adapters. A Microsoft Azure IaaS VM by default has only a single network adapter, and its IP address is allocated by the Microsoft Azure fabric using DHCP. There is some control of the virtual networks in Microsoft Azure that I cover later, but you can never specify a static IP address within the VM. The IP address must be allocated by Microsoft Azure. Additionally, a single adapter can have only a single IP address—the one set by Microsoft Azure. If you set the IP address statically, at some point you will lose access to your virtual machine. The good news is that using Azure virtual networks, you can do some clever things to make sure that a virtual machine always gets the same IP address within ranges that you configure. For communication, you can use TCP, UDP, and any IP-based protocol within the virtual network in Microsoft Azure, but you cannot perform broadcast communications.

Hopefully, at this point it is clear that Microsoft Azure IaaS is giving you various-sized virtual machines with which you can do pretty much anything you wish, provided that you stay within the capabilities of Microsoft Azure IaaS that I briefly covered earlier. The next question is, "How much does it cost?"

Azure is not broken into separate buckets of credit. You have a certain amount of Azure credit, and you can use it however you want: for storage, VMs, websites, SQL databases, services, and so on.

You are charged for the services that you use under your Azure account, and different services and different sizes of service vary in price. The easiest way to understand the cost of various services is to use the Microsoft Azure pricing calculator available at `azure.microsoft.com/en-us/pricing/calculator`. The calculator allows you to specify the quantity of services you need, and then it shows the monthly price. Note that discounts are available as part of various plans and agreements with Microsoft. Figure 12.8 shows part of the virtual machine section of the pricing calculator, where I have requested pricing to run 10 small Windows and 10 small Linux virtual machines along with 1TB of geo-redundant storage. I also specified 200GB of egress (outbound) traffic from Microsoft Azure. It shows me the estimated monthly price of the requested virtual elements.

FIGURE 12.8
Sample of the
Microsoft Azure
pricing calculator

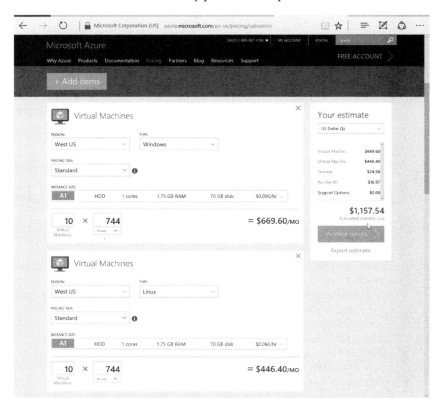

You may wonder why the price of a Linux virtual machine is less than the price of a Windows Server virtual machine if all that is being provided is the virtual machine. You are actually getting more than that with a Windows Server virtual machine. The Windows Server license is part of the price of the VM instance, which means that you don't need to separately license the Windows Server operating system running in Microsoft Azure. Note that as your Windows Server licenses are covered by Software Assurance, the Hybrid Use Benefit (HUB) enables a discount to be applied to Azure usage equivalent to the price difference between a Linux and Windows VM, which essentially boils down to enabling you to bring the Windows Server licenses that you own on-premises over to Azure. More details on this offer can be found at `https://azure.microsoft.com/en-us/pricing/hybrid-use-benefit/`.

That is not the case for any paid Linux distributions or other applications such as SQL Server. These have to be separately licensed unless when creating the virtual machine, you select a SQL Server or BizTalk Server image that includes the SQL Server/BizTalk Server license as part of the virtual machine price. Also note that if you want to manage virtual machines running in Microsoft Azure with System Center, you need to license System Center accordingly.

If you intend to host a long-term SQL server deployment in Microsoft Azure, it is likely cheaper to install a regular Microsoft Azure Windows Server virtual machine and then install SQL Server and use your own SQL license. If you need SQL Server short term, such as for a specific project, then using the Microsoft Azure SQL image with included SQL Server license is likely more cost-effective than buying a license.

There is an important point about virtual machines and how the billing works. Prior to June 2013, a virtual machine was charged while it existed, whether it was running or not. A big change was announced in June 2013 at TechEd related to Microsoft Azure—stopped virtual machines would no longer be billed, and billing would be per minute instead of rounded to the nearest hour. This makes it sound like all you have to do is to shut down the virtual machine and you stop paying for it, but this is not the case.

There are two types of shutdowns for a Microsoft Azure IaaS VM. A virtual machine can be stopped and it can be deallocated. It's only when a virtual machine is deallocated that billing stops, but this also affects the IP address of the virtual machine.

If you stop a VM from within the guest OS of the VM, or you use the `Stop-AzureRmVM` cmdlet with the `-StayProvisioned` parameter, the VM stays allocated in the Microsoft Azure fabric. The VM still has reserved resources, and it will keep the IP address it was dynamically assigned via DHCP (Dynamic IP, or DIP). A VM shut down this way is considered stopped, but not deallocated, which means that it will continue to be billed. Its status in the Microsoft Azure portal will show as Stopped.

If you stop a VM from the Microsoft Azure portal by using the Shut Down button, the VM is actually deallocated from Microsoft Azure resources. It no longer has resources reserved, and it loses its network configuration and therefore its IP address lease. When you start the VM, it is reprovisioned in Microsoft Azure, resources are assigned, a network adapter is added, and it gets a new IP lease, which means that its IP address will change. This type of deprovisioning also happens when the `Stop-AzureRmVM` cmdlet is used without the `-StayProvisioned` parameter. The VM will show as Stopped (Deallocated) and VMs in this status will not incur any billing.

Here's a summary:

◆ Shutdown within the VM or `Stop-AzureVM -StayProvisioned`: Billing continues for the VM, and it keeps resources reserved, including keeping its leased IP address.

◆ Shutdown from Microsoft Azure portal or `Stop-AzureVM` without `-StayProvisioned`: Billing stops for the VM, and all resources are deprovisioned, including network adapters, which means that the IP address lease is lost.

This is critical to understand, because when using cloud services, you will use VMs differently from how you use them on premises. On-premises VMs run 24/7—since you have the hardware, why wouldn't you run them all the time? If VMs are shut down and consolidated, it would be possible to power down certain hosts, which would save some electricity. However, the additional work required to orchestrate this behavior and understanding of when services are required is not a worthwhile investment of effort for 99.9 percent of organizations. In the cloud, the behavior has to change, as you pay for the time that the VM is running. In the pricing calculator example, I showed that the VMs were set as running 744 hours a month, which means running 24 hours a day, every day of the month. However, it's unlikely that every VM has to run every minute of every day. Consider a website that consists of 20 IIS VMs. All 20 may be needed during the day, but at night maybe only half are needed, which in Azure means that you would shut them down and save that money. If your services are not needed during the weekend, they would be shut down so that you don't pay for them. An assessment would be performed on the environment to understand the real resource requirements throughout the month so that instances can be stopped and started to optimize spending. The Microsoft Assessment and Planning toolkit can assist you with this in addition to scaling capabilities in Azure.

One scenario that commonly comes up is desktop as a service (DaaS), offering desktop environments in the public cloud. Microsoft Azure has its own application publishing service called *Azure RemoteApp*, which can publish Office applications through a provided template or your own custom application through your own custom template, and there is nothing to stop you from creating your own deployment for your organization. Microsoft has guidance on the configuration of Remote Desktop Services (RDS) in Microsoft Azure, which will give you a session-based desktop experience. This guidance can be found at the following location:

http://msdn.microsoft.com/en-us/library/windowsazure/dn451351.aspx

What you cannot do is run Windows client operating systems in Microsoft Azure (or any other public cloud service, for that matter). This is not a technical limitation but rather a licensing one. There is no way to license a Windows client to run in a public cloud environment. That is why any DaaS offerings that you see are based around sessions running on Windows Server as opposed to connections to an actual Windows client operating system. Even if a Windows client could be run in Azure, you would still not be able to run a VDI solution, as VDI requires agents to run on the hosts to help manage the state of VMs, and it is not possible to deploy agents on Azure hosts. The good news, as discussed in the previous chapter, is that using session-based services gives the same end-user experience and a higher density of users, so it's a win-win. Also, Windows Server 2016 has Personal Session Desktops, which provide a way to give specific users a specific hosted desktop, and it does not require an agent on the compute host.

Creating Virtual Machines in Azure IaaS

Now that you understand the basics of Microsoft Azure IaaS, let's focus on some key aspects of using the Microsoft Azure management portal, explain some of the options, and then walk you through a simple creation using PowerShell.

As previously mentioned, the management of Microsoft Azure can be performed through the Microsoft Azure management portal at https://portal.azure.com. Through the portal, you have access to all of the various datacenters that can host Microsoft Azure services, and where you wish to host your Microsoft Azure infrastructure is one of the first things that you need to decide. You should pick the location closest to where the services will be consumed because this will result in the lowest network latencies.

If you followed the video on creating a Minecraft VM, you would have seen that two constructs are required to create a virtual machine: a virtual network on which to place the VM's NIC and a storage account to host the VHD file that will be used by the virtual machine. During the creation of the virtual machine, you can use an automated virtual network and an automatically generated storage account, or you can create them in advance manually. In most cases, you should create the virtual network and storage accounts in advance along with the Resource Groups. Otherwise, every VM will be siloed in its own network, thereby limiting communication. Both the virtual network and the storage account can and often should be used by more than just the virtual machines, but they can also be used for the other types of roles available within Microsoft Azure. A VM can use a virtual network and storage account only in the same region as where the VM is being created. It would not be efficient to have virtual machines running in one datacenter using storage in another datacenter, hundreds of miles away.

The Microsoft Azure management portal is intuitive, and the only information needed to create a VM is the name of the VM and a region in which you wish to create it. Creating a storage account is a similar intuitive process; simply give a unique name for the storage account URL and pick the location. Because the storage account name must be unique throughout all of Azure, simple names are unlikely to be available, so focus on using something containing an aspect of your organization's name. You can also select the replication options for the storage account, which can be locally redundant or geo-redundant. A virtual network is also easy to create; the only critical information is the region and the IP address space, which must not overlap with any IP address space used on premises or in other virtual networks.

When I am starting in Azure, I think about creating resources in the following order:

1. How will I create subscriptions? Will I have an Enterprise Agreement (EA) and delegate department and account administrators to create the subscriptions for various projects?

2. Plan the Resource Group model that will be used (heterogeneous vs. homogeneous) and the role-based access control used. Create the Resource Groups.

3. Create virtual networks in the regions required in the pre-created Resource Groups.

4. Create storage accounts in the regions required in the pre-created Resource Groups with the desired resiliency option configured.

5. Agree on how resources in Azure will be accessed. Will a site-to-site VPN or ExpressRoute be used for access to VMs via their private IP addresses? For services published to the Internet, will Public IPs be assigned directly to VMs or to a load balancer that can use forwarding rules to VMs?

6. Create virtual machines using the existing resource groups, virtual networks, and storage accounts.

7. How will services be provisioned by normal users? Will I leverage PowerShell or JSON templates with an existing service catalog to provide a single portal for all types of requests?

8. How will services in Azure be backed up? Services such as Azure Backup can be leveraged and replicated to other regions.

There are other considerations, but I consider these to be the absolute key minimums in order to get running. Note that after you create resources, you cannot just move them between regions. You would need to export out the resources and import them into the new region, so pick your regions carefully when creating new services.

Notice at the top of the Microsoft Azure management portal is a status bar that has the actions related to configuration of the portal experience, such as customizing tiles, changing the theme, and modifying the subscriptions that will have objects shown in the portal if your account has access to multiple subscriptions. There is also a bell icon, which shows any current actions being performed. Click the icon to get details such as those shown in Figure 12.9. Some of the notifications can be dismissed, and others will show more details via an information icon.

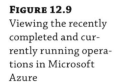

FIGURE 12.9
Viewing the recently completed and currently running operations in Microsoft Azure

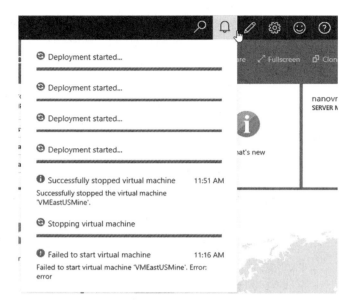

Availability Sets

An *availability set* is an important concept if you want high availability in Microsoft Azure and want virtual machines in Azure to be covered by an SLA. Consider that Microsoft Azure comprises many datacenters, and those datacenters have many racks of servers. Each rack can be considered a point of failure, a fault domain, which includes the servers, power, networking, and so on. While Microsoft takes every precaution, there is the chance that a rack could fail, which will cause a brief interruption of virtual machines/services running on that rack before the Azure fabric can perform healing and reinstantiate the VM on another host in another rack.

Additionally, Microsoft does perform maintenance, which will result in virtual machines on hosts being shut down for maintenance. While Hyper-V fully supports Live Migration, this is not performed in Azure. When an Azure host has to be rebooted for maintenance, the VMs on the box will be unavailable. Microsoft does not patch hosts in Azure; it would take too long. Instead, hosts are simply rebooted to a new image that contains the updated OS. There has been a lot of work to minimize this downtime, including VM Preserving Host Update (VMPHU), which enables a host to reboot without wiping the memory content that enables VMs to be paused, the host to be rebooted, and the VMs unfrozen with their memory intact.

To avoid a single point of failure, you may deploy a minimum of two instances of a service (for example, deploying two domain controllers into Microsoft Azure or two SQL servers in an Always On configuration), but you have no guarantee that those two instances are not running in the same rack. Therefore, a rack failure would affect both instances. By placing virtual machines in an availability set, you place the virtual machines into separate fault domains and therefore separate racks, and thus prevent a single failure from affecting all of the instances in the availability set.

Additionally, VMs in an availability set are distributed over multiple update domains. For IaaS, the update domains are used when the fabric goes through routine maintenance such as applying new boot images for the blades that make up the Azure fabric, ensuring that not all instances of the service are taken down at the same time. By default, with Azure Resource

Manager, an availability set is spread over three fault domains and five update domains, as shown in Figure 12.10. (You can increase the update domains to twenty, although three is the maximum for fault domains.) PaaS utilizes update domains when updating the code deployed to PaaS instances to avoid taking down the entire service during an update.

FIGURE 12.10
Properties of a new availability set

Figure 12.11 shows example availability set content with four VMs. Note that the VMs are spread over three fault domains, with the first and last VM in the same fault domain, while all are in their own update domain.

FIGURE 12.11
Viewing the fault domain and update domains for an availability set

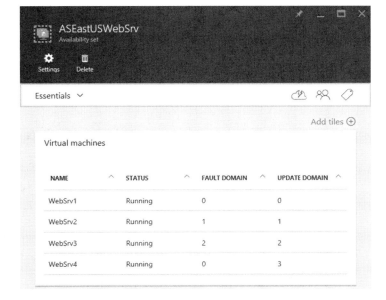

NAME	STATUS	FAULT DOMAIN	UPDATE DOMAIN
WebSrv1	Running	0	0
WebSrv2	Running	1	1
WebSrv3	Running	2	2
WebSrv4	Running	0	3

This information can also be seen with PowerShell:

```
PS C:\> $AS.VirtualMachinesReferences | ForEach { $VMResource =(Get-
AzureRmResource -Id $_.id); $VM= Get-AzureRMVM -Name $VMResource.Name –
ResourceGroup $VMResource.ResourceGroupName -Status;
[PSCustomObject]@{"Name"=$VM.Name;
"FaultDomain"=$VM.PlatformFaultDomain;"UpdateDomain"=$VM.PlatformUpdateDom
ain;}}

Name    FaultDomain UpdateDomain
----    ----------- ------------
WebSrv1           0            0
WebSrv2           1            1
WebSrv3           2            2
WebSrv4           0            3
```

With Azure Resource Manager, a VM can be added to an availability set only at the time of creation. If you need to change the availability set membership of a VM, you would need to delete and re-create it. Note that the storage of a VM does not have to be deleted, which is the actual state of the OS. Instead, a VM is deleted, but its storage is kept. A new VM is created using the existing VHDs, which essentially re-creates the old VM. It's important to make sure that availability sets contain only virtual machines that are performing exactly the same function. If you mix the functions of virtual machines into a single availability set, the virtual machines performing the same function could end up in the same fault domain, which would be a very bad thing. I would create one availability set for my domain controllers, another for a specific SQL Always On cluster, another for a different cluster, another for one web application, and so on. Never mix workloads in an availability set, as Azure has no knowledge of the actual function of each VM. It is blindly distributing the VMs between fault domains and update domains in a round-robin fashion with no consideration of other factors.

Azure Storage

While aspects of Azure Compute have been covered, I also want to focus on other key elements. The usage of Microsoft Azure Storage is a great benefit for virtual machines for multiple reasons. The Hyper-V host has a virtualized storage driver that works with a component, RDSSD, which consists of local cache, and then it communicates to Microsoft Azure Storage (xStore), which has a number of BLOBs (Binary Large Objects). The BLOBs are formatted as fixed VHDs and exist within specific storage accounts. Microsoft Azure holds an infinite lease on the BLOBs that are considered disks in the storage account, to prevent them from ever being accidentally deleted. The fact that fixed VHD is used may cause concern, because you pay for used storage, and you may create a 1TB VHD but initially use only a small amount of storage. The good news is that the BLOB is sparsely stored; only blocks written to it are stored, so you pay only for data written rather than for the total size of the VHD. This means that you can safely always use 1TB as the size for your VHDs. Additionally, if you delete content, TRIM is supported, which means that when data is deleted, the TRIM command is sent to the storage subsystem on the Hyper-V host, which then marks the blocks as no longer needed, and in Microsoft Azure Storage, the blocks are deallocated so you stop paying for the deleted data.

Microsoft Azure Storage ensures that, at minimum, every piece of data is replicated three times to provide protection from data loss. Asynchronous data replication is also available to replicate the data to another datacenter, and it's then replicated three times at that datacenter, which is known as *geo-redundant storage (GRS)*. Another advantage of using Microsoft Azure Storage is that all existing tools for Microsoft Azure Storage work without modification with the page BLOBs that contain the VHD, making management simple.

Microsoft has a free tool available that enables easy interaction with Azure Storage, *Microsoft Azure Storage Explorer*, which is available from http://storageexplorer.com/. Figure 12.12 shows the tool browsing the VHDS container, which shows the various page BLOBs used to store the VHD files that are used by virtual machines. The tool also enables the copying of storage in addition to downloading and uploading data.

FIGURE 12.12
Interacting with Azure Storage by using Microsoft Azure Storage Explorer

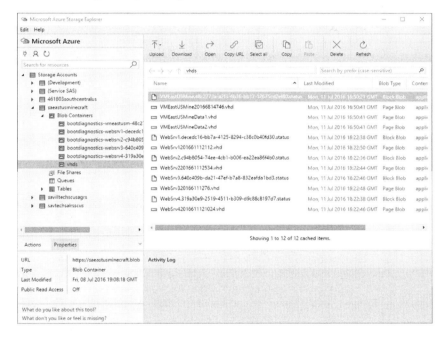

When a virtual machine is created in Microsoft Azure IaaS, it has the operating system VHD. However, you likely don't want to store application data on this disk because by default it has read and write caching enabled, which is not desired for most application data workloads but is beneficial for OS disks. Additional disks can be added to a virtual machine, and a reboot is not required because the disks are added to the virtual SCSI controller, which supports hot-adding storage.

Additional disks are added via the Disks menu item from the VMs Settings blade. Through the blade, either a new empty VHD can be attached or a new VHD created and attached. When you add a disk, it will be a data disk type. You can specify a name for the disk and a size up to 1TB (although 1,023GB is the maximum size, not 1,024 as would be expected). The type of caching can also be configured, as shown in Figure 12.13. Notice that the type of storage account can be selected, but only xS series VMs can use Premium Storage accounts, such as the DS, FS, and

GS series VMs. Once the options are configured, click the OK button to complete the addition, which will generate a new page BLOB in Microsoft Azure Storage and attach the disk to the virtual machine.

FIGURE 12.13
Options for a new
data disk attached to
a virtual machine

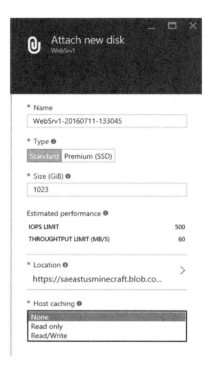

There are two types of disks: the OS disk used to store the operating system and a data disk used to store data. With Azure Resource Manager, the cache options are the same. (This is different from ASM, which did not allow no caching for the OS disk.) With Azure Resource Manager, while I have talked about OS disks and data disks, these are not actual constructs. Instead, they are just page BLOBs and are disks only in terms of their relationship with an Azure VM. Therefore, configurations (such as changing cache information of the size of disks) are performed through the actual Azure RM VM object that is using the page BLOB as a VHD. The first step is to retrieve the VM object that has the disk connected:

```
$vm = Get-AzureRmVM -ResourceGroupName RGEastUSMinecraft -Name VMEastUSMine
```

Once you have an object to the VM, the OS and data disks can be enumerated through the `StorageProfile` model property. The OS disk is `OsDisk`, and the data disks are in the `DataDisks[]` array. For example, this sets Read and Write caching on the OS disk and no caching on the first two data disks (which are the defaults anyway). Once these changes are made, the VM object must be updated for the changes to take effect.

```
$vm.StorageProfile.OsDisk.Caching = 'ReadWrite'
$vm.StorageProfile.DataDisks[0].Caching = 'None'
$vm.StorageProfile.DataDisks[1].Caching = 'None'
Update-AzureRmVM -ResourceGroupName RGEastUSMinecraft -VM $vm
```

The number of disks that can be attached to a virtual machine varies depending on the size of the virtual machine, as shown earlier in Table 12.1. The full specifications for all VMs is listed at `https://azure.microsoft.com/en-us/documentation/articles/virtual-machines-windows-sizes/`, with the most being 64 with the G5. Suppose that you add 16 disks, 1TB in size, to a virtual machine. You will have 16 separate disks in the virtual machine. But what if you want an actual 16TB volume? The Windows operating system has the ability to create striped volumes that effectively join multiple disks together by creating a simple Storage Space. Make sure that you select the Quick Format option to minimize the time to format and keep the sparse nature of the underlying Azure Storage. Once it's created, you will have a single volume of 16TB that can be used, which has not only aggregated the size but also the IOPS, creating an 8,000 IOPS disk. For Linux operating systems, you can use the MD capability or LVM to get the stripe. You don't need to use any kind of RAID, such as mirroring or parity, because each disk is already fault-tolerant through the three copies stored in the Microsoft Azure datacenter.

Regular Azure Storage provides a maximum of 500 IOPs per disk, but that is not guaranteed. The actual IOPS delivered may be slightly less, depending on other workloads on the compute and storage stamps. An Azure Premium Storage offering is also available and differs in three key ways:

◆ You are billed based on the size of the disk and not data written. Therefore, from a billing perspective, it is not sparse storage.

◆ There are various disk size options that have different amounts of IOPS.

◆ The IOPS delivered are predictable and will be the amount specified.

As an example at the time of this writing, Premium Storage disks come in three sizes, and each has a different number of associated IOPS, as shown in Table 12.2.

TABLE 12.2:   Azure Premium Storage Disk Types

Premium Storage Disk Type	P10	P20	P30
Disk Size	128GB	512GB	1024GB
IOPS per Disk	500	2,300	5,000

Source: `https://azure.microsoft.com/en-us/documentation/articles/storage-premium-storage/`

Notice that the larger the disk purchased, the higher the number of IOPS. Therefore, typically you will buy the disk based on the IOPS required. If you need more than 5,000 IOPS, you can still add multiple disks and aggregate them together inside the guest OS in the same manner as with the regular Azure Storage. To use Premium Storage, you must use the xS series VMs, such as the DS, FS, and GS series, and it is possible for those series VMs to mix disks from both regular and Premium Storage accounts.

At this point, you have a virtual machine with numerous configurations available. If a virtual machine is no longer required, you can use the Delete option within the virtual machine's actions. When you delete a VM, its storage will not be deleted automatically. Instead, the page BLOBs that contained the VHDs will need to be manually deleted. Note that other resources, such as public IP addresses, Network Security Groups, and vmNICs, are also not automatically deleted. While the Microsoft Azure management portal is a great interface for managing Microsoft Azure virtual machines, if users also access virtual machines in a private cloud, remember that you can leverage System Center Orchestrator to integrate with Azure and then offer those services out via Service Manager.

LEVERAGING AZURE STORAGE OUTSIDE OF VMS

This chapter has gone into a lot of detail about using Microsoft Azure Storage on Microsoft Azure IaaS virtual machines. This section briefly covers other ways that Microsoft Azure Storage can be used. Specifically, I want to tell you about two key uses that I've found to be the most interesting for my customers.

The first is backup, because with Microsoft Azure Storage, you effectively have a limitless amount of offsite storage, and Microsoft Azure provides the ability to create backup vaults that can then be used by backup applications, including Windows Backup (which is built into Windows Server) and System Center Data Protection Manager (DPM). In the case of System Center DPM, the Microsoft Azure backup acts as a secondary, offsite backup target in addition to the disk-based primary backup target.

Microsoft has detailed instructions on configuring the Microsoft Azure backup vault, creating the certificate required, and downloading and installing the Microsoft Azure backup agent at the following location:

```
www.windowsazure.com/en-us/manage/services/recovery-services/
configure-a-backup-vault/
```

My goal is to ensure that you know about the capability, because it's an easy way to get offsite backups and architect a backup solution whereby a certain number of days' backups are kept onsite and then an additional duration is kept in the public cloud.

Using Microsoft Azure Storage for backups is a great use case. Nonetheless, if things go well, you will never use it, and it's not helping solve organizations' number 1 pain point regarding data, namely, that there is too much of it and it's getting harder and harder to store and manage it. Figure 12.14 shows a typical organization's amount of data over time, and as you can see, it is exponentially increasing. However, also notice that the actual working set of data that is used is much smaller and grows much more slowly.

FIGURE 12.14
Typical organizational
data volume over time

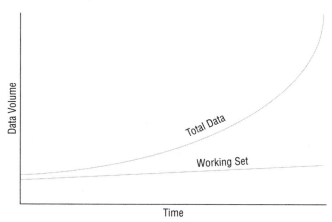

Microsoft acquired StorSimple, which is a storage appliance that has a certain amount of local storage, both HDD and SSD, but it can also leverage Microsoft Azure Storage. The StorSimple appliance acts as an iSCSI target and then at a block level leverages tiers of storage, including using deduplication and compression to store the data. The more frequently accessed data will be stored on a higher tier; for example, the most-used data will be stored in the SSD tier, less-used data would be stored in the HDD tier, while rarely used data will be stored in Microsoft Azure Storage. This reorganizing of data happens automatically by using algorithms built into StorSimple. All of the data that exists, but that is rarely used, would be uploaded to Microsoft Azure Storage and then deleted from the local storage, keeping the most-used data local (as well as storing it in Microsoft Azure for protection), which gives the highest performance while providing essentially an infinite total capacity size. To the end user, all of the data looks like it's available locally on the StorSimple appliance because even data that has been moved to Microsoft Azure Storage keeps a local thumbprint (representing the Microsoft Azure stored data) on the StorSimple storage appliance, like a stub file but at a data block level.

If data that has been offloaded to Microsoft Azure is accessed, the StorSimple device will automatically download it and make it available, but obviously this would impact storage performance because the data has to be downloaded over the Internet. It is also possible to pin certain data always to be kept locally (near) or configure it to be offloaded to Microsoft Azure as soon as possible (far). StorSimple uses storage in different ways, in that there is SSD Linear (not deduplicated), SSD Dedupe (deduplicated), and then HDD (which is deduplicated and compressed). What is not shown is the final Microsoft Azure Storage tier. Data stored in Microsoft Azure Storage is not only deduplicated and compressed, but also encrypted using a key known only to the StorSimple appliance. Initially, data is written to the SSD Linear tier and then over time deduplicated in SSD, and then, depending on its usage, it may get moved to the HDD tier or even Microsoft Azure Storage.

This automatic tiering may sound familiar. Storage Spaces in Windows Server 2012 R2 does something similar with its HDD and SSD tiers. Initially, StorSimple was based on Linux, but this changed with the recent release now to be Windows based. I also don't think it would be much of a "leap" for the StorSimple algorithms used to offload to Microsoft Azure to find their way into some future version of Windows Server and become part of Storage Spaces, adding the Microsoft Azure Storage tier to Storage Spaces. This is all pure conjecture on my part, but it would make complete sense because Microsoft pushes Storage Spaces and it now owns StorSimple.

The StorSimple appliances come in different sizes. To help you use Microsoft Azure Storage more easily, Microsoft is giving them away if you purchase certain amounts of Microsoft Azure credit. StorSimple is a great solution in certain key scenarios. It's great as a storage for file servers and archive servers. It can be used for low- to mid-range Hyper-V VM storage and SQL workloads, including SharePoint. It should not be used for high disk IOPs Hyper-V and SQL scenarios because it will not deliver the storage performance that is required. It should also not be used as a backup target because once it hits a certain threshold percent full of its local storage, all future writes basically have to go directly to Microsoft Azure, which means at that point the storage performance would be terrible during the backup.

Microsoft Azure Storage can be used in many other ways, especially when combined with ExpressRoute to provide fast, low-latency connectivity such as through custom applications and more, but the backup scenario and StorSimple are powerful and easy ways to quickly get real benefits.

Virtual Networks

Microsoft Azure Virtual Networks enables networks to be defined that have the following benefits:

◆ You can use a private IPv4 space that you specify, and different virtual subnets can be created within the virtual network.

◆ The virtual network can be connected to your on-premises network by using site-to-site VPN and/or ExpressRoute, and it can also support point-to-site VPN connections.

◆ You have the ability to use custom DNS, such as an on-premises DNS server, a DNS server deployed to Microsoft Azure IaaS, or even a public DNS service. This allows DNS resolution outside just those resources within a cloud service.

When you put these capabilities together, your on-premises network can be extended into Microsoft Azure, bringing seamless connectivity that is not using Internet-facing public IP addresses and removing the need to use the public IPs for the virtual machines unless specifically required to publish services out to the Internet, such as for a web server. Figure 12.15 shows the new connectivity when using a virtual network.

FIGURE 12.15
Connectivity
when using
virtual networks

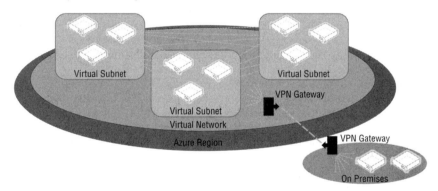

A virtual network cannot cross regions and exists within an Azure subscription. If you wish to create services in different regions or different subscriptions, separate Azure virtual networks will be required. Make sure that all virtual networks use a unique IP address space. The valid IP address ranges that you can specify to use for a virtual network are those defined in RFC 1918, which are the private, non-Internet routable addresses, as follows:

◆ 10.0.0.0 to 10.255.255.255 (10/8 prefix)

◆ 172.16.0.0 to 172.31.255.255 (172.16/12 prefix)

◆ 192.168.0.0 to 192.168.255.255 (192.168/16 prefix)

Additionally, you can bring a portion of other ranges, such as from a class B network your organization acquired in the early days of the Internet. When deciding which IP network to use in Microsoft Azure, always consider that even if you don't want to connect Microsoft Azure to your on-premises network today, you may want to do so in the future. Therefore, use an IP network that is not used on premises so that connectivity and routing will be possible in the future.

If my organization used the 10.0.0.0/8 IP range on premises, I would like to use the 172.16.0.0/12 range in Microsoft Azure to avoid any risk of overlap. Once you decide on the IP address range you wish to use for the Microsoft Azure network, you can divide it into subnets for use by different types of services. For example, I like to create different subnets for my Microsoft Azure infrastructure servers, such as domain controllers, and another for my Microsoft Azure application services, such as SQL servers. The Microsoft Azure gateway to provide VPN also requires its own IP subnet. A subnet can be as large as /8 and as small as /29 (using CIDR subnet definitions). Remember, this is showing the number of bits in the IP address that defines the network. A /8 means a subnet mask of 255.0.0.0, and I don't think you would ever have a subnet anywhere close to this size. Gateway functionality between subnets in a virtual network is provided automatically by the virtual network, but you cannot ping the gateway for each subnet, nor will tracert-type utilities work.

Within a virtual network subnet, the first and last IP addresses of a subnet are reserved as part of the protocol for network addresses (host ID all 0s) and broadcast addresses (host ID all 1s), respectively. Microsoft Azure also reserves the first three IP addresses in each subnet (binary 01, 10, and 11 in the host ID portion of the IP address). This can be seen in Figure 12.16, where I show an example virtual network I have defined that has three subnets. Note that in the example, my virtual network has a Subnet3 with a /29 address space. Although this should give eight usable IP addresses, note that only three are available, because five IPs are lost, as previously discussed.

FIGURE 12.16
Viewing available IP addresses within a virtual subnet

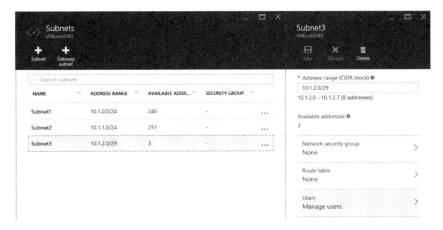

Once you define subnets and add virtual machines to a subnet, the virtual machine's IP address will be allocated from the IP address range from that subnet as an infinite lease. Even though DHCP is used to assign the IP address to the virtual machine, the actual IP address will never change while the virtual machine is provisioned; that is, while you are paying for it. This does mean that you have to be careful never to deprovision the virtual machine, such as shutting it down from the Microsoft Azure management portal, because this will result in the virtual machine getting a new virtual network adapter and a new MAC when it is subsequently started, and therefore a new IP address. If you want to ensure that your virtual machine's private IP address never changes, configure its private IP address as static, which tells the Azure fabric always to give the VM the same IP address even if it has been deprovisioned. If you leverage static private IP addresses, the best practice is to have a subnet just for IP addresses that will be statically assigned rather than mixing them in a subnet that also dynamically assigns IP addresses.

Within a virtual network, most IP-based protocols—such as TCP, UDP, and ICMP—will work. However, multicast, broadcast, IP-in-IP encapsulated packets, and GRE packets are blocked. The GRE blocking is logical when you consider that behind the scenes Microsoft Azure is leveraging Hyper-V Network Virtualization, which itself uses GRE.

This really is all a virtual network is. You have an IP address space that you define and then divide into subnets, and virtual machines are then assigned to the subnets when they are created. You cannot move existing virtual machines into a virtual network or move a virtual machine out of a virtual network without deleting and re-creating the VM. Note that the subnet the VM is in can be changed. The virtual network configuration must be done at the time of virtual machine creation. I am referring exclusively to virtual machines, but PaaS web and worker roles can also leverage virtual networks.

If you have multiple virtual networks and you want the VMs in those networks to be able to communicate, you have to link them together. This can be done through the site-to-site VPN or ExpressRoute (as covered in the next section), but instead of connecting a virtual network to on premises, you simply connect multiple virtual networks.

Linking On-Premises Networks with Azure IaaS

I previously discussed public IP addresses, which are Internet-accessible addresses that can be assigned directly to VMs or to a load balancer that can distribute traffic between VMs. A public IP can be dynamic or static in nature, and it can have an optional DNS name to reference it. Using a public IP address, services can be published out to the Internet. If a VM is created through the Azure portal by default, a public IP is added, and the automatic Network Security Group that is created, which restricts the types of traffic, has an exception for RDP traffic that enables connectivity to the VM via the Internet. However, this is added only as a "lowest common denominator" action to ensure that people can connect to their VM. In the real world, very few services should publish RDP out to the Internet; instead, the services should be connected to via a secure link between an organization's on-premises network and the Azure virtual network. This enhances security and removes the need to have public IPs, except in cases where a service needs explicitly to be published to the Internet, such as for a web service.

Once your virtual networks are created in Microsoft Azure, it's easy to enable the site-to-site VPN feature to bring cross-premises connectivity. A subnet is added to the virtual network for the gateway VMs that are automatically created and managed to leverage, and then the actual gateway is created and your local network space is defined, which enables Azure to know the IP address space used on premises to allow it to route traffic correctly that should be sent via the site-to-site VPN connection. Once the Azure side of the gateway is created, it has the option to generate a script that contains information such as its IP address and key that is used for the IPsec-based encryption of the traffic, which is used to configure the VPN gateway device on your network to complete the connection. Microsoft has a full walk-through of the process at https://azure.microsoft.com/en-us/documentation/articles/vpn-gateway-howto-site-to-site-resource-manager-portal/.

The standard VPN gateway has a theoretical maximum speed of 100Mbps, but I've never seen an implementation reach higher than 80Mpbs. This is not a connectivity limitation but rather, on the Azure side, a pair of VMs is used in an active-passive configuration. These VMs are single-core VMs, and IPsec is heavily computationally expensive, which maxes out the CPU, and this is where the bandwidth maximum originates. There is also a High-Performance gateway option, which increases the throughput to 200Mbps by leveraging bigger VMs. It is possible to connect a gateway to multiple on-premises locations and/or multiple other virtual networks, but there is only one gateway per virtual network, which means that when multiple partners are added, they share the throughput. If 10 site-to-site partnerships are created for a single gateway, each VPN would have only 8Mbps of bandwidth if all were running at maximum capacity. This may change in the future, but at the time of this writing, the one gateway per virtual network is a hard limit. For a basic gateway, 10 is the maximum number of IPsec tunnels, and for a high-performance gateway, 30 is the maximum.

The site-to-site VPN is a good first step to establish connectivity between on-premises and the Azure virtual network, and it makes Azure an extension of your datacenter. Nevertheless, there are challenges with the site-to-site VPN, including the following:

- The maximum available bandwidths may not be fast enough.

- The latency can be high and unpredictable, because the connection is over the Internet and the actual route packets change and the equipment between your location and the Azure datacenter is unknown.

- The connection is over the Internet, which although secure through the use of IPsec is still a challenge for some organizations due to compliance requirements.

- Only services in a virtual network can be accessed over the connection and not other services such as Azure Storage.

To address these challenges, Microsoft also offers an ExpressRoute connectivity option. ExpressRoute offers a private layer 3 connection between an organization's on-premises network and the Azure service. Microsoft has ExpressRoute partners all over the world to enable organizations throughout the globe to connect to Azure services by using the ExpressRoute connectivity option. ExpressRoute has two flavors: Exchange Provider and Network Service Provider.

With an exchange provider/Internet exchange point (IXP), a dedicated connection is established, such as a dark fiber connection, between an organization's location and the IXP. The IXP has resilient, high-bandwidth connections to Azure, and it establishes the direct connection from the customer to Azure. With a network service provider (NSP), the provider connects your network using MPLS, which is especially useful if an organization has multiple locations already connected via MPLS, in which case the Azure connection just becomes a node on that MPLS connection. In both cases, ExpressRoute offers numerous benefits over site-to-site VPN:

- High bandwidth with offerings up to 10Gbps

- Low and predictable latency—since the path is known, the latency is consistent

- Redundancy in the connectivity through dual connections

- An SLA

ExpressRoute is purchased for a particular speed and also as metered or unmetered. With metered, the customer is charged for network egress (traffic leaving Azure), whereas with unmetered, there is no egress charge but the monthly ExpressRoute charge is higher. The

ExpressRoute partners can be found at `https://azure.microsoft.com/en-us/documentation/articles/expressroute-locations/`, which are broken down by provider and location. The pricing details can be found at `https://azure.microsoft.com/en-us/pricing/details/expressroute/`. Note that when dealing with ExpressRoute, the Microsoft price is just Microsoft's side of the pricing to allow the connection to Azure via the provider. There are other costs, including these:

◆ The service provider's costs

◆ The cost of the gateway on the Azure virtual network (this is still required, just as with site-to-site VPN)

◆ Network egress if a metered plan is selected

When connecting via ExpressRoute, even though a connection may be to the local ExpressRoute partner location, services in Azure regions throughout the geo-political region can be accessed through that ExpressRoute connection. For example, if I establish an ExpressRoute connection in Dallas, I can access Azure services not just in the South Central United States but in all U.S. regions via the Microsoft Azure backbone network. If the ExpressRoute Premium add-on is also purchased, all Azure services throughout the globe can be accessed via the Azure backbone network through the ExpressRoute local connection.

Another major difference between a site-to-site VPN connection and ExpressRoute is peering. With a site-to-site VPN, private peering is used; the on-premises network is connected to an Azure virtual network. That type of peering is also available with ExpressRoute, but so are other kinds. Public peering with ExpressRoute enables nearly all Azure services to be accessed via ExpressRoute, which would otherwise be accessed over Internet endpoints. Consider services such as Azure Storage, Azure Backup, and Azure SQL Database as just a few examples of useful services that can be used in new ways when not accessed over the Internet and instead accessed over a secure, low-latency connection. There is also Microsoft peering, which connects to Office 365 and CRM Online services via the connection, but this is only recommended in specialized scenarios.

For organizations using Azure for production tasks, ExpressRoute is highly recommended over site-to-site VPN. However, organizations can still have site-to-site VPN as a fallback connectivity option, as it can coexist with ExpressRoute.

A point-to-site VPN capability is also available to give specific machines connectivity to Microsoft Azure. It leverages a special client component that is downloaded from the Microsoft Azure management portal, and the clients connecting using the VPN client component receive an IP address from a pool defined as part of the Microsoft Azure point-to-site VPN configuration. If you need this kind of point-to-site VPN, it is available as an option, and Microsoft has plenty of documentation. The primary documents are available at `https://azure.microsoft.com/en-us/documentation/articles/vpn-gateway-howto-point-to-site-rm-ps/`.

Managing with PowerShell

I went into detail on the creation of virtual machines using the Microsoft Azure web-based management portal. Virtual machines can also be created using PowerShell and JSON templates. Where possible, avoid the portal, because you cannot automate provisioning by using the portal; it's thus not repeatable. It's great to look around and experiment with Azure, but it should not be the tool used for production provisioning. Choosing between JSON and

PowerShell is tricky. JSON has the benefit of being immutable; I can run a template, and if there is a problem, I can fix the problem and rerun the template, and only what is different or missing will be created. This is not the case with standard PowerShell. If I have a PowerShell script creating many resources and it crashes halfway through, I cannot simply rerun the script, because it will err, as many resources would already exist. However, for administrators who are familiar with PowerShell, it will probably be preferable over learning a completely new way of defining resources. If you want to look at JSON templates, I recommend looking at the GitHub repository at `https://github.com/Azure/azure-quickstart-templates`, which has a whole series of templates starting with simple ones (prefixed with 101) to more complicated, multitier deployments. While the JSON templates are verbose, they are also fairly simple, consisting of blocks of input parameters, constants used throughout the template (although they are called variables), and then the actual definition of resources to be created along with dependencies between them. A good start is the simple Windows VM at `https://github.com/Azure/azure-quickstart-templates/blob/master/101-vm-simple-windows/azuredeploy.json`. As an infrastructure person, and because PowerShell is used throughout the book, I'm going to spend a few pages looking at using PowerShell to manage Azure resources.

Two separate sets of Azure PowerShell modules are available: one for Azure Service Manager (Azure) and one for Azure Resource Manager (AzureRM). In this section, I focus on using the AzureRM module with Azure Resource Manager resources. Installation is covered in detail at `https://azure.microsoft.com/en-us/documentation/articles/powershell-install-configure/`, but it can easily be installed from the PowerShell Gallery by using the following command from an elevated PowerShell session:

```
Install-Module AzureRM
```

The `Install-Module` command utilizes the NuGet provider, and you will be prompted if the NuGet provider can be installed. Select Yes, and the installation will continue. Microsoft updates the Azure modules frequently. To update to the latest version at any time, use this command:

```
Update-Module AzureRM
```

After they are imported, if you run the following command, you will get some idea of the scope of the AzureRM cmdlets:

```
Get-Module –ListAvailable Azure*
```

You will notice that a huge number of modules were installed, related to all aspects of Azure, including Backup, Compute, Networking, storage, and more. There is no need to perform an `Import-Module` manually with PowerShell 3 and above, as modules are autoloaded as required.

The first step is to authenticate to Azure to enable access to your resources. For AzureRM, this is achieved via the `Login-AzureRmAccount` cmdlet that will open a dialog box to enable credentials to be entered.

Once you have authenticated to Azure, you can view the list of subscriptions to which you have access and select one as the default, which is what future cmdlet operations will be performed against.

```
Get-AzureRmSubscription
Select-AzureRmSubscription -SubscriptionId <ID>
```

Azure is made up of resource providers to provide services. These can all be directly viewed with the code that follows, and then the actual services within a resource provider, such as for the Compute resource provider.

```
Get-AzureRmResourceProvider
Get-AzureRmResourceProvider -ProviderNamespace Microsoft.Compute
```

The resource providers can be used to check where services are offered. For example, to check where IaaS VMs are available:

```
PS C:\> $resources = Get-AzureRmResourceProvider -ProviderNamespace
Microsoft.Compute
PS C:\> $resources.ResourceTypes.Where{($_.ResourceTypeName -eq
'virtualMachines')}.Locations
East US
East US 2
West US
Central US
North Central US
South Central US
North Europe
West Europe
East Asia
Southeast Asia
Japan East
Japan West
Brazil South
Canada Central
Canada East
West US 2
West Central US
```

Using an image from the Marketplace is a little more complex than in the past with Azure Service Manager. The process consists of selecting a region, viewing the available publishers, viewing the images offered by the publisher, viewing the SKUs of the published image, and then selecting an image. Here is an example of selecting a Windows Server 2012 R2 image:

```
$loc = 'SouthCentralUS'
#View the templates available
Get-AzureRmVMImagePublisher -Location $loc
Get-AzureRmVMImageOffer -Location $loc `
    -PublisherName "MicrosoftWindowsServer"
Get-AzureRmVMImageSku -Location $loc `
    -PublisherName "MicrosoftWindowsServer" -Offer "WindowsServer"
Get-AzureRmVMImage -Location $loc `
    -PublisherName "MicrosoftWindowsServer" `
    -Offer "WindowsServer" -Skus "2012-R2-Datacenter"
$AzureImage = Get-AzureRmVMImage -Location $loc `
    -PublisherName "MicrosoftWindowsServer" -Offer "WindowsServer" `
    -Skus "2012-R2-Datacenter" -Version "4.0.20160617"
```

```
$AzureImage
```

An easy way always to get the latest version of an image is the following:

```
$AzureImageSku = Get-AzureRmVMImage -Location $loc `
    -PublisherName "MicrosoftWindowsServer" -Offer "WindowsServer" `
    -Skus "2012-R2-Datacenter"
$AzureImageSku = $AzureImageSku | Sort-Object Version -Descending
$AzureImage = $AzureImageSku[0] #Newest
```

At this point, a VM can be created by using PowerShell. The following code uses an existing virtual network and storage account based on the names in the variable, along with the image selected, using the previous example that found an image and assigned to the variable $AzureImage. The VM creates a new public IP address and assigns it to the VM.

```
$rgname = 'RG-SCUSA'
$vmsize = 'Standard_A2'
$vmname = 'VM-TestVM'
# Setup Storage
$stoname = 'sa-lrsscussav'
$stotype = 'Standard_LRS'
# Virtual Network
$virtname = 'VN-Net1'

$stoaccount = Get-AzureRmStorageAccount -ResourceGroupName $rgname `
    -Name $stoname

# Create VM Object
$vm = New-AzureRmVMConfig -VMName $vmname -VMSize $vmsize

#Get the network object
$vnet = Get-AzureRmVirtualNetwork -Name ($virtname) `
    -ResourceGroupName $rgname
$subnetId = $vnet.Subnets[0].Id

#Create a Public IP address
$pip = New-AzureRmPublicIpAddress -ResourceGroupName $rgname `
    -Name "vip1" -Location $loc -AllocationMethod Dynamic `
    -DomainNameLabel $vmname.ToLower()
#Create a new NIC using the virtual network and the Public IP
$nic = New-AzureRmNetworkInterface -Force -Name ('nic' + $vmname) `
    -ResourceGroupName $rgname -Location $loc `
    -SubnetId $subnetId -PublicIpAddressId $pip.Id

# Add NIC to VM configuration
$vm = Add-AzureRmVMNetworkInterface -VM $vm -Id $nic.Id

#Setup the OS disk
$osDiskName = $vmname+'_osDisk'
$osDiskCaching = 'ReadWrite'
```

```
$osDiskVhdUri = "https://$stoname.blob.core.windows.net/vhds/"+$vmname+"_os.vhd"

# Setup OS & Image
$user = "localadmin"
$password = 'Pa55word5'
$securePassword = ConvertTo-SecureString $password -AsPlainText -Force
$cred = New-Object System.Management.Automation.PSCredential ($user,
$securePassword)
$vm = Set-AzureRmVMOperatingSystem -VM $vm -Windows `
    -ComputerName $vmname -Credential $cred
$vm = Set-AzureRmVMSourceImage -VM $vm `
    -PublisherName $AzureImage.PublisherName `
    -Offer $AzureImage.Offer -Skus $AzureImage.Skus `
    -Version $AzureImage.Version
$vm = Set-AzureRmVMOSDisk -VM $vm -VhdUri $osDiskVhdUri `
    -name $osDiskName -CreateOption fromImage -Caching $osDiskCaching

# Create Virtual Machine
New-AzureRmVM -ResourceGroupName $rgname -Location $loc -VM $vm
```

Once all of the PowerShell runs, you will have a new VM. To view all VHDs in a storage account, use the following code:

```
#View all VHDs
Get-AzureRMStorageAccount -Name <store account> `
    -ResourceGroupName <RG Name> |
    Get-AzureStorageContainer | where {$_.Name -eq 'vhds'} |
    Get-AzureStorageBlob | where {$_.Name.EndsWith('.vhd')}
```

To stop and start VMs, use the Start and Stop-AzureRmVM cmdlets along with the VM name and resource group name.

There is no action that can be performed in the Azure portal that cannot be performed with PowerShell. As new capabilities are added to Azure, those capabilities are first surfaced via the REST API, then in PowerShell, and finally in the Azure portal.

Migrating Virtual Machines Between Hyper-V and Azure IaaS

A huge "better together" factor with Microsoft Azure and Microsoft Hyper-V on premises is the compatibility aspect of the virtual machines, enabling virtual machines to be moved between on-premises and Microsoft Azure and back again. Here are some considerations:

◆ At the time of this writing, Microsoft Azure does not support VHDX, so your virtual hard disks should be VHD.

◆ At the time of this writing, Microsoft Azure has a 1,023GB size limit, so keep the VHD files at 1,023GB or less.

◆ Microsoft Azure supports only fixed VHD files, but dynamic VHDs can be converted by using the Convert-VHD cmdlet.

◆ Microsoft Azure virtual machines can have only a single network address, and its IP must be configured using DHCP.

◆ Microsoft Azure is currently based on Windows Server 2012 R2 Hyper-V.

◆ Microsoft Azure does not currently support generation 2 virtual machines; use generation 1 virtual machines only.

Primarily to move virtual machines, the VHD file(s) for the virtual machine will be uploaded or downloaded from Microsoft Azure and then a new virtual machine will be created that uses the VHD file(s). The process to perform an on-premises to Microsoft Azure migration is as follows:

1. Upload the VHD(s) to Microsoft Azure by using the `Add-AzureRmVhd` cmdlet. For example, here I create a test VHD and then upload it:

```
$sourceVHD = "D:\Temp\vhdtst.vhd"
$destinationVHD =
https://masteringhyperv2016.blob.core.windows.net/vhds/vhdtst.vhd"
New-VHD -Path $sourceVHD -Dynamic -SizeBytes 10GB
Add-AzureRmVhd -ResourceGroupName <RG Name> `
        -LocalFilePath $sourceVHD -Destination $destinationVHD `
        -NumberOfUploaderThreads 5
```

2. The disk can now be used with a VM. If it was going to be the OS disk, it can be used with a new VM as follows:

```
$vm = Set-AzureRmVMOSDisk -VM $vm -VhdUri $osDiskVhdUri `
  -name $osDiskName -CreateOption attach -Windows `
  -Caching $osDiskCaching
```

If the disk was to be added as a data disk, use the following:

```
Add-AzureRmVMDataDisk -VM $VM -Name $VHDNameShort -Caching None `
-CreateOption Attach -DiskSizeInGB 1023 -VhdUri $dataDiskVhdURI
```

To retrieve a VHD from Microsoft Azure, the process is similar. Download the VHD and then create a virtual machine locally that uses it. To download the VHD, perform the following:

```
$sourceVHD = `
"https://storact10.blob.core.windows.net/vhds/test1.vhd"
$destinationVHD = "D:\temp\test1.vhd"

Save-AzureRmVhd -Source $sourceVHD `
        -LocalFilePath $destinationVHD -NumberOfThreads 5
```

Hopefully, this showed that it's fairly simple to move VHDs into and out of Microsoft Azure. PowerShell is just one option, but you can use it in pretty much any other environment, including automated processes to bulk-move virtual machines. This was performing a manual migration of VMs. The other, preferred approach would be using Azure Site Recovery, which would replicate the storage and create the VM in Azure with a minimum amount of downtime.

The Bottom Line

Explain the difference between platform as a service and infrastructure as a service. The key difference relates to who is responsible for which elements of the solution. With platform as a service, solutions are written for a supplied platform within certain guidelines. The platform then ensures availability and protection for the application, and no operating system or fabric management is required. The key point is that the application must be written to work with the PaaS platform. With infrastructure as a service, a virtual machine is provided, which means that the provider manages the compute, storage, and network fabric, but the user of the virtual machine is responsible for the operating system and everything within it as well as patching it. The benefit of IaaS is that you have complete access to the operating system, so normal applications can run in IaaS without requiring customization. A key principal of IaaS is that you should not have to modify the application to work on it.

Master It What is software as a service?

Connect Microsoft Azure to your on-premises network. Creating connectivity between Microsoft Azure and your local network has several requirements. First, virtual networks need to be defined in Microsoft Azure within a region. Virtual machines are created and configured at the time of creation to use a specific subnet in the virtual network. A site-to-site gateway is created between Microsoft Azure and your on-premises network, which permits seamless connectivity via a site-to-site VPN or ExpressRoute.

Master It Can Windows Server 2012 RRAS be used on the local premises side of the VPN gateway?

Move data between on-premises and Microsoft Azure. Microsoft Azure is built on Windows Server Hyper-V and specifically leverages the VHD format currently. A virtual machine that uses VHD can be copied to Microsoft Azure storage and used with a new Microsoft Azure virtual machine or added to an existing virtual machine. Similarly, VHD files used in Microsoft Azure virtual machines can be downloaded to on-premises and used with Hyper-V virtual machines.

Master It What PowerShell cmdlets are used to copy VHDs to and from Microsoft Azure?

Master It Can dynamic VHDs be used in Microsoft Azure?

Chapter 13

Bringing It All Together with a Best-of-Breed Cloud Solution

Many technologies have been covered in this book so far—on-premises technologies and those that are available through the public cloud. It can seem daunting to know which technology to use in different scenarios. This chapter covers all of the technologies and provides guidelines for when to use them. You'll also see what other companies around the world are doing related to virtualization and hosting services.

In this chapter, you will learn to:

◆ Identify the best overall architecture for your organization.

Which Is the Right Technology to Choose?

The most important step in choosing the right technology is to determine a direction for your organization. Does your organization want to focus on the public cloud first and have a minimal on-premises infrastructure? Is it investing in brand-new datacenters and servers and looking to maximize that investment by focusing its on-premises infrastructure? Or does it want to achieve best of breed with a hybrid approach?

Having a direction is important, but it's also critical to know your limits. By this I mean, what can your organization realistically implement and support with its given resources, including its budget? It's doubtful that a 50-person company with a single "IT guy" could operate a complete on-premises infrastructure and have the facilities, resources, and budget to have its own disaster-recovery, off-site location. At this point, the company has to evaluate where its IT resources should be focused, and for some IT services, look at external solutions. A great example that I see a lot in the industry, even for the very largest organizations, is using software as a service (SaaS) for email and collaboration, such as the Microsoft Office 365 service. Messaging can be complex. It's considered a tier 1 application for many companies, which means that it must always be available. Thus, rather than try to architect what can become complex messaging solutions, it's easier and more effective for organizations to outsource this.

Take the time to understand the types of IT services that your organization needs to provide. Understand the data retention, backup, and compliance requirements and regulations for your business. Understand the criticality of the system and the services upon which it depends. Then look at your resources and what you can support, because this will certainly help guide your direction. You may have services on premises today that would be an appropriate fit for the cloud because contracts are ending, hardware could be reused for other projects, and so on. Many organizations today spend huge amounts of time, effort, and expense on applications and services that consume way more than they should, especially in relation to their benefit to the organization.

Microsoft also offers organizations something that strangely is fairly rare in today's solutions—a choice. Microsoft is a leader in the Gartner magic quadrant (explained at www.gartner.com/technology/research/methodologies/research_mq.jsp) in many areas including x86 virtualization, infrastructure as a service (IaaS), and platform as a service (PaaS), allowing customers to choose how they deploy their solutions. The actual solutions are different, depending on whether they are on-premises or public cloud, which may mean rearchitecture if an organization changes its mind on how to host the solutions at a later time.

With the introduction of Windows Server 2016 and Microsoft Azure Stack, this scenario changes. Now an organization writes an application by using the Azure Resource Manager model, and that application can run in the Azure public cloud, it can run on-premises with Microsoft Azure Stack, or with a hosting partner that utilizes the Microsoft Azure Stack platform without any change. I can create a JSON template to deploy a service and run that same template to deploy anywhere. This flexibility and mobility is huge for customers, and it no longer restricts them from getting maximum benefit from hybrid scenarios where their workloads can easily cross clouds and be freely moved if the organization's cloud goals change.

Consider the Public Cloud

Looking at the public cloud services available, if I'm a new company, I would be thinking about using them where possible. Email, collaboration, application platforms, and customer relationship management—these are all critical areas that require large initial investments to get running. Using a public cloud solution, such as SaaS or PaaS, allows you to "pay as you go." You pay a small amount when your company starts, and the amount you pay grows as your company grows. That's perfect for a growing startup.

If I'm an established company and I'm looking at ways to cut down on my IT expenses or diversify them, moving some services off premises and to the cloud may make a lot of sense, particularly if I'm looking for new features or site disaster-recovery capabilities. Using a cloud service like Office 365 instantly gives an organization enterprise email, communication, and collaboration resources that are replicated across multiple sites with a per user, per month fee structure. When I talk to organizations, more and more I hear the desire to move from capital expenditure (cap ex) to operational expenditure (op ex), and using a pay-as-you-go public cloud service removes the cap ex part almost completely. Keep in mind that moving services to the public cloud is not "free." Most likely, you will need help from a consulting organization to enable a smooth migration process, because there will likely be a period of time that you will have a hybrid solution, such as for email (some mailboxes may be on premises while others are in the cloud). Some services will remain hybrid services. For example, I've seen some organizations that host Exchange mailboxes on premises for office-based workers but use Office 365 for other workers, such as those in retail locations that have a higher turnover or can function with a lower quality of service. I've also seen the opposite, where the most important people in a company have their email hosted on Office 365 to ensure its availability, while everyone else stays on premises. Another big benefit of this type of cloud solution is rate of innovation. Microsoft can update services such as Office 365 whenever it wants to, constantly bringing new functionality. This is often referred to as *cloud cadence*. Additionally, because of the scale of the public cloud and its compute power, it can offer services that would not be practical on-premises to anyone other than the largest enterprises, but now they can be available to all.

If a new application is needed for the short term, or if high availability and growth potential are a requirement, hosting it on Microsoft Azure would be a great choice. Development scenarios are a great fit because they have high turnover (also referred to as *churn*), with environments constantly being created and deleted; without a private cloud on premises, that could result in a lot of work for administrators.

Familiarize yourself with the public cloud solutions available, and use them in the right way. Use them where it makes sense, but don't use them just to sidestep internal provisioning processes or their shortcomings. Some organizations that I have worked with took six weeks to provision a new virtual machine. Because of this long delay, business units decided to use the public cloud instead, and often not officially. The business units have a credit card and simply purchase public cloud services without IT approval or oversight, commonly known as *Bring Your Own IT (BYOIT)*. This BYOIT by business units can lead to security, discovery, and retention requirements not being met, which is a huge problem. That is a poor reason to use the public cloud. Fix the internal process-using capabilities such as self-service and the private cloud that I've talked about in detail in earlier chapters.

Moving services to the public cloud has additional advantages. Typically, those solutions will ensure the availability of the service and perform the backups. It's also easy to scale up and down as you pay for what you use, but consider that many services are consumed from anywhere. I check my email at home, on my phone, and on a laptop at a restaurant, which means that my company would have to provide Internet-based access to at least a portion of the corporate infrastructure if the service was housed on premises. By leveraging a public cloud solution, the organization does not have to provide that access. The service is already being offered on the Internet.

If you are creating a new custom application, consider whether it is a fit for a PaaS solution such as Microsoft Azure. Something like this will minimize the ongoing IT overhead required, because the only work to do is to maintain the application. Remember, as I mentioned earlier, that when an application is written on the Azure Resource Manager, it can be run not just in the public Azure PaaS, but on-premises or with hosters via Microsoft Azure Stack. For other applications and workloads that you want to run in the public cloud using IaaS, most should work without modification, which is a key principle of IaaS.

If your organization utilizes Microsoft Azure for just development, testing, and stand-alone projects, then no communication may be required between Azure and your on-premises network outside of the standard Internet-based communications via load balancers with NAT rules or VMs with public IPs. More commonly, seamless connectivity between Microsoft Azure and the on-premises network is required to enable cross-premises connectivity. To enable the cross-premises connectivity, you need either to configure the Microsoft Azure VPN gateway site-to-site functionality over the Internet or leverage ExpressRoute for dedicated connectivity over a private network.

Before implementing connectivity to Microsoft Azure, you need to have created a virtual network with subnets defined that will be used by virtual machines created after you create the virtual network. The use of a virtual network is mandatory when using Azure Resource Manager, but it is optional (although always recommended) for the older Azure Service Manager. It is important to use an IP scheme for the virtual network in Microsoft Azure that does not conflict with any on-premises IP allocation. When you use a different IP address range in Microsoft Azure, IP traffic will be able to be routed cross-premises. If the on-premises gateway device that is used to connect to Microsoft Azure is not the default gateway for on-premises, you will need to add manual routes so that on-premises traffic that is destined for

Microsoft Azure will route correctly. Also make sure that all on-premises IP scopes are defined within Microsoft Azure correctly, to ensure correct routing of traffic from Microsoft Azure to the on-premises network.

When using the site-to-site VPN connection option, multiple on-premises locations can be connected to the single Azure gateway. This helps connect multiple locations not only for normal operation, but also for disaster-recovery scenarios. For organizations that utilize a primary and a disaster-recovery location, both locations can be connected, avoiding the need for gateway reconfiguration in the event of an actual disaster and required failover. If using ExpressRoute, the exact connectivity will vary depending on the type of ExpressRoute leveraged. However, whether an Exchange provider or network service provider ExpressRoute vendor is utilized, it is always possible to connect to multiple on-premises locations. Typically, the network service provider option is simpler, as it can use existing multilocation connectivity solutions such as MPLS (Multiprotocol Label Switching). Nevertheless, I've also seen exchange providers apply some ingenious solutions, and so I always encourage my customers to talk to their current communications partners about how they can help with connectivity to Azure and always to keep an open mind.

Once network connectivity is established cross-premises, some operating system instances running in Microsoft Azure will most likely need to be domain joined. This introduces various considerations. One requirement is name resolution via DNS. Initially, configure the virtual network in Microsoft Azure to use on-premises DNS servers for name resolution, which will allow machines to locate domain controllers and join the domain. Using a shared DNS infrastructure between on-premises servers and Microsoft Azure will also allow cross-premises name resolution.

Within Active Directory, create a separate Active Directory site for the IP ranges used in Microsoft Azure and create a site link to the actual on-premises location that has connectivity. Make sure to set the site link cost and replication interval to values that meet your requirements. The default replication of every 3 hours is likely not fast enough.

The next decision is whether Active Directory domain controllers should be placed in Microsoft Azure. Initially, many organizations have security concerns about placing a domain controller in Microsoft Azure for fear of directory or security compromise, which would potentially expose the entire contents of the directory service. As previously discussed, the Microsoft datacenters likely have far more security than any normal company could hope for. It is more a question of trust, and that trust has to be built over time. However, Microsoft has been very public about its security, including its fights to protect customer data from government requests, and they offer numerous options for customers to encrypt their data so that access by Microsoft is not possible. When the domain controller in Microsoft Azure is configured, care is taken to make sure that endpoints, which aren't required, are not exposed and to ensure that firewall services and monitoring are in place. These are the same steps that you would take for an on-premises domain controller, but you need to be aware if any endpoints defined for the virtual machine are directly accessible on the Internet. Most likely, the domain controller would also be a global catalog, or at least one of them if you place multiple domain controllers in Microsoft Azure. For a small number of domain-joined machines in Microsoft Azure, the authentication traffic and other directory services data could be facilitated by the on-premises domain controllers and accessed using the VPN gateway. However, as the number of domain-joined Microsoft Azure resources grows, it will become necessary to have a local domain controller.

Companies often consider using a read-only domain controller (RODC) in Microsoft Azure because an RODC has passwords for only a subset of the users cached, and it cannot make changes, which minimizes damage if the RODC is compromised. The decision depends on which services are running in Microsoft Azure and whether they work with an RODC. If a service does not work with RODCs, there is no point in placing an RODC in Microsoft Azure, and you will need a regular domain controller or will need to accept that the Active Directory traffic will need to traverse cross-premises. Another option is to create a child domain for Microsoft Azure.

Once a domain controller is running in Microsoft Azure and it is configured as a DNS server, the virtual network can be modified to use the domain controller(s) in Microsoft Azure as the primary DNS server. Remember not to deprovision the domain controller(s), because this could result in an IP address change. However, using a small, separate subnet just for domain controllers can help alleviate this problem by reducing the possible IP addresses that can be allocated to those domain controllers and stopping other VMs from using those IP addresses.

If an organization wishes to run services in Microsoft Azure that require Active Directory, but that organization does not have Active Directory available in Microsoft Azure, there is another option: Azure AD Domain Services. Azure AD is primarily an identity solution that enables a single sign-on across many cloud services with multifactor authentication, machine learning backed reporting, and more built in, but it is not a traditional directory service that machines can be joined to and have policy applied, like standard Active Directory. Azure AD Domain Services is a feature that can be enabled on an Azure AD instance, which allows Azure AD to emulate a traditional Active Directory. This enables VMs running on a specific virtual network that has been configured with a specific Azure AD Domain Services DNS configuration in Azure to "join" the Azure AD instance, have policy applied, and authenticate to Azure AD using Kerberos and NTLM, which typically is not possible. Now services that need AD can run in Azure by utilizing Azure AD and save the cost and management of standing up regular domain controllers. Note that if you do have an AD instance, it is generally better just to extend that into Azure and think of Azure AD Domain Services as functionality when no such AD availability is possible.

With cross-premises connectivity and Active Directory services, you can really open up the services that can be placed in Microsoft Azure. I see many organizations using a hybrid approach. Often, they start with testing and development in Microsoft Azure, and once the technology is proven and trusted, it is expanded. Remember to look constantly at what new capabilities are available. Although initially you could, for example, deploy an IaaS VM running SQL Server databases, over time those databases may be able to be moved to SQL Azure instead, reducing your management overhead.

An interesting use case that I have seen is to use Microsoft Azure as the disaster-recovery site. At the time of this writing, Microsoft Azure can be the target for replication from many sources, including Hyper-V, VMware, and even physical systems via Azure Site Recovery (ASR). This protection is at an OS level and not application "aware." In the case of Hyper-V, the replication is performed at the VM level via Hyper-V Replica, and for VMware and physical systems, the replication is achieved through an in-OS agent that captures writes to the filesystem and sends them to the target replica. While this type of VM/OS replication is fairly simple and generic enough to be used across many types of services, it may not be the best option because it is not application aware. You need to look at each service and how to replicate. Here are some approaches. Keep in mind that there is not one right answer; it will depend on the workload.

◆ For Active Directory, deploy domain controllers to Microsoft Azure and use Active Directory multimaster replication to keep the Microsoft Azure domain controllers up-to-date.

◆ For file data, one option is to use Distributed File System Replication (DFS-R) to replicate data to a file server running in Microsoft Azure IaaS. Distributed File System Namespaces (DFS-N) could be used to give users transparent access to the data. Another option is to use StorSimple, which will also store data in Microsoft Azure. In the event of a disaster, a virtual StorSimple appliance is started in Azure and can enable access to the Azure-backed data. Windows Server 2016 introduces Storage Replica, which, via its asynchronous replication, or possibly synchronous replication, if latency was low enough via ExpressRoute, replication configuration, may be a great fit to copy all kinds of data. Another option is to copy data periodically using Robocopy or PowerShell.

◆ SQL databases can be replicated using SQL Server AlwaysOn, which should be used in asynchronous mode. This requires stretching a cluster between your premises and Microsoft Azure.

◆ SharePoint instances are mainly SQL Server data. Therefore, deploy SharePoint instances in Microsoft Azure and use SQL Server AlwaysOn to replicate the SharePoint data. For data not stored in SQL Server, use another process to replicate filesystem configuration periodically or as part of a change-control process.

◆ Exchange and Lync are supported to run in IaaS with various caveats. However, the best solution is to migrate users to Office 365 if you need offsite capabilities. This type of migration will likely be a major undertaking, and you will run in a hybrid mode during the migration.

◆ Other applications will need to use a combination of technologies. If the application uses a SQL database, use SQL replication to replicate the database. Use filesystem replication to replicate other filesystem assets.

◆ For replication of anything running in an operating system that is not covered by an application-aware solution, you can look at the replication provided by Azure Site Recovery that was previously mentioned.

To ensure mobility between on-premise infrastructure and Microsoft Azure, make sure that for those workloads that need to be transportable, you use only features common to both environments, such as the following:

◆ Generation 1 virtual machines

◆ VHD disk format of 1023GB maximum size

◆ No requirement on IPv6 communications

There is also an interesting licensing consideration for placing workloads in Microsoft Azure. Your organization may already have a large number of Windows Server licenses, but they are not required when using Microsoft Azure because the Windows Server license is included. It may be possible to repurpose licenses for other on-premises workloads. Your organization may have multiyear agreements for licenses, in which case you may be able to negotiate converting elements of the agreement to cloud-based services.

Ultimately, the public cloud offers many capabilities. Your organization should look at each one and decide whether it is a good fit for some workloads. Then your organization should deploy its choices in a carefully planned manner to maintain service availability and supportability.

Decide if a Server Workload Should Be Virtualized

While the public cloud is great, you'll want to keep many workloads internally on your company's systems. As you read this, your company probably has some kind of server virtualization. It could be VMware ESX, it could be Microsoft Hyper-V, it could be Citrix XenServer, or it could be something else, and likely your organization is using multiple hypervisors. The most common scenario that I see is organizations using ESX and Hyper-V, as they were originally a pure ESX shop, but as Hyper-V functionally has matured, they have begun migration of some, if not all, workloads for reasons including cost, management, and compatibility with the cloud.

The default for most organizations is virtual first for any new server workload except for servers with very high resource requirements and some specialty services, such as domain controllers that provide the Active Directory domain services for the environment. (Typically, though, only one domain controller is a physical server, while all others are virtualized. However, even this is not really required thanks to clustering changes with Windows Server 2012, which enables VMs to start in a cluster even if a DC cannot be contacted, a feature known as *AD-less cluster bootstrapping*.) Most of these exceptions are based on limitations of the previous generation of hypervisors.

The reality is that with Windows Server 2012—and the ability to run very large virtual machines with 64 vCPUs, NUMA topology projected to VM, 1TB of memory, Direct Access to network cards using SR-IOV if needed, 64TB VHDX virtual storage, shared VHDX, and access to both iSCSI and Fibre Channel storage where necessary—very few workloads cannot run in a virtual machine and run the same as on bare metal, including high-resource workloads such as SQL Server. Windows Server 2016 takes this even further with the Discrete Device Assignment (DDA) feature; hardware such as GPUs can be mapped directly to a VM, enabling the native hardware drivers to be used and the full capability lit up within the VM. This had been one scenario, even with Hyper-V 2012 R2, in which physical servers were still leveraged that required massive GPU compute availability.

Even if you had a physical server that had only one virtual machine running because it needed all of the resources, virtualizing is a good idea because all of the other benefits of virtualization would still apply:

◆ Abstraction from the underlying hardware, giving complete portability

◆ Ability to move the VM between physical hosts for hardware maintenance purposes (although DDA does break this ability, since the VM is not tied to specific hardware in a specific host)

◆ Leveraging the high availability and replica features of Hyper-V where needed

◆ Consistent deployment and provisioning

There may still be some applications you cannot virtualize, either because they need more than the resource limits of a virtual machine or, more likely, because of supportability. Some application vendors will not support their applications running in a virtualized manner. Some have not had time to test the application, and others may have their own virtualization solution and so will support only its product on its hypervisor. For example, Oracle supported only its products on its own Oracle VM hypervisor, but this changed in 2013, and Oracle now supports its products on Hyper-V and Microsoft Azure.

Prior to this shift in support, organizations had to make a decision at this point on how to proceed. Remember, applications don't really know they are running on a virtual operating system. To the application, the operating system looks exactly the same as if it were running on bare metal, except that certain types of devices, such as network and storage devices, will be different because they are virtual devices, so virtualizing an application should not introduce problems with today's hypervisors.

Carrying on with the Oracle example, in my experience, even before the supportability update, the Oracle products worked just fine on Hyper-V, and Oracle support would even try to assist if there was a problem with it running on a non-Oracle hypervisor on a best-effort basis. However, organizations have to be prepared, because if a problem cannot be fixed, the application vendor may ask for the problem to be reproduced on a supported configuration, such as on a bare-metal system without virtualization or on a supported hypervisor. Technology can help here. There are third-party solutions that normally help with physical-to-virtual conversions when organizations want to move to a virtual environment and can also take a virtual machine and deploy to bare metal. This could be an emergency backup option for organizations that want to standardize on one hypervisor and run all applications on virtual operating systems, even when not officially supported.

The decision comes down to an organization's appetite for some risk, however small, and how critical the application is should it run into a problem. If you have a noncritical application, then virtualizing in a nonsupported configuration that has been well tested by the organization is probably OK. If it's a critical system that would need instant support by the vendor if there was a problem, then running in an officially unsupported configuration is probably not the best option.

In the past, there were concerns about virtualizing domain controllers. That is not the case with Windows Server 2012 and Windows Server 2012 Hyper-V, which have special capabilities directly related to Active Directory, VM-GenerationID, as covered in Chapter 6, "Maintaining a Hyper-V Environment." Most companies I work with today virtualize domain controllers, and in Windows Server 2012 Failover Clustering, there is even protection from the cluster not being able to start if a domain controller was not available, which was a previous concern. Essentially, prior to Windows Server 2012, if all the domain controllers were running on a cluster, there was a problem if you shut down the cluster. Normally, virtual machines cannot start until the cluster service starts. The cluster service could not start without contacting a domain controller. Therefore, if the domain controller was a virtual machine, nothing could start. Windows Server 2012 Failover Clustering removed this dependency.

I've focused on Windows workloads and how Windows can be virtualized, but many organizations have some non-Windows servers as well. Hyper-V has great support for Linux distributions. Even Linux distributions that are not officially supported will likely still work and can use the Hyper-V integration services to give you a great experience. This applies equally to Microsoft Azure, which has a wide range of Linux support. Just because a workload is not a Windows Server workload does not mean it cannot be virtualized. Some Linux/Unix workloads cannot be virtualized on any x86 hypervisor, because they are using a non-x86 architecture. A good example is Solaris running on SPARC. This cannot be virtualized on an x86 hypervisor because SPARC is a different hardware architecture. If you are using the x86 version of Solaris, it would probably run on Hyper-V. However, at the time of this writing, it's not a supported Linux distribution for Hyper-V, and if you are running this Solaris workload, it's probably pretty important, so running in a nonsupported manner may not make sense for you.

When you are using clustering within virtualized environments that require shared storage, you have numerous options. Where possible, use Shared VDHX, because this maintains complete virtualization of the storage and removes direct storage fabric visibility for the virtual machines. If Shared VHDX is not an option—if you're not running Windows Server 2012 R2 Hyper-V or if you have a mixed cluster of virtual and nonvirtual operating systems—then virtual Fibre Channel or iSCSI can be used and perhaps even an SMB 3 file share if the service supports it.

Remember that just because Hyper-V has a great replication technology with Hyper-V Replica, this should not be the first choice. It is always better to use an application- or service-aware replication technology such as Active Directory replication, SQL AlwaysOn, Exchange Database Availability Groups, and so on. Only if there is no native replication solution should Hyper-V Replica be used. Remember that replication is not a replacement for backups.

Do I Want a Private Cloud?

I talk to many customers about the private cloud, and some are open to it and some just hate the idea. This is largely because of a misunderstanding about what the private cloud has to mean to the organization. Instead of asking whether they want to use a private cloud, I could ask the following questions and get very different responses:

◆ Do you want easier management and deployment?

◆ Do you want better insight into networking and storage?

◆ Do you want to abstract deployment processes from the underlying fabric, enabling deployments to any datacenter without worrying about all of the underlying details like which SAN, VLAN, IP subnet, and so on?

◆ Do you want to track usage better and even show and charge back to business units based on this usage?

◆ Do you want to be able to deploy multitiered services with a single click instead of focusing on every virtual machine that is needed?

◆ Do you want to simplify the process of creating new virtual environments?

I would get "Yes" answers to these questions from pretty much everyone. And I could take it a step further by asking, "Do you want to enable users to request their own virtual environments or service instances through a self-service portal with full-approval workflow within quotas that you define, which are automatically enforced, including virtual machine automatic expiration if required?"

I may start to get some headshaking on that one. IT teams may have concerns about letting users have self-service portals even with quotas, even with approval workflows, and even with full tracking. That's OK. As with using public cloud services, when implementing end-user self-service solutions, it can take some time for IT to trust the controls and process and see that it won't result in VM sprawl and a wild west of uncontrolled VM mayhem. In reality, with the private cloud, there will be better tracking and more controls than with the processes used in most organizations today. I've seen many organizations that hate the idea of users having quotas and self-service, but they actually have no tracking or limits for user requests, and it's simply the fact the VMs take so long to create in environments that slows the sprawl of VMs. Ultimately the sprawl happens, however, and they have no idea of who owns what and if it's still needed. This would not happen with a private cloud!

The key point is that adopting a private cloud brings only benefits to IT departments and the organization as a whole. The private cloud, allows far greater utilization of the resources that the company already has, better insight into those resources, much better responsiveness to the requirements of the business (such as provisioning new environments), and the ability for everyone to focus on what they care about—the application.

Go back to those first questions I asked. If your answers to any of those are "Yes," then a move to the private cloud model makes sense. Also, remember that you don't have to expose all of its capabilities to end users—you can have self-service capabilities but let only the IT teams use them to better enable provisioning processes. It's still helping the environment.

Remember that the private cloud provides a foundation on which you can offer many types of services. You can offer basic virtual machines as an in-house IaaS. You can offer environments with certain runtime environments like .NET or J2E to enable PaaS where business units can easily run their applications. You can even have complete services that model an entire multitiered application through service templates, thus offering SaaS. It's really whatever makes sense for your organization. Typically, organizations will start with basic IaaS, offering virtual machines, and then build up from that point on as confidence and experience grows. Also, with Microsoft Azure Stack, you may want that flexibility for applications to be able to run anywhere, which may also drive an Azure Stack private cloud implementation on-premises.

My recommendation is to get your organization on the latest version of Hyper-V. The new capabilities make it the best virtualization platform out there. It adds support for far larger virtual machines and larger clusters. It has better replication and availability features and better support for Direct Access to network hardware and network virtualization. It has full PowerShell management and guest-level Fibre Channel access, which means more workloads can be virtualized and therefore you can have a simpler datacenter. And that's just scratching the surface.

It probably seems daunting. There seems to be a lot of change going on, and if you are struggling to keep things running—either by not patching servers or by patching them manually and always installing servers by running around with a DVD or ISO—this will seem like a huge difference. But it's a good difference. A large time investment is required initially to get these processes and solutions in place, so some organizations may need to bite the bullet and use a consulting company to help them get up-and-running. If that's the case with your company, make sure that the consultants don't work in isolation. Work with them, and be part of the decision and planning. That way, when they leave, you understand *why* things were done as they were and can carry on any best practices that were implemented.

Enabling Single-Pane-of-Glass Management

Virtualization does not have to change the way that you manage your datacenter. It would be possible to carry on managing each operating system instance, deploying each instance by booting to an ISO, but you are not getting the most from the technologies available and are making life far harder than it needs to be.

One of the biggest changes that virtualization introduces to the datacenter initially is the way you provision new servers. Instead of installing operating systems via an ISO file, you use virtual machine templates that can include customizations, join a domain automatically, and install applications and run scripts. Most likely you will have a few virtual hard disks that can be used by many different templates that can be tailored for the exact needs of the organization.

The longer-term goal is to shift from creating virtual machines to deploying instances of services that are made up of many virtual machines and service templates. Using service templates is a big change in the way services and virtual machines are provisioned. The benefits they bring—such as easy deployment, updating of deployed instances by updating the template, server application virtualization, and automated configuration of network hardware—make the use of service templates something that should be a goal. This is not to say that normal virtual machines will never be deployed. Service templates are great to enable the deployment of services within an organization, but there will always be those applications that just need to be deployed once, and often the additional work in creating a service template does not make sense.

What is important, though, is that you *don't* end up with two completely different management solutions or even potentially more:

◆ One management solution for virtual machines

◆ One management solution for physical machines

◆ One management solution for the virtual infrastructure, such as the hypervisor

◆ One management solution for the public cloud resources, such as Window Azure IaaS virtual machines

The goal is to manage your environment as simply and with as few tools as possible. Look for management solutions that enable complete management without having to put in lots of point solutions for different aspects of your datacenter. Patching is a great example: there are solutions that will patch just virtual machines, and there are different solutions to patch hypervisors, and other solutions for patching desktops. A solution such as System Center Configuration Manager (SCCM) will provide patching for all servers, physical or virtual, and your desktops. Also, with Hyper-V, because it's part of Windows, SCCM can patch the hypervisor itself. One solution is to patch everything. SCCM can also integrate with many third parties to be able to apply updates to hardware (such as firmware and BIOS) plus deploy updates for Microsoft and non-Microsoft applications.

The same idea applies to all aspects of your datacenter. Try to stay away from point solutions. System Center Operations Manager (SCOM) can monitor your physical servers, the virtual servers, the operating system, applications, custom .NET and J2E applications, networking equipment, and even non-Windows workloads in addition to monitoring and integrating with Microsoft Azure. This gives you a complete view, from soup to nuts as they say. The same applies for backup, for service management, and for orchestration; keep it simple and minimize the number of separate tools.

From a virtual machine management perspective, Windows Azure Pack or Microsoft Azure Stack can provide a single view of on-premises virtual machines that are managed by System Center Virtual Machine Manager (SCVMM) or Microsoft Azure Stack and of virtual machines running in Microsoft Azure and even of virtual machines running with hosters that leverage Service Provider Foundation (SPF) or Azure Stack with the right configuration and third-party add-ons. The same can apply to provisioning with more complex workflows using System Center Service Manager (SCSM) to provide a service catalog fronting many services, including virtual machine provisioning and management.

Orchestration is where I would like to finish because it brings together everything about the datacenter. As organizations use more and more IT, and your organization will have more and more operating system instances to manage, technologies like service templates help to bring the focus to the application instead of the operating system. However, many operating systems will still require management. To truly scale, you must look at automation capabilities and working with multiple operating system instances at the same time.

PowerShell is a key part of enabling automation. Especially in Windows Server 2012 and above, basically everything that can be done with the GUI can also be done with PowerShell. Actions can be scripted, but more important, they can be executed on many machines concurrently and in an automated fashion. Building on orchestrating tasks and beyond just PowerShell, takes some time to look at System Center Orchestrator. Every client I talk to gets very excited about Orchestrator in terms of its ability to connect to any system that exists through various methods and then to create runbooks based on PowerShell workflows, which are sets of actions that should be performed in a sequence and based on results from previous actions across all of those connected systems. Start with something small, some set of actions that you perform manually each day, and automate them in Orchestrator. Another good way to learn is to take a simple PowerShell script that you have and integrate it in Orchestrator instead. Note that Orchestrator historically was based around graphical runbooks built from actions defined in integration packs. It has now shifted, however, to be built on PowerShell workflows, which has the benefit of not requiring separate packages of actions to be built for a single product and instead can leverage PowerShell modules that are widely used. Because of this shift, I advise my customers to build most of their logic using PowerShell, which can be used in a .NET activity, even if using the older Orchestrator product.

For organizations taking a hybrid approach, providing a seamless experience for the users of services is vital. Although using Windows Azure Pack or Azure Stack provides the seamless pane of glass, it's key for the IT organization to own the process of deciding whether new virtual machines will be deployed on-premises or in Microsoft Azure. I've had great success using System Center Orchestrator with runbooks that utilize PowerShell to receive a provisioning request made via System Center Service Manager. The logic of whether to deploy to on-premises or in Microsoft Azure is made by the logic built into the Orchestrator runbook and based on the target use for the new environment, the available capacity on premises, the predicted length of usage of the environment, and the capabilities requested. Once the logic provisions the virtual machine, either on-premises or in Microsoft Azure, the requesting user receives an email with an RDP file to enable connectivity, or the new service is added to their list of services. The point is that the provisioning process and ongoing interaction is the same no matter where the virtual machine is actually hosted.

The Bottom Line

Identify the overall best architecture for your organization.   As this chapter has shown, there are a lot of thing to consider when choosing a cloud-based solution for an organization. It's important to take the time to understand the organization's strategic direction, its resources, and the needs of its workloads. Only then can an architecture be created that utilizes the strengths of the various options.

Master It   What is the most important first step in deciding on the best architecture?

Appendix

The Bottom Line

Each chapter's "The Bottom Line" section suggests exercises to deepen your skills and understanding. Sometimes an exercise has only one possible solution, but often you are encouraged to use your skills and creativity to create something that builds on what you know and lets you explore one of many possibilities.

Chapter 1: Introduction to Virtualization and Microsoft Solutions

Articulate the key value propositions of virtualization. Virtualization solves the numerous pain points and limitations of physical server deployments today. Primary benefits of virtualization include consolidation of resources, which increases resource utilization and provides OS abstraction from hardware, allowing OS mobility; financial savings through less server hardware, less datacenter space, and simpler licensing; faster provisioning of environments; and additional backup and recovery options.

Master It How does virtualization help in service isolation in branch office situations?

Solution Virtualization enables the various roles required (such as domain controllers and file services) to run on different operating system instances, ensuring isolation without requiring large amounts of hardware.

Understand the differences in functionality between the different versions of Hyper-V. Windows Server 2008 introduced the foundational Hyper-V capabilities, and the major new features in 2008 R2 were Live Migration and Cluster Shared Volumes (CSV). Windows 2008 R2 SP1 introduced Dynamic Memory and RemoteFX. Windows Server 2012 introduced new levels of scalability and mobility with features such as Shared Nothing Live Migration, Storage Live Migration, and Hyper-V Replica in addition to new networking and storage capabilities. Windows 2012 R2 Hyper-V enhances many of the 2012 features with generation 2 virtual machines, Live Migration compression and SMB support, new Hyper-V Replica replication granularity, and Hyper-V Replica Extended replication. Windows Server 2016 builds on this with shielded VMs providing new levels of security for virtual environments, containers for new ways to deploy and manage applications, SDNv2, and other features and management enhancements.

Master It What is the largest virtual machine that can be created on Windows Server 2012 Hyper-V, and does this change for Windows Server 2016 Hyper-V?

Solution The largest virtual machine possible in Windows Server 2012 R2 is 64 vCPUs with 1TB of memory. This changes in Windows Server 2016 to 240 vCPUs and 12TB of memory.

Master It What features were enabled for Linux virtual machines in Windows Server 2016 Hyper-V?

Solution A key feature enabled for Linux in Windows Server 2016 Hyper-V is Secure Boot. Additionally, many other features new to Windows Server 2016 work with Linux, such as hot-add of memory.

Differentiate between the types of cloud service and when each type is best utilized.
There are three primary types of cloud services: software as a service (SaaS), platform as a service (PaaS), and infrastructure as a service (IaaS). SaaS provides a complete software solution that is entirely managed by the providing vendor, such as a hosted mail solution. PaaS provides a platform on which custom-written applications can run, and it should be used for new custom applications when possible because it minimizes maintenance by the client. IaaS allows virtual machines to be run on a provided service, but the entire OS and application must be managed by the client. IaaS is suitable where PaaS or SaaS cannot be used and in development/test environments.

Chapter 2: Virtual Machine Resource Fundamentals

Describe how the resources of a virtual machine are virtualized by the hypervisor. The hypervisor directly manages the processor and memory resources with Hyper-V. Logical processors are scheduled to satisfy computer requirements of virtual processors assigned to virtual machines. Multiple virtual processors can share the same logical processor. Virtual machines are assigned memory by the hypervisor from the memory available in the physical host. Dynamic Memory allows memory to be added and removed from a virtual machine based on resource need. Other types of resources, such as network and storage, are provided by the management partition through a kernel mode memory bus known as a VMBus. This allows existing Windows drivers to be used for the wide array of storage and network devices typically used.

Master It How is Dynamic Memory different from Memory Overcommit?

Solution Dynamic Memory allocates memory in an intelligent fashion to virtual machines based on how it is being used by processes running inside the virtual machine. Memory Overcommit technologies work by telling a virtual machine that it has a large amount of memory and allocating the memory only as the virtual machine writes to it. However, this approach does not work well with modern operating systems that try to use all memory available, even if it's only for cache purposes.

Correctly use processor and memory advanced configuration options. The compatibility configuration of a virtual machine processor should be used when a virtual machine may be moved between hosts with different versions of the same processor family. The processor compatibility option hides higher-level features from the guest operating system, enabling migrations without downtime to the virtual machine. Processor reserve and limit options ensure that a virtual machine coexists with other virtual machines without getting too many or too few resources. Dynamic Memory configurations allow the startup, minimum, and maximum amounts of memory for a virtual machine to be configured. It's important to note that the maximum amount of memory configured is available only if sufficient memory exists within the host.

Master It   When should the NUMA properties of a virtual machine be modified?

Solution   Hyper-V will configure the optimal settings for virtual machines based on the physical NUMA configuration of the hosts. However, if a virtual machine will be moved between hosts with different NUMA configurations, then the NUMA configuration of the virtual machine should be changed to match the smallest NUMA configuration of all of the hosts it may be moved between.

Explain the difference between VHD/VHDX and pass-through storage.   VHD and VHDX files are virtual hard disks that are files on a filesystem or share accessible to the Hyper-V host. They provide abstraction of the storage seen by the virtual machine and the underlying physical storage. Pass-through storage directly maps a virtual machine to a physical disk accessible from the host, which limits Hyper-V functionality and breaks one of the key principles of virtualization: the abstraction of the virtual machine from the physical fabric.

Master It   Why would VHD still be used with Windows Server 2012 Hyper-V?

Solution   VHDX is superior to VHD in every way. However, if you need backward compatibility with Windows Server 2008 R2 Hyper-V or Microsoft Azure IaaS (at the time of this writing), then VHD should still be used.

Chapter 3: Virtual Networking

Architect the right network design for your Hyper-V hosts and virtual machines by using the options available.   There are many different networking traffic types related to a Hyper-V host, including management, virtual machine, cluster, Live Migration, and storage. While traditionally separate, network adapters were used with each type of traffic; a preferred approach is to create multiple vNICs in the management partition that connect to a shared virtual switch. This minimizes the number of physical NICs required while providing resiliency from a NIC failure for all workloads connected to the switch.

Master It   Why are separate network adapters no longer required if SMB is leveraged and the network adapters support RDMA?

Solution   RDMA is not compatible with NIC Teaming, which would have been used as the foundation for the connectivity of the virtual switch prior to Windows Server 2016. However, in Windows Server 2016, a new teaming technology called Switch Embedded Teaming (SET), which is implemented within the VMSwitch, is utilized. This means that, unlike Windows Server 2012 R2, which required separate adapters for RDMA traffic and those used with the VMSwitch, converged NICs can now be used with the VMSwitch, avoiding the need for extra NICs dedicated to RDMA traffic.

Identify when to use the types of gateways.   There are three types of gateways supported by the SDNv2 multitenant gateway: basic layer 3 forwarding to connect virtual networks to other networks, GRE tunneling to other GRE endpoints or MPLS, and site-to-site VPN to connect different locations. The SDNv2 multitenant gateway supports multiple active and multiple passive instances, and it is designed to support multiple tenants using shared physical infrastructure.

Leverage SCVMM for many networking tasks.   While Hyper-V Manager enables many networking functions to be performed, each configuration is limited to a single host and is hard to manage at scale. SCVMM is focused on enabling the network to be modeled at a physical level, and then the types of network required by virtual environments can be separately modeled with different classifications of connectivity defined. While the initial work may seem daunting, the long-term management and flexibility of a centralized networking environment is a huge benefit.

Master It   Is SCVMM required for network virtualization?

Solution   SCVMM is required for SDNv1, which was the only SDN solution in Windows Server 2012 and Windows Server 2012 R2. It is still part of Windows Server 2016 for backward-compatibility reasons. SDNv2 has a new controller plane, the Network Controller, which is part of Windows Server 2016. Through the Network Controller, different management solutions can interact and manage. SCVMM is one possible management solution for SDNv2, but not the only solution. PowerShell and Microsoft Azure Stack can also be used. If you are utilizing SCVMM for your Hyper-V management, then utilizing it for SDNv2 management is logical.

Chapter 4: Storage Configurations

Explain the types of storage available to a virtual machine.   Windows Server provides various types of storage to a virtual machine. VHDX files provide a completely abstracted and self-contained virtual container for filesystems available to virtual machines, and 2012 R2 and above allow a VHDX file connected to the SCSI bus to be shared between multiple virtual machines, providing shared storage. Additionally, storage can be exposed to virtual machines that are hosted in SAN environments through the use of iSCSI running inside the guest operating system or through the new virtual Fibre Channel capability.

Master It   Why is MPIO required?

Solution   When multiple paths are available to storage for resiliency purposes, the storage will be seen multiple times by the operating system. MPIO makes the operating system aware of the multiple paths to the storage and consolidates the storage view to one object for each storage instance.

Identify when to use Virtual Fibre Channel and when to use VHD Sets and the benefits of each.   Virtual Fibre Channel allows virtual machines to be directly connected to a Fibre Channel SAN without the host requiring zoning to the storage, but it requires knowledge of the storage fabric. A VHD Set provides shared storage to the virtual machine without requiring the users of the VHD Set to have knowledge of the storage fabric, which is useful in hosting the type of scenarios where all aspects of the physical fabric should be hidden from the users. VHD Sets also maintain features such as host-level backup and replication, which are not available when using Virtual Fibre Channel.

Articulate how SMB 3 can be used.   SMB 3 went through a huge upgrade in Windows Server 2012, providing an enterprise-level file-based protocol that can now be used to store Hyper-V virtual machines. This includes additional storage options for Hyper-V environments, including fronting existing SANs with a Windows Server Scale-Out File Server cluster to extend the SAN's accessibility beyond hosts with direct SAN connectivity.

Master It Which two SMB technologies enable virtual machines to move between nodes in an SoFS without any interruption to processing?

Solution SMB Transparent Failover and SMB Scale-Out enable the movement of SMB clients between servers without the need for LUNs to be moved and with no loss of handles and locks.

Chapter 5: Managing Hyper-V

Identify the ways to deploy Hyper-V. Windows Server 2016 Hyper-V can be deployed using numerous methods. The traditional approach is to install a server from setup media, which could be a DVD, USB device, or even files obtained over the network. Enterprise systems management solutions such as System Center Configuration Manager and Windows Deployment Services can be used to customize deployments. System Center Virtual Machine Manager can also be used to deploy Hyper-V hosts using Boot-to-VHD technology, providing a single management solution for deployment of hosts and virtual machines. Nano Server deployments are deployed in a different manner, as custom images are created and leveraged.

Master It What other types of servers can SCVMM 2016 deploy?

Solution In addition to deploying Hyper-V hosts, SCVMM 2016 can deploy Scale-out File Servers to act as storage hosts for Hyper-V virtual machines.

Explain why using Server Core is beneficial to deployments. Windows Server and Windows client operating systems share a lot of common code, and a typical Windows Server deployment has a graphical interface, Internet browser, and many graphical tools. These components all take up space, require patching, and may have vulnerabilities. For many types of server roles, these graphical elements are not required. Server Core provides a minimal server footprint that is managed remotely, which means less patching and therefore fewer reboots in addition to a smaller attack surface. Because a host reboot requires all virtual machines also to be rebooted, using Server Core is a big benefit for Hyper-V environments in order to remove as many reboots as possible. Nano Server is a completely refactored deployment of Windows Server, which is also a good choice for Hyper-V Servers but may not be compatible with an organization's management toolset.

Master It What was the big change to configuration levels between Windows Server 2012 R2 and Windows Server 2016?

Solution Windows Server 2012 introduced configuration levels, which allow the graphical shell and, separately, management tools to be added and removed at any time, requiring only a reboot to change configuration level. Windows Server 2016 changes this, requiring the configuration level to be set at installation time; this setting cannot be changed post installation. In Windows Server 2016, the configuration levels available at setup are Server Core and Server with Desktop Experience. Nano Server is deployed by using custom images and not via the standard setup process.

Explain how to create and use virtual machine templates. While it is possible to create the virtual machine environment manually and install the operating system for each new virtual machine, it's inefficient, considering the virtual machine uses a file for its virtual storage. A far more efficient and expedient approach is to create a generalized operating system template VHDX file, which can then be quickly deployed to new virtual machines. A virtual machine template allows the virtual hardware configuration of a virtual machine to be configured, including OS properties such as domain join instructions, local administrator password, and more. The configuration is then linked to a template VHDX file. When the template is deployed, minimal interaction is required by the requesting user, typically just an optional name, and within minutes, the new virtual environment with a configured guest operating system is available.

Chapter 6: Maintaining a Hyper-V Environment

Explain how backup works in a Hyper-V environment.   Windows features the VSS component that enables application-consistent backups to be taken of an operating system by calling VSS writers created by application vendors. When a backup is taken of a virtual machine at the Hyper-V host level, the VSS request is passed to the guest operating system via the backup guest service, which allows the guest OS to ensure that the disk is in a backup-ready state, allowing the virtual hard disk to be backed up at the host and be application consistent.

Master It   Is shared VHDX backed up when you perform a VM backup at the host level?

Solution   No. Shared VHDX, iSCSI, and Fibre Channel–connected storage are not backed up when performing a VM backup at the host level. To back up these types of storage, a backup within the virtual machine must be performed. If VHD Sets are used, which are the Windows Server 2016 implementation of Shared VHDX, then the VHD Set content is backed up when performing a host-level backup.

Understand how to best use checkpoints and where not to use them.   Checkpoints, previously known as snapshots, allow a point-in-time view of a virtual machine to be captured and then applied at a later time to revert the virtual machine back to the state it was in at the time the snapshot was taken. Windows Server 2016 introduced a new type of checkpoint, the production checkpoint. Production checkpoints interact with the VSS infrastructure inside the guest OS that provides an application-consistent checkpoint. Production checkpoints can be used in production environments. Standard checkpoints that do not interact with VSS and save the complete state of a VM, including memory, are useful in testing scenarios but should not be used in production, because the effect of moving a virtual machine back in time without the OS knowledge can cause problems for many services. It can even cause domain membership problems if the computer's AD account password changes after the checkpoint creation.

Understand the benefits of service templates.   Typically, a virtual machine is created from a virtual machine template, which allows a single virtual machine to be deployed. A service template allows a complete, multitiered service to be designed and then deployed through a single action. Additionally, each tier can be configured to scale up and down as workloads vary, which enables additional instances of the virtual machine for a tier to be created and deleted as necessary. Deployed instances of a service template retain their relationship to the original service template, which means that if the original service template is updated, the deployed instances can be refreshed and updated with the service template changes without losing application state.

Chapter 7: Failover Clustering and Migration Technologies

Understand the quorum model used in Windows Server 2012 R12 and above.   Windows Server 2012 R2 removed all of the previous models that were based on the way votes were allocated and the type of quorum resource. In Windows Server 2012 R2, each node has a vote and a witness is always configured, but it's used only when required. Windows Server 2012 introduced dynamic quorum, which helps ensure that clusters stay running for as long as possible as nodes' votes are removed from quorum because the nodes are unavailable. Windows Server 2012 R2 added dynamic witness to change the vote of the witness resource based on whether there are an odd or even number of nodes in the cluster.

Identify the types of mobility available with Hyper-V.   Mobility focuses on the ability to move virtual machines between Hyper-V hosts. Virtual machines within a cluster can be live-migrated between any node efficiently, since all nodes have access to the same storage, allowing only the memory and state to be copied between the nodes. Windows Server 2012 introduced the ability to move the storage of a virtual machine with no downtime, which when combined with Live Migration enables a Shared Nothing Live Migration capability that means a virtual machine can be moved between any two Hyper-V hosts without the need for shared storage or a cluster, with no downtime to the virtual machine.

Shared Nothing Live Migration does not remove the need for Failover Clustering but provides the maximum flexibility possible, enabling virtual machines to be moved between stand-alone hosts, between clusters, and between stand-alone hosts and clusters.

> **Master It**   Why is constrained delegation needed when using Shared Nothing Live Migration with remote management?

> **Solution**   Windows does not allow a server that has been given a credential to pass that credential on to another server. Constrained delegation enables credentials to be passed from a server to another specific server for defined purposes. This enables management to be performed remotely, including migration initialization.

Understand the best way to patch a cluster with minimal impact to workloads.   All virtual machines in a cluster can run on any of the member nodes. That means before you patch and reboot a node, all virtual machines should be moved to other nodes by using Live Migration, which removes any impact on the availability of the virtual machines. While the migration of virtual machines between nodes can be performed manually, Windows Server 2012 Failover Clustering provides Cluster-Aware Updating, giving you a single-click ability to patch the entire cluster without any impact to virtual machines' availability. For pre-Windows Server 2012 clusters, SCVMM 2012 also provides an automated patching capability. Configuration Manager 2016 provides a cluster-aware patching capability for organizations that leverage Configuration Manager for patching.

Chapter 8: Hyper-V Replica and Cloud Orchestration

Identify the best options to provide disaster recovery for the various services in your organization.   When planning disaster recovery, application-aware disaster recovery should be used first where possible, such as SQL Always On, Exchange DAG, Active Directory multimaster replication, and so on. If no application-aware replication and DR capability is available, another option is to look at the replication capabilities of the SAN, such as synchronous replication. Additionally, replicating at the virtual machine disk level, such as with Hyper-V Replica, provides a replication solution that has no requirements on the guest operating system or the application.

Master It   Why is Azure Site Recovery useful?

Solution   Hyper-V Replica provides the replication of the virtual machine but does not provide any enterprise management or failover orchestration. Azure Site Recovery provides a cloud-based portal to enable enterprise-level configuration, management, and execution of failover plans in a structured manner. Azure Site Recovery also provides a target for replication with Microsoft Azure instead of an on-premises location, if required, enabling DR to the cloud.

Describe the types of failover for Hyper-V Replica.   There are three types of Hyper-V Replica failover. A test failover is performed on the replica server, and it creates a clone of the replica virtual machine that is disconnected from the network and allows testing of the failover process without any impact to the ongoing protection of the primary workload as replication continues. A planned failover is triggered on the primary Hyper-V host and stops the virtual machine, ensures that any pending changes are replicated, starts the replica virtual machine, and reverses the replication. An unplanned failover is triggered on the replica Hyper-V host and is used when an unforeseen disaster occurs and the primary datacenter is lost. This means that some loss of state may occur from the primary virtual machine. When possible, a planned failover should always be used.

Master It   In an unplanned failover, how much data could be lost?

Solution   The Hyper-V Replica configuration specifies a time interval to perform replication, which can be 30 seconds, 5 minutes, or 15 minutes. This relates to the recovery point objective (RPO), which is the amount of data that can be lost. A replication of 15 minutes means that potentially up to 15 minutes of data could be lost, while a replication of 30 seconds means that the maximum amount of data loss should be 30 seconds, provided that there is no network bottleneck that is slowing down the transmission of replica log files.

Explain the automated options for Hyper-V Replica failover.   Hyper-V Replica has no automated failover capability. To automate the failover steps, PowerShell could be used, System Center Orchestrator could be used, or, for a complete solution, Azure Site Recovery could be used. The key point is that the decision to use failover should not be automatic, because many conditions (such as a break in network connectivity) could trigger a false failover. The automation required should be the orchestration of the failover after a manual action is taken to decide whether a failover should occur.

Chapter 9: Implementing the Private Cloud, SCVMM, and Microsoft Azure Stack

Explain the differences between virtualization and the private cloud.   Virtualization enables multiple operating system instances to run on a single physical piece of hardware by creating multiple virtual machines that can share the resources of the physical server.

This enables greater utilization of a server's resources, reduction in server hardware, and potential improvements to provisioning processes. The private cloud is fundamentally a management solution that builds on virtualization but brings additional capabilities by interfacing with the entire fabric, including network and storage, to provide a complete abstraction and therefore management of the entire infrastructure. This allows a greater utilization of all available resources, which leads to greater scalability. Because of the abstraction of the actual fabric, it is possible to enable user self-service based on their assignment to various clouds.

Master It Do you need to change your fabric to implement the private cloud?

Solution Typically, no. Provided your storage supports SMI-S to enable it to be communicated to and from SCVMM and your compute and network resources meet your needs in terms of your desired levels of capability, there should be no need to change the actual fabric—only the management will change.

Describe the must-have components to create a Microsoft private cloud. The foundation of a Microsoft private cloud solution comprises virtualization hosts using Hyper-V and then SCVMM and Windows Azure Pack to provide the core fabric management, abstraction, cloud creation, and end-user self-service functionality. Orchestrator and Service Manager can be utilized to build on this core set of private cloud functionality to bring more-advanced workflows, authorization of requests, and charge-back functionality.

Chapter 10: Containers and Docker

Explain the differences between Windows containers and Hyper-V containers. Windows containers provide a user-mode level of isolation from other containers. Hyper-V containers run the Windows container in a dedicated, utility VM that is automatically managed and provides kernel-mode-level isolation from other containers.

Master It When would Hyper-V containers be used over Windows containers?

Solution Anytime other containers on the same container host may not be trusted is a good use case for Hyper-V containers to gain complete isolation.

Manage Containers Containers are managed using the docker CLI. While a PowerShell module is available this module utilizes the Docker REST API and the same management structure as the docker CLI. This means management performed either with the docker CLI or PowerShell is working on a single management platform,

Master It Can Linux applications run on Windows containers?

Solution No. Containers provide isolation. However, the applications within the container run on the shared kernel, which is Windows. This means that a Linux application cannot run on a Windows container, as Linux applications are not compatible with a Windows kernel.

Master It Can the Docker client on Windows manage Linux containers?

Solution Yes, the Docker client works across platforms, meaning that both the Windows Docker client and the PowerShell can manage Windows and Linux container instances.

Chapter 11: Remote Desktop Services

Explain the types of desktop virtualization provided by RDS. Windows Server 2016 provides two main types of desktop virtualization: session-based desktops and VDI-based desktops. There are two types of VDI deployments: pooled and personal.

Master It When should VDI be used over session-based virtualization?

Solution The primary difference between session-based virtualization and VDI desktops is one of isolation. If particular users require a high level of isolation from other users, such as needing to customize the operating system or reboot it, then VDI is a good fit. For other users, such as task-based ones who are more locked down, session-based virtualization is a good solution.

Describe the benefits of RemoteFX and its requirements. RemoteFX brings various technologies such as USB port-level redirection and improved codecs that with Windows Server 2012 and above are available separately from GPU virtualization, which is the other primary RemoteFX technology that allows a physical GPU to be virtualized and assigned to VDI virtual machines running client operating systems. Using RemoteFX vGPU enables virtual machines to have local graphical resources, which enables the ability to run rich graphical applications, specifically those that leverage DirectX. To use RemoteFX vGPU, the graphics card must support DirectX 11 or newer and have a WDDM 1.2 driver or newer. The processor must also support SLAT.

Master It Is RemoteFX vGPU a good solution for OpenGL applications?

Solution Prior to Windows Server 2016, the answer would be no, as there was only very limited OpenGL 1.1 support using the CPU and not utilizing the vGPU. This changes, however, with Windows Server 2016, which adds virtual GPU support for OpenGL 4.4 and OpenCL 1.1 through RemoteFX vGPUs making it a great fit for OpenGL and OpenCL applications.

Articulate the other technologies required for a complete virtualized desktop solution. The complete user experience comprises numerous layers. The operating system provided by VDI or session virtualization is just the foundation for the user experience. The users need access to their profiles, their data, and their applications. To provide data access, the most common technology is folder redirection. For a user's profile, while historically roaming profiles were used, a better and more granular solution is UE-V, which provides application-level setting replication. For the applications, technologies such as App-V and RemoteApp can be leveraged, while specific core applications could be installed on the RD Session Host or VDI virtual machine template.

Master It Why is it best to minimize the number of applications installed in the VM VDI template image?

Solution Every application installed in a reference image will eventually need to be updated, which is additional maintenance on the template. This is not a simple process, because any change will require running Sysprep again, which has its own complexities. Additionally, the more applications installed in the template, the bigger the template and the more resources consumed that would be wasted unless the application is used by every single user. With App-V and RemoteApp, there are better ways to enable applications in the environment.

Chapter 12: Microsoft Azure IaaS, Storage, and Networking

Explain the difference between platform as a service and infrastructure as a service. The key difference relates to who is responsible for which elements of the solution. With platform as a service, solutions are written for a supplied platform within certain guidelines. The platform then ensures availability and protection for the application, and no operating system or fabric management is required. The key point is that the application must be written to work with the PaaS platform. With infrastructure as a service, a virtual machine is provided, which means that the provider manages the compute, storage, and network fabric, but the user of the virtual machine is responsible for the operating system and everything within it as well as patching it. The benefit of IaaS is that you have complete access to the operating system, so normal applications can run in IaaS without requiring customization. A key principal of IaaS is that you should not have to modify the application to work on it.

> **Master It**   What is software as a service?
>
> **Solution**   Software as a service requires no infrastructure management from the user of the service because a complete, maintained solution is provided that is accessible, typically over the Internet. The only administration relates to basic configuration and administration of users of the service. A good example of SaaS is Office 365, which is Microsoft's Exchange-, Lync-, and SharePoint-based service in the cloud.

Connect Microsoft Azure to your on-premises network.   Creating connectivity between Microsoft Azure and your local network has several requirements. First, virtual networks need to be defined in Microsoft Azure within a region. Virtual machines are created and configured at the time of creation to use a specific subnet in the virtual network. A site-to-site gateway is created between Microsoft Azure and your on-premises network, which permits seamless connectivity via a site-to-site VPN or ExpressRoute.

> **Master It**   Can Windows Server 2012 RRAS be used on the local premises side of the VPN gateway?
>
> **Solution**   Yes. Windows Server 2012 RRAS can be used for the on-premises side of the VPN connection, and the Microsoft Azure management portal will generate the full configuration script required to enable automatic configuration.

Move data between on-premises and Microsoft Azure.   Microsoft Azure is built on Windows Server Hyper-V and specifically leverages the VHD format currently. A virtual machine that uses VHD can be copied to Microsoft Azure storage and used with a new Microsoft Azure virtual machine or added to an existing virtual machine. Similarly, VHD files used in Microsoft Azure virtual machines can be downloaded to on-premises and used with Hyper-V virtual machines.

> **Master It**   What PowerShell cmdlets are used to copy VHDs to and from Microsoft Azure?
>
> **Solution**   `Add-Azure[RM]Vhd` and `Save-Azure[RM]Vhd` are used.
>
> **Master It**   Can dynamic VHDs be used in Microsoft Azure?

Solution   No. All VHDs must be fixed, and the `Add-AzureVhd` cmdlet converts dynamic VHDs to fixed VHDs during the upload. However, Azure Storage stores files sparsely, which means that only blocks with data written to them are stored and therefore billed.

Chapter 13: Bringing It All Together with a Best-of-Breed Cloud Solution

Identify the overall best architecture for your organization.   As this chapter has shown, there are a lot of thing to consider when choosing a cloud-based solution for an organization. It's important to take the time to understand the organization's strategic direction, its resources, and the needs of its workloads. Only then can an architecture be created that utilizes the strengths of the various options.

Master It   What is the most important first step in deciding on the best architecture?

Solution   Have a clear direction for your IT organization. Is it cloud first? Is it geared toward focusing on best-in-class datacenters? This will guide the architecture design and final solution.

Index

Note to the Reader: Throughout this index **boldfaced** page numbers indicate primary discussions of a topic. *Italicized* page numbers indicate illustrations.